Risk Management in Health Care Institutions

Jones and Bartlett Related Titles of Interest

Corporate Compliance in Home Health: Establishing a Plan, Managing the Risks
Fay Rozovsky

Ethical Challenges in the Management of Health Information
Laurinda Harman

Infection Control in Home Care
Mary Friedman and Emily Rhinehart

Institutional Review Board: Management and Function
Robert J. Amdur and Elizabeth A. Bankert

Institutional Review Board Member Handbook
Robert J. Amdur

Managed Care Success: Reducing Risk While Increasing Patient Satisfaction
James Saxton

Medication Errors: Causes, Prevention, and Risk Management
Michael R. Cohen

Quick Reference to Outbreak Investigation and Control in Health Care Facilities
Kathleen Arias

Contents

SECTION 2 General Risk Management Strategies

CHAPTER 6 Total Quality Management, Continuous Quality/Process Improvement, and Evaluation of the Risk Management Program 133

Robert Stanyon

About the Authors

Florence Kavaler, MD, MPH, is Professor of Preventive Medicine and Community Health, State University of New York (SUNY), Health Science Center, College of Medicine, Brooklyn, New York, and Principal Clinical Coordinator, IPRO, New York. She was formerly Assistant Surgeon General and Director of the U.S. Public Health Service Hospital, Staten Island, New York; Study Director, Milbank Memorial Fund Commission for the Study of Higher Education for Public Health; and Assistant Commissioner for Health and Medical Insurance Programs, New York City Health Department.

Dr. Kavaler was educated at Barnard College (BA), SUNY, Downstate Medical Center (MD), and Columbia University School of Public Health and Administrative Medicine (MS, MPH). She is a Diplomate, American Board of Quality Assurance and Utilization Review Physicians; a licensed nursing home administrator (New York); and a licensed health care risk manager (Florida Agency for Healthcare Administration). Dr. Kavaler formerly was President, Institute of Medical Law, Inc. (New York), and President, Medical Network Care Managers, Inc. (New York).

Her consultation skills capitalize on extensive experience in hospital administration, ambulatory care services, health insurance, HMOs, long term care, and malpractice analysis.

Her many publications address the areas of medical care evaluation in multiple settings, administrative public policy dynamics, and research activities in drug addiction, hospital cost control, aging, public health, and history of medicine. Recent books include *Computers in Medical Administration; Higher Education for Public Health; Foster-Child Health Care;* and *Cost Containment and DRGs: A Guide to Prospective Payment.*

Allen D. Spiegel, PhD, MPH, is Professor of Preventive Medicine and Community Health, State University of New York, Health Science Center, College of Medicine, Brooklyn, New York. His experience includes a wide range of activities in medical and health care services, comprehensive health planning, public health education, and health and medical communications. Formerly, Dr. Spiegel was with the New York City Health Department and The Medical Foundation, Inc., of Boston. He was also a Special Research Fellow at Brandeis University.

Dr. Spiegel received an AB from Brooklyn College, an MPH from Columbia University, and a PhD from Brandeis University. He also earned a Special Diploma from New York University in radio and television.

served as Law Secretary to the Administrative Judge of Supreme Court, Bronx County, Criminal Part; became Appellate Counsel to District Attorneys in more than 20 counties; and managed disciplinary investigations, trials, and appeals in the New York City Department of Sanitation as Deputy Inspector General. Mr. Greenblatt conducts training in supervisory skills, sexual harassment prevention, and cultural diversity, and speaks on various topics in employment law. He has investigated allegations of discrimination for several New York State agencies, contributed to the new curriculum on sexual harassment prevention for the Governor's Office of Employee Relations, and taught Personnel Administration in the S.U.N.Y. College of Health-Related Professions as Adjunct Assistant Professor in the Health Information Systems Program. Mr. Greenblatt received his law degree from New York Law School and his Masters of Laws in Labor Law from New York University School of Law.

Gary H. Harding, BS, BMET, is Director, Technical Services, Greener Pastures, LLC (Durango, CO), and has more than 20 years of consulting and clinical experience serving diverse clients in the health care industry. His areas of specialization include professional liability management, strategic planning, product development and liability consulting, accident investigation, forensic engineering, and FDA consulting assistance in new products, government regulations, and product recalls. Mr. Harding is professionally active with the Association for the Advancement of Medical Instrumentation, Laser Institute of America, and Institute of Electrical and Electronics Engineers. He graduated *magna cum laude* from Temple University with a BS in Biomedical Engineering Technology and has completed courses in the Law and Social Policy program at Bryn Mawr College.

Robin A. Maley, MPH, RN, is President of Maley Health Care Strategies, an independent health care risk management consulting firm. She was previously Senior Vice President, CNA Insurance Company, in charge of risk management. Prior to that, she was a consultant at Johnson Higgins and the director of risk management at Beth Israel Hospital (New York). As an adjunct professor at Columbia University School of Public Health, Ms. Maley lectures on risk management. In addition, she has spoken on managed care, home health care, occupational risk management, and integrated health care delivery systems at national professional meetings. Ms. Maley is co-editor of *High Technology Health Care: Risk Management Perspectives*. She received a nursing degree from Skidmore College and a graduate public health degree from Columbia University.

David E. Manoogian, JD, is a senior partner in the Health Department of Epstein, Becker and Green (Washington, D.C.), a national health law firm. In 33 years of law practice, he has handled approximately 350 cases involving a wide variety of issues for managed care organizations. Mr. Manoogian graduated from Dickinson College and received his law degree from George Washington University. After a judicial clerkship, he entered the private practice of law, specializing in health litigation and the defense of medical malpractice.

Kevin M. McLaughlin, CPCU, AIC, is Senior Vice President, Risk Management Division, with International Planning Alliance, LIC, and has held insurance positions in claims, sales, sales management, operations, public relations, and underwriting. Mr. McLaughlin frequently lectures at universities on risk management topics and was on the faculty of the Institute of Medical Law. He graduated from Seton Hall University (BA), was top in his class at the College of Insurance (New York), and attained advanced education at the Insurance Institute of America (Associate in Insurance, Associate in Claims, CPCU).

David Metz, MPA, is an insurance and health services executive and educator with over 30 years of public- and private-sector experience in health services administration, managed care, medical education, consulting, employee benefits, and risk management. He formerly was President and CEO of CapitalCare, CEO of George Washington University Health Plan, and Vice President of Operations and Finance at Georgetown University Health Plan. In New York City, he was Assistant Health Commissioner for Communicare. He was health resource advisor to the City of New York, and currently consults similarly with business coalitions. Mr. Metz has held academic appointments at Schools of Medicine at the University of North Carolina at Chapel Hill, Georgetown University, George Washington University, and Columbia University.

Kathleen E. Powderly, PhD, is Acting Director, Division of Humanities in Medicine and Clinical Assistant Professor of Nursing and Obstetrics/Gynecology at the State University of New York, Downstate Medical Center. Dr. Powderly teaches clinical ethics to students and practitioners in medicine, nursing, and allied health professions. She is the Vice Chairperson of the Kings County Hospital Center/UHB Ethics Committee, an ethics consultant to the Long Island College Hospital, and an Adjunct Associate at The Hastings Center. Dr. Powderly was educated at the Niagara University (BS), Yale University (MSN), and Columbia University (PhD). Her PhD is in Sociomedical Sciences.

Joanne K. Singleton, PhD, RN, CS, FNP, is Professor at Pace University and Co-Director of the Institute for Health Aging. Previously, she was Associate Professor, Chairperson and Director, Nurse Practitioner Programs, State University of New York, Health Science Center at Brooklyn. Dr. Singleton has her own practice at University Hospital, Brooklyn. Her experience over 25 years has included direct patient care, clinical supervision, nursing administration, education, and long term care research. She is a Fellow in the National Academies of Practice. She has received a diploma in nursing (St. Clare's Hospital School of Nursing), a BA (Marymount Manhattan College), an MA (New School for Social Research), a BSN (Regents College), and a PhD (Adelphi University).

Robert Stanyon, MS, BSN, is Assistant Vice President, Risk Management and Research, FOJP Service Corporation, which is the risk management advisor to the UJA Federation of New York, its hospitals, and its agencies. He is responsible for the risk management and safety and security services to nine hospitals, 10 nursing homes, and approximately 50 social service agencies. Key aspects of these programs are data services specific to risk management and interactive online professional staff education initiatives. He is past President and a member of the Board of Directors of the Association for Healthcare Risk Management of New York. He holds degrees from Syracuse University (BS), the University of New Hampshire (MS), Quinsigamond Community College (ASN), and St. Peter's College (BSN).

Amy Wysoker, PhD, RN, APRN, BC, is a certified clinical specialist in adult psychiatric mental health nursing and a psychiatric nurse practitioner. She is a psychiatric/mental health consultant and medical legal nurse consultant in private practice, and is an Associate Professor of Nursing, C.W. Post Campus of Long Island University. Active in professional organizations, Dr. Wysoker has been chair of the psychiatric/mental health clinical practice unit of the New York State Nurses Association and chair of the Mandatory Outpatient Treatment Taskforce of the American Psychiatric Nurses Association. Dr. Wysoker writes for a national psychiatric journal on legal and ethical issues pertaining to the psychiatric/mental health nurse and is a frequent guest lecturer at national conferences. She has received a BS (Nursing) from SUNY College of Nursing, an MA (Nursing) from New York University, and a PhD (Nursing) from Adelphi University.

Introduction to Second Edition—Risk Management

In the years since the first edition of this book, the critical importance of a sound risk management program in health care institutions has continued and increased unabated. Human frailty will always play a major part in the management of risks. Research studies, such as one by the Institute of Medicine,[1] continue to show that medical errors and incompetence kill thousands of people each year. Inadvertent administration of overdoses of medications and wrong medications still result in tragic outcomes. Inappropriate behavior by professionals and ancillary staff continues to incur legal action for assault, battery, lack of informed consent, malpractice, negligence, and wrongful death. Sexual harassment, wrongful termination, and discrimination by age, disability, gender, race, and sexual orientation plague the employees of health institutions. Issues of safety and security require a constant alertness so that adverse incidents can be avoided. Accusations of fraud still arise from improper billing for services and inappropriate use of research funds. Adaptations of medical therapies based on recent research pose potential risks when there are conflicting opinions as to the appropriate therapy.

Sophisticated technology has introduced new liability areas and uncharted concerns for risk management, such as the use of robots in medical and surgical care; telemedicine for diagnosis and therapy; human and mechanical organ transplantation; and the therapeutic use of stem cells. In evaluating medications and devices, the powerful role of the federal Food and Drug Administration is evident in the frequency with which it mandates recalls. With the new emphasis on privacy, the federal Health Insurance Portability and Accountability Act (HIPAA) requires attention to the management of risks related to the huge amounts of medical, personal, and financial data collected about patients in health institutions. Emerging concepts of enterprise liability further expand risk potential in health care institutions engaged in associated activities such as ambulance or oxygen services, real estate interests, and home care.

After the horrific events of September 11, 2001, when hijacked airplanes were used as missiles to destroy the World Trade Center in New York City, the reality of terrorism was made clear to health care institutions. Additionally, the distribution of anthrax spores via the U.S. mail highlighted the risk of bioterrorism and the potential use of smallpox as an agent of such terrorism as well. Health care institutions were stimulated, as were many other organizations throughout the nation, to review and update their disaster plans and to increase their participation in emergency preparedness.

During the past few years, the continuous avalanche of risk management problems awaiting resolution has led to a focus on patient safety. Protecting the public became a rallying cry, waking up state governments responsible for licensing health professionals and professional societies organized for the common good of their practitioners. Physicians are being charged with malpractice, malfeasance, fraud, patient abuse, and negligent practice. Problems such as alcoholism, drug abuse, and incapacitation among physicians and other health care practitioners are being uncovered.

Increasingly, the actions of licensing authorities result in suspension of practice, revocation of license, and limitation of practice. Hospital and health facilities are mandated to inquire of the National Practitioner Data Bank to check the backgrounds of physicians. Consequently, this curbs the movement from state to state of identified miscreants. Rights of physicians, rights of institutions, and rights of patients are in challenging competition.

New data has evoked changes in diagnosis and appropriate therapy guidelines as promulgated by the American Medical Association, medical specialty societies, health insurance companies, and governmental agencies. These utilize the best available knowledge at the time and are updated as new research data is released or technology evolves. Of course, controversy is engendered by proponents of one or another guideline and those who are reluctant to abandon their customary practices. Opponents of the experts who define appropriate community standards and practices complain about the imposition of "cookbook medicine."

In our multicultural society, citizens are better educated, knowledgeable, and armed with information when they utilize the services of health care professionals and institutions. They ask questions and want intelligent answers, in their own language, that they can understand. They have rights, need to consent to their treatment, must be told the risks and benefits of available alternatives, and consent to participation in research. This is not a silent generation. Only the best outcomes will be tolerated in obstetrics, orthopedics, and other surgical specialties. Expectations are high for appropriate medical care rendered in a humane manner with compassion, dignity, and privacy.

The unending need for risk management may be attributed to a number of variables. Certainly, the recent difficulties in the overall economy of the nation have not helped. Health care institutions have ceaselessly struggled to contain ever-rising costs. In addition, there is ubiquitous access to the Internet and to lawyers. Individuals have maintained a persistent, rapid propensity to initiate litigation against health care institutions. Even though our society is prone to litigation, frequently there may indeed be justification for legal action against the inadvertent errors and incompetence of health care professionals. However, monetary awards from litigation drastically reduce the resources available to render high-quality health care to those in need. Reacting to the huge increase in malpractice coverage premiums, some obstetricians have even abandoned the delivery of babies.

Risk management operates in this dangerous minefield. Programs attempt to ensure that institutional administration, policies, and procedures provide a safe and secure environment for patients, visitors, health professionals, support staff, and employees. Every organizational department, service, unit, committee, and employee must be involved in daily activities that assure that the patient/institution, patient/health care provider, and patient/employee interactions are beneficial ones.

Plainly put, risk management for health care institutions involves the protection of the assets of organizations, agencies, and individual providers. To achieve that financial well-being, risk managers strive to eliminate, to mitigate, to prevent, and to defend against errors. Balance sheets reveal that risk management activities yield cost savings for all types of institutions and organizations.

Risk management requires a strategic approach to addressing these issues, and this approach should be integrated with the institution's strategic plan, mission, long-term objectives, strategies, and policies with an understanding of the community in which it operates. In general, the risk management process consists of five steps:

1. Identifying and analyzing the exposures to loss.
2. Examining the feasibility of alternative techniques, risk control to stop losses, and risk financing to pay for losses.
3. Selecting the apparent best technique(s).
4. Implementing the chosen technique(s).
5. Monitoring and improving the risk management program itself.

This book offers governing boards, chief executive officers, administrators, and students of health professions the opportunity to organize and devise a successful risk management program. Section 1 introduces risk management and covers five areas of generic concern: operation dynamics, regulations, employer risks, patient communications, and financing. In Section 2, there are three chapters on strategic approaches to evaluation, ethics, and safety and security. Lastly, Section 3 deals with specific strategic risk areas in seven chapters: malpractice, liability reduction strategies, psychiatry, long term care and home care, high-risk areas in hospitals, managed care, and integrated health care delivery systems.

To emphasize actual situations, almost 200 real-life case studies are highlighted throughout the book, along with practical guidelines for risk managers. At times, relevant material is briefly repeated in these case studies because the information is appropriate to the material. There is also a comprehensive index to guide readers to their desired data.

Considering the volume of material cited in this book, it's apparent that this hasn't been a solitary accomplishment. Our contributors deserve our sincere thanks for an inclusive approach to their subject matter. These experts in the field synthesized current subject matter to assist health care providers with practical risk management strategies. A number of consultants reviewed the material for accuracy and relevance. For their efforts, we thank James E. Allen, PhD; Matthew J. Avitable, PhD; Angela A. Bennett, MD; Alvin M. Berk, PhD; Harry F. Blair, JD; Delores Bowman, RN; Charles Blum, JD; Vincent J. Cardozo; Denis B. Collins; Daniel Cowell, MD; M.P. Demos, MD, JD; Ivan R. Durbak; Leonard Glass, MD; Joseph Hayden; Edward J. Hinman, MD; Pascal J. Imperato, MD; Lorraine E. Jenkins, RN; Franklin Kavaler, JD; Gregory E. Kliot, MD; Spencer Lubin, MD; Jack Lubowsky, PhD; Joseph Lynaugh; Jane C. McConnell, RN, JD; Sheila McCullagh, RN; Karol L. Murov, RN; Stephen N. Rosenberg, MD; Andrea M. Spiegel; Terry Straub, RN, MBA; Peter B. Suskind; Gloria Valencia, MD; and Cecelia E. Yeaton. While these consultants graciously read parts of the manuscript, commented, or made suggestions, we remain responsible for the content.

Ann Cohen provided critical editorial assistance. Research associates Ester E. Bown, Gary W. Chien, MD, Yevgeniy Kaplan, Amy B. Lemel, Hester Suh, Christopher R. Springer, and Anthony Ugligloro supplied countless hours locating and analyzing the relevant literature and preparing drafts of material. Jeanny Brodsky, Lois A. Hahn, Eudelle P. Marshall, Jean C. Russell, and Cynthia F. Skeete effortlessly and efficiently handled the secretarial tasks as the need arose. This book has been a cooperative task and we deeply appreciate the work of our contributors and all the others who helped us.

Florence Kavaler, MD, MPH
Allen D. Spiegel, PhD, MPH

March 2003

Reference

1. Kohn, K., Corrigan, J., Donaldson, M., eds. (1999). *To Err Is Human: Building a Safer Health System.* Committee on Quality Health Care in America, Institute of Medicine, National Academy of Sciences, National Academy Press: Washington, D.C.

Risk Management in Health Care Institutions

SECTION 1 | Introduction to Risk Management Strategy

CHAPTER 1 Risk Management Dynamics

Florence Kavaler
Allen D. Spiegel

Risk management for health care institutions is not a new socially and/or legally ordained program. About four thousand years ago, the Babylonian Code of Hammurabi ordained severe punishment for physicians who caused death or harm through their own malpractice:

> If a physician operates on a man for a severe wound with a bronze lancet and causes a man's death, or opens an abscess in the eye of a man with a bronze lancet and destroys the man's eye, they shall cut off his fingers.[1]

In the 1970s, an upsurge in malpractice suits created a crisis situation for health care providers. Faced with the threat of lawsuits involving huge dollar amounts, the health care institutions and agencies employed risk management personnel and initiated activities designed to prevent adverse patient outcomes (APOs) and potentially compensable events (PCEs).[2] In this prevention mode, focusing on the organization's bottom line, a governmental risk manager earned a place on the 1994 Business Insurance Risk Management Honor Roll for effecting programs that attacked losses on several fronts (see Box 1-1).

RISK MANAGEMENT DEFINED

Risk management for health care entities can be defined as an organized effort to identify, assess, and reduce, where appropriate, risks to patients, visitors, staff, and organizational assets. Another definition is:

BOX 1-1

Ronald J. Guilfoile, risk manager, city of St. Paul (MN) saved at least $20 million: $10 million through workers' compensation activities and $10 million by setting up an open-ended health maintenance organization.[3]

a program designed to reduce the incidence of preventable accidents and injuries to minimize the financial loss to the institution should an injury or accident occur.[4]

From a managed care viewpoint, the risk management definition can be expanded to encompass a comprehensive rationale:

> Risk management is the process of assuring that covered persons (members) receive all of the health care services they need, to which they are entitled under the contract, no more and no less at the most cost-effective level possible by reducing or eliminating untoward incidents (occurrences) that might lead to injury or illness of patients, visitors or employees.[5]

Untoward or adverse outcomes tend to yield a broad spectrum of possible explanations. A research scientist argued that there was no such thing as a medical accident. As a caveat for the doctors, he quoted from Shakespeare's *Julius Caesar*: "The fault . . . is not in our stars, but in ourselves." He concluded that more precise medical terminology would help physicians reduce harm. "Accident conveys a sense that bad outcomes are to be explained in terms of fate and bad luck rather than a set of understandable, and possibly changeable, antecedents."[6]

PROGRESSIVE STEPS IN THE RISK MANAGEMENT PROCESS

In straightforward terms, risk management is the protection of assets. Risk management personnel usually accomplish this goal by following four steps in progression or combination: risk identification, risk analysis, risk control/treatment, and risk financing.[7] In slightly different wording, the risk management process can move from (1) identifying exposures to accidental loss that may interfere with an organization's objectives, to (2) examining feasible alternative risk management techniques for dealing with these exposures, to (3) selecting the best risk management techniques, to (4) implementing the chosen risk management techniques, to (5) monitoring the results of the chosen techniques to determine effectiveness. Arguing that this risk management process needs refinement to reflect reality, Burlando[8] opts for the **5i** system, a measured application of five descriptors:

- **Investigate:** observe or study by close examination and systematic inquiry.
- **Inform:** present in material form.
- **Influence:** affect or alter by indirect or intangible means.
- **Interpret:** explain or tell the meaning of; present in understandable terms.
- **Integrate:** form or blend into a whole; unite with something else.

Furthermore, Burlando declares that the mission of risk management "is to select, coordinate and efficiently apply interdisciplinary skills to harmful uncertainties which may diminish the future value of public, private or personal resources."

A physician/lawyer operating a risk management firm advises clients to adhere to the "Big A" strategy. "Big A" means to "anticipate" what can go wrong and to be prepared to handle that possibility. Even if a patient specifies no allergy to penicillin, prudent risk managers find it appropriate to be ready if an unanticipated reaction occurs.[9]

A Veteran's Administration needle-stick risk potential can focus operational steps (see Box 1-2).

Risk Identification

Risk identification involves the collection of information about current and past patient care occurrences and other events that present potential loss to the institution. In alphabetical order, such risks can be identified as antitrust violations, breach of

> **BOX 1-2**
>
> In one year, the VA Medical Centers reported 4,791 needlestick injuries. There are more than 40 safe, approved needle and sharps devices in the United States. Questions to be considered: (1) the extent to which safer devices are needed and (2) whether the devices will reduce the number of percutaneous injuries.[10]

contract, casualty exposure, defamation, embezzlement, environmental damage, fraud and abuse, general liability, hazardous substance exposure, professional malpractice, securities violations, transportation liability, and workers' compensation. It is vital to realize that risk identification is not a one-time static analysis. The continuous identification of possible liability risks, such as unexpected treatment outcomes, patient complaints about care, and adverse events that did, or could, cause harm, must be an ongoing process. Early warning data can occur in security reports, quality assessment studies, accreditation and/or licensure surveys, and patient complaints. Risk managers should receive a steady stream of information from specific departments, such as when attorneys seek chart information from medical records in preparation for a suit; billing offices, following up on delinquent statements, hear aggravated complaints; volunteers hear complaints because patients don't regard them as employees; and quality assessment activities yield data connected with their screening and review procedures. Furthermore, statistical data from insurers can identify the high-risk individuals and services involved in the payment of claims.

Risk Analysis

Risk analysis entails the evaluation of past experience and current exposure to eliminate or limit substantially the impact of risk on cash flow, community image, and employee and medical staff morale. Seriousness of the risk must be considered in terms of the probable severity to the individual and to the organization, the number of people possibly harmed, and the likelihood and/or frequency of occurrence. Closed claims data are most helpful in gaining an insight into the evaluation of current risks. A priority of high-risk activities for the risk manager logically develops from risk analysis information.

Risk Control/Treatment

Risk control and/or treatment is the organization's response to significant risk areas, as well as its rejoinder to limit the liability associated with incidents that have occurred. This is the most common function associated with risk management programs. Loss control activities within an institution should not be viewed as a single formal program, because of the varied interrelated and overlapping elements. Often, loss control activity is equated with safety management, since the basic objectives are similar. At times, the quality assessment functions also cloud the specifics of loss control. It is not unusual for a loss/risk control program to be a collaborative effort involving risk management, quality assessment, and safety management. Ideally, a risk control/loss management program should categorize the potential liability problems into four areas: bodily injury, liability losses, property loss, and consequential losses. Exhibit 1-1 illustrates some elements of risk exposure. Note that the health care organization's governing board and the chief executive officer (CEO) are responsible for the overall risk control system. In the second circle surrounding the board and the CEO are the administrative personnel who

EXHIBIT 1-1 RISK CONTROL SYSTEM

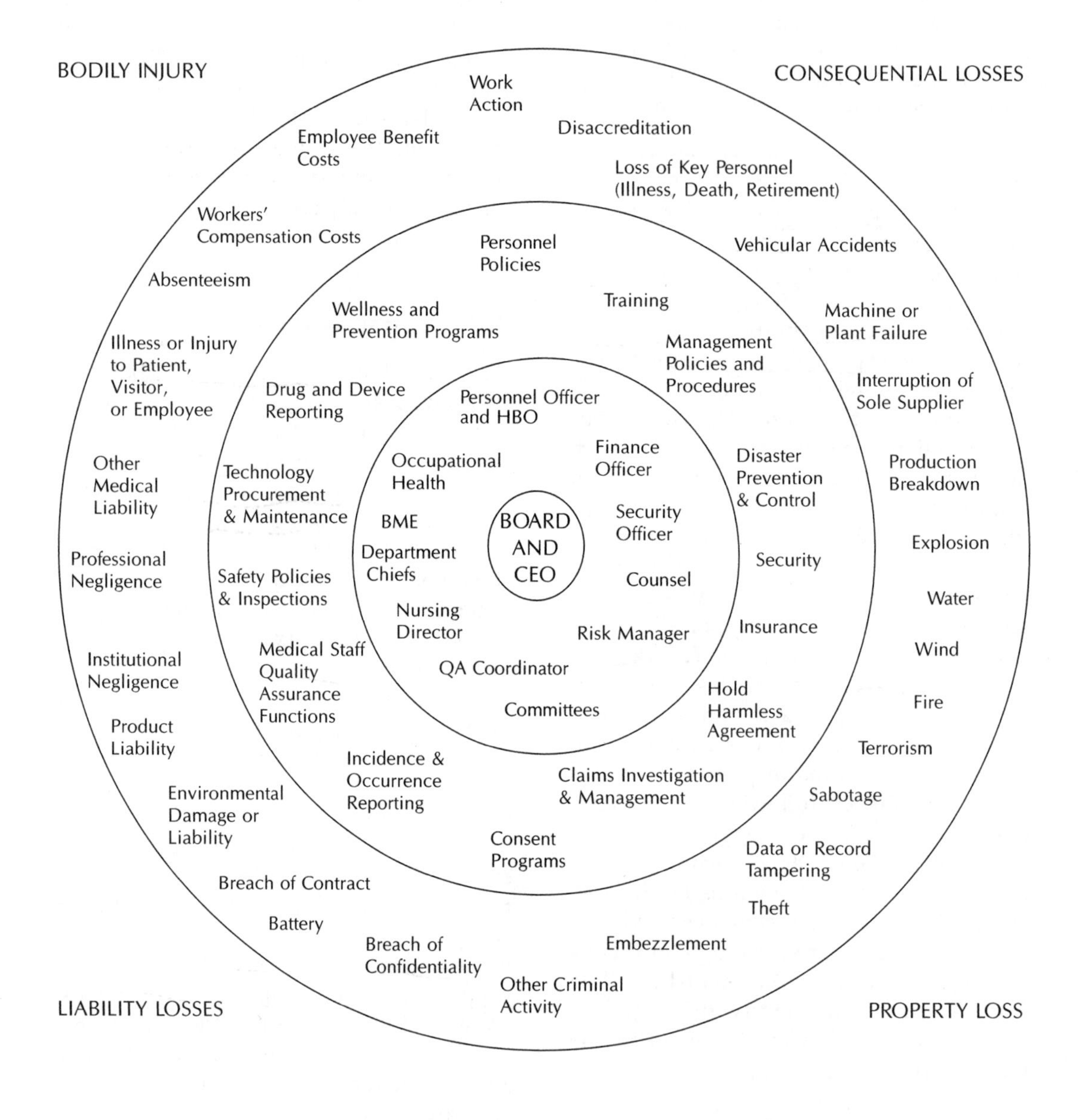

implement the programs. Specific elements in the third and fourth circles illustrate bodily injury, liability losses, property loss, and consequential losses.

There are a variety of methods and a combination of techniques for controlling the risks: risk acceptance, exposure avoidance, loss prevention, loss reduction, exposure segregation, and contractual transfer.

Risk Acceptance

Essentially, risk acceptance means that the facility decides not to purchase insurance against specific adverse events because the risk cannot be avoided, reduced, or transferred. In addition, the probability of loss is not great and the potential fiscal consequences are within the institution's capabilities to resolve.

Exposure Avoidance

After he investigated a hospital's major liability losses, a consultant advised: "Eliminate the emergency room!" In theory, exposure avoidance aims to rid the institution of the service, personnel, or equipment that may cause the loss, or to advise the institution never to be involved in providing the service or program at all.

Loss Prevention

Using early detection and investigation, risk managers examine the medical records, incident reports, patient complaints, and patient billing to pinpoint loss prevention areas. Some losses in specific services can be prevented by the involvement of medical and ancillary staff in educational programs and preventive maintenance. Some even advise keeping the patient fully informed of all mishaps, thereby relying on the satisfied patient not to sue the institution.

Loss Reduction

Although there may be loss prevention activities, loss reduction usually involves the management of claims and ensures that all records are preserved and that all personnel are prepared in the event of a loss. Settlements and releases conclude loss reduction efforts. Without abandoning high-risk services, loss reduction or minimization aims to control adverse events by focusing on activities such as staff education, revisions of policy, and procedures.

Exposure Segregation

Administrators can decide to separate out or to duplicate the specific offending services, personnel, or activities identified as exposure risks to the institution. Risk managers can suggest intensive control actions; for example, to reduce medication errors in a hospital, all pharmaceuticals can be disbursed from a central location. If the problem appears to be the distance between medication source and delivery, satellite pharmacies can be established on selected floors.

Contractual Transfer

A facility can transfer or shift the risk to the organization that provides the service through insurance or contract. This allows the institution to provide a high-risk service while avoiding liability loss. If a contracted company operates the emergency room of a hospital, the facility avoids risk by ensuring that the contract includes the assumption of all risk by the contractor. Although private insurance premiums can handle contractual liability coverage, the facility may still be responsible for selecting a qualified contractor.

Risk Financing

Appropriate indemnification of risk requires a comprehensive prospective and retrospective organizational analysis of the direct expenditures associated with quantifying and funding losses and risk management activities. Financing choices are self-insurance, commercial insurance coverage, insurance premiums, and funding for any related risk management activities and liability payouts. While risk financing may be the responsibility of the institution's or agency's financial office, risk managers can make a valuable contribution to the deliberations by communicating effectively with the finance department, using terminology that finance personnel can understand.[11]

RISK MANAGEMENT ACTIVITIES

An examination of the eight minimal components of a risk management program, as defined by the American Society of Healthcare Risk Management (ASHRM), engenders a fuller understanding of a risk management program:[12]

1. There must be a designated, trained, and experienced risk manager who must obtain at least eight hours of continuing risk management education annually.
2. Risk managers must have access to all necessary credentialing, management, and medical data.
3. Institutions must commit the necessary resources to risk management through a written policy statement that is adopted by the governing body, medical staff, and administration.
4. Facilities must have a system in place for the identification, review, and analysis of unanticipated adverse outcomes.
5. Organizations must have the means to centralize risk management data and to share and integrate data collection and analysis with other clinical and administrative departments.
6. Periodically, at least annually, risk managers must provide the organization's governing body a report that reviews and evaluates risk management program activity.
7. Risk managers must ensure that medical staff and new employee educational programs on minimizing patients' risks and addressing high-risk clinical areas are provided.
8. Risk managers must forward information on individual practitioners, such as malpractice claim history, knowledge of adverse outcomes, and incident reporting data, to the committees that evaluate the competency of medical staff.

Strictly from a business-oriented approach, risk management aims to accomplish three major functions:

- Reducing the organization's risk of a malpractice suit by maintaining or improving the quality of care.
- Reducing the probability of a claim being filed after a potentially compensable event (PCE) has occurred.
- Preserving the institution's assets once a claim has been filed.

Without doubt, risk management includes quality assessment and related activities, such as medical staff credentialing, occurrence screening, incident reporting, and peer review. In addition, risk management seeks to promote effective communication and a positive attitude between patients and staff, and to make patients less likely to sue for malpractice.

Physicians agree on three ideal attributes for a professional risk manager: the ability to present facts rather than feelings, the ability to be concise in writing or stating the situation; and the wherewithal to understand the facts and to respond to critical questions. In contrast, nurses identify three common qualities of a good risk manager: a demonstrated willingness to listen, an understanding of the other person's responsibilities and problems, and a team approach to problem solving that involves asking input from others in forming solutions. These responses lead to the conclusion that a risk manager's basic skills must include the art of persuasion, the expertise to be a keen listener, and knowledge about team building.[13] Importantly, risk managers must realize that the board of directors or governing body is part of the team, even though that directorate is not the immediate supervisor. Communicating effectively with the board requires the use of these basic risk management skills.[14] Risk events, PCEs, and APOs are quite diverse, as revealed in a survey of more than two thousand corporate executives who identified the 15 most important risk management areas (see Box 1-3).

Legislative and regulatory mandates also guide risk management activities to focus on preventive maintenance of equipment and devices, on patient safety measures, and on enhancing the safety of employees and visitors. Examples of such measures include ensuring that equipment is clean, properly calibrated, and in good repair; that a nurse call system is functional; and that security personnel patrol well-lighted parking lots and hallways.

CLASSIFICATION OF RISK LIABILITIES

Risk events include a multitude of sins: untoward incidents occurring to patients (clients), employees, or visitors; use of inadequate equipment or procedures to perform a task; use of improperly trained or qualified individuals to perform a task; improper manufacture of a product; and contamination and/or pollution of the environment. Failure to perform a service may prevent the achievement of a desired outcome or lead to an undesired outcome, may cause harm or injury, and may result from an error of omission or commission.

BOX 1-3

The Fifteen Most Important Risk Management Areas[15]

Caps on noneconomic and/or punitive damages	85%*
Spiraling health care costs	83
Modification of joint and several liability doctrine	77
Managed care programs	73
Workers' compensation cost shifting	71
Unpredictable price swings in the insurance market	70
Self insurance regulation and taxes	68
Workers' compensation health reforms	68
Workers' compensation claims proof and benefits payable	67
Workplace safety	67
Comprehensive disaster plan	65
Liability for court-ordered cleanups	64
Workers' compensation cost containment	64
Use of alternative dispute resolution mechanisms	64
Liability for transfer of contaminated property	64

*Percentage total includes "high importance" and "above average importance" ratings.

Some specific examples of risk events, classified by type, are:

Property risks: structural damage; vehicular accidents; technological obsolescence; theft; sabotage; production breakdown; and consequential losses.

Casualty/liability risks: professional negligence (PCEs and APOs); workers' compensation; directors and officers liability; environmental liability; and product liability.

Employee benefit risks: cost of benefit plans; disability claims; and Employee Retirement and Income Security Act (ERISA) violations.

Risks can be identified through the use of records and files, flowcharts, personal inspections, expert consultations, surveys, questionnaires, and financial statements. Risk analysis considers the frequency and severity of the loss as related to profit, stable earnings, growth, continuous operation, legal requirements, and humanitarian concerns. A comparative assessment combines cost-benefit analyses with frequency of risk events and with populations affected to yield a weighted risk analysis. Interestingly, people may accept new technology with perceived injury risks or reject the technology because of a minimal risk of injury.[16] Using a mortality standard, researchers identified comparative risk data (see Box 1-4).

From an expenditure viewpoint, the median cost of a life saved by childhood immunizations or prenatal care is negligible—less than zero. Other interventions can be calculated in terms of the cost of a life saved: flu shots ($600); heart disease ($14,000); breast cancer screening ($17,000); kidney dialysis ($46,000); and heart transplant ($104,000). Medical care generally saves lives at less cost than workplace safety or environmental measures do.[18] Substantial resources may be devoted to problems that are relatively minor. Since the viability of the institution is at stake, efforts must be made to evaluate and weigh the risk to preserve assets and to restrict the loss.

RISK RED FLAGS

One or more "red flags" in connection with a patient's care should alert health care providers to take actions to remedy the situation. Appropriate care and treatment should be provided, and patient records should reflect that care. In addition, the risk management department should be notified. Some specific red flags are:

Treatment conditions: poor treatment results; repetition of the problem; lack of follow-up care; and equipment malfunction.

Patient relations: dissatisfied patient; antagonistic patient or family members; complaining relatives; patient discharged against medical advice; intimidated patient; poor physician/patient relationship; and poor staff/patient relationship.

Practice management: poorly maintained medical records; lack of critical policies and procedures; and excessive volume of patients.

BOX 1-4

Comparative Risk of Death per Million People per Year[17]

Twenty-one cigarettes in a lifetime	10
Airline crash in ten trips	10
Appendectomy operation	200
Auto accident	210
At least one pack of cigarettes per day	3,000
All risks, age 45–54	5,840

Conduct of staff: acting outside the scope of training; lack of qualified supervision; performance of a procedure for the first time without supervision; outspoken or rude behavior; personality conflict; and poor physician/staff relationship.

RISK MANAGEMENT TOOLS

Prompt identification of injuries and accidents to patients, visitors, and staff members has been a primary concern of risk management programs since they were first used in hospitals. In this manner, institutions address potential problems and correct their causes before they can occur again. In addition, administrators can take immediate action to avoid or lessen the cost of a lawsuit. Three systems are used to accomplish prompt identification: incident reporting, occurrence reporting, and occurrence screening.

Incident Reporting

Incident reporting systems were developed in the late 1940s and early 1950s to identify events that were not consistent with the routine operation of the hospital or the routine care of particular patients or visitors, such as malfunctioning equipment or medication errors. Box 1-5 illustrates the use of an incident reporting system.

BOX 1-5

Nurse Jones enters Mrs. Smith's room and finds her sitting on the floor next to her bed. Mrs. Smith says she slipped and fell, but she thinks she's okay. Nurse Jones appraises her condition and helps her back into bed. Mrs. Smith's doctor is notified and Nurse Jones reports to her supervisor. She is told to fill out an incident report.[19]

Incident reporting systems have incorporated computer technology. Calgary General Hospital (Alberta, Canada) devised a computer program that identifies five major incident categories: falls, medication errors, treatment/procedure errors, assaults, and computer errors.[20] Another computer system focuses on the early identification of patterns and trends in the "how" and "why" of untoward events. Coded vulnerability indicators include the following specific options: system failure (22 choices); diagnostic tests (12 choices); consultation (28 choices); documentation (37 choices); patient rapport (7 choices); clinical conduct (50 choices); human factors (14 choices); and a miscellaneous narrative section. Analysis of the adverse events yields an awareness and a basis for improved clinical practice and professional risk avoidance.[21]

Reporting systems rely on facility personnel to recognize and report an incident to a risk manager, a quality assurance coordinator, or a member of the management team. Reports tend to focus on treatment procedures, medication, intravenous and blood errors, infections, birth injuries, falls, burns, and equipment problems that could result in claims against the organization. By themselves, the reports do not produce a complete picture of the number of incidents that occur in a facility. According to some estimates, incident reports identify about 5 to 30 percent of adverse patient occurrences at a hospital. Staff may not report incidents for several reasons: lack of understanding of what a reportable incident is, fear of punitive action, concern that incident reporting exposes them to personal liability, reluctance to report incidents involving physicians, lack of time for paperwork, and lack of knowledge about the results that an effective incident reporting system can achieve.

Only the person who witnessed the incident, or first discovered it, should file and sign an incident report. Anybody else with firsthand knowledge should file a separate report. Critically, anybody filling out an incident report should keep in mind that the written report will be available to lawyers, and any admissions or accusations could be damaging to the reporting individual, as well as to the employer. There are several dos and don'ts regarding the filing of an incident report:[21]

- **Do** record the details in objective terms, describing exactly what was seen and heard and nothing else: Jones writes that she found Mrs. Smith on the floor beside the bed, not that she fell.
- **Do** describe what actions were taken at the scene: helping patient back into bed; assessment findings; any instructions to patient.
- **Do** document the time of the incident, the name of the doctor notified, and the time notified, and have the supervisor review the report.
- **Don't** include names and addresses of witnesses, even if the form requests such information. Such data make it easier for attorneys to sue the institution. Check with the supervisor on supplying this information.
- **Don't** file the incident report with the patient's chart. Send the incident report to the person designated by the organization to collect and review such matters.
- **Don't** admit liability or blame or identify others as responsible. Obviously, this incrimination could be harmful to the agency if a lawsuit ensues.

Occurrence Reporting

Some states and insurers require or encourage institutions to develop lists of specific adverse patient occurrences (APOs) that must be reported by staff, physicians, or both—that is, occurrence reporting. APOs could include maternal or infant death, a surgical patient's unplanned return to the unit, or an allergic reaction to medication. Although the lists vary at the discretion of the organization, the insurers, or the states, specifying the reportable events increases the APO identification process by 40 to 60 percent. Because the system depends on individuals for reporting, however, many incidents still may not be written up. To promote better reporting, some states grant immunity from legal action to persons who provide or evaluate risk management information. There are also efforts to protect against the possibility that documents generated by the risk management program will become public information.

Occurrence Screening

Occurrence screening systems identify deviations from normal procedures or expected treatment outcomes and may be used in both risk management and quality assessment. An occurrence screening system uses criteria to identify APOs but does not rely on staff members to report the adverse events. Typical examples of APOs that can be identified using such a system include transfer from a general care unit to a special care unit, nosocomial infection, or unplanned return to an operating room. Medical record analysts or trained data screeners systematically review patient records using the prespecified criteria to discover APOs. Peer reviewers then determine whether a deviation from acceptable standards of care occurred. This screening can be conducted during or after the patient care, or at both times. An estimated 80 to 85 percent of APOs can be identified by occurrence screening—a much higher percentage than obtained through incident reporting systems. Furthermore, a risk management program that combines occurrence screening with other data sources, such as incident reporting, infection surveillance, antibiotics use review, and medical staff peer review, can identify 90 to 95 percent of APOs—a greater proportion than any individual method can identify.

RISK AND QUALITY OF CARE

Any risk management process may sound harsh and lead to the conclusion that the health care industry is adopting a businesslike, bottom-line approach without consideration for the humane aspects of providing care to people in need. This perception is not accurate, although even charitable and well-meaning organizations must maintain financial viability to continue their worthwhile endeavors. Significantly, governmental and voluntary nonprofit health care agencies must compete with proprietary health care providers in an open marketplace. That fact is a major stimulus in moving all health care providers to reduce their losses and to attract patients to the services being offered. For this reason, risk management by health care institutions becomes an integral tool of sound management. Effective risk management strategy "should be judged not just in terms of whether it saves the provider money, although that certainly is a legitimate and important goal, but also should be judged against the fundamental objective of contributing to the quality of services."[22] It is possible, however, that some patients covered by different insurance programs receive differential care. A study of problems in the quality of care among Medicare and Medicaid patients came to a startling and disturbing conclusion:

> Of great concern is the fact that premature death directly resulted from confirmed quality problems in 53 (7.4%) of 706 Medicare and in 42 (27.2%) of 154 Medicaid patients. These deaths were avoidable and were directly due to departures from accepted standards of medical care. Also of concern is the fact that readmission occurred in 60 Medicare and 18 Medicaid patients, resulting from confirmed quality of care problems during the previous admission.[23]

These connections are affirmed by the accreditation standards of the Joint Commission on Accreditation of Healthcare Organizations (JCAHO). Effective January 1, 1989, every applicable institution that seeks JCAHO accreditation must show substantial compliance with several standards that apply only to the quality of care and patient safety aspects of risk management:

- A hospital's governing body must provide resources and support for the quality assurance and risk management functions related to patient care and safety.
- A hospital's chief executive officer, through the management and administrative staff, must assure appropriate medical staff involvement in and support for
  - — the identification of areas of potential risk in patient care and safety.
  - — the development of criteria for identifying cases with potential risk re patient care and safety and the evaluation of these cases.
  - — the correction of problems in patient care and safety identified by risk management activities.
  - — the design of programs to reduce risk in patient care and safety.
- A hospital's management must establish and maintain operational linkages between risk management functions related to patient care and safety, and quality assurance functions.

- A hospital's management must ensure that existing information relative to the quality of patient care is readily accessible to both the quality assurance and the risk management functions.

RISK MANAGEMENT/QUALITY ASSURANCE FUNCTIONS AND ACTIVITIES

In 1980 the American Hospital Association (AHA) formed the Interdisciplinary Task Force on Quality Assurance and Risk Management to define the relationship of hospital risk management (RM) to quality assurance (QA). There is a causal connection between risk management, the quality of care, and quality assurance programs. A quality-risk continuum exits, and quality assurance and risk management programs must work together to achieve their own goals. Four dicta emerge from the quality-risk spectrum:

- Quality control is the process of assuring that standards are met. The objective is 100 percent met, or zero defects.
- Risk control assures that losses due to property, casualty, or employee benefit risks are prevented, reduced in frequency and/or severity, or transferred.
- Quality control is doing what you want to do: meeting standards.
- Risk control is not doing what you don't want to do: preventing errors.

RM and QA Comparisons

The AHA task force established in 1980 concluded that risk management and quality assurance are two activities whose functions sometimes overlap. When that overlap occurs, their purposes and methods are almost indistinguishable. During their deliberations, the task force identified the functions of RM and QA, as well as the major differences between them (see Box 1-6). An examination of the comparison between RM and QA leads to the relevant conclusion that a close working arrangement between the two activities is unavoidable. The AHA task force concluded that integrating RM and QA, where feasible, could achieve the following results:

- Maximization of the use of limited resources.
- Elimination of duplication because data sources for both activities are the same.
- Creation of a means for developing new solutions to problems.
- Facilitation of the development of training programs.
- Improvement of the budget process by identifying and consolidating budget requirements for both activities.

A requirement of the JCAHO mandates that hospitals seeking approval have programs that link risk management with quality assurance.[24] The question is whether this linking of quality assurance and risk management increases the proclivity of physicians to order an excessive number of diagnostic tests and/or procedures. A review by the U.S. Congress Office of Technology Assessment (OTA) concluded that the QA-RM link "may promote quality-enhancing rather than wasteful defensive medicine."[26]

ADMINISTRATION OF RISK MANAGEMENT PROGRAMS

Goals and Prime Objectives

A risk management system aims to identify, evaluate, and reduce risks to patients, visitors, employees, and professional staff involved in the provision of health care services. There should be a written description of the program, periodic revisions and review, and amendments when changes are

BOX 1-6

A Comparison of RM and QA Functions[25]

RISK MANAGEMENT	QUALITY ASSURANCE
• Protects the institution's financial assets. • Protects human and intangible resources. • Prevents injury to patients, visitors, and property. • Reduces loss by focusing on individual loss or on single accidents. • Prevents incidents by improving the quality of care through continuing and ongoing monitoring of agency activities. • Reviews each incident and the pattern of incidents through the application of the risk management process: risk identification; risk analysis; risk control; and risk financing.	• Reflects the institution's caring philosophy. • Improves the performance of all professionals and protects patients. • Focuses on the quality of care delivered by the organization. • Sets the quality of care rendered according to standards and measurable criteria. • Prevents future losses or patient injuries by continuous monitoring of problem resolution areas. • Searches for patterns of nonconformance with goals and standards using the following quality assurance processes: problem identification; problem assessment; corrective action; follow-up; and report of findings.
Differences	
• Concerned with acceptable levels of care from a legal standpoint. • Directed toward all persons, events, and environs in the health care setting. • Focused on legal, insurance, and risk financing activities.	• Concerned with optimal level of care. • Directed toward patient care. • Focused on improving care.

Source: Adapted from *Hospitals,* Vol. 55, No. 11, by permission, June 1, 1981, Copyright 1981, American Hospital Publishing, Inc.

made. All federal, state, and local legislation and regulations should be complied with and documented. Incidents such as fires, equipment malfunction, poisoning, strikes, disasters, and termination of vital services should be reported to the proper authorities.

With the help of a Risk Management Committee responsible to the Board of Directors, Mt. Sinai Hospital (Toronto, Canada) identified three objectives for its risk management program:[27]

1. To reduce the frequency of preventable adverse occurrences that lead to liability claims.
2. To reduce the probability of a claim's being filed after an adverse event has occurred.
3. To help control the costs of claims that do emerge.

Initiatives integrated into this risk management program included acting on the risks identified in the recommendations of a coroner's jury, in departmental reports, in incident analysis, in occurrence reporting, and in a claims summary database.

Responsibilities of a Risk Management Committee and/or Coordinator

Because a risk manager's activities involve the entire institution and all its programs and services, the responsibilities can evolve into a long, overwhelming list of tasks.[28] Many tasks overlap with other units and are cooperative in nature. Grouping the responsibilities delineates the descriptive scope of a risk manager's job.

Purpose, Accountability, and Authority Functions:

- Coordinate and carry out risk management activities in line with the program objectives.
- Secure written statements affirming the support of the governing body, the administration, and the medical staff for the risk management program.
- Describe the organizational reporting lines and the relationships between the risk manager and the rest of the institution.
- Prepare a written statement detailing the involvement of every department and service and their responsibilities in risk management activities.
- Provide for the flow of information among quality assurance, credentialing, peer review, and any risk management committee.
- Monitor all incidents related to patient care.
- Define the responsibility to recommend and implement corrective actions.
- Prepare a statement assuring the confidentiality of all data collected for the risk management program.

Specific Functions:

- Review the potentially compensable events (PCEs).
- Investigate the PCEs.
- Analyze and pinpoint trends in PCEs.
- Report appropriate PCEs to the insurance carrier.
- Assist in the resolution of conflicts among patients, physicians, and institution to avoid claims.
- Settle claims, obtaining liability releases, at the authority level approved by management. Adjust or write off bills as necessary within authority approved by management.
- Maintain files of all lawsuits.
- Assure protection of records and other evidence.
- Prepare the necessary material and people for a legal defense under the guidance of the insurance company and defense counsel.
- Represent the institution in legal proceedings within defined parameters.
- Assist and monitor the activities and charges of defense counsel.
- Provide risk management support/input to appropriate medical staff and institutional committees.
- Act as the institution's resource for risk management topics.
- Prepare reports to the board, the health care system, management, and other entities as directed.
- Comply with applicable regulatory codes and professional standards.
- Provide risk management education for institutional personnel, medical staff, and residents.
- Maintain professional competence through participation in seminars, conferences, and so on, and through membership in appropriate professional societies.

- Develop the annual risk management budget.
- Determine general, short-term, and long-term objectives.
- Evaluate the program regularly and update it as necessary.

Functional Relationships:

- Biomedical engineering re new products, equipment involved in PCE, record keeping, and risk management alerts.
- Quality assurance re PCE, professional staff, and incidents.
- Safety/fire/disaster committees.
- Employee health services.

Risk Management Committee

Programs should include a risk management committee to assist in prioritization of risk reduction activities and to act as a liaison to the various professional staffs in the hospital. A typical risk management committee has a physician chairman, as well as representation from the major medical and surgical services, the nursing department, the technical staff (biomedical engineering, radiology, respiratory services, clinical laboratory), the quality assessment department, and the risk manager. One or more members of the governing body and hospital counsel may be members. A risk management committee reviews key risk exposure information: all claims; all state-reported incidents; internal incidents of concern because of either the extent of injury or the potential for injury; emerging treads in delivery of care that present new avenues of exposure; and any other issues or events that may occur, or be averted, that may have the actuality or potential of heavy loss of financial resources or good reputation. A mix of clinical and technical personnel on the committee provides for multifaceted examination of loss potential and risk exposure of any situation. This committee reports to the medical staff, governing body, and administration and frequently serves as the primary source of ongoing education on loss prevention in a facility.

The goals of the risk managers and the administration in working within this committee are to facilitate information flow among various departments and services and to provide a central focus for collaborative loss control and risk reduction actions.

Responsibility of the Governing Body

A commitment, including accountability, to an institutionwide risk management program must be adopted in a written governing board policy. Governing body bylaws should include mechanisms for the approval of medical staff bylaws, including the appointment and reappointment of physicians. A mechanism must be established for reporting risk management activities to the board. If possible, a governing body member should be appointed to any risk management advisory group or committee.

Under the guidance of the governing board, one risk manager suggested that "chaos theory" offers an opportunity to enhance risk management. Chaos theory is "based on the simple principle that order can be found in disorder."[29] This theory concentrates on events that do not adhere to established principles, are unpredictable, do not result in a rational aftermath, and appear to disregard a lucid explanation. At a minimum, chaos theory provides a few buzzwords for risk managers. At most, chaos theory presents a unique prototype that has direct application to the risk management process. Five chaos theory concepts forge links to risk management practices:

1. Predictable patterns exist in apparent random events, since the nature of risk is universal; only the scale changes. Risk managers need to change their perspectives to study the larger universe, need to examine parallel systems, and need to avoid the isolation of increasing specialization.
2. There is a sensitive dependence on initial conditions. Small initial events need to be studied and related to larger outcomes. Could the minuscule wind from a butterfly's wings cause severe weather changes elsewhere in the world?
3. Risk managers usually deal with apparently discrete or chance events. Over time, specific patterns begin to materialize as the random repetitive behavior produces information. Risk managers need to know where to look for this information and extract the data to apply in their activities.
4. Risk managers must comprehend the intricate interconnected network of forces and external influences that determine the variety of eventual outcomes. Predictably, these forces include the institutional values, goals, and rules, such as a smoke-free workplace, a policy of hiring the handicapped, or a mandate to recycle waste products.
5. To move from the conspicuous and make connections to the improbable, risk managers must adopt new ways of looking for risks using a combination of intelligence and perspicacity.

SPECIFIC RISK MANAGEMENT FUNCTIONS

Incident Identification, Reporting, and Tracking

An identification and reporting process must exist to identify any circumstance or occurrence that may be injurious to a patient or that may result in an adverse outcome to a patient. Mortality, morbidity, infections, complications, errors in diagnosis, transfusions, results of treatments, and unimproved cases other than those related to the natural course of disease or illness should be reviewed. Each institution must define and list what constitutes a reportable incident and transmit that information to all employees and all regulatory bodies. A management system should include these elements:

- A time frame within which incidents must be reported.
- Designation of the individual to receive incident reports.
- Requirement that any employee or medical staff appointee who is aware of an incident must report it to the appropriate person.
- The sharing of information, at a minimum, between quality assurance and risk management.

Utilizing general purpose computer software, a multihospital group developed an automated quality assessment incident tracking system.[30] This computer program provided an efficient and effective mechanism to control and organize multiple staff assignments, to track tasks through due dates and participants, and to manage multiple objectives over the resolution cycle associated with hospital incident reporting. An individualized record of the incident's progress helped to identify useful and dysfunctional patterns in the resolution of the incident. Importantly, the system used existing computer hardware and software (WordPerfect and Lotus Agenda) while avoiding expensive resources and staff increases.

A successful program depends on the risk management staff's skill in obtaining relevant information. In any risk management program, the keystone to information gathering is the incident report. Originally designed by the insurance industry, the incident report is a tool that is the mainstay for risk assessment in all risk management programs in all industries.

Incident report forms are usually custom-designed for a health care facility by the risk management department, taking into consideration the type of information and the amount of detail for any event that needs to be collected for adequate computer tracking. To foster use, most risk managers prefer to sacrifice detail in favor of quick notification of an incident. Incident report forms should be devised so that they are unlike any other forms in use in the facility, and they should be easy to complete. User-friendly forms have frequently occurring incidents listed in alphabetical order, with a checkoff box, allowing space for a brief description of any detail the reporter thinks may be relevant to the situation. Some facilities include a space for physician's comment if the event required medical intervention. On prompt notification of a serious event or situation, risk management staff can conduct their own investigation immediately and institute any needed loss control measures simultaneously.

Routing of the incident report must be clearly defined. In some facilities the incident report is sent immediately to the risk management office. In most hospitals, if a report is completed by nursing staff, it is routed through nursing administration before being transmitted to the risk manager. An industry standard for transmitting the incident report is no later than twenty-four hours, with telephone notification to the risk manager as soon as possible after any serious injury or other significant event. A combination of user-friendly forms, staff education, and feedback through risk management trend reports will encourage information flow that meets or exceeds the standard of 4.5 incident reports per licensed bed per year.

Incident reports can be categorized by type of events and severity of situation for computer tracking. A severity index or scale might be based on the type of injury and/or the type of breach of procedure. On a scale of 0, 1, 2, or 3, the 0 represents "no injury" and 3 may be an injury requiring significant "therapeutic intervention," or significant "breach of procedure," such as giving medication to the wrong patient. This information can easily be developed into a graphic report to accompany the risk manager's analysis and recommendations of loss exposures and risk activities as reported in monthly, quarterly, and annual reports to the safety committee, the quality assessment committee, and the CEO and finance officer.

State-Mandated Incident Reporting

Some states have recognized the utility of risk management programs for the identification of major areas of patient vulnerability within the health care system and mandate the reporting of "incidents" to a state regulatory agency, but details vary considerably from state to state. New York State mandates reporting of hospital staff strikes; disasters or emergency situations affecting hospital operations; termination of any vital services in the hospital, such as telephone, laundry services, and pest control; and poisoning occurring within a hospital. When the peer review process finds that the standard of care was not met and a patient death or impairment of bodily function unrelated to the normal disease process occurred, the incident must also be reported to the state Health Department. In addition, events requiring police or other legal notification are reportable. In contrast, Massachusetts mandates quarterly and annual reporting of adverse patient events to the

Board of Registration in Medicine. Events that are reportable in Massachusetts are defined as incidents of patient harm or death as an outcome of medical intervention. Meeting the standard of care is implied but not explicit in the regulations, leaving facilities to make their own interpretations as to whether or not an incident is reportable. Both states reserve the right to conduct an on-site review of any incident, including examination of the credentials of any personnel involved in an event.

At least ten states (Arkansas, Colorado, Florida, Kansas, Maryland, Massachusetts, New York, North Carolina, Rhode Island, and Washington) have legislative mandates for risk management programs. These state regulations relate to the administration of a risk management program, investigation and analysis of identified risks, education programs, patient grievance procedures, and confidentiality of risk management data. Obviously, it is incumbent on risk managers to be aware of specific legislation in their own states. Risk managers and quality assessment professionals can use statewide statistical data to compare the type and severity of events by region and/or type of health care facility to "improve" modalities of care.

Incident Review and Evaluation

There must be an incident review and evaluation process that provides for:

- Investigation of all incidents, even if no injury results.
- Identification of trends among incidents.
- Referral of incidents and trend summaries to be evaluated to determine whether further action is necessary.
- Referral of incidents requiring further action to the appropriate institutional individuals, departments, services, and committees.

Actions to Prevent Recurrence of Incidents

Any actions taken by quality assessment, peer review, or medical staff committees regarding referred identified problems must be documented in a written record. These actions can be classified by the acronym **PACED**: preventive, administrative, corrective, educational, and documentary.[31]

- Preventive activities could include a patient relations program; an employee newsletter; a formal safety and security program; a community input effort; and ongoing planning, coordination, and review functions.
- Administrative actions relate to an active process, involvement of department heads, and a formal philosophy regarding administration.
- Corrective activities focus on the encouragement of problem identification, the monitoring of problem situations, the existence of internal audit functions, and the expeditious resolution of problems.
- Educational programs concentrate on creating an interdepartmental educational services unit, upgrading medical and technical skills, having a patient education program, and maintaining records of educational activities.
- Documentary activities include attention to personnel files, financial records, medical charts, regulatory requirements, and written policies and procedures.

Examples identify a host of work area concerns that could be involved in risk management actions. Examples include:

Hazards at work
Fire safety
Disaster plans
Electrical safety
Central services safety
Employee/patient safety

Nursing safety
Malpractice/legal liability
Medical staff
Anesthesia personnel
Surgery personnel
Surgical suite hazards
Surgery and anesthesia
Nursing treatment
Dietary safety
Housekeeping safety
Pathology safety
Respiratory safety
Radiology/laser safety
Nursing/pharmacy errors
Nursing and law

Internal Documentation

Institutions must maintain complete files of all risk management documentation, along with malpractice liability coverage documentation, individual malpractice case files involving the institution, and records of all expenses involved in safety programs to reduce or eliminate patient injuries. Documentation should be contained in the recorded minutes of appropriate bodies, as well as in reviews of credentials and personnel files of staff.

Credentialing and Privileging

Professional staff credentialing aims to ensure that institutions are staffed only by qualified individuals and that their performance is maintained at an acceptable level. Credentialing activities consist of a complete review of the licenses, education, and training of all applicants seeking appointment or employment. In addition, physicians must regularly have their privileges updated. This process of recredentialing involves an evaluation by the institution of the physician's clinical experience, competence, ability, judgment, and demonstrated performance in specified functions, such as open heart surgery, before any reappointment. Specifically, a profile of each physician and dentist must be compiled from at least the following data sources:

Morbidity and mortality review
Blood utilization review
Safety committee review
Peer review organization data
Medical care evaluations
Incident report review
Liability claims data
Continuing education programs and training
Utilization review
Infection control review
Surgical case review
Tissue review
Medical record review
Complaints
Prescription review
Medical case review

In addition, hospitals are mandated under the Health Care Quality Improvement Act of 1986 to make inquiries to the National Practitioner Data Bank concerning each physician, dentist, and others. Inquiry of the Federation of State Medical Boards, individual state medical boards and societies, and the insured's malpractice insurance carrier provide additional information on adverse professional actions, discipline, and sanctions. This legislation also mandates reports to the National Practitioner Data Bank of disciplinary actions or dismissals of medical staff from hospitals and institutions based on peer review activities and adverse situations.

In terms of risk management, credentialing and privileging is critical because it is the primary mechanism available to hospitals, agencies, managed care organizations, and other institutions to help ensure that only competent personnel are employed and that they perform only those clinical duties and procedures for which they are deemed clinically competent. This evaluation process, in turn, reduces the likelihood of the occurrence of any negligent acts that could result in a claim against the organization. A facility or agency with a nonexistent or ineffective credentialing or privileging process could find itself in a nondefensible position if a malpractice claim were filed, since the absence of such a process might indicate that the institution was negligent in ensuring that it employed only competent health care providers.

Patient Complaint Program

A copy of the patients' "Bill of Rights" should be given to each patient on admission and be available in the patient's own language. These rights should be posted in conspicuous areas throughout the institution or agency. There must be a formal written program for addressing patient complaints, as well as documentation of any action taken to resolve grievances. All complaints must be investigated promptly and thoroughly. Patients must be provided with the name and phone number of the representative designated to respond to such complaints. Representatives must treat complaining patients with dignity, courtesy, and due regard for their privacy while providing information about the following:

- Whom the patient may contact regarding the complaint.
- Whom the patient may contact if dissatisfied with the resolution.
- Procedures for investigating the complaint.
- When the patient can expect a verbal or written response or resolution to the complaint.

Tracking patients' complaints and identifying trends in those complaints should be routine and reported to the risk management and other committees as necessary.

Risk Management Education 

Risk management education should be included in orientation and annual in-service training programs for all institutional employees and professional staff in the following areas:

- Organization and goals of the risk management program.
- Patients' "Bill of Rights."
- Patient relations and complaint program.
- Incident-reporting program.
- Reporting responsibilities for alleged professional misconduct.
- Safety program and department-specific safety practices.

On the basis of the theory that "happy patients do not sue," a California insurance company initiated a mandatory loss prevention seminar for physicians in June 1984.[32] By 1993, almost ten thousand physicians had attended the 472 seminars and received three hours of continuing medical education credits. Core educational units fall into four categories. Opening with the perceived reasons for the malpractice problem, the seminar covers the public patient, plaintiff attorneys, laws, the standard of care, and the role of physicians in iatrogenic injuries and defensive medicine. Second, the seminar focuses on loss prevention strategies, including rapport between physician and patient, communications, satisfaction, informed consent, office staff strategies, relationships between physician and hospital, and medical record documentation. Third, the seminar highlights litigation awareness, emphasizing the dos and don'ts if physicians are sued. Finally, arbitration details the alternate dispute resolution forum, the binding legal resolution, and the advantages and disadvantages of each method. In theory, these seminars may prevent claims, conserve the institution's financial resources, prevent patient injury, and improve the quality of patient care delivered. About 95 percent of the participating physicians stated that they would change their behavior based on the information presented at the seminar.

Insurance Companies and Risk Management

Insurance companies offer their insured institutions a variety of risk management services, including consultation, educational programs, publications, closed-claim studies, and computer software packages. Consultations between insurance company representatives and institutional risk management personnel aim to help the organization minimize the risk of malpractice claims. Services may include claims auditing, chart review, policy review, and evaluation of specific clinical areas. Individual insurance company personnel may spend time in loss prevention and loss control activities. In this role, these individuals keep up to date with changes in laws and standards of practice having implications for facility liability, including lessons learned from cases involving actual losses and case law decisions. Sometimes, the problem is a misunderstanding of the insurance policy. Box 1-7 illustrates an insurance policy misinterpretation.

Educational services seek to help organizations minimize the frequency and severity of malpractice claims. Programs can be provided in several formats, including national, regional, local, and institutional seminars and individualized focused training workshops. Seminars allow representatives of all the insured organizations to meet and discuss clinical, administrative, and legal risk management issues. Focused workshops give individual risk managers a more in-depth examination of issues that directly affect their specific facility. Companies may offer formal certificate programs for risk managers in areas such as an overview of risk management, risk exposure identification and evaluation, or functions of risk management. Each course may consist of self-study, specified readings, study questions, and projects. At the end of each course, participants may be tested and evaluated by qualified faculty.

Publications are designed to aid the insured institution to manage and reduce their liability risks. Material can vary from pamphlets on a single issue to workshop proceedings to multi-volume books to a combination of mass media approaches. Often, insurance companies publish and distribute regular newsletters, case alerts, and bulletins. Available videotapes, audiotapes, films, and slide presentations may deal with topics such as malpractice in the emergency department, medication errors, and minimizing risks in surgery.

Claims are studied continuously by the insurance companies. A database of open and closed claims filed against their insured organizations and individuals is routinely analyzed to identify lessons learned, so that future claims can be avoided. Professional

BOX 1-7

About thirty-seven thousand Humana Health Insurance Company of Florida customers "paid anywhere from a few dollars to several thousand dollars more than they should have under the terms of their insurance policies." Without admitting wrongdoing, Humana agreed to pay $4.4 million in consumer refunds and $1.9 million in investigative costs.[33]

liability representatives periodically analyze claims to identify factors that may have caused their submission. These factors are evaluated jointly by insurance company representatives and institution officials in an effort to correct the situations that led to the claims. This process is facilitated by computer reports that pinpoint the frequency and severity of malpractice claims.

While none of the insurance companies require a prescribed risk management program, the surveys of the agency or institutional program and the data analysis may reflect on the adequacy of the program and variation in the premium. Continuing professional liability coverage may be conditional on implementing corrective action based on recommendations for improvement in the program or in specific situations that can cause liability.[10]

Computer software packages may be provided by the insurance companies to enable their insured to analyze physician performance in areas such as adverse patient occurrences, infection rates, and pharmaceutical complications. New analysis software emerges from the claims studies to track the identified risk factors as they are discovered. This is a dynamic service, and risk managers will be exposed to creative and innovative software applications from insurance companies and others to limit liability.

Dos and Don'ts of Risk Management: A Claims Perspective

Small things that hospital employees, departmental supervisors, and medical staff members do—and don't do—can have a significant impact on the frequency and severity of claims made against a hospital. Risk management experts urge hospitals to enforce dos and don'ts relative to documentation, product malfunction, contracts, confidentiality, and conflicts (see Box 1-8).

Computer Use in Risk Management

Next to an involved risk management committee, the most valuable asset for any risk management program is a one-gigabyte computer and all the software the risk management department can afford.

Although smaller agencies and facilities (with fewer than two hundred beds) can manage data for trend analysis manually, the need for long-term trend analysis of incidents, claims, equipment problems, and internal disasters (for example, floods occurring from broken pipes only on weekends) cannot be overemphasized. While there are many software packages available that provide for central entry of data and specialized modules for RM, QA, or utilization review, the purchase decision should be based on a thorough analysis of the risk management data needs. Standard database software can be selected and customized to a particular program's needs at a significant savings over the special risk management packages available. In selecting software, the type of information the risk manager will be analyzing and the type of reports that will be generated from the analysis are the key factors in making the purchase decision.

Data that risk management most frequently analyzes for trends are events with patient injury, with financial loss to the institution (floods, fires, theft), malpractice suits naming the facility, dates and allegations of malpractice suits filed against medical staff members (obtained on appointment and reappointment), and "indicators"—specific events with potential for patient injury or financial loss, such as a missing surgical consent, antibiotic given to the wrong patient, a patient chart missing, or narcotic cabinet keys missing from the pharmacy. It is common to track hospital incidents and events by date, time, and location. Malpractice claims are usually

BOX 1-8

Dos and Don'ts of Risk Management

DOCUMENTATION[34]

- **Do** follow all policies and procedures pertaining to documentation.
- **Do** document any changes in patient's status, attempts to contact patient's physicians or family members, and other activities relevant to patient's care. The absence of such documentation makes defending a medical malpractice action against the hospital difficult. In the words of one plaintiff attorney: "If it's not in the chart, it never happened."
- **Do** complete documentation entries contemporaneously. If changes or updates are necessary, they should be documented in a timely manner, with the date, reason for the change or update, and the initials of the person making the change included.
- **Don't** alter records out of fear of litigation or disciplinary action. Altered records discovered by a plaintiff attorney can make a case practically indefensible.
- **Don't** make changes to documentation days after an event occurs. Outline in memo form the situation surrounding the need for a change and discuss it with the hospital risk manager.

PRODUCT MALFUNCTION

- **Do** contact risk management whenever a product malfunctions, regardless of the perceived consequences at the time of the malfunction.
- **Do** notify the manufacturer of the malfunctioning product as soon as possible.
- **Don't** return the malfunctioning product to the manufacturer after it has caused an injury.
- **Don't** discard the malfunctioning equipment, product, or disposable accessories. Store it in a secure location until the hospital's professional liability company can be notified. Without the product as evidence, securing a contribution from a manufacturer would be very difficult if the incident ultimately warranted settlement, and the hospital could be solely liable.
- **Don't** attempt to recreate the malfunction to discover what or how something happened. A report from an independent third-party investigation will be less credible if the product has been altered in any way.

CONTRACTS

- **Do** review all vendor contracts to ensure that the hospital is not exposed to additional risks.
- **Do** have all contracts reviewed annually by the hospital attorney.
- **Don't** sign a contract without reading it and understanding it first.

CONFLICTS

- **Do** keep conflicts involving physicians and the hospital out of the public arena.
- **Do** familiarize all hospital personnel with hospial policies and procedures that affect their daily jobs. Lack of knowledge of hospital policies is not a viable defense.
- **Don't** allow or engage in open criticism of health professionals' treatment of a patient. Any documented conflicts over patient care would not only make a case very difficult to defend, but could also raise the ultimate value of the judgment.
- **Don't** enact policies or procedures that are unrealistic. The hospital will be held to its stated policies and procedures as standards of care.

CONFIDENTIALITY

- **Do** hold professional discussions about patients in hospital settings, not in public areas.
- **Don't** discuss patients' problems outside of the hospital.

tracked by date, allegation, person(s) involved, and damages requested, and are followed through the entire defense process, listing information collected and individuals deposed for the defense, to judgment, settlement, or dismissal of the case. The amount of the judgment or settlement is tracked, as are the expenses incurred. Any one of the many risk management packages currently on the market or one of the database software packages would handle this type of information readily.

Whether or not a facility is self-insured, consideration should also be given to purchase of a spreadsheet package, for analysis of claims payments and costs of defense. For a facility that traditionally has purchased insurance coverage, a four-year cost analysis, if readily available, may point the way to cost savings by self-insurance. This is rapidly becoming an industry trend; the risk manager should prepare for the possibility that this move will occur as a natural outcome of the shifts in delivery of and payment for health care.

TOWARD THE FUTURE

Usually, risk managers aim to reduce preventable adverse events and to minimize financial loss to their organizations should such events occur. In a rapidly changing business environment, risk managers must be able to accurately determine where their health care organization is headed and effectively plan methods and techniques to mitigate the risks to their institutions. Within these goals, risk managers, along with everybody else, from top management to the lowest level employee, appear to be involved in almost every aspect of the health care delivery system. Health care organizations that survive the constant turmoil in the industry will be abetted by an effective, strategic risk management program.

References

1. Dawson, B. (1932). *The History of Medicine. A Short Synopsis.* New York: Macmillan, pp. 14–16.
2. Challan, B., McConnell, J., and Walsh, A. (1993). Risk management in health care: Where did it come from and where is it going? *Mt. Sinai Journal of Medicine* 60(5):359–362.
3. Lenckus, D. (1994). Risk management honor roll: Ronald J. Gulifoile. *Business Insurance* 28(16): 137–138.
4. Smith, D. G., and Wheeler, J. R. C. (1992). Strategies and structures for hospital risk management programs. *Health Care Management Review* 17(3):9–17.
5. Hinman, E. J. (1995). Risk management: An overview. Presentation notes for lecture for Institute of Medical Law, Inc., course on risk management.
6. Evans, L. (1993). Medical accidents: No such thing? *British Medical Journal* 307(6917):1438–1439.
7. Youngberg, B. J. (1994). *The Risk Manager's Desk Reference.* Gaithersburg, Md.: Aspen, pp. 13–26; Harpster, L. M. and Veach, M. S., eds. (1990). *Risk Management Handbook for Health Care Facilities.* Chicago: American Hospital Publishing, pp. 28–30.
8. Burlando, A. J. (1990). The 1990s: The decade of risk management. *Risk Management* 37(3):50–56.
9. Soper, D. (1994). Risk manager offers legal and medical talents. *New Orleans CityBusiness* April 11:18.
10. Baine, D. P. (1994). *Purchase of Safer Devices Should Be Based on Risk of Injury.* GAO/HEHS-95-12. Washington, D.C.: Government Printing Office.
11. Marta, M. R., and Hornback, M. (1993). Risk management and finance: The link. *Journal for Healthcare Quality* 15(2):11–13.
12. Hagg, S. R. (1990). Elements of a risk management program. In *Risk Management Handbook for Health Care Facilities*, edited by L. M. Harpster and M. S. Veach. Chicago: American Hospital Publishing, pp. 23–33.
13. Hine, C. (1993). Doctors, nurses differ on RM communication. *National Underwriter* 97(43):10–11.
14. Kurland, O. M. (1994). Communicating effectively with the board room. *Risk Management* 41(4): 116–120.

15. Alexander & Alexander Government & Industry Affairs, Inc. (1994). *Risk Management Survey*. Washington, D.C.
16. Gregory, R., and Lichtenstein, S. (1994). A hint of risk: Tradeoffs between quantitative and qualitative risk factors. *Risk Analysis* 14(2):199–206.
17. Weighted risks: Trying to put worst things first. (1994). *Governing* 7(7):62–64.
18. Stipp, D. (1994). Prevention may be costlier than cure. *Wall Street Journal* July 6, B1:3.
19. Clinical Skillbuilders. (1992). *Write Better Documentation*. Springhouse, Pa.: Springhouse Corporation.
20. Pesaud, D. D., and Dawe, U. (1992). Personal computers and risk management. *Hospital Topics* 70(3): 11–14.
21. Hazen, S., and Cookson, J. (1990). A database tool for centralized analysis of untoward health care events. *Military Medicine* 155(10):492–497.
22. Kapp, M. B. (1990). Health care risk management: The challenge of measuring costs and benefits. *Quality Review Bulletin* 16(5):166–169.
23. Nenner, R. P., Imperato, P. J., Silver, A. L., and Will, T. O. (1994). Quality of care problems among Medicare and Medicaid patients. *Journal of Community Health* 19(5):307–318.
24. Joint Commission on Accreditation of Healthcare Organizations. (1995). *Accreditation Manual for Hospitals*. Oakbrook Terrace, Ill.: JCAHO.
25. Orlikoff, J. E., and Landau, G. B. (1981). Why risk management and quality assurance should be integrated. *Hospitals* 55(11):54–55.
26. U.S. Congress, Office of Technology Assessment. (1994). *Defensive Medicine and Medical Malpractice*. OTA-H-602. Washington, D.C.: Government Printing Office, pp. 32–33.
27. Freedman, T. J., and Gerring, G. (1993). Focus on risk management. *Leadership* 2(3):29–33.
28. Murov, K. L. (1995). Implementation of a risk management program. An educational presentation for the Institute of Medical Law, Inc., New York Health Care Risk Management Program; Monagle, J. F. (1985). *Risk Management: A Guide for Health Care Professionals*. Gaithersburg, Md.: Aspen.
29. Burlando, T. (1994). Chaos and risk management. *Risk Management* 41(4):54–61.
30. Kirtland, A. B. (1991). Quality assurance tracking or "finding the needle in the haystack." *Journal of Medical Systems* 15(2):183–196.
31. Rowland, H. S., and Rowland, B. L. (1995). *Hospital Risk Management. Forms, Checklists & Guidelines*. Gaithersburg, Md.: Aspen.
32. Oppenberg, A. A. (1993). A mandatory physician loss prevention seminar. *Journal of Healthcare Risk Management* 13(2):714.
33. Humana Inc., agrees to pay $6.3 million to settle allegations. (1994). *Wall Street Journal* February 25, p. B8:4.
34. MAG Mutual Insurance Company. (1994). *Hospital Risk Manager* 2(3):3.

CHAPTER 2 Regulatory Environment

Standards and Risk Management

Allen D. Spiegel
Florence Kavaler

Health care is one of the most regulated industries in the United States. A regulatory environment is generated by the establishment of standards by legislative acts, by regulations administered by official executive agencies, and by standards of professional organizations. Violations of the law and/or regulations or standards could considerably interrupt revenue stream and even result in jail time for high-level management personnel. An understanding of the regulations is vital for individuals and institutions engaged in health care risk management.

A STANDARDS PRIMER

In a health care milieu, standards are statements concerning proper procedures and/or actions to be taken in given clinical or administrative situations. Using juxtaposed terms, standards can be created within the following boundary dimensions:[1]

- Explicit or implicit
- National or local
- Validated or consensual
- Used or ignored
- Periodically updated or static

Explicit standards are written guidelines to ensure that everyone follows the same specific procedures in given clinical or administrative situations. Implicit standards, on the other hand, are usual and customary or based on collective experience but are unwritten, understood, assumed, or implied. Standards that are documented by scientific testing are verifiable and replicable; thus, their validity can be authenticated. Consensual standards develop by mutual agreement among involved parties.

Government jurisdictions, professional associations, or voluntary organizations at national, state, or local levels may develop and promulgate standards that may be incorporated into codes of ethics or separate guidelines, or be embedded in legislation and regulations. Excellent standards may be in force when the precepts are first established, but without a dynamic process of periodic review and updating, standards can fall into disuse and be ignored.

PROMULGATION AND IMPLEMENTATION OF STANDARDS

Standards may be promulgated in four classifications: legal, regulatory, reimbursement, and practice guidelines. To compound matters further, there may be crossovers between the classifications (see Box 2-1).

Three particularly troubling areas for health care institutions illustrate the conflicting legislative interplay: Occupational Safety and Health Administration (OSHA) standards provoke conflicts with the Americans with Disabilities Act (ADA) relative to preemployment medical examinations. Health insurance guidelines evoke interplay between the Employee Retirement and Income Security Act (ERISA) and ADA regarding health insurance plans that exclude or limit benefits for disabling conditions. State workers' compensation laws may conflict with the ADA by using examinations of the back to screen out injury-prone job applicants.[6]

BOX 2-1

Examples of Regulatory Interplay and Conflicts

- The Equal Employment Opportunity Commission (EEOC) wants to extend employment discrimination protection to obese people under the ADA (Americans with Disabilities Act) and the Rehabilitation Act of 1973.[2]
- The EEOC declared chronic obesity a protected category under the ADA. Obesity is defined as being twice the normal weight for one's size.[3]
- A jury awarded 5′2″, 320-pound Bonnie Cook $100,000 for a discrimination violation of Section 504 of the Rehabilitation Act of 1973. A prehire physical exam by the Rhode Island Department of Mental Health, Retardation and Hospitals found her "morbidly obese" and denied her a job.[4]
- Under three court decisions, obesity, sexual obsession, and tobacco smoke allergies do not amount to disabling conditions protected by law.[5]

LEGAL STANDARDS

Legislatively, standards have been required relative to a broad spectrum of health care issues, such as public health rules, disease reporting requirements, utilization of immunizations, workers' compensation, health insurance, and licensing of institutions, agencies, and professionals. Usually, legislation is followed by regulations issued by the appropriate executive department.

A judicial system provides the primary legal initiative for implementing standards. If disagreements arise, the parties involved meet in a courtroom to decide the issue before a judge and / or a jury. Subsequently, the decision of the court yields a basis in law for future actions. Statutes and court orders constitute the framework for the legal implementation of standards. These legal renderings provide the foundation for health care institutional policies relative to alternative directives, living wills, informed consent, access to medical records, and information about practitioners.

FEDERAL MANDATES

Mandatory regulations cover a multitude of activities in the health care industry. A health care institution must meet the Conditions of Participation (COP) established by the federal Health Care Financing Agency (HCFA) before they can be reimbursed for treating people covered by the Medicare health insurance program. Like members of any other industry, health care providers must meet the mandates of federal regulations, such as those required by OSHA. One official at a large hospital summed up the effect of federal regulations on the health care industry as follows:

> Although workplace regulations are serious, time-consuming and expensive, in the scheme of things, federal workplace regulation is not the worst thing.[7]

The sections that follow look at some examples of federal regulation of the health care industry.

Occupational Safety and Health

Legislative mandates that apply to the workplace illustrate the complex spectrum of conceivable risk management activities in health care institutions. Exhibit 2-1 lists the legislative chronology of almost thirty federal acts from the 1920s into the 1990s. Most of the statutes and the one executive order that form the framework of federal workplace regulations were put in place during three periods: 1931 to 1940; 1963 to 1974; and 1986 to 1993. Although seven statutes had been enacted by 1940, only eight major statues were in place as of 1960. Congress initiated a second wave of legislation during the 1960s that addressed civil rights issues and regulated new areas, such as employee pensions. During the 1980s and 1990s, Congress passed a series of labor standard statutes focusing on narrower workplace issues. OSHA-related laws and regulations have continued to evolve, protecting the working public, creating substantial costs for implementation, and increasing potential liabilities for businesses. Exhibit 2-2 lists examples of regulatory statues, giving details about each law and enumerating the civil and criminal, monetary and nonmonetary, enforcement sanctions and remedies available under the statute. However, enforcement agencies commonly negotiate settlements with employers even when not required by the regulation.

On a federal level, the Occupational Safety and Health Act of 1970 requires employers to furnish each employee with work and a workplace free from recognized hazards that can cause death or serious physical harm (see Exhibit 2-3). By itself, this law contains a myriad of regulations required of health care facilities that apply to accidents, blood-borne pathogens, drug testing for employees, ergonomics, hazard communication, infection control, inspections by OSHA, lasers, maintenance and sterilization of medical equipment, medical wastes, medication safety, radiation, record keeping, reproductive hazards, safety and health committees, self-audits, staff training, and violence in the workplace.[8] Furthermore, new rules can be adopted as the federal government emphasizes the enforcement of standards in the health care workplace. As of February 9, 1994, OSHA rules were put into place, requiring facilities that use nonsolid prescription drugs, such as aerosols, liquids, and powders, to maintain material safety data sheets (MSDSs) for these drugs and to use the MSDSs in training.

In late 1993, new guidelines for controlling the spread of tuberculosis (TB) were mandated, with particular attention given to the high risk of TB exposure in health care facilities and nursing homes. Federal Centers for Disease Control and Prevention (CDCP) recommendations called for the use of improved masks, the use of ultraviolet light to kill airborne TB germs, ventilation standards, and tightened record keeping.

EXHIBIT 2-1 LEGISLATIVE CHRONOLOGY, 1920s–1990s

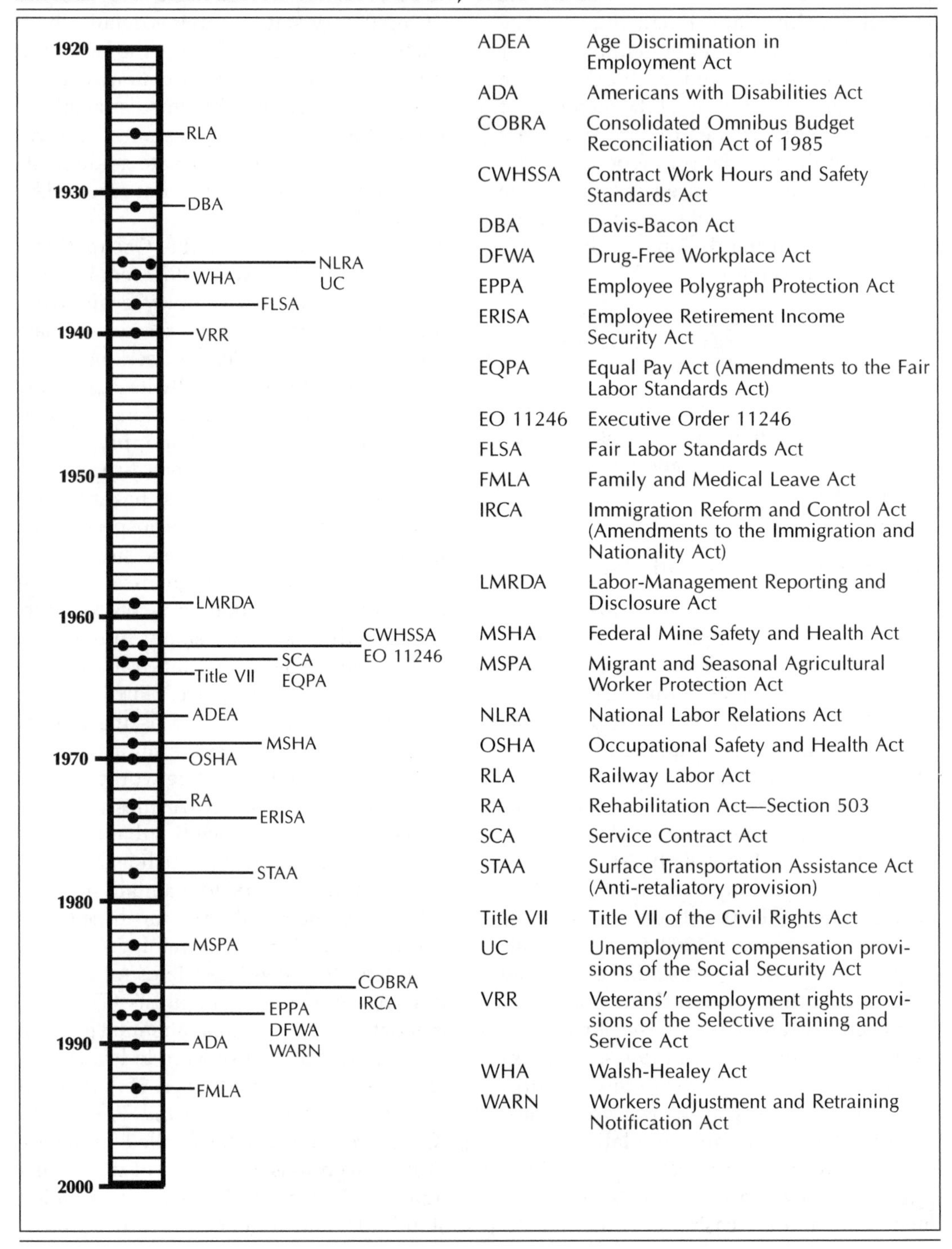

EXHIBIT 2-2 EXAMPLES OF REGULATORY STATUTES, DESCRIPTIONS, AND PENALTIES[9]

OCCUPATIONAL SAFETY AND HEALTH ACT (OSHA)

Description
Requires employers to furnish each employee with work and a workplace free from recognized hazards that can cause death or serious physical harm.

Penalties
$5,000 to $70,000 for each willful violation; up to $70,000 for each repeat violation; up to $7,000 for serious, other-than-serious, or posting violation for each day of failure to abate hazard; abatement of hazard; imminent danger situations: $500,000 for a corporation and $250,000 and/or six months imprisonment for an individual for a willful violation that results in death of an employee; one year imprisonment if prior conviction; $200,000 for an organization and $100,000 and/or six months imprisonment for an individual for false statements in a required certified document.

DRUG-FREE WORKPLACE ACT (DFWA)

Description
Requires recipients of federal grants and contracts to take certain steps to maintain a drug-free workplace.

Penalties
Debarment; restraining order or injunction.

CONSOLIDATED OMNIBUS BUDGET RECONCILIATION ACT (COBRA)

Description
Provides for continued health care coverage under group health plans for qualified separated workers for up to eighteen months.

Penalties
$100 per day for failure to comply with notice requirements; elimination of tax deductibility of plan contributions.

TITLE VII OF THE CIVIL RIGHTS ACT

Description
Prohibits employment or membership discrimination by employers, employment agencies, and unions on the basis of race, color, religion, sex, or national origin; prohibits discrimination against women affected by pregnancy, childbirth, or related medical condition.

Penalties
$100 for each willful violation of posting requirements, unpaid wage, liquidated or punitive damages.

EXHIBIT 2-3 CATEGORIES OF POTENTIAL HAZARDS FOUND IN HOSPITALS[10]

Hazard category	Definition	Examples found in the hospital envionment
Biological	Infectious/biological agents, such as bacteria, viruses, fungi, or parasites, that may be transmitted by contact with infected patients or contaminated body secretions/fluids	Human immunodeficiency virus (HIV), vancomycin resistant enterococcus (VRE), methicillin resistant staphylococcus aureus (MRSA), hepatitis B virus, hepatitis C virus, tuberculosis
Chemical	Various forms of chemicals that are potentially toxic or irritating to the body system, including medications, solutions, and gases	Ethylene oxide, formaldehyde, glutaraldehyde, waste anesthetic gases, hazardous drugs such as cytotoxic agents, pentamidine ribavirin
Psychological	Factors and situations encountered or associated with one's job or work environment that create or potentiate stress, emotional strain, and/or other interpersonal problems	Stress, workplace violence, shiftwork, inadequate staffing, heavy workload, increased patient acuity
Physical	Agents within the work environment that can cause tissue trauma	Radiation, lasers, noise, electricity, extreme temperatures, workplace violence
Environmental, Mechanical/ Biomechanical	Factors encountered in the work environment that cause or potentiate accidents, injuries, strain, or discomfort	Tripping hazards, unsafe/unguarded equipment, air quality, slippery floors, confined spaces, cluttered or obstructed work areas/passageways, forceful exertions, awkward postures, localized contact stresses, vibration, temperature extremes, repetitive/prolonged motions or activities, lifting and moving patients

New standards proposed in 1997 and 2002 have further expanded interest in risk assessment.[11]

OSHA indicated that hazards could be minimized in several ways: engineering and work practice controls, personal protective equipment, HBV vaccination, training and education, and appropriate use of signs and labels.[12] In 1993, OSHA reported 2,064 violations of the blood-borne pathogen regulations by health care industry organizations. This regulation was the most frequently violated standard in the industry that year. Specific blood-borne pathogen standards that were violated fell into five deficiency areas: exposure control plan (28%), methods of compliance (24%), communication of exposure to employees (23%), hepatitis B vaccination and postexposure evaluations and follow-up (19%), and record keeping (6%).[13]

In 1991 OSHA published the Occupational Exposure to Bloodborne Pathogens standard because of the significant health risk associated with exposure to viruses and other microorganisms that cause blood-borne diseases. Of primary concern are the human immunodeficiency virus (HIV), hepatitis B (HBV), and hepatitis C (HCV). Many of these diseases are fatal or chronically disabling.

The Centers for Disease Control and Prevention (CDC) reported 56 documented cases of occupationally acquired HIV infection in health care workers between 1985 and 1999, and an additional 136 cases of possible transmission. They also reported 8,700 cases of HBV infection in 1987, but only 800 new cases in 1995. Health care workers' risk of exposure to HCV is much higher than the risk of HIV, mostly because of the high frequency of HCV in the general population, which therefore makes it a more significant threat through needlestick and sharp injuries.[14]

In 2000, the Needlestick Safety and Prevention Act (H.R. 5178)[15] was promulgated to specifically address the 600,000 needlesticks and other sharps injuries each year. This updated revision to the bloodborne pathogens standard emphasizes the importance of reviewing institutions' exposure control plans annually, and of implementing engineering controls and use of safe medical devices such as retractable syringe needles, sliding needle shields, needleless connectors for IV delivery systems, self-blunting phlebotomy, and winged-steel needles.[16] Employee input into the plan and the selection of safe medical devices to be utilized is emphasized and requires documentation. Record keeping and a sharp injury log, along with maintenance of information on first aid, medical care, and subsequent follow-up of medical illnesses, are important aspects of reducing the sequelae of these injuries.

The Joint Commission on the Accreditation of Healthcare Organizations has added adherence to the federal Needlestick Safety and Prevention Act to its accreditation process, which has speeded hospital compliance preparation.[17]

Health Insurance Portability and Accountability Act of 1996, Public Law 104–191[18]

In 1996, President William J. Clinton signed the Health Insurance Portability and Accountability Act (HIPAA). This broad legislation deals with a wide set of health policy issues and mandates action that seeks to: (1) ensure continuity of health care coverage for individuals changing jobs; (2) impact on the management of health information; (3) simplify the administration of health insurance; and (4) combat waste, fraud, and abuse in health insurance and health care. The new rules, the first comprehensive federal standards for medical privacy, will affect virtually every doctor, patient, hospital, drugstore, and health insurance company in the United States.[19]

Title II of the HIPAA law (also known as Administrative Simplification) includes requirements for ensuring the security and privacy of individuals' medical information. The standards aim to maintain the right of individuals to keep information about themselves private. Hospital compliance is now required by April 2003.

The regulations protect medical records and other "individually identifiable health information" (communicated electronically, on paper, or orally) that is created or received by covered health care entities that transmit information electronically. Covered entities include health care providers (such as hospitals), health care insurers, and organizations that process health care transactions on behalf of providers and insurers. Individuals' medical records relating to their past, present, or future physical or mental health condition, the provision of health care, or the payment for such care are considered private and are protected under the new laws.

Institutions engaged in the processing of electronic medical records and claims submissions will be required to assess the potential risks to and vulnerabilities of the individual health data in their possession in electronic form, and to develop, implement, and maintain appropriate security measures. They must also document these security measures and keep them current.

The laws also specify standards for a "security matrix," which depicts a minimum level of security for electronic health information. Institution- and agency-wide attention needs to be focused on specifying authorization to access information, developing a contingency plan, reporting of untoward incidents, and training employees on security and privacy concerns.

The new rules specify that information from a person's medical records cannot be disclosed to an employer unless the patient specifically authorizes the disclosure. Also, patients can review their medical records and request changes to correct errors, and researchers can use medical records to track an outbreak of disease if they strip the records of the patients' identities.

The rules appear to set strict standards on using personal data from patients for marketing purposes. They prohibit drugstores from selling personal medical information to drug companies or other businesses that want to sell products or services. In the past, some drug companies have paid pharmacies for customer health information and used it to try to sell products to individuals with conditions like osteoporosis, diabetes, or depression.

Enforcement, Compliance, and Penalties

OSHA attempts to control or shape the behavior of a regulated community through the enforcement of certain rules or commands monitored by compliance inspections, administrative adjudication, or the courts.

Obviously, employer compliance is influenced by the employer's awareness of the regulatory requirements. A randomly selected mail survey of almost 2,000 employers found that more than 50 percent reported little or no awareness of OSHA's Hazard Communication Standard (HCS) or were not knowledgeable about its key requirements.[20]

Significantly, the effectiveness of command and control regulation is influenced by the level of available regulatory resources and the sanctions for noncompliance. There are only about 2,000 compliance offices to enforce standards in more than 6.5 million workplaces. Historically, OSHA penalties have been inconsequential: the average penalty for a serious violation was $750 in fiscal year 1993; criminal sanctions are infrequent, and a conviction is rare. In comparison, the allowable legislative sanctions are quite severe. Maximum civil monetary penalties under OSHA are substantial (see Box 2-2): from thousands of dollars to a half million, plus imprisonment in more severe cases.[21]

In addition to setting standards for the workplace, federal legislation affects individual health care providers. Seeking to improve the quality of health care, legislators have created some potentially high-liability risks for institutions that employ or contract with licensed health care practitioners.

Emergency Medical Treatment and Labor Act of 1986

This law bars hospitals and physicians from ordering transfers of emergency patients or women in active labor until they are stabilized. "Dumping patients" through inappropriate transfers (see Box 2-3), such as diverting patients via radio messages to ambulances or denying services to psychiatric patients, could incur fines of up to $50,000 per violation. Repeat offenders could be terminated from the Medicare program.[22]

BOX 2-2

An Ohio children's hospital was cited and fined $21,250 for failure to require protective eye equipment where there was "reasonable probability" for injury . . . failure to use engineering and/or work practice controls to eliminate employees' exposure to hazardous substances . . . and failure to include the physical and health hazards of workplace chemicals in employee training.[23]

BOX 2-3

An uninsured patient arrived at the hospital in labor, with signs of fetal distress. She waited almost 12 hours without being admitted, was allegedly stabilized, and discharged. She returned 18 hours later, was transferred to a general hospital, underwent a cesarean section, and delivered an anemic baby who died within a few days. A federal court for Virginia ruled that the hospital had violated the anti-dumping statute and the baby had died as a direct and proximate cause of the hospital's negligence.[24]

Six hospitals have been terminated since the law went into effect, but four of those have been recertified. A report from the Public Citizen's Health Research Group claimed that enforcement of the dumping law lagged behind the increased complaints about the practice.[25] Extending the regulation, several courts ruled that this law applies not only to patient dumping but also to the more general allegations of inadequate care of insured patients.[26]

Mammography Quality Standards Act of 1992

Public Law 102-539 requires national uniform quality standards for mammography facilities, whether in a hospital, physician's office, mobile van, military base, or any other public or private enterprise. By October 1, 1994, all mammography facilities had to be certified by the Food and Drug Administration (FDA) or alternatively by the American College of Radiology. Facilities must apply for accreditation annually and submit to several procedures: a periodic review of clinical images; an annual survey by a medical physicist; and compliance with quality standards for equipment, personnel qualifications, quality assessment programs, record keeping, and reporting.[27,28]

Enhanced mammography regulations effective since April 28, 1999 are directed at ensuring that physicians and personnel are adequately trained and qualified to conduct mammography examinations and interpret mammograms. There are requirements for reporting the results of mammograms quickly to physicians and patients (in lay terms) in order to avoid delay in follow-up testing and treatment.[29]

There are almost 9,800 mammography facilities performing 40 million mammograms per year. For teaching hospitals, there are additional requirements for diagnostic residency training programs that specify the interpretation, under direct supervision, of 240 mammographic examinations within six months of qualifying as an interpreting physician.[30]

Recent studies suggest that "radiologists are missing far more tumors than previously assumed." There are 20,000 physicians who interpret mammograms, and their skills vary widely. Opportunities exist for double-reading mammographies to uncover missed cancers and for physician failures to be interpreted appropriately. Federal emphasis has not been on the quality of physicians' practice, but on equipment design and performance characteristics.[31]

Safe Medical Devices Act of 1990

A report from the National Committee for Quality Health Care (NCQHC), a coalition of providers and manufacturers, urges mandatory federal FDA-like premarket review of emerging technology involving modified tests and treatments. From the viewpoint of its vested interest, the NCQHC seeks to curb inappropriate use of medical technology.[32] This group recommended that medical and surgical procedures be required to demonstrate their clinical efficacy before being adopted outside the research setting. Currently, new drugs and devices must undergo rigorous FDA premarket review. However, no such requirements exist for emerging medical tests and treatments that do not involve a new product.[33] Critics of such requirements believe that a formal regulatory system could impede providers and delay access to promising new technology and procedures.

There are 13,000 manufacturers of medical devices, with revenues of $78 billion a year, that depend on the Food and Drug Administration for approval of their products. Responsive to critics who have demanded speedier action, the FDA Modernization Act of 1997 allows many new devices to be marketed before they have undergone full-scale clinical trials. However, some devices have had little data available and some manufacturers have submitted false data, hiding injuries, deaths, and malfunctions, and providing inadequate financial disclosures.[34]

Manufacturers of medical devices aver that liability concerns threaten their implant research activities. Since "there are no inert materials," the climate of litigation in the United States may "ultimately push device manufacturers to introduce their new devices in countries less prone to litigation."[35] Furthermore, in light of cost containment restraints, health care organizations are considering the reuse of disposable medical devices. However, the FDA says that "providers that reuse disposable devices are liable for the products' safety and effectiveness."[36]

In the past decade, more than two million implants have been recalled. Heart implants like pacemakers, defibrillators, valves, and stents comprise 800,000 (40%) of the recalls, and bone screws and plates comprise 470,000 units (23%). In addition, 66,000 breast implants and 27,000 penile implants were recalled.[37]

Risk managers must contemplate possible causes of injury relative to medical devices: design defects, manufacturing defects, random component failure, packaging errors, user errors, idiosyncratic patient reaction, sabotage, faulty repair, or maintenance or calibration errors. Estimates attribute 50 to 80 percent of medical-device accidents directly to user error, on the part of patient, technician, physician, nurse, or other professional.[38]

Corporate giants in American medical device production have been involved in regulatory sanctions invoked by the FDA.[39] In February 1994, for example, Siemens Medical Systems, Inc., signed a consent decree stating that it had improperly manufactured certain devices, such as hearing aids, pacemakers, patient monitors, and ultrasound monitors. Siemens was granted time to correct the violations,[40] and by November 1994, Siemens had received approval from the FDA to resume marketing of its devices.[41] Box 2-4 gives other examples.

Nearly 25 million Americans have one sort of implant or another, and medical devices continue to raise the specter of huge liability risks. For example, Sulzer Orthopedics of Austin, Texas, agreed to a $1 billion settlement in 2002 because of failed replacement hip joints. In addition, Boston Scientific Corporation currently faces more than 500 lawsuits from women who say they were injured by problems resulting from an implant to control incontinence.[42]

MEDWatch

In June 1993, the FDA announced a new program, MEDWatch: The FDA Medical Products Reporting Program.[43] Because many health professional do not routinely report adverse events, MEDWatch was designed to encourage the voluntary reporting, by professionals and consumers,[44] of serious adverse events caused not only by medical devices but also by biologics, dietary supplements, and drugs. Problems such as defective devices, inaccurate or unreadable product labeling, packing or product mix-up, contaminations or stability problems, and particulate matter in injectable products should be reported promptly.

Eight months after MEDWatch was launched, 4,625 adverse events had been reported; 2,270 were drug reactions (64%), 856 were device problems (20%). Pharmacists were the overwhelming source of reporting (2,531, or 55%), distantly followed by physicians (683, or 16%). Importantly, many hospitals and physicians still do not report malfunctions of medical equipment as the law requires.[45]

Of concern to risk management, up to 10 percent of hospital admissions in the United States are due to adverse reactions. If an adverse event occurs in the hospital, approximately two additional inpatient days, costing about $1,000 per day, are needed.

BOX 2-4

- Pfizer Inc. and Shiley, Inc. agreed to pay $10.75 million to settle claims and to monitor patients who had received a heart valve device.[46]
- Federal marshals impounded more than 2,000 sphygmomanometers from the Surgical Instrument Company of America because these devices allegedly had defective pressure gauges and leaking and torn inflator bladders.[47]
- Wire leads on 22,000 pacemakers manufactured by Telectronics Pacing Systems, Inc. (Englewood, CA) were declared a potential lethal risk for patients with cardiac problems because of possible fractures in the wire leads, causing severe heart injury or death.[48]

Critically, up to 75 percent of adverse drug reactions are preventable.[49] On a less positive note, a medical marketing trade journal alerted its readers in 1994 to the hidden negative aspects of MedWatch relative to their business concerns.[50]

On July 20, 2001 the FDA issued an advisory to hospitals and nursing homes concerning the misconnecting of oxygen delivery systems. From July 1997 to July 2001, the FDA received reports of seven deaths and 15 injuries associated with medical gas misconnections (see Box 2-5).

Currently, there is also a proposal by the FDA for a new format for prescription drug product labeling, also known as the package insert. The current labeling has been criticized as being too lengthy, complex, and hard to use, and changes are designed to be more user-friendly, in the hope of reducing medical errors.[51]

Baycol (Cerivastatin), a cholesterol-lowering drug, was pulled off the market by Bayer Corporation in response to 31 deaths due to severe rhabdomyolisis, an adverse muscle reaction reported to the FDA. More than 700,000 people take Baycol, which was approved in 1997.[52]

BOX 2-5

Medical Gas Mishaps[53]

- At the Hospital of St. Raphael's in Connecticut, two women died during diagnostic catheterization when they were given lethal doses of nitrous oxide instead of oxygen. A safety feature on the oxygen flow meter was missing.
- At a hospital in Ohio, two patients died after a medical gas deliverer used a wrench to disconnect the fitting on a vessel of nitrogen that he believed to be oxygen, and replaced it with an oxygen fitting.

The Centers for Disease Control (CDC) and the FDA have been investigating CryoLife Corporation after 27 people developed serious infections and one died after receiving soft-tissue implants processed by the company. About 650,000 people each year in the United States have surgery involving soft-tissue implants, and CryoLife supplies 15 to 20 percent of the market. The company processes 70 percent of the nation's heart valves and 90 percent of vascular tissue from human cadavers; it also supplies soft tissues such as tendons, ligaments, and cartilage for elective orthopedic surgery.[54]

Medical Waste Tracking Act (MWTA) of 1988

This legislation was a political response to the highly publicized hysteria over hypodermic needles that washed up onto the beaches of three states. Although the MWTA was a federal law, the mandates were limited to two years and applied only to Connecticut, New Jersey, New York, Rhode Island, and Puerto Rico. Participation was voluntary for any other state. The MWTA requires tracking of seven types of waste: cultures and stocks, pathological wastes, human blood and blood products, sharps, animal waste, isolation waste, and unused sharps. By 1991, when the MWTA expired, the problem had evaporated.

Regulations for hazardous waste, such as mercury or radioactive wastes, are developed by the federal government. Potentially infectious medical waste, sometimes referred to as Regulated Medical Waste, is generally covered by state regulations.

The MWTA required the Environmental Protection Agency to investigate various treatment technologies available at the time for their ability to reduce the disease-causing potential of medical waste. The technologies that the EPA examined in 1990 included incinerators and autoclaves (both on-site and off-site), microwave units, and various chemical and mechanical systems. From the information gathered during this period, the EPA concluded that the disease-causing potential of medical waste is greatest at the point of generation and naturally tapers off after that point, thus presenting more of an occupational concern than a generalized environmental concern. Risk to the general public of disease caused by exposure to medical waste is likely to be much lower than the risk to the occupationally exposed individual.[55]

Environmental Protection Agency (EPA)

Although individual hospital incinerators are relatively small, an EPA report stated that collectively, medical waste incineration by hospitals may be the largest source of airborne dioxin emissions in the United States.[56] Such emissions constitute a risk because the EPA has concluded that dioxin causes cancer in animals and is a probable human carcinogen. Hospitals use many disposable medical products typically made of chlorinated plastics. These waste materials, high in chlorine, are burned, freeing the element during combustion to form dioxin. Often, medical waste incinerators lack technologies to reduce, control, and monitor toxic emissions into the air. Opponents of this method of waste disposal vehemently assert that medical waste should not be incinerated under any circumstances.[57] As of 1996, new EPA regulations require hospitals using medical waste incinerators to eliminate toxic emissions and to monitor compliance. As a result, hospitals have changed the way they handle medical waste. In Florida, high-volume regional incinerators have replaced smaller on-site units. Since 1989, about 90 small hospital incinerators, 75 percent of Florida's total, have shut down. In 1994, the Mayo Clinic in Rochester, Minnesota, opened a $10.6 million, state-of-the-art incinerator 10 miles north of the clinic. Advanced incineration technology is combined with an aggressive recycling program to reduce the volume of waste burned. This incinerator also accepts waste from other area hospitals.

Currently, over 90 percent of potentially infectious medical waste is incinerated. In August 1997, the EPA promulgated regulations concerning emissions from medical waste incinerators (MWI). These regulations include: (a) stringent air emissions guidelines for states to use in developing plans to reduce air pollution from medical waste incinerators built on or before June 20, 1996; and (b) final air emission standards for medical waste incinerators built after June 20, 1996. These guidelines and standards will substantially reduce MWI emissions. The EPA estimates that mercury emission will decline by 94 percent, particulate matter by 90 percent, hydrogen chloride by 98 percent, and dioxin by 95 percent.

On June 24, 1998, the EPA entered into a voluntary partnership with the American Hospital Association (AHA) and its member hospitals to: (a) virtually eliminate mercury waste generated by hospitals by 2005; (b) reduce overall hospital waste volume by 33 percent by 2005, and 50 percent by 2010; and (c) jointly identify additional substances to target for pollution prevention and waste reduction opportunities.[58]

Regulatory Implementation Mandates

Legislation allows governmental agencies to audit and survey health care facilities to determine whether the institution is abiding by regulatory standards. These audits and surveys can be accomplished through personal visits, written questionnaires, or telephone inquiries. They may be by appointment or random, without notice to the agency, such as by the state health department.[59]

Inspectors have the power to review the physical plant and the operations of facilities, and to examine documentation. Serious violations can result in a loss of a license to operate, as well as in monetary fines. Risk managers must ensure that the organization is prepared at all times for an unannounced or unexpected audit or survey.

STATE LEGISLATION AND REGULATIONS

Historically, general health regulation has been a matter of local concern.[60] Health care facilities such as hospitals, skilled nursing facilities, intermediate nursing facilities, and managed care entities require a license before they can become operational. Individual professionals such as physicians, dentists, registered nurses, physical therapists, and psychologists must have a state license or state registration before they can render care to their clients.

Reacting to "oppressive health care regulations," in 1994 New York's governor revised 16 edicts, including those mandating on-site inspections, hospital social work departments, the education and experience requirements for emergency room staffs, the explanation to all patients of their rights, and the indicators for reporting adverse events.[61] A *New York Times* editorial labeled the plan "a modest easing of hospital regulations."[62] This action by a state governor follows the example set at the federal level of reducing the government's involvement in the regulation of industry. New Jersey legislators also considered reforming 25 years of a tight rein over health care facilities and services,[63] but not before flexing regulatory power again (see Box 2-6).

The sections that follow look at some examples of state regulation of the health care industry.

BOX 2-6

Blue Cross/Blue Shield of New Jersey was fined $106,000 for setting up a string of family health centers without prior approval from the state health department. These centers were part of a $13 million network of 10 centers to serve 200,000 managed care policyholders.[64]

Licensure and Registration of Professional Institutions

State governments have always had the responsibility of licensing health care professionals and defining the parameters of their practices. All the states license professionals such as physicians, dentists, and registered nurses. However, not all the states license or register providers such as physical and occupational therapists. Licensing or registration remains a state prerogative and is subject to change. In addition, legislation concerned with professional malpractice is embedded in state tort law that deals with civil and criminal injury and harm. Box 2-7 raises a malpractice question and answers with a real example.

Smoke-Free Workplace

More than 40 states have enacted legislation to restrict smoking in public places, including health care facilities, and 11 states regulate smoking in the workplace. Civil court judges in California, Georgia, and Ohio

BOX 2-7

Should an insurer deny malpractice coverage to a nurse who rendered a service that, under statute, is defined as "medical" practice? Nurse Valerie Tomlinson was suspended from the Royal Cornwall Hospital for operating on a patient.[65]

have found that "battery," which usually entails touching people against their will, can apply to secondhand cigarette, cigar, or pipe smoke (see Box 2-8).

Although many states and cities have adopted laws restricting smoking in public places, when it comes to enforcement, such laws are usually regarded as self-policing.[66] Efforts to eliminate the risk of secondhand cigarette smoke were stimulated by a 500-page 1992 report from the Environmental Protection Agency that estimated 3,000 deaths per year from such exposure.[67] Even small amounts of smoke can endanger nonsmokers and may double or triple their risk of heart disease.[68] Indoor air quality regulations are evolving to protect workers from various outdoor contaminants and to control microbial contaminants by routine inspection.[69,70]

Violence Prevention

California passed a law requiring all hospitals to provide training and education in security measures. All hospitals were required to initiate violence prevention programs by July 1995. This legislation was prompted by statistics revealing that almost 60 percent of the hospitals in the five largest cities in the state had reported attacks on staff, patients, and visitors.[71] Beefing up security was particularly critical for emergency rooms. A survey by the journal *Topics in Emergency Medicine* reported that 43 percent of hospitals experienced at least one physical attack per month on a medical staff member.[73]

BOX 2-8

Bank receptionist Bonnie Richardson claimed that a colleague maliciously directed pipe smoke at her. She went to the hospital twice for severe headaches, nausea, and weight loss. She sued and won. A judge for the Georgia State Appeals Court declared: "Pipe smoke is visible. It is detectable through the senses and may be ingested or inhaled. It is capable of touching or making contact with one's person in a number of ways."[72]

STATE-MANDATED RISK MANAGEMENT LEGISLATION

Several states have passed legislation or promulgated regulations requiring hospitals to implement risk management programs. A federal government study[7] compared the major characteristics of ten state programs: Alaska, Colorado, Florida, Kansas, Maryland, Massachusetts, New York, North Carolina, Rhode Island, and Washington. Legislative and regulatory requirements of Maryland and New York that apply to health care are relatively comprehensive. Maryland is unique because it is the only state in which the requirements represent a consensus of the hospital industry, legal interests, and the state government. New York mandates reveal detailed requirements for a combined risk management and quality assessment program supported by an extensive survey process to monitor compliance.

In most of these states, risk management requirements are specifically designed to interrelate with other quality assessment initiatives in the hospital environment. Significantly, the requirements are made a condition for the hospital's licensure by the state. Generally, the mandates focus on preventing and controlling risk to patients, rather than on risks such as fire prevention, equipment maintenance, safety, and security. A 10-state comparison illustrates the considerable variabilities among the mandated risk management regulations.

Not every state mandates every risk management characteristic. Nevertheless, a framework emerges for implementing a basic risk management program in all instances. These nine main legislative and regulatory attributes are compared in Exhibit 2-4 and examined further in the sections that follow.

Risk Management Responsibility

Depending on the state, hospitals must assign risk management responsibility to a single risk management coordinator or to a committee. In some instances, states can choose between the two. Two states (Arkansas and Rhode Island) do not assign such responsiblity.

Governing Body Involvement

When state regulations require governing body involvement, emphasis ranges from ensuring that governing bodies provide an adequate level of resources and support systems to a minimal requirement that the governing bodies formally approve a risk

EXHIBIT 2-4 GENERAL CHARACTERISTICS OF STATE RISK MANAGEMENT REQUIREMENTS

CHARACTERISTICS	AK, 1976	RI, 1979	FL, 1985	NY, 1985	KS, 1986	MD, 1986	WA, 1986	MA, 1986	NC, 1987	CO, 1988
Assigned responsibility for risk management program	—	—	X	X	X	X	X	X	X	X
Governing body involvement in risk management	—	—	X	X	X	X	X	X	X	X
Risk identification system	—	X	X	X	X	X	X	X	X	X
Investigation/analysis of risks	X	—	X	X	X	X	—	X	X	X
Education programs on risk management	X	X	X	X	—	X	X	X	X	—
Sharing of risk management information	—	—	—	X	—	X	X	X	X	X
Patient grievance procedure	X	X	X	X	—	X	X	X	—	—
Provisions for immunity and confidentiality	—	X	X	X	X	X	X	X	—	—
Follow-up of risk management activities	X	—	X	X	—	X	—	X	X	X

management plan. States can require that the governing board or hospital administrator receive reports on the risk management program. Reporting varies from a general statement to specific language calling for quarterly reports. A few states mandate that a member of the governing body also be a member of the risk management and/or quality assessment committee.

Risk Identification

Most states require systems to identify risks to patients. Legislative wording can be general, without establishing procedures, or it can be specific. Sometimes the legislation specifies the types of incidents to be reported by hospital staff, the patient grievance data required, and the additional quality assessment information demanded. Colorado commands its hospitals to submit for state approval a general description of the types of cases, problems, or risks to be reviewed, and the criteria to be used for identifying potential risks. Massachusetts' detailed requirements call for three risk identification methods: incident reporting, occurrence reporting, and occurrence screening. Exhibit 2-5 compares seven state-mandated requirements for risk identification systems.

Risk Analysis

Legislative mandates for risk analysis can range from a general obligation to specifics such as what to include in such analysis (for example, frequency and causes of injuries, time, place, persons involved). Exhibit 2-6 indicates the scope of analysis of identified risks by state.

Risk Management Education

State legislation can specify topics to include in risk management activities, can compel annual risk management education for designated staff, or can merely call for educational programs without giving a time frame. Examples of relevant subject matter include injury prevention, patient safety, principles and techniques of infection control, incident reporting or staff responsibility to report professional misconduct, legal aspects of care, causes of malpractice claims, patients' rights, improved communications, and topics related to employees' job responsibilities. Staff education can be for all staff, for appropriate staff, or for staff engaged in patient care activities. One state excludes physicians from the education requirement.

Sharing of Information

Colorado obliges hospitals to coordinate all pertinent case, problem, or risk review information with other applicable institutional quality assessment or risk management activities. Maryland requires "a flow of information" among quality assessment, credentialing, peer review, and any risk management committees. North Carolina dictates "operational linkages" between risk management and other functions relating to patient care, safety, and staff performance. New York orders hospitals to review extensive information, including quality assessment data, complaints, incident reports, and utilization review data to identify problems in patient care. Massachusetts indicates that credentialing, quality assessment, risk management, and peer review functions should be strongly and thoroughly integrated. Maryland, New York, and Washington have legislative requirements on credentialing information. New York, Washington, Maryland, and Kansas specifically require that a quality assessment or peer review committee be responsible for acting to correct identified problems.

EXHIBIT 2-5 RISK IDENTIFICATION SYSTEM REQUIREMENTS

	AK	RI	FL	NY	KS	MD	WA	MA	NC	CO
Risk identification required, but no specific system mandated	—	X	—	—	—	—	X	—	X	—
Incident reporting system	—	—	X	X	X	—	—	X	—	X
Occurrence reporting system	—	—	—	—	—	X[a]	—	X	—	—
Occurrence screening criteria required	—	—	—	—	—	—	—	X	—	—
Patient grievance data required	X	X	X	X	—	—	X	—	—	X
Other quality assurance data required	—	X	—	X	—	X	X	—	—	X
No risk identification required	X	—	—	—	—	—	—	—	—	—

[a]Although Maryland law refers to an "Incident Reporting" requirement, its hospitals must list and describe incidents to be routinely reported. Thus, Maryland law, in effect, imposes an occurrence reporting system.

EXHIBIT 2-6 ANALYSIS OF IDENTIFIED RISKS

	AK	RI	FL	NY	KS	MD	WA	MA	NC	CO
Requirement to investigate/analyze identified risks	X	—	X	X	X	X	—	X	X	X
Trending of identified risks is required	—	—	X	—	—	X	—	X	—	X
Investigation or analysis of patient complaints by hospital is required	X	—	X	X	—	X	—	X	—	—
Hospital investigation reports required	—	—	X	X	—	—	—	—	—	—
No investigation/analysis required	—	X	—	—	—	—	X	—	—	—

Patient Grievance Procedures

Most states regard patient grievance data as an important element in their risk management requirements. Maryland detailed its mandates for a patient complaint program with four specifics:

- Risk management programs must include a formal written program for addressing patient complaints.
- Patients must be given information about the program, including the name and phone number or address of a hospital representative whom the patient may contact to register a complaint.
- A hospital representative must treat the complaining patient with dignity, courtesy, and due regard for privacy and must provide the patient with certain information about the complaint-handling process.
- A hospital representative must document the complaint and any action taken as a result of it.

Massachusetts requires that all patients receive written notice of their rights within 24 hours of admission and be informed as to how to file complaints. Alaska's general requirement orders the hospital to have a procedure to investigate, analyze, and respond to patient grievances related to patient care.

Immunity and Confidentiality for Providers of Risk Management Information

Seven states grant immunity from liability to those who provide information on incidents; six provide for confidentiality. Immunity and confidentiality provisions have two goals: to shield those who report or evaluate risk management information; and to protect privileged risk management records from subpoena, discovery, or other public disclosure. Exhibit 2-7 reveals the extent of state legislation.

Risk Management Follow-up Procedures

Legislation and/or regulations may require a follow-up or review of a hospital's specific risk management actions and can include a summary report of risk management actions to the governing body. New York and Colorado oblige hospitals to institute a method for evaluating the effectiveness of actions taken to address risks or problems. Maryland mandates that hospitals establish an internal committee structure to conduct reviews and evaluations of risk management activites. Massachusetts obligates hospitals to create a system to ensure compliance with incident reporting requirements.

LOCAL CITY AND COUNTY LEGISLATION CONTROLS

Regulations and rules that affect risk management may be created at city and county levels. Although city and county legislative bodies often adopt and/or adapt federal and state requirements, there may be local variants. A city health department may enact its own regulations, such as procedures for the reporting of tuberculosis or communicable diseases of a sensitive nature (for example, positive lab results for sexually transmitted diseases), guidelines for sanitation and disposal of hazardous waste, restrictions on the transport of radioactive and/or nuclear materials through city streets, and the functions of patient advocates. A county water department may set thresholds for purification chemicals added to drinking water or to be found in waste water. Building codes, fire safety regulations, and occupancy permits are generally a function of local government. A risk man-

EXHIBIT 2-7 IMMUNITY AND CONFIDENTIALITY INCLUDED IN LEGISLATION AND REGULATIONS

	AK	RI	FL	NY	KS	MD	WA	MA	CO	NC
Specifically prohibits retaliation/discrimination against employees who report incidents	—	—	X	—	X	—	—	—	X	—
Immunity from liability for those who provide risk management information in good faith	—	X	X	X	X	X	X	X	—	—
Immunity from liability for members of peer review, quality assurance, or risk management committee	—	X	X	X	X	X	X	X	—	—
Risk management documents generally confidential	—	—	X[a]	X	X	—	X	—	—	—
Proceedings of medical staff/peer review meetings confidential	—	—	—	—	X	X	—	—	—	—
Confidentiality specifically not provided for data obtained from other sources	—	X	—	—	—	—	—	X	—	—

[a]Some documents are discoverable (that is, may be revealed to opposing counsel but are not admissable in court).

ager should be aware of the major laws and regulations at all levels of government.

REIMBURSEMENT REQUIREMENTS

Third-party insurers set their own standards for reimbursement to providers and to the insured parties. Usually, the insurers establish an indemnification system wherein the providers agree to reimbursement standards such as accepting whatever fee schedule the insurer establishes as the total payment, accepting predefined amounts for specific services but billing the patient for any differential from their regular fee, or agreeing to a discount off their usual and customary fee. Some variations on these standards involve a patient out-of-pocket copayment or co-insurance, and private insurance companies set their own standards for the types of services for which they will pay and for when the services are appropriate.

Managed care organizations negotiate their reimbursement fees with individual practitioners, with clinical groups, and with hospitals. Significantly, these reimbursement guidelines can include financial incentives or disincentives. If practitioners reduce their referrals and hospitalizations, they may receive a bonus from any surplus funds. On the other hand, if practitioners use too many resources in rendering care, the potential bonus could be reduced. However, such financial awards or punishments are within the standards for quality of care that the managed care entity establishes. Despite their critics, health maintenance organizations (HMOs) and preferred provider organizations (PPOs) maintain that their subscribers receive whatever medical care is appropriate; no medically necessary care is denied. There are serious arguments about the financial incentives in health care, and the money/care relationship raises liability issues for risk management.

Reimbursement by public entities requires adhering to their respective standards as well. Medicare is an insurance program; Medicaid is a type of welfare. Since Medicare is a federal program, the standards are uniform for the entire nation. Fees are calculated based on federal determinations. Medicaid, on the other hand, is a combined federal/state/local financing program with 50 different standards as established by each of the states. Each state also makes its own determination of reimbursement policies.

Through a prospective payment system using a payment mechanism of diagnosis-related groups (DRGs), the federal Health Care Financing Administration (HCFA) requires that every Medicare patient be classified into one of the approximately 500 DRGs in order for the institution to receive payment for services rendered. Furthermore, the HCFA sets a length of stay for each DRG, and providers must explain why patients are remaining in the facility if the outside limit of the length of stay is exceeded.[74]

A resources-based relative value scale (RBRVS) is another reimbursement mechanism for services rendered by providers. An RBRVS aims to set fees for ambulatory care provided by physicians. Generally, the reimbursement relies on a written calculation of the relative value of specific procedures as compared to an initial base service. In essence, a price is set by agreement with the insurers, and standards are implemented to follow the rules. Violations could disqualify the facility and/or the individuals from providing care to people covered by that insurer.

FALSE CLAIMS

In reimbursement, "bundling" and "unbundling" refer to the manner in which services are billed. When care is rendered as a package with all the resources included in the billed amount, the services are said to be bundled together. Unbundled services are itemized and billed for separately. Regulations need to be checked to determine whether revenue flow can be increased by unbundling individual items of care. Whereas inpatient care services may be bundled together in a set fee for each DRG, outpatient care may not be reimbursed in a similar fashion. To enable unbundling, facilities could convert selected inpatient services to outpatient services, assuming that such conversions were feasible and posed no harm to patients.

Anti-fraud activities of the federal government under the regulations of the False Claims Act (FCA) range from audits of hospitals, nursing homes, medical care organizaations (MCOs), and practicing health professionals to targeted medical care claims. It is estimated that there is a direct monetary return of $8 for each $1 invested in FCA enforcement activities.[75] Regulatory actions have resulted in both a $30 million settlement with the University of Pennsylvania and a $5.3 million fine at Georgetown University.[76]

Under July 1996 regulations for teaching hospitals, the federal government started PATH (Physicians at Teaching Hospitals) audits (see Box 2-9).

The FCA allows the government, as well as private citizens, to sue individuals or companies that are defrauding the government, and to recover three times the damages plus additional penalties. In Pennsylvania, 11 hospitals and their consultants were charged with upcoding, unbundling, and rebundling Medicare claims to increase their reimbursement. Physicians or institutions can be excluded from participation in Medicare, Medicaid, and other federal programs.

The reward provision under FCA allows whistleblowers a 15 to 25 percent share of the total amount the government recovers. Whistleblowers are encouraged and protected, and could be employees or competitors. Lawsuits initiated by whistleblowers are called *qui tam* cases.[76]

PRACTICE GUIDELINES

Voluntary regulatory programs, such as the Joint Commission on the Accreditation of Healthcare Organizations (JCAHO), the National Committee for Quality Assurance (NCQA), and board certification by professional specialty societies, have a decided impact on risk management considerations. Health care institutions may be denied reimbursement by government programs and third-party insurers if they are not accredited by the JCAHO.[78] With the increased competition in the health care field, voluntary accreditation can be used in marketing and advertising activities, since the public views such accreditation as evidence of high-quality care.

JCAHO's nationwide prominence in promoting high-quality health care has influenced most state regulatory agencies to accept its findings when considering accreditation and/or licensure applications. Third-party insurers rely on JCAHO decisions in reimbursement matters. On the federal level, the Department of Health and Human Services (HHS) accepts the JCAHO accreditation as evidence that the institution meets the Medicare conditions of participation. That recognition allows the provider to bill for services rendered to individuals having Medicare coverage. Disturbingly, a 1992 validation sample by the federal HCFA of hospitals accredited by the JCAHO revealed that one of three failed to meet Medicare/Medicaid standards. The October 1994 *Health Letter* of the Public Citizen's Health Research Group reported that 57 (34%) of 167 hospitals failed to meet one or more of the federal conditions of participation. Profound questions can be raised about the safety and quality of care rendered. This validation suggests that between 1,000 and 1,900 hospitals may have placed millions of patients at risk without timely intervention by the JCAHO, raising serious questions as to whether government regulators should continue to rely on the JCAHO for hospitals' accreditations.[79]

Accreditation programs for seven different types of health care are sponsored by the JCAHO: ambulatory health care, home care, hospice care, long term care, psychiatric facilities, hospital care, and managed care.

BOX 2-9

Thomas Jefferson University paid $12 million to settle charges that faculty claimed reimbursement for patients treated by residents.[77]

Each of these accreditation programs develops standards and uses a peer-based consultative and educational survey process to stimulate the provision of high-quality patient care. In addition, each accreditation program encompasses a variety of organizations and providers:

Ambulatory care: clinics, surgery centers, college or university health services, community health centers, emergency care centers, group practices, primary care centers, and urgent care centers.

Home care and hospice care: independent programs, home health care agencies, hospital-based programs, long term care organizations, and psychiatric agencies. Areas covered include home visits by health care professionals, setting up equipment, education of family members providing care, homemaker services, drug administration in the home, personal services such as shopping, and support services such as lawn mowing.

Long term care: hospital-based care, freestanding care, nursing homes, rehabilitation centers, and custodial facilities.

Psychiatric facilities: community mental health services, programs for the developmentally disabled, forensic psychiatric services, substance abuse programs, and psychiatric services.

Hospital care: about 75 percent of the general and specialty hospitals in the United States accredited by the JCAHO.

Managed care: a variety of developing managed care entities, such as HMOs, PPOs, and Individual Practice Associations (IPAs).

Standards may be implemented within an institution, and apply only in that facility, through utilization management, quality assessment, and peer review. Utilization management tends to focus on the efficacy and effective use of resources. Quality assessment aims to ensure that the procedures followed abide by the internal standards and guidelines. New criteria for reporting an occurrence as a sentinel event have been issued by the JCAHO.[80] Failure to comply with the reporting requirement will place the facility on accreditation-watch status. Incidents must be reported to the JCAHO when a patient is affected by circumstances such as the following: an event resulting in an unanticipated death or major loss of function not related to the natural course of the patient's illness or underlying condition; suicide during continuous care; infant abduction or discharge to the wrong family; rape; hemolytic transfusion involving the administration of blood or blood products having major group incompatibilities; or surgery on the wrong patient or body part. Peer review occurs in tissue committees, mortality conferences, infection control committees, and quality improvement committees. In addition to these activities that implement standards, organizations usually have their own mandates regarding admissions, readmissions within a brief time period for the same condition, appropriate laboratory and diagnostic tests, repeated surgery for the same problem, length of stay, the process of care, and discharge planning (see Box 2-10). Risk managers must be alert to any violations of internal standards,

BOX 2-10

The Department of Veterans Affairs issued an advisory to its physicians recommending that they no longer perform arthroscopic surgery on the knee. A study by V.A. researchers concluded that it was no more effective than placebo arthroscopy.[81]

since there is a direct relationship to outside regulatory requirements. Most of these internal guidelines could have an impact on reimbursement from third-party insurers.

To complicate the situation, internal requirements may be duplicated by outside organizations. Notable examples include the JCAHO, the Medicare and Medicaid programs, the Institute of Medicine, the Agency for Health Care Policy and Research, the National Committee for Quality Assurance, and a variety of specialty professional societies. A directory of practice parameters, titles, sources, and updates delineates about 1,600 practice guidelines developed by 70 organizations.[82] Risk management programs can use the outside standards as a minimum to establish their internal guidelines. If internal standards are better than the outside guides, violations and penalties are less likely.

What If Practice Guidelines Are Not Met?

Failure to fulfill the legal obligation to provide a quality of care that meets professional standards constitutes a breach of standards. Although medical malpractice awards may occupy the mass-media headlines, however, the majority of Americans do not sue their health care providers. Legislation noted in Box 2-11 attempted to raise the mandated level of physician competence.

BOX 2-11

A legislative bill sought to change the physician competence standard from requiring "a preponderance of credible evidence" to requiring "clear and convincing evidence," a tougher standard. A newspaper editorial noted that the doctors would move from the same standard as lawyers to a more stringent level.[83]

Falls are the most common adverse event reported by health care institutions. An elderly patient may fall from a bed because its railings are missing, an employee or a visitor may slip on a wet floor when a warning sign is absent, and a nurse may be stuck by a needle if syringes are not disposed of correctly. All of these incidents are covered in the practice guidelines and training of health care workers. All are preventable.

Potential damages from these breaches of standards could result in physical, emotional, social, and/or environmental harm. An individual could receive merely bumps and bruises, or could be permanently disabled or even die. Embarrassment, humiliation, and mental distress are typical allegations included under "pain and suffering." Breakage and structural damages may also be involved. Damages appear to be limited only by the creativity of the people suing the health care facility. Several examples in Box 2-12 illustrate potential risk situations.

A broad range of possible damage outcomes includes censure, personnel action, monetary loss from fines, loss of individual practitioner privileges, facility closures and/or reductions, loss of licensure, loss of accreditation, a professional or criminal negligence lawsuit, imprisonment, loss of confidence in the facility, revenue stream disruption, mergers, bankruptcy, and corporate dissolution.

IGNORANCE OF THE LAW IS NO EXCUSE

Numerous complicated laws, regulations, and standards seriously affect the management of risks in health care institutions. Violations of the mandates can result in fines and penalties that could damage the health care facility's financial well-being. Risk management personnel help prepare for

BOX 2-12

- A dentist was granted provisional hospital staff membership and placed under observation of designated proctors. Unfavorable reports claimed that the dentist spent too much time on certain procedures, that blood loss in some patients was excessive, and that too many patients needed follow-up and repeat procedures. A hospital decision denied the oral and maxillofacial surgeon privileges beyond tooth extraction.[84]
- Antonio Benedi, a special assistant to ex-President George Bush, habitually drank wine with his dinner. To combat the flu, he took Tylenol for several days. There was no warning on the box or bottle about the danger of mixing alcohol with the drug. Benedi lapsed into a coma and was hospitalized. Later, he had a kidney transplant and expects to start kidney dialysis. Benedi claimed that his liver had been "sensitized" to react to Tylenol. A jury awarded him $7.855 million for compensatory damages and $1 million for punitive damages.[85]

regulatory or voluntary inspections, maintain documentation relative to administrative and clinical issues mandated by good operations, and establish appropriate oversight of the medical care provided by the agency or hospital. To carry out these functions effectively, risk managers must initiate mechanisms to learn about all the laws, regulations, and standards, on federal, state, and local levels, and to implement risk prevention and control activities.

References

1. Speigel, A. D., and Backhaut, B. H. (1980). *Curing and Caring: A Review of the Factors Affecting the Quality and Acceptability of Health Care.* New York: SP Medical & Scientific Books, pp. 22–27.
2. Joint Commission on Accreditation of Healthcare Organizations. (2001). *Device vise: Joint Commission enforcing OSHA needle mandate, hospital infection control.* October.
3. Allerton, H. (1994). Price per pound. *Training & Development* 48(5):144.
4. Murphy, B. S., Barlow, W. E., and Hatch, D. D. (1994). Discrimination against the obese violates Rehab Act. *Personnel Journal* 3(2):35–36.
5. Moskowitz, E. (1994). In the courts—Am I disabled? *Hastings Center Report* 24(3):4.
6. Skoning, G. D., and McGlothlen, C. A. (1994). Other laws shape ADA policies. *Personnel Journal* 73(4): 116–118.
7. Bain, D. P. (1989). *Initiatives in Hospital Risk Management.* GAO/HRD-89-79. Washington, D.C.: Government Printing Office, pp. 6, 20–27.
8. Wilson, T. H. (1994). *OSHA Guide for Health Care Facilities.* Tampa, Fla.: Thompson Publishing Group.
9. Shikles, J. L. (1994). *Workplace Regulation: Information on Selected Employer and Union Experiences.* GAO/HEHS-94-138. Washington, D.C.: Government Printing Office, pp. 26–28, 42–44.
10. U.S. Department of Labor, Occupational Safety and Health Administration. (2001). *Hospital Hazards.* Revision date: November 20, 2001.
11. U.S. Department of Labor, Office of Public Affairs. (2002). *OSHA Reopens Tuberculosis Rulemaking Record.* January 14.
12. Udasin, I. G., and Gochfeld, M. (1994). Implications of the OSHA's bloodborne pathogen standard for the occupational health professional. *American Journal of Occupational Medicine* 36(5): 548–555.
13. Thompson Publishing Group. (1994). Brochure for Wilson book (see reference 10), pp. 2–3.
14. U.S. Department of Labor, Occupational Safety and Health Administration. (2000). Congressional Testimonies: Bloodborne Pathogens. (June 22, 2000). The Subcommittee on Workforce Protections House Education and the Workforce Committee, Statement of Charles N. Jeffress, Assistant Secretary of OSHA.
15. Needlestick requirements take effect April 18. (2001). OSHA national news release, April 12.
16. NIOSH alert: Preventing needlestick injuries in health care setings. Publication No. 2000-108.
17. Sentinel Alert. (2001). Preventing needlestick and sharps injuries. Joint Commission on Accreditation of Healthcare Organization. August, Issue 22. *http://www.jcaho.org*.

18. *Health Insurance Portability and Accountability Act of 1996*, Public Law 104-191, Title II, Subtitle F, *Administrative Simplification and Privacy Provisions*. (28 December 2000). In Pear, R. (2002). Bush rolls back rules on privacy of medical data. *New York Times*, August 10, p. 1.
19. Associated Press. (2002). Efforts abound to limit pharmaceutical marketing. East Brunswick (New Jersey) *Home News Tribune*. August 4, p. E10.
20. Occupational Safety and Health Administration. (1991). *OSHA Action Needed to Improve Compliance with Hazard Communication Standard*. GAO/HRD-92-8. Washington, D.C.: Government Printing Office.
21. Litvan, L. (1994). OSHA sharply increases fines for serious safety violations. *Nation's Business* 82(9):8.
22. COBRA—A summary of final regulations. (1995). *Hospital Risk Manager* 3(4):1–2.
23. Bernstein, S. (1994). Advertising letter re Wilson book (see reference 8), p. 3.
24. Patient not formally admitted but "dumped" all the same. (1995). *American Medical News* 38(9):20.
25. McCormick, B. (1994). Dumping law enforcement lags. *American Medical News* 37(42):37.
26. Felsenthal, E. (1994). Patients skirt states' malpractice limits. *Wall Street Journal* August 30, p. B2, col. 3.
27. Segal, M. (1994). Mammography facilities must meet quality standards. FDA Consumer 28(2):8–12; Quality standards compliance for mammography facilities. (1994). *Journal of the American Medical Association* 272(10):763.
28. Fintor, L., Alciati, M. H., and Fischer, R. (1995). Legislative and regulatory mandates for mammography quality assurance. *Journal of Public Health Policy* 16(1):81–103.
29. *Mammography Quality Standard Act*, Federal Register Notice; Direct Federal Rule. June 17, 1999.
30. Doctors falling short in mammogram skills. (2002). *New York Times* News Service, June 27.
31. In Denver, a mammogram team learns from its errors. (2002). *New York Times* News Service, June 28.
32. Oberman, L. (1994). Group backs FDA-like review of tests and treatments. *American Medical News* 37(40):6–7.
33. Cohen, R. (1995). Medical device industry wants a private, European-type FDA. *Star-Ledger* (Newark, N.J.), February 10, p. 3, col. 4.
34. Roane, K. (2002). Replacement parts. *U.S. News & World Report*, July 29, pp. 54–59.
35. Service, R. S. (1995). Liability concerns threaten medical implant research. *Science* 266(4):726–727.
36. Scott, L. (1995). Researchers test safety of medical device reuse. *Modern Healthcare* 25(17):78.
37. Cohen, R., and Orr, J. S. (2002). A hipmaker's billion dollar mistake, *Star-Ledger* (Newark, N.J.), August 13, p. A1.
38. Bruley, M. (1991). Investigating equipment-related accidents. Presentation at the American Health Risk Management Association, New York, December 6.
39. Rudolph, R. (1994). Ousted J&J exec files suit to regain his post. *Star-Ledger* (Newark, N.J.), November 8, p. 24, col. 3.
40. Siemens unit in U.S. to halt some output to correct problems. (1994). *Wall Street Journal* February 25, p. B8, col. 1.
41. Taylor, I. (1994). FDA clears the way for Siemens Medical. *Star-Ledger* (Newark, N.J.), November 8, p. 45, col. 4.
42. Cohen, R., and Orr, J. S. (2002). Often the patient is the last to know. *Star-Ledger* (Newark, N.J.), August 11, p. 9.
43. Kessler, D. A. (1993). Introducing MEDWatch. A new approach to reporting medication and device adverse effects and product problems. *Journal of the American Medical Association* 269(21):2765–2768.
44. Monitoring medical products. You can help. (1994). *People's Medical Society Newsletter* 13(3):6.
45. Burton, T. M. (1994). Law concerning medical devices is often ignored. *Wall Street Journal* May 2, p. B1, col. 3.
46. Meier, B. (1994). Pfizer unit to settle charges of lying about heart valve. *New York Times* July 2, p. A33, col. 1; Defective implants can slip past FDA's checkpoints. (1995). *Staten Island Advance* (N.Y.), January 30, p. B8, col. 1.
47. Rudolph, R. (1994). U.S. seizes blood pressure devices at firm cited for failing FDA rules. *Star-Ledger* (Newark, N.J.), November 4, p. 71, col. 1.
48. Leary, W. (1995). Remedy sought for 22,000 patients with risk pacemakers. *New York Times* January 16, p. A9, col. 1; Leary, W. (1995). Government urges testing for pacemakers with wiring problem. *New York Times* January 25, p. A13, col. 1.
49. Horton, R. (1994). MEDWatch moves forward. *The Lancet* 343(8893):285–286.

50. Dickinson, J. G. (1994). Hidden negatives in FDA's MedWatch efforts? *Medical Marketing & Media* 29(3):34, 36.
51. Food and Drug Administration, Office of Public Affairs. (2000). Physicians labeling proposal, *HHS News*, December 21.
52. *http:/www.civilrights.com/baycol.html.*
53. Hospital where 2 died says it failed to shut a gas line. (2002). *New York Times*, January 19, p. B5.
54. Blakeslee, S. (2002). Recall is ordered at large supplier of implant tissue. *New York Times*, August 15, p. 1.
55. U.S. Environmental Protection Agency. Medical Waste: Frequently Asked Questions, *http://www.epa.gov/epaoswer/other/medical/mwfaqs.htm.* Website updated June 24, 2002.
56. Hearn, W. (1994). EPA calls hospital incinerators key dioxin emission source. *American Medical News* 37(40):19.
57. Charlton, A. (1995). Advisory panel voices opposition to incinerating medical waste. *Star-Ledger* (Newark, N.J.), April 16, p. 40, col. 4.
58. U.S. Environmental Protection Agency. Medical Waste: Frequently Asked Questions. *http://www.epa.gov.* June 24, 2002.
59. Leusner, D. (1994). Coalition beats back legislation to replace state inspection of hospitals. *Star-Ledger* (Newark, N.J.), December 2, p. 35, col. 1.
60. Johnsson, J. (1995). Supreme court lowers barrier to health reform. *American Medical News* 38(19):1, 28, 31.
61. Fisher, I. (1995). Pataki will lift some regulations for health care. *New York Times* April 5, p. 1, col. 6.
62. A modest easing of hospital regulations. (1995). *New York Times* April 12, p. A24, col. 1.
63. Leusner, D. (1995). Debate begins on easing health service rules. *Star-Ledger* (Newark, N.J.), March 19, p. 21, col. 2.
64. Whitlow, J. (1995). Blue Cross fined $106,000 for failing to get clearance on HMO centers. *Star-Ledger* (Newark, N.J.), February 8, p. 7, col. 1.
65. *The Lancet.* (1995). Who is a surgeon? 345(8951): 663–665.
66. Rigotti, N. A., Stoto, M. A., and Schelling, T. C. (1994). Do businesses comply with no-smoking law? Assessing the self-enforcement approach. *Preventive Medicine* 23(2):223–239.
67. U.S. Environmental Protection Agency. (1992). *Respiratory Health Effects of Passive Smoking: Lung Cancer and Other Disorders.* EPA/600/6-90/006F. Washington, D.C.: Government Printing Office.
68. Smoke said to take greater toll on nonsmokers. (1995). *New York Times* April 5, p. A21, col. 1.
69. Murphy, B. S., Barlow, W. E., and Hatch, D. D. (1994). OSHA proposes indoor air quality regulations. *Personnel Journal* 73(6):32–35.
70. Swoboda, F., and Hamilton, M. M. (1994). No-smoking push ignites firestorm of controversy. *Star-Ledger* (Newark, N.J.), December 4, Sec. 3, p. 1, col. 1.
71. Dunkel, T. (1994). Newest danger zone: Your office. *Working Woman* 19(8):38–41.
72. Woo, J. (1994). Blowing smoke around others may be battery. *Wall Street Journal* April 11, p. B6, col. 6.
73. Kahn, S. (1994). Risk of violence a chronic problem in many hospitals. *Business Insurance* 28(37):1, 12.
74. Spiegel, A. D., and Kavaler, F. (1986). *Cost Containment and DRGs: A Guide to Prospective Payment.* Owing Mills, Md: Rynd Communications.
75. Meyer, J. and Anthony, S. (2001). Reducing health care fraud: An assessment of the impact of the False Claims Act, Oct. 1. *Legislative and Policy Issues in the Year 2001*, Legislative Update of the False Claims Act Legal Center. *http://www.tat.org/legislative.html.*
76. Phillips, J. R., and Cohen, M. L. (1997). How to avoid liablity under the False Claims Act. *American Medical News*, Feb. 10.
77. Compliance in Medical Research and Academic Centers Forum, St. Louis University School of Medicine, Nov. 29–30, 2001. http://www.hcca-info.org/documents/acad-comp.pdf.
78. Altman, L. K. (1995). Federal official cites deficiencies at Harvard hospital. *New York Times* May 31, p. A16, col. 1; Hospital official resigns over drug overdoses. (1995). *New York Times* May 12, p. A16, col. 1.
79. 34 percent of JCAHO-accredited hospitals failed Medicare standards in 1992. (1994). *Medical Benefits* 11(21):11.
80. JCAHO sentinel event reporting detailed at E&A Conference. (1998). *AABB Weekly Report* 4(25):6–7.
81. Kolata, G. (2002). V.A. suggests halt to kind of knee surgery. *New York Times*, August 24, p. A9.

82. Office of Quality Assessment and Utilization Management. (1995). *Directory of Practice Parameters, Titles, Sources, and Updates.* Chicago: American Medical Association.

83. Rx for competence (editorial). *Star-Ledger* (Newark, N.J.), November 19, p. 32, col. 1.

84. Berry, R. (1994). Court finds no malice in hospital privileges case. *Journal of the American Dental Association* 125(3):324–325.

85. Verdict against Tylenol upheld. (1994). *News Tribune* (Woodbridge, N.J.), December 4, p. A3, col. 1.

CHAPTER 3 Identifying and Controlling Risks as an Employer

Steven J. Greenblatt
Diana J. Goldwasser

We live and work in a litigious society, and therefore we must develop and enact policies and procedures in the workplace that will protect institutions, employees, clients, and the public not only from harm, but also from litigation. There is a need for risk management techniques and oversight both in the administration of human resources and in facility management. The procedures by which an institution selects, appoints, promotes, demotes, disciplines, and separates employees demonstrate to its employees and the community its corporate conscience and climate, as well as its vulnerability/susceptibility to risk and litigation. The management of human resources is governed by many federal, state, and city laws relating to wrongful discharge, racial or religious discrimination, sexual harassment, age discrimination, disability law, AIDS, workers' compensation, accidents and injuries, and even the provision of medical treatment.

WRONGFUL DISMISSAL OR DISCHARGE

A new and rapidly growing area of employer liability centers around the allegations of wrongful dismissal or discharge.[1] Approximately 65 to 70 percent of the workforce are considered employees-at-will,[2] meaning that "an employer may dismiss an employee hired for an indefinite period of time for any reason or no reason at all without incurring liability to the employee."[1] However, an employer may not discharge an employee for an unlawful reason, such as racial discrimination. Historically, employers had broad powers to dismiss employees. In recent years, courts and state legislatures have whittled away at this unrestricted doctrine.[3] Exceptions to the employment-at-will rule have been expanding based on a variety of legal concepts, including claims in contract, torts (civil wrongs), and the fact that a particular termination violates public policy.[2]

A number of courts have found an implicit contract assurance of job security in employer communications such as employer policies, handbooks, oral assurances, industry customs, employer conduct, and the duration of employment. Most commonly, the claim is based on a personnel manual or handbook.[4] Although courts do not always find that these documents establish contracts between an employer and its employees (see Box 3-1), employment contracts have been inferred from them in some instances, and the more detailed the document's descriptions of disciplinary procedure, the more likely it will be found to be an implied contract.[2] Furthermore, courts have used the legal concept of an implied covenant of good faith and fair dealing to find an existing contractual relationship restricting an employer's decisions to dismiss an employee.[5]

Intentional infliction of mental distress can be used as the basis for a wrongful discharge claim. However, this type of claim has been confined to employer conduct that is outrageous or extreme.[2] To qualify as intentional infliction of mental distress, employer conduct must result in behavior that no reasonable person could be expected to endure, or in embarrassment, fright, or intense humiliation (see Box 3-2).[6] The positions of both employer and employee illustrate the complexity of a wrongful dismissal situation.

Terminations of employment may embroil an employer in claims of defamation. Defamation occurs where, purposely or carelessly, an employer disseminates incorrect or derogatory information about an employee. An employee alleging defamation must show that the information concerned the employee, that it was published or disclosed to others, that it is false, that it damages the employee's reputation, and that the employer either acted negligently or had malicious intent (see Box 3-3).[2]

An employee claim that discharge violates a public policy and may be wrongful has gained some acceptance.[1] To prove this claim, employees must show clear and convincing evidence that they carried out an act encouraged by public policy or refused to act in a way discouraged by public policy,

BOX 3-1

Despite a statement in the United Parcel Service employee handbook that it would not demote employees without just cause, plaintiff Workman's reliance on this as a binding promise was superceded by a later, unambiguous statement in the manual that declared the document was not a contract of employment and does not affect the rights of employees.[7]

BOX 3-2

Cheryl Conner, the sole woman holding a blue-collar position in a manufacturing plant, was assigned to machines and shifts that were designed to make her ability to work intolerable, and was subjected to comments about her sexual experiences. She was also forced to display bloodied panties to her supervisor when she requested permission to leave early.[8]

BOX 3-3

Where a bank officer inserted poor evaluations into the file of Mr. Gaia, an employee with whom he had a strained relationship, and used them as a basis to slander Mr. Gaia to examiners during a routine audit, actual malice can be inferred and damages will be upheld.[9]

and that employer retaliation for this act was the factor motivating the discharge.[2] To qualify as a discharge in violation of public policy, the issue at stake must affect the public at large, not only the individual employee. Moreover, the public policy relied on must be unambiguous, and in some jurisdictions, must be based on a statute. Elsewhere, it is considered sufficient that the policy be clear from a statutory scheme. Generally, the employee must have acted in good faith; the employee need not report correct information to invoke this legal protection. An employee may be found to have been discharged in violation of public policy if the discharge resulted from the employee's refusal to commit illegal or unethical acts, or from the employee's filing of a workers' compensation claim.[1,2]

Arbitration in Wrongful Dismissal

Arbitration may be an effective remedy to decide wrongful dismissal cases without litigation and within the legal framework. Utilization of existing organizational and/or union contract procedures should precede arbitration, and state legislation determines whether arbitration is allowable. Investigators conducted a comprehensive review of state laws, developed a model employment termination act, selected court decisions covering both sides of the issue, and concluded that trying wrongful dismissal arbitration was a proper approach for health care organizations.[10] In a variation of arbitration, a risk management director suggests an alternative dispute resolution method, such as employment dispute resolution, as a way to reduce employment-related litigation risks.[11]

Due Process in Wrongful Dismissal

Wrongful discharge law is diverse and changing rapidly. Any alteration in the traditional employment-at-will principle may drastically increase an employer's liability for terminations. Risk managers should make their employers aware that discharging employees for exercising certain rights is best avoided. However, problems that appropriately point to potential discharge include absenteeism, tardiness, carelessness, negligence, inappropriate dress or grooming, insubordination, theft, falsification of records, substance abuse on the job, or any deviation from practice standards (see Box 3-4). As a litigation prevention measure, there should be progressive discipline protocols that include verbal warning and written reprimands before a termination. These protocols should be characterized by due process that is consistent and predictable. Courts have been favorable in cases where the employer followed progressive disciplinary procedures bolstered with due process for the employee. When due process is not followed and an employee is fired, however, the court can rule for the employee.

BOX 3-4

Malena Cervantes, an import supervisor, complained about racial and national origin discrimination and harassment based on criticisms supervisors made both privately and publicly. Despite receiving virtually regular annual raises for years, she was terminated for excessive tardiness and poor work product. The courts found that since the criticism was based on long-standing documented performance issues, and management directed the same kind of criticism to Japanese workers with similar records (the majority of employees were Japanese in national origin), no discrimination or harassment was found. Cervantes suffered no adverse employment action as well.[12]

If termination is necessary, employers should consider safeguarding against sabotage initiated by a disgruntled employee. Keys, computer codes, and access to vital information should be secured as soon as the employee is discharged.[13]

DISCRIMINATION LAW

Most of the law against employment discrimination is about 30 years old. Although the law is based on a variety of sources, the primary federal statute is Title VII of the Civil Rights Act of 1964.[14] Title VII prohibits discrimination on the basis of race, color, sex, religion, pregnancy, and national origin affecting the terms and conditions of employment. This statute was modified in important ways by the Civil Rights Act of 1991 (Public Law 102-166). A significant change was the provision for jury trials in cases pursuant to Title VII. For the first time, the 1991 act allowed punitive damages for Title VII violations, with monetary recoveries capped on the basis of the size of the employer: a $50,000 ceiling for employers having 15 to 100 employees, and a $300,000 ceiling for employers with 300 or more employees.[15] Because of these changes, the potential verdicts in Title VII lawsuits can be much higher than those of the past.

Based on past experience, risk managers should be particularly wary of jury trials. A majority of jury trials of employment discrimination claims are decided in favor of the plaintiff. Juries tend to favor the "little guy" against any adversary and may award large sums.[16] To prevail on a claim of race discrimination, though, the "little guy" must satisfy four requirements: (1) he must belong to a protected class, (2) he must have performed his job in accordance with his employer's legitimate expectations, (3) he must have suffered an adverse employment action, and (4) similarly situated employees not in the same protected class must have received more favorable treatment. The potentially devastating outcomes of jury trials motivate many employers to consider out-of-court settlements and other means to reduce their potential costs when discrimination complaints are filed.

Sources of employment discrimination law, in addition to Title VII, include state laws, local ordinances, the federal civil rights legislation of 1866 and 1871, the Equal Pay Act, the Americans with Disabilities Act, and the Age Discrimination in Employment Act. As Box 3-5 illustrates, substantial monetary awards have resulted from federal equal employment opportunity suits.[17]

Risk managers should be sufficiently aware of discrimination law to assist their organization in preventing lawsuits and to be able to participate when a suit does occur. In today's diverse workforce, many employment decisions create the potential for a discrimination claim; these have to be recognized and evaluated. Risk managers

BOX 3-5

Troy Swinton worked in the shipping department of a picture frame company and was the only African American out of the 140 employees in the entire organization. Upon applying for unemployment, he stated that his reason for leaving was the racial jokes and epithets that pervaded the atmosphere, told mainly by his fiancée's uncle, who had assisted him in obtaining the position. However, other co-workers engaged in similar banter, and Swinton's supervisor witnessed these episodes and "laughed along." Despite the fact that Swinton did not formally complain to his superiors, he was awarded back pay, damages for emotional distress, and $1 million in punitive damages.[18]

can take proactive steps to minimize liability. Potential legal issues can be identified for employers, and the involvement of the organization's counsel can be suggested when necessary. An informational program about the extent of discrimination prohibitions can make supervisors and managers aware of actions that may involve legal issues.

Discrimination law covers more than a lawsuit brought on the basis of a particular promotion or dismissal. Claims of discrimination can include problems arising on the job, such as religious bias (see Box 3-6). While the scope of unlawful discrimination varies from state to state, state laws frequently prohibit more forms of discrimination than do federal laws.[19] In addition to the familiar prohibitions against discrimination based on race, religion, sex, and national origin, many states ban discrimination based on pregnancy, age, handicap, or disability. Several states prohibit discrimination based on sexual orientation, which is not prohibited by the major federal antidiscrimination statutes. Other prohibitions include discrimination based on family responsibility or obligations, association with protected groups, personal appearance, height, weight, arrest or conviction records, and status with regard to public assistance.[19]

Since there is such diversity among state antidiscrimination laws, risk managers must become familiar with state and local mandates and know which groups are protected, to allow for an analysis of whether an employer's position is precarious in a specific situation.

BOX 3-6

- A nurse asks for every Saturday off because that is her sabbath. Her colleagues usually have only two weekends off per month. This request raises the issue of religious accommodation.
- Employees refuse to shave facial hair for religious reasons, despite requirements instituted to protect them from tuberculosis. Specifically, facial hair may result in an inaccurate reading of a test to determine whether masks used when working with tuberculosis patients fit well enough to protect the employee.
- An ordained minister in the Church of the Nazarene who was denied a federal prison chaplaincy position on the grounds that he lacked the required degree failed to provide sufficient statistical evidence to establish a *prima facie* disparate impact religious discrimination claim against the government. The government provided evidence that 65 percent of the federal prison agency's chaplains were Protestant and six were members of the Church of the Nazarene, all of whom had the required Master of Divinity degrees.

Three Primary Discrimination Theories

Different theories underlie the three primary types of employment discrimination lawsuits: the individual disparate treatment case, the disparate impact case, and the disparate treatment pattern and practice case.

Individual Disparate Treatment

These cases require the plaintiff to prove that the employer's actions resulted from a discriminatory motive.[16] An employer's motive can be proved directly—for example, through statements by the employer—or indirectly. Most often, the means of indirect proof is evidence that similarly situated persons who are not in the protected class have received better treatment than members of the protected group. When a plaintiff presents evidence of a discriminatory motive, the defendant must respond that the challenged action was the result not of discrimination but of a legitimate, nondiscriminatory motive. The plaintiff's task is to show that the employer's stated reason is only a pretext, a cover-up for a discriminatory motive (see Box 3-7).

Disparate Impact

A disparate impact case, in contrast, does not require proof of intent. An employment practice that is neutral on its face but has an adverse effect on a protected group is unlawful. Employers must defend the practice by showing a business necessity for it.[16]

Disparate Treatment Pattern or Practice

In these cases, the plaintiff is required to show that discrimination was the employer's standard operating procedure. Usually, plaintiffs use statistical evidence to make this showing. Defendants have two basic arguments to make in response; either or both may be advanced. The defendant may try to show that the statistical evidence is flawed and/or that the challenged employment practice is a business necessity.[16]

BOX 3-7

Joann Duble, a teacher in a nursery school, was involuntarily discharged. She sued, claiming that the basis for her dismissal was age discrimination. In response, the school demonstrated that other teachers had been warned for speaking harshly to children, as the plaintiff was, and had been discharged for physically harming a child, as was the plaintiff. The court held that even if the employer's decision was mistaken, ill-considered, or foolish, "so long as the employer honestly believed those reasons, pretext has not been shown."[16d]

Burden of Proof

A notable amount of litigation and legislation has focused on the key legal concept of burden of proof in Title VII cases. Litigants having the burden of proof are required to prove that their position is more correct than that of their adversaries. Where both sides have equally credible positions, the party who has the burden of proof is said not to have established his or her case. A variety of standards are used to measure the burden of proof. "Beyond a reasonable doubt," the standard placed on the prosecution in a criminal case, is the most familiar. In civil litigation, the burden of proof generally is on the plaintiff, who must show by a "preponderance of the evidence" that his or her position is more convincing. A preponderance of the evidence is a majority, or more than half. However, this decision is not made mechanically by weighing the volume of evidence submitted. Decisions involve analysis of the evidence and assessment of the credibility of witnesses. For the most part, legislation and judicial decisions have settled the technical issues of burden of proof as they relate to Title VII cases.

In each of the three types of discrimination cases, the plaintiff has the burden of coming forward with what is termed a *prima facie* case. A *prima facie* case is evidence that raises a reasonable inference that an employer's action, if unexplained, was based on unlawful factors.[16] It is relatively simple to establish a *prima facie* case of discrimination. In a disparate treatment case, plaintiffs must show that (1) they are a member of a protected group; (2) they either performed a job satisfactorily or were qualified for a job being sought; (3) they were disciplined, terminated, or rejected for a position despite having the objective qualifications for it; and (4) either other employees of another Title VII class were disciplined less severely, or after rejecting an application, the employer continued to accept applications of people who were no better qualified.

These principles make the employers' rationales for their actions highly significant, since reasons must be plausible and consistent. An employer who maintains that the reason for discharge is poor performance, rather than discrimination, will face credibility problems if all the plaintiff's evaluations are highly positive. Although a jury as a whole may rely on legal principles, individual jurors are likely to evaluate an employer's reasons according to their own concepts of fairness. In reality, many cases are decided solely on the jury's idea of fairness.

Proof and Discrimination Suits

Are there ways in which employers can prepare for their potential burden in discrimination litigation? Certain steps may be helpful. Generally, employers are better protected if their decisions are based on objective, measurable criteria. Subjective decisions are more easily challenged as a pretext concealing discrimination. An employer is not well protected if an employee's termination is based on the unsupported subjective statement of a supervisor, such as that the employee has a poor attitude or demeanor, is not a team player, or has poor interpersonal skills. Although decisions based on subjective reasons are not illegal, the more subjective the reason, the easier it will be for a jury to decide that discrimination is the real reason.

A health care employer's documented reasons for putting someone on the fast track may include terms such as "dedication to work" or "good team spirit." If the rationale is based on personality factors rather than on performance, an employer will find it more difficult to convince a jury that the distinction between the favored and the less favored employee is not race, sex, or age. Plaintiffs can characterize such evidence as demonstrating that the favored individual is part of the club because of a difference in race, national origin, gender, age, or disability. This potential vulnerability leads some lawyers specializing in employment law to advocate that management eliminate or reduce subjective factors in their decision-making.

Companies that consistently apply a policy of progressive discipline and maintain records of employees' performance and deficiencies are in a better position to defend themselves against discrimination claims than those that do not observe these practices. Clear policies on the nature of unacceptable employee conduct also assist with the burden of proof.

In health care, as in every other industry, there are pressures that tend to favor leniency toward those who are in the decision-making hierarchy of the workplace. If the workplace has the traditional racial composition, favoritism of this kind tends to excuse white males while other groups are held accountable. If highly placed and lower level employees are not treated consistently for the same conduct, lawsuits by minorities and women are bound to raise knottier questions than they would otherwise. A risk manager seeking to protect an organization against liability would do well to keep the necessity for consistent treatment in the forefront of the minds of management.

AFFIRMATIVE ACTION

Affirmative action and reverse discrimination embody two concepts that are controversial and require definition. Often these terms are used to represent different concepts in the workplace.

Voluntary Affirmative Action

Voluntary affirmative action plans by employers are permissible if they have the same remedial purpose as Title VII and open employment opportunities for protected groups in traditionally closed occupations.[20] Plans must not unnecessarily infringe on the rights of others. Affirmative action plans must be justified by a demonstrable imbalance in historically segregated job categories. To determine whether an imbalance exists, an employer compares the proportion of women and minorities in its workforce to the area labor market, or if appropriate, to the general population. Many employers have affirmative action requirements that mandate the reporting of workplace statistics to government agencies. A review of these available reports allows for an organizational comparison of the racial, sexual, and ethnic composition of the workforce. Since 1989, the federal government has paid its employees at least $87.4 million, mostly for back pay, as a result of equal opportunity lawsuits.[21]

Reverse Discrimination

Reverse discrimination is "discrimination against groups historically favored in employment, such as whites or men." Importantly, reverse discrimination is lawful only if it is pursuant to a valid affirmative action plan.[22]

SEXUAL HARASSMENT

Sexual harassment law is relatively new, has grown in importance, and has imposed completely new obligations on employers. Specifically, sexual harassment law emphasizes the employer's obligation to anticipate and to prevent illegal behavior. Employers are required to have an explicit policy addressing sexual harassment; a general policy on harassment is not sufficient to meet the employer's responsibility.[23] Generally, an employer is well advised to make efforts to prevent sexual harassment and to address actual cases of harassment. Employer-initiated efforts can reduce liability. Court decisions have found the employer not liable if prompt, effective steps to investigate and stop sexual harassment were taken.

To guard effectively against the risks of sexual harassment, we must understand what sexual harassment means. As defined by the Equal Employment Opportunity Commission, sexual harassment is unwelcome sexual advances, requests for sexual favors, or other verbal or physical conduct of a sexual nature when

- Submission to such conduct is made either implicitly or explicitly a term or condition of employment.
- Submission to or rejection of such conduct by an individual is used as the basis for employment decisions affecting that individual.
- Such conduct has the purpose or effect of unreasonably interfering with the individual's work performance or creating an intimidating, hostile, or offensive working environment.[24]

A nationwide survey of hospitals documented a rapidly increasing rate of sexual harassment charges within the health care industry.[25] Although the vast majority of sexual harassment complaints are made by females, the concept applies equally to males. In addition, sexual harassment may occur between members of the same sex as well as across genders.

Frequently, there is a fine line between sexual harassment, and flirtation or romance. The same behavior can be illegal if unwelcome, or legitimate if the affected person is gratified by the behavior. If that person is displeased by the behavior, and the behavior is repeated, it will generally be considered sexual harassment.[26] Harassment actions run the gamut from the use of seemingly innocuous terms such as "honey" or "babe"; to unwelcome printed material in the workplace such as sexual posters, photographs, or calendars; to physical conduct such as sexual assault or even rape.[27] Subtleties involved in distinguishing sexual harassment from welcome sexual attention make this issue difficult for an employer to recognize and address.

When confronted by a possible case of sexual harassment, the employer's representative should attempt to determine whether the behavior was welcome. If the allegedly harassed individual was pleased to receive sexual attention from the particular person accused of harassment, the attention was welcome. On the other hand, if the individual merely tolerated the sexual behavior and went along with it voluntarily, sexual harassment occurred.[23] Even if the questionable behavior was welcome to the direct recipient, it may offend other persons, such as employee bystanders, who have the right to challenge the conduct.

Two Categories of Sexual Harassment

In 1998 the United States Supreme Court revised its utilization of the concepts of *quid pro quo* and hostile environment harassment. In *Burlington Industries, Inc. v. Ellerth*,[28] the Court stated:

> This Court nonetheless believes the two terms are of limited utility. To the extent they illustrate the distinction between cases involving a carried-out threat and offensive conduct in general, they are relevant when there is a threshold question whether a plaintiff can prove discrimination. Hence, Ellerth's claim involves only unfulfilled threats, so it is a hostile work environment claim requiring a showing of severe or pervasive conduct. This Court accepts the District Court's finding that Ellerth made such a showing. When discrimination is thus proved, the factors discussed below, not the categories quid pro quo and hostile work environment, control on the issue of vicarious liability.[28a]

Those factors, the Court found, focus on agency principles, not on state law. The Court observed that while the general rule is that sexual harassment by a supervisor is not within the scope of employment, if an employer is negligent or reckless with respect to that supervisor's exertion of authority, then liability based on negligence or vicarious liability can be imposed. Therefore, to avoid liability, the employer must demonstrate that the plaintiff did not suffer an adverse employment action, which is defined as a significant, tangible employment action, i.e., a significant change in employment status, such as discharge, demotion, or undesirable reassignment. In the absence of such an action that would warrant the imposition of vicarious liability, the employer should be able to show that it has a well-publicized anti-harassment policy in place that specifically provides avenues workers can use to complain about various types of illegal discrimination. This affirmative defense is based on two necessary elements outlined by the Court: (a) that the employer exercised reasonable care to prevent and correct promptly any sexually harassing behavior, and (b) that the plaintiff employee unreasonably failed to take advantage of any preventive or corrective opportunities provided by the employer or to otherwise avoid harm.[28b]

The Court's reasoning extends to hostile environments cognizable as illegal discrimination of all kinds. Employers should be alert to the significant likelihood that courts will find hostile environments, without the need to find discrimination per se, based on disability, race, national origin, age, gender, sexual orientation, and even ancestry.

Quid Pro Quo Harassment

This type of harassment involves a bargain or exchange of sexual conduct to obtain a workplace benefit or avoid a workplace detriment (see Box 3-8). Areas of concern for health care facilities include "operating rooms where sexually abusive remarks are exchanged in tense moments; labs, in which hugging and kissing are commonplace; medical staff that have little respect for nurses; and work units where sexual graffiti is present."[25]

Hostile or Abusive Environment Harassment

This type of harassment is a more difficult concept to grasp than *quid pro quo* harassment. A 1993 U.S. Supreme Court decision, *Harris v. Forklift Systems, Inc.*, explained the standard to be followed in deciding whether a particular case constitutes hostile or abusive environment harassment: "When the workplace is permeated with 'discriminatory intimidation, ridicule and insult' . . . that is 'sufficiently severe or pervasive to alter the conditions of the victim's employment and create an abusive working environment,' . . .Title VII is violated."[29]

To prove hostile environment harassment, an employee need not suffer any tangible economic loss. Employees can sue their employers for harassment even when they have benefited from the harassment.[30] Victims need not show that they suffered psychological harm to make a case. However, hostile environment charges may be more difficult to prove, since subjective interpretations are involved. For example, males and females may have differing notions about what is hostile, intimidating, or offensive.[25]

A hostile or abusive sexual harassment environment occurs when a person writes unwelcome love letters or sends unwelcome gifts to a colleague, when groups of males congregate near an entrance lobby to make unappreciated comments about the body parts of women entering the building, when supervisors brag about their sexual prowess, and when off-color jokes are allowed to continue in the office after employees com-

BOX 3-8

- A supervisor insists that an employee have sex as a condition of receiving a positive evaluation, a promotion, or a favorable work assignment.
- A supervisor threatens to fire someone who will not go out on a date or refuses to reveal details of his or her sex life to the supervisor.

BOX 3-9

A supervisor called his employee "vulgar names," intimated to others that she provides him with sexual favors, showed and described pornography to her, told others she is incompetent, stalked her at home, and attempted—more than once—to touch her breasts. After many months of suffering, she called an employee hotline 14 times and complained to his manager after her supervisor informed a customer that she was a "whore". She claims the company then selectively enforced its disciplinary policies against her. She is suing for a hostile environment and retaliation.[31]

plain that this conduct makes them uncomfortable (see Box 3-9).

Since sexual harassment includes so many routine behaviors, how can a health care employer be expected to control such behavior or be held liable for it? Realizing the breadth of the problem, persons learning about the law of sexual harassment for the first time often suggest that employers adopt no-fraternization rules as a means of avoiding illegal conduct. However, laws against sexual harassment do not require employers to adopt no-fraternization policies. Employers are not responsible for stopping all flirtation and romance in a work environment.

Nevertheless, risk managers should make sure their organization takes certain steps in this regard. Employers should have a specific sexual harassment policy indicating that sexual harassment will not be tolerated. This policy should provide that more than one person is authorized to receive sexual harassment complaints. Among the most important steps an employer can take to minimize liability is to ensure that employees and supervisors understand sexual harassment and believe that the company is serious about controlling it.

- Managers and supervisors should be informed that they may be held personally liable for acts of sexual harassment.[32]
- Employers must respond promptly and effectively to harassment complaints. It is essential to investigate all complaints as soon as an employer becomes aware of them.
- Any sanctions imposed on harassers should be calculated to bring the harassment to an end.

While an employer need not demonstrate success in deterring further unwelcome conduct, but only an appropriate and prompt response, this option is available only when there has been no adverse employment action taken.[28] Under these circumstances, unless the victim takes steps to put the employer on notice, the employer may escape liability.[33]

Even if the employer's actions do not prevent liability in a particular instance, a credible enforcement program should have a deterrent effect on the workforce. Fear of potentially costly sexual harassment lawsuits has spawned a new cottage industry in education about sexual harassment. This education is accomplished at a fraction of the cost of using professional trainers.[34]

The development of sexual harassment law makes it advisable for an employer to take proactive measures to publicize the company's anti-harassment stance and to enforce its rules. In addition to legal liability, there is a significant public relations risk. A manager's worst nightmare concerns accusations of sexual harassment in the mass media. Prevention and quick remedial action are the best approaches.

AIDS AND THE HEALTH CARE WORKPLACE

Disability discrimination is a developing area of legal concern. Inevitably, the subject of disability leads to questions about AIDS and HIV in the workplace environment. Because of morbidity and mortality statistics, employers have become increasingly concerned about the effects of AIDS on the workplace. AIDS carries a special set of issues and obligations in the health care context because there are patient-related treatment implications as well as employment concerns. These obligations stem not only from the Americans with Disabilities Act (ADA), a relatively new statute, but from a variety of other sources as well.

Many states have passed legislation prohibiting employers from discrimination based on AIDS or HIV status. A majority of states have passed laws protecting the confidentiality of persons who are HIV positive or who have AIDS.

Obviously, an employer's first question is whether the ADA or other antidiscrimination statutes apply to individuals who are HIV positive or who have AIDS. In discussions about the ADA legislation, Congress debated this question and decided in favor of coverage of AIDS and other contagious diseases.[35] In 2002, the Supreme Court held that to be substantially limited in performing manual tasks, and come within the ADA's purview, an individual must have an impairment that prevents or severely restricts that individual from doing activities that are of central importance to most people's daily lives.[36]

ADA regulations indicate that someone who is HIV positive is not automatically considered a person with a disability.[37] However, individuals who are suffering physical effects are apparently covered. Persons who are HIV positive may fit the definition of individuals with a disability if they are perceived as disabled. Depending on the circumstances, a full range of possible accommodations must be made available to HIV- or AIDS-infected employees. When an HIV-positive employee is a person with a disability, what is the employer's obligation to accommodate that individual?[38]

Applicable accommodations include, but are not limited to:

- Making facilities used by employees readily accessible to and usable by individuals with disabilities.
- Job restructuring; part-time, modified work schedules; or reassignment to a vacant position.
- Acquisition or modification of equipment or devices.
- Appropriate adjustment or modification of examinations.
- Training materials or policies.
- Provision of readers or interpreters.
- Other similar accommodations for individuals with disabilities.[39]

Prejudice and fear among other individuals in the workplace does not justify an employer's discriminating against those who are HIV positive or who have AIDS. The safest recourse for employers, including health care employers, is a comprehensive program to educate employees. To dispel the myths and rumors, employers can provide employees with scientific information confirming that they are unlikely to contract AIDS through casual contact with someone who is infected. Of course, a health care employer has the added obligation to adopt reasonable protective measures to prevent HIV transmission from patients to employees. Failure to initiate appropriate preventive measures can cause a health care employer to be held liable for negligence. Generally, health care employers must comply with standards promulgated by the federal Occupational Safety and Health Administration (OSHA) to prevent the transmission of HIV.

A major controversy among health care employers is whether employees who are HIV positive or who have AIDS should be prevented from performing invasive procedures. This argument also applies to the private practice of medicine and dentistry. Steadfastly, the American Medical Association (AMA) has refused to require health care professionals to disclose their HIV status to patients before undertaking specifically identified invasive procedures. Similarly, the federal Centers for Disease Control and Prevention recommends leaving disclosure up to each doctor's professional judgment.[40] In 1990, the Centers for Disease Control reported on a dentist whose AIDS virus had been linked to six patients who developed the disease. According to the CDC, "further studies of more than 22,000 patients of 63 health care providers who were HIV-infected have found no further evidence of transmission from provider to patient in health care settings."[40] But, in the case *Waddell v. Valley Forge Dental Associates*, 276 F. 3d 1275 (11th Cir. 2001), a dental hygienist's HIV-positive status was held to pose a significant risk to patients' health and negated the employee as a "qualified person" under the ADA. These standards may change as the law regarding AIDS develops in the legislatures and in the courts.

WORKERS' COMPENSATION

Workers' compensation is a mutually beneficial social insurance system whereby the employer agrees to underwrite an injured employee's medical costs and a significant portion of a worker's salary in exchange for the waiver of the employee's right to sue the employer.[41] In a 10-state comparison, the most commonly specified injuries in workers' compensation claims were strains (38%), fractures (14%), ruptures (9%), sprains (7%), and other (16%). By percentage of injuries to the body, the most common workers' compensation claims involved lower back (40%), complex joint (15%), upper extremity (14%), multiple body parts (12%), lower extremity (6%), trunk (6%), head (3%), neck (3%), and central nervous system (1%). About 40 percent of injuries were caused by strain-related jumping, carrying, lifting or pushing, pulling, reaching, or using a machine or tool. Slips and falls (30%) and being struck by falling objects (11%) were the next most frequent causes. Almost 63 percent of the cases involved surgery, and 68 percent of the costs were attributed to inpatient care.[42] A total of 5.7 million workers' compensation injuries were reported in 2000, about the same number as in 1999. Costs have risen on a yearly basis, from $43.1 billion in 1999 to $45.9 billion in 2000. However, the increases vary widely from state to state, and the overall costs have declined relative to wages.[43] From a cost containment point of view, with these statistics in mind, workers' compensation emerges as a topic of increasing importance to risk managers.

Workers' compensation is a social welfare program that exists in every state. Although the programs differ in specifics, the basic concept is constant throughout the nation: Employees who are injured or become ill as a result of an accident arising out of and in the course of employment receive compensation, regardless of fault. This concept of no-fault compensation is fairly new to the U.S. legal system. Traditionally, the law allowed recovery from another person when that person had caused an injury to someone else. Workers' compensation is an exception to this traditional approach because the program reimburses for medical expenses incurred as a result of the accident and provides limited income to the disabled employee. Typically, the income benefit is one-half to two-thirds of the employee's salary. The program's objective is not to fully compensate the employee for all losses connected with the injury or illness, but to give employees enough sustenance to prevent them from requiring public assistance.[44] In return for these modest but definite workers' compensation benefits, employees sacrifice the right to sue their employer for their injuries.

Whether the injury is caused by the employee's own negligence, the employer's negligence, or an act of God, the employee is entitled to workers' compensation benefits. Employees are not permitted to waive workers' compensation coverage, choosing instead to sue their employer for a particular injury, or for all injuries. Generally, workers' compensation is the exclusive remedy available against an employer for injuries caused by accidents arising in the course of and as a result of employment. This concept of exclusivity provides an employer with a defense to many actions that employees attempt to bring on the basis of workplace injuries.

Certain exceptions to the exclusivity of workers' compensation are built into most versions of the program. First, if an employer intentionally inflicts injury on an employee, the employee may sue the employer. Intentional acts of the employer are not covered by workers' compensation, since they are not considered to be "accidents" within the meaning of the law. Usually, this exception is confined to instances in which the employer had a "specific intent" to cause injury (see Box 3-10).

Where a wrong is committed that does not have a significant connection to the work itself, such as defamation and retaliatory discharge,[46] and in some jurisdictions, sexual harassment,[46] a plaintiff may be permitted to sue the employer. Another traditional exception to the concept of the exclusivity of workers' compensation coverage is the private feud that causes injury in the workplace.

Employers may be liable for employee injury if they had actual or constructive knowledge that certain equipment was unsafe and, despite that information, required the employee to do the work, because the job necessitated the use of the unsafe equipment.[46] An injury that is not intentionally inflicted usually is covered by workers' compensation if it arises out of and in the course of employment. This means that the injury and/or illness must occur during the time and at the place of work while the employee is engaged in an employment-related action.[47]

Workers' compensation, as an employee's exclusive remedy against an employer, does not always mean that the individual cannot sue. An employee injured at work by a piece of equipment may have a basis to sue the manufacturer for negligence. An individual who is injured in a contractor's parking lot may sue the contractor for damages.

Risk managers are actively involved in controlling workers' compensation costs. Before efforts to contain medical costs, workers' compensation was a bastion of uncontrolled health care expenditures. The cost of workers' compensation insurance soared so high that a number of insurers stopped writing compensation policies.[48] Experts maintained that the lack of cost controls had resulted in ballooning workers' compensation costs, in contrast to intensive efforts to monitor health care costs overall. This financial squeeze, along with related factors, motivated states and employers to

BOX 3-10

When an employer deliberately puts an employee at risk, this social and legal contract is torn asunder. Such a collapse occurred in *Laidlow v. Hariton Machinery Co., Inc.*, wherein the New Jersey Supreme Court held that routinely tying up a safety guard on a machine, but discontinuing the practice during an OSHA inspection, presented the kind of circumstances that permitted the employee, who suffered serious, debilitating injuries, to sue his employer. Other aggravating factors beside the systematic deception included ignoring previous complaints by the employee and a history of several "near-misses."[45]

adopt workers' compensation cost containment measures. These measures include steps to reduce accidents and injuries, and to monitor treatment and administrative costs.[49]

Preventing Accidents and Injuries

The best advice employers can follow to achieve fewer accidents and lower workers' compensation costs is to minimize safety hazards and investigate all accidents with a view toward future deterrence.[50] Each accident should be viewed as evidence of "prevention failure" and should be used to focus on future safety initiatives.[51] Ergonomic equipment should be considered a preventative aid.[52]

Employee training is highly recommended on topics such as safe lifting practices, safe work techniques, protective equipment, and safety rules. In some states, legislation requires employers to provide safety education. Training can begin with employee orientation and include continuing refresher courses. Safety committees to review workplace hazards, including committees that incorporate line employees, also are recommended and, in some sates, required. An independent audit is one method of assessing safety practices; the audit may be provided by a state agency, the compensation insurer, or a private company.

To prevent injuries, changes in safety rules, work equipment, protective equipment, and job structure may be necessary. From a medical viewpoint, attention should be given to the detection, treatment, and prevention of technology-related work injuries and illness such as exposure to electromagnetic radiation, repetitive use syndromes, ear and eye injuries, respiratory difficulties, and skin disorders. Ergonomic changes to reduce hazards can include remedies such as the redesign of work areas and/or lighting or the institution of frequent, short breaks to address a host of work-related problems: computer workstation eyestrain, chronic headaches, and fatigue; cumulative trauma disorders; and repetitive strain injuries.

Another prevention technique offers incentives for adherence to safe practices. Usually such incentives are monetary and include prizes for periods with no injury. Another way to create incentive is to make adherence to safety rules a criterion included in employee and supervisor evaluations.

Monitoring Treatment and Administrative Costs

To minimize the adversarial environment that often permeates workers' compensation claims, employees should be informed about this benefit during their orientation. If they lack such knowledge when an adverse event occurs on the job, employees may be frightened and become antagonistic.[54] In addition to assisting with this educational effort, risk managers can be helpful to an employer by developing a program to return disabled employees to the workplace at the earliest possible date. Studies indicate that employees are more likely to return to work if the employer maintains caring communications with the injured worker.[55] Often, the most effective contact is from the employee's supervisor. Sending cards, visiting an employee in the hospital, calling the employee in the hospital, calling the employee periodically, requiring the regular submission of medical documentation, and providing transitional light-duty assignments all appear to have a salutary impact on an employee's early return to work.[56]

The most effective method for reducing administrative costs requires a multidisciplinary approach, incorporating the knowledge and concerns of all the players: operations manager, first-line supervisor, risk manager, training department, and recruiting department.[57] Direct access to health care specialists has also produced significant results in lowering costs and returning employees to productivity.[58] Research has begun to demonstrate that utilization management using skilled nursing case managers should be an integral part of a cost-conscious program.[59,60]

Financial savings can result from steps to control administrative insurance costs. Risk managers can assist in evaluating insurers by comparison shopping for premiums and by examining insurance company reserves, the amount of money needed to cover open claims. An insurance company that overstates its reserves may overcharge an employer as a result. In states where it is permitted, some employers opt for self-insurance. Some states allow employers to self-insure in combination with a pool of other companies.

Fraud in Workers' Compensation

Although workers' compensation laws favor employer coverage of employee reports of injury, claims should nonetheless be scrutinized. Workers' compensation fraud is not an uncommon practice, and it carries significant costs for health care employers, with some estimates ranging as high as $20 billion annually (see Box 3-11).[61] The best deterrent of fraud is an effective communication network that obtains as much information as possible about a claim as soon as possible, and combines this with a well-publicized capability to investigate even the slightest evidence of fraud or overreaching. Employers should be alert to telltale signs of fraud such as inconsistent data; unwitnessed accidents; reports made soon after returning to work from a holiday or a weekend, or the day after payday; accidents occurring outside the employee's regular work area; and employees who fail to appear for physical examinations. Often a co-worker or supervisor will become aware that a colleague on workers' compensation leave is working, even part-time, elsewhere; these unsolicited offerings can provide fertile ground for investigation. Another likely indication of fraud occurs when the first notice to the employer comes through a health care provider, often someone associated with workers' compensation claimants, or from an attorney. Failure to report a claim for a protracted time is another clue to possible fraud. Employers should be very wary if an employee cannot be reached, is often not at home, or is unavailable for other reasons.[62]

BOX 3-11

Thirty-five percent of respondents in a 1999 Insurance Research Council survey, Public Attitude Monitor 99, stated that overstaying your workers' compensation leave is perfectly acceptable. This figure represents a 100 percent increase over a similar conclusion based on a 1992 survey. The 1999 survey also found that one out of five employees said they were aware of incidents of workers' compensation fraud where they worked. Such notoriety denotes a practice that likely exceeds current estimates of fraud in this system.[61]

Wellness Programs

Employees are an institution's most valuable asset.

Based on a study of over 4,500 employees of Johnson & Johnson over the course of three years, "targeted and intensive health management initiatives can be powerful agents in influencing" employee health.[63]

That analysis determined that intervention services provided before, during, and after major health-related incidents of illness, accident, or injury resulted in improvement in eight of 13 risk categories; i.e., tobacco use, aerobic exercise, and high blood pressure. This particular study benefited from a $500 incentive for each employee who participated, resulting in 90 percent of the employees agreeing to do so. However, the effects of programs in weight loss, stress reduction, and smoking cessation often wear off after a short time as participants become acclimated to a new benefit scale, which may increase health care costs.[64]

Most research surveys conclude that "utilization and expenditures may be reduced by better coordination of existing health and productivity management programs, with many of these benefits occurring in later years."[65,66] "Laser-targeted" programs may result in greater savings, pinpointing specific categories of employees who are at risk and, similarly, are redeemable at great savings to the company.[67] For example, a 1998 study concluded, based on an analysis of 10 modifiable health risk factors, that employees suffering from depression were 70 percent more expensive than their non-depressed colleagues.[68] Moreover, "the synergistic relationship of depression and high stress resulted in costs 147% more than control employees."[68] Focusing on employee populations that may be most at risk for depression and high stress may produce significant gains for the employer and its human resources.

There are ever-increasing costs resulting from mental illness. Losses in productivity and sick days totaled $75 billion in 1996, with over $69 billion spent on diagnosing and treating mental disorders—more than seven percent of total health spending.[69] These indirect cost estimates (i.e., losses in productivity, disability insurance, and sick days) are conservative because they do not capture some measure of the pain, suffering, disruption, and reduced productivity that are not reflected in earnings.[70] Considering the disparities in access, quality, and availability of mental health services that exist for racial and ethnic minority Americans, employers have an opportunity to play a significant role in increasing the equality of these services and to simultaneously improve employee health, morale, and productivity.[70,71]

Employers should provide training programs for workers on how to spot health issues and respond to them effectively. Regular screenings and stress management education, with referrals to professional health care providers and follow-ups to ensure compliance, round out the prescription for employers.[72]

EMPLOYEE ASSISTANCE PROGRAMS

Employee Assistance Programs can be a potential boon to employers and employees alike, if they are truly designed to assist the employee and are administered with care. The programs may offer services ranging from substance abuse prevention and treatment, to emotional support and treatment, to aid with financial and other burdens that may impact on the workplace. Effective EAPs guarantee a degree of confidentiality that creates potential liability for the employer.[73] The reality is that physicians and other health care providers, including EAP counselors, have a dual loyalty in their competing roles as confidantes and employees of management. Therefore, this risk may be diminished through a written agreement with the employee, or through some published understanding that critical information, such as severe mental illness that may endanger the employee or others, or a disability that may imperil the safety of workers, may be related to those with a need to know.[74] Written agreements under EAP auspices may also provide for drug testing and consequent discipline for failure to adhere to treatment protocols.[75] The viability of the EAP is at stake in these decisions, since employees must invest trust in the persons involved and in the process. The employer must weigh this dilemma carefully to determine the potential benefits of an effective program compared to the need to know critical information.

AMERICANS WITH DISABILITIES ACT

The Americans with Disabilities Act of 1990 (ADA) provides broad-ranging protection against employment discrimination for individuals with disabilities.[76] A fundamental provision is the following "general rule":[77]

> No covered entity shall discriminate against a qualified individual with a disability because of the disability of such individual in regard to job application procedures, the hiring, advancement and discharge of employees, employee compensation, job training and other terms, conditions and privileges of employment.

If found guilty of violating the ADA, employers face civil damages of up to $50,000 for the first infraction and $100,000 for subsequent violations.[78] What constitutes a disability will require legal and judicial interpretations, since the U.S. Bureau of the Census estimates that 49 million Americans have a disability.[79] The examples in Box 3-12 illustrate some of the complexities of disability issues.

Recent decisions of the United States Supreme Court have significantly reduced the effective reach of the Americans with Disabilities Act. For example, the Court has held that states may not be sued for money damages by private parties under the Act.[80] The Court also has continued to handicap plaintiffs by limiting the definition of "disability" under the Act.[81] Another decision reiterated that seniority systems generally supercede claimed rights under the ADA.[82] Punitive damages are also unavailable to private plaintiffs that sue state and local governments and federal fund recipients.[83]

Along these lines, courts have generally supported employers' contentions that attendance is an "essential element" of the job,[91] although this holding is not a foregone conclusion.[92]

BOX 3-12

- A bus company's medical standards prohibited persons with hypertension or epilepsy from working as bus drivers. Obviously, the employer's main concern was to lower the risk that sudden heart attacks or seizures would affect a driver, causing an accident. However, a person with controlled hypertension or epilepsy may present only a very remote risk to bus passengers. That risk may be no greater than that of the average person, who may be subject to an unpredictable heart attack or seizure at any time.
- In 1955, Herb Ditzel III was diagnosed with a rare kidney cancer, Wilms' tumor, before he was one year old. He survived life-threatening surgery and illness and in 1988 was manager of publications for the University of Medicine and Dentistry of New Jersey (UMDNJ). Almost all of his performance ratings were superior. On January 31, 1994, he was fired for allegedly poor work. Ditzel claimed that UMDNJ fired him on a pretext because it no longer wanted to pay cancer survivors' health insurance. He sued for $4.5 million for violation of his ADA rights.[90]

Medicaid and the ADA

Aiming to control the rising costs of Medicaid, Oregon devised an approach bordering on rationing. An ADA analysis concluded that the plan rested "on the premise that the value of the life of a person with a disability is less than the value of the life of a person without a disability." After revision, Oregon eliminated mentioning an individual's functional limitations when considering the medical effectiveness of treatment.[84] This Medicaid discrimination issue still has to be played out.[85]

As with most complicated legislation, regulations, and standards, risk managers can consult available resource material. the article "A Core Collection of ADA Information" provides a guide to resources,[86] and a videotape is also available.[87]

The ADA mandates require employers to consider each person with a disability on an individual basis to determine whether the person is capable of performing the job in question.[88] Making a distinction between individuals on a basis other than their ability to carry out a job is clearly not permissible under the statute.[89]

A disability is defined as a physical or mental impairment that substantially limits one or more major life activities, or a record of such impairment, or being regarded as having such an impairment. Major life activities are defined as "functions such as caring for oneself, performing manual tasks, walking, seeing, hearing, speaking, learning and working."[93] A person is not covered by the ADA merely because a disability prevents him or her from performing one specific job.[94] Any physiological disorder or condition, including cosmetic disfigurement, is included. Mental and psychological disorders, including mental retardation, special learning disabilities, and many forms of emotional or mental illness, are also covered.[93]

Psychological Stress as a Disability

A study of about 3,500 people indicated that an employee will be absent from work 3.2 to 9.4 days per year for an emotional reason. Depression and panic disorders (44% each) constituted the largest percentage of these instances.[95]

Once identified, personnel who pose a potential stress liability can be aided by a six-component claim prevention model: an employee assistance program (EAP); job selection and placement programs; concrete personnel policies and record keeping; communication policies regarding employees' job expectations; supervisor training; and a strategy for treating an existing stress claim as a form of valuable feedback. Many leading corporations are helping workers meet the needs of their children, parents, or other dependents through non-job-related activities such as providing support for day care, childcare centers, and before- and after-school programs.[96]

Exclusions and Other Conditions

Psychoactive substance disorders resulting from current use of illegal drugs are excluded from the definition of a disability.[93] Although alcoholism is a covered disability, employers are entitled to impose the same performance standards on people with alcoholism as on any other employee. If alcoholism impairs the individual's ability to do the job, the person does not at that time qualify as disabled.[94]

About 96 percent of organizations have had direct experience with employee substance abuse, alcohol, cocaine, or marijuana on the job.[97] A person under the influence of illegal drugs is not covered by the ADA, but a person who has a history of addiction to drugs but who is not currently using them cannot be excluded from employment. Personal characteristics are not covered disabilities. Height, hair color, or a preference for a slow pace of work would not be termed disabilities under the ADA.

Essential Functions

If an individual meets the criteria for disability, employers must consider whether that person can perform the essential functions of the job with reasonable accommodation. In deciding whether a duty is essential, the following specific questions should be asked:[94]

1. Would removing the function fundamentally change the job?
2. Does the job exist to perform a particular function?
3. Are there a limited number of employees available to perform the function?
4. Is the function highly specialized?
5. How much time is spent doing the task?
6. What are the consequences of not requiring a person in the job to perform a function?
7. Are there applicable terms in the collective-bargaining agreement? (Information in the agreement may be evidence of a position's essential functions.)
8. What is the experience of people who currently perform similar jobs or who have performed a job in the past? (Answering this question should involve observation of employees doing the job.)
9. Are there any other relevant factors? Examples include the nature of the operation and the organizational structure. In an assembly line operation, the essential function may be one task only. By contrast, a team structure may require all team members to carry out different functions on a rotating basis.

Although the ADA does not define "essential functions" specifically, there are certain factors to consider in deciding whether reasonable accommodation is possible.

Reasonable Accommodation

A Job Accommodation Network survey found that about 67 percent of business respondents stated that it cost less than $500 to meet the ADA mandates; only 4 percent said it cost more than $5,000.[98] Under the law, employees must make reasonable accommodations to enable an otherwise qualified job applicant to perform his or her duties.

Employers must use an interactive process to determine reasonable accommodation. First, they must determine the job's purpose and its essential functions. Next, they must find out the individual's specific limitations and determine whether there are barriers to performing essential functions. Employers are entitled to request written documentation of the individual's limitations to support an accommodation request. Part of the accommodation process must involve a discussion with the employee in question.[94] An employer must consult with the individual to identify appropriate accommodation and to assess its effectiveness. Technical assistance may be useful at this stage in the process.[99] A list of possible accommodations from the ADA Technical Assistance Manual enhances a practical understanding of accommodation:[94]

- Making facilities readily accessible to and usable by an individual with a disability.
- Restructuring a job by reallocating or redistributing marginal job functions.
- Altering when and how an essential job function is performed.
- Instituting part-time or modified work schedules.
- Obtaining or modifying equipment or devices.
- Modifying examinations, training materials, or policies.

- Providing qualified readers or interpreters.
- Reassigning the employee to a vacant position.
- Permitting the use of accrued paid leave or unpaid leave for necessary treatment.
- Providing reserved parking for a person with a mobility impairment.
- Allowing an employee to provide equipment or devices that an employer is not required to provide.

Employers need not accommodate employees if such accommodation would mean undue hardship, but the ADA does not define "undue hardship." Factors that should be considered in determining whether an undue hardship exists are the employer's size, the resources available, and the nature of the operation. Notices of ADA provisions, including reasonable accommodation, must be conspicuously posted.[100] Medical examinations for employment are prohibited until after a conditional offer of employment is made. Furthermore, medical examinations are permissible only if they are given to all persons in the same job category. In addition, all medical information must be treated as confidential and kept in a separate medical file.[93] Even though the ADA considers alcohol testing a medical examination, the testing is not preempted where it is a business necessity. Courts have supported alcohol testing in regulated industries, safety-sensitive positions, and private sector workplaces. A legal expert contends that "the ball is rolling toward making alcohol testing an accepted part of all workplace substance abuse programs."[101]

During any medical examination following an offer of employment, an employer may ask wide-ranging questions. However, any information obtained during the examination may be used to disqualify an applicant only if there is a high probability of substantial harm to that employee or to others, as documented by current medical evidence. An employee's personal physician may challenge such medical disqualification.[93]

Employment Interview

Many questions commonly asked during preemployment screening are prohibited by the ADA's rules. Whether on a written job application or during an oral interview, the employer may not inquire about any disability, the number of sick days the person took at another job, treatment for any physical or mental conditions, periods of hospitalization, or the person's workers' compensation history.[102]

An interviewer may ask if the applicant can perform the essential or marginal functions of the job, with or without reasonable accommodation. An applicant also may be asked to describe and/or demonstrate how he or she would perform those functions.[102]

If the examination following the job offer reveals a disability, the employer may refuse to hire the person. Importantly, acceptable rationales for not hiring someone on the basis of a disability must relate specifically to the job, must demonstrate why the absence of such disability is necessary to the business, and must show that no reasonable accommodation is possible or that accommodation would impose an undue hardship on the employer. An applicant who poses a direct threat to the health and safety of others may be disqualified from the job.[103]

Suggestions for ADA Compliance

Risk managers can minimize ADA liability by making sure that a written statement of policy on the ADA exists and that it is distributed regularly to all employees. Employers can initiate a review of job descriptions to identify essential functions in advance of any controversy.[104] Policies on interactions with disabled employees should be evaluated in light of the ADA mandates. Policies and practices pertaining to the medical documentation of physical examinations should be reassessed in view of ADA regulations. If a collective-bargaining agreement exists, it is useful for unions to negotiate a provision stating that nothing in the contract will prevent the employer from complying with the requirements of the ADA. Without such a provision, the act's requirements may very well conflict with seniority stipulations.

Significantly, the ADA compels health care employers to be careful to fit the individual's abilities to the job in question. Risk managers must try to ensure that the ADA provisions are understood and enforced throughout the organization. During 2001, 16,470 ADA complaints were filed with the Justice Department.[105]

TELECOMMUTING

In an effort to recruit and retain employees, or in response to requests for reasonable accommodation under a variety of laws, health care employers may consider telecommuting arrangements with employees. These agreements may also free up precious hospital, office, and parking space, while reducing employee stress. This last provision often appears most appealing to employees, and some research indicates that productivity significantly increases under the telecommuting structure.[106] However, employers should take into account that potential workers' compensation liability cannot be satisfactorily monitored when the employee is not routinely subject to supervision in the workplace.[107] Other possible risks include liability under the Occupational Safety and Health Act, the Fair Labor Standards Act, and the Americans with Disabilities Act,[108] as well as potential responsibility for negligence in regard to visitors to the employee's home and loss of control over intellectual property.[109] In consultation with legal counsel, employers should create standards that preserve management's prerogative to grant or deny the opportunity to telecommute. These criteria must carefully delimit the availability of the arrangement and impose strict criteria as to qualifications, particularly with respect to time, attendance, and length of time of the arrangement.[110] Furthermore, health care organizations should be wary about extending telecommuting privileges to one employee and denying them to another who is similarly situated,[111] since such a disparity could serve as a predicate for a claim of discrimination, particularly where an employee claims a statutorily protected status.[112]

DOWNSIZING

While downsizing of the workforce is often necessary, it also presents several potential perils. One is the impact on older workers and the consequent invitation to claims of age discrimination. When a seniority system results in workers of a protected class being adversely impacted as a result of fewer years on the job, the employer may be vulnerable to claims of disparate impact.[113] Employees who are on leave pursuant to a statutory protection, such as the Family Medical Leave Act[114] or workers' compensation, or who have filed complaints internally, with an administrative agency, or in court,[115] may also cloak themselves with a colorable claim that the action in force as applied to them may be linked to granting or denying their leave.[116] Each case must therefore be individually analyzed to determine whether there is a nexus between the adverse employment action and the leave status (see Box 3-13).[117]

BOX 3-13

"Insofar as Title VII is concerned, an employer can hire or fire one employee instead of another for any reason, fair or unfair, provided that the employer's choice is not driven by race, gender, pregnancy, or some other protected characterisitic. . . . The flip side of the coin, however, is that an employer who selectively cleans house cannot hide behind convenient euphemisms such as 'downsizing' or 'streamlining.' Whether or not trimming the fat from a company's organizational chart is a prudent practice in a particular business environment, the employer's decision to eliminate specific positions must not be tainted by a discriminatory animus."[116]

Downsizing carries other pitfalls as well. The Federal Workers' Adjustment Retraining Notification Act (WARN),[118] the Older Workers Benefit Protection Act (OWBPA),[119] and similar state laws contain generous notice provisions, and failure to comply may result in back pay and other liability. Reservists who are called to duty also receive liberal protections under the United States Employment and Re-Employment Rights Act of 1994[120] and similar state statutes. Employers should consult legal counsel before taking any adverse action in these circumstances, including planning for a downsizing or modifying the returning reservist's position.

RETALIATION AND WHISTLEBLOWING

In 2001 the United States Equal Employment Opportunity Commission reported that approximately 25 percent of all Title VII cases, and approximately one in five age and disability cases, are eventually accompanied by retaliation charges.[121,122] Employees who oppose discrimination or participate in some related proceeding are protected under various statutory enactments.[123] Health care employers are well advised to train supervisory personnel on the elements of retaliation and ways to avoid it.[124] Higher-level executives must monitor adverse employment actions and neutralize managers' tendency to react defensively to charges of discrimination or a hostile environment. It is suggested that enforcing policies that hold supervisors and managers accountable for this type of misfeasance would send the right message to those personnel and to the courts, and would most likely result in fewer changes. To do so, a policy declaring the importance of a prompt supervisory response should be adopted and published.

CO-EMPLOYMENT

Employers are often unaware that they may be responsible to contingent workers, or temporary workers, as if they were employees of the health care organization. Potential benefit, tax, and discrimination implications loom, amongst others.[125] This possibility increases with the integration of temporary worker functions with the regular workforce and with the exercise of direct control over the performance of the contingent worker.[126] Microsoft's managers learned this lesson as a result of the decision in *Vizcaino v. Microsoft Corp*,[127] when they were forced to offer stock options to these contingent workers after the I.R.S. determined that its actual control over them transformed the "contingent workers" into employees. In the Microsoft case, some "temporary" employees worked for continuous periods of two years, working in teams with regular employees on ongoing projects under the same supervisors. Therefore, the existence of a second employer, such as an employment agency, does not exempt the organization from liability for the awarding of benefits to the temporary worker, claims of discrimination, or a host of other possibilities limited only by the universe of rights and privileges that full-fledged employees may enjoy.[128]

Health care employers often hire temporary staff to circumvent health insurance, tax, and retirement charges while retaining the discretion to terminate the relationship at will. Employers that rely on contingent workers should be aware that they may try to organize collectively within a unit made up of the employer's regular staff. This reality was sanctioned by the National Labor Relations Board in *M.B. Sturgis, Inc., v. Jeffboat Division*,[129] wherein the Board held that workers that are co-employed and share a "community of interest" with regular employees may be jointly represented in the same bargaining unit. Despite the advantages of temporary workers, therefore, prudence requires that employers take steps to minimize liability for co-employment. With respect to these contingent workers, employers must scrupulously avoid the hallmarks of employment that may transform the contingent worker into one who cannot be distinguished from regular employees: issuing a paycheck to the free-lancer, directly supervising the temp, permitting complaints to be made directly to those charged in the organization rather than to the involved staff, directly changing the pay rates of the contingent worker, and, perhaps most lethal, listing the temporary worker in the company directory.[130]

VIOLENCE IN THE WORKPLACE: BACKGROUND CHECKS

The responsibility to exercise prudent judgment in the hiring and retention of employees applies a fortiori in the context of patient care, where ill patients may be vulnerable to violence committed by employees, family members, the public, and other patients.[131] The employer must attempt to anticipate these perils and respond promptly and effectively when signs of potential or inchoate violence appear.[132] An employer that fails to do so may be found liable for negligent hiring[133] or negligent retention or supervision.[134]

The obligation to identify potentially violent employees begins before hiring takes place.[135] To reduce the possibility of liability for negligent hiring or retention, employers should use every available legal means to check references and network with other people who may have information about a candidate. Generally, the more reliable information one can obtain, the better. This effort should be recorded and preserved during and past the tenure of the employee. Since fraudulent statements in resumes are rampant,[136] the employer's application forms[137] should also require a step-by-step recounting of the candidate's educational and employment history, and should include a blanket waiver of claim, to be signed by the applicant, as to the employer and any potential reference that the employer may contact. The application should clearly state, in bold letters, that any omission, misrepresentation, or false information may result in rejection of the application or in termination of employment at any time that it is discovered. Every applicant should be required to fill out an application form, even if a resume is also submitted. Moreover, employers should consider conducting periodic checks of current employees to provide a safe workplace and demonstrate a diligent effort to determine continued employability. These checks could be limited to employees who have contact with patients; nonetheless, they may require consultation and negotiation with employee organizations.[138]

The *New York Times* determined in a 2000 study that signs of latent violent tendencies in workers, including pronouncements of intentions to do harm, were not credited or were routinely ignored by those in authority and by co-workers prior to aggressive acts in the workplace that eventually took place; many of them could have been prevented.[139] Employers are well advised to have a policy on violence in place that requires early identification and reporting of problems, together with a well-publicized procedure to follow when physical hostilities occur or when an employee's conduct or statements create a hostile environment or indicate the need for further inquiry.[140] Policies are not adequate by themselves; employees also should be required to undergo training to heighten awareness. Generally, as in other bases of discipline, if an employer determines the basis for termination or discipline of an employee in good faith, basing its decision on reliable information and clear reasoning before an adverse employment action is taken, then the employer should be shielded from liability for wrongful discharge.[141]

MANDATORY ARBITRATION

In its *Circuit City Stores v. Adams*[142] decision, the United States Supreme Court accelerated the trend toward requiring employees to submit to an arbitration process in lieu of litigation, generally upon entering a new employment relationship. "In the view of the Court, an individual worker who agrees to submit a statutory claim to arbitration does not give up any substantive rights afforded by law. A worker merely shifts the forum for resolving a dispute from a court of law to an arbitration proceeding."[143] Research has demonstrated that this system brings tangible benefits to employers.[144]

Several courts have responded by holding that employers can force workers to sign agreements as a condition of employment.[145] Nonetheless, health care employers should be wary about overreaching, since a one-sided agreement, particularly one that circumvents hallmarks of due process or attempts to leave unbridled discretion to amend the agreement or choose the arbitrator to the employer, will be deemed illusory or a contract of adhesion.[146]

At the other end of the employment process, when an employee agrees to leave and signs a release that waives certain rights, the employer is well advised to provide consideration for the departure (i.e., some tangible benefit in exchange for the waiver), in order to allow the employee time to consider the offer and to document fully the basis for seeking the separation.[147] Federal law, however, imposes strict limitations on waivers of claims based on age, which should be vetted through legal counsel. An employee may not waive an ADEA claim unless the waiver or release satisfies the requirements of the Older Workers Benefit Protection Act (OWBPA).[148] These restrictions address the time allowed for reconsidering the settlement agreement and impose duties of disclosure on the employer.[149]

Health care employers may also want to initiate mandatory arbitration agreements with their current employees. This process should not be regarded as within the employer's unbridled purview, as is a change in the organization's policies and procedures that may be completely discretionary.[150] Consideration in exchange for the agreement and some grace period are advisable, as are negotiations with union organizations and fee-sharing.

ENHANCING EMPLOYEE SATISFACTION

Health care institutions must protect workers because of legal requirements and the need to limit liability. But employees and health professionals are also valued members of the health care team, and deserve to be protected and nurtured. While patient satisfaction is a primary goal of health care institutions, every effort should be made to create and maintain a safe, healthy, and welcoming environment for employees.

References

1. Courts have been expanding the parameters within which a claim for wrongful discharge may be brought. See, e.g., *Shick v. Shirey*, 716 A.2d 1231 (1998), in which the Pennsylvania Supreme Court carved an exception to the at-will rule permitting an employee to state a claim when he has been terminated for exercising his rights under the Workers' Compensation Law. This doctrine was extended to shield an employee who refused or failed to persuade a co-worker to withdraw a workers' compensation claim. *Rothrock v. Rothrock Motor Sales, Inc.*, 53 Pa. D. & C. 4th 411 (Pa. Com.Pl. 2001).
2. Ahern, A. M. (2002). Fight back against retaliation. *Trial*. June 1. Vol. 38. Issue 6. See, e.g., U.S. ex rel. *Yesudian v. Howard University*, 153 F.3d 731 (D.C. Cir. 1998).
3. See, e.g., *Guz v. Bechtel National, Inc.*, 8 P.3d 1089 (Cal. 2000). Some state statutes also empower employers to hold employees accountable for off-hours recreational activity while they purport to restrict employers in penalizing employees for political activity, use of substances off the job, or legal recreational activities. See, e.g., New York Labor Law Section 201(d)(2) (McKinney 1986 and Supp. 2002); and *State of New York v. Wal-Mart Stores, Inc.*, 621 N.Y.S.2d 158 (3d Dept. 1995). See *Bilquin v. Roman Catholic Church*, 286 A.D.2d 409 (2d Dept. 2001), in which an employee was terminated for an off-duty affair with a married man; and *Anderson v. State Personnel Board*, 239 Cal. Rptr. 824 (1987), in which the court upheld the termination of an employee for appearing nude in his home and backyard. But see *Pasch v. Katz Media Corp.*, 95 WL 469710 (S.D.N.Y. 1995), which found that a romantic relationship may be a protected recreational activity under the New York statute. Public embarrassment alone, without a further nexus to the ability to carry out one's responsibilities, may also invite defamation or wrongful discharge claims. See *Deegan v. Mountain View*, 84 Cal. Rptr.2d 690 (1999).
4. See, e.g., *Guinn v. Bosque County*, 58 S.W.3d 201 (Tex. App.—waco 2001, pet. filed) in which the court found that a personnel manual may modify the at-will rule only if it specifically and expressly restricts the employer's right to terminate the employee); *Gaudio v. Griffin Health Services Corp.*, 733 A.2d 197 (Conn. 1999); and *Kuhn v. Lockheed Aeromed Center, Inc.*, 134 F.3d 378 (9th Cir. 1998), which was based on Standard Practice Instructions. But see *Lobosco v. New York Telephone/NYNEX*, 727 N.Y.S.2d 383 (New York 20). Relying on the "Code of Conduct," which assured staff that no reprisals would be taken, an employee refused an employer's alleged demand to testify falsely. The code was held not to be a contract of employment in light of the unambiguous disclaimer.
5. *Lobosco v. New York Telephone/NYNEX*, 727 N.Y.S.2d 383 (New York Court of Appeals 2001). See also *D'Sa v. Playhut, Inc.*, 102 Cal. Rptr.2d 495 (Second District 2000), in which the employer that terminated an art director who refused to sign an incomplete agreement was found to have violated public policy based on a state statute that renders void any contract that restrains people from engaging in a lawful profession, trade, or business.
6. *Harris v. Pameco Corp.*, 12 P.3d 524 (Ore. Ct. App. 2000).
7. *Workman v. United Parcel Service*, 234 F.3d 998 (7th Cir. 2000).
8. *Conner v. Schrader-Bridgeport International, Inc.*, 227 F.3d 179 (4th Cir. 2000); cf. *Moysis v. DTG Datanet*, 278 F.3d 819 (8th Cir. 2002).
9. *Rockwood Bank v. Gaia*, 170 F.3d 833 (8th Cir. 1999).
10. Crane, D. P., and Gerhart, P. F. (1994). Wrongful dismissal arbitration: What can the parties expect? *Labor Law Journal* 45(5):315–319; Gerhart, P. F., and Crane, D. P. (1993). Wrongful dismissal. Arbitration and the law. *Arbitration Journal* 48(2):56–68.
11. A Dose of ADR for the Health Care Industry. (2002). *Dispute Resolution Journal*. Vol. 16. February–April.
12. *Cervantes v. Nippon Express Co., Ltd.*, 2002 WL 1722404 (Cal.App. 2 Dist. 2002).
13. Bergstein, B. (2001). HG Claims Employee Sabotage. Associated Press, November.

14. *Employment Coordinator: Employment Practices.* (1995). Deerfield, Ill.: Clark, Boardman & Callaghan, 7:70,051.

15. 42 U.S.C.A. Sec. 1981 a(b)(3)(d). See, e.g., "Annual Survey Confirms Trend of Large Jury Awards," 6 NO. 3 Wash. Employment L. Letter 2 (April 1999). The United States Supreme Court recently fortified the trend of ballooning jury verdicts by determining that front pay damages, the amount an employee who demonstrates that he was wrongfully discharged would have earned in the future, are not included in the $300,000 cap and must be calculated separtely. See also *Pollard v. E.I. du Pont de Nemours & Co.*, 121 S.Ct. 1946 (2001). The number of discrimination cases in federal courts nearly tripled between 1990 and 1998, from 8,413 to 23,735, and the cases that were resolved by way of jury verdicts rose from 48 percent to 77 percent. See also Corman, K. and Green, Gary II. (2002). Employers Should Insure Against the Coming Storm. 24 *National Law Journal* No. 34. April 29. Employers may wish to consider Employment Practices Liability Insurance as a means to reduce potential liability. Id.

16. *Employment Coordinator: Employment Practices.* (1995). Deerfield, Ill.: Clark, Boardman & Callaghan, 9:99,736 and 9A:98,603–604, 604A, 621–623. (a) Reference to *Little v. Illinois Dept. of Revenue* N.D.III., 2002. *Curry v. Menard, Inc.*, 270 F.3d 473, 477 (7th Cir. 2001). (b) Reference to the need to show that an adverse act resulted from discriminatory motive and reference to the need to show the business a reason for the act: *Harrison v. Metropolitan Gov't of Nashville and Davidson County*, 80 F.3d 1107, 1115 (6th Cir. 1996); *Garcia v. Richard Stockton College of New Jersey*, 210 F.Supp.2d 545 D.N.J., 2002. (c) Reference to disparate treatment reference in reference 16: Tucker v. Reno, 205 F.Supp.2d 1169 D.Or., 2002. (d) *Duble v. Aramark Educational Resources, Inc.*, Slip Copy, p. 6 (N.D.III. 2002).

17. The EEOC has collected almost $750 million in cases it has litigated since 1992. See "EEOC Litigation Statiscs, FY 1992 through FY 2001," the U.S. Equal Employment Opportunity Commission web site: *http://www.eeoc.gov/stats/litigation.html.*

18. *Swinton v. Potomoc Corp.*, 270 F.3d 794 (9th Cir. 2001). The Court rejected the argument that exclusion of the employer's post-complaint remedial measures constituted, in that case, a basis for reversal of the award of punitive damages. Id. at 814–817.

19. *Employment Discrimination Coordinator.* (1995). Deerfield, Ill.: Clark, Boardman & Callaghan, 5: 80, 105, 127–128, 130. As of 1993, at least 15 states had laws prohibiting discrimination based on sexual orientation: California, Connecticut, District of Columbia, Hawaii, Massachusetts, Minnesota, New Jersey, New Mexico, New York, Oregon, Pennsylvania, Rhode Island, Vermont, Washington, and Wisconsin.

20. *Le Doux v. District of Columbia*, 820 F.2d 1293 (App. D.C. 1987).

21. "EEOC Litigation Statistics, FY 1992 through FY 2001"; and "Comprehensive Litigation Report," U.S. Equal Employment Opportunity Commission, August 13, 2002. *http://www.eeoc.gov/stats/litigation.html.* In 1999 alone, the federal government paid $8,521,713 in compensatory damages, most in the form of back pay. Between 1992 and 2001, the EEOC collected monetary benefits in excess of $610,000,000 overall. The EEOC is responsible for federal and private-sector cases of discrimination.

22. *Bass v. Board of County Commissioners*, 256 F.3d 1095, 1110 (11th Cir. 2001).

23. This requirement stems from the U.S. Supreme Court's decision in *Meritor Savings Bank, FSB v. Vinson*, 47 U.S. 57, 91 L. Ed. 2d 49, 106 S.Ct. 2399 (1986). See, e.g., *Gaines v. Bellino*, 801 A.2d 322 (N.J. 2002), which stated that effectiveness of policy and procedure is the key. See *Courtney v. Landair Transport, Inc.*, 227 F.3d 559 (6th Cir. 2000), in which prompt, effective action to arrest harassment by coworkers avoided employer liability.

24. 29 C.F.R. Sec. 1604.11a.

25. Little, B., and Kinard, J. (2002). Sexual Harassment in the Health Care Industry: A Follow-Up Inquiry. *Health Care Supervisor* Vol. 20, No. 4. June 1.

26. Turner, R. (2001). Book review of *The Unwanted Gaze: The Destruction of Privacy in America*, by Rosen, J., Random House, 2002. In *University of Pennsylvania Journal of Labor and Employment Law* 243, 263 (Fall 2001). See generally Reasonable person vesus reasonable woman: Does it matter? 10 *American University Journal of Gender, Social Policy and the Law* 633 (2002).

27. See *Autoliv ASP, Inc. v. Dept. of Workforce Services*, 29 P.3d 7, 12–13 (Utah app. Ct. 2001), which deals with e-mail transmission of sexually explicit material such as jokes, pictures, and videos; *Curry v. District of Columbia*, 195 F.3d 654 D.C. Cir. 1999, which discusses staring; *Coakley v. International Double Drive-Thru, Inc.*, 1998 WL 157517 N.D.III.,

1998 Reference 5, which says that gifts may represent evidence of a sexually charged atmosphere. Of course, the acts that form the basis of the comlaint must be viewed in the totality of the circumstances, as discussed in *Grant v. Murphy & Miller, Inc.*, 149 F.Supp.2d 957 (N.D.III. 2001). See generally, Eyres, P. (2002). Harassment Measures. 39 *Los Angeles Lawyer* July/August. But see *Mendoza v. Borden, Inc*, 195 (11th Cir. 1999), which deals with staring and suggestive remarks insufficient to create hostile environment.

28. See, e.g., *Richardson v. New York State Dept of Corr.*, 180 F.3d 426, 436 (2d Cir. 1999), on the issue of race; *Gregory v. Daly*, 243 F.3d 687 C.A.2 (2001), on sex; *Little v. National Broadcasting Co. Inc.*, 210 F.Supp.2d 330 S.D.N.Y., 2002, on race and sex; *Fox v. General Motors Corp.*, 94 F.Supp.2d 723 (N.D.W.Va. 2000), on disability; *Walton v. Mental Health Ass'n*, 168 F.3d 661, 666–667, 9 A.D. Cas. 34 (3d Circ. 1999), also on disability; *Thomlison v. Sharp Electronics Corp.* (S.D.N.Y. 2001), on national origin; *Hafford v. Seidner*, 183 F.3d 506, 512 (6th Cir. 1999); *Venters v. City of Delphi*, 123 F.3d 956 (7th Cir. 1997), on religion; and *O'Gorman v. Holland*, S.D.N.Y. 2000 (2000 WL 134514), on pregnancy. See also *Schmedding v. Tnemec Co.*, 187 F.3d 862, 865 (8th Cir. 1999). According to the Court, this claim based on "perceived sexual preference" states a claim for hostile sexual environment, not because the plaintiff was homosexual but because the ridicule he endured was based on the false rumor that he was and his co-workers' image of masculinity. See also *Fairmont Specialty Services v. West Virginia Human Rights Commission*, 522 S.E.2d 180, 188 (W.Va. 1999), on the issue of ancestry; cf. *Cruz v. Coach Stores, Inc.*, 202 F.3d 560, 566 (2d Cir. 2000), on retaliation; *Bennington v. Caterpillar, Inc.*, 275 F.3d 654 (7th Cir. 2001), on age. 118 S.Ct. 2257 (1998). (28a) Id. at 2264–65. (28b) Id. at 2268–70. However, "Congress did not condition Title VII liability on employees' use of internal grievance procedures, so it is unclear why such limitations should apply to sexual harassment cases." Tipping the scales of justice in sexual harassment law, 27 *Ohio Northern University Law Review* 517 (2001); Title VII's retaliation jurisprudence: Litigation despite Faragher and Ellerth, 68 *Defense Counsel Journal* 83 (January, 2001); Sexual harassment of employees by customers and other third parties: American and British views, 31 *Texas Tech Law Review* 807 (2000); Blair, Anita K. (1998). Harassment law: More confused than ever. *Wall Street Journal* p. A14, July 8.

29. 126 L. Ed.2d 295, 114 S.Ct. 367, 370.

30. In the *Meritor* case (see reference 23), the plaintiff received several promotions after beginning an affair with her supervisor. "The critical issue . . . is whether members of one sex are exposed to disadvantageous terms or conditions of employment to which members of the other sex are not exposed." 523 U.S. 17, 80, quoting *Harris v. Forklift Systems*, 510 U.S. at 25 (Ginsburg, J., concurring).

31. *Hansen v. Genuine Parts Co.*, 2001 WL 586722 (D.Minn., 2001).

32. Although the general rule is that there is no personal liability under Title XII unless the party is an "employer," under certain circumstances state statutes will be used to impose supervisory liability. See, e.g., *Winarto v. Toshiba America Electronics Components, Inc.*, 274 F.3d 1276 (9th Cir. 2001) (California's Fair Employment and Housing Act's anti-retaliation provision). See also *Heap v. County of Schenectady*, 2002 WL 1892775, *7 (N.D.N.Y. 2002), in which a supervisor who aided and abetted discrimination was held personally liable under State Human Rights Law; and *Nowak v. EGW Home Care Inc.*, 82 F.Supp.2d 101 (W.D.N.Y. 2000), in which failure to take action to deter sexual discrimination and hostile environment triggered liability under State Human Rights Law.

33. *Caridad v. Metro-North Commuter R.R.*, 191 F.3d 283 (2d Cir. 1999); *King v. Village of Gilberts*, Slip Copy (N.D.III. 2002); *Madray v. Publix Supermarkets, Inc.*, 208 F.3d 1290, 1299 (11th Cir. 2000).

34. Training of managers, supervisors, and even of line staff may fall within the range of mandatory education and must be available to all employees of the organization. *Gaines v. Bellino*, 2002 NJ LEXIS 1083 (July 24, 2002); *Martin v. Philips Chevrolet, Inc.*, 269 F.3d 771, 778 (7th Cir. 2001). The latter case stated that "ignorance of the basic features of the discrimination laws is an 'extraordinary mistake' for a company to make, and a jury can find that such an extraordinary mistake amounts to reckless indifference." In any case, it is a good business practice and probably should be extended to all forms of illegal discrimination.

35. 28 C.F.R. § 36.104 (I)(iii).

36. *Toyota Motor Mfg., Kentucky, Inc., v. Williams*, 122 S.Ct. 681 (2002).

37. 29 C.F.R. § 1630.2(g)–(h)(1), (i)–(j).

38. In *Blanks v. Southwestern Bell Communications*, the court found that HIV did not limit the employee's reproduction or working abilities, and a lower-paying job constituted reasonable accommodation. Employment: Disability defined. (2002). 26 *Mental*

and Physical Disability Law Reporter 255. March–April.

39. *Cain v. Hyatt,* 739 F.Supp. 671.
40. Are patients in a dentist's or doctor's office at risk of getting HIV? (2002). National Center for HIV, STD and TB Prevention, Divisions of HIV/AIDS Prevention. Frequently Asked Questions. *http://cdc.gov/hiv/pubs/faq/faq29.htm.*
41. *Patterson v. Mobil Oil Corp.*, 241 F.3d 417, 418 (5h Cir. Feb. 2001), explained in S. Adrogue, "Business Torts," 33 *Texas Tech Law Review* 635, 641–642 (2002).
42. National Council on Compensation Insurance. (1994). *Claims Costs: An Interstate Comparison.* Boca Raton, Fla.: NCCI.
43. *Workers' Compensation Benefits Decline Relative to Wages for Eight Years in a Row.* National Academy of Social Insurance 2002 Study, May 22, 2002. See also Walter, F. (2001). Safety by the numbers. 12 *OSHA Job Safety and Health Quarterly* 4, p. 14. Summer; See also Rivera, P. (2002). Comp costs at issue: Meeting to target high fees Texas employers face for workers claims. *Dallas Morning News*, April 11, p. 1D. See also Anderson, T. (2002). County workers' comp costs up 65% in 5 years; Yaroslavsky cites "obvious" abuse of insurance system. *L.A. Daily News*, January 10.
44. See Fontana, T. J. (2000). Proving employer intent: *Turner v. PCR, Inc.* and the intentional tort exception to the worker's compensation immunity defense. *Nova Law Review* p. 365. Fall.
45. Hardberger, P., Chief Justice. (2000). Texas workers' compensation: A 10-year survey—Strengths, weaknesses and recommendations. 32 *St. Mary's Law Journal* 1.
46. See *Laidlow v. Harlton Machinery Co., Inc.*, 790 A.2d 884 (2002), which discusses injury from removal of safety guard on machinery; and *Urban v. Dollar Bank,* 725 A.2d 815, 817 (Pa. Super. Ct. 1999), on defamation and malicious process.
47. E.g., *Horodyskyj v. Karanian,* 32 P.2d 470 (Colo. 2001). See generally "Proving employer intent: *Turner v. PCR, Inc.* and the intentional tort exception to the worker's compensation immunity defense," note 44 above.
48. Carter, R. (2002). Comp source total premium rises 48.6 percent. *Oklahoma City Journal Record,* July 24.
49. Giordano, G. (2002). OSHA inspections not just a cost of doing business. *New Jersey Law Journal.* July 26.
50. "Lost Time Work Injuries Decline in 1999," 4 Cal. Workers' Comp. Appeals Bd. Rep. 10,046 (Feb. 8, 2002). "The decline has been ascribed to numerous factors—including the economy, shifts in the workforce, improved safety, anti-fraud efforts, and changes in reporting patterns—all of which are likely to have played a role."
51. Position Statement/Committee Report, "ACOEM's Eight Best Ideas For Workers' Compensation Reform," Vol. 40 No. 3 *Journal of Occupational and Environmental Medicine* (March 1998).
52. Fragala, G. The new ergonomic program standard and work-related injuries in health care: Part 3—Training, engineering controls, and the five-step approach. Vol. 4 No. 7 *Journal of Healthcare Safety, Compliance and Infection Control* 318–322 (August/September 2000).
53. Kertesz, L. (1994). Control costs by investigating accidents. *Business Insurance* 28(18):21–22.
54. Spitz, K. (2002). Computer-related aches, pain being reported by younger useres. *The Sun News,* July 29.
55. Bureau of National Affairs. (1991). Experts recommend steps that employers can take to avoid problems. *Workers' Compensation Report* 2:424–425.
56. Juliff, R. J., and Polakoff, P. L. (1994). An integrated approach to disability management. *Risk Management* 41(4):91–98.
57. Atkinson, W. (1999). Curbing workers' comp claims and costs (the new direction in disability management). *Business and Health* (August).
58. Atcheson, S., Brunner, R., et al. (2001). Paying doctors more: Use of musculoskeletal specialists and increased physician pay to decrase workers' compensation costs. Vol. 43 No. 8 *Journal of Occupational and Environmental Medicine* (August).
59. West Group, Inc. Direct access to specialists may reduce workers' compensation costs. 18 No. 22 *Employment Alert* 10 (Oct. 25, 2001).
60. Bailey, L. Managed care and workers' comp: A success story? Vol. 48 No. 4 *Business & Economic Review,* found at 2002 WL 10852547 (July–Sept. 2002). See, e.g., Wickizer, T., Lessler, D., et al. Vol. 41 No. 8 *Journal of Occupational and Environmental Medicine* 625–631 (August 1999).
61. Fraud Awareness Week August 5–11 Prompts Tips for Preventing Workers' Compensation Fraud. PR Newswire (July 23, 2001). See also It's OK to stay home and collect workers' compensation benefits—even when your doctor says you are able to

return to work. PR Newswire Association (August 1999).

62. Foley, J. Is your workers' compensation program a leaking pipeline? 3 *Journal of Healthcare Safety, Compliance & Infection Control* 28–30 (January 1999).

63. Goetzel, R., Ozminkowski, R., Bruno, J., Rutter, K., Isaac, F., and Wang, S. The long-term impact of Johnson & Johnson's Health & Wellness Program on employee health risks. 44 *Journal of Occupational Environmental Medicine* Number 5, pp. 417–424 (May 2002). See also Ozminkowski, R., Goetzel,R., Smith, M., Cantor, R., et al. The impact of the Citibank, NA, Health Management Program on changes in employee health risks over time. 42 *Journal of Occupational Environmental Medicine,* pp. 502–511 (2000).

64. But see Stein, A., Shakour, S. K., and Zuidema, R. Financial incentives, participation in employer-sponsored health promotion, and changes in employee health and productivity: HealthPlus Health Quotient Program. 42 *Journal of Occupational and Environmental Medicine* 12 (December 2000), pp. 1148–1155.

65. Ozminkowski, R., Ling, D., et al. Long-term impact of J&J's Health & Wellness Program on health care utilization and expenditures. 44 *Journal of Environmental Medicine* No. 1, pp. 21–29, at 28 (January 2002). See Freudenheim, M. Employers see cost savings in trimmer employee waistlines. *New York Times* (Sept. 20, 1999).

66. Freudenheim, M. (1999). Employers see cost savings in trimmer waistlines. *New York Times,* Sept. 20.

67. See, e.g., Foster, S. Stanford researchers present employee presenteeism scale. Stanford Report (Jan 30, 2002); Burton, W. The real measure of productivity. *Business and Health* (November 1999). Burton proposes a formula, the "Worker Productivity Index," for calculating productivity. The formula incorporates absenteeism, short-term disability, and presenteeism, i.e., the productivity loss when employees are on the job but are not fully functioning.

68. Goetzel, R., Anderson, D., Whitner, R., et al. The relationship between modifiable health risks and health care expenditures: An analysis of the multi-employer HERO health risk and cost database. 40 *Journal of Occupational Environmental Medicine* 843–854 (1998).

69. Mental Health: a Report of the Surgeon General. U.S. Department of Health and Human Services, Substance Abuse and Mental Health Services Administration, and National Institutes of Health, Bethesda, MD (1999).

70. Goetzel, R., Ozminkowski, R., Sederer, L., and Mark, T. The business .case for quality mental health services: Why employers should care about the mental health and well-being of their employees. 44 *Journal of Occupational Environmental Medicine* No. 4, pp. 320–330 (April 2002).

71. Mental Health: Culture, Race and Ethnicity: A Supplement to Mental Health: A Report of the Surgeon General. U.S. Department of Health and Human Services, U.S. Public Health Service (Aug. 2001).

72. Silberman, R. Employee benefit offerings growing, but vary by company size. 6 No. 11 *Compensation & Benefits Update* (May 29, 2002).

73. See *Oleszko v. State Compensation Insurance Fund,* 243 F.3d 1154 (9th Cir. 2001), wherein the court held that privileged information for licensed mental health advisors also applied to unlicensed EAP counselors.

74. See *Williams v. Houston Lighting & Power Co.,* 980 F.Supp. 879 (S.D. Tex. 1997); Gostin, L., Health information privacy, 80 *Cornell Law Review* 451, 528 (1995). See, e.g., *Bratt v. International Business Machines,* 785 F.2d 352 (1st Cir. 1986), on publishing participation in the program, without details of confidential disclosures having been discussed. But see *Davis v. Monsanto Co.,* 627 F.Supp. 418 (S.D.W.Va. 1986).

75. See *Ellerbee-Pryer v. State Civil Service Commission,* 803 A.2d 249 (Pa. Commonwealth 2002); and *Bosshard v. Hackensack University Medical Center,* 783 A.2d 731 (N.J.Super.A.D. 2001).

76. On July 26, 1990, the ADA was signed into law. Employers with 25 or more employees became subject to the act on July 26, 1992. Employers with 15 or more employees were first covered by the act on July 26, 1994.

77. 42 U.S.C. 12112, § 102(a).

78. Weiland, R. (1995). Equal rights. *Successful Meetings* 44(1):31–36.

79. Baker, D. (1994). One in five Americans is defined as disabled. *Nation's Cities Weekly* 17(10):20.

80. *Board of Trustees of the University of Alabama v. Barrett,* 121 S.Ct. 955 (2001), which barred private suits against states. Employers must be wary, however, that state statutes may neutralize the impact of this federally recognized immunity.

81. *Sutton v. United Airlines,* 119 S.Ct. 2139 (1999), which held that "a person whose physical or mental impairment is corrected by medication or other

measures does not have an impairment that presently 'substantially limits' a major life activity." See also *Toyota Manufaturing, Kentucky, v. Williams,* 122 S.Ct. 681 (2002), which held that a limitation on a major life activity must exceed merely limiting the ability to perform tasks at work; the impairment must prevent an individual from doing activites that are of "central importance to most people's daily lives."

82. *U.S. Airways v. Barnett,* 122 S.Ct. 1516 (2002). However, if an employer makes exceptions to the seniority system, plaintiffs may be able to insinuate a further incursion that would not inordinately upset employees' expectations.

83. *Barnes v. Gorman,* 122 S.Ct. 2097 (2002). Again, local statutes must be checked in this regard. E.g., *U.S. E.E.O.C. v. AIC Sec. Investigations, Ltd.,* 55 F.3d 1276 (7th Cir. 1995). AIC terminated the plaintiff, knowing that he had inoperable metastatic lung and brain cancer, and claimed that the reason for the executive's dismissal was that he could no longer drive. The court saw through this fiction and upheld a significant damage award.

84. Marzen, T. J., Sullivan, L. W., Avila, D., and Flanagan, T. B. (1994). ADA analyses of the Oregon health care plan. *Issues in Law & Medicine* 9(4): 397–424.

85. Pear, R. (1994). Saying Medicaid experiments cut services to poor, clinics sue U.S. *New York Times* June 12, Section 1, 30:1.

86. O'Donnell, R., Gunde, M., Rosen, J., and Pontau, D. (1994). A core collection of ADA information. *RQ: Reference Quarterly* 33(3):328–334.

87. Norlin, D. A. (1994). A video for all—and access for all: ADA and your library. A videotape and resources guide about the ADA. *Library Journal* 119(6):140.

88. *Federal Register.* (1991). 56, no. 144, p. 35739. Appendix to Part 1630—Equal Employment Opportunity Commission's interpretive guidance on Title I of the Americans with Disabilities Act. Washington, D.C.: Government Printing Office.

89. Enforcing the ADA: Looking Back on a Decade of Progress. A Special Tenth Anniversary Status Report from the Department of Justice. (2000). U.S. Department of Justice, Civil Rights Division, Disability Rights Section. June 27.

90. Loder, C. M. (1994). Cancer survivor sues UMDNJ over dismissal. *Star-Ledger* (Newark, N.J.), October 12, p. 25, col. 1.

91. See *Earl v. Mervyns, Inc.,* 207 F.3d 1361, 1366 (11th Cir. 2000); *Vaughn v. Nationsbank Corp.,* 137 F.Supp.2d 1317 (N.D.Ga., 2000).

92. E.g., *Dutton v. Johnson County Board of County Commissioners,* 859 f.Supp. 498 (D.Kan. 1994).

93. 29 C.F.R. 1630.2(g), (g)(1), (h), (i), (r), 3(d), (d)(3), 14(b), (b)(1).

94. Equal Employment Opportunity Commission. (1992). A Technical Assistance Manual on the Employment Provisions (Title I) of the Americans with Disabilities Act. Washington, D.C.: Government Printing Office, pp. I-6; II-6, 10, 13–18, 24; II-4, 6, 8–9, 12_13; IV-9, 11; VIII-1.

95. Kouzis, A. C., and Eaton, W. W. (1994). Emotional disability days: Prevalence and predictors. *American Journal of Public Health* 84(8):1304–1307.

96. See, e.g., Freudenheim, M. (2000). Employers seek new route to cutting health costs. *New York Times,* April 17.

97. U.S. Department of Health and Human Services. (2002). *The NHSDA Report: Substance Use, Dependence or Abuse among Full-Time Workers.* See also Center for Substance Abuse Prevention, U.S. Department of Health and Human Services. (1999). *Substance Abuse Prevention in Workplaces Is Good Business.*

98. Bowers, B. (1994). Government watch, ADA compliance. *Wall Street Journal* September 16, p. B2, col. 5.

99. A free consultant service, the Job Accommodation Network, provides information on workplace accommodations and can assist with public programs such as incentives for barrier removal. To discuss ADA issues, particularly accommodation and accessibility, the Network can be reached at 800-ADAWORK (232-9675). For accommodation information in West Virginia, the telephone number is 800-526-4698. For out-of-state callers, the number is 800-526-7234.

100. The Equal Employment Opportunity Commission will provide posters for this purpose.

101. Evans, D. (1994). Employers face difficult questions in initiatives against alcohol abuse. *Occupational Health & Safety* 63(9):58–60.

102. Equal Employment Opportunity Commission. (1994). Enforcement guidance of pre-employment medical inquires under the ADA. In *Bureau of National Affairs Americans with Disabilities Act Manual.* Washington, D.C.: BNA, Inc. 29:70:1103. Hoffman, S. (2001). Preplacement examinations and job-relatedness: How to enhance privacy and

diminish discrimination in the workplace. 49 *University of Kansas Law Review* 517 (April).

103. *Chevron U.S.A. Inc. v. Echazabal*, 122 S.Ct. 2045 U.S. (2002).

104. According to the ADA Manual (see reference 84), an employer's job description is viewed as evidence of a position's essential functions, particularly if the description is prepared in advance of the position's being advertised. In addition, the employer's judgment about essential functions is viewed as evidence supporting the proposition that the functions are essential.

105. The U.S. Equal Employment Opportunity Commission.

106. Oregon Office of Energy. Health care organizations credit telecommuting with product gains, cost savings and reduced traffic. *http://www.energy.state.or.us/tleework/telehlth.html.* (updated June 20, 2002). But see Westfall, R. D. Does telecommuting really increase productivity? Fifteen rival hypotheses. AIS Americas Conference, Indianapolis, IN, August 15–17, 1997. This work concludes that (a) this work option is underutilized; (b) productivitiy is engendered by factors unrelated to telecommuting; and (c) it may not increase net productivity.

107. See Dutrow, K. (2002). Working at home at your own risk: Employer liability for teleworkers under the Occupational Safety and Health Act of 1970. 18 *Georgia State University Law Review*. Summer.

108. See, e.g., *Davis v. Guardian Life Insurance Co.*, 2000 WL 1848596 (E.D.Pa.), in which discrimination was found based on ADA and retaliation, where an employer retracted the formerly successful accommodation of telecommuting.

109. See Swink, D. R. Telecommuter law: A new frontier in legal liability. 38 *American Business Law Journal* 857, 899–900 (Summer 2001); D'Ambrosio, N. Telecommuting doesn't relieve employer of liability. *The Business Review*, Feb. 25, 2000.

110. See *Tarin v. County of Los Angeles*, 123 F.3d 1259, 1265 (9th Cir. 1997); and *Stembridge v. City of New York*, 88 F.Supp.2d 276, 279 (S.D.N.Y. 2000).

111. *Davis v. Lockheed Martin Operations*, 84 F.Supp.2d 707, 713, Fn. 2 (D.Md. 2000), which discusses comparison to like employees who were not engaged in telecommuting.

112. E.g., *Young v. Sprint Corp.*, 173 F.R.D. 309 (D. Kan. 1997).

113. *Thiessen v. General Electric Capital*, 267 f.3d 1095 (10th Cir. 2001); and *Smith v. City of Des Moines*, 99 F.3d 1466, 1469–70 (8th Cir. 1996). Contra, *Adams v. Fla. Power Corp.*, 255 F.3d 1322 (11th Cir.), cert. granted, 122 S.Ct. 643 (2001), cert. dismissed, 122 S.Ct. 1290 (April 1, 2002).

114. See 29 U.S.C. 2601, et seq. (2001).

115. E.g., *Dugan v. CBS Broadcasting, Inc.* 2002 WL 338142 (S.D.N.Y.).

116. E.g., *Lacey-Manarel v. Mothers Work, Inc.*, No. 01 Civ. 0235, 2002 WL 506664, at *2 (S.D.N.Y. March 29, 2002) (FMLA) Cf. *Smith v. F. W. Morse & Co., Inc.*, 76 F.3d 413 (1st Cir. 1996). See generally Lester, M., and Hollender, L. How employers can reduce the risk of litigation during downsizing. *Law Journal Newsletters* (2001).

117. See generally Blumrosen, A., Blumrose, R., Carmignani, M., and Daly, T. Downsizing and employee rights. 50 *Rutgers Law Review* 943, 976–981 (Spring 1988). It should be noted that this plaintiff must not only demonstrate a nexus between the application for leave and the adverse action, as in *Texas Dep't of Cmty. Affairs v. Burdine*, 450 U.S. 248, 253 (1981); and *Smart v. Ball State Univ.* 89 F.3d 437, 441 (7th Cir. 1996), but he must show that the employment action is objectively adverse.

118. Worker Adjustment and Retraining Notification Act, 29 U.S.C.A. §§ 2101–2109 (West 1999 & Supp. 1999).

119. 29 U.S.C. 626(f), Pub. L. No. 101–433 104 978 (1990).

120. 29 U.S.C. 2102, et seq. (2001); 38 U.S.C. 4301, et seq. See Brown Castronovo, A. Military leave obligations: A new issue for employers. *Metropolitan Corporate Counsel* 17, Vol. 10, No. 4 (April 2002).

121. Klein, J. S., and Pappas, N. J. Retaliation: A potent claim in litigation. *N.Y.L.J.*, Feb. 1, 1999, at 3. See also Neil, M. Drawing the line. 88 *ABA Journal* 38 (May 2002).

122. See EEOC web site statistics at *http://www.eeoc.gov/docs/retal.html.*

123. See, e.g., *Stone v. City of Indianapolis Public Util. Div.*, 281 F.3d 640 (7th Cir. 2002); and *Nichols v. Azteca Rest. Enterprises*, 256 F.3d 864, 869 (9th Cir. 2001). See Occupational Safety and Health Act, 29 U.S.C. § 660 (1994); Family and Medical Leave Act of 1993, 29 U.S.C. § 2615 (1993); Americans with Disabilities Act of 1990, 42 U.S.C. § 12203 (1990); Welfare and Pension Plans Disclosure Act, § 301

(1974); Occupational Health and Safety Act of 1970, 29 U.S.C. § 660(c) (1970); Age Discrimination in Employment Act of 1967, 29 U.S.C. § 623(d) (1967); Civil Rights Act of 1964, 42 U.S.C. § 200e–3(a) (1964); and Fair Labor Standards Act of 1938, 29 U.S.C. § 215(a)(3) (1938). The majority of states also provide whistleblower protection. See, e.g., Mich. Comp. Laws § 15.361 (2000); N.J. Stat. Ann. § 34; 19–1–8 (Lexis through 1999 Reg. Sess.); N.Y. Lab. Law § 740 (McKinney 1988 & Supp. 1999); Minn. Stat. Ann. § 181.931–935 (West 1996 & Supp. 1997); Cal. Lab. Code § 1102.5(a) (West 1989). Public employees are often protected by such provisions, although to varying effect. See, e.g., N.Y. Lab. Law § 740 (McKinney 1988 & Supp. 1999), which limits claims to complaints related to public health and safety. The National Labor Relations Act of 1947, 29 U.S.C. § 201 (1947), provides shelter to those who experience retaliation for protected collective activity.

124. Delikat, M. (2002). Litigating employment discrimination and sexual harassment claims. 676 *Practising Law Institute* 49, June. Failure to train may result in the loss of the good faith defense available under *Kolstad v. American Dental Ass'n.*, 119 S.Ct. 2118 (1999), as in *Anderson v. G.D.C. Inc.*, 281 F.3d 452 (E.D. Va., 2002).

125. *Perry v. Harris Chernin, Inc.*, 126 F.3d 1010, 1013 (7th Cir. 1997), in which the standard for co-employer liability for sexual harassment was held to sound in negligence.

126. McGee, J. (2000). Benefits for contingent employees. 63 *Texas Bar Journal* 870 (October).

127. 120 F.ed 1006 (9th Cir. 1997).

128. Malloy, N. (2001). Defensive staffing in the new economy. 9 *Metropolitan Corporate Counsel* 4 (April). See also Ellis, E. (2001). Defining the term 'employee' under federal statutes relating to employment. American Law Institute-American Bar Association Continuing Legal Education 1063, 1080 (July 26–28).

129. 331 NLRB No. 173 (Aug. 25, 2000).

130. Mazares, G. (1999). Tips for avoiding co-employment liability. 7 *Metropolitan Corporate Counsel* 12 (December).

131. See Department of Health and Human Services (NIOSH). (2002). *Violence: Occupational Hazards in Hospitals*. Publication No. 2002–101 (April 2002). See also U.S. Department of Labor. (1996). *Guidelines for Preventing Workplace Violence for Health Care and Social Service Workers*. OSHA 3148.

132. Lest, M., and Maccone, M. (2001). Prevent violence in the workplace: The work environment must be physically secure with communication and evacuation plans in place. 166 *N.J.L.J.* 497 (November 5).

133. See *American Guarantee and Liability Ins.*, 273 F.3d 605 (5th Cir. 2001).

134. *Jaslowski v. Cello Partnership* Slip Copy (N.D. Ill. 2002), which discusses negligent retention. See also *Hazel v. Medical Action Industries*, 2002 WL 1917661 (W.D.N.C.), on negligent retention; and *Brock v. United States*, 64 F.3d 1421 (9th Cir. 1995), on negligent supervision.

135. See Ballam, D. (2002). Employment references–speak no evil, hear no evil: A proposal for meaningful reform. 39 *American Business Law Journal* 445, 450 (Spring). See also Befort, S. (1997). Pre-employment screening and investigation: Navigating between a rock and a hard place. 14 *Hofstra Lab. L.J.* 365, 367–379.

136. One-third of applicants lie on job resumes. (2000). Federal Human Resources Weekly. (Feb. 10). Available at LEXIS, Legal Research Library, Legal News File. See, e.g., *Johnson v. Honeywell Information Systems, Inc.*, 955 F.2d 409 (6th Cir. 1992).

137. The application form itself shold be in compliance with all legal requirements. For example, in most cases it may not ask for date of birth, previous workers' compensation claims, or arrest information.

138. See, e.g, Booth, M. (2002). Ocean County jury tags nursing care provider with $40.6 million bill for deadly assault. 167 *N.J.L.J.* 760 (February 25). See also Challenge expected against Illinois law requiring background checks on health care workers, 1996 WL 258014.

139. Goodstein, L., and Glaberson, W. (2000). The well-marked roads to homicidal rage. *New York Times* (April 9, 10).

140. See Piesco, J. and Jachera, J. (2001). Violence in the workplace. 9 *Metropolitan Corporate Counsel* No. 24 (col. 1) (November).

141. See *Braithwaite v. Timken Co.*, 258 F.3d 488, 493–494 (6th Cir. 2001).

142. 532 U.S. 105 (2001).

143. Snow, C. J. (2002). Collective agreements and individual contracts employment in labor law. 50 *American Journal of Comparative Law* 318, Section III (Fall).

144. Abraham, S., and Voos, P. Empirical data on employer gains from compulsory arbitration of employment disputes. *http://www.lawmemo.com/arb/res/empirical.htm.*

145. *E.E.O.C. v. Luce, Forward, Hamilton & Scripps,* 2002 WL 2004340 (9th Cir. 2002). See also *Martindale v. Sandvik, Inc.,* 800 A.2d 872 (N.J. Supreme Court, July 2002).

146. *Ferguson v. Countrywide Credit Industries, Inc.,* 298 F.3d 778 (9th Cir. 2002). See also *Circuit City Stores, Inc. v. Adams,* 273d 889 (9th Cir. 2002), in which a contract was held procedurally and substantively unconscionable; *Armendariz v. Foundation Health Psychcare Services, Inc.* 99 Cal. Rptr. 2d 745 (2000), which also found a contract procedurally unconscionable as cast in a "take-it-or-leave-it" fashion and substantively void as unfairly one-sided in the scope of matters covered by the agreement; *Penn v. Ryan's Family Steak Houses, Inc.,* 269 F.3d 753 (7th Cir. 2001), in which an illusory service provision rendered a contract void; and *J. M. Davidson, Inc. v. Webster,* 48 S.W.3d 507 (Tex.App., Corpus Christi 2001), which discusses the one-sided ability to modify the agreement, and lack of consideration, i.e., something of value given to the current employee to enter into the agreement.

147. See, e.g., *Smith v. Amedisys, Inc.,* 2002 WL 1484494 (5th Cir.).

148. Age Discrimination in Employment Act of 1967, § 7(f)(1), 29 U.S.C.A. § 626(f)(1).

149. *Flick v. Bank of America,* 197 F.Supp.2d 1229 (D.Nev. 2002).

150. Kramer, A., Copus, D., and Baskin, S. (1999). Mandatory arbitration as an alternative method of resolving workplace disputes. American Law Institute—American Bar Association Continuing Legal Education, ALI-ABA Course of Study, VLR994 ALI-ABA 177 at 202 (September 14).

CHAPTER 4

Patient/Consumer Communications to Reduce Risk

Allen D. Spiegel
Florence Kavaler

An editorial in the *Journal of the American Medical Association* commented that "breakdowns in communication between patients and physicians and patient dissatisfaction are critical factors leading to malpractice lawsuits."[1] An earlier Harvard Medical Practice Study found that about one percent of hospitalized patients suffer significant harm because of an adverse event and negligence. However, less than three percent of these patients or their families instituted a malpractice claim.[2] Logically, risk managers need to examine why patients sue, observe the therapeutic milieu, listen to patients, and use communication skills. Applying appropriate communication skills to informed consent procedures and to patient education can result in meeting patient expectations and satisfying the customers. Satisfaction also raises the burgeoning issue of grading health care providers via "report cards." With these aspects in mind, it is relevant to remember that some communication difficulties may be the result of changes in the health care industry.

A NEW AGE IN HEALTH CARE

Health care providers seem to be adopting the culture of corporate America as they utilize the commercial creativity flowing from the nation's business schools.[3] Critics of the "medical-industrial complex" argue that the profit motive is inappropriate and corrupts the entire health care industry. With competition in mind and the business approach touted as the answer, supporters declare that they will have to go out of business if they don't keep pace. If health care is a business, it is logical to assume that not all health care consumers are patients. Is it time to re-label the patient a customer?[4] If patients are customers, it is reasonable to assume that they would prefer that their health care facility be part of a shopping mall, as illustrated in Box 4-1.

Insured customers/patients may pay little out-of-pocket money for health care. Some people have the attitude that the insurer's money is being spent when health care resources are used.[5] However, health care is not subject to the usual business/customer relationship. Does a health care customer ultimately reign supreme? As César Ritz, the famed luxury hotel magnate, stated: "Le client n'a jamais tort."[6]

WHY DO PATIENTS/CUSTOMERS SUE?

If health care is a business and the customer is never wrong, why is there a need for malpractice insurance? In talking about rude physicians, Dr. Sidney M. Wolfe of the Public Citizen's Health Research Group stated: "A doctor can't get away with being a technical whiz and an interpersonal jerk."[7] This quote was a reaction to an American study concluding that doctors are more likely to be sued if a patient feels they are rude, rush visits, or fail to answer questions.[8] A plethora of additional litigation rationales are identified in *Medicine on Trial,* "the appalling story of ineptitude, malfeasance, neglect, and arrogance." Using professional literature, authors from the People's Medical Society, a voluntary association primarily of *non*physicians, cited evidence and expert testimony related to abuse of patients.[10] An investigation in England of why people sue doctors highlighted four familiar themes as reasons for litigation:[11]

Concern with standards of care: Both patients and relatives wanted to prevent similar incidents in the future.

A need for an explanation: People wanted to know how the injury happened and why.

Compensation: People wanted compensation to cover actual losses, pain, and suffering or to provide care in the future for an injured person.

Accountability: People believed that the staff or organization should have to account for their actions.

An editorial in *The Lancet* rephrased the rationales into blunter, if skeptical, language: "Suing the doctor: altruism, naked truth, or recompense?" using anecdotal reports from Action for Victims of Medical Accidents.[12] Examples of specific incidents indicate that the underlying issue is still communication, or the lack thereof (see Box 4-2).

More than 500 potential plaintiffs in malpractice litigation were interviewed in a study of four risk factors: (1) being kept in-

BOX 4-1

Medical City in Dallas, Texas, is part of a mall-hospital that has 22 retail stores including a dry cleaner, a bank, an auto mechanic, a bookstore, an optician, a clothing store, a pharmacy, and several resaurants. There are two atria with water fountains and marble floors with bright lighting and airy spaces.[9]

BOX 4-2

"After the death of my grandchild, the obstetrician said by way of an explanation, 'It was just one of those things.' That's not good enough—people need more than that—I hope they [my son and daughter-in-law] get the answers they need.

"They [the doctors] have admitted negligence, they have offered compensation, they want to make amends—but they won't give me an apology—'Yes, we did it but we're not sorry!' sums up their attitude."[11]

formed by provider; (2) rapport with provider; (3) availability of provider when needed; and (4) referral when needed. These litigation risk factors were related to 11 medical specialties, as well as dentistry and nursing. Patients felt that none of the 13 provider groups kept them well informed. Obstetrics, family practice, and pediatrics were rated highest for attaining rapport with their patients; nursing, orthopedic surgery, emergency medicine, and radiology were the worst. Emergency medicine physicians and pediatricians ranked as most available, and nurses were rated as least available. When patients felt that a referral was appropriate, all the providers were rated poorly except for internal medicine, pediatrics nursing, and neurosurgery. More than half (53%) of the potential plaintiffs griped, frequently in irate terms, about a poor relationship that existed with the health care provider even before the alleged negligence incident. Researchers concluded that "miscommunication between patient and provider is clearly a major contributor to calls received by attorneys."[13]

In New York City, the Health and Hospital Corporation decided to spend at least $1 million in a mass media campaign to recruit 300,000 Medicaid patients into a managed care entity. If the multiyear goal is achieved, the MetroPlus Health Plan would gain $60 million a month. MetroPlus's advertising slogan is "We Really Care" and reflects praise for city hospitals documented in marketing studies. This publicity blitz aims to attract Medicaid patients, who often receive second-class treatment at private health care facilities.[14] Professional literature is replete with references confirming that the synergistic interaction between curing and caring yields a more satisfied patient and/or customer.[15] If a caring physician is so important to patients, it is understandable that patients, in conjunction with physicians, would sue a managed care organization to keep their preferred doctors from being deleted from the specified providers. This litigation risk factor emanating from patients is known as "deselection" and entails alleged antitrust and consumer protection violations.[16]

Syndicated columnist Ann Landers commented on lawsuits for damages that address a diverse range of issues: injury from a cup of hot coffee, bleeding to death while undergoing cosmetic surgery, exposure to secondhand cigarette smoke defined as a form of battery.[17] With possible litigation risk factors so directly correlated to the consumer/patient/customer trilogy, what can providers do to reduce the risk? How can risk managers assist health care providers in this endeavor?

OBSERVE, LISTEN, AND COMMUNICATE

Malpractice researchers identified four types of communication problems present in more than 70 percent of plaintiff depositions:[18] (1) deserting the patient; (2) devaluing patients' views; (3) delivering information poorly; and (4) failing to understand patients' perspectives. These communication problems require health care providers to listen and talk to patients and to do so in a nonnegative manner. In a study of 160 adults, Lester and Smith[19] demonstrated that the use of negative communication behaviors by the physician increased litigious intentions. Participants were shown two videotapes of office visits to a physician. In each videotape, the patient had an identical complaint, and the physician made the same diagnosis and performed identical treatments. The only difference was the communication behavior of the physician (see Box 4-3).

BOX 4-3

Positive communication: Physician behavior included eye contact, a friendly tone of voice, smiling, shaking hands, appropriate praise, information presentation and requests for information, acknowledgment of verbalizations, and a five-minute, 25-second encounter.

Negative communication: Physician behavior included no eye contact, harsh and clipped tones of voice, criticism, nonsmiling expressions, no friendly physical contact, no praise, minimal shared information or request, and a two-minute, two-second encounter.[19]

Fiesta[20] agrees that words and attitude are important aspects of positive patient communication that establishes rapport and reduces liability. After an adverse event, Fiesta recommends an apology to the patient and family, without admitting negligence. Such apology is set forth as a matter of good manners, common sense, and an extremely important risk management tool.

Language barriers in medical settings cause misdiagnoses, medication errors, and complications leading to needless illness, hospitalization, and deaths. At the time of the 2000 census, 28.4 million Americans (10.4 percent) were foreign-born, and more than half came from Latin America and speak Spanish.[21] The federal legal authority mandating language assistance and the provision of information and services in languages other than English to Limited English Proficient (LEP) individuals derives from the Civil Rights Act of 1964 and Title VI regulations.[22] The Department of Health and Human Services issued guidelines on December 12, 2000 that offered suggestions regarding the use of oral interpreters and the translation of written materials for use in facilities where a specific language is spoken by 10 percent or 3,000 people of the persons served.[23] Use of patients' relatives or friends and bilingual staff (such as nurses) as informal translators poses risks and burdens staff in areas in which they are not proficient or trained.[24]

Under the Americans with Disabilities Act (ADA), medical treatment for patients with hearing impairments must be assured. Institutions need to have interpreting services available (see Box 4-4). If institutions are not in compliance with these regulations, they face fines, potential loss of federal funding, and substantial negative publicity in their communities.

Engaging the Patient

Engaging the patient results in improved diagnostic ability, an understanding of the patient's perspective, and the development of a physician/patient partnership. Owen urges providers to listen to what is not said, by observing body language, voice inflection, appropriateness of complaints, and nonverbal responses to questions.[25] Physicians tend to interrupt patients within 18 seconds after the initial complaint. When appropriate, the doctor should ask the patient, "Is there anything else you would like to talk about?"

BOX 4-4

The New York State Attorney General's Office has entered into consent decrees with Montefiore Medical Center, New York Community Hospital, and United Medical Associated in Brooklyn, requiring them to comply with the ADA to:

- contract with interpreting services
- establish a TYY telephone line
- train staff in ADA requirements
- provide general education about the needs of the deaf and hard of hearing communities.[26]

Three skills aid in securing information:

Knowing terminology: Medicine has its own language, and providers must adapt their words to the level of the patient with appropriate questions and explanations. In addition, the cultural background of the patient must be integrated into the terminology.[27]

Taking the funnel approach: Encourage the patient to communicate freely during the interview. Follow up with closed-ended questions designed to garner specifics and to organize the data.

Bridging the information: Acknowledge everything the patient said and explain which symptoms are most important or pertinent.

Displaying Empathy

Empathy can be communicated verbally and nonverbally. Patients can be greeted by name, preferably while they are still fully clothed. Avoiding inhibiting behaviors, such as sitting behind a desk or holding and reading a medical record, improves rapport. To show acceptance, for example, the doctor might say, "I understand how important it is for you to get back to work." Although a display of empathy generally elicits a positive response, providers must balance their concern for a patient's emotional needs with objectivity. If a patient feels that the physician has heard and understood their aches and pains, that individual is likely to confide in the provider. By displaying empathy, the health care provider lowers patient anxiety, increases compliance, and achieves higher levels of patient and provider satisfaction.

Educating the Patient

A random survey of the health-promoting behavior of 1,262 people revealed that a large percentage of Americans need to be educated, ideally by their health care providers, about maintaining good health. Nearly seven out of 10 adults (68 percent) exceeded the recommended weight range for their age, sex, and body type. Only 37 percent exercised strenuously for 20 minutes or more at least three days per week. Overall, the "Prevention Index" of 21 health-promoting behaviors was only 65.6 out of a possible 100.[28] "Consumer information is the most basic of all consumer rights," according to an American Association of Retired Persons publication that suggested opportunities and recommendations for lightening the load.[29] Health care experts contend that an informed consumer is the key to quality, cost, and competitiveness.[30] If people exit a provider/patient encounter without having had their questions answered, the result is anger and dissatisfaction. An angry, dissatisfied patient may certainly be a lawsuit waiting to happen. While information desires vary among patients, anticipating and answering basic general questions about procedures and outcomes will meet the information needs of most patients.

Enlisting the Patient

Noncompliance with therapeutic regimens is more the rule than the exception. Obviously, if harm results to the patient, litigation risk factors arise. Five communication techniques can improve adherence to the physician's instructions and reduce the risk of lawsuit:

1. Arrive at an agreed-upon physician/patient diagnosis through open discussion.
2. Keep the regimen as simple as possible.
3. Give the patient written instructions in understandable language.
4. Motivate the patient with benefits, personal goals, and individual ability to achieve them.

5. Discuss potential risks, possible side effects, and costs.

As a risk management tool, effective communication becomes a powerful tool to reduce litigation and improve patient satisfaction.

Communication Skills and Malpractice History

Most cases of patient dissatisfaction stem from deficient communication on the part of medical care institutions and providers, rather than from patients' personality quirks.[31] Relating this fact to the choice of an injury prevention approach or a human relations approach gives risk managers reason to reflect. It has been suggested that the malpractice problem is essentially a human relations problem and that greater attention to the human components is the only sure solution. Communication is a basic human component.

In a poll of 70,000 readers, *Consumer Reports*[32] identified five conclusions critical to the physician/patient relationship:

1. Physicians' communication skills were faulted as poor.
2. Physicians did not discuss the side effects of prescriptions.
3. Patients with chronic diseases were the most dissatisfied.
4. Female physicians performed better in terms of caring, communication, and thoroughness.
5. Patients were noncompliant when communication was poor.

The article told patients to ask crucial questions about the problem, the diagnosis, the prognosis, the diagnostic tests, medications, treatments, side effects, lifestyle changes, and preventive actions. The following specific guidelines for patients in encounters with physicians suggest a proactive communication skills strategy for risk managers:

1. Be prepared. Plan the visit. Bring a list of problems.
2. Bring memory aides such as a notepad or small tape recorder.
3. Reserve time to talk. Request no interruptions.
4. Clear up uncertainties. Ask the physician to repeat, to define, to use diagrams.
5. State your doubts. Ask for alternatives.
6. Ask to see your medical chart.

Investigators examined the relationship between patients' opinions of their physician's communication skills and the physician's malpractice history. This study, which included 107 physicians and 2,030 of their patients, revealed a complex relationship. Women and better-educated patients gave higher ratings on communications and explanations to physicians with fewer claims. In contrast, men and lesser-educated patients rated physicians with more claims higher on these two dimensions. Patients gave higher ratings to general surgeons and obstetrician/gynecologists and poorer ratings to orthopedists and anesthesiologists. In conclusion, the researchers stated, "Physicians must learn to adapt their communications to the individual variations in their patients' intellectual and emotional needs."[33] This leads to an exploration of the risks associated with informed consent.

CONSENT, INFORMED OR OTHERWISE

"The subject of informed consent is to a hospital risk manager what the concept of a black hole is to an astronomer."[34] Risk managers should advise physicians that informed consent is an unequivocal, nondelegatable duty. Consent implies a discussion of all the elements. As comprehensive as the informed consent process seems, the patient is not entitled to the entire body of medical knowledge. A court ruling in Box 4-5 sheds light on this doctrine.

An expanded checklist, marketed under the name PREPARED®,[35] helps physicians cover the essential points that enable patients to make informed decisions. Guidebooks and videotapes augment the checklist where each letter in PREPARED® is associated with a discussion point (see Box 4-6).[36]

Kapp proposed expanding the informed consent concept to allow the patient to decide about the provider's "defensive medicine" practices, thereby shifting the decisions about "unnecessary" medical tests and procedures from the physician to the patient.[37] A *New England Journal of Medicine* editorial commented on defensive medicine: "There can be no doubt that fear of litigation drives many physicians to wasteful styles of practice."[38]

Misconceptions of providers may blur their perceptions of informed consent and lead to increased risk situations, as indicated by some of their typical quotes:[38]

- "Patients don't want a lot of information. It only makes them anxious."
- "If patients want to know more, they will ask."
- "I know what's best in this situation."
- "This patient needs and wants me to make the tough decisions."

BOX 4-5

In *McGeshick v. Choucair*, a federal appellate court in Wisconsin said that the doctrine of informed consent was meant to apprise a patient of risks inherent in a proposed treatment. It did not require that a physician provide a patient with all the knowledge he may have regarding the patient's condition or all other possible methods of diagnosis.[39]

BOX 4-6

The Basic PREPARED® Checklist

- Recommended **Procedure**, **Plan**, or **Prescription**.
- **Reason** for the recommendation.
- **Expectation** of preventing or reversing the harm stated in terms of the patient's reason for wanting the procedure.
- **Probability** of achieving the patient's expectations.
- All reasonable **alternatives** to what has been recommended.
- All significant **risks** associated with what has been discussed.
- Direct and indirect **expenses** associated regarding the recommendation and alternatives.
- An informed collaborative **decision**.

Regarding the content of what a physician tells a patient, the California court decision in the *Arato v. Avedon* case (Box 4-7) instigated informed consent debates.[40] In arriving at the decision in Box 4-7, the court referred to a prior ruling in *Cobbs v. Grant* that the doctrine of informed consent is anchored in the following four propositions: (1) Patients are generally ignorant of medicine. (2) Patients have a right to control their own body and thus to decide about medical treatment. (3) To be effective, consent to

BOX 4-7

Miklos Arato had cancer of the pancreas, underwent surgery to remove the tumor, and died about a year later. His family sued, claiming that the physicians breached their duty to obtain informed consent by failing to tell the patient the statistical data about his projected life expectancy. Had the patient known, he would have foregone costly therapy and gotten his finances in order.[41]

treatment must be informed. (4) Patients depend on their physicians for truthful information and must trust them (making the doctor/patient relationship a "fiduciary" or trust relationship rather than an arm's-length business relationship).

In reviewing this case, Annas felt that the court ruling was "an affirmation of information sharing and patient-centered decision-making in the context of a physician-patient relationship based on trust."[41] Nonetheless, Annas argued that existing law and good medical practice required that the critically ill patient be told the success rate of the proposed treatment relative to survival, as well as to the anticipated quality of life. He declared that the issue is not *whether* to tell, but *how* to do so. In American immigrant cultures, certain immigrant groups saw such directness as being cruel and bypassing family involvement.[42] Nevertheless, patients and/or significant others must be given adequate information to make an informed decision. A related informed consent issue concerns people consenting to participate in experimental research therapies.

Informed Consent in Experimental Research

Does misinformed consent take place in research experiments? Federal regulations mandate that eight key elements be included in the consent forms: (1) details of the research study; (2) any reasonably foreseeable risks; (3) likely benefits; (4) alternative treatments; (5) extent of confidentiality; (6) rules governing compensation; (7) a contact point for further questions in the event of research-related injury; and (8) a note indicating the voluntary nature of any participation and the ability to withdraw.[42]

Rarely do informed consent guidelines mention an investigator's potential conflict-of-interest financial disclosure to patients (see Box 4-8).

Types of Informed Consent

Emergency situations when the patient is unable to give consent have led to several alternatives to informed consent: deferred consent, compassionate use, implied consent, consent at hospital admission, and waiver of consent.[43]

In deferred consent, consent is given after the individual enters into the research study, and it is not real consent. Compassionate use without informed consent applies in emergency and/or life-threatening situations for which recognized treatment is available. Implied consent, a similar concept, is based on the rationale that a reasonable person would give consent in an emergency.

In recognition of the difficulty in some cases of obtaining informed consent prospectively, facilities may seek a waiver of consent. Health and Human Services permits the waiver of informed consent, provided that:

> (1) The research involves no more than minimal risk to the subjects; (2) The waiver or alteration will not adversely affect the rights and welfare of subjects; (3) The research could not practicably be carried out without the waiver or alteration; and

BOX 4-8

In a clinical trial, 80 of 82 patients who were recipients of bone marrow transplants at a Seattle cancer center died. The deaths resulted from graft failures and leukemic relapses stemming from the treatment. The class action suit filed by families of the patients alleges that researchers misrepresented the risks to patients and had direct financial interest in the outcome of the experiemt.[44]

(4) Whenever appropriate, the subjects will be provided with additional pertinent information after participation.[45]

FDA regulations are akin to emergency situations:

(1) The human subject is confronted with a life-threatening situation necessitating the use of the test article; (2) Informed consent cannot be obtained from the subject because of an inability to communicate with, or obtain legally effective consent from the subject; (3) Time is not sufficient to obtain consent from the subject's legal representative; and (4) There is generally no alternative method of approved or generally recognized therapy that provides an equal or greater likelihood of saving the life of the subject.[46]

Problematically, health care providers may apply liberal innovative definitions of regulatory wording to explain a waiver of informed consent[47] (see Box 4-9).

Potential payoffs from improved informed consent can be substantial in terms of compliance, outcomes, and satisfied patients. If informed and educated patients have more realistic expectations, they are less likely to be disappointed and less likely to sue. Risk managers might do well to promote patient education activities. In addition, risk managers should assure periodic physician and house staff education regarding informed consent, to reduce potential liability from misunderstandings and ineffective communications with patients.

BOX 4-9

Physician's Perspective

"Patient autonomy often seems to be more important to doctors than to patients. As a first-year cardiology fellow, a big part of my job is to obtain 'informed consent' for procedures. I tell patients the risks—bleeding, infection, heart attack, death—but rarely does this prompt a meaningful discussion. Instead, I am invariably told, 'You're the doctor, I'll go along with whatever you say' . . . Most of my patients seem to think 'informed consent' is a sham, either asking them to ratify decisions that have already been made or to make decisions they are not prepared to make. Informed consent, as it is practiced today, is very different from the way ethicists envisioned it. It was supposed to protect patients from doctors. Instead, it is used to protect doctors from patients or, rather, from the hard decisions that patient care demands. Doctors today sometimes use informed consent as a crutch to abdicate responsibility, as I probably did that afternoon."[49]

TRADITIONAL PATIENT EDUCATION

A professional conference on communicating risk to patients suggested that risk information should be (1) provided in writing, (2) tailored to the patient, and (3) prioritized by the health care provider.[48] A review of patient education in the health care industry concluded that "patient education is good patient care and good business."[30] An analysis of 25 patient education programs found that for every dollar spent, the institutions saved an average of $3.50.[50] In addition to saving money, patient education can influence whether or not litigious situations arise.

Barriers to patient education from the physician's point of view include lack of time, lack of adequate reimbursement, provider forgetfulness, physician doubt, and the effects of the provider's personal life.[51] Computer programs allow physicians to generate inexpensive customized patient handouts to deal with drug information, health risk appraisal, diet planning, anatomy, and the question "What's wrong with me?"[52] Electronic data links allow physicians to monitor the patient's health automatically and to provide proactive care to individuals with problems such as asthma, diabetes, heart ailments, high-risk pregnancy, and kidney failure.[53] Providers can help patients become medication risk managers, actively participating in their own care, by following these guidelines:[54]

1. Encourage patients to keep a list (medication log) of their medications, their over-the-counter nutritional supplements, and/or other remedies.
2. Remind patients to tell providers about allergies and/or sensitivities.
3. Remind patients to tell providers how they take their current medications.
4. Encourage patients to be active partners in care by asking the name and purpose of medications.
5. Explain how to prepare each day's medications in advance and to review and check them.
6. Encourage patients to examine medications for size, color, shape, and dosage form.
7. Remind patients to ask questions before any intervention.
8. At discharge, verify patients' understanding of medications by asking questions.
9. Advise patient to select a single pharmacy and to know the pharmacist.

According to Kinnard,[55] nurses classify patients into six categories of people who are likely to sue:

- Patients who take notes and write everything down.
- Patients who have a lawyer in the family.
- Patients who are lawyers, accountants, or other professionals.
- Patients with certain injuries or illnesses (e.g., head injuries, backaches).
- Patients who have serious injuries or illnesses.
- Patients who always want to know more.

Patient education offers an opportunity to prevent the patient from becoming dissatisfied, disappointed, and/or enraged.[56] Robert White, director of claims and loss prevention for the Physicians Protective Trust Fund, appraised the situation bluntly: "Patient rapport and good documentation are the only two things that matter in loss prevention."[55] Relative to documentation, Cordell devised a streamlined form to document the patient teaching that was being done but not being charted.[57] Providers can check off appropriate boxes or add brief comments in three areas: educational assessment, educational goals, and knowledge or skill criteria to be met by discharge. Each item is dated and initialed when taught.

Patients' Rights

Do patients have any rights similar to the usual consumer/manufacturer/retail store relationship? Toward that end, the American Civil Liberties Union (ACLU) published a guide to the rights of patients. Annas discussed the patients' rights movement, informed consent, human experimentation, medical records, confidentiality, organ donation, malpractice, living wills, refusal of treatment, and how to use medical and law libraries.[58] Regarding risk management, Annas pointed out that risk managers should educate health care personnel about the issues of patients' rights and patient safety to benefit patients generally. European countries have also identified the rights of patients.[59,60]

Under expanded sections of the Social Security Act (1154e and 1879) that covers Medicare patients, hospitals have the authority to issue notices of non-coverage when they determine that the admission of a patient is not medically necessary, is inappropriate, is custodial in nature, or that continued stay after a physician's written discharge order is no longer necessary. Medicare beneficiaries have the right to appeal decisions to deny or limit payment for their medical care after they are provided with a written notice of non-coverage from the hospital or HMO. Technically, the patient receives a written Notice of Discharge and Medicare Appeal Rights (NODMAR), may request a review within three days of the notice, and must be responded to in two days with either a denial or a notice explaining that the care would be, or is, covered. Even after discharge, the Medicare beneficiary still has appeal rights and can request another review of coverage. These appeal rights are operative if health coverage of the Medicare beneficiary is through an HMO.[61]

Several states have similar independent review laws protecting patients' rights concerning assessment of medical necessity and coverage issues. In New York, an external review process for appealing an insurance carrier's decision was instituted, and the HMO is bound by the reviewers' decision. As of August 2002, the state had received 4,000 appeals, and about 47 percent of the HMO denials had been overturned.[62]

In addition, the Supreme Court has ruled in *Rush Prudential HMO, Inc. v. Moran* (U.S. No. 00-1201, 6/20/02) that patients can demand a second opinion when their HMO refuses to approve surgery or treatment.[63]

Access to the information in the federal National Practitioner Data Bank (NPDB) could allow consumers to see which physicians have been sued and/or disciplined by professional boards. U.S. Congressman Ron Wyden contends, "At the very least, consumers have a right to know which health care providers they should avoid or ask more questions about."[64] Believing that the data may be misinterpreted, the AMA opposes public disclosure, while the Public Citizens' Health Research Group favors disclosure, so that "the public can be warned about a potentially dangerous practitioner."[65]

After a series of hospital mistakes in Florida that seriously harmed or killed patients, the Association for Responsible Medicine was formed. This patient advocacy group urged state legislators to face disclosure and to impose criminal penalties on physicians and hospitals. Legislators responded and proposed a Patients' Right to Know bill.[66]

Patient education leads directly to the topic of patient satisfaction, again integrating the rationales for lawsuits: communication and informed consent.

SATISFYING THE PATIENT STOPS THE SUITS

Patient satisfaction may be a measure not of what *actually* happened during the physician/patient encounter, but more of an individual's *perception* of what took place. Critics of patient satisfaction as an evaluative measure argue that patients lack the scientific background to evaluate care, that patients' health status may make them incapable of judgments, that patients don't have a comprehensive grasp of their care, that providers and patients have different goals, and that definitions of quality care vary greatly. With these conflicting views and vagaries in mind, studies identify three measures of health care that consumers value:

- **Science of medicine:** technical competence, knowledge, and skills to resolve the problem.

Art of care: interpersonal, expressive, and communicative attributes of "caring" for the individual.

Amenities of care: comfort, courtesy, privacy, and promptness in the setting in which care is rendered.[3]

"Satisfied patients will heal better, complain less, be more likely to return, and less likely to sue."[67] A marketing professor at a business college advises that the quality of care provided and the level of patient satisfaction are emerging as the core of many marketing strategies in health services. Strategic marketing by health care providers should aim to establish, in the minds of consumers, that their institution's service quality and customer satisfaction is the "best in the world."[68] To achieve that lofty "best" status, a 34-chapter, 400-page book,[69] reminiscent of high-powered sales manuals, takes providers through a step-by-step approach to prove that patient satisfaction pays. Four key elements are identified for a patient satisfaction effort: "The *customer* is the reason for all your efforts. Without *commitment*, you will achieve nothing that is meaningful. You must know your patient's *expectations* to satisfy, manage, or exceed them. Service demands *continuity* through daily attention and continual improvement."[69] Payoffs include a reduced risk of a malpractice suit and greater profitability, in addition to improvement in referrals, compliance, productivity, collections, and efficiency. *Medical Economics* reported that "more than two hundred Texas physicians who have never been sued for malpractice credit their flawless records to positive patient relations."[70]

Why are positive patient relations important? Joel, a former president of the American Nursing Association, unflatteringly described the health care provider environment as one where "people feel intimidated, overwhelmed, and victimized as they try to muddle through a mean-spirited delivery system."[71] She recounted that customers "encounter unjustified paternalism, heavy-handedness, and confusing explanations." Patients can react violently to a provider's behavior (see Box 4-10).

PATIENT EXPECTATIONS AND PATIENT SATISFACTION

As expectations often have not been met, Freed asserts that society has become very dissatisfied with medical technology's cost and ineffectiveness.[72] Public expectations of medical technology must be tempered by the following three considerations: (1) Medical technology does not behave by itself. (2) The ideology underlying medical technology does not operate independently of the availability of resources. (3) The expectation that medical technology is guided by an objective, omniscient medical establishment needs to be redefined. Medical technology, just like the health care system, can no longer can meet every expectation of society. Initially, medical technology can satisfy consumers, but it bears the liability brunt when the technology fails. For example, Dow Corning Corporation was forced to file for bankruptcy after thousands of women who had received silicone breast implants filed lawsuits for injuries.[73]

At the Harvard Medical Institutions, malpractice claims involving surgeons of all

BOX 4-10

Dr. Marcus Edelstein, a Brooklyn (NY) ophthalmologist, was shot and seriously wounded outside his office by a disgruntled patient. Mike Lombard said he had been treated three years earlier and was dissatisfied with the care he had received.[74]

specialties have increased significantly over the last several years. From 1994 to 1996, the probability of a surgeon being named in a lawsuit was one in 30, as compared to one in 19 from 2000 to 2002. The possible causes include "increased complexity of the surgical cases as well as unrealistic patient expectations, and communications breakdowns among providers and patients."[75]

Conceptually, explanations for patient satisfaction can fit into discrepancy, fulfillment, and equity theories.[76] These three theories measure differences between a patient's desires and experiences, between rewards desired and those received, and a consideration of a balance of inputs and outputs. Exhibit 4-1 details common patient expectations. Regardless of the theories about patient satisfaction, in 2001 a National Research Corporation national survey of 10,000 households ranked 12 characteristics for a satisfaction report card.[78] The results are summarized in Exhibit 4-2. An additional 120,000 interviews were analyzed later in the year, with similar overall results.

Satisfaction as a Risk Management Tool

Abeln assumes that consumers view the quality of their care on the basis of their own values and preferences. To the point, she contends that ensuring patient satisfaction does provide an edge in managing the

EXHIBIT 4-1 TYPICAL PATIENT EXPECTATION AND REQUESTS FOR GENERAL MEDICINE SERVICES[77]

- I had some tests done and I would like to find out my test results.
- I want the doctor to prescribe medications or refills for me.
- I would like the doctor to write a letter or fill out some forms for me.
- I want something to be done to relieve my physical discomfort or symptoms.
- I would like to be referred to a specialist or other doctor for treatment of my problem.
- I want the doctor to do something or have some tests done to find out what's wrong.
- I would like to tell the doctor my ideas and concerns about my problem (what I think my problem might be, what I think caused it, or how it's affecting my life and family).
- I would like to know more about my problem (what the name of my problem is, what caused it, what I can and can't do while I have the problem, whether it will get better or get worse).
- I would like some advice about how to stay healthy (diet, exercise) or about some personal health habits (how to lose weight, stop smoking, control my drinking).
- I want to tell the doctor about problems I'm having taking my medications on time.
- I would like to know more about my medications (how they work, what are the possible side effects).
- I want to tell the doctor about side effects or problems I think are caused by my medications.
- I want the doctor to make some changes in my medications (type, amount, schedule).
- I want something to be done to relieve my emotional discomfort (nerves, stress, worry).
- I would like help for some personal family, marriage, or emotional problems I'm having.
- I want to talk with the doctor about increasing or decreasing how often I come to the clinic.

EXHIBIT 4-2 CUSTOMER SATISFACTION WITH HEALTH CARE

Satisfaction by Health Plan Type[78]

Variable	Total	FFS	HMO	POS	PPO
Overall satisfaction with plan	51.39%	58.30%	49.73%	51.23%	50.83%
Recommend plan	84.88%	86.65%	3.09%	82.54%	82.19%
Intend to switch plan	85.74%	90.36%	82.22%	83.56%	82.82%
Time on paperwork	67.11%	69.39%	68.38%	67.36%	65.31%
Problem resolution	48.09%	58.84%	47.24%	47.02%	45.99%
Ease of choosing doctor	61.63%	79.85%	54.84%	62.91%	62.45%
Choosing specialist	56.31%	78.06%	47.25%	57.35%	58.17%
Freedom to change doctor	57.56%	78.31%	48.52%	57.99%	59.85%
Information on how to use plan	45.67%	61.19%	44.13%	43.27%	43.06%

Source: 2001 NRC Healthcare Market Guide, National Research Corporation, Lincoln, NE

FFS — Fee for Service
HMO — Health Maintenance Organization
POS — Point of Service
PPO — Preferred Provider Organization

risk of medical negligence claims. According to Abeln, consumers look for providers who quickly recognize a commonsense nursing care approach that uses four strategies for meeting, and even exceeding, patient expectations:

- Don't just assess your patients' needs; reassess them.
- Try to exceed your patients' expectations.
- Recognize that you own the problem, even if it's not your fault.
- Remember that patients are health care consumers—and like all consumers, they want good service.

A professional management consultant advocates a patient-centered practice to achieve patient satisfaction. Three aspects of care quality on the part of the provider are identified: technical (clinical skills); humanitarian (caring people skills); and transmissible (responsiveness and enthusiasm). All three elements can be measured by patient satisfaction surveys.[79] Risk managers should help devise questionnaires and cooperate in surveys to investigate dissatisfaction issues in specific services or with particular providers. Once the dissatisfactions and potential liabilities are identified, risk management activities should be initiated to alleviate the problems.

With reference to older patients, satisfaction in initial medical encounters revealed positive associations with the length of the encounter, the physician's engagement with the patient, the provider's use of questions worded in the negative, shared laughter during the encounter, physician orientations to the visit, and physician satisfaction. Furthermore, there was a positive relationship between the quality of the physician's questions and topics raised by the patient, physician support on questions raised by both the patient and the physician, and provision of information to the patient on topics raised by both the patient and the physician.[80]

Responding to the market influences in the health care industry, factors such as patient satisfaction, communication, informed consent, and patient education have led to the concept of "report cards" for consumers.

GRADING HEALTH CARE: CONSUMER REPORT CARDS

Health care providers can be rated in a similar manner, with a "report card" that helps consumers make informed choices about a provider's reputation and about disenrolling in a particular group. Measurements on the report card may include mammography, prenatal care, cesarean section, hypertension, asthma (adult and child), and mental health (admissions and days). Additional criteria include the rate at which the plans perform childhood immunizations, PAP smears, cesarean sections, eye exams for people with diabetes, and mammographies.

The Health Plan Employer Data and Information Set 2001 Quality Report Card for Aetna U.S. Healthcare for reporting year 2000 indicates declining member satisfaction with the New York health plan. In 1994, members gave the plan an overall satisfaction rating of 96 percent, compared to only 59 percent in 2000. Also in 2000, members gave Aetna's New York physicians and specialists a satisfaction rating of about 75 percent. As for annual retinal eye examinations for members with diabetes, there was a decline in satisfaction from 53.7 percent in 1994 to only 49 percent in 2000.[81]

Report card measurements by the providers include clinical and administrative performance variables such as mortality rates for surgery, immunization rates, cancer survival rates, patient satisfaction, and claims experiences. Presumably, consumers would use these report cards to choose health care providers with the best performance for the least cost. Although report cards could pose a threat to health care businesses, the president of the Group Health Association of America, the nation's largest managed care association, wholeheartedly endorses the evaluation concept.[82] State legislative governing bodies also generally approve, and since 1991, California, New York, and Pennsylvania have released report cards to the general public about certain vital services provided in their states. With assistance from federal agencies, Oregon aims to build a better report card.[83] After a typographical error misled people into believing that there was a list of "death hospitals," Florida issued an updated corrected version of their report card.[84]

On a voluntary basis, the Joint Commission on Accreditation of Healthcare Organizations (JCAHO) offers performance reports on providers accredited by them.[85]

Although it has been difficult to define the quality of health care, most experts now agree that assessing quality includes measuring attributes related to three variables:[86]

Appropriateness: providers giving the right care at the right time.

Accessibility: patients being able to obtain care when needed.

Acceptability: patients being satisfied with care.

These attributes are measured using indicators that represent (1) the structure of care—resources and organizational arrangements in place to deliver care; (2) the process of care—physician and other provider activities carried out to deliver the care; and (3) the outcomes of care—the results of physician and provider activities. Outcomes are the most difficult to interpret, and "research has not clearly demonstrated correlations between some commonly used measures of structure and process and desirable outcomes.[87]

It is commonly accepted that a board-certified physician provides better care than a non-board-certified physician. However, an Office of Technology Assessment review of seven studies indicated that "no one has proven that the patients of board-certified physicians have better results than other patients."[87] Clinical factors and patient characteristics such as age or prior health status could affect the results significantly. Risk adjustment methods may be necessary to rectify the outcomes.

No matter what attributes are used in health care report cards, the data will not be comparable unless the performance indicators are standardized. Under the aegis of the National Committee for Quality Assurance (NCQA), the Health Plan Employer Data and Information Set (HEDIS) emerged.[88] More than 60 indicators are included in HEDIS that describe performance in five areas: quality, access and patient satisfaction, membership and utilization, finance, and health plan management activities. These indicators include:

- Childhood immunization rates, low birth-weight rates, and asthma inpatient admission rates.
- Number and percentage of primary care physicians accepting new patients.
- Percentage of members who are "satisfied" with the plan, according to health plan survey information.
- Membership enrollment and disenrollment information.
- Frequency and average cost of certain high-occurrence, high-cost procedures.
- Inpatient utilization rates.
- Compliance with statutory requirements.
- Descriptive information about provider recredentialing.
- Financial liquidity.
- Premium trend information.

In 1997, 60 percent of HMOs used HEDIS to evaluate their own performance. The United States Quality Assurance Health Services Research Program reviews treatment and performance, and determines outcome measures for patients suffering from almost 65 chronic diseases. The Ford automotive company insists that its insurers provide real-time data on patient care and outcomes that allow trending quality and improvements in care.[89]

Administrative databases and medical records constitute the primary sources of information for health care report cards. These sources might be inaccurate, incomplete, or misleading. Administrative data are designed to speed accurate and timely payment to providers; limitations in such a database may be that it is (1) incomplete because information about a patient's condition or the results of services rendered required for report card indicators are not collected; (2) misleading because numerical codes are used to represent undefined diagnoses, procedures, and treatments; and (3) inaccurate because data have been entered carelessly.

In medical records, providers may knowingly or unknowingly enter incorrect information or neglect to document certain information. A variety of health care professionals can type, write, or scribble clinical and non-clinical notes on the voluminous pages of a medical record. Trained personnel are required to retrieve report card indicators from medical records. This data collection process can be expensive and time-consuming and still not deal with the underlying problem of misleading or inaccurate information.

Investigators at the University of Nebraska analyzed 40 studies of patient judgments on general practice care.[90] Measurements dealt mainly with the accuracy of the practitioner's professional performance, humaneness, informativeness, and availability. Minimal data were collected on effectiveness, mutual trust and cooperation, accountability and autonomy, and continuity of care.

In contrast to the emphasis on the quality of care, consumers do have enlightening opinions regarding a choice of a health plan. A national public opinion poll found that they consider a provider's reputation among friends, neighbors, and co-workers more important than satisfaction surveys and standardized quality ratings.[91] This consumer attitude was reinforced in a JCAHO marketing investigation using a focus group. Participants revealed that "a gap existed between the kind of information employers and policy makers consider important and what consumers want."[92]

In view of the diversity of professional desires, the views of policy makers, and the stated needs of consumers, report cards could raise troubling questions. A commentary in *American Medical News* was filled with speculative queries and exclamations related to patient satisfaction polling. Pointedly, Adelman highlights the dilemma: "Will the surveys turn an encounter with a doctor into a popularity contest? Will doctors have to be good-looking, dressed in suits and smiling?"[93]

INFORMATION TECHNOLOGY

Access to the Internet has increased the amount of health information available for consumers to use as a supplement to health care education materials usually available in physicians' offices, hospitals, and clinics. Support groups and alternative therapies can be explored in addition to resources for care. However, because the Web is unregulated, not all information may be accurate, and this poses a problem for professionals interacting with patients who have obtained dubious advice online or have been in chat rooms whose quality is suspect.[93]

However, many volunteer organizations (American Heart Association, American Cancer Society), along with HMOs, managed care companies, insurance companies, and hospitals, use the Internet to provide services to the patient populations they treat. Kaiser Permanente Health Facts and the Mayo Health Advisor have programs designed to answer questions about common health problems.[88]

Significant growth has occurred in telemedicine—the use of electronic information and communications technology to provide and support health care when distance separates the participants. As an aid to decision-making, telemedicine makes available experts and databases to help in diagnoses and treatment decisions. Systems are available for transmittal of electrocardiograms, X-rays, and other records to use in collaborative consultations, as well as in grand rounds and teleconferencing for continuing education.[94] For risk management, this raises important issues of referral and payment arrangements, staff credentialling, liability, and licensure potentially crossing state lines (see Box 4-11).

BOX 4-11

Potential Online Risk Situations

- Threatening suicide
- Threatening harm to others
- Unknowingly revealing a potentially serious health problem
- Reporting a circumstance that may constitute sub-standard care
- Inappropriate, inadequate, and perilous self-care

STRATEGIC CAVEAT

Risk managers must navigate the boundaries separating professionals, politicians, policy makers, and consumers in the communication quagmire. Specific occurrences such as the following require immediate attention: an increase in malpractice claims, a decrease in cash flow, a diminished reputation of the organization in the community, an increase in the movement of patients to other providers, a decrease in provider participation in the plan, the aftermath of quality assessment reviews, unfavorable information collected for data banks, and the impact of varied surveys. Strategically, all the vested interests have to be satisfied while the financial stability of the institution endures. Risk management activities must be integrated into the responsibilities of personnel in quality assessment, education, medical records, and administration. Scientific report card measurements will be required to meet professional demands and to ensure reimbursement. If the consumer opinion polls are reliable, a combined, cooperative effort will be required to maintain a bottom line profitability and to enhance the institution's reputation in the community. As the Internet continues to play a large role in daily life, this technology will hopefully enhance consumer knowledge and confidence in the doctor–patient relationship.[95]

References

1. Levinson, W. (1994). Physician-patient communication. A key to malpractice prevention. *Journal of the American Medical Association* 272(20):1619–1620.
2. Brennan, T. A., Leape, L. L., and Laird, N. M. (1991). Incidence of adverse events and negligence in hospitalized patients: Results of Harvard Medical Practice Study 1. *New England Journal of Medicine* 324(6):370–376.
3. Spiegel, A. D., and Hyman, H. H. (1991). *Strategic Health Planning: Methods/Techniques Applied to Marketing/Management*. Norwood, N.J.: ABLEX, pp. 261–262, 400–402.
4. Henry, W. F. (1993). Need vs. want. Will consumers decide? *Hospitals & Health Networks* 67(20):56.
5. Post, S. C. (1994). Ax middleman: Insurance (letter to editor). *Wall Street Journal* August 18, p. A13, col. 1.
6. Augarde, T. (1991). *The Oxford Dictionary of Modern Quotations*. New York: Oxford University Press, p. 181.
7. Studies show that rude doctors are more likely to face lawsuits. (1994). *New York Times* November 25, p. B14, col. 1.
8. Hickson, G. B., Clayton, E. W., Entman, S. S., et al. (1994). Obstetricians' prior malpractice experience and patients' satisfaction with care. *Journal of the American Medical Association* 272(20):1583–1587.
9. Rudavsky, S. (1994). Designing a new hospital? Let malls be your muse. *Wall Steet Journal* August 1, p. B1, col. 5.
10. Inlander, C. B., Levin, L. S., and Weiner, E. (1988). *Medicine on Trial*. New York: Prentice Hall.
11. Vincent, C., Young, M., and Phllips, A. (1994). Why do people sue doctors? A study of patients and relatives taking legal actions. *Lancet* 343(8913): 1609–1613.
12. Suing the doctor: Altruism, naked truth, or recompense? (1994). *Lancet* 343(8913):1582–1583.
13. Huycke, L. I., and Huycke, M. M. (1994). Characteristics of potential plaintiffs in malpratice litigation. *Annals of Internal Medicine* 120(9):792–798.
14. Mooney, M. (1994). City hosps set to show they care. *New York Daily News* November 14, p. 5, col. 3.

15. Spiegel, A. D, and Backhaut, B. (1980). *Curing and Caring. A Review of the Factors Affecting the Quality and Acceptability of Health Care.* Jamaica, N.Y.: Spectrum.

16. McCormick, B. (1994). Patients, doctors sue CIGNA in deselection flap. *American Medical News* 37(36):3, 24.

17. Landers, A. (1994). Lawsuits are popping up everywhere. *News Tribune* (Woodbridge, N.J.), October 30, p. L9, col. 3.

18. Beckman, H. B., Markakis, K. M., Suchman, A. L., and Frankel, R. M. (1994). The doctor-patient relationship and malpratice: Lessons from plaintiff depositions. *Archives of Internal Medicine* 154(7): 1365–1370.

19. Lester, G. W., and Smith, S. G. (1993). Listening and talking to patients. A remedy for malpratice suits? *Western Journal of Medicine* 158(3):268–272.

20. Fiesta, J. (1994). Communication—Are you Listening? *Nursing Management* 25(9):15–16.

21. Schroeder, D. G. (2002). Limited English Proficiency (LEP) Regulations: Implications and Guidance for U.S. Hospitals Serving Minority Populations. Emory University School of Public Health, June.

22. Officially, Title VI of the Civil Rights Act of 1964, U.S.C. 2000d et seq., and its implementing regulation at 45 CFR Part 80. *Federal Register* 65, no. 169 (August 30, 2000).

23. U.S. Department of Health and Human Services. *Strategic Plan to Improve Access to HHS Programs and Activities by Limited English Proficient (LEP) Persons. http://www.hhs.gov/gateway/language.languageplan.html.* (December 12, 2000).

24. Sussman, D. (1999). Diversity Rx. American Translators Association Newsletter. *www.nurseweek.com.* (August 12, 1999).

25. Owen, K. (1994). Listen to what patients don't say. *RN* 57(1):96.

26. New York State Attorney General's Office. (2000). Press release: Agreement provides hospital interpreters for deaf. May 2.

27. Pachter, L. M. (1994). Culture and clinical care. Folk illness beliefs and behaviors and their implications for health care delivery. *Journal of the American Medical Association* 271(9):690–694; Wynter, L. (1994). Medical group considers patients' culture. *Wall Street Journal* February 2, p. B1, col. 2.

28. Lalik, M., and Hugick, L. (1995). *The Prevention Index. A Report Card on the Nation's Health.* Emmas, Pa.: Rodale Press, p. 4.

29 Mayer, R. N., and Brady, J. T. (1994). *The Consumer Information Research Burden.* Washington, D.C.: AARP, p. iii.

30. Metz, D., Kavaler, F., and Bunn, M. D. (1991). The informed consumer: Key to quality, cost, and competitiveness. In *The Contemporary HMO: Managing Care in the Modern Market.* Proceedings, Group Health Institute, GHA of America, Inc., June 23–26, New York, pp. 189–205.

31. Bartlett, E. E. (1991). Injury prevention vs. patient communications. *Risk Management* 38(1):40–43.

32. You and your doctor. How to get the best care. (1995). *Consumer Reports* 60(2):81–88.

33. Adamson, T. E., Tschann, J. M., Gullion, D. S., and Oppenberg, A. A. (1989). Physician communication skills and malpractice claims—A complex relationship. *Western Medical Journal 150(3):356–360.*

34. Romero, R. C. (1993). Informed consent: Health care RM's black hole. *National Underwriter* 97(43): 13–14.

35. Great Performance, Inc., 14964 Greenbrier Parkway, Beaverton, OR 97006.

36. Skelly, F. J. (1994). The payoff of informed consent. *American Medical News* 37(29):11–12.

37. Kapp, M. B. (1993). Informed consent to defensive medicine. *Pharos of Alpha Omega Alpha* 56(2):12–14.

38. Relman, A. (1989). The National Leadership Commission's health care plan. *New England Journal of Medicine* 320(3):314–315.

39. Medicolegal decisions. (1995). *American Medical News* 38(23):16.

40. Letters to the Editor from Miyaji, N. T.; Espinosa, E., Zamora, P., and Barón, M. G.; Ferris, T.; Holcombe, R. F.; Price, F. V., Kelley, J. L., and Edwards, R. P.; and a reply from Annas, G. J. (1994). *New England Journal of Medicine* 331(12):810–812.

41. Annas, G. J. (1994). Informed consent, cancer, and truth in prognosis. *New England Journal of Medicine* 330(3):223–225.

42. Mydans, S. (1995). Should dying patients be told? Ethnic pitfall is found. *New York Times* September 13, p. A24, col. 3.

43. Olson, C. M. (1994). The letter or the spirit. Consent for research in CPR. *Journal of the American Medical Association* 271:1445–1447.

44. Cancer center accused of violating ethics. *Healthcare Risk Management*, newsletter of the American Health Consultants. 2(5):58.
45. C.F.R. Sec. 46.116d.
46. 21 C.F.R. Sec. 50.23a.
47. McCarthy, M. (1994). Consent and U.S. emergency room studies. *Lancet* 343(8905):1093.
48. U.S. Pharmacopeial Convention. (1995). *Communicating Risk to Patients*. Rockville, Md.: U.S. Pharmacopeial Convention, p. 107.
49. Jauhar, S. (2002). Cases: Advice rejoins consent. *New York Times*, July 2.
50. Lumsdon, K. (1994). Getting real: Study finds success factors in patient education. *Hospitals & Health Networks* 68(8):62.
51. AAFP issues white paper on patient education. (1994). *American Family Physician* 49(3):673.
52. Doyle, E. (1995). For the personal touch in patient education—computers? *ACP (American College of Physicians) Observer* 15(2):8–9.
53. Borzo, G. (1995). Reaching out to patients electronically. *American Medical News* 38(26):19.
54. Davis, N. M. (1994). Teaching patients to prevent errors. *American Journal of Nursing* 94(5):17.
55. Kinnard, L. S. (1993). Managing risk through patient education. In *Managed Hospital-Based Patient Education*, edited by B. E. Giloth. Chicago: American Hospital Publishing, pp. 115–128.
56. Giloth, B. E. (1993). *Managing Hospital-Based Patient Education*. Chicago: American Hospital Publishing.
57. Cordell, B., and Smith-Blair, N. (1994). Streamlined charting for patient education. *Nursing94* 24(1): 7–59.
58. Annas, G. J. (1992). *The Rights of Patients. The Basic ACLU Guide to Patients' Rights*. Totowa, N.J.: Humana Press.
59. Sheldon, T. (1994). Europe backs new declaration on patients' rights. *British Medical Journal* 308(6935): 997.
60. Sheldon, T. (1994). Dutch law defines patients' rights. *British Medical Journal* 308(6929):616.
61. U.S. Department of Health and Human Services. (1999). HCFA (HealthCare Financing Administration) *Medicare Peer Review Organization Manual*, Transmittal no. 79, November 1999, Sections 7000–7055.
62. Court rule: Patients can demand second opinions on HMO denials. (2002). *News of New York Medical Society of New York State* 57(8):13.
63. ERISA: Divided U.S. Supreme Court rules that state HMO law is not preempted. (2002). *Legal News, Health Plan and Provider Report*. Bureau of National Affairs, June 26, 8(26):757.
64. Montague, J. (1994). Should the public have access to the National Practitioner Data Bank? *Hospitals & Health Networks* 68(11):52–56.
65. Wolfe, S. M., and Steiber, J. (1994). Medical consumers need malpratice data. *New York Times* June 7, p. A22, col. 4.
66. Patient advocacy group formed. Mistakes at Tampa hospital prompt request to legislators. (1994). *Sun Sentinel* (Tampa, Fla.), March 17, p. A18, col. 3.
67. Press, I. (1994). Patient satisfaction. The last word. *Hospitals & Health Networks* 68(5):60.
68. Taylor, S. A. (1994). Distinguishing service quality from patient satisfaction in developing health care marketing strategies. *Hospital & Health Services Administration* 39(2):221–236.
69. Brown, S. W., Bronkesh, S. J., Nelson, A., and Wood, S. D. (1993). *Patient Satisfaction Pays. Quality Service for Practice Success*. Gaitherburg, Md.: Aspen.
70. Mangels, L. (1991). Tips from doctors who've never been sued. *Medical Economics* February 18, pp. 56–64.
71. Joel, L. A. (1994). Changing standard in consumer-provider relations. *American Journal of Nursing* 94(6):7.
72. Freed, D. H. (1994). Toward redefining expectations about medical technology. *Trends in Health Care, Law & Ethics* 9(2):21–28.
73. Labaton, S. (1995). Don't sue, they say. We went bankrupt. *New York Times* May 21, p. E16, col. 6.
74. Kennedy, R. (1995). Doctor is shot in Brooklyn. *New York Times* April 13, p. B5, col. 1.
75. Insight on claims data: Surgeons getting sued more. (2001). *RMF Quarterly Risk Management Foundation of the Harvard Medical Institutions*. Winter.
76. Williams, B. (1994). Patient satisfaction: A valid concept. *Social Science in Medicine* 38(4):509–516.
77. Joos, S. K., Hickam, A., et al. Parents' desires and satisfactions in general medicine clinics. *Public Health Reports* 108(6)751–759.

78. National Resources Corporation. (2001). *2001 NRC Healthcare Market Guide*. Lincoln, Nebraska.

79. Capko, J. (1994). Patient satisfaction helps you with managed care. *American Medical News* 347(34):29.

80. Greene, M. G., Adelman, R. D., Friedman, E., and Charon, R. (1994). Older patient satisfaction with communications during an initial medical encounter. *Social Science in Medicine* 38(9):1279–1288.

81. *www.USQA.com/Clinical Performance Report/ What We Do/perform.html*. Aetna Insurance. (2002).

82. Cerne, F. (1994). Interview with GHAA president Karen M. Ignagni. *Hospitals & Health Network* 67(23):62.

83. Oberman, L. (1995). Feds, Oregon work together to build a better report card. *American Medical News* 38(8):4.

84. Florida looks to make the grade on hospital report cards. (1995). *Clinical Data Management* 1(11):1–2.

85. Oberman, L. (1994). Top accreditor goes public on new hospital report cards. *American Medical News* 37(38):3, 10; Reports will give hospitals grades. (1994). *News Tribune* (Woodbridge, N.J.), October 28, p. S12, col. 5.

86. Baine, D. P. (1994). *"Report Cards" Are Useful but Significant Issues Need to Be Addressed.* GAO/HEHS-94-219. Washington, D.C.: government Printing Office, p. 13.

87. U.S. Congress, Office of Technology Assessment. (1988). *The Quality of Medical Care: Information for Consumers*. OTA-H-386. Washington, D.C.: Government Printing Office.

88. Bergman, R. (1994). Making the grade. Report cards will be used to measure the performance of health plans: How might they work? *Hospitals & Health Networks* 68(1):34–36.

89. Chekuri, L., and Schumacher, F. (2001). Health systems: Improving with information technology. Case Western Reserve.

90. Wensing, M., Grol, R., and Smits, A. (1994). Quality judgements by patients on general practice care: A literature analysis. *Social Science in Medicine* 38(1):45–53.

91. Harvard Community Health Plan. (1994). *Annual Report*. Brookline, Mass.: HCHP.

92. Winslow, R. (1994). Health-care report cards are getting low grades from some focus groups. *Wall Street Journal* May 19, p. B1, col. 3.

93. Adelman, S. H. (1994). Clinton's satisfaction reporting plan raises questions. *American Medical News* 37(5):16.

94. Eshleman, A. M. (2002). Quality assurance and risk management in on-line medical discussion groups. *American Journal of Medical Quality* 17(3):89–93.

95. Scannell, K., Perednia, D. A., et al. Telemedicine: Past, present, future: January 1966 through March 1995. U.S. Department of Health and Human Services, Public Health Service, National Library of Medicine CBM 95-4.

CHAPTER 5 Financing of Risk and Insurance

David Metz
Kevin M. McLaughlin

Health care institutions and other types of businesses typically use several strategies to control the financial consequences of the risks associated with their operations. Among these are avoiding certain high-risk exposures and initiating quality control and other techniques to prevent or mitigate the frequency and severity of losses. Often, these institutions also transfer all or portions of the cost of their losses to an insurer, or they self-insure, depending upon their size, financial strength, and culture regarding assumption of risk.

The availability of acceptably priced, insured alternatives is a key factor in the cost/risk calculation and is influenced by the institution's claim experience, trends, competition in the primary and reinsurance markets, and insurance company investment performance.

The events of September 11, 2001, and their consequences for the property and casualty (P&C) insurance industry, poor investment performance, and a prolonged period of relatively stable insurance rates resulted in almost $8 billion worth of losses for the P&C industry in 2001, compared with $20.6 billion in P&C industry earnings in 2000.[1] The reaction of insurers to these kinds of losses is predictable: many have dropped out of the market, and several others don't insure specific risks, are very selective and strict with underwriting requirements, and have raised their rates high enough to cover the anticipated costs as well as the unexpected costs (see Box 5-1).

Generally speaking, health care facilities should be aware of the cyclical nature of insurance markets. High-profile facilities, particularly in high-profile communities such as New York City and Washington, D.C., need to pay particular attention to the impact on their risk management budgets of the events of September 11, and to other

BOX 5-1

The terrorist attacks on the World Trade Center are expected to result in estimated financial losses of $340 million to hospitals in the New York City, Long Island, Westchester County, and Hudson Valley areas, according to the Greater New York Hospital Association.[2]

factors of market consolidation, competition, cost trends, investment performance, and profitability. These factors are all likely to influence primary and reinsurance carrier underwriting and pricing strategies (see Box 5-1).[2]

Health care institutions that may not be eligible for or able to afford terrorism insurance, due to market conditions or other circumstances, may also find themselves unable to get bond or other long-term financing for capital projects; or they may find that they are in technical default on existing debt if they are without coverage.[1]

Risk management budgets for medical malpractice insurance are a unique concern for health care institutions. "Premiums are doubling, hospital deductibles are tripling, claims-free physicians are not being renewed, and insurers are leaving (markets) en masse."[3,4]

Carrier payment results for medical malpractice coverage since 1990 illustrate the trends, the cyclical nature of the health care insurance industry, and the financial consequences that result when insurance companies focus on increasing market share and premium income at the expense of underwriting and pricing for profitability. The combined ration trend for 2000 has been estimated to be 140 percent, which means that insurance carriers were paying out $1.40 for every premium dollar collected, as compared to $1.01 in 1990 and 96 cents in 1995.[3] There is no reason to believe that the factors influencing the cost of medical malpractice claims (i.e., increasing litigation, increasing costs for medical care, high cost of legal settlements, etc.) are likely to abate in the near future.

Since external market factors and trends are beyond a health care institution's control, its investment in loss control efforts has become increasingly important in recent years, as insurer underwriting practices focus more and more on the institution's ability to manage its risk exposures.[5] It should not be expected, however, that quality improvement and other risk prevention efforts will, in the short term, pay off in the form of lower expected claims costs or lower medical malpractice premium increases.[6] As health care institutions focus on loss control and risk financing issues in the aftermath of the catastrophic events of September 11, the necessity of examining all of their risk exposures (financial, operation, general business hazard, medical malpractice, general liability, business interruption, etc.) as a key component of their overall business strategy has become increasingly important to assuring long-term enterprise viability.

This strategic approach to risk management, generally referred to as Enterprise Risk Management (ERM), is an evolving concept and has been defined as "an approach to assessing and addressing risks from all sources that either threaten the achievement of an organization's strategic objectives or represent opportunities to exploit competitive advantage and is designed to raise the responsibility for risk management to the senior management and board levels."[7]

ERM does not ignore specialized departments, activities, or functions, but rather takes into account their interrelationships and interdependencies and then attempts to build a quantitative decision-making and organizational matrix and process that facilitate and enhance the institution's ability to evaluate and formulate responses to all risk exposures efficiently and effectively.[8,9]

The importance of risk management's ability to identify a health care institution's internal and external interdependencies becomes critically obvious in light of the consequences of the September 11 disruptions to organizations' supply chains. Health care institutions have begun to diversify; decentralize; outsource professional, administrative, business, and other services; and leverage their working capital through demand inventory and supply. As this happens, the operational and financial consequences of business disruptions to a health care institution or its business dependents becomes an issue for heightened focus and planning[10] (see Box 5-2).

In the opinion of insurance industry leaders and the International Risk Management Institute, "standard and non-standard war risk exclusion (will) not operate to deny coverage under property and casualty insurance policies for claims arising from the terrorists' attacks on September 11, 2001." Risk managers should, however, evaluate the language of any non-standard form policy and of their various coverages from an enterprise perspective on a current basis and for future risk management planning.[12]

A New York health care institution reviewed its property insurance on November 1, 2001, and was able to obtain only 20 percent of the expiring policy's coverage limit with a broad terrorism exclusion, a tighter "occurrence" definition, and a premium three times higher than that of the previous year.[13]

Crafting a risk financing program sensitive to market cycles can entail risk transfer in a soft market, or the unbundling of lines of coverage, utilizing various pooling and captive arrangements, deciding on self-

BOX 5-2

Immediate Impact on Hospitals of September 11 Attack
(Survey conducted from September 11, 2001 to October 6, 2001)

Actions Resulting in Unreimbursed Standby Costs

- Activated emergency command centers
- Cancelled all possible elective surgeries, medical admissions, and scheduled procedures
- Closed ambulatory care clinic services
- Transferred or discharged hospitalized patients

Increased Costs

- Disaster-related property loss
- Incremental labor and overtime
- Incremental security
- Emergency supplies, pharmaceuticals, and blood
- Disaster crisis counseling services
- Emergency food, housing, and transportation
- Emergency structural repairs and debris clean-up
- Emergency telecommunications, generators, purchases, and rentals
- Emergency morgue

insurance exposures and limits, and establishing "intricate layers of primary and excess insurance covering the self insured/policyholder and other persons or entities."[14]

Although multiple factors influence a health care institution's risk management program, each institution has a unique approach to the decision matrix, according to its unique circumstances and culture. Some factors that nevertheless have general applicability and are worthy of priority consideration in the aftermath of September 11 follow:

- Identify, evaluate, and manage the risks arising from internal and external interdependencies and organizational infrastructures that could be affected by catastrophic events.
- Consider decentralizing where possible in order to obtain a spread of risk and reduce the operational and financial consequences of a catastrophic event.
- Choose insurance companies that are financially strong and have a history of experience and commitment to the health care industry.
- Continuously review and rehearse organizational, operational, and community disaster and recovery programs.
- Back up critical information systems and records.
- Review and strengthen safety, security, and communications activities and programs.
- Avoid being surprised by significant rate increases. Plan ahead by reviewing risk transfer and financing options on an ongoing basis.
- Develop benchmarks and implement plans for improvement in key areas. Prioritize these plans.
- Integrate risk management into the strategic thinking of the institution.

Risk managers must identify each of the many areas of risk exposure and determine how best to manage their financial consequences.[15] Identification of these various exposures is an organized process that includes using insurance company loss data, in-house adverse incident reports, Occupational Safety and Health Administration (OSHA) reports, complaints from guests and visitors, financial statements, accreditation and licensure inspections, and professional periodicals. A matrix of incidents can be distinguished and coordinated based on variables such as employee shift, location in the facility, type of incident, and outcome. Once a pattern is recognized, appropriate solutions can be identified and implemented. Cooperation of the administration and the medical staff is essential for effective implementation. Any risk reduction plan also includes the education and training of medical care personnel, executives and administrators, nonprofessional staff, and volunteers in the procedures for controlling loss, for reducing incidents of patient injury, and for identifying and avoiding potentially injurious events and taking appropriate corrective actions.[16] An appropriate risk management plan that includes a mission statement and a policy statement should be developed.[17]

When formulating a plan, risk managers must carefully evaluate the potential loss in terms of frequency of adverse events and severity of financial consequences. This analysis is central to the choice among the alternatives for dealing with risk exposure. This process is now evolving into Enterprise Risk Management, which is an integrated approach that combines both traditional property/liability and financial risk. Generally accepted accounting practices (GAAP) and health care risk management integration will not be easy, but it is coming.[7]

Frequency refers to the number of times an event occurs and can be gauged in relation to any relevant period of time or area—per patient day, per discharge, per year, per procedure or in the emergency room area, per operating suite, or per intensive care unit. Areas of the organization should be studied individually and comparatively over periods of time. Typically, the most frequent adverse occurrences are of a minor nature, such as the loss of eyeglasses or false teeth. One of the difficulties in gathering accurate data is that many very minor occurrences may go unreported. However, an "occurrence screen" procedure that requires employees to report specifically listed events may yield increased data about minor incidents. In essence, the "occurrence screen" is an integration of quality assessment and risk management.[15]

Severity refers to the cost of the loss in dollars. Financial payouts can range from insignificant to catastrophic. A risk exposure that is infrequent and catastrophic can be one of the most difficult and time consuming to assess. Losses of that nature are difficult to plan for because their likelihood always seems remote and the size of the loss may distract attention from preventing other more prevalent, though less costly, potential losses.

Daniels and Lynch[18] argue that all reasonably predictable losses should be retained and covered by the health care organization using financial ratio analysis, actuarial review, and cost benefit analysis to determine the optimal risk retention. This disciplined methodology to calculate the amount of risk to self-insure or retain should replace the notion of applying unscientific "rules of thumb" in the decision-making process.

Traditionally, a facility that suffers from a combination of high-frequency and high-severity financial losses will generally find itself facing high costs and limited options unless the administration makes significant changes in the scope and manner in which it operates.

Currently, all risk managers are facing the same crisis—increasing liability premiums, despite good claims histories. Those institutions with prior losses are doomed to the ever-increasing combined ratios suffered by the insurance industry. This is due primarily to the loss of several insurance companies—Frontier, Reliance, and P.I.E. Mutual. The most recent casualty is PHICO, one of the 10 largest insurers in the United States. The problem is not only causing hospitals concern, but is affecting all health care providers.

What can be done? Risk managers must now look at various risk management techniques, including high retentions, self-insurance, internal loss controls, claim procedures, and protocols. Failure to do this may result in an unaffordable risk transfer program that will force change.[4]

OPTIONS IN IMPLEMENTING A PLAN

Traditionally, the purchase of insurance has been the key ingredient in a risk management program.[19] Insurance is an effective alternative and can be implemented quickly; the cost is fairly predictable, major exposures are usually covered, and the insurance company offers services that complement its programs. However, the cost of insurance tends to be the highest among all alternatives because insurance companies pool premiums from all participants to pay claims. Exposures not covered by the insurance carrier are not the carrier's responsibility or concern. If such events occurred, the facility could still be exposed to substantial financial loss. In addition, part of the cost goes to insurance company expenses and profit, which are increasing.

In addition to fully insured guaranteed cost programs, there are other various "loss-sensitive" plans available from insurance companies—with deductibles, retrospectively rated plans, and dividend plans, to name a few. Loss-sensitive plans may respond to a good loss experience with return of a dividend to reduce the premium.

Before choosing any insurance plan, the organization should undertake a historical analysis of claims and premiums for a period of five years, if possible. This analysis should consider the time value of money and loss costs, prospectively and retroactively. To properly assess funding levels and acceptable amounts of risk, an actuary should be consulted.

One of the techniques in analyzing the potential financial loss in terms of frequency and severity is "benchmarking." A benchmark is comparable to a standard or norm. Flores concluded that "benchmarking should be . . . a problem identification tool, not a performance indicator."[20] His company utilized the frequency rate published by the U.S. Bureau of Labor and Statistics (BLS) and each operating plant was compared to BLS statistics. Certain statistics predicted financial losses that could be incurred as a result of medical care, employee time off, and productivity reductions. Each accident has ramifications beyond the immediate incident. With the benchmarks in use, improvement was possible because a measurable standard existed, allowing management to evaluate performance. The *Benchmarking Exchange* suggests "benchmarking a company that serves as a good model."[21]

INSURANCE OPTIONS BASED ON PREMIUM SIZE

An anticipated premium level can be determined by the size and complexity of the health care organization or facility. In addition, the premium depends on factors such as payroll, physical plant, number of beds, utilization statistics, specific programs, and other variables. Health care consultants commented on the risks of ignoring insurance risk management and the factors contributing to the resulting uncertainty: "Health care insurers face financial risks when they assume liability for the difference between premium revenues and their estimates of future claims costs for a group."[22] Although there is no definitive rule that states when each alternative is feasible, the greater the premium, the more alternative risk financing methods are available. The number of types of plans that can be considered increases as the premium levels advance. In a small hospital with a premium of $200,000 to $450,000 for workers' compensation alone, many alternatives are available. However, if the premium is at $50,000—for example, at a home health agency—then fewer alternatives are realistically available; certainly self-insurance and captives are excluded. In addition, at higher premium levels the cost becomes less predictable as the cost savings opportunity increases, because in larger insurance programs the costs are driven by losses rather than by premium payments (see Box 5-3).

Captive Insurance Companies

A single owner captive is an insurance company owned solely for the benefit of an individual health care organization to insure its own risks, whereas a multiowner captive is established jointly by more than

BOX 5-3

- Bacon Hospital in Alma, Georgia, a facility with 80 beds, took out a loan to cover a premium that more than tripled.[28]
- Memorial Hospital and Manor in Bainbridge, Georgia, operates a hospital and nursing home and was faced with a 600 percent increase in its premium.[28]

one health care organization of like size and exposure for the purpose of insuring the risk exposures of the participating institutions.[23] In exchange for the policy, the health care organization is charged a premium reflecting the charges to issue the policy and to pay the claims.

Typically, the domicile of the captive insurance company is Bermuda or the Cayman Islands because the capitalization costs and assets needed for operation are much lower there than those required in the United States, and there are certain tax advantages. By the end of 2003, 50 percent of the U.S. commercial market will migrate to the alternative risk market, up 40 percent in 2001.[24]

Self-Insurance

When a health care organization assumes the risk of a loss within its own financial structure, it is considered self-insured. Simultaneously, the health care organization develops a plan to accumulate reserve funds in escrow to pay for any loss that occurs. Most organizations combine an escrow account with an "excess insurance" policy purchased from a commercial carrier. Up to a specified dollar amount, the self-insured organization pays the claims, and the insurance carrier picks up the losses in excess of the designated expenditure level.

Pools, or Self-Insured Groups

A group of similar health care organizations may pool their funds to finance a trust fund that is used to pay claims. This single entity trust fund develops, adopts, and follows a formal financial plan to accumulate funds with which to pay the cost of loss-producing events of the members of the pooled self-insurance fund.[25] These pools are attractive to small or medium-size organizations, which may not be able to self-insure economically and have the advantage of group pooled experiences. Pools are not legal in all states.

Large Deductible Insurance Policies

These insurance contracts provide "coverage" from the first dollar. Insurance companies handle the claims and then assess the insured up to the agreed-upon deductible. This is not self-insurance, but it helps the insured meet the requirements of statutory coverage (for example, workers' compensation) without having to be a licensed self-insurer. The amount assessed tends to be $50,000 or more; thus it is considered "large deductible."

Retrospectively Rated Dividend Plans

For retrospectively rated plans, the loss experience of the current year is evaluated. If there are few losses (a "good" experience), there is a potential credit or dividend. If the losses are high (a "poor" experience), there is a potential debit to be assessed. At the initiation of the contract, the rating formula is agreed upon and usually includes commissions, taxes, assessments, loss adjustment expenses, and administrative costs.

CONSIDERATIONS IN CHOOSING AN ALTERNATIVE INSURANCE PROGRAM

In any review of the financial consequences of these alternative insurance programs, the philosophy of the health care organization's management should be considered. If the health care organization is conservative, a gradual approach should be used. Additional considerations involve portability, flexibility, services, and protection. To assist in structuring any contemplated alternative insurance, costs should be evaluated.

Portability

For multistate organizations or networks, the portability feature is extremely important. If the insurance coverage is statutory in nature, such as workers' compensation or automobile liability, the ability to operate with a single insurance plan program in multiple states outside of conventional insurance is limited. In self-insurance, the states require the insured to become licensed in each state for statutory coverage and to comply with all state laws. An alternative is to be "fronted" by a licensed insurance carrier, which would issue the policy and then reinsure with the self-insured program. Captives and their variations also can be used to address portability.

Flexibility

Many financial programs, including some insured programs, require letters of credit or a bond to guarantee that the claims will be paid by the insured. Typically, the letters of credit must be collateralized. Often, programs require that each policy period have its own letter of credit or bond until all claims are liquidated. This makes changing insurance carriers more difficult. Additionally, there should be a consideration of whether there is flexibility when services are purchased individually.

Services

Evaluation of the claim handling, investigation, claim payment, and loss control services is critical. Except for full insurance programs, the health care organization has an opportunity to choose the company, or third-party administrator, to service its claims or to perform loss control services.

CHOOSING A THIRD-PARTY ADMINISTRATOR

Since claim costs are key in all programs, an effective pre-loss and post-loss plan must be in place. Factors to consider in choosing a third-party administrator include:

Experience: Line of coverage, type of business, and references should be provided.

Staffing: Consider the number of claims per adjuster, turnover, presence of RNs or nurse practitioners on staff, and geographic location.

Technology: Are they fully computerized? Can they tie into the facility's system? Is there a 24-hour reporting system?

Procedures: Is there 24-hour turnaround? Is the reporting system cumbersome? Can they modify for each facility? What are their short term and long term case management procedures?

Costs: Per-claim and flat-cost projections should be analyzed. Third-party administrators should offer a proposal that provides service until the agreement is severed and adjust claims until they are closed.

Protection: Since all the risk financing alternatives involve elements of insurance, the contractual obligations set forth affect the scope of coverage. These include the definition of retention, how the limits are applied per event or per occurrence, and what the limits are. In addition, the financial strength of the carrier, claim practices, and reputation should be evaluated. A comparison among all competitors should be comprehensive.

STRUCTURE OF RISK EXPOSURE MANAGEMENT

A risk manager has the task of identifying exposures to loss and managing the potential effects of those exposures. This is a dynamic process that must be systematically approached on a daily basis. The nine key areas of exposure are:

Property: structures, their contents, and goods in transit.

General liability: injuries to third parties arising from operations.

Professional liability: injuries to third parties arising from medical incidents.

Automobile liability and physical damage: usual automobile coverage.

Employee/volunteer injury and illness: occupational accident and disease, as well as disease or injury transmitted to family members.

Directors and officers liability: management errors and omissions.

Fiduciary liability: financial injury to others arising from an employer's acting in a fiduciary capacity. Most arise from employee benefit plans.

Aircraft liability: injuries sustained while loading or unloading aircraft.

Crime: employee dishonesty and theft.

The risk manager must understand each area of exposure. Obviously, this is not a solo task; other professionals in administration and finance will be needed and should be available to assist in assessing the risks.

Property

For many institutions, physical property is the largest asset. Before examining insurance programs or alternatives, property insurance underwriters usually require basic information about buildings, contents, electronic data processing equipment, valuable printed material and documents, unusual property, personal property of others, boiler and other machinery, and business income. A property insurance contract should be for "all risks" of physical damage. Without this stipulation, the carrier can decline the loss if it is specifically excluded from the contract. Another way to insure property is on a "named peril" basis. This requires the insured to identify perils *before* the loss and to link the exposure to the financial loss when an adverse event occurs. A court ruling in *Garvey v. State Farm Insurance*[26] clarified the issue:

> In determining whether insurance coverage exists under an "all-risk" homeowner's policy, when loss to an insured property can be attributed to two causes, one of which is a nonexcluded peril, and the other an excluded peril, the courts are to find coverage only if the nonexcluded peril is the efficient proximate cause of the loss, rather than finding coverage whenever a nonexcluded peril is a concurrent proximate cause of the loss.

In large organizations, the insurance valuation of various types of property can be a very difficult task. An initial review has to identify the types of property to be protected and the various risk exposures to be insured against. The following sections address each type of property individually.

Buildings

Valuation of the physical plant is primarily a function of the total square footage and the cost per square foot. Generally, the cost per square foot is based on the type of construction, local labor costs, and safety features such as automatic sprinklers. A facility's engineering department should be able to provide the analysis of square feet by fire division, by the age of each part of the building, and by how the building is protected against loss. Factors to be considered are: "(1) specifications, (2) materials, (3) labor, (4) overhead, and (5) profit."[27] With this information, an engineer from the loss control service or insurance company can usually determine the value of the building. However, the insurance company appraisal is not guaranteed by the company. Prudent risk managers will consider an independent appraisal. Risk managers need to select insurance coverage based on replacement cost or depreciated value in the event of loss. A survey of business owners revealed that although 76 percent thought they had purchased replacement cost insurance coverage, only nine percent actually had such coverage.[16]

Contents

Since the contents of buildings are so variable, this type of property is difficult to value, especially in a large facility. In part, the reason for the difficulty is that the amount of materials purchased and deleted is hard to track. In addition, either the replacement cost or the original cost must be determined and verified. Physical contents of buildings include materials such as furniture, fixtures, and equipment. Disposable contents include inventories of medical supplies, spare parts, and housekeeping materials. Typically, the valuation of these contents is set at replacement cost. An appraisal company can help place a value on contents. However, special contents may prove more difficult to insure.

Electronic Data Processing (EDP) Equipment: Hardware, Software, and PCs

Electronic data processing is the "nerve center," if not the "brain,"[16] of the health care organization. Every part of the organization is affected, and EDP is vital in a risk management program. Valuation difficulty stems from the rapidly changing technology, which causes obsolescence in a short period of time. Data processing managers must constantly calculate the cost of purchasing state-of-the-art equipment. As the organization becomes more dependent on computers, there is a greater exposure to loss. Furthermore, the types of losses the computer can suffer compounds the insurance coverage difficulty.

A computer data system is best insured on a specific EDP "floater" to the policy. This floater addresses the specific valuation and causes of loss associated with computer equipment.

Valuable Papers, Books, and Documents

This risk includes the re-creation of critical documents such as medical records. Loss control companies can make a pre-disaster assessment of the cost to restore valuable papers, books, and documents. Of course, a simpler alternative is to maintain a duplicate set of records.

Experience indicates a special need to protect records that have been requested by a plaintiff attorney or government agency. If these records are scheduled to be used in a hearing or trial, they must be complete and unaltered. Risk managers should consult with the director of medical records concerning the state of the art in record protection and retrieval.

Unusual Property

Some general examples of unusual property are items of sophisticated technology, of extremely high value, of an essential nature, or of intrinsic value; high technology communications equipment; movable property; and exhibits. Specific examples include magnetic resonance imagers, linear accelerators, paintings and collectibles, satellite dishes and mobile radios, and equipment on ambulances. Property that emits X-ray radiation or has the potential of nuclear exposure should be insured for contamination and toxic remediation of the occurrence site. After these items are identified, they must be appraised appropriately. If the property is essential, a replacement or backup must be locatable and available prior to a loss. Unique property should be insured separately on an inland marine "floater." This coverage is usually broader and easier to adjust in the event of loss.

Personal Property of Others

This category consists primarily of leased equipment and the personal property of patients, guests, employees, and volunteers. Risk of such loss can be controlled by not allowing patients to keep highly valued personal property on the premises. Guests and volunteers should be alerted to protect their valuable belongings. Employees should accept full responsibility for their own goods.

Boiler and Other Machinery

Boilers or pressurized machinery that is located in the basement or the main building represents a potential catastrophic exposure. Proper maintenance and an effective backup system are an absolute necessity. If the boiler is insured separately from the general property coverage, the property carrier and the boiler carrier should sign a "joint loss agreement." This agreement resolves any discrepancies between the two carriers in the event of a loss.

Pressurized machinery is frequently under-insured, because an inspection service is the primary focus and the law does not require other equipment to be inspected.[18] In most cases, insurance is the best way to meet this risk exposure because of the relatively low rates and the low-frequency, high-severity nature of boiler losses.

Business Income

An organization can suffer a loss in business income as a direct consequence of a physical property disaster. In addition to a general loss of revenue, losses include continuing operation costs, extra costs (overtime, rented telephones, heaters, etc.), and opportunity costs. These potential business income losses should be identified and quantified in a written disaster plan.

Additional Property Exposures

Risk exposure related to construction activities and in connection with rental property are common liability risks for health care organizations. The initial process is to design the structure and to hire a contractor. Model contract forms[18] contain specific wording regarding "hold harmless" and "assumption of liability" conditions. Such wording transfers the risk to the architect and the contractor. "Builders Risk" is the insurance policy that addresses this situation and sets dollar limits based on the completed value of the construction.

Along with the building, off-site property, property in transit, contractor's equipment, and installed equipment must have proper coverage. Since either the contractor or the building owner is responsible, the construction agreement should indicate acceptable coverage limits for automobile liability, workers' compensation, and general liability, naming the facility as an additional insured. If this is not done, the health care organization will be responsible for supplying the protection.

When renting property from another entity, the terms of the lease should delineate who is responsible for damage or injury. In many leases, a partial demise of the premises does not necessarily decrease the rent.

General Liability

A health care organization faces exposure to loss from various areas arising from the law of torts. A tort is a failure to act in a responsible, prudent manner. This standard of prudence constantly changes as society changes, a dynamic process that must be constantly monitored. Risk managers should strive to be continuously aware of laws and court decisions that affect the health care industry. When a tort is committed, various subdivisions of the law can impose a penalty. Jurisdiction is determined as follows:

Common law: judicial interpretation of law.

Statutory law: legislative acts.

Civil law: suing another for damages.

Criminal law: societal punishment for intentional violations of law.

Contract law: violation of written or oral agreements.

Civil actions are the most common actions taken against health care facilities. To be awarded damages, a plaintiff must show negligence on the part of the defendant. Costs for the health care institution involved with any civil action may be divided into at least five categories:

Settlement or judgment: Three awards may be determined: *general*, noneconomic loss such as pain and suffering; *specific*, such as medical bills or lost income; or *punitive*, such as punishment for acts considered reckless or unusually harmful by the courts.

Defense costs: Defense costs may exceed the settlement and may include lawyers' fees, court costs, transcription fees, and various other legal costs.

Loss reduction: These are the costs to change work practices to avoid future losses.

Morale: Continuous losses cause employees to question work safety, the professionalism of the health care facility, and the management. Thus, the institution may need to spend money to boost morale.

Opportunity costs: When a facility takes too long to decide on new projects or abandons them altogether, the opportunity dissipates and incurs costs.

Although criminal actions can have ramifications of tremendous proportion, they are typically uninsurable. In some cases, unintentional criminal acts can be insured. Risk managers can address only imputed liability to the organization. Internal controls and procedures can deal with this type of exposure. Loss of public or consumer confidence as a result of real or perceived safety concerns can lead to a significant loss of business and income.

Risk Transfer

Organizations generally arrange for some form of insurance, either primary or excess, to cover the catastrophic cost potential associated with general liability. Key terms and conditions in the insurance contract need to be fully examined. For a health care organization, the following will typically be included in the contract, and should be applied *per location*: bodily injury and property damage; product/completed operations; fire damage legal liability; employee benefits liability; and patients' property. General aggregate coverage applies to everything except products/completed operations/employee benefits. Medical payments should be endorsed in the policy to cover guests and volunteers, on and off the premises. Professional liability limits are usually stated separately on a per loss or aggregate basis.

Insuring Agreements

Insuring agreements state that the insurance company "will pay those sums that the insured becomes legally obligated to pay." This means that the law imposes an obligation on the insured. Further, the insurer responds to bodily injury or property damage inflicted upon a third party. Even if the lawsuit alleges uninsured acts along with a covered act, the insurance company has a "right and duty to defend" the health care organization. Inclusion of an insured act obliges the insurance company to defend the entire lawsuit (see Box 5-4). However, the insurance company reserves the right to settle or to defend. Exclusions enumerate the coverages specifically taken out of the contract, such as work-related injuries, pollution, aircraft, and automobile liability. Personal and advertising liability in the general liability contract covers offenses such as libel, slander, invasion of privacy, and false arrest. When allegations affect a loss of reputation or loss of employment status, the employee may claim that unfounded slanderous or libelous remarks of various insureds caused the termination.

BOX 5-4

An ice cream manufacturer produced a contaminated product, and a settlement in the resulting lawsuit of $24 million was reached with the U.S. Food and Drug Administration. This firm supplied its own defense because the primary general liability carrier and excess carrier denied coverage. A court ruled that the carriers must pay the policy limits, but not the cost of the defense. An appeals court decided that the insurers had breached their duty to defend. It said that the insurers were contracted to defend the entire action, even though some allegations might be out of the scope of coverage.[29]

Because of the dynamic and complicated legal structure of a health care organization, the "named insured" can include the entity, its owners or active directors, officers and stock-holders, employees, and real estate managers. A conditions section of the policy outlines the "named insured's" duties, rights, and responsibilities and the rights of the health care organization under the contract. Failure to properly review the conditions could mean restriction or denial of coverage.

Professional Liability

Professional liability coverage can be written either as an endorsement or as a separate contract. To avoid "gray areas" in the event of a claim, the general liability and the professional liability insurance are often written by a single carrier. Liability coverage is triggered by a "medical incident." This term is explained in the definitions section of the policy and should include at least the following four types of liability:

- Liability from finding by an accreditation survey, review board, or committee.
- Liability arising from any and all services provided or not provided by an insured or someone for whom the insured can be held liable.
- Liability from the dispensing of drugs and supplies.
- Liability from any and all postmortem procedures.

These liabilities can result in "injury," but bodily injury is not a requirement for coverage.[30] If physicians are included in the program, dollar limits can be applied per location or per provider. Provided that a legal liability exists, the duty to defend still applies.[20]

A "consent" provision in an insurance contract relates to whether or not the insurance company needs the insured's consent to settle a claim. This clause obligates the insurance company to pay up the covered amount of any pretrial settlement or post-trial judgment. If the insureds refuse to settle, they are personally responsible for any judgment amount in excess of the proposed settlement. This option can cause a tremendous personal liability to the health care provider (see Box 5-5).

Liability insurance differentiates between "occurrence" and "claims made" coverage. "Occurrence" policies cover all injuries that occurred during the policy period, regardless of when they were reported. "Claims made" policies cover injuries reported during the policy period that occurred after the retroactive date stated on the policy's declaration page (see Box 5-6).

An advantage of an occurrence policy is that it will cover all injuries during the policy period until the agreement is exhausted. A disadvantage is that medical malpractice claims may be made many years after the event. Any awards resulting from such claims are applied against dollar limits that seemed adequate at the time the insurance was purchased, which may be woefully inadequate at the time of settlement. Occurrence limits should be negotiated with the realization that their financial adequacy may be tested 20 years later.[35]

BOX 5-5

- A 6-year-old boy died in an unexpected MRI accident when a hospital staff member brought a metal oxygen cylinder into the room. The machine's powerful 10-ton electromagnet pulled the oxygen tank through the air and into the machine, fracturing the boy's skull. The medical center assumed full responsibility.[31]
- Parkway Hospital was fined $32,000 by the New York State Health Department for its failure to prevent and address unnecessary urologica surgeries performed on 12 patients from a home for the mentally ill.[32]
- Two patients died from a laboratory error in the calculation of prothrombin time, leading to excessive doses of Coumadin and resultant intracranial hemorrhages. Another 932 hospitalized patients received incorrect test results and 100 received incorrect doses of Coumadin.[33]

BOX 5-6

Without having been properly notified of a lawsuit resulting from a complicated birth, a hospital changed its insurance coverage to a claims made policy. The incident in question had occurred prior to the retroactive date of the new inusrance. Solely on the basis of the dates of coverage, the carrier denied coverage. In its defense, the hospital relied on the fact that the carrier knew that the hospital had poor risk management procedures.[34]

Automobile Liability

Health care organizations can use conventional automobile liability insurance to provide coverage for vehicles. Only vehicles licensed for road use qualify for coverage. Service vehicles used solely on the premises are covered under the general liability policy. Unless the organization has an automobile fleet that generates enough premiums to justify alternative risk techniques, it is not cost effective to go beyond conventional insurance. Auto liability is statutorily required, and evidence of financial responsibility must be documented.

A business auto policy has several sections. In all states, auto liability is mandated, and some states require uninsured motorist and personal injury protection. Auto liability is offered on a per occurrence basis with no aggregate limit. A large emergency ambulance fleet has a much greater exposure to severe loss than does a fleet of autos for executives. Automobile physical damage is an optional coverage that can be purchased for any vehicle.

Employee/Volunteer Injury and Illness

Workers' compensation is statutorily required in all states. This insurance policy is composed primarily of two coverage parts. Part A affords statutory benefits as allowed by state law. This policy covers medical payments, indemnity, and legislatively mandated benefits. Part B insures employees not included under part A and covers injuries to family members arising from the employee's injuries. In a health care setting, Part B is critical coverage, since a disease could be transmitted from employee to family members.

Litigation regarding injury and illness of employees and volunteers is increasing on the basis of two legal arguments: (1) Dual capacity "means that the employer can be held liable for supplying the means to incur the injury in the course of doing business." For example, an employee is injured mowing the lawn while using a lawn mower manufactured by his own employer. (2) "Third party over" means that an employer has improperly instructed an employee on how to use a particular product. If an employee is injured while using the product and sues the manufacturer, in turn the manufacturer enters the employer as a codefendant in the lawsuit. Health care organizations, in some states, may purchase coverage "ex-medical," which allows the organization to provide the required medical services.

Experience modification is another factor that must be reviewed. Experience modification is an actuarially determined premium factor that applies either a debit or a credit to the premium. A mistake, such as an overstatement of an insured loss, can result in unnecessary premiums. Loss information and the workers' compensation experience data worksheets must be reviewed on a periodic basis. In a fully insured program, the procedure takes four steps:

1. A claim is reported to the insurance company by the employer.
2. An insurance company adjuster receives the claim and sets a reserve. This reserve represents the estimated gross severity of the claim and is called an incurred loss.
3. Incurred losses are reported to the state workers' compensation bureau.
4. On the basis of the first three of the previous four years, the workers' compensation bureau makes calculations. Earned premiums and incurred losses

are used to determine the experience modification. Other factors in the formula include a loss limitation and frequency.

Risk managers should check the state laws regarding the reporting of small claims. If legal, small claims should be paid directly to the employee by the employer. This will keep claim frequency down and reduce overall costs. In fact, any cost controls allowed by law should be implemented immediately. Box 5-7 illustrates an unusual example of court-determined cost control.

Directors and Officers Liability

Directors and Officers (D&O) liability is risk exposure insurance covering personal management decisions, misuse of assets, and errors or omissions of the members of the board of directors, the officers, and the chief executive of the health care organization. D&O coverage can be expanded to include additional administrative personnel. Box 5-8 gives some examples in which D&O liability is at issue.

Significantly, risk managers should be aware that "D&O insurance is the only coverage that is triggered solely by an action against an individual" of the health care institution.[37] Since D&O contracts are not standardized, all contract proposals must be scrutinized carefully. Risk managers should be aware that a D&O contract does not include the coverage normally found in a general liability policy. There are additional distinctions between D&O coverage and general liability insurance:

- Typically, D&O insurance does not "pay on behalf" of the insured any legal defense costs. The insured must pay the settlement and legal costs first and then wait for reimbursement.[38]
- D&O insureds employ their own legal counsel, and the insurance company has no "duty to defend." Since there is no duty to defend, the company can "allocate" defense cost and coverage based on the allegations in the lawsuit. These allocated legal defenses can be costly and cause an additional lawsuit against the company.
- A D&O contract covers only nonphysical injury, and aims to protect against management errors and omissions. An action that alleges pain and suffering is different from a suit that claims wrongful acts not involving bodily injury. Lawsuits must be evaluated carefully with the aid of legal counsel, because allegations can be categorized into the general liability and/or workers' compensation

BOX 5-7

A ranch foreman was seriously injured and left with a permanent partial disability. Unable to return to physical activity, he refused to be retrained, despite strong academic and mental abilities. A district court denied him a lump sum payment for permanent and total disability, finding that the benefit was only economic. An appeals court upheld the denial, on the basis of his unwillingness to be retrained.[35]

BOX 5-8

- Beneficiaries of a hospital association established to provide benefits to railroad employees sued the hospital board of trustees to prevent the dissolution of the association.
- Trustees of a charity sold an old building used to house the homeless and invested in a newer, better building. They were sued for wasting the trust's assets.[36]

policy, or into the D&O policy, depending on the type of claim.

- A D&O contract is on a "claims made" basis, and an extended reporting period is offered after the policy is canceled or not renewed. The cost, the duration, and the terms of the extension should be checked.
- A D&O insurance application contains warranties by the purchaser. An application for a D&O policy requires the insured to guarantee specific facts to be literally true, to their best knowledge and belief. Failure to do so voids the coverage. Warranties relate to prior and/or pending litigation, knowledge of circumstances that could result in a claim, and whether prior D&O insurance had been canceled or was not renewed.

D&O insurance came into prominence in the United States in the 1980s. Today it is a worldwide problem. In an international review of D&O liability, three top financial management executives cited examples of litigious societies in Australia, Canada, China, France, Germany, Hong Kong, Japan, Taiwan, and the United Kingdom.[39]

If a health care organization plans to offer stock to the public, the organization should have a three-year Securities and Exchange Commission (SEC) liability contract along with the D&O policy. This SEC liability agreement protects the health care organization from lawsuits that arise from misstatements in its prospectus.

Fiduciary Responsibility

In another burgeoning area of litigation and risk exposure, fiduciary responsibility liability addresses risk exposures that the health care facility faces as a result of the handling of money for employees. Primarily, the insurance covers employee payroll deductions for pension plans, savings plans, and various employee benefit options. Exposures arise from the loss of funds or benefits by the implementor and/or fiduciary of the plans, the employer. Even in fully insured plans, a failure of a designated provider of a benefit can result in a vicarious loss. An employer must select benefit providers that are not only financially sound, but also operationally adept.

Aircraft Liability

A general liability insurance policy excludes bodily injury arising from the loading or unloading of any aircraft. Since many health care organizations have helicopter landing pads on site, it is prudent to have a helipad liability policy to cover the loading and unloading of patients, supplies, and passengers.

Crime Insurance

A crime insurance policy can be included with the property contract or written separately. In its most common form, the blanket crime contract includes five insuring agreements:

1. An **employee dishonesty agreement** covers theft by an employee and is in the form of a bond. A bond is written as a guarantee of an employee's faithful performance of duties. Should a loss occur, the bond carrier tries to recover the value of the stolen items or money from the individual(s) responsible. If necessary, a bond endorsement can cover theft by an employee from third parties. If the health care organization has employees rendering services to patients in their own homes or in the community, or performing similar off-site activities, this is necessary coverage. To comply with the federal Employee Retirement and

Income Security Act (ERISA) regulations, the amount of the bond should be at least $500,000 or 10 percent of pension assets. As an insured plan, the exact name of the pension plan should appear on the bond.

2. A **loss on premises agreement** covers robbery or theft.
3. A **loss off premises agreement** also covers robbery or theft.
4. A **counterfeit money orders and currency agreement** loss is extremely rare and may be unnecessary for many health care organizations.
5. A **depositors forgery agreement** covers the theft and alteration of negotiable instruments.

PROTECTION FOR A RAINY DAY

Health care organizations cannot operate without a cash flow and a positive profit-and-loss accounting. Risk managers can assist in protecting the financial assets of their organizations against devastating liability losses. A knowledge of the options and key areas of risk transfer and insurance helps build a comprehensive risk management program. Within health care organizations, there are experts who can help with everything from overviews of insurance coverage to an entire restructuring of the risk management program. These experts could be personnel of the health care organization itself, such as financial and accounting managers, plant engineers, electronic data processing managers, nurse supervisors, directors of volunteers, organizational auditors, insurance brokers, and numerous others who have the expertise in some or most of what the risk management plan proposes to do.

A risk management process affects every aspect of the health care organization in varied ways. Finances of the organization can be crippled by an uninsured or underinsured loss. Benefits can accrue through cost-effective improvements in the overall program. Employee morale increases if losses go down. Operational efficiencies are realized when the health care organization's assets are properly protected. If a health care organization has a commendable safety record and reacts to losses with little, if any, effect on the services, the community recognizes that the organization is well run.

Top management must be solidly behind risk management efforts. A demonstration of visible, quantifiable results is the best way to garner management support. If results are presented in general terms, management may not fully understand the impact of proper risk management. As a technique, "benchmarking" creates optimistic outcomes and shows quantifiable results that demonstrate quantifiable financial outcomes.

As complex as the risk management mission in financing and insurance seems currently, the dynamic nature of the health care industry can only lead to a higher level of sophistication with newer options to minimize losses.

References

1. Cohn, M. (2002). Insurers put businesses state in bind. *Baltimore Sun*, July 21.
2. *http://www.advanceforot.com/previousdnw/otdnw1008.html*
3. Kolodkin, C. (2001). Medical malpractice insurance trends? Chaos! International Risk Management Institute, Expert Commentary (September). *http://www.irmi.com/expert/articles/kolodkin00/asp.*
4. American Association of Health Plans E.C.H.O. Chamber. (2000). Medical malpratice lawsuits by the numbers. *http://www.aahpechochamber.tv/malpractice/numbers.htm.*
5. Bausom and Associates, Inc. (2001). So where do insurers go after 9/11? International Risk Management Institute Expert Commentary (September 2001).

6. Burstin, H. R., et al. (1999). Benchmarking and quality improvement: The Harvard Emergency Department Quality Study. *American journal of Medicine* 107:437–447.
7. Tillinghast-Towers, P. (2000). Enterprise risk management: What's behind the talk? International Risk Management Institute Expert Commentary (May). *http://www.irmi.colm/expert/articles/miccolis001.asp.*
8. Tillinghast-Towers, P. (2001). ERM and September 11. International Risk Management Institute Expert Commentary (November). *http://www.irmi.com/expert/articles/miccolis005.asp.*
9. Tillinghast-Towers, P. (2002). Implementing enterprise risk management: The emerging role of the chief risk officer. International Risk Management Institute Expert Commentary (January). *http://www.irmi.com/expert/articles/miccolis006.asp.*
10. Bausom and Associates, Inc. (2002). The importance of contingent business interruption. International Risk Management Institute Expert Commentary (August). *http://www.irmi.com/expert/articles/bausom009.asp.*
11. *The Fiscal Impact of the World Trade Center Attack on New York Hospitals, Preliminary Estimate.* (2001). Greater New York Hospital Association. October 2.
12. Attack on America: The insurance coverage issues, part I: General coveage provisions; Part II: War risk exclusions. (2001). International Risk Management Institute Insights (September). *http://www.irmi.como/insights/articles/gibson008.as*p and *009.asp.*
13. Serio, G. V. Testimony given by Superintendent of Insurance, New York State Insurance Department, U.S. House of Representatives Committee on Financial Services, Subcommittee on Oversight and Investigation. February 27, 2002.
14. Self insurance primary insurance and excess insurance: Adventures in contract interpretation. (2002). Expert Commentary, Causality Risk Consultants, LLC (February). *http://www.irmi.com/expert/articles/Wollner003.asp.*
15. Sagner, J. S. (1995). Financial system risks to watch for in 1995. *Healthcare Financial Management* 49(1):94–95.
16. Youngberg, B. (1990). *Essentials of Hospital Risk Management*. Gaithersburg, Md.: Aspen, p. 6.
17. How to manage risk. (2001). *Risk Management Reports* 28(8). *www.riskinfo.com/rmr/rmrsep01.htm.*
18. Daniels, G. L., and Lynch, P. M. (1994). Determining optimal risk retention in the healthcare industry. *Healthcare Financial Management* 48(4):48–54.
19. Parett, J. T. (1983). *Insurance Buyers Guide—A Manual for Risk Managers*. Chicago: Cudahy, pp. 1–16, 111–112, V-1–2.
20. Flores, D. T. (1994). Benchmarking: A traditional approach with an alternative perspective. *Risk Management Quarterly* 4(4):3.
21. What is benchmarking? *www.benchnet.com/web.htm.*
22. Jones, S., Cohodes, D. M., and Scheil, B. (1994). The risks of ignoring insurance risk management. *Health Affairs* 13(2):108–122.
23. Do-it-yourself insurance. (1995). *Economist* 333: 119–121.
24. Captives and other risk-financing options. (2002). Hot Topics and Insurance Options, Insurance Information Institute. June. *www.ii.org/media/hottopics/insurance/test3.*
25. Reynes, R. (1995). Do-it-yourself workers' comp. *Nation's Business* 83:26–28.
26. *Garvey v. State Farm Fire & Casualty Co.,* 48 Cal. 3d 395, 257 Cal. Rptr. 292, 770 P. 2d 704 (1989).
27. Thomas, P. I., and Reed, P. B. (1977). *Adjustment of Property Losses,* 4th edition. New York: McGraw-Hill, pp. 237–245.
28. Bryant, J. (2002). Malpractice rates sicken hospitals. *Business Chronicles.* (March 25).
29. *U.S. Fire Ins. Co. v. Good Humor Corp,* 496 N.W. 2d 730 (Wis. App. 1993).
30. Rowland, H. L. (1993). *Law of Liability Insurance, vol. 2: Medical Malpractice Liability Insurance.* New York: Matthew Bender, pp. 66–80, 102–106.
31. Hospital fined $22,000 in fatal MRI accident. (2001). *Healthcare Risk Management,* American Health Consultants 23(11):127.
32. NY hospital fined for unnecessary surgeries. (2001). *Healthcare Risk Management,* American Health Consultants, 23(11):129.
33. Lab error kills two patients. (2001). *Healthcare Risk Management,* American Health Consultants, 23(10): 119.
34. *American Continental Ins. Co. v. Marion Memorial Hospital,* 773 F. Supp. 1148 (S.D. III. 1991).
35. *Schiff v. N.D. Workes Comp. Bureau,* 480 N.W. 2d 732 (N.D. 1992).
36. Brunoli, T., and Gundersen, J. (1994). Non-profits can protect themselves. *Fund Raising Management* 25(3):16–18.
37. Kurland, O. M. (1994). Towards a better understanding of the D&O coveage process. *Risk Management* 41(4):20.

38. Monteleone, J., and McCarrick, J. F. (1993). *Directors and Officers Developments*. Presentation at Society of CPCU, Woodbridge, N.J. December 1.
39. Kelly, W., Ryan, J., and Kawamoto, B. (1994). The directors & officers dilemma. *Risk Management* 41(7):72–81.

SECTION 2 | General Risk Management Strategies

CHAPTER 6 Total Quality Management, Continuous Quality/Process Improvement, and Evaluation of the Risk Management Program

Robert Stanyon

No challenge in risk management is more immediate than the imperative of demonstrating that the evaluation of the risk management program makes a difference to the organization and its bottom line. An evaluation process helps determine how well risk management is doing within the organization, while the processes of total quality management and continuous quality improvement enable institutions to make the transition to higher levels of performance. Risk management focuses on an institution's exposure to financial loss. In minimizing this exposure, risk managers make a contribution to quality patient care by assuring that hazards and injuries are less likely to occur.

MEDICAL INJURIES ARE NEITHER NEW NOR UNCOMMON

Injury resulting from a medical procedure or event is nothing new. Kaiser Wilhelm II, as emperor of Germany and Prussia, was the architect of World War I. The young Kaiser suffered an Erb's palsy at birth, during which chloroform anesthesia was used.[1] Today, Wilhelm's withered arm, hyperactivity, and emotional instability would certainly have resulted in a medical malpractice lawsuit. Even in 1859, the year of his birth, medical malpractice litigation already was an established process in the United States[2] (see Box 6-1). More recently, medical malpractice has become an international phenomenon extending well beyond the United States to such decidedly non-Western cultures as Japan.[4]

Modern medical knowledge and practice have conferred the extraordinary benefit of wellness on today's citizens, but medical accidents still happen. The Harvard Medical Malpractice Study estimated that roughly one percent of patients discharged from New York State hospitals were victims of medical negligence resulting in injury.[5] A

BOX 6-1

Between 1840 and 1850, medical malpractice became a recognized cause of action in the U.S. courts. The most common cases were procedure-related and resulted in poor medical outcomes. Prior to the 1840s, a physician would generally amputate a limb that had a compound fracture. As the century progressed, the improved training and experience of the best doctors resulted in attempts at realignment of these fractured limbs. The outcome often was an intact limb that was deformed. Gratitude did not always flow to the practitioner in these cases. Often, the best of them were sued.[3]

larger number of patients experienced an injury not caused by negligence, but obviously resulting in patient dissatisfaction. This study concluded that injuries happen with significant frequency during hospitalization.

INJURIES AND LAWSUITS

Most of the injured patients in the Harvard study did not initiate a lawsuit. Most of the actual claims did not result from adverse events caused by negligence.[6] Paradoxically, many claimants that are not really appropriate candidates for compensation seek redress in the courts for injuries. One rationale for the rapid rise in malpractice lawsuits could be the steady increase in the number of lawyers—about 50,000 new attorneys each year.[7,8] Compared to other countries, the United States has more than three times the number of lawsuits. Generous awards from professional liability insurance coverage create a major incentive for malpractice litigation.

Injuries happen and so do lawsuits. A challenge for risk managers is to effectively minimize the injury side of the equation. Claims do require skillful management, but control of the future lies in prevention.

AN OUNCE OF PREVENTION

What is clear is the importance of communication within the physician-patient relationship. Physicians who used more effective communication techniques and spent a little more time with the patient were less likely to be sued,[9,10] and they included the patient in the decision-making process.[11,12,13,14] The process of improving the understanding of the stakeholders, i.e., the patient and the physician, depends upon mutual communication. The patient understands the risks, benefits, and alternatives of treatment, and the physician understands the "rich conceptualization of risk" entertained by the patient.[15] Informed consent is one of the tools used to facilitate this mutual understanding. The risk manager must understand this complex process and incorporate the informed consent concepts into the proactive risk management program.

THE CHALLENGE OF PREDICTION

If science and mathematics eventually permitted predictions about hazards and malpractice, risk management would be very different. Risk or hazard could be appreciated before the fact and eliminated before an adverse event. Importantly, predictive methods are statistical in nature. An equation cannot tell you that something *will* happen, only that there is an increased likelihood that it *might* happen.

A patient who likes a particular practitioner is less likely to sue that physician in the event of a bad outcome.[16] To some extent, a physician's likability is determined by cultural attributes, although the reason could be as simple as giving a patient quality time. Cultivating a personal style acceptable to patients is an important loss prevention technique for today's physician. Physicians need to be enlightened, and the risk manager is in a unique position to identify those who need help, because the risk manager knows which physicians have been sued.

STATISTICAL PREDICTIVE MODELS

Gibbons developed a statistical model for predicting medical malpractice claims for individual physicians.[17] Insurers can use this model to "predict an individual's claim vulnerability." Investigation revealed the following:

- A sizable random physician effect exists.
- Risk of a claim increases for physicians between the ages of 40 and 60 years.
- Surgical specialists are at increased risk of a claim.
- Male physicians are at greater risk for a claim than their female colleagues.
- Following an initial claim, risk increases, particularly in the first year after the claim.
- Risk management education has beneficial effects on physicians with a prior claim history, particularly in anesthesiology and obstetrics/gynecology.

In addition, the researchers noted that even if the risk management education did not reduce the number of claims, the payout was often less because the education "may equip the physician to be a better defendant in the event of a claim."

How can this information be utilized? Should middle-aged male physicians in surgical specialties be targeted for intensive review and remedial education? Given the lag time between an adverse event and the receipt of a claim, it's likely that the damage or injury alleged in subsequent claims occurred prior to the arrival of the first claim. If a risk management program is to be proactive rather than reactive, the risk management activities to be emphasized must be predetermined. Post-claim risk management education for professional staff seems like a good bet, but don't expect to see immediate positive results.

Hazard and Dread

Cindynics, literally "the science of danger," is concerned with the discipline of hazard identification. This technique attempts to describe the basic assumptions about the "operating systems" of complex organizations and to identify mechanisms that allow risk management professionals to understand the nature of the hazards. The methods used in cindynics are mathematical and involve complex reasoning to describe hazards and catastrophes.[18]

For the individual, hazard is more than a scientific method. It includes a "fear factor," or a certain quantity of dread.[15] Patients do not want a complex process presented to them. Patients view risk in more concrete terms: How bad could it be and what are the odds that something bad will happen to me? A list of risks will need to be presented, but the patient will want to know when each of them could happen (e.g., during a procedure or a week later), and how permanent a negative result might be (e.g., resulting in death vs. an infection easily treated with antibiotics).[19] Most patients want to know what their chances of hazard are—either as a statistical number derived from a population or as a relative value such as "poor" or "excellent." The challenge is to explain how one might be in the one percent risk group, rather than the 99 percent risk group.

EFFECTIVENESS OF RISK MANAGEMENT

Risk managers may have to prove the value of the services they provide.[20] Does a risk management program in health care have value? Assuming merit, which programs are the most valuable? It is vital to illustrate that a risk management program materially contributes to an institution's survival and to the quality of care delivered. A study in Maryland hospitals demonstrated significantly better claims experiences in hospitals with certain risk management policies or activities.[21] One pivotal activity for the risk manager focused on regular formal education programs to teach physicians and nurses about risk management and the role of the risk manager. A key to success involved the handling of information and interventions following an adverse event. Information must get to the upper-level administration and, most importantly, to the clinical chief or chiefs as quickly as possible. Although controversial, the study supported the beneficial influence of a policy to inform affected patients and families of adverse events. Investigators identified "highly productive" areas for quality review and risk management oversight in ambulatory care that included hospital discharge diagnosis, procedure codes, length of stay, and cancer staging.[22]

The definitive research to demonstrate conclusively that risk management makes a difference has yet to be undertaken. Given the diffuse nature of the tasks and responsibilities of risk management, as well as the lengthy tail introduced by statutes of limitation, it would be enormously expensive to design and implement a controlled study that would be relevant. More importantly, the Maryland study used baseline data from a time period when risk management interventions were not so widely accepted. Even the controversial idea of informing patients of adverse events is now necessary if Joint Commission on Accreditation of Healthcare Organizations (JCAHO) accreditation is expected.

The well-designed risk management program will, at the least, have the systems and the data necessary to show the history and trends in claims and adverse events that could be utilized as indicators for planned interventions. The fundamental reason risk management is necessary is that adverse events and claims do happen.

RISK MANAGEMENT PROCESS

Traditionally, the risk management process consists of five steps that are similar in other disciplines, such as quality assessment or nursing:[23]

1. Identify and analyze the exposures to loss.
2. Examine the feasibility of alternative techniques: for example, risk control to stop losses, risk financing to pay for losses.
3. Select the apparent best technique(s).
4. Implement the chosen technique(s).
5. Monitor and improve the risk management program.

In the last step, the program is evaluated as the particular operation, assumptions, and interventions are reanalyzed. Subsequent improvement of the process can follow this evaluation.

To ensure excellence, Penchansky developed a reconceptualization of the linkage between quality assessment, risk management, and utilization review.[24] The "organization must have continuing processes to (1) define and/or change the desired goals and related standards of performance; (2) measure performance; and (3) maintain performance and/or change inadequate performance." There can be no doubt of the direct linkage between the risk management process and quality assessment.

QUALITY MANAGEMENT

"As a systems approach to preventing malpractice claims, organized risk management identifies, analyzes, and treats risks which quality assessment works to eliminate."[25] However, quality care may be influenced by ulterior motives and result in blaming others. In blaming the "bad apple," the traditional view indicated that problems of quality are caused by poor intentions (see Box 6-2).[26]

Historically, JCAHO has defined quality assessment (QA) as a "formal, systematic program by which care rendered to patients is measured against established criteria."[28] The concept of QA has broadened considerably to encompass a management process of monitoring and evaluating quality issues, followed by changes in the system of healthcare. This process has become known as Quality Management (QM). Ongoing monitoring of systems is necessary to ensure that problems are identified early and appropriate intervention is initiated. Inspection improved quality and established thresholds for acceptability. Under specific circumstances, oversight and disciplinary measures are necessary. There must be a mechanism for identifying dishonest or poorly performing practitioners. Sanctions or limitations in privileges may be necessary. Standards of care cannot be left to chance when a patient's safety is at stake. If health care is to improve beyond these artificial thresholds that discourage peak performance, the concept of quality improvement must be introduced.

Although quality assessment is individualized for each patient, QA professionals routinely seek to aggregate information to identify recurring quality problems. Data from QA, utilization review (UR), infection control, and risk management departments must be reviewed as a whole. This synergistic amalgamation of data enhances the common desire to improve quality. LDS Hospital (Salt Lake City) combined the QA, UR, and risk management departments into a single unit, the Quality Management Department, to simplify the task of information management.[29] A group of 13 registered nurses accomplishes the department's shared functions. Anyone involved in assessing the quality of patient care requires a basic understanding of quantitative methods and information management systems.[30]

BOX 6-2

In a series of articles beginning with one titled *Nursing Mistakes Kill, Injure Thousands: Cost-Cutting Exacts Toll on Patients, Hospital Staffs,* Michael Berens of the *Chicago Tribune* made national headlines. This often-sensational series established a balance between the good and the less-than-good in nursing practice. Most importantly, inadequate staffing and insufficient training are singled out as important determinants in the "error equation." The hospital's cost-cutting strategies targeted their greatest expense—that of nursing. According to Berens, blaming individual practitioners would never solve the problems in these hospitals. Rather, the fundamental systems responsible for hiring, training, and retaining qualified nurses needed to be fixed.[27]

TOTAL QUALITY MANAGEMENT

After World War II, the modern quality movement began with the work of W. Edwards Deming in Japanese industry.[31] His 85-15 rules states: "When something goes wrong, 85 percent of the problem is related to systems failures; 15 percent is the fault of the people involved." This powerful concept rejects the traditional approach to problem solving that aims to identify those at fault and punish them. While the threat of dismissal or of a poor evaluation can be motivational, the 85-15 rule posits that such interventions may not be the most effective way to solve a problem or to prevent its recurrence.

A better approach, total quality management (TQM), focuses on the system and not on the individual. Stratton urged management not to give employees the impression that they are responsible for the 15 percent.[32] Management must take responsibility for the entire problem. However, employees may have a good idea of how to fix the process or system, the other 85 percent of the problem. Suggestion boxes have proved that it pays to ask employees. Three working premises about quality emerge:

- Quality is important and can be measured.
- People are a critical part of the solution and not necessarily the problem.
- Change is fundamental and always present, but change can be managed to improve any organization.

Kim discussed implementing TQM in the health care industry[33] while Goonan described applications,[34] with an emphasis on clinical quality management, along with practical advice for establishing a TQM program.

Total quality management is a broad business concept that includes the continuous quality improvement (CQI) process. CQI initiatives occur simultaneously in many areas and are overseen and guided by the TQM process.

Lynn stated that TQM is the process organizations use to improve their ability to satisfy customer expectations.[35] A key to understanding TQM changes in health care is the recognition of the central importance of the customer. In business, a customer buys services from a vendor and is free to choose to buy—or not to buy. Patients/customers of health care institutions can select services that meet their expectations and reject services that do not. This approach will be the measure of the health care organization's success in the future. The following fundamental beliefs form the basis of the TQM approach:[35]

- TQM is a positive strategy for growth and should be integrated into the organization's strategic business plan.
- Top management must be committed to and actively involved in the TQM process.
- TQM is a process, not a program.
- Quality improvement processes must be applied to all levels of the organization.
- Quality improvement benefits everyone, both internal and external audiences.

BARRIERS TO QUALITY MANAGEMENT INITIATIVES

Organizational culture of health care institutions may create obstacles to implementing CQI initiatives.[36] Separation of administrative functions that are usually performed by nonclinicians from the medical functions performed by professional staff makes efforts to involve physicians in CQI more challenging. Physicians tend to focus their attention on patients and not on what they perceive to be administrative responsibilities. It is imperative for the success of CQI to help physicians understand how the process will benefit their patients. Furthermore, the hierarchical and bureaucratic structure of larger health care organizations makes the empowerment of the employees on CQI teams, a fundamental tenet of CQI thinking, even more difficult. "Hot groups"[37] may allow an organization to bypass resistance to change. Hot groups are those that managers cannot control; individual members are self-motivated and see themselves as moving beyond their own limits. Neatly organized institutions often suffocate the initiative of this kind of group, but these groups are well worth cultivating as quality improvement teams. An entrenched cadre of middle management, resistant to change, further hinders the process.

CONTINUOUS QUALITY/PROCESS IMPROVEMENT

As a management tool, the concepts of continuous quality improvement and process improvement (PI) are an integral part of the thinking of health care administrators. CQI directs attention to the fundamental mechanism that drives a process or system being reviewed. Furthermore, CQI focuses on techniques to accomplish positive change by assessing a process that leads to an intervention.[38] In selected hospitals, CQI actions have decreased unnecessary intravenous catheter use,[39] improved preventive services in primary care,[40] decreased hospital costs for patients with chest pain,[41] and improved the timeliness of preoperative radiologic reports.[42]

Birnbaum discussed the use of sentinel events as an important component in managing the quality of care through CQI.[43] A sentinel event is a single occurrence of sufficient concern to trigger a systematic response. Parisi urged implementing a CQI approach to incident reporting to improve health care systems and processes.[44] Regardless of the technique, evaluating the process after the intervention to further refine or change the strategy beings the cycle again. This cycle should be viewed as a spiral through time, rather than as a static circle. After each subsequent turn, the intervention will never be quite the same.

TOOLS FOR EVALUATION: ROOT CAUSE ANALYSIS AND FAILURE MODE, EFFECT, AND CRITICALITY ANALYSIS

Through JCAHO mandates, new tools have become available for the analysis and management of adverse events. Root cause analysis is one of these. The central importance of the root cause analysis (RCA) for evaluation of adverse events cannot be overemphasized. Accurate information about the causes of serious events is critical for use in prevention programs. The RCA identifies not only the direct causes, such as user error, but also brings to light the indirect causes or latent errors. As an example, JCAHO specifies 12 factors that must be addressed in an RCA for a medication error, and these factors go far beyond the error of omission or commission that directly caused the mistake. They include staffing levels, orientation and training, credentialing, supervision, and physical environment, among others.[45]

One study examined the use of RCA for a 29-month period. The root causes most commonly identified were related to patient census, patient acuity, and staffing issues, primarily in nursing. Subsequent interventions focused on early response to the census / acuity / staffing issues, as well as on the use of constraining functions, such as removal of concentrated potassium solutions from patient care areas.[46]

JCAHO now requires that health care organizations select one high-risk process a year and subject it, prospectively, to Failure Mode, Effect, and Criticality Analysis (FMECA). The FMECA process examines the steps in the system that failed and led to the adverse outcome. Flow charts are used and errors at each step are rated according to their criticality or influence on the final event. Finally, solutions and redesign are planned and implemented. An RCA is conducted at those steps in the process where failure is critical to the outcome.[47,48]

Quality Improvement Team

In the improvement process, the Quality Improvement Team (QIT) is the effector of change. Staff members appointed to a team should be the employees who actually do the work within the company or institution. A QIT should be of manageable size, with one member designated as recording secretary to ensure a written record of the proceedings. Traditional group dynamics theory projects that the ideal team has five to seven, and generally no more than 10, members. A QIT may need to be somewhat larger to encompass the organization's various areas and disciplines. In addition, the team needs a leader to provide direction and vision for the group. In experienced groups that have developed a cohesive structure, any member can serve as the leader.

A facilitator, who is not a member of the QIT or part of the problem in the organization, acts in a guiding role when the team loses its focus or veers off track.[49] This key role combines the traditional task roles of clarifier, summarizer, and reality tester with maintenance roles of harmonizer, consensus taker, and compromiser. The facilitator is primarily an observer and is in a unique position to provide feedback to the group regarding its progress or lack of progress. A QIT should meet regularly to carry out the CQI process.

With the prospect of numerous teams simultaneously moving in many directions, central guidance certainly is necessary. There is a need to coordinate the QITs, to focus team efforts on strategic priorities, to transfer learning from one set of projects to another, and to focus quality improvement work on the organization's strategic priorities.[36] A steering committee should approve QIT projects and monitor the teams' progress. This committee can help remove obstacles to implementation and change.

CQI Questions

As a process, CQI implies that an organization knows what needs to be improved. If resources are limited, making the correct choice may be unlikely. The following pertinent questions need to be asked:

1. Is there a corporate strategic plan or mission statement that sets the organization's general direction?
2. Which operations are fundamental or critical to the organization?
3. What are the needs of the external (community) and internal (employees, volunteers, attending physicians) customers? What do they expect from the organization?
4. How is the organization spending its money? Where is the money going? Can less be spent?
5. What existing problems have been identified?
6. From current data, what can be done better and more efficiently?

7. Which activities would benefit from simplification? Which activities seem so complicated that it is obvious there must be a better way?
8. Where can the organization put its resources and expect a reasonable outcome or return?

Undoubtedly, more than one problem will be isolated in the group's initial brainstorming session. Deming listed questions contributed by an executive of the Ford Motor Company to help a QIT start the process (see Box 6-3).[30] Those questions provided initial direction in thinking about the organization's structure, what the organization does, and where the individual team members fit into the organization, and they are directly applicable to health care institutions and agencies.

An Organization's Mission Statement

A CQI team begins by reviewing the organization's mission and/or vision statement, such as the following:

> Beth Israel Medical Center will be recognized as a premier health care system in New York City. We will strive consistently to surpass professional quality standards, exceed patient and physician expectations and promote an exceptional work and healing environment.[50]

By focusing on the critical few objectives, rather than on the trivial many, this CQI review ensures that the organization's design for its future and direction is incorporated into the team's planning. Then, the quality improvement team can write its own mission statement to set its direction. Next, the team's goals and objectives must be developed. In particular, the objectives must be specific to the problem, and they must be measurable (see Box 6-4).

A FOCUS ON THE CUSTOMER IS VITAL

Driven by the needs of the organization's customers, the quality improvement process recognizes the customer as being central to its purpose. Nine quality improvement factors define the process:

1. **State the objectives:** Decide what your mission will be, consistent with that of the company; state your objectives in relation to this mission.
2. **Identify the customers:** Determine what the customers want. What are their needs? What do they require from the organization to meet those needs?
3. **Understand how the process works now:** Identify the process components and perform a flow analysis to locate the problems within the system. Problems may be identified for further study and subjected to CQI.
4. **Collect the data:** Focus on the problem and subject the data to analysis to determine cause and effect.
5. **Decide on a solution:** Develop an appropriate plan of action to solve the problem.
6. **Implement the plan:** Initiate actions to solve the problem.
7. **Evaluate the plan:** Determine the success or failure of the plan of action.
8. **Improve the process:** Redraft the objectives or mission, if necessary; determine the effect on the customer; and reconsider the plan.
9. **Create a new plan:** Incorporate learning from prior efforts.

Juran created a quality planning road map that was customer-driven and designed to meet the needs of the organization.[52] He explained the flow process:

- Identify our customers.
- Determine the needs of those customers.

BOX 6-3

Initial Quality Improvement Team (QIT) Questions

CONCERNING ORGANIZATIONAL STRUCTURE

- Where do specific departments fit into the total organizational structure?
- What products and services does the organization provide?
- How does the organization provide these products and services? That is, what processes are used?
- What would happen if the organization (unit, section, department) stopped producing its products and services?

CONCERNING INDIVIDUAL EMPLOYEES

- Where do you fit into your department? What is your job?
- What do you create or produce? That is, what are the results of your work?
- How do you do this? (Give a general description of what you do.)
- How do you know if you produce good results or poor results? That is, are there standards or criteria of good performance?
- If so, how were these standards established?

CONCERNING CUSTOMERS

Immediate Customers

- Who directly receives the products or services that are produced? That is, who are the customers?
- How do customers use what's produced?
- What would happen if employees did not do their jobs correctly?
- How do employee efforts affect the organization's customers?
- How does the organization determine that the needs or requirements of their customers are not being met?

Intermediate and Ultimate Customers

- How far beyond the immediate customer can the organization trace the effect of what it does?

CONCERNING ORGANIZATIONAL SUPPLIERS

- How is work initiated (for example, assigned from boss, requested by customer, self-initiated)?
- Who supplies materials, information, services, and whatever else is needed to do your job (for example, boss, customer, coworker in the same group, people in other areas)?
- What would happen to employees if suppliers did not do their jobs?
- Do suppliers have performance standards?
- How do the efforts of suppliers affect the organization?
- How do suppliers discover that they are *not* meeting the organization's needs or requirements? Who works with them and fulfills obligations to them?

BOX 6-4

Pilot Program Uses Quality Improvement to Achieve Glycemic Control in Diabetics

Using a team approach to quality improvement can benefit both the patient and the organization. One outpatient network improved glycemic control in chronic diabetics by using QI methods. A team undertook the change project and developed the Diabetes Care System, an organized network of processes designed to address:

1. Prescriptives (medications, diet, and exercise)
2. Psychosocial support
3. Information provided to diabetics
4. Monitoring of diabetic data
5. Self-management promotion

The pilot study showed the feasibility of the interventions and of using CQI across organizations. One benefit was that the HbA1c monitoring improved glycemic control. Perhaps the most important determinant for success was the commitment and involvement of upper-level leadership.[51]

The CQI team might have phrased its mission, goals, and objectives as follows:

Team Mission: Establishing high-quality medical care for chronic diseases produces better patient outcomes.

Team Goals:

1. Assure delivery of interventions found to be effective.
2. Empower patients to assume responsibility for care management.
3. Provide information, support, and resources to these patients.

Team Objective: Establish a program to achieve improved glycemic control, as measured by HbA1c levels.

- Translate those needs into our language.
- Develop product features that can optimally respond to those needs.
- Develop a process that optimally is able to produce the product features.
- Transfer the process to the operating forces.

It is important to know who the customers are, as well as their relative importance to the operation. Specific operations must be examined in some detail to identify all of the customers. Internal customers belong to the organization, either as employees or through some other relationship, such as volunteers or private contractors (for example, attending physicians). These people help produce the product: health care. External customers, such as the community, do not belong to the organization but use or purchase its goods and services or are affected by the organization in some other way. In health care, the patient is the primary external customer. Juran described customers as belonging to two groups:[52]

The **vital few**, all of whom are of "great importance," because of the amount they buy (for example, a health maintenance organization) or because of the amount they contribute (for example, a successful surgeon who brings many patients into a hospital).

The **useful many**, who are a relatively large number of customers, but each of whom is of only "modest importance" to the organization (for example, a patient or a nurse).

How does the organization discern a customer's needs? Simply, customers can be asked about their likes and dislikes either in an interview or through a written questionnaire. Indirectly, an organization can examine the products or services that customers actually use and in what relative quantity. In the case of a product, analysis of what is returned or discarded is helpful. A customer may have a need that has not yet been perceived; these needs may be discovered in the details as the process is subjected to flow analysis. A pilot project can be instituted to meet the unperceived need. If successful, the pilot program results in the identification of a particular customer need. Juran contended that customers' needs are a "moving target": not static, but requiring continuous evaluation and prioritization over time to ensure that they are met.[52]

Juran referred to the concept of replanning to give direction to the retrospective analysis performed at the conclusion of a project.[52] This "Santayana Review," as Juran labeled it, reinforces positive actions and prevents the repetition of mistakes.

THE PATIENT WAS RIGHT!

Our customer in health care, the patient, always knows the answer. We simply don't always ask the right questions. To find out why some patients sue their health care providers, one study evaluated patient complaints and coded them according to the quality of the physician's communication, humaneness, care and treatment, access and availability, environment, and billing. This was compared to the number of risk management records, either incidents or lawsuits, each of the physicians had on file. Not surprisingly, the physicians with the most complaints tended to have more risk management records.[53]

This tells us that it is important to systematically collect the patients' evaluations of their experiences with individual practitioners. An angry patient is not necessarily responding to negligence when consulting an attorney. The real issue is medical error, for that is what ultimately will drive a lawsuit. We must look to reducing errors, rather than to placating patients.[54] Lawsuits occur one at a time. The unhappy patient is an indicator for improvement, one physician at a time.

A SAMPLING OF POTENTIAL RISK MANAGEMENT CQI PROJECTS

Health care institutions might benefit from the application of CQI intervention to analyze the following readily identifiable potential risks:[55]

- Excessive delay in responding to fetal distress.
- Excessive number of missed emergency room diagnoses of cerebral or spinal injuries, myocardial infarction, appendicitis, ectopic pregnancy, or meningitis.
- Slow response time to trauma patients requiring surgery for orthopedic, abdominal, or head injuries.

- High, unplanned return rate to the operating room within 48 hours of initial surgery.
- Intubation mishaps, such as failure to maintain an airway.
- High suicide rate among psychiatric patients.
- Frequent failure to monitor/observe adverse effects of psychiatric or other medications.
- Improperly obtained informed consent.
- High rate of central nervous system complications during or within two days following administration of anesthesia.
- High rate of adverse occurrences/claims involving HIV/AIDS patients.
- Inadequate credentialing and privileging policies and procedures.
- High rate of institutional review board-related occurrences/claims.
- High rate of claims for which the risk identification/reporting system failed to provide warning.
- Numerous claims in which physician-patient communication issues were identified.[9]
- Numerous claims involving patients for whom English is a second language.[56]
- Several claims of uterine rupture in patients who chose a trial of labor following a prior Caesarean section (VBAC).[57]
- Several claims involving miscommunication in e-mail or other telemedicine vehicles.[58]
- Several claims involving alternative medicine therapies such as chiropractic medicine, herbal medicine, or massage therapy.[59]
- Several claims in which nurse staffing or supervision issues are identified.[60,61]

QIT RISK MANAGEMENT EXAMPLES

The initial selection of CQI projects that evaluate processes of direct concern to the medical staff may engender participation. If physicians realize that CQI makes their work more effective and less frustrating, they may become willing participants in the CQI process. In one institution, a CQI team that included physicians significantly decreased the time between ordering and performing diagnostic imaging scans.[20]

Team members must be clear with themselves and others about why they are interested in the activity of a particular team. To promote individual self-awareness of these factors, the team should discuss the issue of self-interest and bias. In addition, a basic tenet of TQM holds that top management must be committed to the process (see Box 6-5).

CQI AND LABOR RELATIONS

Two decisions by the National Labor Relations Board (NLRB) raise the possibility that TQM/CQI employee management teams may violate the National Labor Relations Act (NLRA) of 1935. Such a violation would occur if the TQM/CQI teams were judged to be labor organizations dominated by the employer.[63] In reality, most employee participation programs, including QITs, are problematic under the criteria set forth in the NLRA. A two-part test would have to be satisfied in any complaint of unfair labor practice: (1) The employer-employee group would have to be consistent with the definition of a labor organization and (2) it would have to be shown to be unlawfully dominated by the employer. To be considered a labor organization, the group would have to meet *all* three of the following conditions:[63] (1) Employees participate. (2) In part, the

BOX 6-5

One health care system's management of Erb's palsies provides an example of a multidisciplinary team approach to solving a classic risk management problem through clinical intervention. This interesting program was developed by the University of Maryland Medical System. The assumption was that an early intervention program would result in lower morbidity rates for Erb's children. Program components include:

- A clinical pathway for management of brachial plexus impairments.
- An Erb's clinic for evaluation, treatment, and follow-up of children with brachial plexus impairment.
- A grading scale for these injuries, as no satisfactory measure was found in the literature.

Regular clinic visits featured evaluation and physical therapy. Children were identified early, and the program began immediately after the infant was discharged from the hospital.

Eighteen children were evaluated during the first year. All children with first visits at less than six months of age improved at least three levels in their grading system. Intervention in the first three months of life yielded a similar benefit. Even older children benefited, although not to the same degree.

Of interest to the risk manager is the fact that the parents of two of the children had initiated lawsuits prior to entering this program. None of the other children's parents have started legal activity after almost two years with the program.[62]

organization exists for the purposes of dealing with management. (3) Dealings concern conditions of work, grievances, labor disputes, wages, rate of pay, or hours of employment; conditions of work can be broadly defined and would include work-related issues with which a CQI team might be concerned.

If the group is identified as a labor organization, the second part of the test is invoked: Is the group dominated by the employer? Unlawful domination exists if only one of the following conditions is met:[63] (1) An employer interferes with the labor organization's formation. (2) An employer interferes with the labor organization's administration. (3) An employer provides the labor organization with financial and other support.

Depending on interpretation, almost any group could be considered to be in violation of any one of these three conditions. Three specific characteristics of CQI programs appear to make them allowable:[63] (1) Information sharing with management is the purpose of the group. (2) Employees, not management, retain the right to make decisions, by majority rule, to implement proposals. Management can participate in the decision but not control it. Management cannot administer the CQI team. (3) The collective bargaining process offers an alternative solution for establishing "legal" CQI teams.

Risk managers should insist that the structure, mission, and objectives of CQI teams be reviewed to be allowable under the NLRA. Care must be taken to avoid even the appearance of management interference in the group process of these teams. In the early planning, the structure, goals, and objectives should be developed in partnership with the employees who will do the work.[64] Team members must be volunteers, not acting on behalf of other employees, and must not address employee discontent. Areas such as those involving safety and health must be approached with caution to avoid conflict with the NLRA.

Congress attempted to broaden the potential for the use of teams in 1996, but the legislation did not survive a presidential veto. In 2001, the NLRB expanded the role of teams to include employee management. The teams in question made up a management system that went beyond the bounds of traditional team management, addressing issues of plant safety, as well as issues of employee discipline, advancement, and pay. Importantly, the teams did not make proposals that management responded to with acceptance or rejection. Rather, these teams were empowered to make changes themselves. Management was represented on the teams, but did not control them or have the final decision authority.[65]

BENCHMARKING COMPARISONS

Benchmarking is a process whereby one organization's operation is compared to that of another, usually an organization that happens to do it better. A limited internal type of benchmarking can compare different units of the same organization to discover the "best" practices. However, there is no assurance that any particular unit will be doing any better than any other unit. To gain the most from benchmarking, it is advisable to go outside the organization to find the best within the industry, or even outside the industry, to find others who excel in similar processes.[66]

Benchmarking is a thoughtful, introspective process that goes beyond simply touring another organization. First, risk managers must know their own organizations and have an idea of what they want to accomplish. Next, organizations that are appropriate for comparison need to be identified, assessed, and compared regarding their operation. Risk managers must then formulate a plan to bring their operations closer to the best practices of the other organization. Evaluation and replanning must follow the implementation of any changes in the organization. This is not a process to be undertaken without a firm commitment in resources by upper-level management.

In health care, such external benchmarking may be difficult because organizations that are geographically close may see themselves as competitors. Internal benchmarking projects would be more likely in this setting. In one example from the litigation process,[67] individual defendants filled out questionnaires following their depositions. The questionnaires addressed the adequacy of preparation of these defendants, as well as who was most helpful at putting the individual at ease. The questionnaire also asked for suggestions on improving the process. Over time, a standard for benchmarking could be expected to develop. Another effort, involving a consortium of health care organizations, compared claims to organizational demographic data.[68] This comparison helped the individual organizations evaluate their claims management methods and identify areas for improvement.

MEDICAL ERROR REDUCTION

The Institute of Medicine cited the results of the Harvard Medical Malpractice Study and others to call for changes in the health care system that would improve safety for all patients.[69] The IOM's goal is to reduce the number of medical errors by 50 percent. There is disagreement about the actual numbers in the report,[70,71] but not about the need to reduce the number of medical errors.

The importance of patient safety and medical error reduction is a unifying theme in risk management and quality management. Interventions to reduce error are given a high priority. The publication of evidence-based information specific to clinical departments focusing on the efforts to reduce medical error is important.[72] Researchers agree that evidence-based data can validate some interventions, but not everyone agrees on the place for interventions that have not been tested by evidence-based methods.[73] For example, it seems common sense that to place a leading zero before a decimal point in a medication order will eliminate some medication errors. Any nurse who has transcribed medication orders knows this intuitively; an expensive study with statistical power would seem unnecessary. The risk manager, understanding these limitations, may find the Agency for Healthcare Research and Quality (AHRQ) report helpful in providing guidance for individual clinical departments.[72]

For the risk manager, injuries resulting from adverse events are only a small part of the total picture. To determine the success of a risk management program, all medical errors will need to be accurately categorized and tracked.[74] A reduction in the number of errors would translate into measurable improvement. Finding error is almost impossible without a functioning error-reporting system. For such reporting to work, the institutional culture must foster blame-free disclosure of events.

PROGRAM EVALUATION ISSUES AND METHODS

In health care risk management, program evaluation traditionally has been considered difficult. Unlike quality management, program evaluation does *not* focus on what is normal. Risk management deals with abnormal events or aberrations that expose financial structures to loss. In health care, a major professional liability exposure may be unrelated, or only slightly related, to the quality of care rendered by a physician to a patient. A jury may disagree with expert reviewers who judge the standard of care to be acceptable. Despite the facts, the well-known sympathy factor contributes to a jury's liberal monetary awards in malpractice cases. These unrelated factors make it difficult to form objective conclusions based on the data. Standards, evaluations, and checklists contribute to resolution of the difficulty.

Standards as Guides

What are the standards? The standards are whatever an organization says they are. It is the responsibility of each institution to determine its own standards. A definition of standards begins with the corporate mission statement or a similar declaration of organizational goals or strategic objectives. To have meaning, standards must be a reflection of the company's goals. A standard must be reasonable, capable of being achieved, and measurable. In health care, specific standards may be imposed by government regulatory requirements. Antidumping provisions of the federal COBRA statute necessitate establishing a standard and monitoring the disposition of patients arriving at the emergency room.

Outcome measures use a standard or norm to arrive at a risk-adjusted expected value for a patient outcome.[75] This expected value is compared to actual patient outcomes to determine whether a problem exists. Outcome measurement ensures that quality has been maintained *or* indicates to what degree quality has been compromised. Problems are identified and referred to quality improvement for a process and systems review. The first step is to review and confirm the accuracy of the data documenting the substandard condition. There is a tendency to assume that data must be correct because the measurements are quantitative, but there may be problems with the measurements. The JCAHO issued a call for collaboration in performance measurement defined "as an interrelated set of process and outcome measures that, when used together, provide a meaningful performance profile of the organization to which the measures are applied."[76]

Standards may be described either as results standards, which refer to what is accomplished, or as activity standards, which refer to the means by which something is accomplished. Outcome measures, such as patient mortality or survival, are results standards. An activity standard could specify the number of staff education sessions on basic or advanced cardiac life support for different levels of professional staff. Carroll classified more than 140 outcome indicators of patient care into 15 clinical areas for quality evaluation review.[77]

Evaluation

Evaluation is the process that determines to what degree the standard was or was not met. Evaluations may be done on a regular basis, as part of the ongoing monitoring of a process, or in response to a problem within a process. In all cases, standards are assessed for compliance, and their reasonableness is reviewed. If a standard is not being met, the fault may be with the standard rather than with individual performance. Systems problems may prevent a reasonable standard from being achieved. For example, even if the standard specifies that single-cut frozen section results will be available to the surgeon in the operating room within a specified time period, specimen transport problems and clerical delays may prevent the meeting of that standard.

Checklists

In evaluating programs, risk managers need assurance that they have incorporated all possibilities into their risk management efforts, such as a checklist for evaluating an incident reporting system.[78] This evaluation gives the risk manager valuable and comprehensive direction. Although part of the evaluation process is qualitative, the assessment may point out areas in which quantitative methods for monitoring are appropriate. A checklist is not a complete description, but rather identifies many components of the process.[79]

Security of the records requires written policies and procedures, as well as methods to identify that the procedures were followed (see Box 6-6). When securing records, it is helpful to use a checklist and include the medical record as well as billing records, fetal monitoring strips, X-rays and radiology reports, photos, films, pathology slides, and any other items that may be relevant to a case.[80]

EXTERNAL EVALUATION

On occasion, the risk management program will be evaluated by organizations outside the health care institution. These external evaluators could include the Joint Commission on Accreditation of Healthcare Organizations (JCAHO), insurance companies, professional organizations, government entities, and legal groups.

JCAHO Evaluation

As part of its accrediting procedure, the JCAHO may examine the risk management program. The JCAHO requires the organization to collect data about risk management activities. Risk managers need a methodology for data collection, data analysis, and data transmittal to other

BOX 6-6

Checklist for Security Evidence

- ❑ Policy and procedure for receipt of a lawsuit includes identification of persons responsible for notifying the appropriate departments to secure evidence.
- ❑ Maintain a contact list of individuals, by department, responsible for security (list maintained by risk manager).
- ❑ Request form for the security of items is filled out and sent to the appropriate department.
- ❑ Make sure there is a procedure in place to validate that the security form was received by the particular department and that the item was secured. A multi-part form or an e-mail system that demands return of a confirmation can be used.
- ❑ Make sure there is a procedure in place to ensure that secured items are returned to the unsecured file or storage location as cases are closed.
- ❑ Each department with a security file must keep a log of secured items inventoried at least annually.
- ❑ The risk management security file should include a copy of the security forms sent to the individual departments.
- ❑ Perform a periodic audit of clinical departmental security procedures to determine their effectiveness (e.g., number of steps in the procedure, number of people responsible for the process, and adequacy of storage, retrieval, and return to storage).
- ❑ Procedures are relevant to the evidence item (e.g., new electronic fetal monitoring and archiving system changes the process of managing fetal monitoring records).

departments and/or committees. Quality, risk, and safety groups are expected to share information toward the goal of improving quality. Aggregate data and information from risk management and these other areas must be applied to organization-wide performance/improvement activities.[81]

Evaluation by Insurers/Underwriters

The primary role of the insurance company underwriter is to act as a gatekeeper.[52] In this role, the underwriter has the greatest control over who will be offered access to the protection offered by his or her insurance company.

Underwriters are concerned about credentialing, peer review, screening systems, compliance with JCAHO standards, and related internal evaluation mechanisms. An underwriter can evaluate the soundness of a risk management program by considering the following vital program elements:[82]

Commitment: senior management involvement.

Centralization and coordination: a designated individual responsible for the program.

Committee structure: issues identified, analyzed, resolved, and monitored.

Quality assessment integration: QA and RM mutually supporting and reinforming.

Medical staff involvement: active physician involvement.

Informed consent: effective in reducing claim frequency.

Patient representation system: handling patient complaints.

Disposition management/discharge planning: posthospital needs addressed (case management).

Incident/accident reporting: essentially a reporting system but also very important to trend and to respond to adverse trends.

Claims management: written policy of procedures to follow after a serious incident occurs or an actual claim is filed.

Biomedical services and medical devices: test equipment prior to use; evaluate and remove defective equipment from service.

Contract review: risk manager should be involved in reviewing contracts.

Educational programs: provide education in risk management issues.

If the health care institution is self-insured, the same evaluation process protects the assets of the self-insured trust fund, captive insurance company, or alternate risk financing mechanism.

Claims experience is one of the most critical elements an underwriter will evaluate.[83] Underwriters want to review a minimum of five to seven years of claims experience, as well as the entire period for which coverage of prior acts is sought. Prior acts coverage insures the institution against events that occurred before the inception date of the policy. At a minimum, the risk manager should have the following information on *every* open and closed claim:[82]

- Date of loss
- Closing date
- Evaluation of the allegations
- Date of notice
- Nature of the injury
- Who's involved; insurance coverage
- Reserve evaluation or final disposition

Practice Guidelines

Practice guidelines set a standard of care to which the practitioner will be held. These guidelines require continuous monitoring and/or evaluation to ensure that the requirements are appropriate for the clinical area, are being used properly, and are reasonable. Risk managers must be aware of departures from the guidelines, because of the potential liability risk exposure. As such, practice guidelines can potentially reduce the number of malpractice cases and the costs of settling those claims.[84] However, practice guidelines may cut in both directions. One study reviewed claims from two malpractice insurers and found that 17 of 259 claims used practice guidelines but that in 12 (71%) of these cases, the physician was implicated in a charge of medical malpractice.[85]

When guidelines are implemented, they should first undergo a multidisciplinary review by the affected clinical departments, risk management team, and in-house counsel. It should be assumed that the plaintiff's counsel will review any guideline in use for their own purposes. Following the institution of standards for minimal monitoring during anesthesia, there was a decrease in anesthesia-related injuries.[84] As intended, that practice guideline appeared to lower liability exposure and resulted in reducing the malpractice insurance premiums of anesthesiologists.

Courts may not view guidelines formulated at the local, rather than the national, level as authoritative, and thus they may be inadmissible as evidence. The court and the state, where applicable, will make this decision.[85]

Malpractice Claims Data

Without access to a voluminous database, it may be impossible to derive statistically significant conclusions from an analysis of malpractice claims data. Nevertheless, the evaluation of malpractice claims is critical. Merely the fact that a physician has a claim may mean that more claims are forthcoming[17] or that the physician's communication style is impersonal or abrupt[16] and needs an overhaul. A physician's prior claim history could reveal the existence of complaints filed with the state licensing board.[87] More importantly, malpractice claims data can be used to identify problem-prone clinical processes and suggest interventions to reduce negligence.[88]

It is important to track many different issues related to a claim. Risk managers should have some form of classification scheme for the risk management issues in claims. The hallmark of a specific risk management issue is that it answers the question: Why would we pay money on this case? Another approach is to look at issues as problems in the medical care that relate to the negative occurrence or may adversely affect the defense of the case.[88] Risk management issues transcend the clinical fact pattern and bring together the diverse problems that we would like to prevent from reoccurring. No patient was ever harmed directly by an altered medical record, but many cases have suffered at time of trial because the record was not as it should have been or it had disappeared (see Box 6-7).

Targeting individual practitioners for education or sanctions on the basis of their malpractice claims histories is problematic from a medical perspective.[90] However, the malpractice insurer may cancel a physician's insurance because of underwriting considerations, on the grounds that someone with numerous claims will cost the program too much money. At the very least, the risk manager needs to evaluate the individual claims to make sure a practitioner is not dangerously incompetent. For issues other than standards of care, a more thorough review is recommended. If physicians do the evaluation, the reviewer's knowledge of the severity of the outcome to the patient could negatively influence his or her judgment regarding the appropriateness of care.[91] It may be advisable to withhold patient outcome information from the reviewers until the quality review process is complete.

In addition to the evaluation of individual claims and discussions with the clinical director, trend data for all malpractice claims should be examined. This tracks individuals, specialties, departments, fre-

BOX 6-7

As part of its risk management database, FOJP Service Corporation categorizes medical records documentation problems in their medical malpractice cases. *Documentation Issues* are subdivided into *Process* and *Content* categories, which are further subdivided. These classifications refer to the quality and the adequacy of the documentation.

The *Health Information Management Issues* in the risk management database have proved to be of great interest to the hospitals in the system. These issues include missing X-rays, X-ray reports, pathology slides, pathology reports, medical records (either all or part), operating room reports, fetal monitoring strips, progress notes, and other items. Tracking these specific items over time permits periodic reports of missing documents to be shared with the risk managers and appropriate department chairmen. Having the baseline data establishes a foundation for improvement.

quencies, severity of injuries, and the nature of claims. At this time, loss prevention issues can be identified. When relevant issues are involved, risk managers may direct their efforts toward education and training.

High-Risk Areas

High-risk activities have accumulated a history of financial loss much greater than that in other areas. Clinical services of obstetrics, surgical anesthesia, and the emergency department commonly appear with greater severity on loss runs. Diagnostic services, such as radiology, require close monitoring by risk management. During a clinical consultation, communication between physicians demands ongoing scrutiny.[92] Frequently, lawsuits mention the lack of informed consent. Other areas that need ongoing evaluation by risk managers include advance directives, do not resuscitate (DNR) orders, the withholding of treatment, credentialing, and confidentiality.

Medical records may be requested by a host of people, such as parties to lawsuits, state regulators, peer review organizations, and law enforcement agencies, and they may be troublesome. These individuals and organizations may not be aware of, or may choose to ignore, the health care organization's obligation to maintain the confidentiality of the medical records.[93] Risk managers need procedures for monitoring medical record requests with respect to appropriateness and liability exposure. Two instances that should trigger risk management evaluation are requests by malpractice law firms before a lawsuit and requests by patients who wish to review their own records. Monitoring trends in requests for medical records, particularly by law firm and by department, is a critical activity for risk managers. Tracking these trends can help identify breaches of confidentiality. Breaches may occur innocently or through leaks to journalists or plaintiffs' attorneys.

The Health Insurance Portability and Accountability Act (HIPAA) adds new responsibilities to these obligations, and the obligations become even more complex with the advent of electronic medical records. The necessity for electronic signature standards, the requirement of an unalterable record that is reliably stored, and the requirement of protection from unauthorized access[94] are just some of the important issues to consider as electronic record systems are put into use.

A risk manager should monitor credentialing policies that might tend to exclude or deny privileges to physicians. If physicians' admitting privileges are withdrawn or denied, the economic impact on their practice could be significant enough to cause them to seek compensation in court.

If a patient is unable to respond, the belief by a patient's family or significant others about the patient's wishes regarding resuscitation or withholding of treatment is paramount. Effective monitoring by risk management can provide an early warning that the family is in disagreement and that litigation is being contemplated.

From a liability viewpoint, the monitoring of high-risk areas by risk management is a vital activity. Information on trends is particularly important for clinical areas because quality of patient care may be an issue. Procedures for monitoring whether informed consent has been obtained properly are necessary. Risk managers can track this through the claims incident reporting process. Auditing procedures also may help determine the frequency of lapses.

RISK MANAGEMENT SELF-ASSESSMENT MANUAL

The *Risk Management Self-Assessment Manual*[63] uses process and outcome measures to aid in evaluating the effectiveness of risk management programs and in planning actions to enhance their effectiveness. A chart in the manual indicates how evaluation and planning for part of the organization of the risk management program includes activities, process measures, outcome measures, and action plans. Process measures assess whether these activities are being carried out as intended. Outcome measures assess whether the program is having the impact it was designed to have. Measures should be quantifiable, derived from experience, describe what should happen rather than what is happening now, and be trackable. When using this self-assessment process, the risk manager first identifies the structural components of the risk management program and the necessary activities for achieving those components. A quantifiable process measure or indicator measure is then identified for each activity. In this way, a risk manager can determine whether the activity was carried out as planned. Finally, an outcome measure is formulated for the activity. This is a goal statement that includes a quantifiable measure of the outcome of the activity if it is successful. An example for the claims management structural component might include:[63]

Activity: Set up a written claims management policy that outlines the institution's claims management process.

Process measure: Senior management develops as a policy that is reviewed at least annually.

Outcome measure: Seventy-five percent or more of the claims are investigated within 24 hours of the report of the incident.

The *Self-Assessment Manual* requires considerable training and resources for effective use. One program that utilized the manual extensively discovered certain barriers to the development of a successful program.[96] They included:

- Many risk managers were unaware of the *Self-Assessment Manual* and how to use it.
- Turnover in responsibility for the risk management function limited the opportunity to implement and follow through on self-assessment.
- Decreased resources and an increased variety of responsibilities for risk managers limited the time available for self-assessment activities.
- Differing organizational philosophy and/or organizational arrangement influenced the conduct of risk management and its priorities.

DEPOSITIONS

In an out-of-court setting, witnesses can be examined and can give testimony under oath before the parties in a lawsuit or their representatives. This examination process is called a deposition and provides an opportunity for the witnesses to tell their stories and to be questioned. Risk managers may assist in the preparation of institutional employees for deposition.[97]

Importantly, risk managers should review depositions, or at least peruse the defense firm's summary, looking for areas of exposure. On the basis of such an investigation, Beckman devised a set of questions for deposition reviews.[98] His study examined 45 patients' depositions and classified 15 categories of "relationship issues" found in the depositions to identify problems. As perceived by the patient, these issues were failures in the physician/patient encounter. Physicians confronting specific problems in patient relationships might benefit from educational intervention. Since depositions are taken under oath, the documents often reveal information about the practitioner's involvement that was not previously understood.

Risk managers should devise a structured approach to deposition review that individualizes criteria to the particular institution and its potential problems. If obstetrical residents are permitted to deliver infants without an attending physician under certain circumstances, all depositions in obstetrical cases should be reviewed to validate the location of the resident and attending physicians during labor and delivery.

EVALUATION IS AN APPRAISAL

Analytical tools may assist in the identification of factors that could predict litigation or hazards that lead to injury. Statistical procedures can identify medical practice problems causing litigation. Cindynics allows for the conceptualization of hazard prediction. TQM is a process, not a program, and must be applied to all levels of the organization. CQI is a business concept and a management technique that views quality as something dynamic that can always be improved in a continuous process of evaluation and change. No matter what the initials—TQM, CQI, or XYZ—an evaluation follows the usual scientific method: defining the problem, collecting and analyzing data, formulating hypotheses, testing the hypotheses, and appraising the outcome before starting all over again.

All activities that reduce the incidence of litigation are of primary concern to risk managers. Of course, existing theories and approaches created or adapted from management experiences can be blended into a risk manager's program. A precarious predicament emerges as risk managers initiate liability reduction activities that may affect the quality and quantity of care delivered to patients. This catch-22 occurs if choices are made for economic reasons rather than for quality of care rationales. A relevant adjudication of this dilemma must consider the best of both approaches—risk management and quality management. Evaluation and change are two constants that permit an organization to reach new levels of capacity. Whether through TQM, CQI, or reengineering, an organization must look at its critical processes, redefine its direction on the basis of that review, and meet the needs of the customers utilizing its services. The critical mass for change has been reached through the public's awareness of the prevalence of medical error. It is the unified program of quality, risk, and safety that will manage the future of reform in health care.

References

1. Ober, W. B. (1992). Obstetrical events that shaped western European history. *Yale Journal of Biology and Medicine* 65(2):201–210.
2. Spiegel, A. D., and Kavaler, F. (1997). America's first medical malpractice crisis, 1835–1865. *Journal of Community Health* 22(4):283–308.
3. Mohr, J. C. (2000). American medical malpractice litigation in historical perspective. *Journal of the American Medical Association* 283(13):1731–1737.
4. Nakajima, K., Keyes, C., Kuroyanagi, T., and Tatara, K. (2001). Medical malpractice and legal resolution systems in Japan. *Journal of the American Medical Association* 285(12):1632–1640.
5. Brennan, T. A., Leape, L. L., Laird, H. M., et al. (1991). Incidence of adverse events and negligence in hospitalized patients. *New England Journal of Medicine* 324(6):370–376.

6. Localio, A. R., Lawthers, A. G., Brennan, T. A., et al. (1991). Relations between malpractice claims and adverse events due to negligence. *New England Journal of Medicine* 325(4):245–251.
7. Barber, H. R. K. (1991). The malpractice crisis in obstetrics and gynecology: Is there a solution? *Bulletin of the New York Academy of Medicine* 67(2):162–172.
8. American Bar Association, *http://www.abanet.org/legaled/statistics/le_bastats.html.*
9. Levinson, W., Roter, D., Mullooly, J. P., et al. (1997). Physician-patient communication: The relationship with malpractice claims among primary care physicians and surgeons. *Journal of the American Medical Association* 277(7):553–559.
10. Carroll, J. G., and Platt, F. W. (1998). Engagement: The grout of the clinical encounter. *Journal of Clinical Outcomes Management* 5(3):43–45.
11. Levinson, W., Gorawara-Bhat, R., and Lamb, J. (2000). A study of patient clues and physician responses in primary care and surgical settings. *Journal of the American Medical Association* 284(8): 1021–1027.
12. Braddock, C. H., Edwards, K. A., Hasenberg, N. M., et al. (1999). Informed decision-making in outpatient practice: Time to get back to the basics. *Journal of the American Medical Association* 282(24): 2313–2320.
13. Barry, M. J. (1999). Involving patients in medical decisions: How can physicians do better? *Journal of the American Medical Association* 282(24):2356–2357.
14. Roter, D. L., Hall, J. A., and Aoki, J. (2002). Physician gender effects in medical communication: A meta-analytic review. *Journal of the American Medical Association* 288(6):756–764.
15. Slovic, P. (1987). Perception of risk. *Science* 236: 280–285.
16. Hickson, G. B., Clayton, E. W., Entman, S. S., et al. (1994). Obstetricians' prior malpractice experience and patients' satisfaction with care. *Journal of the American Medical Association* 272(20):1583–1587.
17. Gibbons, R. D., Hedecker, D., Charles, S. C., and Frisch, P. (1994). A random-effects probity model for predicting medical malpractice claims. *Journal of the American Statistical Association* 89(427):760–767.
18. Kervern, G.Y. (1995). Cindynics: The science of danger. *Risk Management* 42(3):34–42.
19. Bogardus, S. T., Holmboe, E., and Jekel, J. F. (1999). Perils, pitfalls, and possibilities in talking about medical risk. *Journal of the American Medical Association* 281(11):1037–1041.
20. Challan, B. (1993). A risk manager's evolving experience with CQI. *Journal of Health Care Risk Management* 13(3):25–30.
21. Morlock, L. L., and Malitz, F. E. (1991). Do hospital risk management programs make a difference? Relationships between risk management program activities and hospital malpractice claims experience. *Law and Contemporary Problems* 54(2):1–22.
22. Macnee, C. L. and Penchansky, R. (1994). Targeting ambulatory care cases for risk management and quality management. *Inquiry* 31(1):66–75.
23. Head, G. L., and Horn, S. (1991). *Essentials of Risk Management*, vol. 1, 2d edition. Malvern, PA.: Insurance Institute of American, pp. 5, 11.
24. Penchansky, R., and Macnee, C. L. (1994). Ensuring excellence: Reconceptualizing quality assurance, risk management, and utilization review. *Quality Review Bulletin* 19(6):182–189.
25. Fiesta, J. (1991). QA and risk management: Reducing liability exposure. *Nursing Management* 22(2): 14–15.
26. Berwick, B. M. (1989). Continuous improvement as an ideal in health care. *New England Journal of Medicine* 320(1):53–56.
27. Berens, M. J. (2000). Nursing mistakes kill, injure thousands: Cost cutting exacts toll on patients, hospital staffs. *Chicago Tribune*, September 10, p. 1.
28. Martin, P. B., and Marder, R. J. (2001). Risk management's role in performance improvement. In *Risk Management Handbook for Health Care Organizations*, edited by R. Carroll. San Francisco: Jossey-Bass Inc., pp. 801–810.
29. Rock, R. C., Barry, D. D., Baldwin, M. M., and Gillespie, K. B. (1991). Integrating QA and QI: Marriage or mayhem. *Quality Exchange* Summer, 1–10.
30. Longo, R. D. and Bohr, D. (1991). *Quantitative Methods in Quality Management: A Guide for Practitioners*. Chicago: American Hospital Publishing, pp. 3–7.
31. Deming, W. D. (1986). *Out of the Crisis, Massachusetts Institute of Technology Center for Advanced Engineering Study*. Cambridge, Mass.: MIT Press, pp. 90–92.
32. Stratton, A. D. (1991). *An Approach to Quality Improvement That Works*, 2d edition. Milwaukee: ASQC Quality Press, pp. 4–5.

33. Kim, P. S., and Johnson, D. D. (1994). Implementing total quality management in the health care industry. *Health Care Supervisor* 12(3):51–57.

34. Goonan, K. J. (1995). *The Juran Prescription. Clinical Quality Management.* San Francisco: Jossey-Bass.

35. Lynn, G. F. (1991). Total quality management: A competitive strategy. *Healthcare Executive* 4(3):1–5.

36. Shortell, S. M., Levin, D. Z., O'Brien, J. L., and Hughes, E. F. X. (1995). Assessing the evidence of CQI: Is the glass half empty or half full? *Hospital & Health Services Administration* 40(1):4–24.

37. Leavitt, H. J., and Lipman-Blumen, J. (1995). Hot groups. *Harvard Business Review* 73(7):109–116.

38. Headrick, L. A., and Neuhauser, D. (1995). Quality health care. *Journal of the American Medical Association* 273(21):1718–1720.

39. Parenti, C. M., Lederle, F. A., Impola, C. K., and Peterson, L. R. (1994). Reduction of unnecessary intravenous catheter use: Internal medicine house staff participate in a successful quality improvement project. *Archives of Internal Medicine* 154(10): 1829–1832.

40. Young, M. J., Ward, R., and McCarthy, B. (1994). Continuously improving primary care. *Journal of Quality Improvement* 20(2):120–126.

41. Weingarten, S. R., Riedinger, M. S., Conner, L., et al. (1994). Practice guidelines and reminders to reduce duration of hospital stay for patients with chest pain: An interventional trial. *Annals of Internal Medicine* 120(3):257–263.

42. Bluth, E. I., Havrilla, M., and Blakeman, C. (1993). Quality improvement techniques: Value to improve the timeliness of preoperative chest radiologic reports. *American Journal of Roentgenology* 160(8):995–998.

43. Birnbaum, D. (1993). CQI tools: Sentinel events, warning, and action limits. *Infection Control and Hospital Epidemiology* 14(9):537–539.

44. Parisi, L. L. (1994). Implementing a CQI approach to incident reporting. *Aspen's Advisor for Nurse Executives* 9(4):4–5.

45. *Minimum Scope of Root Cause Analysis for Specific Types of Sentinel Events.* (2002). The Joint Commission on Accreditation for Healthcare Organizations, Oakbrook Terrace, Ill.

46. Rex, J. H., Turnbull, J. E., Allen, S. J., et al. (2000). Systematic root cause analysis of adverse drug events in a tertiary referral hospital. *Joint Commission Journal on Quality Improvement* 26(10):563–575.

47. Feldman, S. E., and Roblin, D. W. (1997). Medical accidents in hospital care: Applications of failure analysis to hospital quality appraisal. *The Joint Commission Journal on Quality Improvement* 23(11): 567–580.

48. Fletcher, C. E. (1997). Failure mode and effects analysis: An interdisciplinary way to analyze and reduce medication errors. *Journal of Nursing Administration* 27(12):19–26.

49. Patten, T. H. Jr. (1981). *Organizational Development Facilitators through Teambuilding.* New York: John Wiley, pp. 157–158.

50. Newman, R. G. (1991). Continuous quality improvement: Working for the highest quality. *Beth Israel Medical Center Newsletter* 4(2):1–2.

51. Solberg, L. I., Reger, L. A., Pearson, T. L., Cherney, L. M., et al. (1997). Using continuous quality improvement to improve diabetes care in populations: The IDEAL model. *The Joint Commission Journal on Quality Improvement* 23(11):581–592.

52. Juran, J. M. (1989). *Juran on Leadership for Quality: An Executive Handbook.* New York: Free Press, pp. 87–88, 90, 101.

53. Hickson, G. B., Federspiel, C. F., Pichert, J. W., and Miller, C. S. (2002). Patient complaints and malpractice risk. *Journal of the American Medical Association* 287(22):2951–2957.

54. Sage, W. M. (2002). Putting the patient in patient safety: Linking patient complaints and malpractice risk. *Journal of the American Medical Association* 287(22):3003–3005.

55. Joseph, D. E., and Meyers, D. (1993). *Risk Management/Total Quality Management—Making the Connection. Lecture and Discussion Guide.* Chicago: Care Communications, p. 29.

56. Schwartzberg, J. G. (2000). Health literacy: Can your patient read, understand, and act upon your instruction? *Forum*, December, pp. 9–10.

57. Harer, W. B. (2002). Vaginal birth after caesarian section: Current status. *Journal of the American Medical Association* 287(20):2627–2630.

58. Field, M. J., and Grigsby, J. (2002). Telemedicine and remote patient monitoring. *Journal of the American Medical Association* 288(4):423–425.

59. Studdert, D. M., Eisenberg, D. M., Miller, F. H., Curto, D. A., et al. (1998). Medical malpractice implications of alternative medicine. *Journal of the American Medical Association* 280(18):1610–1615.

60. Needleman, J., Buerhaus, P., Mattke, S., Stewart, M., et al. (2002). Nurse-staffing levels and the quality of care in hospitals. *New England Journal of Medicine* 346(22):1715–1722.

61. Steinbrook, R. (2002). Nursing in the crossfire. *New England Journal of Medicine* 346(22):1757–1766.

62. Rubeor, K., Keane, V., and Cross, E. (2001). *Neonatal Brachial Plexus Impairment Program*, Annual Report to Maryland Medicine Comprehensive Insurance Program, Baltimore, Md.

63. Robinson, R. K., Fink, R. L., and Fink, L. A. (1995). Employee participation programs in the health care industry: Are they unlawful under recent labor rulings? *Hospital & Health Services Administration* 40(1):124–137.

64. Abrams, J. (1995). Lessening your professional liability risk. *Occupational Safety and Health* 63(1): 35–39.

65. Crown Cork and Seal, Inc., 334 NLRB No. 92 (July 20, 2001).

66. Plsek, P. E. (1995). Advancing process improvement: Techniques for managing quality. *Hospital & Health Services Administration* 40(1):50–79.

67. Roman, K. M. (2001). Benchmarking. In *Risk Management Handbook for Health Care Organizations*, 3d edition, edited by R. Carroll. San Francisco: Jossey-Bass, pp. 811–836.

68. Youngberg, B. J. (1998). Benchmarking in risk management. In *Risk Manager's Desk Reference*, 2d edition, edited by B. J. Youngberg. Gaithersberg, Md: Aspen, pp. 56–60.

69. Kohn, K. T., Corrigan, J. M., and Donaldson, M. S., eds. (1999). *To Err is Human: Building a Safer Health System.* Washington, D.C.: Committee on Quality of Health Care in America, Institute of Medicine, National Academy Press.

70. McDonald, C. J., Weiner, M., and Hui, S. L. (2000). Deaths due to medical errors are exaggerated in Institute of Medicine Report. *Journal of the American Medical Association* 284(1):93–97.

71. Brennan, T. A. (2000). The Institute of Medicine Report on Medical Errors—could it do harm? *New England Journal of Medicine* 342(15):1123–1125.

72. Shojania, K., Duncan, B., McDonald, K., and Wachter, R. M., eds. (2001). *Making Health Care Safer: A Critical Analysis of Patient Safety Practices.* Rockville, Md: Agency for Healthcare Research and Quality. Evidence Report/Technology Assessment No. 43; AHRQ publication 01-EO58.

73. Leape, L. L., Berwick, D. M., and Bates, D. W. (2002). What practices will most improve safety? Evidence-based medicine meets patient safety. *Journal of the American Medical Association* 288(4):501–507.

74. McNutt, R. A., Abrams, R., and Aron, D. C. (2002). Patient safety efforts should focus on medical errors. *Journal of the American Medical Association* 287(15): 1997–2001.

75. Goldfield, N., Pine, M., and Pine, J. (1995). *Measuring and Managing Heatlthcare Quality Procedures, Techniques, and Protocols.* Gaithersburg, Md: Aspen, pp. 2–3.

76. Loeb, J. M., and O'Leary, D. S. (1995). A call for collaboration in performance measurement. *Journal of the American Medical Association* 273(18):1405.

77. Carroll, J. G. (1995). *Monitoring with Indicators. Evaluating the Quality of Patient Care.* Gaithersburg, Md: Aspen.

78. Rowland, H. S. and Rowland, B. L. (1995). *Hospital Risk Management Forms, Checklists, & Guidelines.* Frederick, Md: Aspen.

79. Eldridge, J., and Conner, C. (2002). *Health Care Facilities Risk Management Forms, Checklists and Guidelines.* Gaithersburg, Md: Aspen.

80. Acerbo-Avalone, N., and Kramer, K. (1997). Writing the Investigation Report, Exhibit 8-2 in *Medical Malpractice Claims Investigation: A Step-by-Step Approach.* Gaithersberg, Md: Aspen, p. 155.

81. Joint Commission on Accreditation of Healthcare Organizations. (1995). *Accreditation Manual for Hospitals*, vol. 1: *Standards.* Oakbrook Terrace, Ill. JCAHO.

82. Barron, B. M. (1989). *How Underwriters Evaluate Risk Management Effectiveness*, in Eleventh Annual Conference of the American Society for Healthcare Risk Management of the American Hospital Association, Orlando, Fla.

83. Zarrella, E. G. (1989). *How Underwriters Evaluate Risk Management Effectiveness* in Eleventh Annual Conference of the American Society for Healthcare Risk Management, Orlando, Fla.

84. Garnick, D. W., Hendricks, A. M., and Brennan, T. A. (1991). Can practice guidelines reduce the number and costs of malpractice claims? *Journal of the American Medical Association* 266(20): 2856–2860.

85. Hyams, A. L., Brandenburg, J. A., Lipsitz, S. R., et al. (1995). Practice guidelines and malpractice litigation: A two-way street. *Annals of Internal Medicine* 122(6):450–455.

86. Mello, M. M. (2000). The role of clinical practice guidelines in malpractice litigation. *Forum*, Fall, p. 1.

87. Sloan, F. A., Mergenhagen, P. M., Burfield, B., et al. (1989). Medical malpractice experience of physicians: Predictable or haphazard? *Journal of the American Medical Association* 262(23):3291–3297.

88. Kravitz, R. L., Rolph, J. E., and McGuigan, K. (1991). Malpractice claims data as a quality improvement tool. *Journal of the American Medical Association* 266(15):2087–2097.

89. Acerbo-Avalone, N., and Kramer, K. (1997). Identifying the medical-legal issues. In *Medical Malpractice Claims Investigation: A Step-by-Step Approach*. Gaithersberg, Md: Aspen, pp. 33–38.

90. Rolf, J. E., Kravitz, R. L., and McGuigan, K. (1991). Malpractice claims data as a quality improvement tool: II. Is targeting effective? *Journal of the American Medical Association* 266(15):2093–2097.

91. Caplan, R. A., Posner, K. L., and Cheney, R. W. (1991). Effect of outcome on physician judgments of appropriateness of care. *Journal of the American Medical Association* 265(15):1957–1960.

92. Gilbert, P. L. (1991). The internist as preoperative consultant: Risk assessment and management. *Mount Sinai Journal of Medicine*. 58(1):3–8.

93. McConnell, J. C., and Praeger, A. M. (1990). Confidentiality of records maintained in a hospital setting. In *Risk Management Handbook for Health Care Facilities*, edited by L. M. Harpster and M. S. Veach. Chicago: American Hospital Publishing, pp. 233–251.

94. Davis, K. S., and McConnell, J. C. (2001). Data management. In *Risk Management Handbook for Health Care Organizations*, edited by R. Carroll. San Francisco: Jossey-Bass, pp. 115–146.

95. Health Services Research & Development Center (1991). ASHRM Risk Management Self-Assessment Manual. Chicago: American Hospital Association.

96. Cassirer, C. (2001). Risk management program evaluation. In *Risk Management Handbook for Health Care Organizations*, edited by R. Carroll. San Francisco: Jossey-Bass, pp. 837–859.

97 Barton, E. L. (1990). Claims and litigation management. In *Risk Management Handbook for Health Care Facilities*, edited by L. M. Harpster and M. S. Veach. Chicago: American Hospital Publishing, pp. 267–294.

98. Beckman, H. B., Markakis, K. M., Suchman, A. L., and Frankel, R. M. (1994). The doctor-patient relationship and malpractice. *Archives of Internal Medicine* 154(7):1365–1370.

CHAPTER 7 Ethical Issues for Risk Managers

Kathleen E. Powderly

A variety of forces have joined together to increase awareness of ethical issues in health care: patient's rights, sophisticated medical technologies, consumer demographics, non-traditional family settings, and the influx of managed-care organizations.[1] On top of all these complicating forces, ethical issues have also evolved related to the control of skyrocketing health care costs, even though "ethics is the discipline of determining right from wrong and is not directly governed by those who benefit and those who do not."[2]

Risk managers will confront many ethical issues in their daily practice. Where federal, state, or local legislation exists, it is vital that the risk manager be familiar with the law. Risk managers may need to develop policies or guidelines to apply the law to specific situations. At other times there will be no law, and the risk manager will have to adapt measures to resolve complex ethical problems. Guidelines regarding ethical issues in health care and examples of related law can help the risk manager develop appropriate procedures.[3]

ETHICAL GUIDELINES FOR RISK MANAGERS

Automomy, beneficence, and justice are three ethical principles that underlie the perplexing decisions that must be made by health care organizations as they render care.

Autonomy

Autonomy, or self-determination, is the core principle of American bioethics. In the United States, the Constitution builds a framework of respect for individual rights, as long as the exercise of those rights does not infringe on the rights of others. In a country as heterogeneous and culturally pluralistic as the United States, this can be quite a challenge. Adults have the right to make their own health care decisions, a change from former determinations based on paternalism. In a paternalistic system, clinicians tell patients what to do relying on what they think is right or best for them. Patients do what they are told to do without asking questions. Yet a clinician's decisions could be grounded in sound medical judgment or could be influenced by the clinician's own personal values or sense of what is right or wrong.

When decisions are based on a respect for autonomy, patients choose from the available options. From the clinician's perspective and values, the patient may make a "bad" decision. Despite the perception of others, individuals have the right to make bad health care decisions about aspects of their lives, such as smoking or driving without a seat belt. However, the clinician has an obligation to inform the patient about available options, including no intervention or treatment, where appropriate. Respect for autonomy does not preclude the clinician's offering information or an opinion about the optimal option(s) for an individual patient. Nevertheless, the ultimate choice belongs to the patient, including "the final autonomy."[4]

Beneficence

In health care, beneficence is interpreted as the obligation to do good for patients. When there are no good options, the clinician should, at least, do no harm, as stated in the Hippocratic tradition of nonmaleficence.[5] At times, a clinician's sense of what is good for a patient is compromised by an autonomous patient's choices. For example, conflicts may arise between a clinician's sense of beneficence and the patient's autonomy when the clinician is caring for a Jehovah's Witness who refuses a blood transfusion or a surgical patient who refuses to consent to the suspension of a do not resuscitate order in the operating room. When respecting the patient's wishes would cause harm, clinicians are not obligated to violate their own set of values and act against their desire to be beneficent. In such situations, clinicians are entitled to a conscience objection. While physicians can't abandon a patient in an emergency, they can refer a patient elsewhere; clinicians can inform their superiors of their objections and ask that the patient be transferred to another provider.

Justice

Ethically, the principle of justice dictates that people should be treated in an equitable, or fair, fashion. Justice is adhered to, or violated, when the allocation of health care resources or access to health care is considered or rationed. In a "just" health care system, people would have access to the resources necessary to achieve a minimally acceptable level of health care. However, it is not clear that health care is a right, or an entitlement, in the United States, and a finite amount of health care resources is inequitably distributed. While resource allocation is important on a societywide level, clinicians are compromised when they have to allocate or deny access to health care resources at the bedside. In reality, providers are constantly allocating resources. When staffing is limited or inappropriate, clinicians may have to struggle with how to apportion their time. Shortages of supplies or critical care beds must also be resolved. Over a considerable period of time, these allocation decisions and the associated stress can contribute to burnout in health care workers. However, a distinction should be made between insufficient resources for optimal care and situations where the resources are so insufficient as to lead to an unsafe health care environment. In the latter situation, the health care institution may be operating in an unethical or even an illegal fashion.

ETHICAL STANDARDS

Ethical standards refer to the ability of adults to make their own decisions. Adults with decisional capacity should make their own decisions. The standards that apply when they cannot participate in decision-making are substituted judgment and best interest:

- Substituted judgment applies when someone previously had capacity for decision-making and has temporarily or permanently lost it.
- Best interest applies when someone never had decision-making capacity or when we have no way of knowing an individual's wishes.

Substituted Judgment

There is a consensus in American society, albeit an uneasy one, that adults with the capacity to make their own decisions have the right to do so. Clinicians have the obligation to respect the patient's autonomy. When the patient lacks the capacity to make an informed decision, the situation becomes more difficult. When a previously capable adult loses capacity to make decisions, the ethical standard of substituted judgment is applied to health care decisions. What would *this* individual have decided, given *this* set of circumstances? Individuals make decisions based on what's uniquely important to them: their own set of values, culture, religion, lifestyle, or life experiences. Examples of patient values include:[6]

- I want to retain my capacity to think clearly.
- I want to avoid unnecessary pain and suffering.
- I want to be treated with respect.
- I want to be treated with dignity when I can no longer speak for myself.
- I don't want to be an unnecessary burden on my family.
- I want to experience a comfortable dying process.
- I want to be with my loved ones before I die.
- I want to be treated in accord with my religious belief and traditions.
- I want respect shown to my body after I die.

An advance directive makes substituted judgment much easier,[7] by legally extending the patient's autonomy beyond the loss of decision-making capacity. A living will specifies a patient's wishes about medical treatment to prolong life and allows individuals to indicate what they would or wouldn't want in critical care situations. Most living wills focus on what the individual would not want to happen. One of the problems with a living will is that the statements are often not clear in relationship to the particular situation at hand. What does it mean when individuals say they wouldn't want to be on a ventilator? People might not want to be maintained on a ventilator if they were in an irreversible, ventilator-dependent state. In contrast, they might not feel the same way about being on a ventilator for a few days after major surgery if their prognosis were good.[8] Since the patient lacks capacity when the living will is consulted, clinicians cannot have a conversation with the patient to clarify the meaning of the statements in the living will.

Sometimes there is uncertainty about whether the patients would have changed their mind, given the specific circumstances. People may not want to live in a quadriplegic state, if given a choice. On the other hand, if there is no other alternative, they might adjust their feelings and live in that state rather than not live at all. In such circumstances, a surrogate decision maker, able to discuss the pros and cons of interventions, would be helpful in providing substituted judgment.[9] Advance directives, such as health care proxies and durable powers of attorney for health care, allow for the designation of a surrogate decision-maker to make medical decisions when the patient cannot. Health care organizations must ask about any advance directives.[10]

Best Interest

When substituted judgment is not possible, the appropriate guideline is the standard of best interest, also known as the objective benefits/burden, or "reasonable person," standard.[11] Best interest applies for individuals who have never had decision-making capacity, such as infants and children. There is no means to determine what a particular infant or child wold have done with no advance directive, no identifiable surrogate decision-makers, and no established set of values. Thus, caregivers must ask the following questions: What is in the best interest of this patient, given the critical circumstances? What would a reasonable person choose to do under the circumstances? Making the decision "requires morally imaginative and empathetic efforts to enter the experimental world of such patients."[11] Despite the difficulties, this determination should be as objective as possible, holding the best interest of the individual uppermost.

CODES OF ETHICS

A code of ethics is one of the defining characteristics of a professional. Traditionally, the Hippocratic oath conveys a sense of the privileged roles and responsibilities of physicians over time. Almost every organization of health care providers has a code of ethics detailing the values, duties, and ethical responsibilities of their chosen professional membership. However, these codes of ethics contain broad statements that provide little assistance to the individual practitioner trying to interpret the applicability of the codes to specific clinical situations. Ethical codes are guiding principles, not directions for action in distinct situations. Although codes of ethics are open to interpretation, they remain important guidelines for health care professionals.

CONFIDENTIALITY AND ETHICS

Every code of ethics emphasizes provider-patient confidentiality. Even though confidentiality is one of the most important ethical obligations of health care providers, it may be one of the most commonly violated. Health care providers have an undeniable obligation to respect the privacy of patients and to keep all information given to them in the strictest confidence. However, hospital visitors riding the elevator or sitting in the cafeteria can attest to breaches of confidentiality.

Violations of confidentiality are always ethically problematic. Breaches are even more unethical if the information is serious, has the ability to stigmatize the patient, or could lead to discrimination. Certainly, a diagnosis of HIV seropositivity should be treated confidentially. There may be individuals, including health care providers, who the patients may not wish to inform. Discrimination against people with a positive HIV blood finding, although illegal in many states and a violation of the Americans with Disabilities Act, does exist. Patients may reasonably fear the loss of friends and support persons, housing, insurance, or job. This discrimination is extremely burdensome for individuals already dealing with a potentially devastating diagnosis. Health care providers and institutions should do everything they can to protect this sensitive information. Obviously, risk managers must be aware of the potential liability of the breach of confidentiality.

Some states have specific laws dealing with strict confidentiality regarding HIV test results. For example, New York State Public Health Law, Article 27-F, mandates the following:[12]

- Keeping information about AIDS and HIV confidential is mandatory.
- Anyone receiving a voluntary HIV test must sign a consent form first.
- The disclosure of HIV-related information is strictly limited.
- When disclosure of HIV-related information is authorized by a signed, special HIV release, the person who has been given the information must keep it confidential.
- These rules apply only to people and facilities providing health or social services, or who obtain the information pursuant to a special HIV release.

In addition, HIV-related information cannot be released in response to a subpoena issued by an attorney. Absent a special HIV release form, a court order is required for disclosure of HIV-related information. The New York law also specifies that persons who test positive will be requested to cooperate with partner notification efforts during required counseling.

INFORMED CONSENT

Clinicians are obligated to provide autonomous adult patients with all the information they need, in a way that they can understand it, to allow them to make a fully informed decision. Patients must be given enough information to weigh the relative benefits and burdens or risks associated with the proposed intervention. Informed consent is a process, not just a signature on a consent form. While the signed consent form serves as documentation of the patient's understanding and consent, the process and dialogue between the clinician and patient are even more important. Can desperately ill patients be expected to weigh all the risks? (See Box 7-1.)

Conceptually, informing a patient about all the possible risks associated with an intervention or treatment is overwhelming to clinicians. How does the professional determine the extent of the discussion to fulfill the obligations associated with informed consent? Risk managers can profit from the court's reasonable approach to this question:

> The discussion need not be a disquisition, and surely the physician is not compelled to give his patient a short medical education; the disclosure role summons the physician only to a reasonable explanation. This means generally informing the patient in nontechnical terms as to what is at stake: the therapy alternatives open to him, the goals expectably to be achieved, and the risks that may ensue from particular treatment and no treatment. So informing the patient hardly taxes the physician and it must be the exceptional patient who cannot comprehend such an explanation in at least a rough way.[16]

Determining what is "reasonably" required remains one of the greatest challenges in obtaining and documenting informed consent (see Box 7-2). In common law, the major case precedent in informed

BOX 7-1

Controversies

- Prostate cancer: Should the patient have surgery or not?[13] Recent studies indicate that there is no difference in the overall death rate of men with prostate cancer who have had surgery compared to those who have not. Seed implantation? Radiation? Hormones? Drugs?
- Hormone Replacement Therapy (HRT) at menopause: After more than 30 years of recommending HRT to control or relieve menopausal symptoms and protect patients from cardiac disease and osteoporosis, new research has shocked the medical community. Data has shown that use of HRT that combines estrogen and progestin (PEMPRO) causes an increase in invasive breast cancer, ovarian cancer, coronary heart disease, pulmonary embolism, and stroke. This combination therapy is currently taken by an estimated six million women to alleviate menopausal symptoms.[14,15] Many health care professionals have become somewhat hesitant to prescribe HRT, and many women are reluctant to take HRT.

Breast cancer

- Early diagnosis—palpation, mammography, sonography, MRI
- Surgical treatment, biopsy, lumpectomy, simple mastectomy, total mastectomy
- Additional hysterectomy? Radiation? Chemotherapy? Tamoxifen?
- Multiple combinations?

consent was decided by the U.S. Court of Appeals for the District of Columbia in 1972 (see Box 7-3).

DECISIONAL CAPACITY TO WEIGH RISKS

Decisional capacity refers to individuals' ability to weigh the relative benefits, risks, or burdens of proposed interventions and their ability to make a decision. In contrast to psychiatric or legal determination of com-

BOX 7-2

Tampa General Hospital paid $1.1 million and the University of South Florida, in Tampa, paid $2.7 million in settlements to plaintiffs who claimed they consented to participate in research studies but did not understand the consent form. The research focused on women at high risk of delivering small, premature babies. The women were in a randomized trial of corticosteroid injection treatments and had to undergo amniocentesis, sometimes repeatedly.[17]

BOX 7-3

Mr. Canterbury consented to and underwent a laminectomy in 1958. Postoperatively, he fell and was subsequently paralyzed from the waist down. He consented to a second operation, but after that he "required crutches to walk, still suffered from urinal incontinence and paralysis of the bowels, and wore a penile clamp." In the court's decision there was a discussion of "true consent," or the obligation of physicians to disclose information to patients. Mr. Canterbury had not been warned about paralysis resulting from falls.

An expanded version of "true consent" in the court's decision provides guidelines for risk managers involved with the informed consent process:

> True consent to what happens to oneself is the informed exercise of a choice, and that entails an opportunity to evaluate knowledgeably the options available and the risks attendant upon each. . . . the physician discharges the duty when he makes a reasonable effort to convey sufficient information although the patient, without the fault of the physician, may not fully grasp it.[16]

petency, decisional capacity is a clinical judgment. Importantly, an individual may have the capacity to make some decisions and not other and/or may have capacity at some times and not at others. Senile individuals may be clearheaded at times and understand and make choices. Sick elderly individuals facing difficult and complicated treatment decisions may understand that they do not have the capacity to make complex decisions but may be able to make simple decisions or designate a surrogate. Extremely sick patients or those undergoing surgery may temporarily lose their decision-making capacity and regain it after treatment or intervent. However, these people may have enough capacity to choose a health care agent or surrogate decision-maker. A court-appointed guardian can also make surrogate decisions. Acting as her guardian, Cindy Wasiek's mother consented to sterilization by laparoscopic tubal ligation for her 26-year-old, severely retarded daughter. A prior legal guardian tried to stop the sterilization and the case went to the U.S. Supreme Court (see Box 7-4).

CLINICAL APPLICATIONS OF ETHICS

There are many clinical situations in which a risk manager should have knowledge about ethical approaches to problem resolution. Critics may contend that violations of ethical doctrines do not incur liability. Yet, as professional organizations publish codes of ethics that include current opinions with legal annotations, liability arguments could be bolstered with the codes of ethics data. A book published by the American Medical Association discusses a broad spectrum of issues and includes about 150 legal citations.[19] Ethical considerations can be applied in routine health care services such as decision-making for adults with capacity, surrogate decision-making, perinatal dilemmas, pediatric care, geriatric care, organ transplantation, medical futility, and end-of-life choices.

BOX 7-4

Judge David Souter found the sterilization appropriate where the woman "may experience severe or life threatening trauma if she becomes pregnant . . . is incapable of understanding reproduction or contraception . . . and is incapable of caring for the child . . . and is likely to engage in sexual activity."[18]

Decision-Making for Adults with Capacity

Adults with capacity have the right to make their own health care decisions, but they do not have the right to demand that clinicians take professional actions perceived as bad medical or nursing practice. In a nonemergency situation, clinicians are not required to do things that violate their personal values, such as perform abortions.

A common conflict arises in the case of capacitated adult patients who are Jehovah's Witnesses and refuse an appropriate blood transfusion. Jehovah's Witnesses believe that it is a serious violation of their religion to accept blood or blood products,[20] and most will risk death rather than imperil their eternal salvation. Clinicians may find their beneficence-based belief in saving lives violated by allowing a Jehovah's Witness to die if a transfusion could be life-saving. These clinicians should remove themselves from the care of Jehovah's Witnesses. They are not justified in transfusing a known Jehovah's Witness who has expressed a conviction against transfusions. Doing so would risk liability, since the doctor would clearly be violating the patient's autonomy. Courts almost never issue an order to transfuse an adult Jehovah's Witness with capacity who refuses a transfusion, or a previously capacitated adult with a relevant advance directive. On the other hand, the courts almost always grant a court order to transfuse the minor child of a Jehovah's Witness against the parents' wishes. Older adolescents who express the same religious beliefs as their parents present a more difficult case; there is no consistent precedent for this situation.

As a risk management initiative, health care institutions should probably identify professionals in surgery, anesthesia, and obstetrics/gynecology who are comfortable with the implications of the Witnesses' religious beliefs. Such planning avoids the ad hoc compromising of health care providers' values and beliefs, while respecting the religious beliefs and values of Jehovah's Witnesses.

Surrogate Decision-Making

When a previously capacitated adult loses capacity, it is helpful to have a designated surrogate decision-maker, even when an advance directive exists. This surrogate can participate in decision-making just as the patient would have, had capacity not been lost. Critics attack the moral and legal rationale for surrogate decision-making for three reasons: (1) Interests of incompetent persons are different from those of the same person during their competent state. (2) Surrogates often project their own desires and needs while neglecting the patient's preferences and values. (3) The lives of vulnerable individuals may be undervalued when instructions are unclear and not comprehensive.[21] A surrogate may have intimate knowledge about the individual that assists in making a substituted judgment. In the absence of such information in an advance directive, the surrogate may participate with clinicians to determine which decisions are in the patient's best interest. Ideally, the surrogate should be chosen by the patient, when capable, and designated in a health care proxy or durable power of attorney for health care document. Appropriate documents vary from state to state. In some states, family members function as surrogate decision-makers and are recognized by the law as such. In other jurisdictions, such as New York State, the family member has no legal authority to make decisions to withdraw or withhold life-sustaining treatment unless properly designated as a health care agent in a health care proxy.[22] Often, end-of-life decisions need to be made for an incapacitated individual. This raises ethical, and sometimes legal, dilemmas in the absence of a designated health care agent or surrogate decision-maker.

Respect for autonomy dictates that clinicians abide by the decisions made by a properly designated surrogate.[23] Risk managers should understand the law in relation to surrogate decision-making within their jurisdictions.[24]

Perinatal Dilemmas

Perinatal issues constitute the most unresolved dilemmas in clinical ethics. While this is certainly true about abortion, it also holds for maternal-fetal conflicts and dilemmas in the neonatal intensive care unit (NICU).

Although not without controversy,[25] abortion is a constitutionally protected right in the United States.[26] Violence at abortion clinics and the debate over training residents in obstetrics/gynecology to perform abortions are evidence of the continuing, emotionally charged controversy.[27] Risk managers should understand the law in their state regarding abortion, including access and consent issues.

In obstetrical care, maternal-fetal medicine remains highly charged with ethical predicaments. Many clinicians practice as if they have two patients, the mother and the fetus, where only one of the patients speaks for herself. This emphasis on two patients was not always the case. In the nineteenth century, there was little discussion among physicians or midwives about the well-being of the fetus. Childbirth was dangerous for the mother, and little could be done for the infant, much less the fetus. During the twentieth century, childbirth became safer for the mother through the use of antibiotics, blood typing, cross-matching, and improved anesthesia. At the same time, technology evolved to intervene with high-risk infants and fetuses. Ultrasound imaging allows for the visualization of the fetus and conveys a real sense of the fetus as an additional patient during the prenatal period.

Maternal-fetal conflicts arise only when the rights or behavior of the pregnant woman are not in the best interest of her fetus. Possible high-risk behaviors of pregnant women include the abuse of drugs or alcohol, the refusal of a cesarean section indicated for maternal well-being and/or fetal distress, the refusal by a pregnant Jehovah's Witness of a necessary blood transfusion, and the failure by a brittle diabetic pregnant woman to adhere to her prescribed diet. These varying behaviors provoke differing emotional and ethical anguish in clinicians. A clinician may be able to accept the decision of a pregnant Jehovah's Witness to refuse a blood transfusion, on the basis of respect for autonomy. Clinicians may have much less tolerance for a pregnant woman addicted to crack cocaine.

A pregnant woman should not be treated any differently from other patients with respect to autonomy. Advocacy for the fetus requires a significant effort to help the pregnant woman understand the consequences if her behavior is not in the best interest of her fetus. Some physicians would seek a court order if a pregnant woman refused a cesarean section necessary for fetal well-being. Even stronger motivation exists if the mother is also at risk, as in placenta previa. On the other hand, some physicians would attempt to get a court order but would not tie the woman down and operate without her consent, even with the court order. These clinicians hope that going to court reinforces, for the pregnant woman, their serious concerns and the seriousness of the situation. From an ethical perspective, it is extremely serious to violate a woman's autonomy simply because she is pregnant.

Case law is inconsistent and not particularly helpful in maternal-fetal conflicts. While some courts have intervened on grounds of fetal interest (see Box 7-5), others have refused to issue court orders. In some cases, the patient has delivered while the court was still deliberating.

BOX 7-5

Mrs. Angela Carder had been diagnosed with cancer as an adolescent, and it was in remission. She was warned that the cancer could be exacerbated by a pregnancy. Nevertheless, she became pregnant and the cancer reappeared and worsened. Early in her third trimester she was dying as a court ordered delivery of her fetus by cesarean section. Her neonate died after birth, and she died shortly after the surgery. Surgery hastened her death by a few days. On appeal, the court reversed the earlier court's order, ruling that Mrs. Carder's autonomy dictated that her wishes be respected. This was particularly true in this case because her fetus was at only borderline viability.[28]

Decision-making in the NICU raises profound ethical challenges. Prior to the regionalization of intensive perinatal care, clinicians and perhaps one or both parents made private decisions about imperiled newborns. Often, these decisions were not subject to public scrutiny or even to professional examination within a hospital. Imperiled newborns include premature infants, those with congenital abnormalities and genetic defects, and those who are very sick.

A landmark article about decision-making in the NICU appeared in the *New England Journal of Medicine* in 1973.[29] Duff and Campbell argued that it is sometimes appropriate to withdraw or withhold life-sustaining treatment from seriously ill or anomalous newborns. They described a methodology employed in the NICU at Yale-New Haven Hospital (Connecticut) to attempt to achieve consensus regarding appropriate treatment for such newborns. Everyone involved with the baby's care or with an interest, such as the parents, was included in those discussions. Duff and Campbell contended that it was fitting to treat some of these severely compromised neonates less aggressively. Furthermore, parents had to be active decision-makers with the team caring for the baby. Infants who were not aggressively treated were supported in a humane way during their dying days. In contrast, critics believed that nonaggressive treatment decisions could be problematic from a legal perspective and that grieving parents might not be in the best position to make such decisions for their children. An active debate regarding decision-making in the NICU ensued among clinicians in pediatrics and neonatology.[30]

In the early 1980s, the federal government became involved in public policy regarding neonatal decision-making when the Baby Doe regulations were issued. On the basis of the Rehabilitation Act of 1973, the regulations established a telephone hotline and investigative procedures to deal with alleged discrimination against or inappropriate treatment of "handicapped" newborns. Although the regulations were overturned by the Second Circuit Court in the New York case of Baby Jane Doe, a public policy debate ensued. In addition, federal legislation was passed that required states receiving federal funds for child abuse and neglect prevention programs to create mechanisms to investigate suspected abuse or inappropriate denial of treatment for handicapped newborns.[30] Legislative amendments defined medically indicated treatment for newborns as "treatment, including appropriate nutrition, hydration, and medication, which in the treating physician's . . . reasonable medical judgment, will be most likely to be effective in ameliorating or correcting all such life-threatening conditions."[31] Three exceptions are allowed in which treatment can be withheld: (1) infants who are irreversibly comatose; (2) infants for whom treatment would merely prolong dying, would not remedy all the infant's life-threatening conditions, and would be useless in ensuring survival; and (3) infants for whom treatment would be "virtually futile" and its provision would be inhumane. Many states utilized existing child abuse reporting measures to implement the federally mandated program. Risk managers should be aware of the specific procedures in their state.

Usually, parents are the appropriate decision-makers for their children. They generally try to make decisions in the best interest of their children, and they live with the consequences. However, parents need information from health care experts to make these difficult decisions. In addition, parents may be comforted if they have a sense that those caring for their infant agree with their decisions. On the other hand, it is quite apparent from the child abuse and neglect statistics that not all parents strive to or are able to make decisions in the best interest of their children. In such rare cases, society has opted to protect the vulnerable child. Such situations occasionally arise with infants in the NICU. When parents are clearly not making decisions in the best interest of their child, an ethics committee should be consulted and ultimately a court order may be obtained. For example, parents could refuse to consent to surgery for an easily correctable gastrointestinal anomaly in an infant with Down's syndrome. In other cases, such as with anencephaly, aggressive treatment clearly is inappropriate. Most would agree that supportive care during the process of dying is the appropriate course for such infants. In the Virginia case of Baby K,[32] however, nonaggressive care was challenged. Baby K's mother demanded aggressive care for her anencephalic infant. Courts supported her request on the basis of legislation prohibiting discrimination against the handicapped and another law prohibiting "dumping" of patients from one hospital to another. Unsuccessfully, clinicians argued that it was medically futile to treat Baby K. The Supreme Court refused to hear the case, and Baby K survived for more than two years.

Many patients in the NICU fall into a gray area where it is appropriate for clinicians and parents to struggle to determine what is in the baby's best interest and to proceed accordingly. Many ethicists and clinicians believe that overtreatment, rather than undertreatment, is the major problem in the NICU. Fear of legal liability, a failure to understand legal requirements, and the inability to accept the limits of technological medicine contribute to overtreatment.

Pediatric Care

Decision-making for children is guided by the same ethical standard as for neonates: the best interest. Identifying the individuals who are optimally suited to determine the child's best interest and the parameters to use can present real dilemmas. Strict objectivity is a vital component of any choice.

Generally, parents are able to determine their child's best interest. As with neonates, parents must live with the consequences for their children. To make fully informed decisions, parents require information from appropriate health care professionals. Children old enough to comprehend data about their health and proposed interventions should also be given information appropriate to their age and developmental level. Chronically ill children may be quite sophisticated about their health status and care. Although the legal decision-making authority generally resides with the parents, children should be given the opportunity to assent, if they are capable.[33] Particularly difficult situations arise when the patients are adolescents. They may have a high degree of understanding and disagree with the decisions of their parents. Some adolescents are considered emancipated or mature by virtue of living independently and/or becoming pregnant or having children of their own. In this area, the law varies among jurisdictions.

In some circumstances, parents do not have the legal right to make health care decisions or their decision-making authority has been removed (see Box 7-6). It is extremely important for risk managers to have a clear understanding of the law in their particular state or jurisdiction. For example, in New York State, parents have a great deal of latitude about how they raise their children in areas such as education and routine health care decisions. However, there is

BOX 7-6

Six-year-old Olivia Pilhar needed chemotherapy to treat her kidney cancer, but her parents rejected the treatment because a former doctor had advised them that cancer was a state of mind. After consulting medical experts, the court stripped the parents of Olivia's custody and decided there must be treatment, even against the will of the parents.[34]

no clear basis in New York State law for parents to make decisions to withdraw or withhold life-sustaining treatment for their children.[35] This ambiguity may leave the child with no clear advocate, short of the courts.

All states have mechanisms for the removal or suspension of parental custody when child abuse or neglect is suspected or verified. The state has an obligation to protect the potentially vulnerable child. In addition, health care providers have an obligation to report suspected child abuse or neglect. Although reporting violates confidentiality and may damage the provider-patient relationship, the protection of this vulnerable population warrants disclosure.

Religion is a variable that may influence the decisions parents make for their children. Freedom of religion is constitutionally protected, and parents are free to raise children as they see fit. Yet sometimes religion interferes with what society perceives to be the best interest of children. Society may intervene and override the decisions of parents, such as when Jehovah's Witnesses refuse to allow a blood transfusion for their child. When parents pursue nontraditional remedies or refuse surgery on the basis of religious beliefs, clinicians or society may label the decisions "medical neglect." Communication with the parents and the child, as developmental level permits, is vitally important, whether or not a court order is pursued and granted.

The participation of children in clinical research and trials is controversial. Obviously, the potential vulnerability of children as research subjects is an ethical concern. Generally, clinical trials are not conducted on children unless the experimental drug has proven to be effective on adults. On the other hand, researchers in areas such as oncology and AIDS argue that ineffective agents in adults may prove to be therapeutic for children because of differences in physiology. Although this is a difficult and ethically problematic dilemma, some children may benefit from being enrolled in particular clinical trials. Risk managers should be certain that all appropriate approvals and consents are obtained and ensure that the clinical trials, as well as the subjects, are carefully monitored. Significantly, children should not be submitted to clinical trials that may increase suffering and hold no hope of benefit, as in last-resort clinical research. This scenario may arise when parents have difficulty accepting the fact that their child is dying. Whereas an adult may choose to participate in a trial for altruistic reasons, children who can't consent should not be subjected to that experience.

Geriatric Care

Elderly people are quite vulnerable, and there is a heightened awareness of elder abuse in the United States. Risk managers must be aware of the legal requirements for reporting elder abuse. Elderly people can be victims of abuse from those caring for them in nursing homes, as well as in residential arrangements with relatives or friends. There are many ethical dilemmas specific to nursing homes and group living situations.

A common problem for elderly patients in hospitals and nursing homes is the inappropriate use of restraints. Confused or senile elderly patients have a tendency to fall, and a fractured hip may result in a total loss of mobility, as well as legal liability for the institution. Elderly patients who have capacity are prone to falls because they may fail to recognize their need for assistance and their limitations in certain situations. Restraining elderly patients thus may seem like a beneficent action. However, there is a clear limitation to mobility and autonomy for patients restrained against their will. This is especially true when patients are restrained inappropriately or for the convenience of the staff. Because of restraint abuses, specific policies and protocols have been established, and restraints often require a doctor's order. Risk managers must be aware of administrative policies and legal guidelines, and work with staff to promote maximum safety for patients with minimal restriction of autonomy and mobility.

Frequently, elderly patients are ignored when health care decisions regarding them are made. Elderly individuals who retain their capacity must be allowed to make their own decisions and should be encouraged to prepare advance directives and to appoint surrogate decision-makers.

The appropriate use of limited health care resources for the elderly presents some quandaries. A large percentage of Medicare money is spent on elderly individuals in the last months of life. Ethicist Daniel Callahan suggested reconsidering the allocation of such resources.[36] In specific cases, the extension of life through technological intervention may be inhumane and, by some standards, unethical. In other situations, a reasonable quality of life may be maintained. There is no societal consensus on guidelines for the allocation of health care resources to the elderly.

Organ Transplantation

The medical ability to transplant organs has contributed to ethical issues such as the determination of "brain death" and the consent process for the donation of organs. Moreover, there may be a fear that the potential donor will be denied care or treatment. Real or perceived religious and cultural prohibitions also play a role in diminishing the number of donors. Mass media promotes awareness of the need for transplantable organs. When celebrities such as baseball star Mickey Mantle or the governor of Pennsylvania receive an organ, public discourse on the subject increases.

Many potential organ donors die each year, many in catastrophic accidents, without actually becoming donors, as potential recipients die while awaiting a transplant. A British study found that although 63 percent of 218 respondents carried organ donor cards, estimates projected that only 40 percent of potential donors actually became donors each year.[37] The low rate of donation is assumed to be due to the reluctance of clinicians to approach the family members of a potential donor. However, a study demonstrated that it is usually the family of the potential donor who is reluctant and refuses the request,[38] as they are grief-stricken and struggling to cope with a sudden catastrophic event.

State laws may "require request" when potential donors are identified, and family members of potential donors must be asked about the donation of organs. That mandate differs from a suggested "presumed consent" policy not routinely adopted, because of the obviously strong public opinion on the subject. Since laws differ among states, it is critical that risk managers be familiar with the relevant laws and policies in their jurisdiction.

In May 2000, there were 69,000 people on the waiting list. In 1999, 22,000 organs were transplanted from 10,505 donors, of which 4,662 were live persons. There has been a tremendous increase in living donor transplantation, but physicians and recipients must also consider the risks, benefits, and ethics of removing organs from healthy people.[39]

A shortage of transplantable organs focuses controversy on how the waiting list is prioritized. The geographic locations of the potential donor and recipient are priority factors, since organs have a short survival time. The severity of the patient's illness is another variable. Social supports available to the patient may be a consideration, given the usually lengthy recuperation period and the need for follow-up care. Although economic considerations play a part in the decision, from an ethical perspective they probably shouldn't. In reality, money must be paid up front or there must be a third-party payer willing to reimburse the hospital for the transplant, as well as for post-transplant care.

An especially acute shortage of organs for infants and small children exists, since they require organs commensurate with their body size and the pool of potential donors is limited. Although not brain dead, anencephalic infants are born without their upper brain, and basic body functions such as respiration and heartbeat may be maintained for a short period of time by the brain stem. These infants are thought to have a universally dismal prognosis. Families of these infants might take comfort in knowing that their child, who will not survive, could benefit other children through organ donation. However, the use of organs from someone who is not brain dead is highly controversial. There is no consensus on anencephalic infants as organ donors, although the American Medical Association recently issued an opinion condoning such donations in certain circumstances.[40]

If transplant services are available in the institution, it is imperative that appropriate policies, procedures, and staff training be in place to avoid risk. Each event should be tracked to ensure that actions were in concert with ethical principles for donor protection, consistent with legal requirements, and with maximum potential for a successful outcome.

Medical Futility

Many health care providers concur with the court's decision in the Gilgunn case (see Box 7-7). "Futile" treatment may deplete a significant amount of scarce health care resources and prolong suffering. On the other hand, determining exactly what is futile remains a real dilemma. Futility is a dangerous "slippery slope" and must be defined explicitly. There are no clear legal guidelines.[42]

Attending physicians could be constantly confronted with families demanding care.

BOX 7-7

Catherine F. Gilgunn became comatose and suffered irreversible brain damage. Her daughter, Joan, told attending physicians that her mother wanted everything medically possible to be done to keep her alive. Over the daughter's objections, doctors issued a do not resuscitate order. Joan sued, saying the doctors were obligated to abide by her mother's wishes. A jury found that the mother would have wanted to stay on life support but that it would have been futile and of no benefit. Therefore, the decision was in favor of the doctors.[41]

An emotional conflict arises between families who want every effort undertaken, no matter how futile, and doctors, applying the beneficence doctrine, wanting to do what's best for their patients and not prolong suffering. Some health care professionals have indicated that it would have been disastrous if the jury had ruled otherwise in the Gilgunn case. Providers would have had to render whatever the family demanded, regardless of whether the treatment was of any benefit to the patient.

In a practical sense, a perplexing problem with the concept of futility is that there is no precise definition or legal clarification of what is futile. In the narrowest sense, if an intervention achieves its desired goal, it may not be viewed as futile. Administering antibiotics to cure an infection that is sensitive to a particular antibiotic may not be futile. On the other hand, if the patient with the infection is terminally ill or vegetative, clinicians may feel that the overall prognosis makes any intervention futile.

End-of-Life Choices

Difficult ethical dilemmas—including the right to refuse, or to request the withdrawal of, life-sustaining treatment—frequently occur at the end of life. Emotional debates about physician-assisted suicide and assisted suicide in general reflect concerns that health care institutions and professionals do not always adequately manage death and dying.[43] Oregon voters approved a "Death with Dignity" law that empowers physicians to prescribe lethal doses of medication to terminally ill patients.[44] Other states have considered physician-assisted suicide bills. However, in 1997, the Supreme Court reversed lower-court decisions in *Washington v. Glucksberg* and *Vacco v. Quill*, holding that there is not a constitutional right to physician-assisted suicide.[45] If pain were managed better, perhaps chronically and terminally ill individuals contemplating suicide to escape a painful death and/or to avoid becoming a burden on their families, might recognize and consider alternatives.[46] Clinicians have improved their pain management abilities. Some physicians remain concerned that if they provide enough analgesics, such as morphine in a terminally ill cancer patient, they will expedite the patient's demise. From an ethical perspective, according to the principle of double effect, the intent of the intervention is of primary importance. A clinician prescribing morphine for the relief of pain is not doing so with the intent to kill but rather to provide comfort. Interestingly, if patients are allowed to self-administer morphine, they often use less, since the anxiety associated with anticipating unrelieved pain is eliminated.

A properly designated surrogate decision-maker should be able to consent to the withdrawal or withholding of life-sustaining treatment for an incapacitated adult. Surrogates and clinicians need to cooperate to form a substituted judgment or to determine what is in the patient's best interest. The standard to be applied is determined by the state's law and the information provided by the patient in an advance directive and in prior statements.

Options available and the process to be followed in regard to end-of-life decision making differs among the states because of a U.S. Supreme Court decision. That ruling allowed individual states to determine what constitutes "clear and convincing evidence" of a patient's wishes. In addition, the court recognized artificially administered food and fluids as treatment subject to withdrawal under certain circumstances. That position on the withdrawal and withholding of nutrition and hydration was supported by the AMA.[19]

BOX 7-8

- Scott Horn suffered a stroke and had surgery. After surgery, he was unable to speak or move his limbs and was fed through a gastric tube. His father and sister asked that the feeding tube be removed. A neurologist found Horn to be in a persistent vegetative state, and the hospital disconnected life support. His ex-wife interpreted Horn's eye blinks as signals that he didn't agree with removing life support. Horn's ex-wife sued for $10 million for trauma and fear experienced by Horn. A jury ruled that the hospital and the doctors were not negligent.[47]
- Nancy Cruzan, a woman in her twenties, existed for a number of years in a persistent vegetative state. Her parents petitioned the court to allow the removal of a feeding tube from their daughter. In an attempt at substituted judgment, they based their request on what they believed Nancy would have wanted. In the only right to die case heard by the Supreme Court, the Court upheld the right of the state to determine, as narrowly or as widely as it chooses, what constitutes "clear and convincing evidence" of a patient's wishes. The parents' request was denied.[48]

The Cruzan decision (see Box 7-8) allowed Missouri to maintain the most conservative standard in the United States regarding the withdrawal or withholding of life-sustaining treatment. New York is the next most conservative state.

End-of-life decisions include choices about the management of pain, resuscitation, and the aggressiveness of interventions. While the treatment plan for a terminally ill patient may be appropriately nonaggressive, each decision must be treated and documented separately. It may be appropriate to discuss a do not resuscitate (DNR) order with the patient or the designated surrogate while the patient is a candidate for palliative surgery or treatment in an intensive care unit.[49] In no case should the patient be denied nursing and basic supportive care by the clinicians on the care team. In contrast, the Baby K court ruling held that respiratory support for an anencephalic infant was "stabilizing care" within the meaning of federal law prohibiting patient "dumping." If such treatment was requested, the law did not allow an exception for comatose patients or medical conditions that could ultimately result in death.[50]

Since no national end-of-life standard exists, risk managers must be familiar with the laws related to end-of-life decision-making in their particular state. For example, New York has specific laws regarding DNR orders.[51] Within the parameters prescribed by law, dying patients and their families should be treated humanely and with dignity. Communication and documentation is vitally important at this time.

RESEARCH ON HUMAN SUBJECTS

Several new developments have potential for effectiveness in institutional review board (IRB) process and research oversight, and in appropriate ethical professional practice. The National Committee for Quality Assurance (NCQA) and the Department of Veterans Affairs (VA) have promulgated standards for the first external accreditation program to protect humans participating in research projects. NCQA will develop and administer the new program, which will apply to more than 120 VA medical centers conducting research with human participants and will set the standard for other federal agencies and private-sector organizations engaged in human research. Accreditation standards address six major areas:

- Institutional responsibilities for human research protection
- Structure and operation of the institutional review board
- IRB consideration of risks and benefits of research
- IRB consideration of recruitment and subject selection for participation in research
- IRB consideration of research-related risks to privacy and confidentiality
- IRB consideration of informed consent for research participants

This program is a response to the suspension of research programs at several universities and affiliated VA medical centers due to shortcomings found by federal oversight agencies.[72]

Eventually, new treatments have to be tested on humans, and these research subjects could be harmed as a result of the experimental therapy. In some cases, investigators have abused participants in their zeal to discover a miracle treatment. To protect the design of a clinical research study, researchers may discuss whether or not to treat subjects or to continue the protocol. Institutional review boards were created to resolve these considerations before the research begins.

Abuses during Research Studies

Scientific organizations such as the Institute of Medicine and the National Academy of Science identify three types of research behavior that must be challenged: "questionable research practices, misconduct in science, and other misconduct."[52] Leaders of these professional groups called for ethical standards to exceed legal mandates.

Whenever the subject of the abuse of human subjects by clinical researchers arises, the medical experiments of Nazi doctors during World War II come to mind. Retrospective investigation of the Nazi atrocities led to the Nuremberg Code and the Declaration of Helsinki, which endeavored to establish high moral standards for the conduct of research on human subjects. Although the abuses of Nazi Germany were outrageous to the extreme, other cases of obvious abuses of human subjects have occurred closer to home (see Box 7-9).

In the Tuskegee syphilis study, conducted by the U.S. Public Health Service from 1932 to 1972, research subjects were poor black sharecroppers in Macon County, Alabama: 399 men in the late stages of syphilis and 201 men who served as controls.[53] For 40 years, these men were studied, initially to observe the course of *undertreated* syphilis, and later of *untreated* syphilis, before and after the discovery of penicillin. This study was well known among physicians locally and was the subject of publications in major national professional journals during those years. Public outrage erupted in 1972 when an Associated Press reporter broke the story to the general public, using information from a whistle-blower who was a former public health worker. Subsequently, the Tuskegee study stimulated emotional public discourse and increased the scrutiny of clinical research involving human subjects in the United States. In the era of AIDS and

BOX 7-9

Mentally defective children at the Willowbrook School (NY) were fed an extract of stool from hepatitis B-infected individuals or were injected with the virus. This 1956–1972 study observed the natural course of the disease and the effectiveness of gamma globulin in treating it. Parents of the children were aware of the study but felt that they had to consent to have their children participate, since it was a prerequisite for admission to the only beds available at the institution.[54]

HIV disease, the Tuskegee study continues to have a legacy. Many individuals from minority communities are suspicious of clinical trials, with good reason. In 1997, President Bill Clinton finally apologized, on behalf of the United States government, to the victims of the Tuskegee syphilis study and their survivors.[55]

Both the Willowbrook and the Tuskegee studies were catalysts for reform in research on human subjects in the United States. A reform measure established the National Commission for the Protection of Human Subjects in the 1970s. This commission produced several volumes of guidelines, including *The Belmont Report*.[56] Another result of reform was the establishment of the Office for Protection from Research Risks, now known as the Office of Human Research Protection, at the National Institutes of Health.

Additional examples of abuse of human subjects in the United States were exposed by Henry Beecher in a landmark article in the *New England Journal of Medicine* in 1966.[54] Many of these studies had a high ratio of harm to benefit and were conducted without fully informed consent.

The discovery and study of possible abuses of human subjects continue, as evidenced by the recent deliberations of the White House Advisory Committee on Human Radiation Experiments concentrating on post-World War II abuses related to radiation exposure (see Box 7-10). Recently, several prominent institutions have come under scrutiny because of harm to research subjects or lack of attention to procedures to protect them (see Box 7-11).

Clinical Trials versus Treatment

Participation in clinical trials must be voluntary and lack of participation must not compromise basic health care. It is an unfortunate reality that participants in clinical trials often receive increased attention from health care providers because of the research design and the data collection methods. Blurring of distinctions between clinical research and treatment in the eyes of prospective participants is a particular consequence of the AIDS epidemic.[60] Early in the epidemic, people infected with HIV, and their advocates, were desperate for any ray of hope and any possible therapy. Since no accepted therapy was available, they demanded access to the few clinical trials showing any promise. This demand moved research goals from primarily protecting human subjects from harm to promoting maximum access to clinical treatment, while at the same time limiting the potential burden or harm and avoiding exposure to poorly designed research. These goals remain a significant challenge for IRBs.

BOX 7-10

Between 1944 and 1947, the U.S. government, fearing liability or embarrassment, deliberately hid several thousand human subject experiments involving plutonium, uranium, iodine-131, and zirconium injections, and testicular and total body irradiation.[58]

BOX 7-11

Jesse Gelsinger, 18 years old, had ornithine transcarbamylase deficiency. He was enrolled in a gene transfer experiment at the University of Pennsylvania Institute for Human Gene Therapy. Within hours after he was infused with trillions of particles of an adenovirus vector delivered by catheter to the liver, he suffered a chain reaction including jaundice, a coagulopathy, kidney failure, liver failure, and brain death. He died the same day.[59]

Institutional Review Boards

A vital institutional safeguard for human subjects in clinical research is the institutional review board, or IRB.[61] The first federal policy requiring review by an investigator's institutional colleagues was issued in 1966. Shortly thereafter, this policy was extended to cover all U.S. Public Health Service grants. In 1974, policies and guidelines were revised and issued as regulations by the Department of Health, Education and Welfare.[62] These guidelines required the IRB to consist of at least five people, including community representation from individuals not employed by the institution conducting the research. An IRB had to review the proposed research for its "legal, professional, and community acceptability."[56]

IRBs are active in all academic medical centers, community hospitals, and organizations involved with the conduct of medical research and clinical trials. With an interdisciplinary membership and representation from the community, IRBs are responsible for reviewing proposals for research involving human subjects, including both invasive and noninvasive studies which may involve patients and/or staff. IRBs are responsible for reviewing the research methodology for soundness and informed consent procedures to make sure that they are clear, understandable, and inclusive. Importantly, the IRB must consider the relative balance of risks and possible benefits to research participants. Studies involving human subjects should not be unduly harmful, and involvement must be voluntary (see Box 7-12). Involvement in a clinical trial must not be a prerequisite for basic health care. In addition, the IRB is responsible for continuous monitoring as the study progresses and for investigating adverse reactions (see Box 7-13).

BOX 7-12

A 24-year-old healthy woman died after inhaling hexamethonium as part of a clinical trial at the Johns Hopkins University asthma study. An inadequate consent from and lack of the specific protocol for permission from the hospital's IRB was cited, as well as failure to seek FDA approval prior to conducting the clinical trial.[63]

Several leaders in academic medicine have recommended guidelines to strengthen research institutions' policies for dealing with financial conflicts of interest that can arise from collaborations between faculty and industry. The Association of American Medical Colleges is reviewing these guidelines, which include requiring disclosure of financial interests to the IRB and requiring

BOX 7-13

- In 1993, R. R. Bard, Inc., one of the world's largest catheter producers, pleaded guilty to 391 charges of health care fraud for submitting false data to the FDA. Critics claim a defect caused some of the catheters to break, leading to at least one death and 22 emergency surgeries.[65]
- The inventor of a flawed medical device was also the product's lead investigator as well as the company CEO. Members of Boston Scientific's urological advisory board authored a paper saying that the (ProteGen) sling material was a "safe, biocompatible substance." Two of the research physicians had received combined compensation of approximately $320,000 from Boston Scientific.[65]
- Duke University is repaying $700,000 in federal grant money that was misspent by two former employees who have been accused of swindling a prominent researcher.[66]

disclosure of financial ties to anyone involved in research—faculty, students, and staff.[64]

ETHICS COMMITTEES

To assist in the resolution of complex ethical dilemmas, health care institutions have established ethics committees with roles, responsibilities, and authority explicitly delineated. In addition, organizations have examined the composition of these committees and the varied guidelines for selecting members. Furthermore, the relationship between risk managers and ethics committees had to be clarified.

Role, Responsibilities, and Authority

Most American hospitals have one or more ethics committees,[67] and the number is likely to increase as accrediting agencies such as JCAHO require attention to patients' rights and ethical issues during their institutional surveys. Utilization and effectiveness of an ethics committee varies greatly and may depend on and reflect its membership. If the ethics committee members are all upper-level administrators, for example, staff members, patients, and families of patients may be reluctant to ask the committee for assistance. On the other hand, the committee needs to have participants who demonstrate credibility at high levels in the health care institution.

The precursors of hospital ethics committees were the dialysis committees in the 1960s,[68] as well as the committees on abortion and sterilization that existed for decades in Catholic hospitals. When the Karen Ann Quinlan 1976 court decision[69] mentioned the use of the hospital's ethics committee, most hospitals did not have one. Ms. Quinlan happened to be a patient in a Catholic hospital in new Jersey that had an ethics committee to consider issues of abortion and sterilization.

As the field of bioethics has grown, the use of ethics committees to consider complex cases has become a stronger recommendation. Federal government recommendations appeared in the Baby Doe regulations,[31] and infant care review committees in neonatology have become common. Ethics committees vary in who they report to: hospital administration, the board of trustees, the medical board, or a specific clinical department.

Usually, ethics committees have three roles in health care institutions: education, policy development, and consultation. Ethics committees spend considerable time educating themselves, their hospital staff, patients, and the broader community served by the institution. This education includes knowledge of basic ethical principles, institutional policy relating to ethical and legal issues, and a basic understanding of the law as it applies to health-related issues in the particular geographical location.

Policy development related to ethical and/or legal issues also concerns ethics committees. For example, the committee might develop a specific policy to implement the federal Patient Self-Determination Act or a state Do Not Resuscitate law.

Many ethics committees assume a consultation role in difficult cases. Usually, the bylaws of ethics committees allow a case to be brought to the committee by a patient, the patient's family, the patient's physician or nurse, or anyone involved with the care of a patient. Often, the dilemma is resolved by simply gathering together all the involved individuals, including the patient or surrogate, and providing an objective, neutral committee or subcommittee to hear the concerns and to facilitate communication. Sometimes the best option for the patient is pinpointed; sometimes the least bad option is identified. This type of group deliberation may provide some comfort, especially if decisions are being made by a surrogate. However, the ethics committee's recommendations are advisory, not binding. In some situations, the patient's physician and / or the institution's administration is in the position of deciding whether to implement the committee's recommendations. Clinicians may decide that the recommendations violate their personal values, based on a conscience objection, and may request that another clinician be assigned to the care of the patient.

Composition of the Ethics Committee

There is no single model for an ethics committee. Committees can include physicians, nurses, social workers, allied health care professionals, ethicists, and at least one community member who is not an employee and can view things objectively from the perspective of patients and their families. Some committees include representatives of the clergy, the hospital attorney, the hospital risk manager, and administrative personnel. In any specific case discussion, appropriate individuals with expertise not represented on the committee can be brought in as necessary.

Clinical departments may choose to have their own ethics committees, in addition to a hospital-wide ethics committee. Departmental committees are most common in departments of nursing, but they may also be found in medicine, pediatrics, and obstetrics / gynecology. One of the most important and unique aspects of an ethics committee is its interdisciplinary nature. On the other hand, departments or professionals may feel more comfortable addressing issues within their own discipline, because they feel the problems are unique to their profession or department. This is a particularly common rationale for the existence of nursing ethics committees. Although these feelings are significant, there must be a communication link between departmental committees and the overall institutional ethics committee, since issues may overlap. In planning educational programs, it makes sense to pool resources and to plan complementary programs.

Relationship to Risk Management

Hospital risk managers are members of ethics committees in many institutions. Some committees include the hospital risk manager as an *ex officio* member without voting privileges. Critics contend that sitting on a committee whose primary role is to protect the patient and serve as an advocate for patients' rights is a conflict of interest for the hospital risk manager, who is responsible for protecting the institution. Putting the voting issue aside, an active communication link between risk management and the ethics committee is very appropriate. Cases that come to the ethics committee are, by definition, complicated. In cases brought before the ethics committee, there may be a need for the patient, patient's family, clinicians, and other members to understand the limits of the law and the hospital's perception of risk and liability—areas of a risk manager's expertise. A clinician may need to know if the hospital will support controversial decisions. Patients or family may also need to understand the hospital administration's position on a deliberation. In addition, when a case is brought to the attention of risk management, coexisting ethical issues may be identified. Thus, ethics committees and risk managers must work together.

ETHICS ARE NOT JUST VALUES

Although ethical behavior is not mandated by legislation, individuals do initiate lawsuits if they feel that health care providers made the wrong decisions.

Recent research studies have shown that there are disparities in how patients are recommended for various treatments. One study revealed that African Americans and women are treated with cardiac catheterization at lower rates than whites and men.[70] For a long time it was observed that African Americans are more likely to die of colon cancer than are white people. However, research at the Dana-Farber Cancer Institute has shown that when both African American and white colon cancer patients are given the same access to chemotherapy, the survival rates are exactly the same.[71] Disparity in the quality of treatment, and therefore in the differential outcomes, has ethical implications for professional practice approaches to patients as well as to medical diseases.

In the face of complicated and perplexing patient care dilemmas, no "right choice" may exist, and varied rationales can justify the deliberate decision. Within a cost containment milieu, health care providers encounter high-risk liability potentials embedded in ethical considerations. Fixed payment reimbursement schemes may promote "quicker and sicker" institutional discharges because money, not therapy principles, dictate early discharge. These cost-saving incentives can place health care professionals and institutions at risk when they violate professionally established ethical concerns about the patient-provider relationship.

As medical science quickly advances, expanded opportunities arise for the President's Council on Bioethics,[73] which provides advice on the complex and often competing moral positions associated with biomedical innovation. The Council includes 18 people: seven PhDs, six MDs, four lawyers, and two people with PhDs in philosophy. It is anticipated that the Council will exercise considerable influence in such areas as human cloning, human genomic research, genetic engineering and embryonic stem cell research, and eugenics. Research using embryonic stem cells[74] holds enormous promise for treating and curing disease. However, in order to get the cells, days-old human embryos must be destroyed, and this practice has stimulated much ethical debate.

Risk managers work to protect their institutions from legal liability. There are many complex situations in the provision of health care in which the application of legal guidelines to the particular patient situation is not clear. Institutional policies and guidelines promoting ethical decision-making are thus vitally important and necessary to render optimal patient care. A risk manager needs to be familiar with basic ethical principles, as well as the law applicable at all levels of government. In addition, extensive communication among health care providers, ethics committees, institutional representatives, patients, and/or surrogates fosters ethical decision-making and reduces legal liability for institutions. An ethics program in a health care institution is certainly more than just values and a good risk management strategy.

References

1. Gesensay, D. (1995). Who's responsible for the ethics in managed care? *ACP (American College of Physicians) Observer* 15(5):18.
2. Tenery, R. M., Jr. (1995). Ethical decisions may not always be politically correct. *American Medical News* 38(9):18.
3. Monagle, J. F., and Thomasma, D. C. (1995). *Medical Ethics: Policies, Protocols, Guidelines & Programs.* Frederick, Md.: Aspen.

4. The final autonomy (editorial). (1995). *Lancet* 349 (890):259.
5. Ahronheim, J. C., Moreno, J., and Zuckerman, C. (2000). *Ethics in Clinical Practice*, 2d edition. Gaithersberg, Md: Aspen, p. 1–98.
6. Schroeder-Mullen, H. (1995). Keeping up with advance directives. *Patient Care* 29(4):12.
7. Brock, D. (1994). Advance directives: What is reasonable to expect from them? *Journal of Clinical Ethics* 5:57–60.
8. Teno, J. M., Lynn, J., Phillips, R. S., et al. (1994). Do formal advance directives affect resuscitation decisions and the use of resources for seriously ill patients? *Journal of Clinical Ethics* 5:23–30.
9. Living, dying and the law (editorial). (1995). *New York Times* June 6, p. A14, col. 1.
10. Rivera, D. (1995). Seminar outlines patients' rights. *Suburban* (East Brunswick, N.J.), April 19, p. 51, col. 1.
11. Fletcher, J. C., and Spencer, E. M. (1995). Incompetent patient on the slippery slope. *Lancet* 345(8945): 271–272.
12. New York State Confidentiality Law and HIV Clinical Resource Public Health Law (Article 27-F). (2000). AIDS Institute and New York State Department of Health.
13. Kolata, G. (2002). Dilemma on prostate cancer treatment splits experts. *New York Times*, September 17, p. F5.
14. Fletcher, S. W., and Colditz, G. A. (2002). Failure of estrogen plus progestin therapy for prevention. *Journal of the American Medical Association* 288(3).
15. Office of Communication, National Cancer Institute, National Institutes of Health. (2002). *Increased Risk of Ovarian Cancer Is Linked to Estrogen Replacement Therapy* (News from the NCI). July 16.
16. *Canerbury v. Spence*, 464 F. 2d 772, 785 (D.C. Cir. 1972).
17. American Health Consultants. (2001). Just because a lawyer can't read consent forms doesn't mean that a patient can. *Health Risk Management* 23(3):3.
18. *C.W. v. Wasiek*, 63 U.S.L.W. 3494 (January 3, 1995).
19. Council on Ethical and Judicial Affairs. (2002–2003). *Code of Medical Ethics. Current Opinions with Annotations.* Chicago: American Medical Association.
20. Gen. 9:3–6; Acts 15:28–29; *Jehovah's Witnesses and the Question of Blood.* (1977). Pittsburgh: Watchtower Bible and Tract Society of Pennsylvania.
21. Dresser, R., and Whitehouse, P. J. (1994). Surrogate decision making rationales. *Hasting Center Report* 24(6):6–12.
22. New York Public Health Law. (1990). Health care proxy, 2980–2994.
23. Gesenway, D. (1995). Finding the right words. How to begin talking to your patients about the tough issue of advance directives. *ACP Observer* 15(5):19.
24. Omnibus Budget Reconciliation Act of 1990. *The Patient Self-determination Act.*
25. *Planned Parenthood v. Casey*, 112 S. Ct. 2791 (1992).
26. *Roe v. Wade*, 410 U.S. 113 (1973).
27. American Committee for Graduate Medical Education. (1995). *Residency Review Committee for Obstetrics and Gynecology.* Chicago: American Committee for Graduate Medical Education.
28. *In re A.C.*, 533 A. 2d 611 (App. D.C. 1989); *In re A.C.*, 573 A. 2d 1235 (App. D.C. 1990).
29. Duff, R., and Campbell, A. G. M. (1973). Moral and ethical dilemmas in the special-care nursery. *New England Journal of Medicine* 289(17):890–894.
30. Imperiled newborns (special supplement). (1987). *Hastings Center Report* 17(6):5–32.
31. 45 CFR 1340, DHHS Part IV. (1995). *Federal Register*. April 15.
32. Capron, A. M. (1994). Medical futility: Strike two. *Hastings Center Report* 24(5):42–43.
33. Leikin, S. L. (1992). Minors' assent or dissent to medical treatment. In *Making Health Care Decisions, vol. 3: Appendices Studies on the Foundation of Informed Consent*. Washington, D.C.: Government Printing Office, President's Commission for the Study of Ethical Problems in Medicine and Biomedical and Behavioral Research, pp. 175–192.
34. Parents overruled on girl's tumor cure. (1995). *Star-Ledger* (Newark, N.J.), July 30, p. 35, col. 1.
35. New York State Task Force on Life and the Law. (1992). *When Others Must Choose: Deciding for Patients without Capacity*. Albany: New York State Task Force on Life and the Law, p. 117.
36. Callahan, D. (1993). *The Troubled Dream of Life: In Search of a Peaceful Death.* New York: Simon & Schuster; Callahan, D. (1990). *What Kind of Life: The Limits of Medical Progress.* New York: Simon & Schuster; Callahan, D. (1987). *Setting Limits: Medical Goals in an Aging Society*. New York: Simon & Schuster.
37. Richardson, R., and Hurwitz, B. (1995). Donors' attitudes towards body donation for dissection. *Lancet* 349(8970):277–279.

38. Kolata, G. (1995). Families are barriers to many organ donations, study finds. *New York Times*, July 7, p. A13, col. 4.
39. Shelton, D. L. (2000). Living donor transplants raise ethical concerns. *American Medical News* 42(21):20:1.
40. AMA Council on Ethical and Judicial Affairs. (1995). The use of anencephalic neonates as organ donors. *Journal of the American Medical Association* 273(20):1614–1618; McCormick, B. (1995). Ethics forum launched. AMA council values input from doctors, patients. *American Medical News* 38(26):3, 21.
41. Kolata, G. (1995). Court ruling limits rights of patients. Care deemed futile may be withheld. *New York Times*, April 22, p. 18, col. 1; Mass. jury: Doctors were right to withdraw life support. (1995). *American Medical News* 38(18):10.
42. Zuckerman, C. (1995). The case of Catherine Gilgunn: The futility debate takes a new turn. *Precepts* 6(1)3–4; Capron, A. (1995). Abandoning a waning life. *Hastings Center Report* 25(4):24–26.
43. Study reveals continuing conflicts over end-of-life care. (1995). *American Medical News* 38(10):17.
44. Pellegrino, E. D. (1995). Ethics. *Journal of the American Medical Association* 273(21):1674–1675; Gesenway, D. (1995). Assisted suicide: It's the law in Oregon, but is it ethical? *ACP Observer* 15(1):12.
45. *State of Washington v. Glucksberg, Vacca v. Quill* No. 95–1858, and Supreme Court of the U.S. 521 US 793, 117 S. Ct. 2293 in same cases.
46. Moore, E. (1995). Doctor, nurse urge helping patients manage pain, not take their lives. *Star-Ledger* (Newark, N.J.), May 18, p. 31, col. 1.
47. Jury: Hospital right to end life support. (1995). *American Medical News* 38(18):10.
48. *Cruzan v. Director, Missouri Department of Health*, 110 S. Ct. 2841 (1990), 497 U.S. 262, 278 (1990).
49. Cassel, C. K. (1995). Finding the right words to talk about DNR. *ACP Observer* 15(7):11.
50. In *re Baby K*, 16 Fed. 590 (4th Cir 1994); Gostin, L. O. (1995). Law and medicine. *Journal of the American Medical Association* 273(21):1688–1689.
51. New York Public Health Law, Sec. 2961 (9) (McKinney Suppl., 1991).
52. Hilts, P. J. (1995). Scientists lament inaction on abuse. *New York Times*, February 5, p. 21, col. 1.
53. Jones, J. (1993). *Bad Blood*. New York: Free Press.
54. Beauchamp, T. L., and Childress, J. F. (1979). *Principles of Biomedical Ethics*. New York: Oxford University Press, pp. 276–277.
55. Remarks by the president in apology for study done in Tuskegee. (2000). In *Tuskegee's Truths: Rethinking the Tuskegee Syphilis Study*, edited by S. M. Reverby. Chapel Hill: University of North Carolina Press.
56. National Commission for the Protection of Human Subjects. (1978). Biomedical and Behavioral Research: The Belmont Report. Ethical Principles and Guidelines for the Protection of Human Subjects of Research. DHEW Publication No. (OS) 78-0012; Appendix I, DHEW Publication No. (OS) 78-0013; Appendix II, DHEW Publication (OS) 78-0014. Washington, D.C.: Government Pringing Office.
57. Beecher, H. K. (1966). Ethics and clinical research. *New England Journal of Medicine* 274(14):1354–1360.
58. Panel suggests apologies, payoffs for radiation test subjects. (1995). *Star-Ledger* (Newark, N.J.), July 18, p. 7. Fadden, R. R. (Ed.). Final Report of the Advisory Committee on Human Radiation Experiments.
59. Stephenson, J. (2001). Studies illuminate case of fatal reaction in gene-therapy trial. *Journal of the American Medical Association* 285(20).
60. Powderly, K., Cox, S., and Sonnabend, J. (1995). Ethics of HIV research in a primary care setting. Unpublished manuscript.
61. Levine, R. J. (1988). *Ethics and Regulation of Clinical Research*, 2d edition. New Haven: Yale University Press, pp. 70–71, 323–325.
62. 45 C.F.R. 46.
63. American Health Consultants. (2001). Consent form blamed in fatality at Johns Hopkins. *Healthcare Risk Management* 23(89).
64. American Health Consultants. (2001). Leading medical schools agree on new guidelines. *Healthcare Risk Management* 23(4):43.
65. *US News and World Report*. (2002). July, pp. 57–58.
66. Zernike, K. (2002). Duke repays $700,000 in grant money and reports a swindle. *New York Times*, August 21, p. A10.
67. Ross, J. W., Glaser, J. W., Rasinski-Gregory, D., et al. (1993). *Health Care Ethics Committees: The Next Generation*. Chicago: American Hospital Publishing.
68. Alexander, S. (1962). They decide who lives, who dies. *Life Magazine*, November 9:103.

69. *In re Quinlan*, 355 A. 2d 657 (N.J. 1976), cert. denied 429 U.S. 1992, 1976. *Star-Ledger* (Newark, N.J.) (1995).

70. Eisenberg, J. M. (2002). The Best Offense is a Good Defense Against Medical Errors: Putting the Full-Court Press on Medical Errors. Duke University Clinical Research Institute. January 20. *www.ahcpr.gov/news/spch012000.htm.*

71. Nagourney, E. (2002). Vital signs, disparities. Care: not biology. *New York Times*, August 13, p. F6.

72. NCQA, VA launch first ever accreditation program for Human Research Protection National Committee for Quality Assurance (NCQA). (2001). *NCQA News.* August 28.

73. Robeznicks, A. (2002). Council explores the ethics of biomedical innovations. *American Medical News* 45(19):13:1.

74. U.S. ruling clarifies stem cell research: Decision helps federally funded scientists. (2002). *Star-Ledger* (Newark, N.J.) August 8, p. 10.

CHAPTER 8 Assuring Safety and Security in Health Care Institutions

Florence Kavaler
Allen D. Spiegel

Ramifications of adverse safety and security incidents combine to create a serious threat to the financial well-being of any health care organization.

Exhibit 8-1 lists a meticulous, yet far from exhaustive, sampling of the occupational hazards present in a health care facility. Prepared by the National Institute for Occupational Safety Hazards (NIOSH),[1] the list is a strong reminder of the potential dangers existing in a health care facility. Risk managers must be aware of and address these potential liabilities every day. Furthermore, employers are required to inform employees of all potential dangers under the Occupational Safety and Health Administration's (OSHA) right-to-know policy. Conspicuously, stress is absent from the hazard list, since stress is reported by workers in all areas and cannot be listed in a single location.

Stress was formally categorized as a job hazard only recently. In 1986, NIOSH identified the following clinical disorders resulting from job stress: affective disturbances such as anxiety, depression, and job dissatisfaction; maladaptive behavior or lifestyle patterns; and chemical dependencies or alcohol abuse.[1] Furthermore, the most stressful job situations in any workplace occur in health care occupations: ranging from dealing with life-threatening injuries and illnesses to dealing with the demands of patients to dealing with the professional authority hierarchy. Isolation and depersonalization are not uncommon circumstances in large health care institutions with bureaucracies that frustrate employees. Employee burnout can result from an administrative failure to recognize the symptoms of workers who feel angry or powerless in such a demanding system.

EXHIBIT 8-1 A SAMPLING OF OCCUPATIONAL HAZARDS

LOCATION	HAZARD
Central supply	Ethylene oxide Infection Broken equipment Soap, detergents Steam Flammable gases Lifting Noise Asbestos insulation Mercury
Dental service	Mercury Ethylene oxide Anesthetic gases Ionizing radiation Infection
Dialysis unit	Infection Formaldehyde
Food service	Wet floors Sharp equipment Noise Disinfectants Ammonia Chlorine Solvents Drain cleaners Oven cleaners Caustic solutions Pesticides Ovens Steam lines Electrical hazards Lifting
House-keeping	Soaps, detergents Cleaners Solvents Disinfectants Glutaraldehyde Infection Needle punctures Wastes Electrical hazards Lifting Climbing Slips, falls
Laboratory	Infectious diseases Toxic chemicals Benzene Ethylene oxide Formaldehyde Solvents Flammable and explosive agents Carcinogens Teratogens Mutagens Cryogenic hazards Wastes Radiation
Laundry	Wet floors Lifting Noise Heat Burns Infection Needle punctures Detergents, soaps Bleaches Solvents Wastes
Maintenance and Engineering	Electrical hazards Tools, machinery Noise Welding fumes Asbestos Flammable liquids Solvents Mercury Pesticides Cleaners Ammonia Carbon monoxide Ethylene oxide Freons Paints, adhesives Water treatment chemicals Sewage Heat/Cold stress Falls Lifting Climbing Strains and Sprains
Nuclear medicine	Radionuclides Infection X-irradiation
Office areas and data processing	Video display terminals Air quality Body mechanics Chemicals Ozone
Operating rooms	Anesthetics Antiseptics Methyl methacrylate Compressed gases Sterilizing gases Infection Electrical Sharp instruments Lifting
Pathology	Infectious diseases Formaldehyde Glutaraldehyde Flammable substances Freons Solvents Phenols
Patient care	Lifting Pushing, pulling Slips, falls Standing for long periods Infectious diseases Needle punctures Toxic substances Chemotherapeutic agents Radiation Radioactive patients Electrical hazards
Pharmacy	Pharmaceuticals Antineoplastic agents Mercury Slips, falls
Print shops	Inks Solvents Noise Fire
Radiology	Radiation Infectious diseases Lifting Pushing, pulling

As far back as 1977, NIOSH[1] documented studies showing health care occupations among the job classifications with the highest rates for mental disorders. Additional research indicated that many health care providers had elevated proportional mortality ratios for suicide. A study of navy personnel emphasized that health care positions, such as hospital food service, should be considered among the high-stress occupations.[1]

INFECTION CONTROL

With the high frequency of needle-stick injuries each year, health care workers are concerned about contracting AIDS or hepatitis from the blood of patients. This life-threatening employee safety anxiety is spurred by mass media stories about health care workers who allegedly contracted disease from blood-borne pathogens.

OSHA regulations concerning needle-stick safety and protection from sharps exposures for health care professionals are described in Chapter 2. While several measures are taken by health care workers to minimize the risk of blood-borne and air-borne pathogens, especially tuberculosis, one of the most effective is the policy of using universal precautions.

Universal Precautions

Universal precautions effectively prevent contamination from all blood-borne pathogens, including HIV and hepatitis. Facilities should adopt universal precautions to reassure employees and to reduce the spread of infections. Importantly, the OSHA regulations concerning blood-borne pathogens require the implementation of a precautions program, put the responsibility for compliance on the facility, and impose heavy fines for failure to comply. In addition, hepatitis B vaccinations are required for all workers with the potential for on-the-job exposure. If a worker is exposed, there is a mandatory investigation of all exposures.

The adoption and use of universal precautions procedures is usually a formal policy and protocol for a health care facility. The precautions are:[2]

1. Wear gloves to prevent the exposure of skin and mucous membranes to potentially infectious materials, including blood.
2. Remove and discard gloves immediately after finishing a procedure; avoid touching anything another person might touch without gloves.
3. Make point-of-use disposal units widely available to prevent sharps injuries.
4. Use gowns and aprons to prevent the anticipated soiling of clothing by blood or body fluids.
5. Wash hands before and after any contact with patients.
6. Use goggles and masks in procedures involving splashes or droplets.

Common sense should make these safety measures second nature for workers. Yet, nosocomial infection is still a leading cause of morbidity and mortality throughout the world. The risk of transmission of pathogens from patient to patient via the hands of health care workers increases as invasive procedures and devices become more common.

In 1847, Ignaz Semmelweiss, a physician in Vienna, demonstrated that antibacterial methods for cleaning hands decreased infection and mortality in hospital wards. Although hand washing is the simplest and most effective prevention strategy, studies find that physicians, nurses, and ancillary workers do not always wash their hands between patient encounters.[3]

Infectious Waste Management Plan

Each health care organization, whether a hospital, ambulatory surgery center, or nursing home, should prepare an infectious waste management plan that:

- Defines and designates those wastes to be considered and handled as infectious material.
- Segregates infectious waste from non-infectious waste.
- Establishes packaging standards for waste disposal.
- Sets storage guidelines.
- Specifies disposal methods.
- Details contingency measures for emergency situations.
- Arranges for staff education.

Infectious wastes originate from various sources: from patients diagnosed with communicable diseases; from laboratory cultures and biologicals; from blood products; from disposables used in treatment in dialysis units; and from sharps and wastes from surgery and autopsies such as dressings, sponges, drapes, tubes, and rubber gloves. To prevent contamination, infectious wastes should be discarded in easily identifiable containers and plastic bags, usually red or orange colored (see Box 8-1). These containers should be able to endure rough handling, lengthy storage, bumpy transportation, and varied treatment prior to ultimate disposal.

Training in universal precautions as well as in infectious waste management are vital elements in a risk prevention program to protect staff, professionals, patients, and visitors from contamination.

BOX 8-1

A Jefferson Regional Medical Center (Pine Bluff, AR) worker was "running late" and reportedly dumped 40 bags of medical waste in a drainage ditch. This tainted waste included sponges and dressings.[4]

INDOOR AIR POLLUTION

Physical plants can affect the health of patients, visitors, and staff. Depending on the extent of services offered in a health care facility, indoor air pollution through contamination by biological or chemical pollutants can be a potential catastrophe. The importance of an inflow of outside air to avoid hazards must be recognized. A lack or blockage of air can produce a variety of ill effects on a building's occupants (see Box 8-2). Complaints are especially common in newer, energy-efficient buildings where windows are sealed shut and fresh air is scarce. The World Health Organization estimates that one out of three employees worldwide is working in a place that is making them sick. Such illnesses are costly in terms of decreased productivity and increased absenteeism.

Air quality deficiencies are often traced to inadequate ventilation resulting from the improper use and maintenance of heating, ventilation, and air conditioning systems. Biological contaminants such as bacteria, molds, pollen, and viruses can breed in stagnant water that has accumulated in ducts,

BOX 8-2

Sick building syndrome refers to a nonspecific cluster of symptoms such as dizziness, nausea, fatigue, and eye or throat irritation. Those afflicted experience a feeling of relief after leaving the premises.

Building-related sickness is any diagnosable illness, such as asthma, that is directly attributable to airborne contaminants in a building.[5]

humidifiers, and drain pipes, and in water that has collected in ceiling tiles, carpeting, or insulation. In addition, chemical contaminants from building materials may seep into the facility's system, and it is not always easy to pinpoint the source of the problems (see Box 8-3).

The outdoor air that enters a building can also be a source of indoor air pollution. Pollutants from motor vehicle exhaust (ambulances, cars in the garage), plumbing vents, and building exhaust (from bathrooms and kitchens) can enter the building through poorly located vents, windows, and other openings.[5]

When no cause seems to be readily identifiable, simple air testing often supplies the answer. For maintenance of optimal air quality, the American Society of Heating, Refrigeration, and Air Conditioning Engineers recommends the following levels: temperature 76°F; relative humidity 40%; air circulation less than 45 feet/minute; and carbon monoxide levels usually 250 to 300 parts per million. These readings should be monitored at regular intervals to quickly identify any problems.

Technological suggestions for achieving clean air include:[6]

1. High-performance filters to remove airborne particles.
2. Adsorbent beds for the removal of specific gaseous particles.
3. Ultraviolet light to kill biological contaminants.
4. Electric air cleaners and ion generators whose electric charges are capable of removing airborne particles.
5. Venting contaminant sources directly to the outdoors.

In operating rooms, employees may be harmed by exposure to nitrous oxide (N_2O). Risks include "decreased mental performance, hearing and visual ability, and manual dexterity, as well as reduced fertility, spontaneous abortion and possible neurological, renal and liver disease."[7] Scavenging systems to vent unused and exhaled gas may create a false sense of security. Control measures to reduce leakage of N_2O from the anesthesia delivery system, training of personnel in appropriate engineering maintenance procedures, protective gear, and monitoring of ventilation and concentrations of gas are advised and explained in the guidelines of the National Institute for Occupational Health and Safety.[8]

"Recreational use" of N_2O is extremely dangerous, but the gas has been subject to abuse because of its psychogenic effects (see Box 8-4). Numbness, loss of balance, and damage to the spinal cord are also attributed to abuse of this gas. Attention to access, storage, and daily accounting for usage will help deter pilferage and misuse.

In an effort to improve air quality and safety, regulatory standards are being imposed on hospital incinerators where medical waste has traditionally been burned. Emission regulations aim to enhance clean

BOX 8-3

An outbreak of Legionnaires' disease at St. Francis Hospital (Wilmington, DE) was blamed on the air conditioning cooling tower. DNA results from two of 23 people treated for the disease matched the strain of the tower's *legionella* bacteria.[4]

BOX 8-4

A housekeeping employee was found dead in the N_2O storage area at St. Margaret's Hospital (Pittsburgh, PA). His face was covered by a plastic mask with a tube leading to a tank. Cause of death was accidental asphyxia from N_2O inhalation.[7]

air for the community and to reduce the spread of pathogens and toxic smokestack emissions. Since compliance with the Environmental Protection Agency's mandates, as well as with state and local laws, is quite expensive, some facilities are hauling the waste to regional incinerators, if available, to avoid being fined.[9]

EMPLOYEE HEALTH INTERVENTION STRATEGIES

With the American population participating in a variety of wellness activities, it makes solid business sense for health care organizations to offer those programs on the job. Investigations conclude that the dollar investment is returned manyfold in the form of lower absenteeism and increased productivity.

Preplacement Physicals and Continuous Monitoring of Employee Health

Health care facilities need to accept responsibility for their workers. This begins with a preplacement physical examination and an occupational history for all new employees. Additionally, there should be periodic health appraisals for workers exposed to a hazardous environment, returning from an absence due to illness or injury, transferring to another department, or retiring. Medical examinations and confidential records need to be maintained in the health unit. In addition to the job orientation, health, safety, and environmental information, selective immunizations should be provided to all personnel on a continuing basis. Information should deal with safe work habits, the use of the occupational health unit for reporting injuries and illnesses, and the availability of employee assistance programs.

Health care facilities need to provide 24-hour medical, psychiatric, or consultative services for staff with counseling programs to handle general problems ranging from substance abuse to HIV infection[10] (see Chapter 3).

Workers' Compensation

If employee health is monitored, protected, and maintained, hazards are controlled, and injuries are avoided or minimized, then the institutional costs for workers' compensation will be much reduced. See Chapter 3 for a full discussion on workers' compensation.

EMERGENCY SITUATIONS

Advance planning for frequent or occasional emergency situations prevents individual or group injury, reduces the spread of contaminants to other people or geographic areas, and limits disability. Appropriate policies and procedures should be enacted and periodically reviewed by the committees that analyze incident reports and the results of concurrent investigations of each emergency.

Each emergency incident, whether fire, spillage, chemical, radiological, or biological, can be handled in a distinct manner with a quick application of absorbent material, use of emergency showers, and isolation of the contaminated areas (see Box 8-5).

FIRE PREVENTION

Fire prevention and disaster plans are critical to the safety of personnel and to liability loss reduction efforts. A meaningful and efficient way to improve safety precautions is to learn from the mistakes of others, particularly when the adverse event is a similar occurrence (see Box 8-6).

BOX 8-5

- A Yale University scientist was accidentally infected when a vial containing the rodent-borne Sabia virus broke in the centrifuge. This virus causes the linings of blood vessels to leak, resulting in massive hemorrhaging. After the scientist was effectively treated, 80 people who had contact with him were closely monitored for three weeks.[4]
- In a Rutgers University (New Jersey) laboratory, a technician inadvertently mopped her forehead with a gloved hand containing trace amounts of phosphorous 32, a radioactive material. A hazardous material team was called, and she underwent a water washdown and returned to work.[11]

The span of time between the two tragedies described in Box 8-6 is about 82 years! However, many organizations today still engage in the same dangerous patterns of blocked exits, inadequate fire detection, and limited fire suppression systems. These deficiencies create an environment of fear and panic when a fire endangers life and limb. Everybody in the health care organization must be involved with the fire control plan, which should include specific policies and procedures to be followed, the assignment of duties to specified personnel, and periodic drills on all shifts (see Box 8-7).

An understanding of prevention, the use of fire fighting equipment, evacuation procedures, and control and containment techniques helps minimize the extension of fires; limit staff, patient, and visitor injury; restrict property damage; and decrease income loss and liability (see Box 8-8). Basic fire prevention steps are represented by the acronym RACE:

Rescue and remove anyone in immediate danger.

Alarm everyone by activating the nearest fire alarm box.

Confine and contain the fire and smoke by closing all doors and windows.

Extinguish the fire with a portable extinguisher, wet sheets, or blankets.

Employees of the facility's management and administrative departments usually are members of the fire safety committees: the fire control team, or fire brigade; the rescue operations team; or the utilities repair team. The duties of these committees are:

BOX 8-6

- In 1911, a raging fire at the Triangle Shirtwaist Company (New York City) claimed the lives of 146 garment workers. Locked exit doors on the eighth and ninth floors forced frightened employees onto the fire escape, which collapsed, sending them plunging to their deaths.
- In 1993, a fire at the Imperial Foods processing plant (Hamlet, NC) caused 24 workers to perish in flames because exit doors were padlocked to prevent employees from stealing chickens. Shortly thereafter, the owner of Imperial Foods was indicted on 24 counts of manslaughter.[12]

BOX 8-7

A 20-month-old baby girl, Terri-Anne Jones, was killed in a fire at a hotel. A court declared the hotel management guilty of unlawful killing. This verdict shows a shift of emphasis, to recognizing inadequate fire safety as the cause of the girl's death.[13]

BOX 8-8

- Four patients were killed and five other patients suffered smoke inhalation in a fire at Southside Regional Medical Center (Petersburg, VA). Investigators believe that the fire was caused by a patient who was smoking in his room. He burned to death, and four others died from smoke inhalation.[14]
- An accidental fire ignited by a patient who was carelessly smoking in bed damaged a room and burned the mattress in the detoxification wing of Bayley Seton Hospital (Staten Island, NY). No patients were injured, but one firefighter received minor injuries.[15]
- A storage room full of diapers caught fire in the newborn unit at Tampa General Hospital (FL). This blaze did not spread but caused the evacuation of 46 hospital employees and patients and closed seven floors while the air was monitored for problems.[16]

Fire control team or fire brigade: initial response and participation in fire control for fires that occur at the facility.

Rescue operations team: rescue and evacuation of all persons trapped in hazardous locations, either before or after an emergency situation.

Utilities repair team: repair and restoration of communication and utility services at the facility.

Teams are flexible in the functions they perform and may be dispatched to execute other significant duties. Primarily, each team protects life and property and extinguishes fires, where possible. Community fire control assistance must also be invoked from the local fire department and is usually directly contacted through the facility's alarm systems.

EMERGENCY PREPAREDNESS AND DISASTER PLANNING

After the April 19, 1995, bombing of the federal office building in Oklahoma City, the local medical community proved it could withstand the challenge presented by what was then the worst domestic disaster in U.S. history (more than 160 people were killed).[17] Physicians and nurses rushed to help the victims minutes after the blast. That incident illustrates the fact that a health care facility needs to be prepared for the chaos of an outside disaster, as well as for any catastrophe arising within its doors. Assuming that injured people are transported to the nearest treatment facilities, any event resulting in a large number of casualties in a single facility's vicinity can be considered a disaster.[18] Primarily, a facility needs to be prepared to handle any situation within its geographic range to prevent additional harm to the community and to minimize the loss and suffering of victims.

The attacks on the World Trade Center in New York City and the Pentagon in Washington, D.C., on September 11, 2001, along with the following anthrax incidents in Florida, New York, New Jersey, Washington, D.C., and Connecticut, have heightened the emphasis on hospital and community disaster preparedness. Hospitals in the vicinity of the September 11 attacks were immediately deluged with both the injured and the worried well, who were fleeing the smoke-choked and debris-laden streets. While New York experienced power outages and disabled communications, health care institutions in New York and Washington, D.C. and their vicinities immediately activated their disaster plans—anticipating mass casualties instead of mortalities. However, these institutions were less prepared in resources and infrastructure for confronting a weaponized biologic agent, such as anthrax or smallpox.[19]

It is imperative that each health care institution identify and evaluate the risk potential of various hazards, along with the probability of their occurrence and how well prepared the institutions are to respond to such incidents (see Exhibit 8-2). There are two types of emergencies, internal and external, and both require coordination within the institution and in the community, at the local, state, and federal levels, for maximum reduction in harm to patients, employees, and the community. The Joint Commission on Accreditation of Healthcare Organizations has promulgated standards for emergency management and promoted the "hazard vulnerability assessment tool," which is published on the web site of the American Society for Healthcare Engineering (*www.ashe.org*).[20] In addition, the American Hospital Association has developed guidelines for bioterrorism readiness plans, including a self-administered bioterrorism survey and a checklist prepared by the Association for Professionals in Infection Control and Epidemiology.[21]

New emphasis on possible terrorist attacks has heightened the need to recognize the threat of bioterrorism and its related health impact. Health practitioners have become more aware of potential threats of the use of biologic agents. In the 1980s, Oregon experienced a rash of salmonella-contaminated salad bars, which sickened 751 people and was attributed to members of the Rajneesh cult. Members of the cult were found to have a bathtub filled with flasks of clostridium botulinum, which was used to poison the salad bars. In the 1990s, Japan's Aum Shinryko cult planned to use anthrax and botulinum toxin. When they were unsuccessful, however, they released sarin nerve gas in the Tokyo subway system. More recently in the United States, the mailing of letters containing anthrax has caused major concern. Similarly, it is feared that smallpox will potentially be used as a terrorist weapon. Questions arise as to whether to vaccinate and immunize all U.S. citizens, or only health care professionals, who will be at the earliest risk of exposure to infected patients.

Risk managers should review these issues with the administration at their institutions, and discuss appropriate internal policies and procedures for diagnosis, treatment, isolation, and use of universal precautions.

Ultimately, the nature, scope, and location of the disaster determine a health care facility's role in treatment, since these factors determine the response and plan of action. A facility must be prepared for a sudden influx not only of patients, but also of visitors and mass media representatives. Since these demanding scenarios tax the entire institution, all departments should restrict third-party visits until after the event. Having areas that are designated for members of the media helps avoid chaos and prohibits unwanted persons in treatment rooms. These measures alleviate excessive strain on a security team occupied with hazards from traffic control, freeing up elevators, and restoring telephone lines. Perioidc disaster drills using simulated patients, visitors, and media provide practice, generate reports for safety committee review, and satisfy government regulation authorities. Exhibit 8-2 illustrates the scope of internal and external disasters.[20]

SAFE ENVIRONMENT

Safety is one area where even a health care business continuously accommodates the

EXHIBIT 8-2 POSSIBLE THREATS TO INSTITUTIONS

Security
- Bomb threat
- Civil disturbance
- Gang-related activity
- Hostage situation
- Infant abduction
- Location in high-crime area
- Terrorist attack, including nuclear, biological, chemical, and explosive threats (internal or external)
- Visiting or injured VIP
- Workplace violence

Utility Failures
- Central medical vacuum
- Central oxygen
- Electrical power
- Emergency generator
- Fire suppression/alarm system
- Heating, ventilating, and air-conditioning (HVAC)
- Information system/computers
- Natural gas
- Overhead paging
- Security system
- Sewage
- Telephone/telecommunications
- Water main break

Weather
- Snowstorm
- Earthquake
- Hail
- High winds
- Hurricane
- Ice storm
- Severe cold
- Severe heat/humidity
- Severe rainfall/flood
- Sinkholes
- Tornado

Structural Implications
- Airplane, bus, or automobile crash into the facility
- Chemical or hazmat spill or release (internal)
- Explosion (internal)
- Fire and smoke (internal)
- Flooding (internal)
- Gas leak (internal)
- Other structural damage to the building

Other
- Airplane, bus, or train crash in the community
- Chemical or hazmat spill or release (external)
- Explosion (external)
- Fire and smoke (external)
- Flooding (external)
- Gas leak (external)
- Other mass casualty incident (including domestic war)

public's expectations for corporate responsibility. Health care facilities need to view themselves as equivalent to major industrial sites or plants when it comes to safety considerations. Unfortunately, "major industrial accidents are just as likely to occur today as they were ten years ago."[22] An effective safety program is concerned with the health and well-being of all employees, professional staff, patients, and visitors. Developing a successful safety program means:[23]

1. Designing programs to cover all potential hazards and to address regulatory requirements.

2. Assigning roles and responsibilities to all staff members.
3. Implementing management processes to develop and maintain policies, procedures, and standards.
4. Being willing to provide appropriate resources such as specialists for advice, specialized equipment, a well-trained workforce, and documentation on proper protocol.

In the event of an unfortunate accident (for example, see Box 8-9), the adverse incident should be investigated and reported to ensure that the injured are properly cared for and restored to full health.

Facility Safety Plan

With the rapidly rising cost of rendering health care, the public focuses its attention on all aspects of the care delivery system. Generally, facility safety and security planning can be viewed as lowering the cost of health care. It should not be difficult for management to decide between increased expenditures to improve safety now or tragic deaths and possible criminal charges later.

BOX 8-9

- A 75-year-old St. Vincent's Medical Center (NY) patient was found dead on the roof of a building. A state Health Department investigation discovered that he had wandered from his room and had fallen out of a window. Authorities cited the hospital for "failing to provide a safe environment."[24]
- A brain-damaged patient, Mr. O'Neil, was burned to death in scalding water that exceeded 160°F. Apparently the hospital maintenance staff, after making a plumbing repair, had failed to check the temperature of the water going into the building.[25]
- An 82-year-old patient died after he was jolted off a gurney when an elevator dropped between floors at the Gouveneur Skilled Nursing Center (NY). As the doors opened, the patient fell and hit his head, suffering "internal multiple trauma."[23]

Risk prevention measures to reduce these liability trends can improve a facility's fiscal standing. Traditionally, safety teams consisting of members from the clinical, ancillary, and administrative departments have addressed risk issues, focusing on improve education and convenience for staff in all risk areas. A simple facilitywide approach serves as the primary intervention strategy to reduce the rising operational costs for a health care facility. Comprehensive facility-wide safety programs should be developed, implemented, monitored, and supported by the administration. The main purpose of the safety program is to reduce losses from occupation-related injuries and illnesses, as well as from harm or property damage affecting patients, visitors, and other professional staff.

Multidisciplinary committee membership should include representation from administration, professional staff, and faculty departments. Additional members to include are the risk manager, quality assessment director, and hospital engineer. A facility safety officer should chair the committee and provide leadership for the organization's safety plan. Many large institutions have subcommittees with specialists and technical staff that are concerned with environmental safety, radiation control, and the health of patients and employees.

Policies and procedures should be developed with the cooperation of the safety committee and the various institutional departments. Essential components in creating the facility safety plan must conform to mandatory government regulations, to voluntary JCAHO standards on life safety, to the standards of other accrediting bodies, to advisories of the National Council on Radiation Protection, and to the National Fire Protection Association's Life Safety Code®.

Reports to the administration and board of trustees should indicate trends and areas of concern to address incidents, infection control, and life safety programs. Full commitment by management is the first step toward successful implementation; the message and example will quickly filter down to every individual. Managers must go beyond legal requirements or appearance concerns.[36] New OSHA rules passed in 1995 can levy fines up to $70,000 per citation. However, even without the threat of OSHA violations, "It's better to spend money . . . on preventing injuries than paying for the injuries themselves."[27,28,29]

Security and Health Care Organizations

Concomitant with the increasing incidence of violent crime and surging litigation costs, a new health care environment is emerging.[30] Despite the dangers, the risk manager is constantly confronted with balancing frugality against the option of even tighter security. How can requirements of the health care facilities be met without compromising the needs of the individuals directly affected? Security plans involve viewing the facility security force as a profit-preserving center with an impact on every department. Adequate security measures can directly affect the facility's fiscal health by protecting existing assets and reducing future losses. Security departments must provide the following services: protection of life and property; prevention and detection of crime; apprehension of offenders; assistance to those who use the facility; and the perception of a safe environment, including visible functions such as keeping the peace, directing and arresting criminals, controlling facility access, directing vehicle traffic, responding to fire alarms, conducting criminal investigations, and maintaining a liaison with local law enforcement agencies.

VIOLENCE ON THE JOB

Considering violent and abusive behavior of patients, visitors, or staff to be "part of the job" is no longer acceptable, nor is it safe, as facilities find themselves confronted with more and more dangerous situations every day.

Although not on the occupational hazard list, violence is a significant concern for health care workers and risk managers alike.[31,32] In an American Management Association survey,[33] about 52 percent of human resources managers reported at least one violent incident involving their companies since 1990. Of the 100 private company managers questioned, more than 30 percent reported multiple occurrences. According to the Bureau of Labor Statistics, 1,063 (17%) of the 6,271 fatal occupational injuries in 1993 were the result of homicides.[34] While health care providers were not among the occupations with the greatest incidence of homicides, they are regarded as a group at an ever-increasing risk for work-related injuries.

As official standards and requirements for policy and legislation are developed to combat this disturbing trend, the importance of the OSHA terminology is apparent. OSHA defines "occupational injury" as:

> . . . an injury which results in death, lost work days, loss of consciousness, restriction of work or motion, termination of employment, transfer to another job, or medical treatment after first aid.[32]

Risk factors detailed in a NIOSH alert on security included: an exchange of money with the public; working alone; late night or early morning hours; valuable property on the premises; and especially community settings in high-crime areas.[34] These risk factors apply particularly to health care institutions that are open 24 hours a day, have employees working alone, have valuable property on the premises, and have locations in dense population settings.

Exhibit 8-3 details the results of the International Association for Healthcare Security and Safety (IAHSS) 10-year crime survey,[35] which included about 250 hospitals from the United States and Canada. This survey is considered to be the best indicator of health care crime available. On their own, the number of incidents and the amount of money in personal and corporate losses are alarming. Of all the possible victims in these hospitals, employees are most affected, specifically in their own work area. Crime is all around the institution and may be committed by fellow employees. In addition, with the decreased length of stay in hospitals and more patients in home health care, there are new risks of potential violence to hospital employees and community health workers.[36]

EXHIBIT 8-3

IAHSS Crime Survey: 10-Year Average Rate Per Hospital 1991–2000[35]	
Murder	0.02
Suicide	0.12
Rape	0.02
Other sexual assaults	0.18
Robbery	0.65
Aggravated assault	0.84
Simple assault	5.40
Larceny theft	53.45
Motor vehicle theft	0.12
Vandalism	10.63

Vulnerability to Violence

Recent data indicate that hospital workers are at high risk for experiencing violence in the workplace. According to estimates of the Bureau of Labor Statistics, 2,637 non-fatal assaults on hospital workers occurred in 1999—a rate of 8.3 assaults per 10,000 workers. This rate is much higher than the rate of non-fatal assaults for all private-sector industries, which is two per 10,000 workers.[80]

Nurses suffer the largest number (and consequently, the highest rate) of non-fatal workplace assaults. Health care patients are the source of more than half of the non-fatal workplace assaults, and former co-workers account for eight percent of the attacks.[80] Such acts of violence in the workplace include threats, physical assaults (rape, homicide, and use of weapons), and muggings.

The potential for violence is a growing concern in all health care facilities. Violent acts may be perpetrated by visitors, patients, employees, or outsiders. Several studies indicate that violence often takes place during times of high activity and interaction with patients, such as at meal times and during visiting hours and patient transportation. Assaults may occur when service is denied, when a patient is involuntarily admitted, or when a health care worker attempts to set limits on eating, drinking, or tobacco or alcohol use. Workplace-related violence as an occupational hazard occurs more frequently in psychiatric areas, emergency rooms, and waiting rooms, and is often precipitated by long waits for services, overcrowded and uncomfortable waiting rooms, patients under the influence of drugs or alcohol, inadequate security, access to firearms, poorly lit corridors, parking lots, and unrestricted movement of the public. Hospital policies such as the open door for visitors aim to project the image that the facility is friendly and homelike. This policy translates into freer access for the public, including criminals, to blend easily into the environment.

Violence prevention plans for increased awareness of potential situations and the procedures and protocols to effectively diffuse, reduce, and control patients and staff in these circumstances is a valuable effort in risk management.[38] Training for all employees should encompass recognizing assaults, resolving conflicts, and maintaining hazard awareness.

Parking Areas Are High Risk

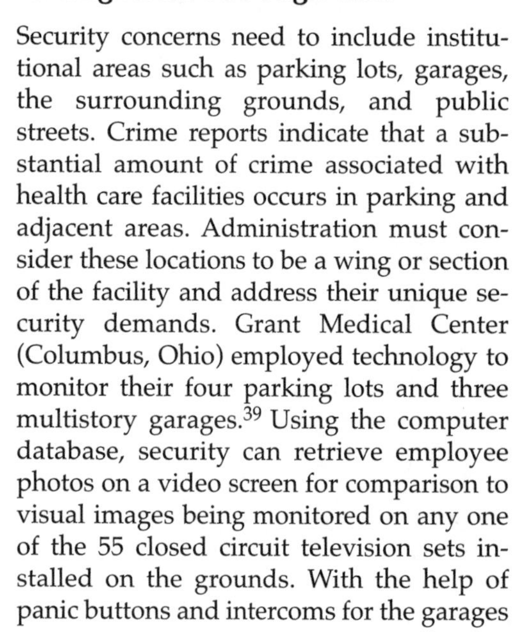

Security concerns need to include institutional areas such as parking lots, garages, the surrounding grounds, and public streets. Crime reports indicate that a substantial amount of crime associated with health care facilities occurs in parking and adjacent areas. Administration must consider these locations to be a wing or section of the facility and address their unique security demands. Grant Medical Center (Columbus, Ohio) employed technology to monitor their four parking lots and three multistory garages.[39] Using the computer database, security can retrieve employee photos on a video screen for comparison to visual images being monitored on any one of the 55 closed circuit television sets installed on the grounds. With the help of panic buttons and intercoms for the garages and parking lots, the facility's security forces can determine the source and extent of any problem that may arise. Children's National Medical Center (Washington, D.C.) went even further in its efforts to fight crime:[40] to bolster the efforts of regular security patrols, pan and tilt cameras and passive infrared motion detectors were installed in the parking structures and in sensitive hospital locations.

Access cards (for staff) and access control gates (for staff and visitors) are recommended safety measures. Employees and visitors have a right to expect that security cameras are being monitored and that there will be a quick response to any incident.[41]

Approaches to Violence

Naturally, emergency rooms are the first to encounter the spillover from any increased violence on the streets. With more than half of the reported violent incidents taking place in the ER, studies have estimated that as many as 10 percent of all patients seen there could be classified as violent.[46]

Waiting time is a primary instigator of violent acts. Frequently, certain behavior while waiting is a telltale sign warning of a violent patient. Clues include how the patient was injured, hints of agitation or anger, apparent stress, and circumstances involving family and friends.[42] Medical residents in emergency medicine in 13 programs in California were "worried about their own safety" (62%) and believed that their hospital program did not provide adequate safety (50%). In addition, these respondents were overwhelmingly in favor of some form of gun control.[43]

Another study concluded that more than 20 percent of violent episodes in hospitals were instigated by nonpatients. Nonpatients should be kept out of the treatment area. Moreover, if they appear disruptive, they should be asked to leave and/or be escorted out of the waiting area. Periodically, staff can interact with family and friends in the waiting area to update them and to answer nonmedical questions.

The number of weapons confiscated from patients has grown as more and more people have begun carrying weapons to protect themselves. "Few people intend to use weapons when they seek medical treatment at emergency departments, but patients and visitors in the ED are often in a highly volatile emotional state."[44]

Although weapon screening is an approach toward the potentially violent patient, it is not always the most effective. Besides furniture, objects commonly used as weapons include writing instruments and eating utensils. Providers need to survey their environments to eliminate as many unnecessary items as possible. To make security and safety procedures unique and applicable to the facility, there has to be an individualized response to the situation. Guidelines[45] for a safer working environment recommended for the emergency department include:

Alarm systems or panic buttons installed at nurses' stations, triage stations, registration areas, hallways, and lounge areas with 24-hour monitoring and a telephone link to the local police department

Metal detection systems installed at all ER entrances.

Seclusion or security rooms designated for confused or aggressive patients.

Bullet resistant glass for protection in triage, admitting, or other reception areas.

Strictly enforced limited access to ER areas enforced by key or code locks.

Closed circuit television monitors to survey concealed areas.

Intervening with Violent Patients

Effective communication strategies[42] facilitate the defusing of a potentially explosive confrontation with violent patients. Calling a patient by name and explaining the reason for a delay or other problems are considerate steps and demonstrate that the facility respects and cares about its patients. While patients have a right to treatment, however, health care workers have a legal right to a safe workplace (see Box 8-10). Reasonable force can be used against patients if necessary to prevent harm or injury to themselves or to others.

BOX 8-10

- After a "verbal dispute" with a hospital attendant at Montefiore Hospital (Bronx, NY), a 66-year-old inpatient being treated for seizures stabbed the attendant with a four-inch-blade folding knife. When the dietician tried to subdue the patient, he stabbed her over her left breast. Both victims were not seriously injured.[46]
- Daniel Alvarez, a murderer being detained as criminally insane, escaped from the Kingsboro State Psychiatric Center (Brooklyn, NY). He returned early the next day and fatally stabbed another patient in the chest with a knife he had apparently obtained while free.[47]
- A discharged airman returned to the Fairchild Air Force Base Hospital (Spokane, WA) with an assault rifle and shot to death his former psychiatrist and psychologist in the hospital annex. He randomly killed two others and wounded 23 patients and staff before being killed by a security patrolman.[48]

The State University of New York Health Science Center at Brooklyn (New York) uses a team approach toward agitated or violent patients in need of control for their own safety or the safety of others. Psychiatric nursing staff and public safety department staff meet and jointly train in appropriate methods of restraint of patients, when necessary, in the psychiatric unit. Policies and procedures have evolved concerning the administrative control of each situation, the physical control of the patient, and the roles of the nurse and safety officer. The staff agreed on prescribed methods of restraint, as well as the team leadership at each stage: medication, protective devices, and physical control. Clues drawn from many sources identify specific populations as violence predictors:

- Adolescent males
- System abusers
- Homeless persons
- Individuals with dementia
- Members of gangs (indicated by tattoos, etc.)
- Individuals traumatized by a recent conflict
- Previously violent individuals

OSHA recommends[49] several educational resources that employers can integrate into their violence prevention programs. One example is the video training program offered by the National Crisis Prevention Institute (Wisconsin). This self-teaching program allows employers to practice safe strategies for de-escalating potentially violent situations.

PROTECTING PATIENT VALUABLES

Patients are usually admonished to leave valuable personal items of jewelry, clothing, and electronic devices such as radios, cassettes, and CD players at home. Despite the warning, many patients bring valuables into the hospital or other facility when admitted. Usually, the loss of patient valuables is blamed on aides and housekeeping staff. Although the dollar value for replacement is usually comparatively small, the inconvenience, sentimental value, and fears generated are high. Reports of such losses to security and risk management personnel result in an investigation, but the stolen items are rarely recovered. Analyzing the data on such incidents to identify trends in location in the facility and shift may help uncover perpetrators. Payments on these claims are within the realm of "petty cash." In these cases, facilities may choose not to invoke their insurance carriers and have options of settling or ignoring these claims.

Documentation of all items belonging to a patient should be detailed, using objective language to describe jewelry, money, dentures, eyeglasses or contacts, hearing aids, prostheses, and clothing (see Box 8-11). Receipts for valuables to be stored in the institution's safe should be noted on the medical chart, as well as in conversations concerning potentially unprotected items to be kept in the room.[50]

BOX 8-11

A woman was admitted to Santa Barbara (CA) Cottage Hospital through the ER because of injuries sustained in an automobile accident. Her valuables disappeared from a bag that also held her clothing. Missing jewelry items included heirloom-quality diamond earrings, a solid gold dolphin bracelet, a diamond and ruby locket, five strands of pearls, a Cartier watch, and other bracelets. If the $100,000–$250,000 valuation can be documented, the hospital will reimburse the value of the jewels.[51]

Patients should be involved in security measures to create a true team effort with a win-win outcome. Encouraging patients to take steps to protect themselves is a preventive measure that benefits both provider and patient. Upon admission, all patients should be given tips and helpful advice.

Patients who wish to protect their valuables should follow these guidelines:

1. Leave valuables and credit cards at home. Anything important should be kept in the hospital safe with a detailed receipt issued to the patient.
2. Make sure any staff in your room is wearing photo identification.
3. Leave your room only if a trusted person is present, if possible.
4. Do not trust other people with valuables or children.
5. Do not get involved in any incidents, particularly in the ER.
6. Make arrangements to have a relative or friend with you in the recovery room after surgery.
7. Use the hospital patients' rights advocate staff to address any concerns or needs.
8. Know and exercise your rights as a patient.

CRIMINAL BEHAVIOR

As hospitals and other health care facilities improve their images by making visiting hours and access less restrictive, more criminal miscreants from the local community enter the premises for unauthorized and unwanted activities. Box 8-12 illustrates the problem.

BOX 8-12

- Dr. Kathyrn Hinnant, a 33-year-old pregnant pathologist, was accosted in Bellevue Hospital (NY) by Steven Smith, a homeless person surreptitiously living in the facility. He raped her and then strangled her.[52]
- As a mother was leaving San Francisco (CA) General Hospital with her two-day-old newborn, a woman she had met during her hospital stay told her that the nurses wanted to reexamine the baby. She left the infant with the woman and went home. Two hours later she telephoned the hospital, and nobody knew where her baby was. Police located the abductor, charged her with kidnapping and child endangerment, and returned the child to the mother.[53]
- A 43-year-old man angered by his mother's death stormed into a hospital and opened fire. He wanted to kill several nurses who he claimed had neglected his mother, but shot other staff members—a pharmacist, maintenance director, and nursing assistant—because they were in the way.[54]
- A 51-year-old woman shot her 75-year-old father to death at Mercy Anderson Hospital in Cincinnati, Ohio, where he was being treated for prostate cancer. This was not considered a "mercy killing," since his disease was not terminal.[55]
- A 26-year-old patient in Gadsden, Alabama was shot by his mother following a domestic dispute in the hospital's locked psychiatric ward, which she had entered for a visit.[56]

Statistics from the National Traumatic Occupational Fatalities Surveillance System revealed that homicides accounted for 20.3 percent of the deaths sustained by health care workers from 1980 through 1990.[33] Of the 106 deaths reported, the greatest number of homicides were among pharmacists (27) followed by physicians (26), registered nurses (18), nurses' aides (17), and other health care workers (18). Firearms, as weapons, contributed to 78 (73.6%) of the health care worker homicides, as compared to about 60 percent for all homicides in the United States. Pharmacists in community pharmacies are at greatest risk, because of the availability of controlled substances as well as of cash. There is an ever-present danger from desperate illicit drug and substance abusers needing both.

It is not always easy to identify people who have unauthorized weapons or who will use knives or instruments for evil purposes. However, every time a weapon is confiscated, an incident report should be filed with the risk manager. This process allows the administration to analyze developing trends before deciding on a risk intervention strategy. Although a reduction in the number of weapons on the premises is a prudent first step, efforts need to be directed toward eliminating all types of confrontation, with or without weapons.

Employee Criminality

Criminal acts in health care facilities are not always perpetrated by outsiders. There is a danger in overlooking another source of crime in health care facilities–employees. Police reports indicate that thefts by employees occur in 76 percent of hospitals nationwide, by far the most common crime by an insider. Budget considerations may curtail an adequate background check as facilities increasingly depend on temporary employment agencies for employees. The turnover rate of hospital employees is now the highest it's ever been. Any attempt to check the backgrounds of such a transient population is basically very difficult. People cross state and country borders and even change their names. Addicts may even apply for hospital jobs to gain easier access to drugs. American Hospital Association reports indicate that nine out of 10 hospital workers who abuse drugs steal them from the hospital where they work.[52]

As a risk, employee theft and embezzlement at health care facilities are often overlooked (see Box 8-13). Prime targets for theft, such as pharmacies or patient rooms, necessitate procedures to prevent criminal actions and to protect individuals.[60]

Criminals are becoming more creative and innovative. Techniques have evolved far beyond the simple stealing of wallets or petty cash. Employers need to be on the alert for forged checks, padded payrolls, the creation of fictitious employees, and varied unique diversions of funds. Reference checks, verification of school attendance, and proof of degrees received help ascertain an applicant's trustworthiness. An operating system of checks and balances needs to be in place to safeguard a facility's assets and to safeguard the financial well-being of

BOX 8-13

- A Veterans Administration (Brooklyn, NY) pharmacy technician, Bruce Weiss, was sentenced to one year in prison plus three years of probation for stealing $60,000 worth of pharmaceuticals to sell to a private pharmacy for resale.[57]
- A radiology technologist at Georgetown University Hospital was observed by a nurse siphoning painkillers from a patient's drug infusion pump and replacing the clear liquids with saline solution. He also utilized discarded needles recovered from infectious waste containers. Approximately 500 patients were potentially infected with HIV, hepatitis A, and hepatitis B while they were receiving medications. He pleaded guilty to tampering with consumer products (a felony) and was sentenced to 51 months in prison.[58]
- $700,000 was embezzled from a research grant at Duke University by two former employees.[59]

a company or institution. Tactics that reduce the opportunity for fraud also ensure the rapid discovery of foul play.

Some actions designed to reduce employee theft include:[60,61]

- Limiting check writing authority.
- Requiring dual signatures on all financial transactions.
- Having employees check each other's work.
- Limiting access to bank accounts.
- Using an outside auditor or accountant for periodic reviews.
- Obtaining a fidelity bond for employees.
- Establishing and maintaining internal controls.
- Accounting for daily cash differences.
- Setting a good example (e.g., not using the company's cash to buy lunch).

Quick, decisive action is imperative when a theft occurs. Investigations should be prompt and thorough, with appropriate attention to due process. Relevant law enforcement agencies and insurers need to be informed of the circumstances, and remedies need to be instituted to prevent similar circumstances in the future.

Violent acts by employees unfortunately threaten health care staff and facilities and all work environments (see Box 8-14). Violence in the workplace is increasing,[62] with incidents, in decreasing order, such as verbal abuse, vandalism, physical fights, stabbings, and shootings.[64] Blamed for this increase in incidents is stress, along with corporate downsizing, alcohol and drug abuse, and the availability of firearms. Damaging acts of violence by employees occur every day and cost businesses an estimated $75 billion each year.[65] Defusing the anger and aggression, rather than trying to confront the violence directly, is the most challenging task.

BOX 8-14

- Bruce Alan Young, a male nurse at Citrus Memorial Hospital (Inverness, FL), was arrested after another nurse caught him having sex with a sedated 15-year-old girl in the recovery room. He was charged with multiple rapes. According to police, Young would prolong female patients' sedation with additional drugs, then rape the women on their hospital gurneys. Lawsuits accused the hospital of negligent supervision and hiring and failure to provide adequate security.[63]
- A former ER physician at Westmoreland Regional Hospital in Pittsburgh, PA has been accused of prescribing OxyContin and Percocet to four women for more than a year in exchange for sex or the expectation of sex.[56]
- A 27-year-old hospital orderly has been charged with rape, sexual abuse, sexual misconduct, and endangering the welfare of a disabled person. He attacked a 37-year-old woman who was receiving chemotherapy for nose and throat cancer, had a breathing tube in her throat, and could not speak or call out when she was attacked.[56]

Varied criminal acts by employees include accepting gifts and gratuities for services; purchasing cigarettes, alcohol, or contraband; gambling; and running prostitution rings (see Box 8-15).

BOX 8-15

At least 10 employees at Woodhull Medical Center (Brooklyn, NY) allegedly sold cocaine and heroin to patients and other employees for use on the premises.[66]

Property Control

Apart from petty theft of small personal items such as radios or jewelry, grand larceny in the form of pilfering of hospital supplies and stealing of major equipment may occur. Appropriate inventory controls are required for monitoring the use of consumable supplies, whether bandages or blood. Protection of these items from unauthorized removal can be aided by locking of storage areas and delegation of personnel for access and accountability. Drugs, biologicals, chemicals, instruments, disposables, and housekeeping and food supplies are all replenishables that may be attractive for personal use or sale by those with criminal intent or inclined to a little "white collar" crime.

The use of stickers or tags on equipment owned by the hospital or facility can help identify items moved within the facility or being taken out of the facility. All large bags, boxes, or equipment moving in or out at doors or loading docks should be scanned to prevent theft of or damage to these items. Prompt distribution of all receivables is a major key to property loss control. If small packages containing highly valuable items, such as computers or technical instruments, are received, they should be delivered to the departmental addressee on the same day, if possible. Otherwise, storage in a secure area is imperative. Certainly, loading docks and storage areas, when not in use, should be specially secured to deter intruders and prevent losses.

SECURING INFORMATION SYSTEMS

Health information systems can be protected with various levels of security approaches, depending on the systems in place and the anticipated breaches of security to be prevented. Sophisticated and well-camouflaged computer viruses that destroy or modify data or render systems inoperable can infect computers from disks, downloaded programs, application software, or even web sites. Problems can arise from theft of computer programs or unauthorized use of the computer networks by employees for their own personal business or by disaffected employees seeking to sabotage the system.[67,68]

The arrival of the computer Internet and its widespread accessibility through generic local area networks (LANs) have exacerbated the complexity of keeping data secure from unwarranted intrusion. Smaller health care organizations and facilities depend on discrete systems for specific functions, such as accounting or personnel or patient care data, with only a few designated people having access and limited ability for computer program interaction. Large institutions no longer use these standalone systems and are now models of system interconnectedness via computer networks for all types of data concurrently entered and retrieved for management and patient care purposes.

Data in such systems can be classified into several categories:

Administration systems: executive information systems, personnel, budget, purchasing, accounts payable, property control.

Patient management data: demographics, admission/discharge/transfer (ADT) information.

Clinical data: medical records, notes, physician orders, laboratory tests and results, treatments, vital signs, clinical reminders.

Ancillary: pharmacy, radiology, ECG.

Facilities operation data: engineering systems, utilities.

In and of themselves, these information systems are large databases, but as part of a network, their interconnectedness complicates security measures. Patient accounts data systems depend on the ADT information as well as on the clinical data for billing and charges, for laboratory tests, for pharmaceuticals, for treatments, for imaging tests, and for operating room use. Similarly, clinical data systems activate and interconnect physicians' orders with laboratory testing and results, orders for medication with pharmacy distribution to the patient care floors, and therapeutic nutrition orders with appropriate dietary response, even to the point of dietary orders of supplies of fruits and vegetables.

Many discrete systems are used for diagnostic and treatment purposes, for research, for physiological monitoring systems used in intensive care units, cardiac care units, the operating rooms, and some treatment step-down units. These systems have on-line real-time capacity for immediate medical care use or trending for patient care. Additionally, other workstations can use clinical data or information from libraries and learning centers.

Unlawful intrusion of computer networks is facilitated by the Internet and by telephone dial-in capabilities of people external to the organization or facility. Data diversion may be used to perpetrate credit card fraud on personnel or patients. Confidential records may be sought in order to modify data, to destroy medical records, or to enter spurious information. Theft of software programs installed on computer terminals attached to the network, by employees or others, for use external to the facility, is another potential risk.

Several counteractive strategies need to be in place to secure the protection of information:[69]

Physical security: physical access limitations and access controls; locked areas to prevent theft of computer hardware, software, and supplies; workstations in secure areas on the premises.

ID and password protection at different levels: restricted access to specified levels of network; restriction of application level for uses of specific programs and/or systems; use of biometric identification devices; restricted access to classes of records (i.e., personnel or patient) and to fields (i.e., name but not social security number); protection of individual user passwords with frequent changes in passwords.

Dial-back systems: confirmation of authorization when there is an internal or external dial-in capacity.

Virus screening programs: utilization on a recurring basis; no disks or programs to be utilized without automated virus scanning protection.

Storage of data in encrypted form and digital signatures: unauthorized retrieval will yield incomprehensible results.

Storage of data on removable disks: encouragement of researchers and students to protect their own data by transferring and storing data on secure "removable disks"; storage of data away from the hard disk at the workstation or the network itself.

Audit trails: incorporation of audit trails in all data systems to document every transaction, including unauthorized use.

Information technology departments will be operating under new requirements and scrutiny when the Health Insurance Portability and Accountability Act (HIPAA) is fully implemented (see Chapter 2). Specific personnel policies and procedures and data security, operations, network, and development methodologies will be required to ensure that medical records, along with general patient information on services, treatment, payment, and other interactions are private and confidential, and that access to them is limited. Methods of access control, event logging, backup, and recovery and contingency plans are all affected, as are the procedures and policies for individual authorization and personal access to medical records, whether electronic, printed, or written. While information technology has created opportunities for abuse of personal information, it also holds the potential to rectify the situation and reduce the risk of intrusion on privacy.

Advanced computer technology to assist administration and patient care givers requires sophisticated countermeasures to reduce unauthorized and criminal access to the use of files for purposes not originally intended. Risk managers will need to rely on the health information specialists to recommend, develop, and implement specific security measures for the the facility's data systems. Reporting of incidents and occurrences relative to these information systems and investigations will require cooperation among risk managers, health information specialists, security personnel, and administrators to analyze trends and to prevent future incursions.[70]

PROACTIVE SECURITY DEPARTMENTS

According to one definition, the role of health care security "is and always will be the protection of people and property, with a secondary role to provide other specifically defined services to the hospital community."[71] Although maintaining the status quo is no longer acceptable, security must stress the dynamic process that is required to allow employees, patients, and visitors to pursue their normal daily activities in a secure manner without creating an armed camp.

Security staff members have access capabilities to allow professionals entry to the pharmacy, laboratory, and radiology in otherwise off-hours. They also respond to major emergencies and both internal and external disasters. In special circumstances, facilities expect cooperation of security staff at sites of cardiac arrest or organ or infant transport. Incident reports are maintained in the security department along with investigation results, and they are reported periodically to the safety committee that also includes a representative of risk management.

With a multitude of decisions to be made regarding security, a facility's director of security[72] is a critical asset in the operations. A security director can rapidly become the trusted colleague of a facility risk manager. A security force protects life and property, detects potential criminals, and prevents crime. When viewed as a proactive police, fire, and safety operation, security force increases in importance dramatically. "Security can no longer be considered a nonrevenue producing part of the company."[72] A facility simply cannot afford to underbudget or understaff this vital department.

Security directors should participate in selecting security staff to meet the agreed-upon managerial expectations. Initially, the administration's objective is to establish a quality security team that will work well and complement the director.

In New York State, all security guards are required to have background checks and eight hours of pre-employment training prior to being granted registration under the provisions of the Security Guard Act of

1992.[73] Individual identification numbers are provided for each security guard independent of their location of employment, health care institution, or other circumstances. Employers must provide 16 to 40 hours of training each year for employees to continue their active registration.

Facilities have a legal responsibility to protect their patients, their visitors, and their workers. Risk managers need to plan how to handle the possible litigation stemming from a violent patient or family member. Administration must be concerned with injuries sustained by individuals being restrained and innocent bystanders unable to escape, and by employees directly in danger. This legal liability demands that security personnel be properly educated and trained. Presbyterian Health Service Corporation's security department requires one year of college, with a law enforcement or security major. One year of college may not seem like a demanding regulation, but it exceeds that of many local police departments. Certification from the International Association of Healthcare Security and Safety is valuable for its emphasis on a wide range of factors, from getting along with staff to restraining patients. Public image has to be considered in the context of an antagonist's perceptions of the facility. In a chaotic ER setting, visible armed police or security can be interpreted as an encouraging symbol of authority.

Security guards pose special risks for organizations, since their mere presence complicates insurance arrangements for a facility. Spurred by widely publicized incidents such as the kidnapping and murder of an Exxon executive, legislators have aimed to formalize minimum standards for the training and licensing of security staff.[74] In 1993, the state of Washington passed a law delineating the authority to license and to regulate private detectives and security guards. New York passed a law setting minimum standards for registration, training, and liability insurance coverage for proprietary and contract guards. These laws and similar legislation have become necessary to push back the rising tide of litigation by outlining reasonable and proper liabilities. Insurers, lawyers, and risk managers alike agree that an essential step in prevention is a thorough background check of applicants for security positions.

A 1979 Illinois court set a precedent in ruling against a detective agency: "The employer knew, or should have known (the guard) was unfit for the position sought to be filled."[74] Consultants advise dealing directly with private security firms, since they are professionals, and elements of the risk and responsibility can thus be transferred and shared. After security guards are hired, they should understand the policies and procedures and the duties expected of a guard in a health care facility. This safeguard reduces the employer's probability of being found negligent in a court.

To screen potential security personnel, employers should:[71]

1. Inform the applicant that a background check will be made, and have the applicant sign a waiver.
2. Take special care with the application form regarding the difference in listing criminal convictions versus arrests.
3. Have the applicant obtain and provide any special information from previous employers.
4. Demand references and check them thoroughly, verifying previous employers.
5. Ask former employers for evaluations on performance; request specific examples on judgment or honesty.
6. Check the validity of all licenses.

7. Start a file on the applicant, documenting calls, references, and checks.
8. Wait until after hiring to administer personality tests; instead focus on background checks.

Cost containment and budget crunching force security staff to accept increased responsibilities and workloads. With security guards forced to double as couriers, record keepers, and bus drivers, their surveillance capabilities and response times will be reduced. However, a team-building approach can develop a unified security force, even in the wake of budget cuts. Proper utilization of manpower is crucial. The creation of an environment filled with enthusiasm and positive feedback strengthens the workforce. As the staff sees visible signs that attention is being paid to their security needs, they are more likely to participate willingly, and tighter security can improve staff productivity and quality of service.

TECHNOLOGY ENHANCED SECURITY

In the wake of the security violence risks facing health care facilities, new innovations and improved security systems are in demand.[75] Institutions have turned to technology to confront their concerns for the security and safety of patients and staff. William Beaumont Hospital (Royal Oak, Michigan) serves as a model for security measures.[76] Alarmed about patient surveillance, infant abduction, violence, pharmaceutical control, and the easy access to the facility by strangers, administrators sought an integrated system to meet all these needs. They selected a fully automated system that incorporates card access, closed circuit television (CCTV), door monitoring, and alarm systems.

In conjunction with CCTV or separately, photo identification badges and access control are two security interventions that go hand in hand.[75] This control enables the monitoring of staff and their movement about the facility and documents the time and date of personnel locations. Electronic tagging of identification bracelets warns of abductions from the nursery or the wandering of the elderly. Antennas with frequency codes can be installed at all exits to emit audio and visual signals to a monitoring station for immediate response if the matching frequencies are detected.

Technology helped Michael Reese Hospital (Chicago, Illinois) administrators to improve security via the BadgePro Video Imaging System.[77] This system creates computer-generated identification cards for employees from a video-recorded display instead of using cut-and-paste laminated cards. These new ID cards can provide access control along with identification. This feature regulates everything from time cards, to building access, to obtaining surgical scrubs, and to entering employee parking areas. A termination date encoded into a magnetic strip limits the access and privileges of temporary workers.

At Bethesda Memorial Hospital in southern Florida, newborn babies wear electronic anti-theft devices developed by Innovative Control Systems (Waukesha, Wisconsin). Several cases of infants abducted from hospitals in the region caused many hospitals in southern Florida to install security systems to safeguard infants. Examples in Box 8-16 pinpoint the abduction problem.

Additional Security Measures

In addition to increased armed security forces, canine teams may patrol and fences may surround the facility grounds.[77] Stam-

BOX 8-16

- An infant was placed in the intensive care unit of San Francisco (CA) General Hospital for security, not health, reasons, under a protective order from the state's Department of Social Services. Although she did not have custody, during a supervised visit the infant's mother was able to walk out of the hospital, thereby abducting the child. She returned the infant about three hours later.[76]
- A drug addicted father swapped a doll for his four-week-old baby lying in a bassinet and vanished with the child in violation of a Child Welfare Department order, depriving the parents of custody. After returning the baby to the hospital, the father said: "I don't know why they didn't catch me. I went down in the elevator with the baby screaming and crying, past the security desk, and I sang all the way out the door."[78]

ford (Connecticut) Hospital opted to add a canine patrol to its security measures. Dogs cost approximately $6,500 each and receive 200 hours of training before patrolling the hospital grounds during swing and night shifts. In addition to police dogs, gentler breeds can patrol inside the facility without intimidating the patients.[79] At Loma Linda Medical Center (California), the canine teams have been a success since their introduction in 1985. Popular with the patients and employees, one dog even stays in the ER at night to add a pacifying effect. Nobody has ever been bitten accidentally. A combination of improved lighting and dog patrols has reduced the hospital's crime rate by 80 percent.

Personal and property crimes are frequent problems because many health care personnel work evening and night shifts at facilities in high-crime areas. However, crime occurs in all locations, from inner-city to rural, and risk managers should not be lulled into inactivity by their tranquil location. Protecting workers from assault in and around health care facilities is a growing problem. Some suggestions for making health care facilities safer include:[1]

- During shift changes, encourage car and van pools and provide security escorts and shuttle services.
- Improve visibility with increased lighting, stairwell and elevator mirrors, and other physical changes.
- Post escape and evacuation routes.
- Install locks on all outside doors to prevent unwanted entrance to, not exit from, the building.

SAFETY AND SECURITY IN OUNCES AND POUNDS

Paraphrasing an old proverb, "An ounce of prevention is better than a pound of cure." Safety and security activities in a health care facility need to focus on the same concept. To achieve their goals, risk managers must make the safety and security programs an integral part of operations, as well as a sound financial investment for the future. Safety and security activities have been practiced throughout industry for many years, and innumerable ideas are waiting to be adapted for health care organizations. Risk managers are supported by major legislation, OSHA and HIPAA regulations, to help provide a safe and secure health care environment. Surveillance and monitoring of potential risks are bolstered by rapid advances in security technology and cooperative team approaches to prevent incidents of unsafe practices, and to react appropriately to incursions on security of people and property. There is no doubt that a prudent safety and security risk management program reduces the potential for liability, while delivering cost savings.

References

1. U.S. Department of Health and Human Services. (1988). *Guidelines for Protecting the Safety and Health of Health Care Workers*. DHHS Publication No. 88-119. Washington, D.C.: Government Printing Office, A3-1, 2; 3-15-17; 5-78, 79.
2. U.S. Department of Health and Human Services, Public Health Service, Centers for Disease Control. (1993). *Guidelines for Prevention of Transmission of Human Immunodeficiency Virus and Hepatitis B Virus to Health Care and Public Safety Workers*. No. 550-147/80031. Washington, D.C.: Government Printing Office.
3. Many doctors don't wash their hands. (1995). *News Tribune* (Woodbridge, N.J.), June 20, p. A7, col. 6.
4. Health hazards. (1994). *Hospital Security and Safety Management* 15(8):15.
5. United States Environmental Protection Agency. (2000). Sick Building Syndrome (SBS) Safety Topic of the Month: March 2000. Washington University School of Medicine, Environmental Health & Safety. *www.ehs.wustl.edu/clinical/topic/top300.htm.*
6. Scaletta, S. E. (1995). Indoor air often tainted. *News Tribune* (Woodbridge, N.J.), February 26, p. R2, col. 1.
7. Employee death from "recreational use" of N_2O at hospital. (1994). *Proactive Risk Management* 1(1):1–4.
8. U.S. Department of Health and Human Services, National Institute for Occupational Safety and Health. (1994). *Request for Assistance in Controlling Nitrous Oxide during Anesthetic Administration*. Washington, D.C.: Government Printing Office.
9. Corn, R. M., and Bader, A. (1994). Pollution liability exposures. *AHRM of NY News* Summer: 11–12.
10. Sandler, H. M. (1995). The changing face of medical surveillance. *Occupational Hazards* 57(3):147–149.
11. Laboratory worker is de-contaminated. (2002). *Star Ledger* (Newark, N.J.), July 19, p. 38, col. 4.
12. Jungels, S. (1993). Eighty years after Triangle fire, safety still lags. *National Underwriter* 97(50):9–10.
13. Ormandy, D. (1995). Burning issue of safety. *Health Visitor* 68(1):34.
14. 4 patients are killed and 5 are injured by fire in a hospital. (1995). *New York Times*, January 2, p. 8, col. 6.
15. Fire damages room at hospital. (1994). *Staten Island Advance* (New York), December 18, p. A14, col. 1.
16. Hospital fire. (1994). *International Association for Healthcare Security & Safety Newsletter* 2(1):1.
17. Hearn, W. (1995). Disaster in action. *American Medical News* 38(18):3, 24–25.
18. Williamson, C. R. (1994). Emergency preparedness: A hospital disaster plan. *Journal of Healthcare Protection Management* 10(2):116–121.
19. Raske, K. (2002). Testimony of the Greater New York Hospital Association on Public Health Emergency State Health Powers Act (MESPHA), New York State Assembly Committee on Health and New York State Assembly Committee on Codes. March 14, New York, N.Y.
20. Special Issue: Emergency Management in the New Millennium (2002). Mobilizing America's Health Care Reservoir *Joint Commission Perspectives.* 21(12).
21. *Bioterrorism Readiness and Response: A Biological and Chemical Disaster Planning Sourcebook for the Health Care System* (2002). American Health Consultants, Inc. *www.ahcpub.com/ahc_root_html/products/sourcebooks/brr01a.html.*
22. Webb, D. A. (1994). The bathtub effect: Why safety programs fail. *Management Review* 83(2):51–54.
23. Van Gelder, L. (1994). Elderly hospital patient dies after elevator accident. *New York Times*, February 21, p. A22, col. 3.
24. Calzolari, A. M. (1995). State cites hospital over patient's death. *Staten Island Advance*, May 17, p. A5, col. 1.
25. Hilts, P. (1995). Inquiry into patient's death finds staff errors. *New York Times*, May 18, p. A20, col. 1.
26. Sells, B. (1994). What asbestos taught me about managing risk. *Harvard Business Review* 72(2): 86–90.
27. Weisman, E. (1995). Safe or sorry? *Health Facilities Management* 8(1):20–25.
28. Blotzer, M. (1995). Virtual reality: Real value for safety training. *Occupational Health and Safety* 64(2): 121–123.
29. Minter, S. (1995). A safe approach to incentives. *Occupational Health and Safety* 64(6):171–173.
30. Bachman, R. (1994). Violence and theft in the workplace. U.S. Department of Justice Crime Data Brief NCJ-148199. Washington, D.C.: Government Printing Office.

31. Goodman, R. A., Jenkins, L., and Mercy, J. A. (1994). Workplace-related homicide among health care workers in the United States, 1980 through 1990. *Journal of the American Medical Association* 272(21):1686–1688.

32. U.S. Centers for Disease Control and Prevention. (1993). *NIOSH Alert: Request for Assistance in Preventing Homicide in the Workplace.* USDHHS Pub. No. 93-109. Washington, D.C.: Government Printing Office.

33. Workplace violence: Policies, procedures, and incidents. (1994). *Medical Benefits* 11(10):11; Simonwitz, J. (1994). Viiolence in the workplace: You're entitled to protection. *RN* 57(11):61–63.

34. Rand, M. (1994). Violence prevention efforts target workplace violence. *Nation's Health* 24(8):1, 6, 10.

35. Anonymous. (2001). The 2000 IAHSS Survey: Crime in hospitals. *Journal of Healthcare Protection Management* 17(2):1–31.

36. Anonymous. (2001). Updates: Protecting home health workers; dealing with abortion violence. *Hospital & Safety Management* 22(4):5–9.

37. Anonymous. (1998). Developing a program for dealing with violence in healthcare facilities. *Hospital Security and Safety Management* 18(11):5–8.

38. Anonymous. (2000). The reality of violence in the workplace: Stop being scared; start acting smart. *Hospital Security and Safety Management* 20(12):5–8.

39. Grant Medical Center invests in better employee access control. (1993). *Hospital Security and Safety Management* 14(7):5–7.

40. Children's National switches to proximity card access. (1993). *Hospital Security and Safety Management* 14(7):7.

41. Applebaum, A. (2002). Meeting the major threats to hospital security within a budget. *Journal of Healthcare Protection Management* 28(1):38.

42. Kinkle, S. L. (1993). Violence in the ED: How to stop it before it starts. *American Journal of Nursing* 93(7):22–24.

43. Anglin, D., Kyriacou, D. N., and Hutson, H. R. (1994). Residents' perspectives on violence and pesonal safety in the emergency department. *Annals of Emergency Medicine* 23(5):1082–1084.

44. Funfhausen, C. (1993). Better safe than sorry. *Minnesota Medicine* 76(8):6–7, 41.

45. Robertson, J. (1995). *Violence in the Medical Workplace: Prevention Strategies.* Chicago: American Medical Association, Young Physicians Section, AMA-YPS Governing Council, pp. 7–8.

46. Patient stabs 2 employees. (1994). *Staten Island Advance* (New York), December 12, p. A3, col. 1.

47. Hynes to convene grand jury on Kingsboro security lapses. (1994). *New York Times,* November 19, p. 19, col. 3.

48. Kertesz, L. (1994). 4 killed, 23 wounded in Wash. rampage. *Modern Healthcare* 24(26):72.

49. National Crisis Prevention Institute, Inc. (1995). Feel safe at work again! Video series. Brookfield, Wis.: National Crisis Prevention Institute.

50. Stephan, A. (1993). Documenting your patient's valuables. *Nursing* 23(10):31.

51. Hospital reimburses for lost jewels. (1994). *International Association for Healthcare Security & Safety Newsletter* 11(1):9.

52. Clavin, T. (1994). The silent epidemic: Crime in hospitals. *Good Housekeeping* 219(3):107, 258, 260–261.

53. Kidnapping attempts. (1994). *International Association for Healthcare Security & Safety Newsletter* 11(1):8.

54. Kelty, J. (2001). California hospitals set uniform emergency codes to ease staff confusion. *Journal of Healthcare Protection Management* 17(2):73.

55. In brief. (2002). *Hospital Security and Safety Management.* 22:11.

56. In brief. (2002). *Hospital Security and Safety Management.* 22:12.

57. Gould, C. (1995). Islander jailed in diversion of pharmaceuticals. *Staten Island Advance* (New York), April 13, p. A2, col. 4.

58. Applebaum, A. (2001). The drug thief at Georgetown University Medical Center. *Journal of Healthcare Protection Management* 17(2):117.

59. Zernike, K. (2001). Duke repays $700,000 in grant money and reports a swindle. *New York Times,* August 21, p. A10.

60. Laredo, M. C. (1994). How to prevent and handle employee embezzlement. *American Medical News* 37(46):25.

61. Koszola, M. (1995). Protecting against losses from employee theft, fraud. *American Medical News* 38(20):14–15.

62. Manigan, C. (1994). The graveyard shift; workplace safety is a full-time job. *Public Management* 76(4): 10–16.

63. Florida nurse is charged with raping 4 women in surgery recovery room. (1994). *New York Times* October 8, p. 30, col. 2; Martinez, J. (1994). Male nurse accused of 5 rapes in hospital. *Staten Island Advance* (New York), October 13, p. A19, col. 3.
64. Losey, M. (1994). Managing in an era of workplace violence. *Managing Office Technology* 39(2):27–29.
65. Nuckols, C. C. (1994). Reducing workplace violence. *Behavioral Health Management* 14(4):5.
66. Hevesi, D. (1994). Woodhull security chief quits in inquiry. *New York Times* September, 18, p. B5, col. 3.
67. Warnock-Matheron, H., Gruending, D. L., and Hannah, K. J. (1993). A risk management approach to the security of hospital information systems. *Canadian Journal of Nursing Administration* 6(2): 22–24, 30.
68. Erlanger, L. (2001). 21st century security. *Internet World* December, pp. 22–32.
69. Hayam, A. (1994). Security audit center—A suggested model for effective audit strategies in health care informatics. *International Journal of Bio-Medical Computing* 35(Suppl. 1):115–127.
70. Jones, J. (2002). Biometrics: No two alike. *Federal Computer Week* 16(21):18–20.
71. Mitcham, J. (1994). Hospital security in the 21st century—A blueprint for survival. *Journal of Healthcare Protection Management* 10(2):41–45.
72. Bagley, G. L. (1994). How can hospitals operate safely? *Journal of Healthcare Protection Management* 10(2):92–96.
73. New York State General Business Law, Article 7, Security Guard Act of 1992.
74. Johnson, N. (1994). On guard against liability. *Business Insurance* 28(2):3, 42–43.
75. Lambert, J. F. (1994). Electronic technology: Building a safe and secure healthcare community. *Journal of Healthcare Protection Management* 10(2): 107–111.
76. Integrated systems at William Beaumont Hospital. (1994). *Hospital Security and Safety Management* 15(8):8.
77. Michael Reese first hospital to employ new ID/access control system. (1994). *Hospital Security and Safety Management* 15(8):2–4.
78. McFadden, R. D. (1994). Drug-addicted infant boy returned to Bronx hospital. *New York Times*, October 14, p. B3, col. 5.
79. Sierpina, D. (1995). A canine corps helps keep the peace at a downtown hospital. *New York Times*, February 26, p. C2, col. 1.
80 Violence: Occupational Hazards in Hospitals. (2002). Washington, D.C.: DHHS (NIOSH) Publication No. 2002-101. *www.cdc.gov/niosh.*

SECTION 3 | Specific Strategies for Specific Risk Areas

CHAPTER 9 A Primer on Medical Malpractice

Arthur S. Friedman

Medical malpractice is controversial and sometimes complex; it affects all health care providers, patients, physicians, lawyers, institutions, and insurers. Numerous investigative reports by the U.S. General Accounting Office (GAO) about medical malpractice related to Medicare, Medicaid, the Veterans Administration, and fraud in the provision of health care services demonstrate the national concern with medical malpractice.

A SCIENCE OF MISTAKES

A Harvard Medical Practice Study in 1984 reviewed more than 30,000 medical records from 51 New York State hospitals and found that adverse events and negligence occurred in 3.7 percent of hospitalizations; 2.6 percent of these instances caused permanent disability, and 13.6 percent resulted in death.[1] This Harvard study echoed the findings of the only other large-scale estimation of the incidence of iatrogenic injury and substandard care, the California Medical Association's Medical Insurance Feasibility Study.[2] In 1977, California researchers reported an adverse event rate of 4.6 percent and a negligence rate of 0.8 percent. Devastatingly, the third Harvard report in the series Localio declared: "Medical-malpractice litigation infrequently compensates patients injured by medical negligence and rarely identifies, and holds providers accountable for substandard care."[1] There is no mention of provider accountability in the case described in Box 9-1.

Brennan found that certain types of hospitals have significantly higher rates of injuries, because of substandard care.[3] Furthermore, Leape's analysis[4] indicated that 67 percent of the adverse events were caused by nonphysician errors, not physician negligence, and he concluded:[5]

BOX 9-1

Matthew Dunn's parents brought their four-year-old son into a hospital for emergency treatment. Dunn's symptoms included fever, coughing, diarrhea, vomiting, and purple blotches on his throat. During five hours at the managed care facility, the doctor on duty examined Dunn, ordered numerous tests, and gave him Tylenol. His condition worsened. He was taken to a hospital, where an antibiotic was administered intravenously, but Dunn died of meningococcal infection one hour later. The doctor was sued for negligence in failing to diagnose the virus. If diagnosed, there was a small risk of death with proper treatment. A jury awarded $625,000 to the parents.[6]

> Physicians and nurses need to accept the notion that error is an inevitable accompaniment of the human condition, even amongst conscientious professionals with high standards. Errors must be accepted as evidence of system flaws, not character flaws.

In a comment related to Leape's article, Blumenthal applied total quality management and opted to redirect medical errors into "medical treasures" because the flaws were exposed and corrected.[7]

A hospital that had experienced mistakes similar to the one described in Box 9-2 devised a plan to prevent future incidents. Administrative orders dictated that any time surgery involved an organ or limb that comes in pairs, staff would write "NO" with a black magic marker on the organ or limb that should be left alone.[8]

A *Lancet* editorial offered advice in a similar vein.[9] What practical lesson does this "science of mistakes" have for providers? To diminish errors, attention should be paid to alterable features outside of the system. Health care providers should attempt to learn as much as they can about people, about how illnesses affect them, and about which treatments work best. "Success in bringing patients to health or relief requires the broadest possible knowledge of anything relevant to the illness."[9]

BOX 9-2

A Texas surgeon admitted negligently removing Benjamin Jones's healthy right lung while leaving a tumor in the left lung. Jones decided against further treatment because doctors told him he would gain a painful few months of life, at best. After his death, the family sued for wrongful death. Even though the hospital admitted no wrongdoing, a settlement gave the family $9 million. Ironically, an autopsy revealed that Jones had a good chance of beating the cancer even after the surgical mistake.[12]

In a unique theoretical approach, Senders concluded that "there are few or no 'medical errors'; there are many errors that occur in medical settings."[10] An error differs from an accident in that the error is a behavioral matter while the accident is an unplanned event. Behavioral errors can involve a misperception, a mistake, a slip, an omission, a commission, an insertion, a repetition, or a substitution, and they may be endogenous or exogenous. Advocating "failure mode analysis," Senders advised evaluation of all incorrect actions and prevention interception. In essence, the technique demands identification of the modes of error in medical settings; prediction of the expressions of those errors; use of training and design to improve self-detection; and the interdiction of their transformation into accidents.

The National Academy of Science's Institute of Medicine (IOM) 1999 Report cited studies showing that between 44,000 and 98,000 people die each year because of mistakes made by medical professionals in hospitals. Thousands of other errors are never detected, and those in nursing homes, home health care, retail pharmacies, physicians' offices, and ambulatory care centers were not included in the report.[11] The IOM said medication errors are among the most widespread and may result in deaths, permanent disability, and unnecessary suffering.

An error, advertent or inadvertent, is one thing, but it has happened that district attorneys have escalated medical mistakes from malpractice into criminal charges. While criminal charges for a medical error are extraordinarily rare, they are not precluded by adverse determinations by state licensure or professional conduct agencies, as illustrated in Box 9-3.

BOX 9-3

- Reckless manslaughter charges were sought against an anesthesiologist who allegedly had failed to monitor vital signs and fell asleep during surgery. His eight-year-old patient died. Colorado revoked his medical license, and the boy's family accepted an out-of-court settlement. Criminal charges are still pending.[13]
- A laboratory in Oak Creek, WI, Chem-Bio Corporation, was charged with "reckless homicide" for allegedly misreading Pap smears that could have saved the lives of two women. Experts testified that there were unmistakable signs of cancer in the slides. A lab technician was paid by the number of samples analyzed. She examined 20,000 to 40,000 Pap smears a year, compared with the maximum of 12,000 recommended under professional standards. The estates of both victims received multimillion-dollar settlements from the laboratory and their health maintenance organization provider, Family Health Plan. The laboratory director and the technician escaped immediate charges under a deal with the prosecutors.[14]

MEDICAL MALPRACTICE LAW—IN BRIEF

Negligence is a civil, as distinct from criminal, wrong and is part of the law of torts. Within the field of negligence, the term "malpractice" refers to negligence as it applies to professionals such as physicians, dentists, nurses, technicians, attorneys, and accountants. "Medical malpractice" relates to professionals within the health care industry, to organizations that provide health care, or to the institutions in which health professionals practice, such as hospitals. An examination of the general principles of negligence provides the foundation for an understanding of medical malpractice.

NEGLIGENCE

Usually, negligence is defined as the failure to exercise ordinary care. But ordinary to whom? If the law set the measuring standard too high, the day-to-day conduct of most of us would, by definition, be negligent. Consequently, lawsuits wold involve standards of conduct that only a small fraction of the population could ever achieve. Defendants would be held to standards that they could not possibly attain. On the other hand, setting the measuring standard too low creates a situation in which the vast majority of injuries caused by "negligence" would go uncompensated, since the conduct would not have fallen below the legal standard. Therefore, the law sets the standard by which it judges the conduct of each of us by "reasonable" person criteria. By legal definition, negligence is a failure to exercise that degree of care which a reasonably prudent person would have exercised under the same circumstances.

Does that mean that every time someone fails to exercise ordinary care, a legal cause of action for negligence is created? An answer to the puzzlement lies in the quintessential explanation of negligence in a famous 1928 decision of U.S. Supreme Court Judge Benjamin Cardozo (see Box 9-4).[15]

Although the New York Court of Appeals recognized that the actions of the LIRR's employees pushing the man may have been negligent, it concluded that that was not enough upon which to base liability.

> Negligence is not actionable unless it involves the invasion of a legally protected interest, the violation of a right. Proof of negligence in the air, so to speak, will not do. . . . In every instance, before negligence can be predicated on a given act, background of the act must be sought and found a duty to the individual complaining, the observance of which would have averted or avoided the injury. . . . Negligence is not a tort unless it results in the commission of a wrong, and the commission of a wrong imports the violation of a right, . . . (H)e must show that the act as to him had possibilities of danger so many and apparent as to entitle him to be protected against doing it though the harm was unintended.[15]

In essence, negligence is founded on the relationship between the actor and the victim. That relationship must be recognized by society as establishing a legal duty between the two. This requirement that a duty exist between actor and victim may produce contrary resolutions of similar factual patterns. A person can commit a single act that inflicts identical injuries on two different victims, but negligence law may bar recovery by one of the victims, while allowing recovery by the other.

Because the law recognizes the relationship between the health care provider and the patient in a situation such as that described in Box 9-5, the professional staff have a duty to warn the patient of such a danger. Not warning her about that danger is considered a breach of that duty, and the conduct of the professional staff is thus negligent to her.

In the scenario of Box 9-6, there can be no negligence. The law does not require that a burglar be warned about the hole in the floor. There is no relationship between the actor and the victim in this case. This is not to say that there is never any duty to a stranger, or even to a lawbreaker. In this illustration, however, no duty was created.

In and of itself, the existence of a duty is only the condition precedent to negligence. Specifically, negligence can occur only when there is a failure, or breach, by the profes-

BOX 9-4

Mrs. Palsgraf suffered injuries while waiting for a train, and a man carrying a package attempted to board a moving train. A Long Island Rail Road (LIRR) employee reached out from the train to pull the man in. At the same time, another employee on the platform pushed the man from behind. This pushing caused the man's package to fall on the tracks. That package contained fireworks, which exploded, causing Mrs. Palsgraf's injuries when a scale fell on her.

BOX 9-5

A patient comes to the office for a scheduled appointment. She slips in a hole in the wooden floor, falls, and breaks a leg. Everybody at the office was aware of the hole but did not warn the patient.

BOX 9-6

A burglar breaks into and enters the same medical office as in Box 9-5 without permission and consent. This individual falls in the same hole in the same wooden floor and also suffers a broken leg.

sional to abide by the applicable standard of conduct established by that duty. Despite the existence of the requisite relationship between the health care provider and the victim, not every injury caused by the provider's conduct will be the result of negligence. If a patient dies from a heart attack during an operation, death may not be attributable to the surgeon's conduct; death may have resulted from the normal risks of the operation and/or from circumstances beyond the control of the surgeon. For the law to recognize the professional culpability, the challenged conduct must have caused the injury or at least have been a causal link in a chain of events.

Four requirements define an act as one of negligence:[16]

- A legally recognized relationship exists between the parties.
- The health care worker has a duty of care to the patient.
- The health care worker breached the duty of care by failing to conform to the required standards of care.
- The breach of duty was the direct cause of harm, resulting in compensable damages for the negligent actions.

Generally, damages are measured by a comparison of the condition of the victim before and after the injury. If the victim is a wage earner, lost wages will be a factor, as will medical expenses and the victim's pain and suffering. Those who earn high wages will be compensated more than the poor. Younger victims are worth more than the elderly. A slow, lingering, painful death is more valuable than an instantaneous one.

In the example in Box 9-7, all the components of negligence, except an injury that produces damages recognized by the law, are present. This woman may have been scared, perhaps trembling with increased anxiety, but she suffered no compensable physical harm or damages.

BOX 9-7

A hospital employee telephoned a woman that her husband had been involved in an auto accident. At the hospital, the woman was shown the X-rays of a crushed head, presumably her husband's. She was not allowed to see the body. An hour later, she saw the driver's license of the dead man. It was not her husband! She sued, but the jury found no basis for liability.[17]

MEDICAL MALPRACTICE

Within the context of medical care, negligence is the improper treatment or neglect of a patient. To constitute medical malpractice, the commission or omission of an action causing the injury must arise from the exercising of professional medical judgment. Failure of a nurse to properly maintain an intravenous tube constitutes professional malpractice, whereas failure to properly supervise the patient in the bathroom is ordinary negligence. Liability for malpractice may be imposed on individual providers of medical treatment or services, such as physicians, surgeons, dentists, nurses, therapists, and technicians, as well as on the facilities where services are rendered. A clear explanation of medical malpractice emerges from a ruling in an 1898 lawsuit:[18]

> A physician and surgeon, by taking charge of a case, impliedly represents that he possesses, and the law places upon him the duty of possessing, that reasonable degree of learning and skill that is ordinarily possessed by physicians and surgeons in the locality where he practices, and which is ordinarily regarded by those conversant with the employment as necessary to qualify him to engage in the business of

> practicing medicine and surgery. Upon consenting to treat a patient, it becomes his duty to use reasonable care and diligence in the exercise of his skill and the application of his learning to accomplish the purpose for which he was employed. He is under the further obligation to use his best judgment in exercising his skill and applying his knowledge. The law holds him liable for an injury to his patient resulting from want of the exercise of knowledge and skill, or the omission to exercise reasonable care, or the failure to use his best judgment. The rule in relation to learning and skill does not require the surgeon to possess that extraordinary learning and skill which belong only to a few men of rare endowments, but such as is possessed by the average member of the medical profession in good standing.

PHYSICIAN-PATIENT RELATIONSHIP

Liability for medical malpractice is predicated on the establishment of a relationship between physician and patient. Legally, a relationship is created when there is treatment, expectation of treatment, or diagnosis for the purpose of treatment.[19] This relationship may by established by express or implied agreement. A patient may verbally agree to treatment or may do so without actually saying the words. Usually, the patient goes to the physician, a relevant interaction occurs between the parties, and there is agreement that the diagnosis, treatment, and consultation will ensure compensation. Yet, the physician-patient relationship and agreement is similarly established by the treatment of an unconscious patient brought into an emergency room.

In the context of this relationship, the physician may be thought to be hired for only a specific limited purpose—to perform a preschool or camp physical examination, for example. Because of the limited nature and scope of such a physician-patient relationship, there is no duty on the physician to give specialized advice or treat the patient for a previously undiagnosed condition.

A person seeking benefits under an insurance policy will often be sent by the insurer to a physician of its choosing, whom it pays for the purpose of conducting an independent medical examination (IME). The purpose of the IME is to substantiate the claimed injuries and the entitlement to benefits. Since no true physician-patient relationship exists,[20] the physician has only a limited duty to the person examined, at least "not to injure a patient during his physical examination."[21]

DUTY TO PERFORM PROFESSIONALLY

Medical practice deals with medical science and skills that are outside the knowledge of the ordinary or average person. Thus, the standard by which conduct is measured must be altered to accommodate the specialized area of medicine. Physicians must possess the skills and knowledge that reasonably competent physicians possess, a standard comparable to the one that applies to lay people, who are legally bound to act as reasonably prudent individuals. A legal duty is imposed on physicians to use ordinary and reasonable care in the exercise of such skill and knowledge, tempered with a duty to use their best judgment. Even though physician incompetence may be easily recognizable, as in the example in Box 9-8, an action for liability may not ensue immediately.

Establishing the "reasonably competent" physician as the standard by which to measure the conduct of doctors may seem un-

BOX 9-8

An anesthesiologist had physical disabilities caused by a stroke and alcoholism. His colleagues allowed him to continue practicing despite his problems. During routine back surgery, the anesthesiologist injected a 44-year-old patient with 10 to 20 times the recommended dose of a sedative. A lack of oxygen followed, and the patient suffered irreversible brain damage and now will require 24-hour nursing care for the rest of his life. A court judgment declared the physician "an incompetent anesthesiologist," and the jury awarded $13.6 million to the patient and his family.[22]

usual. However, a comparison with the law of ordinary negligence demonstrates the wisdom of the standard. If all physicians were required to possess the skill and knowledge possessed by "excellent" doctors, 85 percent of the physicians would fail the test. On the other hand, if the standard were the skill and knowledge of the "fair" doctor, society wold be condoning treatment and conduct that produces injuries for which there would be no compensation.

Since medicine is an inexact science, the mere possession of the requisite skill and knowledge is not enough. Through the law, society imposes a duty on physicians to always use their best judgment. There is no liability when physicians make an error in judgment, provided they have not deviated from accepted medical practice.

At times, the line of demarcation between malpractice and an error in judgment is difficult to ascertain. Moreover, the duties to use "best judgment" and to follow "accepted medical practice" often conflict with each other. If a patient can demonstrate that the decision to follow accepted medical practice was a violation of the duty to exercise best judgment, the physician may have been guilty of malpractice.

Traditional doctrine states that a physician should be held only to that degree of skill and knowledge possessed by the same reasonably competent physicians of the specific area of practice. Several courts have expanded the original restrictive definition to require that physicians must keep up with advances in their respective field, in addition to conforming to community standards. Moreover, the notion of community or locality against which conduct will be measured is not fixed, but may fluctuate according to the nature of the particular part of the country involved.

If physicians practice as specialists, they are held to the standard of the skill and knowledge possessed by reasonably competent similar specialists. This level of skill and knowledge is greater than that possessed by general practitioners.

Sources of Professional Standards

Although it is understood that health care professionals will be judged by standards of behavior, no universal statement of professional standards applies to every possible provider in all possible situations. In addition to the opinions of experts and the actual practices of health care providers, there are several sources of professional standards:

- Government statutes and regulations on licensure, certification, and professional conduct.
- Standards developed by professional societies and credentialing agencies.
- Voluntary accrediting agency standards such as techniques to minimize risks of infection, or staffing norms for intensive care.
- Administrative policies and rules of a hospital or other institution.

ADDITIONAL THEORIES OF LIABILITY

Several other theories of liability are common, and risk managers should be aware of legal actions related to these theories of informed consent, strict liability, *res ipsa loquitur*, and vicarious liability.

Informed Consent

Court decisions affirm that a patient has the right "to determine the course of his own medical treatment" and to "decline medical treatment."[23] A physician has a duty to explain to the patient the diagnosis, the prognosis, the proposed treatment, the treatment alternatives, and the risks and benefits of each (see Box 9-9). These are the legal elements of informed consent.

In a lawsuit claiming lack of informed consent, the plaintiff has the burden of proving that the defendant failed to disclose material risks that would have been disclosed by a reasonable physician under similar circumstances.[24] That the treatment was medically sound is no defense. A patient still has the right to decide whether or not to consent to the treatment.

BOX 9-9

An orthopedic surgeon performed back surgery after a patient's auto accident injury. Pain continued and two more operations were performed. A jury found that the patient had not given informed consent to the three operations. He was not told of the possibility of surgical failure or that his pain might not be relieved. Informed of the risks, a reasonable person might have chosen to forego the surgery. There was no evidence that the surgeon had been negligent. There was an award of $170,000.[25]

Strict Liability

Under normal theories of malpractice and negligence, professionals are liable if their conduct is "at fault." In the doctrine of strict liability, however, liability is assessed irrespective of fault in certain limited areas. This doctrine has its greatest impact on the sale of products. A manufacturer of a product sold on the open market ordinarily is strictly liable for any injuries caused by a defect in the item, without regard to questions of improper or negligent conduct. Since the manufacturer is in the best position to control the product and to ensure its safety, the risk of loss is viewed as another cost of doing business. Strict liability may be applicable in connection with the ingestion of pharmaceuticals, radiological diagnostic services, and the utilization of medical devices. This doctrine of strict liability has not been widely applied with respect to the mere rendition of medical services.

Res Ipsa Loquitur

Res ipsa loquitur means "the thing speaks for itself." Courts relying on this doctrine require a plaintiff to demonstrate the following four elements:[26]

- The injury would not ordinarily occur in the absence of negligence.
- The injury was caused by the actions or instrumentality within the exclusive control of the defendant.
- The injury is not due to any action on the part of the plaintiff.
- The evidence surrounding the circumstances relating to or concerning the injury is mostly within the control of the defendant.

Vicarious Liability

In medical malpractice, the doctrine of holding one person liable for the acts of another depends on the theories of agency and control. Courts have held that where two physicians jointly participate in the diagnosis and treatment of a patient, each is liable for the other's negligent treatment.[27] As opposed to the rule with respect to a partnership, membership in a professional corporation does not in itself make one physician shareholder vicariously liable for the malpractice of another physician shareholder. In the absence of supervision or control, the referral of a patient from one physician to another does not make the referring physician liable for the malpractice of the other physician.

HOSPITAL LIABILITY FOR MEDICAL MALPRACTICE

A court ruling summarizes the legal responsibility of the hospital:[28]

> Present day hospitals . . . do far more than furnish facilities of treatment. They regularly employ on a salary basis a large staff of physicians, nurses and interns, as well as administrative and manual workers, and they charge patients for medical care and treatment. . . . Certainly, the person who avails himself of "hospital facilities" expects that the hospital will attempt to cure him, not that its nurses or other employees will act on their own responsibility. . . . Hospitals should, in short, shoulder the responsibility borne by everyone else. There is no reason to continue their exemption from the universal rule of *respondeat superior.*

Hospital liability is based on two theories: (1) *respondeat superior* and (2) ostensible agency, or agency by estoppel.

An institution may be responsible for the conduct of the physicians who practice there, as well as for its own actions. However, a hospital is an artificial entity, usually assuming a corporate form. As a corporation, a hospital cannot act except through its employees or other agents. Given this situation, the law adopts the practical approach that the employer is in the best position to control its employees, and applies liability to the employer through the doctrine of *respondeat superior*. Vicarious liability of the employer means that employers are responsible for the negligent conduct of their employees when those employees are acting on behalf of the employer. At one time, the law exempted charitable organizations from vicarious liability, but modern legal theory has eliminated that immunity.

Respondeat superior is manifest in individual employees of the hospital, such as nurses, therapists, technicians, service personnel, and other administrative personnel. Even though the nonmedical staff may not provide professional services, the hospital is liable for their conduct by the ordinary rules of negligence (see Box 9-10).

A complex problem arises when hospitals contract with third parties to provide medical and other professional services. This legal situation is most commonly encountered in connection with the rendering of anesthesia, pathology, radiology, or emergency room services, as illustrated in Box 9-11.

The appellate court ruling in the case described in Box 9-11 commented that the contract mandated that the physician comply with the rules of the hospital, that the physician use a fee schedule set by the agreement, and that the physician be guaranteed a minimum income. In addition, the hospital provided the administrative support for the emergency room. Within these basic attributes, an employer-employee relationship existed. Perhaps seeking a broader base to establish its ruling, the court also held that the nature of the relationship of the parties barred the hospital from denying liability. This court ruling recognized that the contractual arrangement between the hospital and its physicians is transparent and invisible to the general public. In such situa-

BOX 9-10[29]

- In November 2001, a transport stretcher carrying a Massachusetts woman collapsed, fracturing the woman's thoracic vertebra and paralyzing her. She was awarded a settlement of $1.03 million.
- Failure to monitor ventilator patient in CTA scan; ventilator ran out of oxygen; persistent vegetative state. Verdict $7,366,000 (Tennessee, February 2000).
- In October 1999, inappropriate respiratory therapy resulted in the death of a 17-year-old quadriplegic in Virginia. He was awarded a verdict of $400,000.
- In August 1998, a therapist improperly set the high pressure alarm on a ventilator, and a Virginia man suffered a hypoxic ischemic brain injury. He was awarded a settlement of $700,000.
- The failure to provide occupational and physical therapy during an extended hospitalization caused several contractures requiring health aide assistance. A verdict of $1.5 million resulted in July 1998 in Washington, D.C.
- In November 1997, a woman in Florida suffered cardiac arrest during paramedic treatment. An endotracheal tube was not properly placed or was dislodged. The ER physician failed to correct the tube placement and brain damage resulted. The settlement was $3.6 million.

tions, courts hold these individuals to be *de facto* employees. Consequently, the hospital is liable for their negligence just as if these professionals were employed by the institution. An alternate theory supporting hospital liability is that the hospital is "holding out" these professionals as if they were employees.

Although the courts have not been uniform in applying the doctrine of *respondeat superior* to these contracted services, they often identify specific indicators in determining liability: How much control does the hospital exert over the person? How does the hospital pay for the contracted services? Are the rendered services normally performed by an employee? Who owns the equipment used? What choices are available to the patients?

BOX 9-11

A plaintiff's decedent was cared for in the hospital by a physician who had a contract to operate the emergency room service. The plaintiff's lawsuit alleged negligence by the attending physician. Because the ER physician was an independent contractor, the hospital sought to escape vicarious liability. Specifically, the contract disclaimed that the hospital was the employer of the physician. An appellate court reversed the dismissal of the lawsuit by the trial court, declared the disclaimer void, and ruled that as a matter of law the physician was an employee of the hospital.[30]

This problem of contracted services may be examined from two perspectives: that of the patient and that of an objective observer. Plaintiffs who hold the hospital vicariously liable for the malpractice of its independent contractors rely on support from both perspectives. Through an examination of the factors appurtenant to the contractual relationship, the plaintiff may attempt to prove that the physician was a *de facto* employee or agent of the hospital. Alternatively, the plaintiff may attempt to demonstrate reliance on the fact that the physician practiced at the hospital. Because of that reliance, the patient did nothing else to verify the credentials of the physician, assuming that the hospital must have verified credentials and specified privileges for any physician who practiced within the institution.

The ostensible agency, or agency by estoppel, theory has been extended to hold the state of New York liable for the malpractice of an independent surgeon (see Box 9-12). After commencement of the lawsuit, the state sought to avoid liability on the grounds that the physician was an independent contractor, not an employee, and thus the state could not be held vicariously liable for his negligence. Citing *Mduba v. Benedictine Hospital*, the appellate division affirmed the lower court denial of the state's motion. Initially, the plaintiff had been examined by a state employee who then had arranged for the surgical consultation; the consultation took place at the facility, the surgery was performed at the facility, and the surgeon was assisted by a facility nurse.

> The applicability of the doctrine [of ostensible agency or agency by estoppel] depends upon whether the plaintiff could have reasonably believed, based upon all of the surrounding circumstances, that the treating physician was provided by the defendant hospital or clinic or was otherwise acting on the defendant's behalf.[30]

As applied to contracted services, the doctrine of vicarious liability has an immediate and direct applicability to the emergency room, where patients are usually "service patients," or patients of the hospital itself (as opposed to individuals who enter the hospital only after referral from a private attending physician). However, vicarious liability also applies to physician services rendered to patients who are placed in the hospital by their private physician.

BOX 9-12

An inmate at a New York State correctional facility underwent a lymph node biopsy excision after being examined by a physician's assistant. Surgery was performed by a semiretired general surgeon who rendered consultations for inmates. Following the surgery, the inmate claimed that the surgeon had committed malpractice by severing a spinal accessory nerve during the procedure.[31]

Anesthesiology is another area of practice that is likely to invoke vicarious liability. Anesthesia services are indispensable to any surgery and, as in the case of emergency room services, are typically contracted by the hospital. One anesthesiology group may provide such services, with each physician within the group having certain distinct responsibilities depending on the time and nature of the surgical procedure. An appellate court sustained a verdict against a hospital based on the alleged negligence of an anesthesiologist,[32] citing *Mduba v. Benedictine Hospital*, a case involving an emergency room physician. Employing the objectivity test, the court held that a jury could, but was not required to, find the hospital vicariously liable on the basis of the degree of control exercised by the hospital over the anesthesiologist. Although the court commented that the patient was not aware of the independent status of the anesthesiology group and instead relied on the hospital, the ruling did not, as a matter of law, hold the hospital vicariously liable pursuant to the estoppel theory. In other words, the court felt that each case should be judged on its own particular facts.

Logically, the courts can apply the same analytic approach to cases involving radiologists and pathologists. Points of discussion can center on the institution's control, the patient's subjective belief, or the patient's reliance on the facility. Ultimately, the court will render a policy decision based on the fact that a patient may enter a hospital through the emergency room, where the patient has no option regarding the treating physicians. That patient places the utmost trust in the institution and in the medical professionals who work there, without regard to the niceties of the financial arrangements between the hospital and those physicians. As recognized by one court:[33]

> Having undertaken one of mankind's most critically important and delicate fields of endeavor concomitantly therewith the hospital must assume the grave responsibility of pursuing this calling with appropriate care. The care and service dispensed through this high trust, however technical, complex and esoteric its character may be, must meet standards of responsibility commensurate with the undertaking to preserve and protect the health, and indeed, the very lives of those placed in the hospital's keeping.

HOSPITAL LIABILITY REGARDING STAFF PRIVILEGES

Hospitals permit doctors to perform professional services at their facilities by granting "staff privileges" that are based upon the specific training and area of practice of the individual physician. Each hospital employs a set of rules and regulations that it uses to measure and evaluate physicians for the purpose of granting or renewing privileges. Based upon the negligence principles discussed above, hospitals may be liable for their negligence in affording staff privileges to incompetent physicians. "While a hospital is not responsible for the actual treatment of a patient by a private physician with staff privileges, the failure of a hospital to develop and adhere to reasonable procedures for reviewing a physician's qualifications creates a foreseeable risk of harm thus establishing an independent duty to such patients."[34]

Using the same reasoning, liability could be assessed against any entity that negligently performs its credentialing function with the result that an otherwise ineligible physician commits malpractice. In this age of managed care, the most pertinent application of this doctrine would be the credentialing process employed by managed care entities such as health maintenance organizations.[35]

Corporate Negligence

Usually, a hospital is not liable for the negligence of its attending staff or nonemployed physicians, since it is assumed that these physicians exercise their independent judgment. Reacting to the realities of practice, however, modern theories of malpractice have developed the doctrine of corporate negligence. Under this doctrine, hospitals are liable for failing to review the credentials of their nonemployed attending physicians, or for failing to monitor the quality of care rendered by such physicians.

A rash of hospital mistakes, as described in Box 9-13, clearly demonstrates the magnitude of the risk manager's task in corporate negligence.

In part, the duty of a hospital to monitor the credentials and performance of physicians and other professionals practicing under its jurisdiction was established and recognized by statute and industry self-regulation. Under the federal Health Care Quality Improvement Act, hospitals and

BOX 9-13

- In a Michigan hospital, a surgeon removed the wrong breast during a mastectomy.
- Three incidents occurred in the same Florida hospital: (1) A patient with diabetes underwent surgery to amputate his diseased right foot; he awoke to find his left foot gone. (2) Another patient had surgery on the wrong knee. (3) A 77-year-old man died when a therapist mistakenly disconnected his ventilator.[8]

other health care entities must review the credentials and malpractice history of all physicians having admitting privileges. In a like manner, state licensure agencies and the standards of the Joint Commission on Accreditation of Healthcare Organizations (JCAHO) detail the responsibility of hospitals to review the credentials of health care professionals.

Contributory Negligence

Given the existence of medical malpractice on the part of a treating physician or institution, the law requires a causal connection between the defendant's wrongful act and the plaintiff's injury. Where the condition of the patient may be severely impaired at the outset, the causal relationship between the injury and the alleged medical malpractice may be difficult to demonstrate.

Frequently, plaintiffs are guilty of some act of negligence that may have contributed to their own injury. In some jurisdictions, a jury finding that the plaintiff's own negligent actions contributed to the injury completely bars any recovery against the defendant. However, most jurisdictions allocate the damages according to the proportionate responsibility of the parties, applying the doctrine of contributory negligence.

In the example in Box 9-14, a jury has the right to apportion relative "blame." If overall damages were assessed at $1 million, with the plaintiff and defendant equally negligent, the plaintiff would recover $500,000 from the defendant.

BOX 9-14

A patient died because the attending physician prescribed a drug that was contraindicated by other medications the patient was taking. Evidence indicated that death was also caused by the presence of illegal substances taken voluntarily by the patient. At no point did the patient inform the physician about the use of illegal substances. A jury found that the patient's conduct made her 50 percent responsible for her death.[36]

LIABILITY THEORIES APART FROM MEDICAL NEGLIGENCE

Additional liability theories in health care institutions may begin with unintentional medical negligence and proceed to intentional torts such as assault and battery, libel and slander, and invasion of privacy.

Intentional Tort or Conduct

Negligence is an unintentional tort because the actor does not intend to cause injury to the victim. In contrast, an intentional tort involves a specific action to cause harm, such as assault and battery. An intentional tort may take place when a physician performs a procedure contrary to the specific directions of the patient, or when a patient's confidential information is improperly released.

Assault and Battery

The words "assault" and "battery" are usually used together, and people perceive them as having the same meaning. However, battery is defined as the nonconsensual, unlawful, or wrongful physical constraint or touching of one person by another. Assault is the perceived attempt at a battery. The examples in Box 9-15 illustrate the distinction.

When a physician performs a medical procedure on a patient without consent, an action for assault and battery may be appropriate. "Any non-consensual touching of a patient's body, absent an emergency, is a

BOX 9-15

- While in an examination room with a woman's infant, a physician kissed the cheek of the young mother. She sued for assault and was awarded punitive damages of $10,000.[37]
- While performing a cholecystectomy, a surgeon called the scrub nurse incompetent, screamed at her, said she had sabotaged the operation, and threw a right-angle clamp at her. She sued for civil battery, slander, and intentional infliction of emotional distress. A trial court dismissed her claims. On appeal, the court held that it was possible to find battery where no injury had occurred but where offensive conduct had taken place.[38]

battery and the theory is that an uninformed consent to surgery obtained from a patient lacking knowledge of the dangers inherent in the procedure is no consent at all."[26]

Libel and Slander

A defamatory written or printed statement is referred to as libel; slander is the speaking of such words to a third party. To be actionable, the words claimed to be defamatory must be false. If a physician discloses patient information that is not true, a defamation suit may be possible if the other elements, such as duty and damages, are provable. However, the physician may be liable under some other theory, such as contract or negligence, for the nonconsensual disclosure of truthful patient information.

Invasion of Privacy

A related cause of legal action to defamation is based on the invasion of privacy of the patient. For example, if a plastic surgeon used photographs of a patient, without the patient's consent, to advertise specialty services or procedures, the patient could sue for damages based on invasion of privacy. Typically, this situation involves the publication of "before and after" photographs.

TYPES OF DAMAGES

Courts may award different forms of compensation in successful actions against physicians, hospitals, or other health care providers:

- Compensatory damage awards cover economic losses for past and future medical and supportive care, or past and future loss of earnings resulting from physical impairment.
- Awards for pain and suffering, mental anguish, and loss of consortium are real and discernible but cannot be measured in economic terms.
- Punitive damage awards in excess of usual compensatory damages reflect gross negligence or deliberate wrongful intent, and are rarely granted except in the most egregious situations. In effect, they serve as an example to deter future similar conduct.

STATUTES OF LIMITATION

Statutes of limitation specify the maximum period of time after the patient's injury during which a lawsuit may be *commenced*, not terminated. If the lawsuit is not filed before this period expires, it is untimely and will be dismissed. The statutory period in the vast majority of states is between one and three years, but the time varies by state. For example, New York State's statutory period is two and a half years. With some exceptions, the statutory period is "tolled" (deferred) during the infancy of a minor patient, and starts to run only on the patient's eighteenth birthday.

THE MOST COMMON AND MOST EXPENSIVE MALPRACTICE ALLEGATIONS

In recent years, the most frequently cited allegations in malpractice suits and the most expensive claims to settle have remained fairly constant.[39] The five most common malpractice allegations are:

1. Surgery/postoperative complications
2. Failure to diagnose cancer
3. Surgery/inadvertent act
4. Improper treatment (birth-related)
5. Failure to diagnose fracture or dislocation

The five most expensive settlements relate to:

1. Improper treatment (birth-related)
2. Failure to diagnose hemorrhage
3. Failure to diagnose myocardial infarction
4. Failure to diagnose infection
5. Failure to diagnose cancer

The study of a nationwide database of 193,500 personal injury verdicts by Jury Verdict Research, a firm that tracks jury awards, revealed that the average jury award in malpractice claims increased from $500,000 in 1995 to $1 million in 2000, and the national settlement median rose from $375,000 in 1995 to $500,000 in 2000. Nearly 60 percent of plaintiffs in medical malpractice cases lose in front of a jury, but if they win the awards are bigger than ever; cases related to childbirth and cancer diagnosis have resulted in the highest jury verdicts.[40]

As of December 31, 2001, Medical Liability Mutual Insurance Company (MLMIC)[41] insured 17,915 New York physicians. The company experienced its highest areas of loss indemnity for obstetricians (an average of $321,713), internal medicine (an average of $218,239), and general surgery (an average of $194,323):

- Obstetrics—66 percent of cases were due to brain-damaged infants, other related injuries, and Erb's Palsy.
- Internal medicine—18.8 percent of cases were due to myocardial infarction and cardiac arrest/heart failure, 10.9 percent were due to colon cancer, and 9.1 percent to other related cancers.
- General surgery—12.2 percent of cases were due to cholecystectomy; nine percent to breast cancer.

The high-cost indemnity areas of the hospital for medical malpractice cases are the labor/delivery room, the ER, patients' rooms, the operating room, and the coronary care unit. The general liability cases primarily concerned the outcomes of slips and falls; in small hospitals this type of injury comprised 68 percent of general liability cases, and in large hospitals 80 percent of general liability cases.[41]

Breast, Colon, and Lung Cancer Risk Applications

Failure to diagnose breast cancer is still the main liability risk reported by the Data Sharing Project of the Physician Insurers Association of America (PIAA). This database includes more than 125,000 malpractice claims filed since 1985 and represents the insurers of 60 percent of the nation's physicians. "Physical findings failed to impress the physician" was the most common reason (35%) for the delay in diagnosis; failure to follow-up was a close second (31%).[42] Physicians named in breast cancer suits in 1995 included radiologists (24%), obstetricians (23%), family physicians (17%), and surgical specialists (14%). A detailed 1994 study of 500 claims found that 60 percent of the plaintiffs were under 50 years of age and that the average settlement was $307,000. PIAA advises physicians to be more aggressive in their diagnosis, especially with younger women.[43] Another PIAA study identified liability mistakes in breast, lung, and colon cancer.[44] In all three cancers, "a serious deficiency" in taking histories from patients was a major problem, as was overlooking signs of cancer in prior X-rays.

Another major problem, likely to be exacerbated when costs are considered, was that physicians did not order diagnostic tests in enough "suspicious" cases. In breast and colon studies, the leading cause of lawsuits was the failure or delay in ordering a specific test. "Inadequate evaluation" followed by failure to respond to an abnormal chest X-ray was the leading cause in lung cancer suits. Failure to perform an endoscopic exam was the major reason for delay in diagnosis of colon cancer, followed closely by failure to perform a barium enema study.

Relative to breast cancer, the study suggested six cautions: (1) perform more careful examinations; (2) order additional studies; (3) explore complete family histories; (4) follow up after lumps are found, even if the mammogram is negative; (5) stress the importance of monthly self-examinations, particularly for women older than 40; and (6) emphasize the importance of an annual or biennial mammogram for women older than 40. Physicians must remember that mammograms are screening devices, not diagnostic tools. Even a fine-needle aspoiration can miss the malignant tumor, and pathologists need considerable experience to interpret the aspirations.

Regarding colon cancer, physicians were urged to be more aggressive in treating younger patients. While it is uncommon for individuals younger than 40 to have colon cancer, the probability goes up after age 45. Key symptoms include bleeding, change in bowel habits, anemia, and weight loss. "Absolute indications for study include multiple polyposis, familial polyposis, ulcerative colitis, and villous adenoma. Failure to pursue a 'remote complaint' is a serious problem."[44]

The study strongly advised physicians to review prior X-ray films when considering a diagnosis of lung cancer. Regarding follow-up, the study said: "The importance of communicating the results of radiographic exams to the treating physician cannot be over-emphasized."[44]

Medication Errors

Between September 1, 1990, and December 31, 1994, 4,215 medication-related physician malpractice payments were reported to the National Practitioner Data Bank. Although 50 percent of the payments were below $30,000, the mean payment was $124,998.[45] In another study based on data from 22 physician-owned professional liability insurance companies, the average settlement per case was $120,722. Analysis of the claim payment data makes medication error the second most frequent and second most expensive claim against physicians. Internal medicine and family practice specialists accounted for 59.3 percent of all the claims and 45.8 percent of all the settlements. Significant injury, such as quadriplegia and brain damage, occurred in 42 percent of the medication errors. In 21 percent of the cases, the patient died, and the medication errors were a major contributing factor in death in

BOX 9-16

The Most Common Medication Errors[46]

TYPE OF ERROR	OCCURRENCE PERCENTAGE
Incorrect dosage	27
Inappropriate for medical condition	25
Failure to monitor for side effects	21
Communication failure between physician and patient	18
Failure to monitor for drug levels	13
Lack of knowledge of medication	13
Most appropriate medication not used	13
Inappropriate length of treatment	13
Failure to monitor for drug effects	12
Inadequate medical history	12
Inadequate charting	10
Failure to note allergy previously listed	10
Failure or delay in ordering laboratory test	8
Inappropriate method/site/route in administration of drug	8
Error in writing prescription	6
Patient noncompliance or error	6
Failure to read medical record	6
Pharmacy error	5
Communication failure between physician and pharmacist	4
Medication contraindicated by other medication	4
Failure or delay in reading laboratory test	4

84.3 percent of the claims.[46] The causes of almost 400 drug-related claims with payments above $5,000 are detailed in Box 9-16. Significantly, most of the claims involved more than one error.

Medication errors involve the interaction and communication between and among the physician, the nurse, and the pharmacist; each party potentially contributes different types of errors leading to liability. In most cases, these medication errors are preventable. Incorrect dosage is the most commonly reported medication error.

In combination, the fame of the newspaper columnist and the well-known good reputation of the treating institution brought considerable notoriety to the case described in Box 9-17. In addition to the disciplinary proceedings brought against physicians, nurses, and pharmacists, the inquiries instituted by the JCAHO uncovered other areas of deficiency needing correction to prevent further casualties. Responding to the resulting recommendations, the hospital committed $1.3 million to an education program concentrating on drug treatment protocols and appropriate medical record documentation.

"Indecipherable prescriptions are causing dangerous and costly illness" according to an American Medical Association report.[47] Cost involves liability payments as well as longer hospital stays, significant illness, or death.

Nurses should not rewrite illegible physician prescriptions or orders, because they could misinterpret the name of the drug or the dosage while copying the prescription. Additionally, the nurse could be charged with practicing medicine without a license.[48] Proper protocol requires the nurse

BOX 9-17

A drug overdose killed Betsy Lehman, 39, an award-winning columnist at the *Boston Globe*. She had breast cancer and was given four times the intended dosage of a highly toxic drug during therapy at the Dana-Farber Cancer Institute. This error went unnoticed by a dozen doctors, nurses, and pharmacists. Another patient suffered heart damage after a similar drug overdose.[49]

to request clarification of all orders directly, to avoid misinterpretation and clinical hazards.

To avoid liability relating to the prescribing of medications, physicians should refrain from ordering unfamiliar medications, or drugs for conditions not normally handled by their own specialty. Medical record documentation should list all of the patient's current prescriptions, enumerate all known medication and other allergies, and detail discussions with patients about their medications. Legible prescriptions and discussions with nurses and pharmacists are important aspects of patient care, especially in cases of unusual treatment protocols (see Box 9-18).[50]

To protect themselves, nurses must acknowledge suspected medication errors, report them to their supervisors and the attending physician, file an incident report, and document the event in the medical record. All adverse reactions of the patient, and notification of the patient and family, should also be documented.[52]

Examining adverse drug events from a systems analysis of medication administration, investigators identified 16 major deficiencies leading to medication errors:[53]

1. Failure to disseminate knowledge about the medication
2. Failure to check the dosage and identity of the medication
3. Failure to provide the patient with information about the medication
4. Failure to accurately transcribe the medication order
5. Failure to prepare for an allergic reaction
6. Failure to track the medication order
7. Failure to communicate with all involved services
8. Incorrect use of devices
9. Lack of standardization of dosages and frequencies
10. Lack of standardization of drug distribution within a unit
11. Lack of standardization of procedures in general
12. Improper preparation of intravenous medications by nurses
13. Problems resulting from transfers or transitions of patients
14. Unresolved conflicts between providers of care
15. Problems with staffing and/or work assignments
16. Lack of feedback about adverse effects of medication errors

These failures of the health care system are directly linked to the most common medication errors ranked by frequency of claims.

BOX 9-18

Medication Errors

- Haldol prescription was 10 times proper dosage. Man with Tourettes Syndrome suffers overdose. Post-traumatic stress disorder. Directed verdict (November 2000). Jury awards $373,300.[29]
- Improper labeling of prescriptions. Overdose of Prednisone leading to avascular necrosis of the hips. Settlement $1 million (New York, June 2000).[29]
- Magnesium Sulfate intravenously injected eight times the prescribed dosage, leading to coma for 10 weeks. Settlement $650,000. (December 1998, Illinois).[29]
- In a neonatal intensive care unit, an eight-pound newborn delivered by caesarean section was recuperating from corrective cardiac surgery. A missing decimal point in a prescription resulted in a tenfold overdose of intravenous potassium and the baby's death. The infant's parents filed a notice of claim for wrongful death.[51]

Drug administration errors are traumatic events for nursing personnel. Their self-esteem and confidence are shaken, and depending on the severity of the disciplinary process, their practice activities may change significantly.[54] The support of professional colleagues is very important, along with the appropriate measures to counteract any adverse consequences of the error. Prevention of further occurrences can be addressed through an understanding of the dynamics of the incident, in conjunction with education and discussions with all pertinent staff.

Causes of pharmacist liability are identified by the Pharmacists Mutual Insurance Company as mechanical or intellectual. Dispensing the wrong drug accounts for 54.9 percent of the claims. More than two-thirds of the claims are for mechanical dispensing errors that can be controlled by the institution of relevant policies and procedures, prescription evaluations, careful computer entry and product handling, labeling, and dispensing. In this complex arrangement, there are several opportunities for cross-checking the appropriateness of the prescribed medication, dosage, administration orders, compounding, and preparation of admixtures and solutions.[55] If prescription legibility is the problem, direct communication with the physician and the nursing personnel who transcribe orders is essential for preventing medication errors.

In *Schroeder v. Lester E. Cox Medical Center, Inc.*, the hospital pharmacy was directly involved in a lawsuit (see Box 9-19).

Risk management responsibilities with regard to medication error incidents focus on diligence in reporting, documentation, and interaction with the physician-nurse-pharmacist triad in order to implement strategies for the future prevention of untoward events. Policies and prodecures need to be continually reviewed, and incidents should be reported to the pharmacy and therapeutics committees. A comprehensive approach to this issue, with an emphasis on trending and education, are known to be successful.

Incidents cited by the U.S. Pharmacopeial Medication Errors Reporting Program reveal confusion between opioid analgesics and drugs with similar generic names, with

BOX 9-19

To permit arterial grafting, Irene Schroeder's doctors stopped her heart during coronary bypass surgery. A cardiplegic solution prepared in the hospital pharmacy was administered to protect the heart. After the procedure, the surgeon attempted but failed to restart the heart and the patient died. A laboratory test of the cardioplegic solution revealed that it did not contain an adequate amount of dextrose, thus causing death. A jury awarded $92,000 in compensatory damages and $400,000 in punitive damages.[56]

BOX 9-20

Medication Errors: Name Confusion in Drugs

Celexa Celebrex Cerebyx	Leukeran Leucovorin Leukine
Acetozolamide Acetazolomida	Zantac Zyrtec
Taxotere Taxol	Flomax Volmax
Lamictal Lamisil	Adriamycin Aredia
Roxicet Roxaol	Hydormorphone Morphine

similar brand names, and with similar labels and packaging, as noted in Box 9-20.

More than 50 percent of the medication error reports are from hospital pharmacists, 4.8 percent from physicians, and 2.3 percent from nurses. Causes of these incidents include unclear and confusing packaging or labeling, suspected subpotency, and contamination. Drug administration dosage forms included injectables (35.5%), tablets (23.0%), and solutions (10.9%).[57] These manufacturing and quality control problems in the pharmaceutical industry present clear opportunities for risk management activities to reduce liability in clinical situations.

In an effort to reduce the improper use of drugs, the Food and Drug Administration has proposed that pharmacists provide patients with easy-to-understand "Medication Guides." More than 50 percent of Americans receiving prescriptions get no written instructions before using powerful drugs. Many patients leave health care facilities with prescription drugs for follow-up therapy but without written instructions. This FDA proposal would supply written patient information on drugs considered to have "serious and significant" health risks.[58]

OBSTETRICIANS UNDER FIRE

Two emerging and continuing trends have serious repercussions for both obstetricians and the patients who utilize their services: (1) the aggressive and sometimes violent activities of the anti-abortion movement, and (2) the flight from practice of skilled obstetricians because of perceived risks of litigation.

One of the tactics employed by the anti-abortion movement is to institute malpractice suits against physicians who perform abortions. In the past 10 years, the Arizona Right-to-Life organization filed nine such actions. Although none resulted in a verdict against the physician, these suits had a demoralizing effect. As one doctor, who has been the object of several such suits, declared: "Even if they lose, they win." Physicians become uninsurable by carriers and their reputations are smeared.[59] In Texas, Life Dynamics, Inc., distributed pamphlets to women leaving abortion clinics listing reasons to initiate malpractice suits against their physicians.[60]

Whereas previously many attorneys had refrained from instituting lawsuits involving abortions, lawyers have become increasingly active in pursuing actions on behalf of women injured during negligently performed abortions.[61] In New York State, criminal charges were lodged against one doctor whose patient died during an abortion (see Box 9-21).

Physicians and hospitals are increasingly unwilling to endure the controversy and costs associated with the abortion debate. Thus, more and more health care facilities are refusing to perform abortions. As a result, residents in obstetrics and gynecology will have fewer opportunities to develop the operative skills necessary to perform successful abortions, and this lack of experience will continue to pose risk problems.

Rising costs of malpractice liability insurance coverage for obstetric services have caused many physicians to stop delivering babies. Several other related factors have contributed to this situation: increases in malpractice claims against obstetric providers; fear of being sued; consolidations

BOX 9-21

Dr. David Benjamin was sentenced to 25 years to life in prison for the murder of a 33-year-old woman who hemorrhaged from a uterine tear during an abortion.[62]

and closures of hospital obstetric services; issues concerning payments and Medicaid; and the daily stress of providing obstetric and gynecological services.[63]

Studies indicate different problems in urban and rural areas. A California study of family practice physicians who discontinued obstetrics demonstrated that even a 25 percent reduction in insurance premium was an insufficient inducement to resume obstetric services. Clearly, other issues were more of a demotivating factor than merely the cost of malpractice insurance.[64]

A review by the Washington State Physicians Insurance Exchange and Association of physicians who had discontinued obstetric practice showed that these physicians were more likely to be older, to be sole practitioners in an urban setting, and to have a higher rate of new obstetric malpractice claims. "Apparently, being named as the target of an obstetrical malpractice claim plays a significant role in the decision of some obstetricians to discontinue obstetrical practice."[65]

In essence, obstetricians are being driven out of business because of the combination of the high risk in this specialty to both the mother and the baby and the relentless pursuit of attorneys.

RISK MANAGEMENT ISSUES IN PROFESSIONAL LIABILITY LITIGATION

Certain personal and professional characteristics may be associated with providers believed to be at high or low risk of vulnerability to malpractice claims. Applying factors relating to the quality of the structure, process, and outcome of patient care, statistical analysis revealed nine variables that predict high or low risk. High risk was associated with increased age, surgical specialty, emergency department coverage, increased days away from practice, and the feeling that the litigation climate was "unfair." Low risk factors were linked to scheduling enough time to talk with patients, answering patients' telephone calls directly, feeling "satisfied" with practice arrangements, and acknowledging greater emotional distress.[66]

Are there common issues surrounding professional liability lawsuits? A survey of defense attorneys in Georgia by MAG Mutual Insurance Company identified six key areas where risk managers could make a difference.[67]

Unrealistic Patient Expectations

About 88 percent of the lawyers stated that the patient and/or the family were surprised by the adverse outcome. Either they had unrealistic expectations, or they were not adequately educated regarding the course of treatment. All written material, personal conversations, and telephone conversations should be documented and updated in the medical record when revised material is distributed. Defense attorneys will then know exactly what the patient was given at the time of treatment.[68]

Research has indicated that risk "appears related to patients' dissatisfaction with their physicians' ability to establish rapport, provide access, administer care and treatment consistent with expectations, and communicate effectively."[69]

No Response to Complaints

A failure by the physician to respond to the specific complaints that had instigated a patient's visit to the physician was cited by more than 80 percent of the attorneys. Health care professionals should maintain eye contact, not interrupt when the patient is talking, and observe a patient's body language. Physicians should document in the medical record that the patient's complaints were considered before a treatment was determined.

Illegible Medical Records

Nothing damages a case more than the hesitant, inarticulate efforts of physician witnesses to read their own illegible handwritten medical record notes. About 77 percent of the lawyers identified illegibility as a significant problem, and this situation seriously inhibits the defense of a lawsuit. Incidentally, the "dictated but not read" annotation is not acceptable and has proven detrimental to the defense.

> "At rest on my desk is a three-inch medical record that defies interpretation. It's part of a latent suit on alleged plastic surgical errors, and I have to send it to the surgeon who wrote the chart entries to have it transcribed . . ."[70]

Insufficient Information in Medical Records

Not only must the information in medical records be legible, but the data should be significant and timely. Almost 70 percent of the lawyers claimed that information relative to medications, allergies, problems, telephone calls, and so on was missing from records and that the operative notes were written more than twenty-four hours after the procedure. A telephone record for each patient can document advice or prescriptions ordered directly from the pharmacy. Juries tend not be believe a physician who has no telephone log.

Comprehensive accounts are needed to describe unusual circumstances, such as a fall. The records should indicate date, time, changes in the patient's condition, follow-up care (X-rays, laboratory data, etc.), patient or family discussions, and instructions.

Any corrections or addendums to medical records need to be made according to hospital-approved procedure (such as the word "error" or "initials"), and it is not appropriate to obliterate, cross out, erase, tamper with, or otherwise change previous notes, either written or electronically entered. Often the medical record is the only evidence of the status of a patient's condition before, during, or after an event that has the potential for legal action.

No Follow-up on Abnormal Tests

In many cases, information from diagnostic tests is not conveyed to the patient in a timely manner. Attorneys indicated that 62 percent of the suits involved the failure to follow up on abnormal test results. A system must exist to ensure that diagnostic reports are received, reviewed by the physician, acted upon, and placed in the record (see Box 9-22). A log of all diagnostic tests should be checked daily and not filed until it has been reviewed and initialed, and action, if required, has been taken.

Professional Miscommunication

The opportunity for miscommunication is always present, and although miscommunication in itself may not be the proximal cause of a lawsuit, the misunderstanding may lead to errors prompting a legal action. About 58 percent of the attorneys stated that

BOX 9-22

Lab Tests

Because of the late delivery of a blood sample and improper testing, there was a failure to detect spina bifida. This Washington, D.C. case resulted in a settlement $1.1 million in August 2000.[29]

miscommunication had occurred in many of their cases. Some common communication errors that can be remedied include:

- Lack of explicit directions or protocols for nursing personnel regarding when to notify the physician of a change in a patient's condition.
- Inadequate communication of a patient's deteriorating condition from nursing personnel to the physician.
- Failure of the covering physician to communicate to the primary physician the services provided to a patient.
- Failure to communicate the degree of urgency to other health care personnel.
- Lack of verbal communication from consultants, radiologists, or pathologists identifying an abnormality.
- Reliance on the assumption that no response from the referral physician indicates that the patient's problem was resolved.

These key risk factors, which are involved in a significant number of lawsuits, can be modified through the practice of the specific risk management techniques already mentioned. Certainly, the techniques are not overly cumbersome and can decrease the likelihood of being involved in a legal action and/or increase the defensibility in court.

References

1. Brennan, T. A., Leape, L. L., Laird, N. M., et al. (1991). Incidence of adverse events and negligence in hospitalized patients. *New England Journal of Medicine* 324(6):370–376; Leape, L. L., Brennan, T. A., Laird, N. M., et al. (1991). The nature of adverse events in hospitalized patients. *New England Journal of Medicine* 324(6):377–384; Localio, A. R., Lawthers, A. G., Brennan,T. A., et al. (1991). Relation between malpractice claims and adverse events due to negligence. *New England Journal of Medicine* 325(4): 245–251.
2. California Medical Association. (1977). *Report of the Medical Insurance Feasibility Study*. San Francisco, Calif.: California Medical Association.
3. Brennan, T. A., Herbert, L. P., Laird, N. M., et al. (1991). Hospital characteristics associated with adverse events and substandard care. *New England Journal of Medicine* 265(24):3265–3269.
4. Leape, L. L., Lawthers, A. G., Brennan, T. A., et al. (1993). Preventing medical injury. *Quality Review Bulletin* 19(5):144–149.
5. Leape, L. L. (1994). Error in medicine. *New England Journal of Medicine* 272:1851–1857.
6. Jones, G. F. (1995). Jury awards parents $625,000 on fatal misdiagnosis of young son. *Star-Ledger* (Newark, N.J.), January 20, p. 28, col. 3.
7. Blumenthal, D. (1994). Making medical errors into "medical treasures," *New England Journal of Medicine* 272:1867–1868.
8. Hampson, R. (1995). Healing place or a horror? Medicial mistakes rock hospitals. *News Tribune* (Woodbridge, N.J.), March 19, p. A10, col. 5.
9. The science of making mistakes. (!995). *Lancet* 345(8954):871–872.
10. Senders, J. W. (1993). Theory and analysis of typical errors in a medical setting. *Hospital Pharmacy* 28(6):505–508.
11. Kohn, K. T., Corrigan, J. M., Donaldson, M. S., eds. (1999). *To Err Is Hman: Building a Safer Health System*. Washington, D.C.: Institute of Medicine, National Academy Press.
12. Wrong lung was removed so hospital pays $9 million. (1995). *Star-Ledger* (Newark, N.J.), April 2, p. 16, col. 5.
13. Bayles, F. (1995). Doctors no longer sacred cows. Rash of criminal charges, indictments seen as evidence of rising public anger. *State Island Advance* (New York), April 12, p. A7, col. 1.
14. Lab charged with homicide for failing to detect cancer in Pap smears. (1995). *Star-Ledger* (Newark, N.J.), April 13, p. 7.
15. *Palsgraf v. Long Island Rail Road*, 248 N.Y. 339, 1928.
16. King, J. H. (1986). *The Law of Medical Malpractice in a Nutshell*. St. Paul, Minn.: West, p. 9.
17. Fiesta, J. (1995). Law for the nurse manager: Legal update. *Nursing Management* 26(3):10–11; *Armstrong v. Paoli Memorial Hospital*, 633 A. 2d 605, *The Citation*, February 1, 1944, 65:3:31.
18. *Pike v. Hornsinger*, 55 N.Y. 201 (1898).

19. *Davis v. Tirrell,* 110 Misc. 2d 889, 443 N.Y.S. 2d 136 (1981).
20. *Savarese v. Allstate Insurance Company,* 287 A.D. 2d 294, 731 N.Y.S. 2d 226 (2d Dept. 2001).
21. *Evangelista v. Zolan,* 247 A.D. 2d 508, 669 N.Y.S. 2d 325 (2d Dept. 1998).
22. Verhovek, S. H. (1994). Medical incompetence: A whispered factor in rising costs. *New York Times,* April 9, p. 8, col. 1.
23. *Matter of Storar,* 52 N.Y. 2d 363, 438 N.Y.S. 2d 266 (1981); see Sec. 2805-d of the New York State Public Health Law, and Sec. 4401-a of the New York State Civil Practice Law and Rules.
24. *Alberti v. St. John's Episcopal Hospital,* 116 A.D. 2d 612, 497 N.Y.S. 2d 57 (2d Dept. 1984).
25. No informed consent to back surgery. (1994). *American Medical News* 37(4):16.
26. *Fogal v. Genesee Hospital,* 41 A.D. 2d 468, 344 N.Y.S. 2d 552 (4th Dept. 1973).
27. *Graddy v. New York Medical College,* 19 A.D. 2d 426, 243 N.Y.S. 2d 940 (1st Dept. 1963).
28. *Bing v. Thunig,* 2 N.Y. 2d 656, 163 N.Y.S. 2d 3 (1957).
29. Healthcare Providers Service Organization. (2002). Case of the Month Archives, All Professions. *http://www.hp30.com/case/case index.lphp3.*
30. *Mduba v. Benedictine Hospital,* 522 A.D. 2d 450, 384 N.Y.S. 2d 527 (3d Dept. 1976).
31. *Soltis v. State of New York,* 172 A.D. 2d 919, 568 N.Y.S. 2d 470 (3d Dept. 1991).
32. *Agustin v. Beth Israel Hospital,* 185 A.D. 2d 2031, 586 N.Y.S. 2d (1st Dept. 1992).
33. *Beeck v. Tucson General Hospital,* 18 Ariz. App. 165, 500 P. 2d 1153 (1972).
34. *Megrelishvili v. Our Lady of Mercy Medical Center,* 291 A.D. 2d 18, 739 N.Y.S. 2d (1st Dept. 2002).
35. *Dykema v. King,* 959 F. Supp. 736 (D.S.C. 1997).
36. Hoffman, J. (1995). Jurors find shared blame in '84 death. *New York Times,* February 7, p. B1, col. 5.
37. Benton v. Scroggie, No. 93-146242, March 1994, p. 4; Fiesta, J. (1995). Law for the nurse manager: Legal update. *Nursing Management* 26(1):30.
38. Snyder v. Turk, 627 N.E. 2d 1053 (Ohio Ct. of App., Aug. 19, 1993); Irritated surgeon throws clamp at nurse in OR. (1995). *American Medical News* 38(20):22.
39. McCormick, B. (1995). Liability rates: Mixed signals. *American Medical News* 38(4):2, 31.
40. Lankarge, V. (2002). Soaring malpractice premiums bleed doctors, rob consumers. *Health Care News Consumer Insurance Guide,* January. *www.heartland.org/health/jan02/malpractice.htm.*
41. Robb, J. H. (2002). *Medical Malpractice Claims Data: A 15-Year Review.* Presentation at 2002 MLMIC Risk Management Seminar, The New York Helmsley Hotel, June 7.
42. Breast cancer leads the list of malpractice suits. (1995). *Star-Ledger* (Newark, N.J.), June 3, p. 2, col. 3.
43. McCormick, B. (1995). Breast cancer still top liability risk: Cost of claims rising. *American Medical News* 38(23):22–23.
44. Clements, B. (1994). The most common causes of lawsuits and how you can protect yourself: Missed cancers. *American Medical News* 37(28):15–16.
45. Oshel, R. E. (1995). Personal communication, U.S. Department of Health and Human Services, Public Health Service, Division of Quality Assurance, National Practitioner Data Bank.
46. Crane, M. (1993). The medication errors that get doctors sued. *Medical Economics* 70(22):36–41.
47. Indecipherable Rx: Danger. (1995). *New York Times,* June 13, p. A22, col. 1.
48. Davino, M. (1995). Poor penmanship can create big legal risks. *RN* 58(3):51.
49. Hospital official resigns over drug overdoses. (1995). *New York Times,* May 12, p. A16, col. 1.
50. Clements, B. (1994). How to avoid medication errors. *American Medical News* 37(27):18.
51. Lambert, B. (2002). Baby dies in hospital, and parents plan to sue. *New York Times,* February 9, p. B6.
52. Parisi, S. B. (1994). What to do after a med error. *Nursing94* 24(6):59.
53. Leape, L. L., Bates, D. W., Cullen, D. J., et al. (1995). Systems analysis of adverse drug events. *Journal of the American Medical Association* 274(1):35–43.
54. Arndt, M. (1994). Research in practice: How drug mistakes affect self-esteem. *Nursing Times* 90(15): 27–30.
55. Fitzgerald, W. L., and Roberts, K. B. (1993). Avoiding legal problems in pharmacy practice. *Drug Topics* 137(21):112–123.
56. LeBlang, T. R. (1993). Punitive damages. *American Druggist* 209(1):21–22.
57. DPPR at a glance. (1995). *USP Quality Review* 47:1–4.

58. FDA wants pharmacists to make prescription medications user-friendly. (1995). *Star-Ledger* (Newark, N.J.), August 24, p. 54, col. 1.

59. Lewin, T. (1995). Latest tactic against abortion: Accusing doctors of malpractice. *New York Times,* April 9, p. 1, col. 2.

60. Schreibman, T. (1995). Sue me, sue me. *New Woman* 25(7):59.

61. Shoop, J. G. (1995). Lawyers enter abortion fray on side of injured women. *Trial* 31(2):12–14.

62. MD gets 25 years for abortion death. (1995). *Star-Ledger* (Newark, N.J.), September 13, p. 5, col. 5.

63. Fondren, L. K., and Ricketts, T. C. (1993). The North Carolina obstetrics access and professional liablity study: A rural-urban analysis. *Journal of Rural Health* 9(2):129–137.

64. Nesbitt, T. S., Arevalo, J. A., Tanji, J. L., et al. (1992). Will family physicians really return to obstetrics if malpractice premiums decline? *Journal of American Board of Family Practice* 5(4):413–418.

65. Rosenblatt, R. A., Weitkamp, G., Lloyd, M., et al. (1990). Why do physicians stop practicing obstetrics? The impact of malpractice claims. *Obstetrics & Gynecology* 76(2):245–250.

66. Charles, S. C., Gibbons, R. D., Frisch, P. R., et al. (1992). Predicting risk for medical malpractice claims using quality of care characteristics. *Western Journal of Medicine* 157(4):433–439.

67. Ostergard, N. (1993). Attorney survey reveals causes of litigation. *Journal of the Medical Association of Georgia* 82(8):414–416.

68. Ridder, W. (2000). Risk tips: Chart what you say. Risk Management Foundation of the Harvard Medical Institution. *RMF Quarterly,* Spring, 3. *www.rmfharvard.edu/publications/quarterly/spr2000/Qspr2000_ab/body.html..*

69. Hickson, G. B., Federspiel, C. F., et al. (2002). Patient complaints and malpractice risk. *Journal of the American Medical Association* 287(22):295.

70. Ridder, W. (2000). Risk tips: Handwriting on the wall for illegible notes. Risk Management Foundation of the Harvard Medical Institution. *RMF Quarterly,* Winter, 3. *www.rmfharvard.edu/publications/quarterly/win2000/Qwin2000_a8body.html.*

CHAPTER 10 Strategies to Reduce Liability

Managing Physicians and Litigation Alternatives

Florence Kavaler
Allen D. Spiegel

To reduce liability, risk managers must consider the scope of management of physicians including the various professional practice acts and the impact of the National Practitioner Data Bank (NPDB) in the collection of adverse action data about providers. Within and without the professions, the legislative and voluntary adoption of clinical practice guidelines creates far-reaching legal implications for risk management programs. In addition, there is a growing movement to enact tort reforms or to offer alternatives to litigation. All these strategies combine to develop an environment where the risk manager must be constantly on the alert for changes affecting liability risks.

PROFESSIONAL PRACTICE ACTS

State legislation defines the scope of professional practice and specifies the powers and functions of the regulatory board for each health care provider group licensed by the state. Usually, the statutes begin with definitions such as distinctions between "registered" and "licensed practical/vocational" nurse. "Collaboration," "direction," "supervision," and "nursing diagnosis" are terms commonly defined. These definitions delineate the scope of practice and the degree of interdependence with other practitioners, especially physicians. State legislation is uniform in granting physicians the power to diagnose and to treat patients. Lawyers frequently refer to the physician as the "captain of the ship" when care is rendered concurrently to sick and ailing patients by a number of different health care professionals.

Regulatory boards for each of the professions are created by statute. Legislation specifies the composition of the board, along with its duties and broad powers to create rules and regulations for specific requirements for professional practice. A process of licensure is detailed and can include state guidelines for mandatory continuing education and the continuous monitoring of the professionals on behalf of the public.

Professional discipline involves investigation and prosecution of allegations of profound misconduct of licensees, as well as the illegal practice of the profession by unlicensed persons. Moral character issues and health-impaired professional licensees are subject to investigation and appropriate action, such as discipline, license revocation or suspension, fines, or referrals for professional assistance.

There are several categories of misconduct that stimulate investigations, hearings, and possible actions against licensees:[1]

- Repeated acts of negligence
- Incompetence
- Aiding or abetting the unlicensed practice of medicine
- Failure to comply with government rules or regulations regarding the practice of medicine
- Exploitation of the patient for financial gain
- Evidence of moral unfitness to practice medicine
- Failure to maintain appropriate patient medical records
- Abandoning or neglecting a patient
- Harassing, abusing, or intimidating a patient, physically or verbally
- Ordering excessive tests or treatments
- Unlawful use of controlled substances

Although the particular procedures for disciplining professionals may vary by jurisdiction, an inquiry usually is initiated by the receipt of a complaint. If an investigation reveals evidence of substantive as opposed to "technical" misconduct, the involved professional will be notified of the nature of the claimed misconduct in a formal charge. At this stage of the proceeding, many cases are settled through a consent agreement. If the case is not settled, a hearing will be held at which the agency will be required to present proof to sustain the charges. In defense, the professional can be represented by counsel and have the right to cross-examine and to present witnesses. In cases where it is deemed that the public would be in danger if the professional continued to practice, the agency has the authority to suspend the practitioner's license immediately.

At the conclusion of the hearing by the fact-finding body, either a panel or an administrative law judge will make recommendations. Adverse actions recommended can include revocation, suspension, limitation, probation, censure, and reprimand. There is usually at least one level of appeal within the administrative agency. A sanctioned professional must appeal within the judicial context, with the understanding that such review is usually limited to whether the decision of the agency was supported by the evidence and the sanctioning action taken was not arbitrary or capricious. This means that the penalty was not disproportionate to the claimed violation. Since violations of professional conduct can lead to disciplinary sanctions and possibly malpractice lawsuits, standards and guidelines have emerged to alleviate potential problems (see Box 10-1).

As an example, there are 70,000 licensed physicians in New York State (58,000 of whom are practicing) and 172,000 physicians with New York State licenses in the United States. The New York State Board for Professional Medical Conduct (OPMC) is composed of 160 members, including 105 physicians, seven physician assistants, and 47 public members. Office of Professional Medical Conduct (OPMC) statistics document that in the year 2000, there were 6,106

BOX 10-1

- Mount Sinai Hospital was fined $66,000 by the New York State Health Department and suspended its live-donor liver transplant program in January 2002. Journalist Mike Hurewitz, age 57, died three days after donating part of his liver to his brother. Inadequate post-operative care was cited.[2]
- The Massachusetts State Board of Registration in MEdicine has indefinitely suspended an orthopedic surgeon's medical license because he left an anesthetized patient with an open incision in his back in the operating room while the surgeon went to deposit his paycheck in a bank several blocks away from the Mount Auburn Hospital,where he was operating. The Board labeled him a "serious threat" to the health, safety, and welfare of the public.[3]
- The New Jersey State Board of Medical Examiners suspended the license of Dr. Jose A. Lopez when a 28-year-old mother of three died after "tummy tuck" surgery in the office. Dr. Lopez is a pathologist who received plastic surgery training in Colombia. He is not board-certified and has no hospital affiliations. Another of his patients was admitted to the hospital three days after liposuction because of abdominal bleeding consequent to excessive doses of lidocaine as an anesthetic. State investigation uncovered many of Dr. Lopez's patients who suffered near-fatal infections, perforated bowels, or torn abdomens.[4]

complaints received and 388 licensees referred for charges. Disciplinary actions against physicians include 97 surrenders, 47 revocations, 105 suspensions, 98 censures and reprimands, and 121 administrative warnings. The Commissioner of Health issued 43 summary suspensions to physicians declared an "imminent danger" to the public.[5]

Impaired Professionals

Health problems, disease, and disability affect health care professionals as they do other members of society. However, when these medical impairments adversely affect professional judgment, patient care, collegial expectations, and social role, private and public interventions become necessary.

In a series of interviews with ill physicians, Spiro,[6] a Yale University medical school professor, found a remarkable ability for denial, continuing to practice despite pain, and reluctance to disclose their diagnosis for fear of losing professional standing. Everybody is concerned with the physiological changes that accompany aging, such as reduced visual acuity, memory lapses, depression, toxic effects of medications, and reduced functional capabilities. Additional risks to professional competence and performance are incurred with alcohol abuse, chemical dependency, and psychiatric diagnoses. Symptoms of impairment should be recognized and appropriate actions taken to help intervene with treatment, rehabilitation, and prevention of untoward professional activities. Examples of symptoms of physical impairment include:[7]

- Making rounds late
- Inappropriate orders
- Complaints from staff
- Frequent accidents
- Hostile behavior
- Unexplained absences
- Mood swings, arguments, violent outbursts
- Deterioration of personal hygiene
- Multiple somatic complaints
- Excessive drinking at staff functions
- Frequent job changes or relocations
- Neglected social commitments

Prompted by a 1973 landmark article on the sick physician in the *Journal of the American Medical Association*,[8] state medical societies and licensing boards have made considerable progress in developing effective programs to identify and treat impaired physicians. Patterned after employee assistance programs (EAPs), a physician assistance committee (PAC) and program were established at the University of Maryland Medical System as a standing committee of the medical board. This PAC accepts referrals from a variety of sources, arranges for specific evaluations, refers physicians to treatment, monitors compliance, and advocates for the physician as long as there is compliance with the treatment agreement. Most of the cases the PAC sees are related to alcohol and/or drug dependence; about 20 percent of the cases involve psychiatric or interpersonal problems.[9]

Established in 1980, the Physician Health Committee of the Medical Society of the District of Columbia reports an 80 percent success rate for impaired physicians. Medical specialists using the program established by this committee include internists (15%), psychiatrists (12%), family and general practitioners (12%), and obstetricians and gynecologists (7%).[10] A program similar to Alcoholics Anonymous, the Impaired Physician Program of the Medical Association of Georgia reported that 77 percent of treatment outcomes for physicians recovering from substance abuse are successful.[11]

The Committee for Physicians' Health (CPH), a division of the Medical Society of the State of New York, monitors approximately 550 physicians recovering from substance use disorders and other psychiatric disorders. Each year, approximately 100 "new" physicians enroll in the monitoring program. In 2001, 32.7 percent of the newly enrolled physicians had a diagnosis of drug abuse or dependence, 22.2 percent had a diagnosis of alcohol abuse or dependence, 15.4 percent had a diagnosis of drug and alcohol abuse or dependence, 28.8 percent had a diagnosis of mental or emotional disorders, and 1.9 percent had a diagnosis of both drug/alcohol abuse or dependence and mental or emotional disorders.[12] Activities of the CPH are confidential and protected by state and federal law, and they are immune from legal challenges. CPH does not report physicians to the OPMC as long as they agree to participate, stay with the program, are helped by treatment, and do not present an imminent danger to the public.

Risks that impaired professionals pose can be extensive and potentially costly. Removal of their practices protects the public and prevents identifiable problems. However, salvaging professional careers should become an important parallel activity with due concern for confidentiality and reduction of the stigma that accompanies official actions against health care professionals.

Sexual Misconduct

Physicians are not unique where sexual misconduct and harassment are concerned. These behaviors occur in all professions. In the health care milieu, such misconduct results from the innate power differential residing in the dependency of the patient on the professional, who exploits the opportunities.[13]

Sexual misconduct and harassment have significant harmful effects on patients, as well as ruinous consequences for the professional. Hospitals experience a three-year average of five rapes per year and about 40 other sexual assaults, according to a survey of the International Association for Healthcare Security and Safety.[14] Two Florida incidents are illustrative (see Box 10-2). Victims in this survey included patients and

BOX 10-2

- A male nurse was witnessed raping a minor female patient at Citrus Memorial Hospital. Police charged him with "five separate counts of rape and interviewed more than 40 women who may have been victims."
- A male occupational therapy aide attacked a mentally disturbed 26-year-old female patient at Memorial Regional Rehabilitation Center. He was charged with sexual battery.[15]

BOX 10-3

Dr. Brij Mohan was charged with 18 allegations of professional misconduct with six female patients between 1991 and 1994. He fondled the breasts and genitals of female patients and asked them for sex during examinations. There were three statutory violations: abusing a patient; moral unfitness; and fraudulent practice of medicine. He admitted guilt and surrendered his license. After a year, he could apply to have his license returned.[17]

visitors; suspects included patients, employees, and one physician.

In 1991, the American Medical Association Council on Ethical and Judicial Affairs considered the sexual misconduct problem extensively and issued a statement: "Sexual contact or romantic relationships concurrent with the physician-patient relationship may be unethical."[16] Subsumed under this ethical standard are a wide range of situations encountered in a professional's daily medical practice:

- Predatory physicians with serious personality disorders who systematically attempt to seduce patients.
- Professionals who claim to use sex for therapeutic purposes.
- Professionals who abuse the physical examination in an inappropriate erotic manner (see Box 10-3).
- Professionals who date patients or encourage or contribute to infatuation, intense lovesickness, or romantic situations.
- Professionals who engage in sexual harassment, making erotic or suggestive remarks to patients.

In 1998 in New York State, there were 26 disciplinary actions involving sexual misconduct by physicians and physicians' assistants: nine revocations of license, 23 surrenders, one suspension, and four censures.[18] There appears to be a growing position of "zero tolerance" for physician sexual misconduct. Physicians with these psychiatric problems or severe personality disorders are dealt with punitively by state licensing agencies and boards of professional medical conduct.

There appears to be a more tolerant and compassionate approach to physicians who experience psychiatric problems attendant to alcoholism, drug or substance abuse, and depression or organic brain disorders than to physicians charged with sexual abuse. Physicians charged with sexual misconduct are regarded as an embarrassment to the professional community and are shunned by the mainstream. Although these physicians presumably also are psychiatrically impaired, their rehabilitation potential is poor. "Currently there is virtually no research regarding the efficacy of therapy for physicians who engage in sexual misconduct."[16]

FEDERATION OF STATE MEDICAL BOARDS

Many health care professionals have licenses to practice in several states concur-

BOX 10-4

The New Jersey Board of Medical Examiners revoked the license of a plastic surgeon who had previously had his license revoked in New York State because of gross negligence, fraud, and "engaging in conduct which evidences moral unfitness." The president of the Board believed that "if the doctor was judged by his peers in New York as not being worthy of holding a New York license, those things would be true in this state, as well."[19]

rently. The Federation of State Medical Boards, Inc., and the federal National Practitioner Data Bank thus help licensing boards share information across state lines concerning adverse actions taken against professionals (see Box 10-4).

Federation membership consists of seventy medical boards, including allopathic, osteopathic, and composite state medical boards, the District of Columbia, Puerto Rico, Guam, Commonwealth of the Northern Mariana Islands, and the U.S. Virgin Islands. Through the Federation, the state medical boards cooperate and share information about physicians to enhance their protection of the public and to improve the quality of care.

The Federation Physician Data Center (FPDC) contains 117,000 Board actions related to 35,000 physicians dating back to the 1960s. This data set is available to licensing and disciplinary boards, and government and private agencies involved in employment and/or credentialing of physicians. In 1999, the FPDC recorded 4,529 actions reported by all of the medical boards. Of these, 3,838 (85%) were prejudicial to the physician and were taken for violations such as quality of care, sexual misconduct, insurance fraud, alcohol/substance abuse, or inappropriate prescribing of controlled substances. The disciplinary actions taken were primarily revocations, suspensions, or consent orders.

The Federation Credentials Verification Services (FCVS), established in 1996, contains physicians' core medical credentials on medical education, postgraduate training, licensing examination history, and board action history, and is a lifetime professional portfolio. The FPDC and FCVS serve to enhance the medical licensing and disciplinary systems.[20]

In 2000, the state medical boards imposed 3,951 punitive actions against the 676,522 licensed practicing physicians, and only 1,725 physicians—or one quarter of 1 percent—lost their licenses. Sidney Wolfe, MD, director of the Public Citizens Health Research Group, has criticized the state medical boards as "grossly ineffective" in ferreting out poor-quality physicians and says he doesn't believe in remedial education for substandard practitioners.[21]

NATIONAL PRACTITIONER DATA BANK

On November 14, 1986, the Health Care Quality Improvement Act (HCQIA), Title W of P.L. 99–660, was signed into law. Congress was prompted to enact the legislation by the burgeoning medical malpractice suits, by the perceived need to improve the quality of care, and by the necessity for effective professional peer review. A major provision of this law created the National Practitioner Data Bank (NPDB), designed to collect comprehensive data on adverse actions taken against health care practitioners, malpractice payments made on their behalf, and Medicare/Medicaid exclusions of practitioners.

There are four classes of adverse actions requiring reporting: those taken against a practitioner's license by a state medical or dental board; those taken against a practitioner's clinical privileges as a result of peer review at a hospital or other health care facility; those taken against membership by a professional society; and those taken by Medicare/Medicaid and the Drug Enforcement Administration (DEA), which excludes practitioners from these agencies. Indemnity is provided to peer reviewers, to individuals who provide information to the process, to hospitals relying on the information they obtain from the NPDB, and to the NPDB itself.

Insurance companies and hospitals are required to report to the Secretary of Health and Human Services (HHS) and to state licensing boards regarding medical malpractice payments resulting from court judgments or settlements. Failure to report the required information results in a civil penalty of $10,000 per claim.

As of December 31, 2000, the end of its 124th month of operations, the NPDB contained reports on 264,065 reportable actions, malpractice payments, and Medicare/Medicaid exclusions involving 164,320 individual practitioners. Of the 164,320 practitioners reported to the NPDB, 69.7 percent were physicians (including M.D. and D.O. residents and interns), 14.1 percent were dentists (including dental residents), 6.2 percent were nurses and nursing-related practitioners, and 10 percent were other health care practitioners. About two-thirds of physicians with reports (65.4 percent) had only one report in the NPDB, 85 percent had two or fewer reports, 97.4 percent had five or fewer, and 99.6 percent had 10 or fewer. One out of every seven United States physicians and one out of every eight dentists has at least one malpractice payment or report with the NPDB. Of the 36,763 reports received by the NPDB in 2000, approximately 53 percent of the reports concerned malpractice payment; 80.3 percent of these concerned physicians and 12.2 percent concerned dentists.[22]

As in previous years, obstetrics-related cases, which accounted for approximately 8.3 percent of all physician malpractice payment reports, had the highest median and mean payment amounts ($225,000 and $417,181, respectively). For all medical malpractice payments made during 2000, the mean delay between an incident that led to a payment and the payment itself was 4.48 years.[22]

Hospitals are mandated to query the NPDB about all new medical staff professionals, and every two years on all staff for recredentialing purposes. In 2000, there were 3,292,157 queries to the NPDB, of which 34 percent were from hospitals, 54 percent from HMOs, PPOs, and group practices, and 0.4% from state licensure and disciplinary boards.[22]

Malpractice report rates vary considerably among the states. Variations could be the result of local factors, such as clinical practice, quality of care, size of the state, and relative number of practitioners. Statutory provisions make it easier or more difficult for plaintiffs to sue for malpractice and obtain a payment. There are differences among states in the statute of limitations provisions governing when plaintiffs may sue, and in the burden of proof requirements. In addition, some states limit payments for non-economic damages (e.g., pain and suffering). These limits may reduce the number of claims filed by reducing the total potential recovery and the financial incentives for plaintiffs and their attorneys to file suit, particularly for children or retirees who are unlikely to lose earned income because of malpractice incidents. The median physician malpractice payment in the United States in 2000 was $125,000. The highest medians for 2000 were found in Maine, Illinois, Massachusetts, Alabama, and Connecticut, all of which had a median payment of $200,000 or more. The lowest median for 2000 was found in California at $55,000. Indiana, Kentucky, and Vermont all had median payments of $75,000.

The reporting of malpractice payments made for the benefit of medical and osteopathic interns and residents is also mandated under the HCQIA, which makes no exceptions for trainees.[22]

Physicians and other health care practitioners are sent copies of all reports received by the NPDB that name them. They may submit a statement for the record and have the right to dispute the factual accuracy of the report with or without an accompanying statement.

At the end of 2000, 4.7 percent (1,755) of all licensure reports, 15.6 percent (1,495) of all clinical privileges reports, and 4.1 percent (7,811) of all malpractice payment reports in the NPDB were in dispute. The data bank is trying to stop insurers and hospitals that allegedly "shield" physicians from being identified in the national repository. This is purportedly done through overt under-reporting, or by naming a hospital or other entity instead of a physician when malpractice payments are reported to the data bank.[22]

Patients want more information about their physicians and other health professionals, and have urged open access to the NPDB. In disagreement, the American Medical Association successfully blocked consumer access and full disclosure. U.S. Representative Ron Wyden (a Democrat from Oregon), the sponsor of the original HCQIA bill, argued for consumer access: "At the very least, consumers have a right to know which health care provider they should avoid."[23] Similar statements by Dr. Sidney M. Wolfe, Director of the Public Citizen's Health Research Group, echo the congressman: "We believe that all information in the data bank should be available to the public—the very people it was created to protect."[24]

To Query Is to Know

Risk managers should review the policies and procedures for credentialing, for granting clinical privileges, and for periodic recredentialing to ensure that all available professional practice data is on hand. The NPDB is an inexpensive source for supplementing data from other queries to assure the health care organization that practitioners are highly qualified and not apt to incur litigious situations for themselves or the institutions.

CLINICAL PRACTICE GUIDELINES

Clinical practice guidelines have been defined as "systematically developed statements to assist practitioners and patient decisions about appropriate health care for specific clinical circumstances."[25] There is a definite intent to influence what clinicians do in order to elevate the quality of care provided by all practitioners and to help reduce waste and abuse and improve cost effectiveness.[26]

Guidelines by Professional Groups

Typically, professional standards begin with the professional associations. Each of the medical specialty societies may develop its own standards for areas that are relevant to its specialty. Practice guidelines developed by these organizations are issued by experts including the American Medical Association (AMA), medical specialty societies, and the federal government. Step-by-step guides help local, state, and regional medical organizations to identify key attributes for practice parameters and to implement the standards.

More than 1,000 guidelines have been contributed by 180 different organizations to the National Guideline Clearinghouse (NGC), which began in 1999. The NGC is a public resource and comprehensive database of evidence-based clinical practice guidelines. The NGC is sponsored by the Agency for Healthcare Research and Quality (formerly the Agency for Health Care Policy and Research), in partnership with the American Medical Association and the American Association of Health Plans. The NGC's mission is to provide physicians, nurses, health care providers, health plans, integrated delivery systems, purchasers, and other health professionals with an accessible mechanism for obtaining objective, detailed information on clinical practice guidelines and to further their dissemination, implementation, and use. For example, the American Society of Colon and Rectal Surgery has issued practice parameters, or guidelines on "prevention of venous thromboembolism" and "identification and testing of patients at risk for dominantly inherited colorectal cancer." The American Academy of Child & Adolescent Psychiatry has 20 guidelines, the American Academy of Pediatrics has 42 guidelines, and the American Diabetes Association has 22 guidelines. The American Academy of Orthopedic Surgeons has developed clinical guidelines on knee surgery and ankle injury. There are 142 guidelines on neoplasms, 96 guidelines on endocrine diseases, 94 guidelines on respiratory tract diseases, 160 guidelines on cardiovascular diseases, and many more.[27]

The National Comprehensive Cancer Network (NCCN) is an alliance of 17 leading cancer centers created to develop and institute clinical practice standards and research on performance outcomes. The National Oncology Outcomes Database established by the NCCN in 1997[28] analyzes the adherence of the centers to the practice guidelines and the outcomes that such practice achieves. The NCCN members attempt to enhance effectiveness and efficiency of care through measurement, management, and research. Their initial focus is on breast cancer, and subsequently will be on non-Hodgkin's lymphoma.

Hospitals and their medical staffs have also adopted or developed clinical practice guidelines as part of their quality improvement efforts. In addition, the American Hospital Association's Medication Safety Initiative provides information on successful practices, tools, and resources, and will track the progress of implementation as a strategy to enhance performance and reduce errors.[29] However, liability concerns are making hospitals reluctant to use the new assessment tool for fear that by using it, they could be held liable for not implementing all of the safe practices recommended.[30]

At the Group Health Cooperative of Puget Sound, Seattle, Washington, a medical care organization, the implementation of two of its own clinical practice guidelines reduced the ordering of lipid-lowering drugs and prostate-specific antigen (PSA) testing, for a cost saving of $800,000 in the first year.[31]

Kaiser Permanente of Ohio has developed a Medical Automated Record System (MARS) to address the business and clinical needs of their system, which includes 220 physicians and 110 allied health personnel. MARS is programmed to generate reminders at the moment of care on compliance with clinical guidelines, and it tracks improvements in such areas as use of aspirin in coronary disease and use of influenza vaccines in patients over 64 years of age.[3]

Private Initiatives

United Health Group, the second largest managed care organization, has demonstrated substantial (albeit decreasing) non-compliance of its contracted physicians with generally accepted clinical practice for treating heart attacks, high blood pressure, asthma, and recurrent heartburn (among other conditions). The company has both the information and clout to significantly impact the economic viabiltiy of those physicians who the company can document are consistent non-compliers. Participating physicians and other caregivers still need to demonstrate their ongoing compliance with the latest standards of practice and technological advance (through their access to evidence-based knowledge bases) to have access to the majority of patients.[32]

Practice guidelines in the Medical Review System of Value Health Sciences, Inc., of Santa Monica, California, are used in claims processing of selected medical and surgical procedures. For their clients, this system is used to precertify hospital admissions for 34 major medical and surgical procedures, which has resulted in a decrease in the number of procedures requested after implementation, and is reported to have saved $200 million since 1990.[34]

Milliman U.S.A. Inc. actuaries and health care consultants estimate that the United States could save 25 percent of total health care costs if efficient medical practices were adopted. Unnecessary services included hospital days (about 40 to 50%), all surgery (10%), all office visits (20%), and all ancillary services (35%). For clients who utilize or subscribe to Milliman U.S.A.'s services, there are available guidelines that describe the best practices for treating common conditions in a variety of care settings. The purpose of these clinical tools is to assist health care professionals in providing quality care, while maximizing efficiency in the use of health care resources. Best practices are a compilation drawn from medical literature, practice observation, and the expert opinions of physicians, nurses, and other providers. Some guidelines are related to inpatient and surgical care, others to home care and workers' compensation.[35]

Merck, AT&T, IBM, Boeing, GE, American Re-Insurance Company of Princeton, General Motors, and Pepsi have joined a coalition now comprised of powerful business members that calls itself the "Leapfrog Group." Employees of these companies are steered to hospitals that have computerized physician order entry systems, critical care-trained physicians in their intensive care units, and agreement to use "evidence-based hospital referral" systems to send patients who need complex procedures (e.g., heart surgery) to the institutions that perform them the most. The Leapfrog Group wants hospitals to make "a commitment to quality" and is supported by the Fortune 500 Business Roundtable. Over the next few years, Leapfrog members will promote the institutions that make this commitment and will hold health plans and their benefit consultants accountable for compliance with the group's practices. This is an attempt to leverage the value of huge employers behind necessary safety improvement processes while supporting employees' health.[36] The group expects health care providers to respond more quickly to the threat of financial losses than to any other motivation.[37]

Government Initiatives

Government organizations, such as the Agency for Health Care Policy and Research (AHCPR), create practice guidelines for use in the huge reimbursement programs. Medicare peer review organizations have published criteria for admission as an inpatient under the Medicare program. Each criterion lists rationales for admission, relevant and nonrelevant diagnostic procedures, and

BOX 10-5

A North Carolina state legislator's husband suffered chest pains, and the hospital diagnosed a pinched nerve. Doctors proposed a two-night stay, saying: "We can't release him. We don't have practice parameters that suggest a different strategy." Three weeks later, this legislator introduced a bill to develop parameters to reduce inappropriate care, cut costs, and boost quality.[38]

discharge status rationales (see Box 10-5). Importantly, government reviewers have used the guidelines to determine reimbursement. Medicaid has adopted the same criteria for reimbursement to its providers.

Each guideline developed by the AHCPR coves a specific disease, such as unstable angina, lower back pain, asthma, cardiac rehabilitation, and colorectal cancer screening, and discusses the most effective methods of preventing, diagnosing, and treating that condition. The financial implications of implementing these guidelines will be studied for five years by Health Economics Research, Inc., of Waltham, Massachusetts at a cost of $3.1 million.[39]

Enhancing the quality of care that Medicare patients receive was the original goal of he AHCPR guidelines, but the ultimate effectiveness is still uncertain. "If guidelines are to work, the federal government will have to develop timely and effective methods of reconciling its payment schedules with its own recommended practice standards."[40]

Several states have passed laws to support the AHCPR clinical guidelines. In 1993, California passed a law that sought to distribute information about the acute care guideline to physicians. Maryland has adopted the urinary incontinence treatment guideline that ties reimbursement to use of the guideline. Minnesota, in its Minnesota Care Act of 1992, cites adherence to these guidelines as a defense against malpractice.[38]

AHCPR guideline development aims to help physicians make better decisions and reduce ineffective and inappropriate services. Some experts argue that the guidelines do not address implementation and need to be simplified so that physicians can understand them more quickly.[41]

Four states (Florida, Maine, Minnesota, and Vermont) have legislated practice guidelines to ensure a high quality of care. These laws were copied or patterned after the criteria developed by the Institute of Medicine,[42] the AHCPR, or specific state guidelines.

Part of Florida's 1992 health care reform law requires the state Agency for Health Care Administration to develop practice guidelines that physicians can voluntarily use as protection against medical malpractice claims. That agency plans to adopt existing standards, especially in areas of high medical utilization and high cost—for example, imaging technology, radiation treatment, and rehabilitation.

Vermont's health care legislation of 1992 allows state-sanctioned practice guidelines to be used as the standard of care in malpractice cases. Minnesota's 1992 health care reform legislation allows the Minnesota health care commissioner to approve and disseminate practice guidelines to use as an absolute defense against malpractice cases for claims arising after August 1, 1993, or ninety days after the commissioner approves the guideline.

The Arkansas Patient Safety Initiative is a forum for discussion of issues, policy, data-driven studies, and dissemination of best practices to achieve quality of care. The participants include the Arkansas Medical Society, the Nurses Association, the Pharmacist Association, the Hospital Association, and the Departments of Health and Human Services for a comprehensive approach with an emphasis on systems.[43]

Almost all of the states have tried to approach the malpractice litigation and defense systems in order to bring perspective and management to the health care industry. For citizens of every state, the federal government has contracted with nonprofit organizations that perform quality assessment, analysis, and improvement services. These quality improvement studies have been based on professional guidelines, utilizing aggregate data from hospitals, health maintenance organizations (HMOs), and medical record reviews. Identified deficiencies are addressed at conferences and individual hospital or HMO consultations promoting best practices, with periodic reanalysis to document change.

At the Island Peer Review Organization (IPRO), the New York State agency the federal government has contracted with to act as a quality improvement organization (QIO), projects are concerned with improving acute myocardial infarction treatment using clinical guides of the American Heart Association and the American College of Cardiology and expert consultants. They also focus on congestive heart failure evaluation and treatment; and on prevention of further transient ischemic attacks in patients with a trial fibrillation using appropriate anti-thrombotic, anticoagulation therapy. For HMOs, the IPRO conducts reviews of denials of care (non-coverage) and beneficiary complaints, and also performs the HEDIS audit evaluation. For contracts with QIOs to be continued by the federal government, the organizations must show improvement in the quality of care, enhancement of the use of guidelines, which involves all levels of professionals, and public education to help individuals cope with their diseases and general health.[44]

Guidelines for Workers' Compensation

To help control workers' compensation payments to employees and health care professionals, several states have adapted existing clinical practice guidelines or have developed their own. In Massachusetts, the Workers' Compensation Reform Act of 1991 granted the Department of Industrial Accidents authority to write guidelines that set limits on the number of reimbursable visits, as well as on payments for costly tests. West Virginia's Physical Medicine Guidelines were written as regulations and are more rigorous in halting visits and controlling payments.

Under the Minnesota Medical Services Review Board parameters, providers are informed about what can be done, what's mandatory, and the therapeutic choices. A guideline for low back pain lists the unreimbursable tests, the mandatory diagnostic modalities, and the treatment choices available, including surgery. "We wanted to put an end to endless treatment with passive modalities that goes on for months or years."[45]

In New York State, the QIO is involved in the Dispute Resolution Program, which tries to intervene and bring workers' compensation issues to closure while avoiding the court systems.

Mandates of Insurance Companies

Medical liability insurers are developing their own practice guidelines. While insurers offer premium discounts to physicians who voluntarily comply with the protocols, some companies require physicians to sign on as a condition of insurance. Companies across the nation are involved: Medical Insurance Company (Arizona); Medical Insurance Company (California); COPIC Insurance Company (Colorado); MAG Mutual Insurance Company (Georgia); Medical Professional Insurance Company (Massachusetts); Medical Mutual Insurance Company (Maine); Medical Assurance Company (Michigan); and Northwest Physicians Mutual Insurance Company (Oregon).[46] Will physicians regard the risk management guidelines as an unreasonable intrusion by insurers into the patient-physician relationship? A physician vice president for medical risk management of a large medical liability insurance company responds: "Physician acceptance has been nearly universal."[47]

Thomasson reports on the Participatory Risk Management Program of COPIC Insurance Company, a physician-owned and -operated medical liability company founded by the Colorado Medical Society in 1983.[47] Guidelines were developed through advisory committees and by consensus of practicing physicians. Physicians are required to comply with the established general and specialty-specific guidelines, which are attached to each new and renewal insurance application, and are expected to attend COPIC risk management seminars. Premiums are adjusted upward for adverse actions against professionals, lack of compliance to guidelines, or nonparticipation in seminars. Premiums in anesthesia and obstetrics have declined consecutively for the past four years, and the trend is expected to continue to reduce losses.

Legal Implications of Practice Guidelines

Risk managers should be aware of these practice standards, since there are legal implications.[48] Tort liability could increase if it is alleged that "defective" practice parameters result in harmful patient outcomes. Antitrust violations could occur if the standards are developed to protect the economic interests of specific groups of physicians. Practice parameters could also become a source of evidence in suits. Despite the legal implications, the development and implementation of practice parameters "do not appear to raise significant liability exposures for physicians, physician organizations, hospitals, payers, or other groups."[49] In court, the issue may reside in how binding the judge considers the standards to be. Codes of ethics and practice guidelines are not legal mandates.

Moniz cautions that "the movement to develop increased standards and guidelines for practice is premature" and suggests that "more studies should be done using outcome criteria in order to determine what actually does make a difference."[50] She fears the legal risks for practitioners who do not quite measure up to published standards, take reasonable short cuts, and / or have differing practice styles based on region or setting. She advocates "minimalist protocols" for "safe care and *not* the maximum for ideal care."

The results of studies on the long-term benefits of clinical guidelines have not yet been published. However, sharp reductions of malpractice losses in anesthesiology have coincided with the implementation of formal written standards in that field at the Harvard Medical Institutions.[51]

Since March of 1985, the Mutual Insurance Company of Arizona has required its insured anesthesiologists to sign a "preferred risk plan" and to agree to comply with underwriting requirements on patient monitoring. Similarly, the Utah Medical Insurance Association in Salt Lake City established malpractice insurance requirements for physicians requesting coverage for obstetric care.[51]

Physician Attitudes toward Guidelines

With the proliferation of clinical practice guidelines, is it possible for practitioners to be familiar with all the standards? Do physicians have confidence in the organizations that are creating the guidelines? What do the clinicians think about the practice parameters?

According to a new study, a surprising percentage of doctors are not following national guidelines that could help them treat patients better because they don't have enough information, time, or readiness to change—or enough confidence in their ability to do everything the guidelines recommend. "Despite the fact that physicians have evidence-based guidelines at their disposal for dozens of conditions, they're having similar problems across the board in implementing them in their own practice."[52] In studies of awareness of particular guidelines, more than 10 percent of doctors said they simply weren't aware of them. An even larger number was not familiar enough with the guidelines to follow their recommendations. In addition, individual doctors may not agree with the guidelines issued by their own peers, leading them to choose a different course of treatment. Some physicians see certain guidelines as being too oversimplified or "cookbook," not practical, a threat to their autonomy, or not completely justified by scientific evidence.[52]

For example, factors such as lack of agreement on guidelines, lack of specific technology training, and lack of expectancy of outcome were considered barriers to guideline usage by pediatricians queried about Asthma Practice Guidelines.[53] In an assessment of internists' familiarity with, confidence in, and attitudes about practice guidelines issued by various organizations, they indicated that they recognized the potential benefits of practice guidelines, but were concerned about possible loss of clinical autonomy, increased health care costs, decreased satisfaction with clinical practice, and legal implications in the disciplinary process.[54]

When physicians were queried about guidelines on the management of Barrett Esophagus, it was discovered that there was low awareness, agreement with, and adherence to professional guidelines promulgated by the American College of Gastroenterology. Even awareness of the guidelines did not predict adherence. Among other methods, it was suggested that structuring payment incentives may help achieve optimal practice of guidelines.[55] One certainty remains: If clinical practice guidelines are to be effective, they must be accepted and followed by practitioners.

PEER REVIEW

At the heart of the peer review process is the philosophy of physicians reviewing physicians, and by extension, health professionals reviewing other like health professionals. Statutes that mandate peer review have been enacted in most states. A comprehensive and equitable evaluation of medical practice to enhance the quality of care and to reduce mortality and morbidity are the goals of the process. Participants in the peer review process are protected from suit, and the law provides protection from discovery for the documents generated during the review. Legal protection ranges from complete immunity to qualified immunity, if action is taken in good faith. Peer reviewers prefer absolute immunity, since abuses of the process could result in unwarranted damage to professional reputations if the information became public. Rules covering document production are elucidated in peer review statutes. Although attorneys may not have access to records created by peer review committees, that rule may not apply to material prepared for other purposes and used during the review. Exceptions exist for practitioners who protest disciplinary action or licensure penalties. Medical practice boards have the authority to examine peer review materials.

Confidentiality is a particularly sensitive issue in peer review procedures. Participants should be cautioned and educated about the vital nature of the peer review process. That reminder should be reinforced by risk management and quality assessment professionals.

Peer review participants have been subject to lawsuits, initiated mainly by physicians whose clinical privileges were revoked or denied. A major charge has been violation of federal antitrust legislation designed to protect free market competition (see Box 10-6). To remedy this situation, the Health Care Quality Improvement Act, Sections 11101 to 11152, included specific liability protection for peer review participants on or after November 14, 1986, when the act was passed. To qualify for immunity, peer review procedures must meet these requirements:

- The action must have been taken with the reasonable belief that it would improve the quality of health care.
- The physician must have been afforded adequate notice and hearing procedures, or other procedures as deemed fair to the physician under the particular circumstances.
- The action must have been taken with the reasonable belief that it was warranted by the facts known.

Components of Peer Review

There are six major reasons for conducting peer review: identified quality concerns, hospital privileging decisions, group practice membership decisions, staff conduct, professional isolation, and education.[57] Peer review's critical role in patient care has been widely accepted in the medical profession. First, a major component of review is the peer evaluation of clinical judgment using written documentation, established clinical guidelines, and patient care protocols. Second, peer review evaluates technical skills, not only in terms of appropriateness, but also regarding performance outcomes. Third, peer review uses practice profiles to assess resource utilization and efficiency of the care process.

Federal and state regulations, insurance companies, and voluntary agencies all use peer review as their processes of licensure

BOX 10-6

After being faced with charges of incompetence and the potential loss of hospital privileges, a surgeon voluntarily relinquished his privileges. Subsequently, he applied for reinstatement of his privileges. His request was denied by the Medical Staff Executive Committee, and the denial was later affirmed by the Fair Hearing Committee and the Board of Governors. The surgeon sued the hospital and peer review physicians under the Sherman Anti-Trust Act, alleging bias in the peer review process and a conspiracy to oust him from the hospital, along with other financial issues. The district court noted that, as a matter of law, a hospital cannot conspire with its medical staff. The staff as an entity had no interest that competed with the interest of the hospital. Therefore, the surgeon could not prove conspiracy between the medical staff and the hospital. There was no concerted action by the defendants.[56]

or accreditation. In addition, state medical boards, nursing boards, and other regulatory bodies use peer review in investigations, on hearing panels, and as part of disciplinary proceedings.

Professional peers have been considered at times too friendly to their colleagues and at other times too adversarial and vindictive. Prosecution lawyers use peers as expert witnesses to support their allegations of malpractice and misconduct. Similarly, defendants counter with their own peer experts to support their allegations. The result is a battle of experts.

Risk management strategies argue for fairness in the evaluative and support processes and attention to peer selection. Charges and allegations should be supported by documentation and peer review. Fairness also means adequate notice to the physician under review, enough time to study the facts presented, and time for discussions, hearings, and presentation of the other side of the story.

Guidelines and System Changes

The importance of "outcomes" as a measure of performance and quality of health care gives an impetus for standardized criteria as a baseline for clinical practice. Practice guideline development is spreading throughout the health care professional community—in dentistry, nursing, rehabilitation specialties, pharmacy, dietary health, long-term care, and so on. Such guidelines effectively reduce extremes and shift the focus toward quality care. Those with practices outside the norm need special attention from risk management. The defense of an unusual or allegedly distinct style that deviates from community norms usually is not very successful.

A survey of 125 academic teaching hospitals has revealed that there is considerable difference in peer review, outcome monitoring, and corrective actions taken in hospitals. Peer review is generally triggered by cases where quality of care is suspected of being substandard. The survey respondents indicated a lack of consensus regarding the best peer review method, and they regarded peer review as only slightly or somewhat effective.[58]

However, some approaches related directly to administrative system changes. In Michigan, a new law restricts the number of mandatory overtime hours that can be required of Registered Nurses. The law limits the hours of mandatory overtime that can be required of RNs to two hours beyond their regular shift and no more than 16 hours in 24-hour period.[59] Understaffed and overworked nursing care may increase the frequency of errors and lessen the quality of care.

Information technology is another area that has a vast potential for improvement of health, access to care, reduction of errors, and increased efficiency in delivering high-quality care. The Institute of Medicine's 1991 and 1997 reports were entirely devoted to the importance of implementing computerized medical record systems, and the 1999 report focused on patient safety recommendations and computerized physician order-entry systems. Since medication errors comprise 20 percent of all medical errors, the impact of such systems would be significant. Studies indicate that reminder systems and computer-assisted diagnosis and management of care improve compliance with professional guidelines. The National Quality Forum has stated that "the inadequate health information infrastructure contributes to substantial inefficiencies and waste, lost productivity, the occurrence of medical errors, and dissatisfaction with the healthcare system of both patients and practitioners."[60]

The New York State Patient Occurrence Reporting Tracking System (NYPORTS) is a reporting system developed by the New York State Department of Health (DOH) to which hospitals must report specific types of adverse occurrences that may or may not represent errors by the hospital. For certain types of serious adverse occurrences, hospitals are required to undertake and submit to the DOH the results of a full analysis of the occurrence. Adverse occurrences include deaths within 48 hours of admission; preoperative and unexpected deaths; and surgical cases with wrong site, procedure, or patient surgery, or retained foreign body. In New York State in the year 2000, there were 114 adverse surgery events, and guidelines were developed and distributed to hospitals and physicians along with possible methods of implementation to reduce such errors.[61]

In New York, some adverse events require the preparation of a root cause analysis. In a six-month data analysis of 120 cases reported as unexpected deaths, the root causes indicated were: ineffective communication (30%), policy or process (system) was not carried out (24%), standard of care was not met (23%), and human error (21%), among other issues.[62] It is anticipated that hospital comparisons will be made, quality improvements will be initiated, and preventable adverse occurrences and medical error will be reduced.

The Joint Commission in Accreditation of Healthcare Organizations (JCAHO) has expanded its interest in "sentinel events," which encompasses voluntary self-reporting of medical errors for aggregations, analysis, and reduction of the risk of future occurrences. A "sentinel event" is any unexpected occurrence involving death or serious physical or psychological injury. Root cause analysis of these occurrences is expected to yield opportunities to alter practices to reduce the frequency and seriousness of mishaps. Of 1,609 sentinel events reported in 6.25 years, the leading causes were: suicide (16.7%), operative/postoperative complication (12.2%), medication error (11.4%), and wrong-site surgery (11.3%). Root cause analyses were submitted in 80 percent of these cases.[93]

The JCAHO has introduced National Patient Safety Goals[63] to address some of these reported occurrences. The 2003 National Patient Safety Goals are:

- Improve the accuracy of patient identification.
- Improve the effectiveness of communication among caregivers.
- Improve the safety of using high-alert medications.
- Eliminate wrong-site, wrong-patient, wrong-procedure surgery.
- Improve the safety of using infusion pumps.
- Improve the effectiveness of clinical alarm systems.

It is anticipated that the JCAHO will incorporate reviews of hospital approaches to these goals as part of the accreditation process.

In several states where health maintenance organizations have high penetration, there have been some successful attempts to provide physicians with incentives or practice that is in accord with guidelines for prevention, diagnosis, and therapies. Where HMOs are not dominant and there are very busy physicians, incentives may not be as effective. There are some HMOs that have translated provider incentives into contracts with individual physicians. Where incentives have been utilized, there has been substantial improvement in performance and physicians have participated in the development of incentive programs. Quality care and quality outcomes will reduce the potential for liability.

LIABILITY ALTERNATIVES: TORT REFORM AND NONJUDICIAL PROPOSALS

Countless physicians around the country are experiencing skyrocketing malpractice insurance rates, making it nearly impossible for them to make a living, let alone run an office. Such hikes are forcing physicians—in particular specialists who perform high risk procedures regularly—to curtail their practices or move to states with lower liability insurance rates to avoid debt or bankruptcy. Some doctors have lost their malpractice insurance altogether and have been forced to shut down their offices. In some areas of the country, patients have to travel to other states in order to be treated by specialists (see Box 10-7).

BOX 10-7

- The only trauma center in Las Vegas, Nevada closed for 10 days in July 2002 after most of its surgeons resigned in protest of the high costs of medical liability and malpractice insurance, and the lack of caps on jury awards for pain and suffering. The trauma unit, at the University of Nevada Medical Center, reopened after an agreement was reached with county officials to temporarily limit the doctors' liability, and the 67 surgeons returned to work.[64]
- The American Medical Association announced in July 2002 that because of astronomical malpractice award increases, 12 states are in a medical liability crisis and 30 other states are on the brink. The AMA concludes that "the U.S. liability system has created a liability lottery, where select patients receive astronomical awards, and others suffer because of it." Congress has been urged to pass medical liability laws to avert a health care crisis.[65]
- Radiologists do not want to read mammograms.[66]
- Some family physicians in Mississippi, Florida, Pennsylvania, and Texas have stopped offering obstetrics care so their insurance premiums will be lower. Obstetricians are also among those giving up obstetrics.[66]
- An Akron, Ohio urologist decided to retire. It would cost seven months of his yearly income to cover the $84,000 premium.[67]

This crisis has raised a ground-swell of demands for "tort reform." A tort is a wrongful act or omission, not based on a contract, that causes injury to another person.[57] Reforms suggest changing certain legal rules, such as imposing limits on the time after an injury or its discovery in which a suit can be filed, or limiting the damages that can be awarded. These "conventional" tort reforms have been labeled pro-defendant because they limit the amounts that plaintiffs can recover, restrict the access of plaintiffs to courts, and, in effect, block the courthouse door.[58]

Tort reform may stem from the physicians' fear of legal liability. The litigation system imposes large indirect costs on the health care system. Defensive medicine that is caused by unlimited and unpredictable liability awards not only increases patients' risk, but also adds costs. The leading study estimates that limiting unreasonable awards for non-economic damages could reduce health care costs by five to nine percent without adversely affecting quality of care.[68] This would save $60 to 108 billion in health care costs each year, and these savings would lower the cost of health insurance.[68]

An Office of Technology Assessment study of defensive medicine and medical malpractice concluded that physicians "tend to over-estimate" their risk of being sued and that malpractice reforms wouldn't significantly reduce the cost of defensive medicine.[69,70] Joining the critics, former U.S.

Senator George McGovern railed against "abusive lawsuits brought by an army of trial lawyers subverting our system of civil justice while enriching themselves.[71]

California has more than 25 years of experience with tort reform. It has been a success. Doctors are not leaving California. Insurance premiums have risen much more slowly than in the rest of the country, without any effect on the quality of care received by residents of California. Insurance premiums in California have risen by 167 percent over this period, while those in the rest of the country have increased 505 percent. This slow increase has saved California residents billions of dollars in health care costs and has saved federal taxpayers billions of dollars in Medicare and Medicaid programs.[72]

Traditional tort reforms within the judicial system can be classified into three groupings: limiting the number of lawsuits, controlling the size of awards, and limiting the access of plaintiffs to the judicial system.

Limiting the Number of Lawsuits

Reform suggestions to reduce the volume of malpractice lawsuits involve attorney fee limits, certificates of merit, pretrial screening panels, penalties for frivolous litigation, and statutes of limitations.

Attorney Fee Limits

To minimize the risk and expenditure for the plaintiff, attorneys are paid on a contingency basis. That is, the attorney receives a portion of the damages received by the plaintiff only if the lawyer wins the case. Often this amount is larger than the portion of the monetary settlement that the injured client receives. A typical contingency fee is one-third of the award, plus expenses. Some states limit the contingency percentage in cases with large monetary damage cases but professional bar associations exert considerable political influence to thwart efforts to limit this fee arrangement.

Certificates of Merit

Before filing a suit, a plaintiff may be required to obtain an affidavit from a qualified physician or medical expert attesting that the malpractice claim has "reasonable and meritorious cause." This requirement may be a moot point in most cases, however, because law firms generally secure expert medical opinions before filing a malpractice claim.

Pretrial Screening Panels

As a prerequisite to filing a suit in court, parties may be required to submit the malpractice claim to hearing before an impartial panel consisting of one or more attorneys and health care providers and, in certain states, a judge or layperson. This panel will render a nonbinding decision on liability and sometimes damages. Parties may choose to accept the panel's findings and settle the case or proceed to file a suit. In some states, the panel's findings may be entered into subsequent legal proceedings. Some states offer panels as a voluntary option.

Penalties for Frivolous Litigation

According to legal definition, a frivolous claim is one that has no hope of success. That definition is too broad, open to varying interpretations, and too vague to apply practically. A "loser pays" system, designed to prevent frivolous claims, requires the losing party to pay the winner's legal expenses. However, sanctions for bringing weak cases to court are seldom applied.

Statutes of Limitations

These statutes prescribe the time period after the injury in which a legal claim may be brought. Usually, the time limits are two to three years (see Box 10-8). In medical malpractice, this time period is measured either from the date of the negligent treatment or from the date the injury could reasonably have been discovered (the discovery rule). Some states have shortened the time period in which a claim can be brought or have limited the application of the discovery rule.

Controlling the Size of Awards

Tort reform proposals may seek to impose "caps" on monetary damages. Recommendations can establish a schedule of damages, lower awards by the amounts collected from other insurance coverage, restrict joint and several liability suits, and schedule periodic payments of damages.

Caps on Damages

Damages can be economic or noneconomic. Economic damages pertain to incurred and future costs arising from the injury, primarily medical and rehabilitative expenses and lost wages. Noneconomic damages compensate for the pain and suffering associated with the injury, the emotional distress, and the lost enjoyment of life, or "hedonic" damages.[74] Certain states have placed caps on the noneconomic amounts the jury can award or on the total of economic plus noneconomic damages. States with limits of $250,000 or $350,000 on noneconomic damages have average combined highest premiums of 12 to 45 percent, as compared to 44 percent in states without caps.[75]

BOX 10-8

After surgery in the hospital, a patient continued taking prescribed anticoagulant medication at home. One month later, she was readmitted, suffering from gastrointestinal hemorrhaging allegedly caused by inadequate monitoring of her condition. Two years and one day later, she filed a malpractice claim, but trial and appellate court rulings found the claim barred by the Georgia two-year statute of limitations.[73]

Schedules of Damages

A schedule of damages could specify the amount of compensation for each type of negligence. Payment for an unnecessary surgical procedure might range from $100,000 to $300,000. Strangely enough, both plaintiffs and defendants oppose this concept. Plaintiffs fear that the schedule's limits will duplicate the law workers' compensation awards. Defendants believe jurors will consistently award the upper limits of any scheduled payment.

Collateral Source Offset

Some states require or permit the jury to reduce the plaintiff's malpractice award by the amount the plaintiff is entitled to receive from collateral sources, such as life, health, and disability insurers.

Restriction of Joint and Several Liability

Plaintiffs have the right to collect from each of multiple defendants in the amount of their responsibility for the injury (joint liability). Alternatively, a plaintiff could collect the entire amount from a single defendant (several liability). The latter circumstance forces the defendant with the "deepest economic pocket" to sue the other defendants for their responsible amounts. Some states have eliminated several liability, usually with respect to noneconomic damages only.

Periodic Payments of Damages

A structured award allows damages for future economic and noneconomic losses to be paid over an extended period on a periodic basis, rather than in one lump sum. Defendants need not pay until the annual installment is due. However, questions do arise. What if the plaintiff dies earlier than expected? Should payments end, or should the plaintiff's estate continue receiving payments?

Limiting the Access of Plaintiffs to the System

Reform measures in this area deal with expert witness requirements, informed consent limits, and *res ipsa loquitur* restrictions. These proposals address the plaintiff's difficulty, or costs, of winning a lawsuit.

Expert Witness Requirements

Regulations may mandate that the expert physician witness be board certified or have meaningful experience in an area of medicine that relates to the subject of the case, as in Box 10-9.

Informed Consent Limits

Did the physician provide adequate information for the plaintiff to make an informed judgment? Adequacy can be judged on the basis of whether a reasonable patient would consider the information provided adequate, or by looking at the practice of other physicians. Often, the former standard is characterized as pro-plaintiff, and some states restrict the use of this patient-oriented standard.

BOX 10-9

Expert witnesses testified that they were familiar with the term "standard of care" but not that they were familiar with the actual standard of care for interns and residents in the Detroit area. On this basis, a $1.3 million verdict to a patient's estate for negligent death was reversed.[75]

Res Ipsa Loquitur *Restrictions*

Some states restrict the use of this doctrine in cases where the injury is obvious to nonmedical trained personnel and expert testimony of negligence is not required.

There are pros and cons for each of the tort reform proposals and no immediate consensus has evolved. An illustration regarding caps demonstrates the extremes. Dr. Nancy Dickey, an AMA official, remarked that liability reform without a cap on economic damages was like "giving an aspirin where what you need is massive chemotherapy." In response, the president of Trial Lawyers of America said, "The cap is grossly unfair because it would force the most seriously injured in our society to, in effect, subsidize the wrongdoers who harm them by capping their responsibility."[74]

REMOVING MALPRACTICE LITIGATION FROM JUDICIAL SYSTEMS

Tort reform proposals to shift malpractice litigation away from of the judicial system include the establishment of special administrative agencies, alternative dispute resolution mechanisms such as arbitration and mediation, and no-fault compensation for injuries. A Robert Wood Johnson Foundation grants program, Improving Malpractice Prevention and Compensation Systems, funds investigations seeking nonadvesarial alternatives to malpractice litigation.[76]

Administrative Agencies

Precedents for administrative agencies to handle malpractice claims exist in workers' compensation agencies that handle occupational accident damages, in labor management agencies that mediate disputes, and in professional sports organizations that use binding arbitration entities. In 1988, the AMA Specialty Society Medical Liability Project proposed that state administrative agencies, consisting of consumers, lawyers, and a few physicians, should handle malpractice claims.[77] Administrative agencies could adapt trial-like procedures but would have much more leeway to avoid time-consuming pleadings. When needed, special expert panels could examine sophisticated medical evidence. Tax money would establish the administrative agencies and also compensate arbitrators, who are not inexpensive. Critics contend that if the agencies followed the example of the workers' compensation agencies, the monetary awards would be "notoriously stingy."[78]

Alternative Dispute Resolution: Mediation and Arbitration

Both mediation and arbitration remove procedure bound litigation from the courtroom to an informal setting where neutral intermediaries work with litigants to resolve the problem. Mediators can only try to negotiate agreements, as illustrated in Box 10-10. In contrast, arbitrators can make judgments and impose awards.

Pretrial screening panels in more than 20 states weed out nonmeritorious claims. About 15 states authorize a form of voluntary arbitration. Some states allow for pretreatment arbitration agreements between physicians and patients. Supporters of alternative dispute resolution argue that this easier and less costly mechanism will open the malpractice system to thousands of people who don't file malpractice suits because the claims are too small or the court system too intimidating. Critics aver that a voluntary alternative dispute resolution system won't solve anything, because people will still sue if they are dissatisfied with the proposed settlement.[77] Since there is not a mandate to accept the arbitration settlement, the practice lacks incentives and appears to be seldom used as an alternative.[80]

NO-FAULT PROPOSALS

Under a no-fault system, any adverse outcome would be automatically compensated without lawsuits, whether or not the outcome resulted from negligence. Some no-fault proposals promise more equitable compensation; others create mechanisms for quality control. Utah's Experiment in Patient Injury Compensation combines a no-fault system with malpractice insurance coverage.[81]

An untested no-fault proposal uses adverse medical outcomes called avoidable classes of events (ACEs) as a mechanism for determining liability for selected injuries. ACEs could be used both to promote high-quality care and to determine quickly and objectively which patients should be compensated. Because patients could be quickly

BOX 10-10

A patient suffered an adverse outcome believing that his physician had told him that the risk of such a result was one in 100. The doctor said he had told the patient one in 10. A Massachusetts Medical Board mediation took only 45 minutes to resolve the dispute. The doctor agreed to reimburse the patient the nominal amount for the care required because of the complication.[79]

compensated through a nonjudicial insurance process, ACEs are also known as accelerated compensation events. Virginia and Florida have implemented ACE programs for a selected set of severe neurological birth-related events.[82] However, both programs stop short of being true no-fault systems.

Accelerated Compensation Events

Applying compensation classification principles, the American Bar Association conducted a feasibility study of designated compensable events in 1979.[83] With a minor language change, the classification became known as accelerated compensation events. Under the ACE system, medical experts identify categories of injuries that are generally avoidable when a patient receives good medical care. Patients experiencing an ACE would be automatically compensated through an administrative system. Compensation would be paid either by the physician's insurer or by another responsible organization.

Because ACEs would not account for all claims, any ACE program would have to operate within a larger injury compensation system, which could be the existing fault-based malpractice system or an alternative fault-based approach. Non-ACE claims could be resolved through the tort system or by an alternative dispute resolution method.

Experts have developed 146 ACEs for general surgery, orthopedic surgery, and obstetrics, and the list is continuously being revised. Examples of ACEs include:[84]

- Complications secondary to anticoagulant therapy in preparation for surgery.
- Consequences of a misdiagnosis of breast malignancy.
- Complications from failure to diagnose and treat hypoglycemia in a new born.
- Complications to infant(s) from syphilis during pregnancy that was unrecognized during prenatal care.
- Complications to infant(s) from fetal distress, including brain damage, that was unrecognized or untreated during attended delivery.
- Certain complications or injuries resulting from surgical procedures, including failing to remove a foreign body from the surgical site.

In a sample of 285 hospital obstetric claims in 24 states, the obstetric ACEs accounted for 52 percent of claims, with a disproportionate number of serious injury claims and paid claims involving ACEs.[85]

In claim disposition, ACEs may promote predictability and consistency. ACEs are developed by medical experts using epidemiological population-based concepts of "relative avoidability." In contrast, negligence is based on a lay jury's judgment. It is quite possible that the same adverse outcome will be compensated by one jury but not by another, because juries differ on whether the standard of care was met.

Enterprise Liability

In a system of enterprise liability, physicians would be immune to malpractice suits. Instead, the institution in which they practiced, or the health plan responsible for paying for the services, would assume the physicians' liability.[86] Although some hospitals and staff-model HMOs already assume such liability, few health care institutions are fully liable for all claims originating within their organizations.

Enterprise liability would eliminate the costs associated with multiple defendant suits and thereby facilitate settlement. It would promote stronger quality control within institutions and health plans while relieving physicians of some of the psychological burdens of a malpractice suit. Institutions bearing the liability risk would have a greater incentive to evaluate physicians' performance. Institutional quality control programs may be a more effective deterrent to poor quality of care than the malpractice system, because the vast majority of patients injured as a result of negligence do not sue.[87]

Some large teaching hospitals have an arrangement known as "channeling," in which the institution and the physicians practicing in the hospital are insured under the same malpractice insurance policy. Physicians pay the hospital for the insurance and are often required to required to agree to a joint defense. In return, the physicians receive favorable malpractice insurance rates and often high coverage limits. Even without true enterprise liability, some of the administrative efficiencies of a joint defense already exist in these settings.

Enterprise liability could increase the number of suits, if patients feel more comfortable suing a corporate enterprise rather than a physician.[88] In return for no personal liability, physicians might find themselves witnesses in a greater number of cases and subject to greater scrutiny from the enterprise in which they provide care.

Both no-fault and enterprise liability demonstration projects have been endorsed by the American College of Physicians.[89]

Other Methods

Early Offers is one innovative approach to liability. This would provide a new set of balanced incentives to encourage doctors to make offers quickly after an injury in order to compensate the patient for economic loss, and for patients to accept such offers. The system would make it possible for injured patients to receive fair compensation quickly and over time if any further losses are incurred, without having to enter into the litigation fray. Because doctors and hospitals would have an incentive to discover adverse events quickly, within 120 days after a claim is filed in order to make a qualifying offer, the system would lead to prompt identification of quality problems. It may also be possible to implement an administrative form of Early Offers as an option for care provided under federal health programs.[90]

Another approach involves medical review boards. Strengthening medical review boards, which have special expertise in the technical intricacies of health care, can streamline the fact-gathering and hearing processes, make decisions more accurately, and provide compensation more quickly and predictably than the current litigation process. Incentives would be necessary for patients and health care providers to submit cases to the boards and to accept their judgments and decisions.

TO TORT OR NOT TO TORT

"Is lawsuit reform good for consumers?" The *Consumer Reports* article suggested that many of the proposed changes would tip the scales of justice against consumers.[91] In another revelation, feminists argued that tort reform would disproportionately hurt women and have a harsh discriminatory impact on women, children, and poor people. Others claim that caps on non-economic damages are unfair to children, the elderly, and stay-at-home mothers.[92]

Physicians argue that the medical liability system is flawed: there is no timely and adequate compensation for injured persons, negligence is not deterred, fear and distrust are promoted, health care providers are not given incentives to prevent and detect injuries, the physician-patient relationship is harmed, and physicians change their behavior because they are vulnerable. If physicians mainly want to avoid jury trials, alternative dispute resolution may be most appropriate. If physicians are distressed when their clinical judgment is questioned, any reform that retains a fault-based system may not result in changes in physician behavior.

Medical liability reform remains uncertain in view of concurrent developments in the health care delivery system and in Congress.

PROACTIVE LIABILITY REDUCTION

Professional practice acts, clinical practice guidelines, and peer review seek to prevent adverse events from occurring in the first place. Tort reform and nonjudicial alternatives aim to resolve conflicts rapidly, equitably, and inexpensively after an injury occurs. Risk managers must be comfortable developing educational programs for health care professionals that evolve from clinical practice guidelines and peer review findings. If administrative actions arising from regulatory professional practice acts or NPDB queries are required, risk managers must ensure that administrators are aware of their options. Regardless of the basis for proactive liability reduction activities, this area of activity can offer significant protection of the organization's financial resources.

References

1. Kern, S. I. (1995). Professional misconduct categories could hold unpleasant surprises. *MSSNY's News of New York* 50(5):3.
2. Polygreen, L. (2002). Transplant chief at Mount Sinai quits post in wake of inquiry. *New York Times*, September 7, p. B3.
3. Surgeon who left an operation to run an errand is suspended. (2002). *New York Times*, August 9, p. A13.
4. Campbell, C. A. (2002). State suspends tummy-tuck MD's license. *Star Ledger* (Newark, N.J.), August 15, 1, p. 1.
5. New York State Department of Health Board for Professional Medical Conduct, Albany, N.Y. 2000 Annual Report, p. 15.
6. Spiro, H. M. (1993). Physician rehabilitation committee. *Straight Forward* 4(2):2.
7. Talbott, G. D., and Benson, E. (1990). Impaired physicians: The dilemma of identification. *Postgraduate Medicine* 68(1):56.
8. AMA Council on Mental Health. (1973). The sick physician: Impairment for psychiatric disorders in cluding alcoholism and drug dependencies. *Journal of the American Medical Association* 233(5):664–667.
9. White, R. K., Schwartz, R. P., McDuff, D. R., and Hartmann, P. M. (1992). Hospital-based professional assistance committees: Literature review and guidelines. *Maryland Medical Journal* 41(4):305–309.
10. Meek, D. C. (1992). The impaired physician program of the Medical Society of the District of Columbia. *Maryland Medical Journal* 41(4):321–323.
11. Gallegos, K. V., Lubin, B. H., Bowes, C., et al. (1992). Relapse and recovery: Five to ten year follow-up study of chemically dependent physicians, the Georgia experience. *Maryland Medical Journal* 41(4): 315–319.
12. Bedient, T. M. (2002). Director, Committee for Physicians' Health, Medical Society of the State of New York, personal communication, September 25.
13. Gabbad, G. O., and Nadelson, C. (1995). Boundaries in the physician-patient relationship. *Journal of the American Medical Association* 273(18):1445–1449.
14. The 2000 IAHSS Survey: Crime in Hospitals (2001). *Journal of Healthcare Protection Management* 17(2): 1–31.
15. Greene, J. (1994). Two arrested in hospital rapes. *Modern Healthcare* 24(43):33.
16. Council on Ethical and Judicial Affairs. (1991). Sexual misconduct in the practice of medicine. *Journal of the American Medical Association* 266(19):2741–2745.
17. Island MD admits sex misconduct. (1995). *Staten Island Advance* (New York), February 24, p. 1, col. 2.

18. Lynch, T. G. (1996). Report of the Subcommittee on Physician Sexual Misconduct Board for Professional Medical Conduct. New York State Health Department, Albany, N.Y.
19. Goldsmith, R. (2002). State rules surgeon is unfit to practice. *Star Ledger* (Newark, N.J.), August 20, 17:1.
20. *www.FSMB.org*
21. Romano, M. (2002). RX for salvaging a career: Special report. *Modern Healthcare*, April 1, pp. 28–32.
22. National Practitioner Data Bank. 2000 Annual Report, United States Department of Health & Human Services. Washington, D.C.
23. Brinkley, J. (1994). You bet your life. Do you know the odds? *New York Times*, May 29, sec. 4, p. 4, col. 1.
24. Wolfe, S. M., and Stieber, J. (1994). Medical consumers need malpractice data. *New York Times*, June 7, p. A22, col. 4.
25. Institute of Medicine. (1990). *Clinical Practice Guidelines: Directions for a New Program*. Washington, D.C.: National Academy Press.
26. Hayward, R. S., Wilson, M. C., Tunis, S. R., et al. (1995). Users' guide to the medical literature. VIII. How to use clinical practice guidelines. A. Are the recommendations valid? *Journal of the American Medical Association* 274(7):570–574.
27. *www.guidelines.gov.ngc*
28. *www.nccn.org/index/wee/care/docdirection.htm*
29. Berman, S. (2000). The AMA Clinical Quality Improvement Forum on Addressing Patient Safety. *Joint Commission Journal on Quality Improvement* 6(7):428–433.
30. Prager, L. O., "Legal system could offer safety incentives." (2002). *American Medical News* 43(22): 11:1. June 12.
31. Naughton, D. (1993). Group health cooperative puts practice guidelines into action. *Report on Medical Guidelines & Outcomes Research* 4(6):9–10.
32. Khoury, A. T. (1998). Support of quality and business goals by an ambulatory automated medical record system in Kaiser Permanente in Ohio. *Effective Clinical Practice* 1(2):78–82.
33. Couch, J. (2001). United Health Group's bold decision to let doctors decide: A glimpse into the future of managed care. *Industry Watch*, December.
34. Leavenworth, G. (1995). Quality costs less. *Business & Health* 12(3):6–11.
35. M&R Care Guidelines. (2001). Milliman USA, Inc.
36. Stewart, A. (2001). Coalition gives hospitals a to-do list. *Star Ledger* (Newark, N.J.), November 15, p. 28.
37. Reducing patients' risk may lead hospitals to bow to pressure. (2001). *American Health Consultants Healthcare Risk Management* 23(1):1.
38. Oberman, L. (1993). States race to whip up practice guidelines; too many cooks? *American Medical News* 36(37):1, 30–31.
39. AHCPR intensifies data collection efforts. (1995). *Clinical Data Management* 1(12):1–3.
40. Blumenthal, D., and Epstein, A. M. (1992). Physician-payment reform—unfinished business. *New England Journal of Medicine* 326(20):1330–1334.
41. Gesensway, D. (1995). Putting guidelines to work—lessons from the real world. *ACP Observer* 15(3):1, 28–30; Gardner, J. (1994). Despite complaints, docs using practice guidelines. *Modern Healthcare* 24(3):36.
42. Institute of Medicine. (1992). *Guidelines for Clinical Practice: From Development to Use*. Washington, D.C.: National Academy Press.
43. Golden, W. E. (2001). *Implementing the Safety Agenda Data and Case-Based Approaches*. Arkansas Foundation for Medical Care.
44. Sheehy, T. S., et al. (2001). Annual Performance Report, Island Peer Review Organization (IPRO), New York, July 31, 2000 to August 31, 2001.
45. Workers' compensation programs climb on guidelines bandwagon. (1995). *Medical Guidelines & Outcomes Research* 6(9):1–3, 5.
46. Oberman, L. (1994). Risk management strategy: Liability insurers stress practice guidelines. *American Medical News* 37(33):1, 31.
47. Thomasson, G. O. (1994). Participatory risk management: Promoting physician compliance with practice guidelines. *Journal on Quality Improvement* 20(60):317–329.
48. Hyams, A. L., Brandenburg, J. A., Lipsitz, S. R., et al. (1995). Practice guidelines and malpractice litigation: A two-way street. *Annals of Internal Medicine* 122(6):450–455.
49. Kelly, J. T., and Toepp, M. C. (1994). Practice parameters: More than 1,500 have been developed since 1989 and more are in the works. *Michigan Medicine* 93(3):36–40.
50. Moniz, D. M. (1992). The legal danger of written protocols and standards of practice. *Nurse Practitioner* 17(9):58–60.

51. Holzer, J. F. (1990). The advent of clinical standards for professional liability. *Quality Review Bulletin* 16(2):71–79.

52. AMA Reports that Many Physicians Do Not Follow Guidelines. (1999). Press release, University of Michigan, October 19. *http://hdlighthouse.org/wee/care/docdiretion.htm.*

53. Cabana, M. D., Ebel, B. E., et al. (2000). Barriers pediatricians face when using asthma practice guidelines. *Archives of Pediatric and Adolescent Medicine* 154(7):685–693.

54. Tunis, D. R., Hayward, R. S., et al. (1994). Internists' attitudes about clinical practice guidelines. *Annals of Internal Medicine* 120(11):956.

55. Cruz-Correa, M., Gross, G. P., et al. (2001). The impact of practice guidelines in the management of Barrett Esophagus. *Archives of Internal Medicine* 161(21).

56. *Urdinaran v. Aarons* No. 99-00540 (D.N.J. September 26, 2000).

57. Wakefield, D. S., Helms, C. M., and Helms, L. (1995). The peer review process: The art of judgment. *Journal of Healthcare Quality* 17(3):11–15.

58. Lindrooth, R. C., Calhoun, E., et al. (2002). Peer review at teaching hospitals: Results of a national survey. *Journal of Quality Care* 1(2):16–19.

59. Legislation and Regulatory Update. (2002). *Michigan Society of Healthcare Risk Management.* March 5. *http://216.239.37.10.../+healthcare+risk+ management.*

60. Raske, K. E. (2001). Testimony on Health Care Information Technology: The Essential Tool for Improving Access to Care, Public Health and Safety. New York State Legislature, Greater New York Hospital Association, July 17.

61. Novello, A. Walking the tightrope. Dr. Bryant Galusha Lecture Federation of State Medical Boards of the U.S. *Journal of Medical Licensure and Discipline* 87(3):111–115.

62. *NYPORTS. News and alert.* (2000). Issue 6. New York State Department of Health, Albany, N.Y.

63. *Joint Commission Announces National Patient Safety Goals.* (2002). News Release, Joint Commission on Accreditation of Health Care Organizaions, July.

64. Madigan, N. (2002). Deal on liability allows trauma center to reopen. *New York Times,* July 13, p. A7.

65. Albert, T. (2002). AMA readies for battle on tort reform. *American Medical News* 45(26):1:1.

66. Albert, T., and Adams, D. (2002). Professional liability insurance rates go up; doctors go away. *American Medical News.*

67. *Akron Beacon Journal* (2002). January. Confronting the new healthcare crisis. U.S. Department of Health and Human Services. July, Washington, D.C.

68. Kensler, D., and McClellan, M. (1996). Do doctors practice defensive medicine? *Quality Journal of Economics* 111(2):353–390.

69. U.S. Congress, Office of Technology Assessment. (1994). *Defensive Medicine and Medical Malpractice.* OTA-H-02. Washington, D.C.: Government Printing Office.

70. Felsenthal, E. (1994). Study downplays cost of malpractice fear. *Wall Street Journal,* June 29, p. B2, col. 2.

71. McGovern, G. (1994). A sneak attack on malpractice reform. *Wall Street Journal,* August 11, p. A12, col. 3.

72. Physician Insurers Association of America testimony on National Association of Insurance Commissioners Profitability by Line by State, 2001. U.S. House Judiciary Committee, June 2002.

73. Anticoagulant-injuries claim barred by time. (1995). *American Medical News* 38(6):19.

74. Perry, C. B. (1995). Hedonic damages and cost containment of health care policy. *Trends in Health Care Law & Ethics* 10(1–2):119–123.

75. Office of the Assistant Secretary of Planning and Research, U.S. Department of Health and Human Services. (2002). Special update on medical liability claims. *Medical Liability Monitor. www.medicalliabilitymonitor.com.*

76. McCormick, B. (1995). Seeking a way out. *American Medical News* 38(1):9, 31.

77. American Medical Association. (1988). *A Proposed Alternative to the Civil Justice System for Resolving Medical Liability Disputes: A Fault-Based Administrative System.* Chicago: AMA.

78. Rosenblum, J. (1993). *Malpractice Solutions.* Knoxville, Tenn.: Whittle Communications, p. 49.

79. Oberman, L. (1995). Board approach tries mediation over litigation. *American Medical News* 38(9):1, 7.

80. Shikles, J. L. (1990). *Few Claims Resolved through Michigan's Voluntary Arbitration Program.* CAO/HRD-91-38. Washington, D.C.: Government Printing Office.

81. Petersen, S. K. (1995). No fault and enterprise liability: The view from Utah. *Annals of Internal Medicine* 122(6):462–463.

82. Va. Code, Sec. 38.2-5008 (1989); Fla. Stats., Sec. 766.302 (1991).

83. American Bar Association. (1979). *Designated Compensable Event System: A Feasibility Study*. Chicago: ABA.

84. Tancredi, L. R., and Bovbjerg, R. R. (1992). Creating outcomes-based systems for quality and malpractice reform: Methodology of accelerated compensation events. *Milbank Quarterly* 70:183–216.

85. Bovbjerg, R. R., Tancredi, L. R., and Gaylin, D. S. (1991). Obstetrics and malpractice: Evidence on the performance of a selective no fault system. *Journal of the American Medical Association* 25(21):2836–2843.

86. Abraham, K. S., and Weiler, P. C. (1994). Enterprise medical liability and the evolution of the American health care system. *Harvard Law Review* 108(2): 381–436.

87. American Law Institute. (1991). *Enterprise Responsibility for Personal Injury*. Philadelphia: ALI.

88. McCormick, B. (1993). In face of doctor onslaught: Enterprise liability backers stand firm. *American Medical News* 36(1):35–37.

89. American College of Physicians. (1995). MICRA (Medical Injury Compensation Reform Act): New ideas for liability reforms. *Annals of Internal Medicine* 12296):466–473; Schmitt, R. B. (1995). Legal beat: Malpractice reform backed. *Wall Street Journal*, March 15, p. B4, col. 5.

90. *Federal Report Endorses Law Professor's Tort Reform Concept that Could Speed Resolution of Medical Malpractice Claims*. (2002). University of Virginia news Service, Office of University Relations, August.

91. Is lawsuit reform good for consumers? (1995). *Consumer Reports* 60(5):312.

92. Gallagher, M. (1995). The law on their side. *New York Times*, June 12, p. A15, col. 1.

93. American Hospital Association Joint Commission on Accreditation of Healthcare Organizations Update. April 2002.

CHAPTER 11 Risk Management in Psychiatry

Amy Wysoker

Risk management in psychiatry poses unique and diverse issues for health professionals and for the institutions providing mental health services. These services could be rendered in a specialty facility, in a small unit in a general hospital, in scattered ambulatory centers, or in private offices. A newspaper article highlights the uniqueness of the liability concerns in a psychiatric setting (see Box 11-1).

BOX 11-1

A psychiatric patient, Gary C. Badger, swallowed pens, coat hanger pieces, metal strips, knives, television antennas, and radio batteries. He had surgery five times to remove material from his stomach. Badger filed suit, claiming that those responsible for his care negligently allowed him access to ingestible objects.[1]

This situation challenges practitioners to offer the safest, most therapeutic care possible to the patient while minimizing obvious and not-so-obvious risks. Psychiatric areas of concern to risk managers include: informed consent; the right to treatment; the right to refuse treatment; clinical risks in psychiatry such as psychopharmacology, electroconvulsive therapy (ECT), suicide, seclusion and restraints, elopement and wandering, discharge and aftercare planning, and child and adolescent psychiatry; confidentiality and stigma; and high risk incidents such as violence, illicit substance use, and sexual misconduct.

INFORMED CONSENT

Unless declared incompetent by the courts, psychiatric patients have the right to select their treatment regimen, as do all other types of patients. Psychiatrists in institutional settings are responsible for evaluating the individual's ability to comprehend the situation and for providing all necessary information. Practice guidelines and professional standards specify each psychiatric discipline's responsibility.[2]

In cases where the patient exhibits psychotic symptomatology, the difficulty is obvious. However, the legal system requires that as much information as necessary be provided to the patient. In legal cases, the courts look for medical record documentation of informed consent throughout the course of treatment.

Competency is a legal term and is decided upon in the judicial system. Decision-making capacity is the ability to make a meaningful, informed decision about participation in treatment or research.[3,4] Although patients may be experiencing psychotic symptoms, they may be able to make decisions about their care. However, some patients exhibiting psychotic symptomatology may not be able to make decisions. Depression, with its symptoms of hopelessness and apathy, and other illnesses can also affect their decision-making ability.[5,6] Wirshing and colleagues found that when adequate informed consent procedures were established, the subjects were able to understand and retain critical components of the information.[7] Carpenter and colleagues concluded that although people with schizophrenia may have difficulty with the cognitive demands of the informed consent process, in many situations educational interventions correct the difficulties.[8] Another study found that most of the psychiatric patients studied were able to provide consent; however, one in five people with schizophrenia had a significantly decreased capacity to do so.[9]

Four legal criteria standards define when a patient can be considered competent to consent to treatment: the patient must be able (1) to communicate a choice, (2) to understand applicable information about the planned treatment and the various options for treatment, (3) to recognize their clinical situation, and (4) to manipulate information rationally.[10]

The MacArthur Competence Assessment Tool-Treatment (MacCAT-T) provides a structured method for clinicians to assess patients' competence to make treatment decisions.[13,14,15,16,17] The American Psychiatric Association (APA) has also formulated guidelines for assessing decision-making capacities.[18] Dunn and Jeste reported that deficits in patients' understanding of informed consent may be related to the consent materials, and that educational interventions could correct these deficiencies.[19]

Galen discussed explaining to the patient the importance of self-disclosure in the therapeutic process.[20] At the onset of treatment, there should be a direct assessment of the patient's understanding of the risks of withholding information from professionals and the benefits of cooperating with the therapist. In the event of subsequent self-injury, appropriate documentation can reduce liability.

Implementing informed consent within the practice of psychotherapy is an issue for therapists to address in their practices.[21,22] Risk managers can review liability variables using a model for obtaining informed consent for long-term psychotherapy. This model focuses on six areas that therapists should cover with patients: (1) the diagnostic model used and the recommendation for treatment; (2) potential risks and benefits of treatment; (3) alternate treatment options, including less expensive short-term approaches; (4) explanation of the necessity for psychotherapy; (5) restrictions of insurance coverage; and (6) plans for evaluating the patient's response to treatment.[23]

Informed Consent and Research

Informed consent procedures involving research with psychiatric subjects must be adhered to with diligence, as illustrated in Box 11-2.

Research guidelines adhere to the general informed consent requirements but are more expansive. The U.S. Department of Health and Human Services provides the specific elements that need to be included in consent forms for research.[25] The National Bioethics Advisory Commission (NBAC) report titled *Ethical and Policy Issues in Research Involving Human Participants* is a document guiding research endeavors.[26] Risk managers in psychiatry need to be well-versed in the guidelines in the document addressing research with vulnerable populations.[26,27,28] The inclusion of a third-party consent in cases where the risk-benefit ratio is increased and the mental capacity of a patient is not certain is crucial.[29] When vulnerable populations are included in research, the appropriateness of using them should be shown.[30] Many states have convened task forces to address research with vulnerable populations and have promulgated state guidelines.[31,32] Researchers need to provide the subject with information about all the necessary components of the research protocol for informed consent, consider employing a third-party consent person, and have all consent forms completed prior to embarking on the proposed project.[33]

BOX 11-2

A ruling by the National Institutes of Health declared that researchers at the University of California at Los Angeles (UCLA) had not adequately obtained informed consent from schizophrenic patients. Subjects in the study were withdrawn from their neuroleptic medications. Although consent forms had been obtained from subjects or family members, sufficient information outlining the potential risks of discontinuing medication had not been provided.[24]

RIGHT TO TREATMENT

In *Wyatt v. Stickney*,[34] the court stated that all involuntarily hospitalized people with mental illness or mental retardation have the right to a psychologically and physically humane setting. A sufficient number of qualified staff to administer active therapeutic treatment and of an individualized treatment plan constitute the rights of treatment. If these legally defined standards are not met, patients need to be discharged unless they choose to remain voluntarily. As increasing numbers of patients are discharged from inpatient mental health facilities, a related liability arises. Supposedly, the patients are discharged to receive follow-up ambulatory care at treatment sites in the community. Who is responsible if the community treatment centers are not available? What if the released patients inflict harm on themselves or on others?

Right to the Least Restrictive Alternative

After evaluating an individual's needs in terms of providing care that permits maximum freedom, the patient is entitled to the right to the least restrictive alternative.[35] *Dixon v. Weinberger*[36] affirmed that right.

"Restrictive" has six conceptual dimensions: (1) *structural* refers to the type of setting; (2) *institutional* relates to the procedures set forth for operating the institution and the degree of patient involvement; (3) *enforcement* concerns the consequences of rule breaking; (4) *treatment* pertains to the type of treatment modalities provided; (5)

psychosocial atmosphere applies to status differences between employees and patients and the level of authority provided; and (6) *patient characteristics* refers to the ability of patients to participate in their care related to their diagnosis.[37] Following through on these concepts allows patients to receive treatment in the least restrictive setting relative to their clinical needs. Caregivers must know the available referral sources when formulating treatment plans.

Right to Treatment and the Closure of Psychiatric Facilities

In response to consumer groups advocating for less hospitalization and more supportive community services, changed laws, and restricted payments from the federal government, most states have deinstitutionalized their mental health systems. In this country, during the past four decades 93 percent of state psychiatric hospital beds have been eliminated.[38] A Department of Justice report in 1999 claimed that approximately 16 percent of the total jail and prison population has a serious mental illness (see Box 11-3). This amounts to approximately 300,000 persons, which is four times the number of people in state psychiatric hospitals.[39] The closure of state psychiatric hospitals, along with the realization that persons with psychiatric illnesses are not getting the treatment they need and then become part of the penal system, brings additional focus on the care (or lack thereof) of the psychiatrically ill in the United States. The return of the state psychiatric hospital and a community health system that provides humane, individualized, coordinated care with appropriate funding would provide options for treatment. However, will communities be accepting of such facilities, and will additional services and monies be available?

BOX 11-3

"One day last month Jesus Portelles, stripped naked and convinced that demons had entered his body, used the broken edge of a plastic spoon to carve open his stomach. By the time the guards at the Dade County, Miami, Florida jail could unlock his cell door and grab him, his guts were spilling out. But the demons stayed."[40]

Right to Treatment: Involuntary Outpatient Treatment

"Involuntary outpatient treatment represents an effort to provide more suitable care for patients who, in the present system, are either overconfined or undertreated."[41] Geller delineated clinical guidelines that must be met in sequential order to ensure a right to treatment.[41] Patients must:

- Verbalize a desire to live in the community.
- Have previously been unsuccessful in living in the community.
- Show evidence of competency to understand the stipulations of their involuntary community treatment.
- Have the ability to comply with the involuntary community treatment plan.
- Have prescribed treatment plans that demonstrate effectiveness when used properly with the identified patient.
- Be capable of administration in the outpatient system.
- Be monitorable by the outpatient treatment agencies providing the prescribed treatments and enforcing their compliance.
- Have public inpatient systems integrated into the community plan and supporting outpatient involuntary community treatment.
- Must not be dangerous while complying with the prescribed outpatient treatment.

Legislation for involuntary outpatient treatment has become a major focus in the United States throughout the past years. Approximately 45 states have enacted some form of legislation for involuntary outpatient commitment, known either as mandatory outpatient treatment, assisted outpatient treatment, or involuntary commitment, to name a few. Some states also have named their laws in memory of a person killed by the act of a mentally ill person, such as New York State's Kendra's Law and California's proposed Laura's Law.[42] The Treatment Advocacy Center, an organization dedicated to eliminating barriers to the treatment of severe mental illness, provides updates on the status of all state laws for involuntary outpatient treatment and provides a model law for implementation.[43] Miller believes that the community practitioner must be involved in the treatment goals prior to the outpatient order.[44]

The controversy surrounding mandating outpatient treatment is at the forefront of psychiatric care. The issue will continue to be addressed by patient rights advocates, civil libertarians, practitioners, and family groups. Challenges to the laws on involuntary outpatient treatment will continue to occur. Potential lawsuits for mandating treatment, as well as for not initiating treatment, are a concern. Risk managers need to be involved in knowing and understanding the laws and stay current. Risk managers need to educate practitioners on the legal implications of their actions and advise them accordingly.

Right to Treatment and "Medical Necessity"

Managed care raises questions about insurance coverage. Who should be covered and for how long? In the United States, physician-ordered "medical necessity" services stimulate the reimbursement system. Sabin and Daniels discuss three models of medical necessity:[45] (1) the normal function model, (2) the capability model, and (3) the welfare model. For a model to be useful, basic criteria should be considered and these questions answered: "Does the model make distinctions that the public and the clinicians regard as fair? Can it be administered in the real world? Does the model lead to results that society can afford?" Investigators concluded that the normal function model best met these criteria for three reasons. First, society recognizes that mental illness should be treated to relieve suffering. Second, professional guidelines, such as the Diagnostic and Statistical Manual of Mental Disorders (DSM-IV),[46] provide an accepted means to diagnose the mentally ill. Last, the normal function model allows society to determine the scope of insurance coverage it will pay. However, the right to treatment and the reimbursement requirement of defined "medical necessity" pose potential conflicts. Individuals requiring a certain type of psychiatric treatment may be unable to secure the care they need. A comprehensive reform of psychiatric care has been recommended, changing the definition of medical necessity from an acute-care model to one that covers both care for acute episodes and long term care for chronic conditions. Long term care would help avoid future acute episodes.[47]

In combination, the closing of psychiatric hospitals, the reduced availability of beds, and the changes in the reimbursement system cause right-to-treatment problems. As these changes occur, the courts will be asked to provide clarification. New definitions of the right to treatment need to be formulated as treatment modalities change and the length of treatment decreases.

RIGHT TO REFUSE TREATMENT

All patients, including the mentally ill, have the right to refuse treatment. In psychiatric care, that right is compounded by the competency status of the patient. A patient may have a diagnosable mental illness and still be competent to make decisions about treatment preferences. In addition, the right to refuse treatment is affected by whether the patient's status as an inpatient is voluntary or involuntary and, more recently, whether outpatient treatment is mandated. Some states have a full-time legal advocate to ensure that patients secure their legal rights.

Right to Refuse Psychotropic Medications

Commonly, the right to refuse treatment involves the refusal to take psychotropic medications. In *Rogers v. Okin*[46] the court concluded that psychiatric patients have the right to refuse psychotropic medications unless such refusal means a threat of danger to themselves or to others. Administration of medications against the will of a patient is permissible only in emergencies and only if the patient is a danger to self or to others. Policies outlining emergency administration of psychotropic medication need to be available in institutional employee manuals. These policies should contain procedures for personnel to follow when patients refuse psychotropic medications.

In instances where medication is clinically indicated, but not as an emergency, court orders may be obtained to facilitate drug administration. Before seeking a court order, it is imperative that treatment personnel attempt a medication education regime. Education should be provided over a period of time so that the patient can gradually comprehend what is being taught and then make an informed decision. These interventions need to be documented in the patient's record. If education proves unsuccessful, a court order may be pursued.

Right to Refuse Involuntary Hospitalization

In psychiatry, the right to refuse treatment includes the right to refuse involuntary court ordered hospitalization. Two basic legal rights provide rationales for a person's right to refuse psychiatric hospitalization: freedom of thought; and the right to live and conduct one's life as long as it does not interfere with the rights of others.[49]

The authority States have to institute involuntary commitment is based on its *parens patriae* power and its police power. *Parens patriae* allows states to intercede in the lives of persons who are unable to care for themselves, including people with mental disabilities, in order to protect them. Police power, on the other hand, is intended to protect society from potential harm. Police power is utilized to commit mentally ill persons whose conditions pose harm to others. Unlike dealings with criminal defendants, police power commitments can be used to detain or confine the mentally ill person without any proof of a violation of criminal law and, in some states, the prediction of dangerous behavior, even without evidence that the individual has previously committed a harmful act, could lead to commitment.

A variety of liability issues may arise from the right to refuse treatment, as illustrated by the Billie Boggs case (see Box 11-4). Institutions need procedural guidelines for their staff when it is clinically necessary to hospitalize patients against their wishes. Adherence to this protocol protects the patient's rights while minimizing the institution's liability. To avoid risk, documentation of the process must be evident in the patient's chart.

BOX 11-4

Billie Boggs, a 40-year-old homeless black woman, panhandled on New York's fashionable Upper East Side for money to buy food. A mental health team decided to forcibly hospitalize her because they determined she was mentally ill and unable to care for herself. On her behalf, the New York Civil Liberties Union brought suit, claiming she was not mentally ill, not dangerous, and her rights were being violated. Mass media reported the battle and thus brought public attention to the problem of the homeless mentally ill.[50]

Right to Refuse Involuntary Outpatient Treatment

The laws mandating involuntary outpatient treatment are just beginning to be challenged in the courts and need close watching. The various laws enacted provide patient protection and allow for patients to be part of the decision-making process, as well as to appeal decisions. Issues relating to patients' refusals to adhere to outpatient treatment plans after they have been mandated and subsequent interventions (i.e., hospitalizations) also bring new liability concerns. Risk managers working in health care institutions subject to outpatient commitment laws need to stay abreast of court rulings and their legal implications.

CLINICAL RISKS IN PSYCHIATRY

There are unique clinical risks associated with the practice of psychiatry, such as the side effects of psychopharmacology, the use of electroconvulsive therapy, patient suicide, the use of restraints, patients who elope or wander, aftercare planning, and therapy for children and adolescents. Each clinical risk has liability issues that apply regardless of the location of the treatment site.

Psychopharmacology and Side Effects

Psychotropic medications are instrumental in the treatment of individuals with psychiatric conditions. Until recently the prescription of medications has been the sole domain of the physician. "Over the years, nurse practice acts changed to allow nurse practitioners and in states like New Jersey, clinical nurse specialists, to obtain prescription privileges."[51] Furthermore, managed care broadens the use of nonphysician prescribers, if allowed by state law. Institutions need to incorporate these changes into their policies along with procedures to ensure patient safety.

Despite the success of psychotropic medications, many patients develop severe side effects such as extrapyramidal symptoms (EPS), a variety of neurological disturbances. To lessen the symptomatology, practitioners may alter the dosage, switch to a different antipsychotic drug, or prescribe an antiparkinsonian drug to reverse the side effect.[52] To reduce the potential for liability, it is important that the approach taken and the rationale for the intervention be documented.

Approximately 20 percent of patients receiving long term treatment with neuroleptic medications develop tardive dyskinesia with long term EPS.[53] Disturbances include abnormal involuntary movements such as tongue writhing, tongue protrusion, chewing motions, lip smacking, choreiform finger movements, and abnormal limb and trunk movements (see Box 11-5).

Administration of the abnormal involuntary movement scale (AIMS), which scores the presence of tardive dyskinesia, is recommended for all patients receiving antipsychotic medications.[52,53]

In 1992, the American Psychiatric Association (APA) task force report on tardive dyskinesia recommended regular examinations of patients treated with psychotropic

BOX 11-5

Marjorie W. sued Middlesex County (NJ) Mental Health Clinic for improperly prescribing medication. After six months she couldn't control her facial movements: her mouth opened, her tongue protruded, her eyes closed, she grimaced involuntarily, and she drooled. Avoiding a possible multimillion-dollar verdict, the county paid and the plaintiff accepted a $700,000 settlement plus $59,587 for her lawyer.[54]

medications at least every three to six months. In addition, the APA report recommended that informed consent be documented by a progress note rather than by consent forms.[55,56]

In the prescription of medications, risk management strategies should monitor the prescribing practitioner's dosages to ensure that the patient is not accumulating an excessive dose over long periods of time. Nursing personnel must be instrumental in monitoring the patient's response to medication and in reporting the reaction to the prescribing practitioner.

The risks and benefits of neuroleptic medications, as well as of alternative treatment, must be explained to the patient and family.[57] Lacro utilizes informed consent forms to ensure patient involvement in treatment decisions and to reduce liability.[58] However, there is controversy regarding the appropriate means of documenting informed consent, such as forms versus record charting. Some states require a written consent form outlining the information. Practitioners and risk managers should check their state laws for legislative mandates.

Electroconvulsive Therapy

Electroconvulsive therapy (ECT) has undergone periods of use, abuse, neglect, and reevaluation as a treatment modality. A low-voltage alternating current of electricity is sent to the brain to produce a therapeutic effect for the treatment of clinical depression. ECT is indicated for severe cases of clinical depression or manic episodes. Generally, ECT is applied following a nonresponsive treatment course of antidepressive/antipsychotic medication, for those with medical conditions preventing the use of medications, and for patients in need of a rapid response. Liability guidelines for the use of ECT include the following:[59]

- Secure proper informed consent.
- Do a comprehensive medical examination.
- Follow emergency management procedures.
- Provide for adequate patient supervision during and after the procedure.
- Review the privileging process of those professionals allowed to conduct the ECT treatment.

The negative connotations that have plagued ECT over the years and the possibility of side effects need to be clarified. Patients' opposition to ECT is frequently based on lack of knowledge. Refusal of treatment may be based on inaccurate information. Informed consent needs to be provided in clear language, explaining the reasons for ECT, alternative treatments, and the benefits and risks associated with the procedure. The patient and family need to be informed of when, where, and by whom the procedure will be administered and the approximate number of treatments expected. Patient and family need to understand that they will be kept informed of the progress as the treatment progresses and that they may terminate the treatment at any time. If the patient is too ill to make decisions and provide informed consent, a court-appointed guardian (usually a family member) needs to be appointed and consent obtained from the guardian before any treatment can begin.[60] Strict adherence to guidelines minimizes the physician's and the institution's liability risk.

Suicide

Suicide remains the leading cause of claims against psychiatrists. The responsibility to monitor or supervise patients has always been higher in inpatient facilities than when patients live in the community, for there is more control over patients in such institutions (see Box 11-6).

Lawsuits for wrongful death suicides began to increase in the 1980s. Between 1984 and 1988, the leading reason for malpractice claims from inpatient psychiatric treatment was self-inflicted injury or suicide. About 30 percent of hospital suicides result in malpractice suits, and the largest number of lawsuits against psychiatrists are linked to suicide.[62] Silverman reviewed inpatient standards of care and the suicidal patient and delineated 10 areas that need standards of care for the treatment of the suicidal patient:[63]

1. Therapeutic contract
2. Treatment planning
3. Comprehensive evaluation
4. Therapeutic milieu
5. Hospital policies and procedures
6. Hospitalization risks and benefits
7. Watch procedures and protocols
8. Clinical risk management and judgment
9. Psychopharmacological agents
10. Discharge and aftercare planning

Alleged failures to meet standards of care for suicidal inpatients can be classified in terms of foreseeability and causation related to the responsibilities and roles of the clinician, the inpatient staff, and the hospital's administration.

A primary intervention for hospitalized suicidal patients is staff observation and monitoring, or 15- or 30-minute checks. These interventions often provide a false sense of security for the institution. Patients may still inflict self-injury. Institutions should periodically evaluate their suicide watch policies. In reality, there may not be enough staff to provide the necessary observation, and when staff-to-patient ratios approach inappropriate levels, liability increases.

Psychiatric care provided by or reimbursed by managed care entities brings new concerns to the treatment of the suicidal patient (see Box 11-7). Inpatient care needs to be justified, and therapists are confronted with dilemmas between cost containment and clinical indications. More recently, the number of lawsuits against psychiatrists and managed care organizations relating to outpatient suicide has increased. The courts

BOX 11-6

A 12-year-old boy was able to hang himself while a patient at a New Hampshire psychiatric hospital, despite expressed suicidal ideation and prior suicidal gestures. The family settled the lawsuit before trial for a confidential amount.[61]

BOX 11-7

A patient of a managed care program was denied certification of additional hospitalization. This patient was discharged and subsequently committed suicide. A court ruled that the treating physician has the responsibility to appeal for an extension of benefits if the patient requires further treatment. All such physician efforts on behalf of the patient need to be documented.[66]

have decided that a physician's duty of care should not be determined by fiscal considerations. As protection against liability, therefore, practitioners repeatedly appeal denials for additional treatment from managed care companies.[64] Rissmiller perceived factors complicating cost containment decisions in the treatment of suicidal patients.[65] Suicide assessment techniques identified a larger number of patients at high risk for hospitalization, but only a small number actually successfully commit suicide. Psychiatrists who fear a lawsuit if a patient commits suicide preventively recommend hospitalization to decrease their own possible professional liability. However, inpatient treatment should be reserved for patients who have made serious attempts at suicide and for those who are at high risk because of other factors. Suicidal patients should be committed to a treatment network allowing for movement between inpatient care, day hospital, and outpatient care depending on symptomatology. The roles and responsibilities of health care workers to suicidal patients are summarized in Box 11-8.

BOX 11-8

Professional Roles and Responsibilities Regarding Suicidal Patients[63]

	RESPONSIBILITIES		
	CLINICIAN	INPATIENT STAFF	HOSPITAL ADMINISTRATION
Foreseeability	1. Correctly diagnose patient 2. Properly anticipate future behavioral difficulties	1. Properly communicate suicidal risk among staff 2. Appraise changes in suicidal risk	1. Properly inform staff of suicidal risk 2. Correctly predict future behavior
Causation	1. Arrange for protection against harm 2. Regulate, supervise, observe, and restrain patient 3. Establish a safe, secure, and protective environment 4. Dispense therapy associated with suicidal behaviors 5. Abide by written treatment orders 6. Properly document clinical decisions 7. Enhance staff communications 8. Maintain patients in hospital until no longer actively suicidal 9. Furnish adequate post-discharge plans 10. Arrange for postdischarge care	1. Appraise changes in patient's condition	1. Ensure a protective environment 2. Design and maintain a safe and secure facility 3. Eliminate all dangerous means of assisting suicidal behavior from patient's access

Suicide is the eighth-leading cause of death for all Americans. Statistics indicate that only 13 percent of Americans are aged 65 and older, yet suicide in that age group accounts for one-fifth of all suicides. The highest at risk are older white men. It is estimated that 33 out of every 100,000 older white men commit suicide every year, amounting to 4,655 suicides in 1998. Suicide is also the third leading cause of death for teenagers and youth aged 15 to 24.[66,67] These statistics indicate an area of possible increased lawsuits if suicidal individuals in these age groups are not identified early on in the health care field. If they are properly identified and referred for treatment, their mental health practitioners need to be aware of the increased risk of suicide in these populations.

Discharge and Aftercare Planning

Litigation risks relate to the appropriateness of the discharge and the follow-up treatment of all psychiatric patients, with a specific emphasis on the suicidal patient. Staff needs to provide instructions about medication and follow-up appointments, and to incorporate the patient and family's full compliance and adherence to aftercare recommendations. Plans and rationales need to be documented in the patient's medical record and discharge summary.

Seclusion and Restraint

The use of restraints and seclusion for the management of violent behavior is a controversial and vehemently debated issue in psychiatry. Mental health advocacy groups actively monitor the use of these treatments and voice their views to professionals and legislators. *The Hartford Courant* in 1998 reported a large number of deaths occurring from the inappropriate use of restraints in psychiatric facilities. It was noted that approximately 50 to 150 deaths from the inappropriate use of restraints or seclusion methods occur each year in the United States.[67] Federal legislation governing the use of seclusion and restraints followed such reports, and in 1999 the Health Care Financing Administration (HCFA) provided guidelines as to how agencies need to comply with the federal rule that regulates the use of these modalities in psychiatric facilities. Risk managers, hospital administrators, and all mental health practitioners working in these settings should be knowledgeable of the Hospital Conditions of Participation in Medicare and Medicaid Programs: Patients' Rights Rule; The State Operations Manual Appendix A; Interpretive Guidelines—Hospitals, provides an excellent source for familiarizing oneself with the specifics of the requirements. Some of the major points include:[68]

- The patient has the right to be free from restraints of any form that are not medically necessary or are used as a means of coercion, discipline, convenience, or retaliation by staff.
- The term "restraint" includes both physical restraints and drugs that are used as restraints.
- A physical restraint is any manual method or physical or mechanical device, material, or equipment attached or adjacent to the patient's body that he or she cannot easily remove and that restricts freedom of movement or normal access to one's body.
- A drug used as a restraint is a medication that is used to control behavior or to restrict the patient's freedom of movement and is not a standard treatment for the patient's medical or psychiatric condition.
- Seclusion is the involuntary confinement of a person in a room or an area that the

person is physically prevented from leaving.

- The decision to use a restraint is driven not by diagnosis but by a comprehensive individual assessment that concludes that for this patient at this time, the use of less intrusive measures poses a greater risk than the risk of using a restraint or seclusion.
- The condition of the restrained or secluded patient must be continually assessed, monitored, and reevaluated.
- All staff who have direct patient contact must have ongoing education and training in the proper and safe use of restraints.
- Seclusion and restraint can only be used in emergency situations if they are needed to ensure the patient's physical safety and less restrictive interventions have been determined to be ineffective. They must be ended at the earliest possible time.
- A physician (or "other licensed practitioner") must order restraint or seclusion. Orders must never be written as a standing order or on an "as needed" basis.
- The hospital must report to HCFA any death that occurs while a patient is restrained or in seclusion, or where it is reasonable to assume that a patient's death is a result of restraint or seclusion.

The following year, the Children's Health Act of 2000 was signed into law, establishing national standards restricting the use of seclusion and restraints in all psychiatric facilities for children and youth that receive federal funds.[69]

Sheridan concluded that behaviors precipitating restraint included verbal threats, threats with an object to be used as a weapon, and physical aggression.[70] These behaviors occurred more frequently in relation to external situations, such as conflict with staff, as opposed to internal psychiatric symptoms. An important finding was that patients viewed conflict with staff as the event most likely to lead to the use of restraints.

Klinge found that staff believed that medication should be used first, followed by seclusion, and finally, by restraints.[71] Higher-educated staff felt that other professionals, not only physicians, should be able to order seclusion and restraints, but they also indicated that these modalities are overused. Finally, gender elicited different views. Female staff commented that patients gained attention from the use of restraints and seclusion, while male staff considered such treatment a negative experience.

Betemps examined hospital characteristics, patient diagnosis, and staff reasons related to the use of seclusion and restraints.[72] Geographic location was the only hospital characteristic associated with the use of seclusion and restraints. Facilities in the Pacific and mid-Atlantic areas used these modalities significantly less than institutions in other geographic areas. Patients with schizophrenic disorders were restrained more often than people with other diagnoses. Staff reasons for the use of restraints and seclusion fell into six major categories; in order of frequency they are: (1) protection of the patient and others, (2) patient agitation, (3) physical violence, (4) verbal violence, (5) psychotic or delusional episode, and (6) intoxicated behavior.

As recently as March 2002, a report titled *Seclusion and Restraints: A Failure, Not a Treatment*, found numerous deficiencies in California health care facilities, despite federal reforms governing the utilization of restraints and seclusions. Senator Wesley Chesbro of California states: "Since 1999, at least 14 people have died and one has become permanently comatose while in seclusion or restraints in California psychiatric facilities. These are dangerous interventions and, despite reforms, people are still suffering from their effects."[73] States such as Pennsylvania, New York, Massachusetts, and Delaware instituted systematic guidelines for the use of seclusion and restraints prior to the federal regulations and have found a reduction in their use. Pennsylvania successfully reduced the use of these modalities by 90 percent between 1993 and 1999.[74] New York has proposed revisions that include the following key points:[41]

- Restraint and seclusion are safety interventions to be used only in emergency situations and only as a last resort.
- A debriefing should follow the administration of restraint or seclusion, so that staff and patient can learn from the episode and prevent future occurrences.
- Patients should be asked what method of calming works best for them.
- Potential negative impacts of these devices should be evaluated when considering their use, especially with patients with a history of sexual abuse.
- Four-point restraint, five-point restraint, wrist-to-belt restraint, and calming blanket are the only permissible forms of restraint.
- One-to-one observation of persons in seclusion should be required.
- Physicians' restraint orders should be reduced from four hours to two hours.

The use of restraints and seclusion is a source of potential liability. Without proper administration and supervision, restraints may restrict body movement in such a way as to seriously harm the patient. Institutional policies must guide personnel regarding the use of restraints and seclusion. Federal and state laws and the dictates of the Joint Commission on Accreditation of Healthcare Organizations provide the specifics for adherence. Guidelines need to specify indications for the use of restraints and seclusion, permissible forms of restraint, how to initiate restraints and seclusion, procedures to safely administer these treatments, written orders, time limits, monitoring care, physical care requirements, and documentation requirements.[75] Case conferences should review and evaluate the necessity and appropriateness of restraint applications. Alternatives and future interventions need to be formulated on the basis of the new information and in consultation with the patient. Documentation of, along with a rationale for, all interventions must be evident in the medical record.

Elopement and Wandering

Psychiatric hospitals are caught between ensuring patient rights and initiating security measures to prevent patient elopement and wandering, leaving the premises without authorization, and straying within the facility (see Box 11-9). This is not an uncommon liability risk.

Allowing patients the opportunity to walk outside the facility is certainly a valued therapeutic intervention. However, if staffing is not sufficient to guarantee safety for patients and staff escorts, the therapeutic goal is not accomplished. Administrators and staff need to comply with the law. Policies need to address both therapy and safety

BOX 11-9

Greystone Park Psychiatric Hospital in New Jersey reported that a patient from a locked ward, but who had grounds privileges, escaped and took the bus to the local mall.[76]

issues. If not, danger results and liability increases.

At two of the five New York State psychiatric hospitals located in the New York City area, one reported 727 patient elopements and at the other 1,188 patients walked away during 1994.[77] This extraordinarily large number of elopements placed these institutions at high risk for a lawsuit.

The scenario described in Box 11-10 raises questions about the ease with which a patient leaves a facility and how a patient is screened upon return. When patients are initially admitted to an institution, their private property is carefully checked. If patients elope and then return, however, they may not go through a similar check of their property. To prevent harm to patients and staff, there must be procedures in place for dealing with elopement returns.

Although patients are classified as violent or homicidal when they first come to the unit, these symptoms may diminish or disappear after treatment. Policies should explain who is eligible for random access to the grounds or to the community. Patients with a history of violence need special attention (see Box 11-11). After a patient elopes the first time, administrative policies should outline the protocol for future privileges. In New York State, all 28 psychiatric hospitals were ordered to secure the wards and tighten up the granting of grounds privileges after the murder at Brooklyn State Psychiatric Hospital in 1995.[79]

BOX 11-10

Daniel Alvarez, a patient at Brooklyn (NY) State Psychiatric Hospital, escaped and roamed the city for 12 hours. He returned at dawn after a night of drinking, was searched, and was placed back with the other patients. Later that day, another patient died after Alvarez stabbed him four times in the chest with a knife he had obtained while free. As a result of this incident, three top executives at the hospital were demoted and transferred.[78]

Child and Adolescent Psychiatry

Risk management in child and adolescent psychiatry is a concern to hospitals and treating practitioners. Related malpractice cases have increased, and the statute of limitations for filing a claim is significantly longer than for those treating adult patients. Child protection laws and the legal mandates for reporting suspected child abuse or neglect have been evident in malpractice litigation. Additionally, an area of increased liability deals with negligent evaluations for child custody and child sexual abuse allegations.[81] In some states, reregistration for professional licensure requires a continuing education child abuse course to keep practitioners knowledgeable.

A national survey pinpointed patterns of malpractice litigation cases in U.S. child and adolescent psychiatric residency programs from 1981 through 1991. Findings indicated that 28 percent of the malpractice cases were a result of suicide and attempted suicide, mainly of adolescent boys with major depression. Secondary to suicide, the most frequent source of litigation was sexual abuse of a prepubescent patient by another patient on the child inpatient service (22 percent).[82]

BOX 11-11

One runaway . . . pushed a grandmother to her death under the wheels of a subway train. At the time of his elopement, Reuben Harris was free to walk the hospital grounds without any escort. When admitted in March, he had been classified as violent or even homicidal. Since March, he had run away four times.[47]

While hospital administration must provide a protective environment to all patients, special emphasis must be placed on the needs of children and adolescents (see Box 11-12). These patients are even more vulnerable than the adult psychiatric population, because of growth and developmental patterns. In this age group, sexual identity is being established and tested, and acting out is common. Institutional policies should mandate a dress code, room limitations, visiting hours, and interventions regarding seductive behaviors. Setting firm limits and maintaining consistency among staff are crucial. Policies should also specify what interventions are available for the children to voice their feelings and concerns around these issues.

Information in medical records concerning children must be entered in a manner than protects the children as well as the confidentiality of parents. Written objective information based on observed behaviors must omit the opinions or attitudes of the observer.[82]

In most states a minor is considered to be any individual who is younger than age 18 and is legally incompetent so that consent for treatment must come from parents or guardian. Exceptions include seeking treatment for drug abuse, consent for contraception, and treatment for psychiatric reasons.[35] The legal rights of children must be protected. However, treatment should be provided when clinically indicated and legally sanctioned. To provide guidelines for practitioners, risk managers must be knowledgeable about applicable state statutes.

Children can be admitted to a psychiatric hospital against their will. If a parent authorizes the child's admission, it is considered a voluntary admission. Safeguards instituted over the years protect children when the parent's decision may not be in their best interest. Many states have modified their statutes by lowering the age of required consent, by requiring consent of the child, or by having a court hearing if the child continues to object to hospitalization.[35]

A new area of concern is the increase in the number of children receiving psychiatric medications. Questions are being raised about the informed consent process and about what information is being provided on the long-term effects of children being on medications and alternative therapies. The potential for lawsuits is increased as more attention is being placed on the diagnosis and psychopharmacological management of children with psychiatric disorders, with specific reference to attention deficit disorders. Risk managers and practitioners need to be aware of the potential liability involved in treating children with psychiatric disorders, and provide patients with the most current information, options for treatment, risks, and benefits. This information should be clearly provided in consent forms and practitioners should document the process utilized to inform the family members of their choices.

BOX 11-12

Within six months, a 13-year-old girl and a 14-year-old boy committed suicide in the Bergen Pines (NJ) Hospital psychiatric unit. An investigative team initiated a management review, scheduled inservice training, and used a crisis team to counsel staff and patients. No negligence was found.[83]

CONFIDENTIALITY AND STIGMA

"Stigmatization of people with mental disorders has persisted throughout history. . . . It deters the public from seeking, and wanting to pay for, care. In its most overt and egregious form, stigma results in outright discrimination and abuse. More tragically, it deprives people of their dignity and interferes with their full participation in society." This comment made by the Surgeon General pinpoints the stigma of mental illness that affects individuals using therapeutic services.[85]

Although strides are being made to change the public's view of mental illness, there is a long way to go. Therefore, the stigma of mental illness places special emphasis on the need for confidentiality. Unauthorized release of medical information is a breach of confidentiality and raises ethical and legal concerns that place the mental health care professional in a precarious situation. As an aid in providing treatment, family members may be questioned to gather relevant information. Although professionals may obtain information from others, they must make a distinct effort not to disclose personal information shared by the patient. There is a distinction between getting information and respecting the patient's right to privacy. Frequently, this is a delicate balancing act that requires concentrated attention.

Patient and mental health professional confidentiality enhances the therapeutic relationship. Patients should have the opportunity to share freely and to work through their concerns. Perceived threats of a breach of confidentiality may compromise the therapeutic relationship. If a patient refuses to allow the mental health professional to communicate with others, the therapist must respect the patient's wishes, despite the inability to obtain needed information. On the other hand, a common breach of confidentiality is the discussion of patients in public areas where others are able to hear. Risk managers need to remind all personnel, through continuing education, of the inappropriateness of careless conversation and the subsequent legal implications.

Continuity of care is imperative and requires referrals to various treatment facilities and resources. For the mental health professional to disclose information, the patient needs to understand what is involved and agree to release the data. Patients must be informed as to who will receive the data and why it is necessary to share the information. Explanations should pinpoint what information is necessary to share, how it will be used, and when the information will be provided to the other source. A signature on a release form should be obtained and secured in the chart.[35]

Institutions must be responsive to the risk issues of confidentiality. Medical records should not be freely accessible to others. Using computers to store medical records data evokes unique problems regarding the right to privacy and to confidentiality. Because of the sensitive nature of the data, psychiatric informational material must be protected using reliable security measures. The Privacy Act, as required by the Health Insurance Portability and Accountability Act (HIPPA) of 1996, provides additional federal regulations that protect the privacy of medical records. Risk managers need to become fully knowledgeable of the new laws, which will be effective in the year 2003.[86]

Privileged Communication

Privileged communication is a legal term applicable in court proceedings. It protects information shared by a patient with certain persons from disclosure in court. The person or institution that obtains the information is bound by law not to disclose the information to any third party. State laws generally hold that communications between clients and attorneys, husbands and wives, patients and physicians, and clergy and parishioners are confidential.[35,87] The

United States Supreme Court decision *Jaffe v. Redmond* (1996)[88] determined that psychotherapist-client confidentiality privileges exist in civil and criminal federal courts under the Federal Rules of Evidence.[89] However, who is considered a psychotherapist is not clearly defined by the court.[90] Professionals must check their individual state laws to clarify the legal dictates of privileged communication.

Although states grant professionals the privileged communication right, there are specified exemptions to that privilege. Most common exceptions include:[35,91]

- When the courts order an examination.
- When civil commitment is sought by the therapist.
- When child abuse is suspected.
- When the patient brings a defense of mental illness into the litigation proceedings.
- When the patient presents a danger to others.

Duty to Protect

In *Tarasoff v. Regents of the University of California* (see Box 11-13), the court established as an exception to privileged communication the "duty to protect" when a patient presents a danger to others. To guide mental health professionals, risk managers should advise their institutions to incorporate pertinent legal definitions into their policies and procedures.

An algorithm proposed by Felthous[93] helps clinicians make critical decisions regarding hospitalization and disclosures to protect others; however, it should not replace clinical judgment. Four questions are of utmost importance:

- Is the patient a danger to others?
- Is this danger due to mental illness?
- Is the danger imminent?
- Is the danger targeted at specific individuals?

All states and the District of Columbia have some type of statute identifying those professionals who are mandated to report child maltreatment, along with the specifics regarding such reporting. Approximately 18 states presently require any person who suspects child abuse or neglect to report it.[94] In addition, elder abuse is a growing concern. Every year, thousands of elderly persons are abused, neglected, and exploited by family members. In response, states have enacted elder abuse laws. All 50 states have passed some type of elder abuse prevention laws. Although the laws and definitions differ, each state has enacted reporting systems.[95] To reduce their liability risk, professionals need to know their own state laws and procedural responsibilities.

BOX 11-13

Tatiana Tarasoff's parents sued the University of California, claiming that a therapist in the university's counseling center knew that his client was threatening to kill their daughter. Their daughter was not warned of the possible danger and was killed. Her parents won the case, and subsequently most states accepted the concept of "duty to protect."[92]

HIGH-RISK INCIDENTS

Since psychiatric treatment deals with emotions, high-risk incidents may be triggered by the volatility of events in the patient's life. These high-risk incidents could involve violence, the use of illicit drugs, or sexual misconduct. Risk managers should be prepared to reduce potential liability of such high-risk areas of concern.

Violence and the Mentally Ill

There is much debate among professionals and mental health advocacy groups regarding the belief that those with mental illness are more prone to be violent than the rest of the population. Earlier professional studies indicate that an association does exist between mental illness and the likelihood of being involved in violent incidents.[96] Approximately 10 to 20 percent of hospital patients physically assaulted others prior to their hospitalization.[97] Blomhoff found that the only discriminating demographic was that the violent group experienced more violence in the family of origin.[98] A history of previous violence by the patient was the best single predictor of violence.

However, the MacArthur Community Violence Study, based on the findings of Steadman and colleagues, made the following conclusions regarding people discharged from psychiatric hospitals and the incidence of community violence:[99,100]

- "People discharged from psychiatric hospitals" is not a homogeneous category regarding violence.
- Those without a substance abuse diagnosis are involved in significantly less community violence than people with a co-occurring substance abuse diagnosis.
- Those without symptoms of substance abuse have about the same prevalence of violence as other people living in their communities who do not have symptoms of substance abuse.
- People with symptoms of substance abuse (those discharged from the hospital and non-patients) have a higher incidence of violence than those without symptoms of substance abuse. Those discharged from a psychiatric hospital have a higher prevalence of violence than others in the community.

In their study, McNiel and Binder found that the symptom patterns of assaultive patients differed from those of nonassaultive patients.[101] Krakowski and Czobor noted that transient violence occurred primarily as a result of paranoid delusions and probably was a symptom of acute decompensation.[102] Chronic, repetitive patterns of violence were related to neurological impairment.

Torrey, a leader in obtaining treatment for the chronically ill psychiatric patient, believes that without treatment the mentally ill do have a higher prevalence of violence.[103] Torrey addressed three predictors of violent behavior in a subgroup of patients with serious mental illness: medication noncompliance, a history of violent behavior, and concurrent drug and alcohol abuse.[104] He recommended steps to decrease violence by the seriously mentally ill, including:

- Involuntary hospitalization.
- Involuntary medication.
- Allowing outpatients to remain in the community only if they comply with treatment and take medication.
- Releasing individuals with serious mental illness into the community only if monitored to ensure oral medication compliance.

Investigators described a decision tree to guide judgments about pharmacological and behavioral treatments of aggression. These decisions depend on where the patient encountered difficulty during the course of the disorder.[105]

Davis outlined individual, situational, and structural factors affecting violence in psychiatric inpatients.[106] Individual variables included drug abuse, stage of illness, psychosis, and a history of violence. Situational factors included staff inexperience, provocative incidents, management's ability to tolerate violence, staff attitudes and behavior, overcrowding, and lack of privacy. Structural factors included changes in mental health policies that make "dangerous" a criteria for hospitalization and a shortage of treatment facilities in the community. Davis claimed that violence is the result of an interaction between the various types of factors and is not simply an extension of individual pathology.

Although additional research is needed to refine predictor variables, Monahan outlined guidelines to assist in violence prevention and in reducing the risk of civil liability.[92] His guidelines address five domains: (1) risk assessment, (2) risk management, (3) documentation, (4) policy, and (5) damage control. The MacArthur Risk Assessment Study attempts to determine markers of violence risk. If these markers prove reliable, clinicians will have specific indicators to guide their clinical practice. If not, the study will confirm the enormous difficulty that clinicians face in addressing the uncertainty of the potentially violent patient.[107,108]

When patients verbally or otherwise express violent intentions, mental health professionals must be aware of their responsibilities. On these occasions, health care workers are exempted from the responsibility of privileged communication.

Violence in the Institution

Violence directed toward staff and other patients is a continuous problem needing institutional attention. "Overwhelmingly, the facilities where risk of assault was highest were psychiatric hospitals."[109] The recent unfortunate death of a psychiatric nurse by a patient in a Florida psychiatric hospital is evidence of this continuous problem.[67]

Nursing personnel are in the best position to assess the potentially violent patient and to intervene accordingly before an outbreak of violence occurs. It is their responsibility to protect their patients and themselves from acts of violence. Institutions are liable for acts of violence directed at one patient by another patient. Patients are in facilities to be treated, not to incur physical harm as a result of another patient's illness. However, hospital administrators must provide the nursing personnel and other staff with adequate resources to provide protection for themselves and the patients they care for. Neglecting proper staffing patterns and violence education protection, to name a few interventions, increases the rate of violence and the liability risk to the facility.

In a study by Ryan and Porter, 61 nurses were asked about being attacked by their patients.[110] In addition to experiencing a variety of feelings such as helplessness, anger, shock, and disbelief, the nurses felt that they should have done something to prevent the attack. Lanza found that nurses were hesitant to share their responses to such attacks.[111] They seemed to blame themselves for not being able to do anything to prevent the attack. Controversy exists as to whether staff members may file charges against patients who intentionally assaulted them. Phelan supports the idea of prosecuting psychiatric patients for assault.[112] However, the question remains as to whether the patient can be held responsible for this violent behavior. If the nurse feels responsible for not preventing the violence, it is unlikely that a legal course of action will be pursued. Nonetheless, institutions need to consider patient violence against staff as potential liability.

What can nurses and other members of the mental health care team do to prevent violence in a psychiatric unit? Gould discussed seven practical ways to reduce levels of violence in a psychiatric ward:[113]

- Provide areas for patient privacy.
- Establish good facilities that value the patients.
- Provide a comfortable and reasonably decorated environment.
- Allow patients to be partners in their care.
- Listen to patient requests and respond accordingly.
- Have a continuity of staff who work well as a team.
- Provide clear leadership to the unit.

Availability of Illicit Substances

Illicit substance use in psychiatric facility units has become a pervasive problem. Family members, visitors, and staff may be a source of illicit drugs, and many facilities have an underground drug source. Use of these substances further complicates the therapeutic process. Policies and guidelines need to state explicit rules about illicit substance use in a unit. Random drug screening procedures and the right to screen for drugs need to be developed in a written statement readily available to staff and patients.

Frequently, illicit substance use in psychiatric units is met with disapproval and disgust. It is easy to forget that substance abuse is an illness. Professionals may view illicit drug use in an inpatient unit as a punitive matter and punish the patient. Although automatic discharge following noncompliance with rules may be indicated, liability issues regarding such discharge may surface. However, liability risk decreases as long as decisions are made on the basis of clinical judgments and are documented accordingly.

Professional Sexual Misconduct

Psychiatric mental health professionals must be cognizant of the ramifications of possible alleged sexual conduct and misconduct (see Box 11-14). Gutheil and Gabbard examined the concept of boundaries and boundary violations in clinical practice.[114] Three principles underlined the relationship among boundaries, boundary crossings, boundary violations, and sexual misconduct:

- Sexual misconduct usually starts with relatively minor boundary violations, such as last name to first name, personal conversation during sessions, some body contact such as pats on the shoulder, and trips outside the office, and ends ultimately in sexual intercourse.
- Not every boundary crossing or violation leads to or represents evidence of sexual misconduct.
- Fact finders, including juries, ethics committees, licensing boards, and professional organizations, usually believe that the presence of boundary violations or crossings is presumptive evidence of, or supports allegations of, sexual misconduct.

Boundary issues that clinicians need to be knowledgeable of include: role; time; place and space; money; gifts, services, and

BOX 11-14

It had all the trappings of a made-for-television movie: a prominent psychiatrist, a patient with multiple personalities, and allegations of sex. In fact, lawyers often referenced Hollywood during the sexual misconduct trial of Dr. Ronald Malave, who was found innocent of charges that he had sex with a woman who has as many as a dozen distinct personalities. But a DeLand, Florida courtroom is a far cry from the studios of Tinseltown. Attorneys for both Malave and his accuser say the case should serve as a cautionary tale for mental health professionals and their patients.[115]

related matters; clothing; language; self-disclosure and related matters; and physical contact. Although guidelines are helpful, the context of the clinical situation must be emphasized. At times, crossing a boundary may be harmless, because clinical judgment dictates the course of action. If such is the case, there must be written documentation of the rationale. Under no circumstances is a sexual relationship between a mental health professional/therapist and a patient a boundary that may be violated. From a risk management approach, a handshake is the only permissible form of physical contact.

To prevent boundary violations of a sexual nature, Epstein and Simon developed an exploitation index providing therapists with a list of questions to answer to monitor their own behavior and to act as a warning indicator of boundary violations.[115] Risk managers can use the index for educational purposes to promote open discussion and self-awareness of boundary issues. Education is the key to the prevention of boundary violations. All health care professions should incorporate professional conduct issues in their educational programs, and risk managers must continue the educational process.[116,117,118]

Staff-Patient Sexual Misconduct

In the claim described in Box 11-15, the hospital was sued for not following its own policies and for not adequately conducting an employee background check. This male employee had been dismissed from previous employment after pleading guilty to a similar sexual assault charge. Furthermore, the prior employer was sued by the hospital for not providing accurate information on a reference. Administrators must be observant of employee hiring policies, conduct background checks, and adhere to legislative requirements.

BOX 11-15

A 22-year-old female ex-patient sued the hospital after being sexually assaulted by a male employee who had attended her while she was an inpatient. Because of her past self-destructive behaviors, the patient's physician had prescribed one-to-one observation. According to hospital policy, the observer should be of the same sex. However, in this case the observer was a male employee.[119]

Recent lawsuits highlight the need for risk managers and hospital administrators to be diligent in preventing sexual abuse and assault among their employees. In a recent case, a worker in a psychiatric facility was sentenced to prison time for assaulting adolescent patients (see Box 11-16). Another court ruled that a hospital has a duty to protect patients against sexual assault by other patients (see Box 11-17).

Screening staff to identify individuals who may engage in sexual misconduct is very difficult and makes risk management strategies demanding. An interpretation of psychological testing, verbal language, or body language cues might indicate potential employees at high risk to engage in sexual misconduct and allow for appropriate intervention. But such evaluative techniques are fraught with possible errors and potential risk liability. Accordingly, educational programs to help staff understand patient dynamics and sexual conduct may be the prudent approach.

BOX 11-16

In Illinois, a hospital worker was sentenced to 15 years in prison for sexually assaulting or abusing five girls who were patients in the adolescent psychiatric unit.[120]

BOX 11-17

The staff of a psychiatric facility permitted a male patient to enter a female patient's room unsupervised. The female patient claimed she was sexually assaulted and brought suit against the hospital. The Virginia court ruled in favor of the female patient, stating "that there is a special relationship creating a duty between a psychiatric patient who is admitted for 24-hour observation and protection and the psychiatric facility where she is housed."[121]

FRAUD AND ABUSE

Fraud and abuse in psychiatry should not be overlooked by risk managers. In a competitive health care market, the desire for and retention of patients is a high priority. In 1991, Texas Senate hearings on complaints from patients brought attention to fraudulent and abusive psychiatric treatment and billing practices. In a settlement, National Medical Enterprises provided $2.6 million in free psychiatric services and paid the state $1.1 million to reimburse the investigative costs.[122] A subsequent federal investigation uncovered allegations against psychiatric hospitals throughout the nation, including the following charges:[123]

- Charging exorbitantly and billing for services never rendered.
- Engaging in overly aggressive and deceptive advertising and marketing.
- Holding voluntary patients against their will without medical justification.
- Unnecessarily hospitalizing patients instead of using outpatient care.
- Paying kickbacks or bounties for the delivery of patients to treatment facilities (see Box 11-18).

BOX 11-18

Psychiatric Institutes of America (PIA) facility administrator Peter Alexis pled guilty to paying kickbacks to physicians and providers for patient referrals. His employer paid the federal government $362.7 million, as well as $16.3 million to 28 states where PIA operated, to resolve potential claims.[123]

Investigators found specific instances of violations in several states. In Wisconsin, a hospital paid kickbacks for patient referrals, billed for services never provided, and included billing days when the patient was not hospitalized. In Georgia, the vice president of a psychiatric hospital chain was indicted for filing false Medicare hospital cost reports. The government is also bringing action against facilities receiving federal funding and providing substandard conditions. Reimbursement is not just for services provided, but for quality care. Likewise, individual insurance companies are monitoring for fraud and have instituted legal action when appropriate.

To prevent allegations of fraud and/or abuse, risk managers in health care facilities should be sure that all employees are cognizant of the institution's referral, treatment, and billing practices. Self-monitoring procedures to eliminate possible fraud and abuse are a necessity. Risk management can curtail possible fraud, such as that depicted in Box 11-19.

At the same time, adhering to Medicare regulations can be daunting, confusing, and not necessarily constitute intent to fraud.[127] Risk managers need to assist professionals and facilities in clarifying confusing regulations and preventing billing errors. Fraud and abuse compromise the care rendered to patients. Professionals need to be alert to fraud and abuse by their colleagues, and initiate appropriate professional and legal remedies (see Box 11-19).

BOX 11-19

- Blue Cross and Blue Shield of New Jersey accused three physicians of billing fraud. A lawsuit detailed how bills were inflated and were submitted for services never performed and for inappropriate treatment.[124]
- In 1998, a psychiatric chain agreed to pay $4.7 million to settle allegations that it fraudulently admitted and lengthened the psychiatric stays of elderly Medicare patients in order to collect millions of dollars of Medicare reimbursement.[125]
- The United States government received $750,000 for fraud committed by an Oklahoma psychiatric hospital that allegedly provided treatment in an unsafe and harmful environment.[126]

PSYCHIATRIC CONCERNS ARE EVERYWHERE

Awareness of the unique potential risk when treating patients with psychiatric problems is not intended to produce paranoia among mental health professionals. Rather, practitioners must be enlightened about occupational realities. With current treatment modalities, patients with mental illness can be cared for in acute care facilities. Even if the facility has a small number of psychiatric beds, the risk manager must be alert to the distinctive potential for liability risks. Only when therapists are informed can optimal care be provided to the patients. In addition, being knowledgeable about risk liabilities protects professionals and institutions while they tend to their patients.

References

1. Rile, B. (1995). Mental patient sues institutions, says workers let him eat objects. *Star-Ledger* (Newark, N.J.), February 4, p. 7, col. 1.
2. Teich, C. (1994). Risk management in the psychiatric setting. In *Risk Management Desk Reference*, edited by B. Youngberg. Gaithersburg, Md.: Aspen, pp. 445–454.
3. Leo, R. J. (1999). Competency and the capacity to make treatment decisions: A primer for primary practitioners. *The Primary Care Companion to the Journal of Clinical Psychiatry* 5:131–141.
4. University of California, San Diego. (2002). Decision Making Capacity Guidelines. UCSD Human Research Protections Program. *http://irb.ucsd.edu/decisional.shtml*.
5. Wysoker, A. (2000). Informed consent: The ultimate right. *Journal of the American Psychiatric Nurses Association* 6:100–102.
6. Appelbaum, P. S., Grisso, T., Frank, E., O'Donnell, S., and Kupfer, D. (1999). Competence of depressed patients for consent to research. *American Journal of Psychiatry* 156:1380–1384.
7. Wirshing, D. A., Wirshing, W. C., Marder, S. R., Liberman, R. P., and Mintz, J. (1998). Informed consent: Assessment of comprehension. *American Journal of Psychiatry* 155:1508–1511.
8. Carpenter, W. T., Jr., Gold, J. M., Lahti, A. C., Queern, C. A., Conley, R. S., Bartko, J. J., Kovnick, J. K., and Appelbaum, P. S. (2000). Decisional capacity for informed consent in schizophrenia research. *Archives of General Psychiatry* 57:533–538.
9. Informed consent among people with schizophrenia. (2002). *American Journal of Psychiatry*, July.
10. Appelbaum, P. S., and Grisso, T. (1988). Assessing patients' capacities to consent to treatment. *New England Journal of Medicine* 319(25):1635–1638.
11. Grisso, T., and Appelbaum, P. S. (1995). Comparison of standards for assessing patients' capacities to make treatment decisions. *American Journal of Psychiatry* 152:1033–1037.
12. Grisso, T., and Appelbaum, P. S. (1998). *Assessing Competence to Consent to Treatment*. New York: Oxford University Press.
13. Grisso, T., Appelbaum, P. S., and Hill-Fotouhi, C. (1997). A clinical tool to assess patients' capacities to make treatment decisions. *Psychiatric Services* 48:1415–1419.

14. Grisso, T., Appelbaum, P. S., and Hill-Fotouhi, C. (1998). *A Clinical Tool to Assess Patients' Capacities to Make Treatment Decisions: The MacArthur Competence Assessment Tool Treatment*. Sarasota, Fla.: Professional Resource Press.

15. Grisso, T., Appelbaum, P. S., Mulvey, E. P., and Fletcher, K. (1995). The MacArthur Treatment Competence Study II: Measures of abilities related to competence to consent to treatment. *Law and Human Behavior* 19:127–148.

16. Grisso, T., and Appelbaum, P. S. (1995). The MacArthur Treatment Competence Study III: Abilities of patients to consent to psychiatric and medical treatments. *Law and Human Behavior* 19:149–174.

17. MacArthur Research Network on Mental Health and the Law. (2001). The MacArthur Treatment Competence Study. *http://macarthur.virginia.edu/treatment.html.*

18. American Psychiatric Association Official Actions. (1998). Guidelines for assessing the decision-making capacities of potential research subjects with cognitive impairment. *American Journal of Psychiatry* 155:1649–1650.

19. Dunn, L. B., and Jeste, D. V. (2001). Enhancing informed consent for research and treatment. *Neuropsychopharmacology* 24(6):595–607.

20. Galen, K. D. (1993). Assessing psychiatric patients' competency to agree to treatment plans. *Hospital & Community Psychiatry* 44(4):361–363.

21. Beahrs, J. O., and Gutheil, T. G. (2001). Informed consent in psychotherapy. *American Journal of Psychiatry* 158(1):4–10.

22. Campbell, T. W. (1999). Issues in forensic psychology-psychotherapy malpractice. *http://www.campsych.com/malpractice.htm.*

23. Wenning, K. (1993). Long-term psychotherapy and informed consent. *Hospital & Community Psychiatry* 44(4):364–366.

24. US researchers fail to get informed consent. (1994). *British Medical Journal* 308(6931):739.

25. U.S. Department of Health & Human Services. (2002). Human Subject Protections. *http://os.dhhs.gov.*

26. The National Bioethics Advisory Commission. (2001). Ethical and Policy Issues in Research Involving Human Participants. Bethesda, Md. *http://www.bioethics.gov.*

27. The National Bioethics Advisory Commission. (1998). Research Involving Persons with Mental Disorders that May Affect Decisionmaking Capacity. *www.bioethics.gov.*

28. American Association on Mental Deficiency. (1998). Center for the Study of Ethics in the Professions, Illinois Institute of Technology. American Association of Mental Deficiency statement on the use of human subjects for research, adopted May 1969, verified on April 21, 1998. *http://www.iit.edu/departments/csep/PublicWWW/codes.*

29. American Association on Mental Deficiency, Legislative and Social Issues Committee. (1977). Consent handbook. Special publication no. 3. Washington, D.C.: AAMD.

30. Morgan, G. A., Harmon, R. J., and Gliner, J. A. (2001). Ethical problems and principles in human research. *Journal of the American Academy of Child and Adolescent Psychiatry* 40(10):1231–1233.

31. Advisory WorkGroup on Human Subject Research Involving Protected Classes. (1998). *Recommendations on the Oversight of Human Subject Research Involving the Protected Classes*. Albany: Department of Health, State of New York.

32. *Final Report of the Attorney General's Research Working Group*. (1998). Baltimore: Office of the Maryland Attorney General.

33. Heinssen, R. K., Perkins, D. O., Appelbaum, P. S., and Fenton, W. S. (2001). National Institute of Mental Health Workshop. Informed consent in early psychosis research. *Schizophrenia Bulletin* 27(4): 571–584.

34. *Wyatt v. Stickney*, 344 Fed. Supp. 373 (1972).

35. Keglovits, J. (1992). Legal issues and clients' rights. In *Psychiatric Nursing*, edited by K. S. Wilson and C. R. Kneisel. Redwood City, Calif.: Addison-Wesley, pp. 930–952.

36. *Dixon v. Weinberger*, 405 Fed. Supp. 974 (1975).

37. Garritson, S. H. (1983). Degrees of restrictiveness in psychosocial nursing. *Journal of Psychosocial Nursing* 21(12):9–16.

38. Hospital Closures and the Medicaid IMD Exclusion. *www.psychlaws.org/Hospital/Closure/Index.htm.*

39. Fact sheet: Criminalization of Americans with Severe Mental Illnesses. *www.psychlaws.org.*

40. Clary, M. (2002). The snake pit: The county jail is one of the largest psychiatric facilities in Florida. *Miami News Times, www.miaminewtimes.com.* July 11.

41. Geller, J. (1990). Clinical guidelines for the use of involuntary outpatient treatment. *Hospital & Community Psychiatry* 41(7):749–755.

42. New York Mental Hygience Law §9.31 (c) §9.01 (c) §9.60 (c).

43. Treatment Advocacy Center (TAC) Model Law for Assisted Treatment. (2000). Arlington, Virginia. *www.psychlaws.org*.

44. Miller, R. D. (1999). Coerced treatment in the community. *The Psychiatric Clinics of North America* 22(1): 183–194.

45. Sabin, J. E., and Daniels, N. (1994). Determining "medical necessity" in mental health practice. *Hastings Center Report* 24(6):5–13.

46. American Psychiatric Association, Committee on Nomenclature and Statistics. (1994). *Diagnostic and Statistical Manual of Mental Disorders*, 4th edition. Washington, D.C.: APA.

47. Ford, W. E. (2000). Medical necessity and psychiatric managed care. *The Psychiatric Clinics of North America* 23(2):309–317.

48. *Rogers v. Okin*, 478 F. Supp. 1342 (1979).

49. Stuart, G. W. (1995). Legal context of psychiatric nursing care. In *Principles and Practice of Psychiatric Nursing*, edited by G. Stuart and S. J. Sundeen. St. Louis: Mosby, pp. 171–197.

50. Brooks, A. (1988). Law and ideology in the case of Billie Boggs. *Journal of Psychosocial Nursing and Mental Health Service* 26(7):22–25.

51. New York State Education Department. (1993). Nursing Handbook. Albany: NYSED, pp. 24–27; Certification of nurse practitioners/clinical nurse specialists. (1993). *New Jersey Register* (Trenton, N.J.), pp. 2829–2833.

52. Laraia, M. T. (1995). Psychopharmacology. In *Principles and Practice of Psychiatric Nursing*, edited by G. Stuart and S. J. Sundeen. St. Louis: Mosby, pp. 663–701.

53. Feltner, D. E., and Hertzman, M. (1993). Progress in the treatment of tardive dyskinesia: Theory and practice. *Hospital & Community Psychiatry* 44(1): 25–33.

54. Malinconico, J. (1995). $700,000 to settle big suit. County paid up to avoid bigger losses. *News Tribune* (Woodbridge, N.J.), April 2, p. A17, col. 1.

55. American Psychiatric Association. (1992). *Tardive Dyskinesia: A Task Force Report*. Washington, D.C.: APA, pp. 217–226, 231–251.

56. Benjamin, S., and Munetz, M. R. (1994). Community mental health center practices related to tardive dyskinesia screening and informed consent for neuroleptic drugs. *Hospital & Community Psychiatry* 45(4):343–346.

57. McElroy, E., Conn, V., and Huff, B. (1994). Persons experiencing the effects of mental disorders: What psychiatric nurses need to know about medication management: The family perspective. In *Psychiatric Mental Health Nursing Psychopharmacology Project*. Washington, D.C.: American Nurses Publishing, pp. 59–61.

58. Lacro, J. P., Sewell, D. D., Warren, K., et al. (1994). Improving documentation of consent for neuroleptic therapy. *Hospital & Community Psychiatry* 45(2):176–178.

59. American Psychiatric Association. (2001). *A Task Force Report on the Practice of Electroconvulsive Therapy: Recommendations for Treatment, Training and Privileging, Second Edition (2001)*. Washington, D.C.: American Psychiatric Association.

60. American Psychiatric Association. (1996). Electroconvulsive Therapy (ECT). Retrieved on August 12, 2002 from *http://ww.psych.org/public_info/ ect~1.cfm*.

61. Medical Malpractice Cases, Inpatient Suicide. (2002). Abramson, Brown and Duga. Retrieved on August 7, 2002 from *www.arbd.com/bases/mm.inpasuic.html*.

62. Bartels, S. J. (1987). The aftermath of suicide on the psychiatric inpatient unit. *General Hospital Psychiatry* 9(3):189–197.

63. Silverman, M. M., Berman, A. L., Bongar, B., et al. (1994). Inpatient standards of care and the suicidal patient. Part II: An integration with clinical risk management. *Suicide and Life-threatening Behavior* 24(2):152–169.

64. Slovenko, R. S. (1999). Malpractice in psychotherapy: An overview. *Psychiatric Clinics of North America* 22(1).

65. Rissmiller, D., Steer, R., Ranieri, W., et al. (1994). Factors complicating cost containment in the treatment of suicidal patients. *Hospital & Community Psychiatry* 45(8):782–788.

66. Doctors study why elderly are so prone to suicide. (2002). Associated Press, July 23. *www.cnn.com/2002/HEALTH/07/023/elderly.suicide.ap/index.html*.

67. The Surgeon General's Call to Action to Prevent Suicide. (1999). *http://www.surgeongeneral.gov/library/calltoaction/fact1.htm*.

68. State Operation Manual, Appendix A. Interpretative Guidelines—Hospitals. *www.hcfa.gov/pubforms/07_som/somap_a_171_to_196.htm*.

69. The Children's Health Act of 2000: A Summary. Title XXXII—Provisions Relating to Mental Health.

http://ww.samhsa.gov/legislate/Sept01/childhealth_title 32.htm.

70. Sheridan, M., Hourion, R., Robinson, L., et al. (1990). Precipitants of violence in a psychiatric inpatient setting. *Hospital & Community Psychiatry* 41(7):776–780.
71. Klinge, V. (1994). Staff opinions about seclusion and restraint at a state forensic hospital. *Hospital & Community Psychiatry* 45(2):138–141.
72. Betemps, E. J., Somoza, J., and Buncher, R. (1993). Hospital characteristics, diagnoses, and staff reasons associated with use of seclusion and restraint. *Hospital & Community Psychiatry* 44(4):367–371.
73. Chesbro, Wesley. (2002). Research, News, and Opinions from the Senate Democrats. Report Released on Seclusion and Restraints in California's Mental Health Facilities. March 19.
74. Statement of Senator Joseph I. Lieberman. (1999). GAO Report on Mental Health: Improper Restraint or Seclusion Use Places People at Risk. September 22.
75. Johnson, V. P. (1994). Psychiatry. In *Risk Management Handbook for Health Care Facilities,* edited by L. M. Harpster and M. S. Veach. Chicago: American Hospital Publishing, pp. 165–176.
76. Ragonese, L. (2002). Another Greystone patient escapes on a public bus. *Star-Ledger* (Newark, N.J.), August 2, p. 32, col. 1.
77. Dugger, C. W. (1995). Slipping through cracks and out the door. Pressures of policy and budget let psychiatric patients just walk away. *New York Times,* January 23, p. B1, col. 2; Dugger, C. W. (1995). Trying to escape a hopeless routine. *New York Times,* January 23, p. B4, col. 2.
78. McKinley, J. C. (1994). 3 officials are demoted after slaying at mental hospital. *New York Times,* November 25, p. B5, col. 1; Harpaz, B. J. (1995). Pataki fires deputy mental health commissioner. *Staten Island Advance* (New York), January 7, p. A3, col. 1.
79. Foderaro, L. W. (1995). At mental hospitals, a tighter rein. *New York Times,* May 28, p. 31, col. 4.
80. Perez-Pena, R. (1995). Subway death stirs call for more curbs on mental patients. *New York Times,* January 6, p. A1, col. 6.
81. Guyer, M. J. (1990). Child psychiatry and legal liability: Implications of recent case law. *Journal of American Academy of Child Adolescent Psychiatry* 29(6):958–962.
82. Wagner, K. D., Pollard, R., and Wagner, R. F., Jr. (1993). Malpractice litigation against child and adolescent psychiatry residency programs, 1981–1991. *Journal of American Academy of Child Adolescent Psychiatry* 32(2):462–465.
83. Guess, T. P. (1995). Hospital faces probe after 2d teen suicide. *Star-Ledger* (Newark, N.J.), July 11, p. 19, col. 4; Guess, T. P. (1995). Hospital not negligent in suicide of teenageer. *Star-Ledger* (Newark, N.J.), July 29, p. 15, col. 5.
84. Breeding, J. (2001). Informed Consent and the Psychiatric Drugging of Children. *http://wildestcolts.com/mentalhealth.*
85. U.S. Department of Health and Human Services. (1999). Introduction and Themes, Chapter 1: The Roots of Stigma. *www.surgeongeneral.gov/library/mentalhealth/chapter1/sec1.html.*
86. U.S. Department of Health and Human Services. (2002). Modifications to the standards for privacy of individually identifiable health information—final rule. *http://www.hhs.gov/news/press/2002pres/20020809a.html.*
87. Levy, R., and Rubenstein. (1996). *The Rights. People with Mental Disabilities: The Authoritative ACLU Guide to the Rights of People with Mental Illness and Mental Retardation.* Carbondale, Ill.: American Civil Liberties Union.
88. *Jaffe v. Redmond,* 64 U.S.L.LW 4491 (1996). *Jaffe v. Redmond,* U.S. 1 (1996).
89. Ciccone, J. R. (1999). The United States Supreme Court and psychiatry in the 1990s. *The Psychiatric Clinics of North America* 22(1):197–211.
90. 20 Rev.Litig. 1 (2000).
91. Wysoker, A. (2001). Confidentiality. *Journal of the American Psychiatric Nurses Association* 7:57–58.
92. Monahan, J. (1993). Limiting therapist exposure to Tarasoff liability. *American Psychologist* 48(3): 242–250.
93. Felthous, A. R. (1999). The clinician's duty to protect third parties. Forensic Psychiatry. *The Psychiatric Clinics of North America* 22(1):49–60.
94. U.S. Department of Health and Human Services. (2001). The Administration for Children and Families, National Clearinghouse on Child Abuse and Neglect Information. Updated May 15, 2001. Child Abuse and Neglect State Statutes Elements. *http://ww.calib.com/nccanch/pubs/stats01/mandrep.cfm.*
95. Administration on Aging. (2000). Elder Abuse Prevention. *http://www.aoa.dhhs.gov/factsheets/abuse.html.*

96. Mulvey, E. (1994). Assessing the evidence of a link betwen mental illness and violence. *Hospital & Community Psychiatry* 45(7):663–962.
97. Otto, R. K. (1992). Prediction of dangerous behavior: A review and analysis of "second generation" reports. *Forensic Reports* 5:103–138; Staznickas, K. A., McNiel, D. E., and Binder, R. L. (1993). Violence toward family caregivers by mentally ill relatives. *Hospital & Community Psychiatry* 44(4): 385–387.
98. Blomhoff, S. B., Seim, S., and Friis, S. (1990). Can prediction of violence among psychiatric inpatients be improved? *Hospital & Community Psychiatry* 41(7):771–775.
99. MacArthur Research Network on Mental Health and the Law. (2002). The MacArthur Community Violence Study. *http://macarthur.virginia.edu/violence.html.*
100. Steadman, H., Mulvey, E., Monahon, J., Robbins, P., Appelbaum, P., Grisso, T., Roth, L., and Silver, E. (1998). Violence by people discharged from acute psychiatric inpatient facilities and by others in the same neighborhoods. *Archives of General Psychiatry* 55:393–401.
101. McNiel, D. E., and Binder, R. L. (1994). The relationship between acute psychiatric symptoms, diagnosis, and short-term risk of violence. *Hospital & Community Psychiatry* 45(2):133–137.
102. Krakowski, M. I., and Czobor, P. (1994). Clinical symptoms, neurological impairment, and prediction of violence in psychiatric inpatients. *Hospital & Community Psychiatry* 45(7):700–705.
103. Briefing paper. Violence and Severe Untreated Mental Illness, updated June 2002. Treatment Advocacy Center. Retrieved on August 21, 2002 from *http://www.psychlaws.or/default.htm.*
104. Torrey, E. F. (1994). Violent behavior by individuals with serious mental illness. *Hospital & Community Psychiatry* 45(7):653–662.
105. Corrigan, P. W., Yudofsky, S. C., and Silver, J. M. (1993). Pharmacological and behavioral treatments for aggressive psychiatric inpatients. *Hospital & Community Psychiatry* 44(2):125–132.
106. Davis, S. (1991). Violence by psychiatric inpatients: A review. *Hospital & Community Psychiatry* 42(6):585–589.
107. Monahan, J., and Steadman, H. J. (1994). Toward a rejuvenation of risk assessment research. *In Violence and Mental Disorder: Developments in Risk Assessment,* edited by J. Monahan and H. Steadman. Chicago: University of Chicago Press, pp. 1–17.
108. Steadman, H., Monahan, J., Appelbaum, P. S., et al. (1994). Designing a new generation of risk assessment research. In *Violence and Mental Disorder: Developments in Risk Assessment,* edited by J. Monahan and H. Steadman. Chicago: University of Chicago Press, pp. 297–318.
109. Sullivan, C., and Yun, C. (1995). Workplace assaults on minority and mental health care workers in Los Angeles. *American Journal of Public Health* 85(7):1011–1014.
110. Ryan, J., and Porter, E. (1989). The assaulted nurse: Short-term and long-term responses. *Archives of Psychiatric Nursing* 3(6):323.
111. Lanza, M. L. (1983). The reactions of nursing staff to physical assault by a patient. *Hospital & Community Psychiatry* 34(1):44–47; Lanza, M. L. (1984). A follow-up study of nurses' reactions to physical assault. *Hospital & Community Psychiatry* 35(5):492–494.
112. Phelan, L., Mills, M., and Ryan, J. (1985). Prosecuting psychiatric patients for assault. *Hospital & Community Psychiatry* 36(6):581–582.
113. Gould, J. (1994). The impact of change on violent patients. *Nursing Standard* 8(19):38–40.
114. Gutheil, T., and Gabbard, G. O. (1993). The concept of boundaries in clinical practice: Theoretical and risk management dimensions. *American Journal of Psychiatry* 150(2):188–196.
115. Haun, M. (2002). Acquittal draws attention to rarity of sexual misconduct by psychiatrists. *The Daytona Beach News-Journal,* April 27.
116. Gabbard, G. O., and Nadelson, C. (1995). Professional boundaries in the physician-patient relationship. *Journal of the American Medical Association* 273(18):1445–1449.
117. Simon, R. I. (1999). Therapist-patient sex: From boundary violations to sexual misconduct. Forensic Psychiatry. *The Psychiatric Clinics of North America* 22(1):31–47.
118. Epstein, R. S. (2002). Post-termination boundary issues. *American Journal of Psychiatry* 159(5):877–885.
119. Spoto, M. (1994). Expatient sues hospitals after sexual assault. *Star-Ledger* (Newark, N.J.), November 18, p. 42, col. 3.
120. Hanson Information Systems (2002). Former Springfield hospital worker sentenced. *www.wandtv.com/ SendPage.asp?2481.* Retrieved on August 20.
121. *Delk v. Columbia/Healthcare Corp.,* 259 Va. 125,523 S.E. 2nd 826 (Va 2000). *http://biotech.law.1su.edu/cases/psyc/DelkvColumbiaHealthcare_brief.htm.* Retrieved on August 20, 2002.

122. Johnsson, J. (1995). Feds expand fraud investigation. *American Medical News* 38(20):3, 27–28.

123. Baine, D. P. (1993). *Psychiatric Fraud and Abuse.* HRD-93-92. Washington, D.C.: Government Accounting Office, p. 3.

124. Jaffe, H. (1995). Blue Cross sues three doctors in billing fraud. *Star-Ledger* (Newark, N.J.), January 22, sec. 1, p. 25.

125. Psychiatric Hospital Chain Settles Allegations of Medicare Fraud. (1998). *http://www.oralchelation.net/data/Psychiatry/data18c.htm*. August 19.

126. U.S. Gets $750,000 for Fraud Claims Against Oklahoma Hospital. (1997). *http:// www.usdoj.gov/opa/pr/1997/February97/062civ.htm.* February 11.

CHAPTER 12 Identifying and Controlling Risks in Long Term Care

Nursing Homes and Home Health Care

Joanne K. Singleton

In 2000, individuals age 65 or older made up 12.7 percent of our nation's total population. By 2020, that percentage will increase by nearly one-third to 16.5 percent—one in six Americans—and will represent nearly 20 million more seniors than there are today, as a direct effect of the aging of the "baby boomers."[1] Currently, of the population aged 65 and over, the highest percentage (18.5 percent) lives in Florida, and Alaska has the lowest percentage (5.6 percent). Iowa has the highest percentage of persons aged 85 and over (2.1 percent). The older a person is, the higher the probability that he or she has disabilities and long term health care needs, both institutional and at home.

In 1999, spending for nursing home and home care was about $134 billion, with over 60 percent of the cost funded through Medicaid and Medicare, 10 percent by health insurance, 25 percent through out-of-pocket expenses of families, and another five percent from other sources. This excludes the costs of unpaid family caregivers and lost wages of family members. Medicare nursing home expenditures have increased from $1.7 billion in 1990 to $9.6 billion in 1999. For home care in 1999, Medicare financing cost $8.7 billion.[2]

Nursing home malpractice costs are rising rapidly because of dramatic increases in both the number of lawsuits and the size of awards. Nursing homes are a new target of the litigation system. Between 1985 and 2001, the national average of insurance costs increased from $240 per occupied skilled nursing bed per year to $2,360 per bed per year. From 1990 to 2001, the average size of claims tripled, and the number of claims increased from 3.6 to 11 per 1,000 beds.[3]

These costs vary widely across states, in relation to whether a state has implemented reforms that improve the predictability of the legal system. Florida had one of the highest per-bed costs in 2001 ($11,000). Nursing homes in Mississippi have been faced with cost increases as great as 900 percent in the past two years. It recently has been reported that "nearly all companies that used to write nursing home liability [insurance] are getting out of the business." Since the costs of nursing home care are mainly paid by Medicaid and Medicare, these increased costs are borne by taxpayers, and they consume resources that could otherwise be used to expand health (or other) programs.[4]

Individuals served by long term care providers include those with chronic, multiple health problems and functional disabilities who require nursing, supportive, or custodial care for extended periods of time. Additionally, long term care aids individuals with acute injuries or illnesses who need treatment or rehabilitation to completely recover or to gain independence. Care can be rendered in institutions that provide varying levels of service, such as skilled care nursing homes, mental health facilities, intermediate care institutions, hospices, and personal or custodial care homes. Long term care can also be provided on an ambulatory basis by home health care services. Distinctive characteristics of long term care include the governing regulations, the residents/patients, the staff, the physical environment, and the program for patients.

Risk management in long term care requires the ongoing identification of situations, policies, or practices that have the potential for financial loss to the facility or agency, and the development and implementation of control strategies to obviate or minimize those risks.

DEMOGRAPHICS OF LONG TERM CARE

Chronic illness and functional disabilities are interrelated and increase with age. Eight percent of persons 65 and older have at least one chronic health problem, and a majority have multiple problems. Predictably, the greatest incidence of disabilities occurs in the fast-growing population group of people 75 years and older, many of whom need long term care.

As people move into their eighties and nineties, the probability of decreased function, dependence upon others, and the risk of institutionalization substantially increase. There has been a gradual expansion of in-home and community-based care, because most elderly and chronically ill people prefer to remain in their own homes. In-home services are generally less expensive than nursing home care. According to the 1997 National Nursing Home Survey, there were 1,465,000 residents age 65 and older in nursing homes (about 4.3 percent of the U.S. population age 65 and older in 1997), but the average age upon admission to a nursing home was 82.6 years. Nearly three-fourths of these residents were women and about one-half were age 85 and older. The average length of stay was 2.5 years and will be decreasing as home care services become more readily available.

In 1997, about 75 percent of all nursing home residents 65 and older required assistance in three or more activities of daily living, including bathing, dressing, eating, transferring from bed to chair, and using the toilet. About 42 percent of nursing home residents were diagnosed with dementia, and 12 percent had other psychiatric conditions, such as schizophrenia and mood disorders.[5]

Furthermore, subacute care is being highly promoted and debated as an unproven level of patient care designed for individuals, of all ages, who are not sick enough to remain in the hospital but are too sick to be transferred to nursing homes or discharged to home health care or to their homes. In advising Congress on potential

Medicare reform areas, the Prospective Payment Assessment Commission (ProPAC) "had difficulty agreeing on the specific definition of subacute care, . . . and, most importantly, whether subacute care is actually beneficial for patients."[6]

LONG TERM CARE PROVIDERS

Nursing homes cover a broad spectrum: from three-bed privately owned adult residential care homes to 20-bed units in acute general hospitals to 1200-bed government operated institutions. In 2001, there were over 17,000 certified nursing homes and 1.81 million beds, which had an occupancy rate of 82.7 percent.[5] Primary medical diagnoses of nursing home residents fall into three major categories: circulatory system disorders (33 percent); mental disorders (22 percent); and nervous system disorders (45 percent). However, the actual reason for admission to a nursing home tends to be functional decline, cognitive impairment, or incontinence, rather than a medical diagnosis.[7]

LONG TERM CARE REGULATIONS

Long term care facilities are licensed by the state in which the facility is located. Each state establishes its own definition of a nursing home, has its own licensing requirements, and establishes its own regulations. In 1987, the Nursing Home Reform Act, which was incorporated into the Omnibus Budget Reconciliation Act (OBRA), made significant changes in how nursing homes are operated and evaluated to conform to Medicare and Medicaid reimbursement requirements. Nursing homes are highly regulated, and the evaluative focus has shifted to the caring process, the resident's feelings, and patient care outcomes. Although there is tremendous concern about the quality of care, the limited budgets of Medicare, Medicaid, and private families clearly demonstrate a lack of funds to comply to the letter or the spirit of the current regulations.

Each regulatory body has its own schedule of on-site facility inspections and reviews of administrative policies, operations, finances, and medical and nursing care services. Credentials of professionals, as well as the credentialing process and minutes of meetings, are reviewed. Strict attention should be paid to the necessary documentation of patient care conferences, meetings of the board of directors, medical staff meetings, adverse incidents and occurrences, and committees on medical records, infection control, and safety. Reports of site visits are presented to the respective facility with an opportunity for the facility to provide corrective action plans to remedy the deficiencies cited.[8] If standards are not met to a significant degree, licensure can be in jeopardy and reimbursements to the facility may be curtailed.

An aggressive presidential strategy was announced in July 1998 to ensure that all nursing home residents are treated with dignity and compassion. Since then, the Health Care Financing Administration (HCFA) has begun to phase in key provisions to strengthen nursing home inspection systems. In addition, the Department of Health and Human Services has issued new instructions to the states to strengthen their nursing home inspections and to take tougher enforcement actions against poor performers (see Box 12-1).

Compliance with the multiple government regulations, federal Medicare and Medicaid, and state licensure is important to maintain the continuing existence and viability of the institution or agency (see Box 12-2).

BOX 12-1

An autistic 14-year-old boy who was restrained died of blood infection and severe respiratory problems. The New Jersey Department of Health and Senior Services fined Bancroft NeuroHealth $127,000, citing violation of 39 state regulations during its investigation.[9]

Risk managers should participate in maintaining appropriate monitoring to ensure the institution's integrity and reputation in the community. A substantial portion of the facility's reputation results from informational material and mass media advertising, and these marketing activities may pose liability risks. "Brochures and promotional information materials that make false or misleading claims or impossible promises can result in liability and costly lawsuits for long term care providers."[11,12]

Facilities that knowingly make misleading or false representations are at risk for a deceptive trade practice lawsuit and possible penalties of triple damages, all attorneys' fees, and costs. Because the action was not based on professional negligence, malpractice insurance may not cover this type of claim. Dos and don'ts of advertising provide liability risk reduction guidelines:

- **Do** limit information in your brochures to verifiable facts about the facility and the care rendered to patients.
- **Do** use factual statements about accommodations, programs, services, and admission procedures.
- **Do** review brochures with regard to state deceptive trade practice statutes and consumer protection laws.
- **Do** revise old brochures and save money in the long run.
- **Don't** use words that imply guarantees, such as "promise" or "ensure."
- **Don't** use phrases that may be misleading if the long term care facility does not deliver, such as "programs are designed to allow each resident to return to independent living."
- **Don't** indicate approval for specialized programs until the approval has been officially secured.

BOX 12-2

Beverly Enterprises, the nation's largest nursing home chain, agreed in 2000 to pay the federal government $175 million to settle allegations of Medicare fraud.[10]

MANAGEMENT OF RESIDENTS

Risk identification and risk management activities must begin with an assessment of the opportunities for problems to arise. Risks may emerge from a variety of sources: from within the resident, as a result of physiological aging or a medical diagnosis; from those who provide care directly or indirectly for the residents; from the type of care the person receives; or from the environment in which residents receive the care.

Recognition of the physiological process of aging immediately suggests a decrease in functional status relative to activities of daily living. That decrease necessitates a need for increased supportive assistance to minimize accidents, both falls and nonfalls. Physiological changes of aging also affect drug therapy in the elderly, pinpointing medications as an area requiring risk management attention. Because the incidence of infection and auto-immune disorders increases with age, the older adult is considered to be immunocompromised. Thus, infection control within long term care facilities is very important.

Documentation in the medical record of admission status, periodic appraisals of physical health and mental status, and all important events and incidents is critical for the care of the patients and the protection of the facility.

A PORTRAIT OF PHYSIOLOGICAL AGING

Physiological aging is universal, progressive, decremental, and intrinsic with an intensification and accumulation of chronic disorders and disabilities.[13]

With aging, there is a decrease in brain weight, accompanied by a change in the proportion of grey to white matter, that may affect an individual's cognitive abilities.[14] Additionally, there are declines in immune response, thermal response, renal and pulmonary function, and glucose tolerance. Physiological changes of aging significantly affect the absorption, distribution, metabolism, and clearance of drugs, resulting in a profound effect on drug therapy in the elderly. Because of the body's inability to detoxify and excrete alcohol, the elderly are more vulnerable to the effects of alcohol.[15]

Age-related changes affect sight, hearing, taste, touch, and smell, as well as physiological patterns and abilities. Older adults experience sleep pattern changes that result in more frequent, and longer, periods of nocturnal waking as compared to those of younger adults. Older adults with mild to moderate organic brain syndrome exhibit "sundowning," or sundown syndrome, which involves behavioral changes that begin in the early evening and range from disorientation to nighttime wandering to hallucinations.[16]

Accidents: Falls and Nonfalls

Accidents are a common problem of the elderly. With physiological aging, there is a decrease in sensory acuity, reaction time, and muscle strength, and balance is impaired.

Falls are the leading cause of fatal and nonfatal injuries in people 65 and older in the United States. The most common resultant injuries are injuries to the head and fractures of the wrist, spine, and hip. The cost of falls among older people is enormous because of the resulting high death toll, disabling conditions, and recovery in hospitals and rehabilitation institutions. The United States spends an estimated $20.2 billion annually for the treatment of injuries to older people after falls, placing additional burdens on Medicaid and Medicare funding.[16]

There is a pattern to falls among the elderly: fear of falling, then the injury, followed by hospitalization and decreased independence and mobility. The majority of the costs that result from falls are for hip fractures, which average $35,000 each. Approximately 25 percent of hip fracture patients make a full recovery, 40 percent require a nursing home admission, 50 percent will be dependent on a cane or a walker, and 20 percent will die in one year.

Significantly, the incidence of falls is affected by the techniques used to gather the data. Kanten investigated three reporting methods: incident reports, chart review, and self-reporting.[17] Researchers found that chart review produced a greater number of documented patient falls than did incident reports or self-reporting. Causes of falls include visual impairment, confusion, dizziness, postural hypotension, weakness, and environmental hazards. Pointedly, Powell's study, using the Situation Specific Indicators of Fear of Falling test instrument, found that individuals fearing falls scored low in perceived balance confidence, and tended to have poorer health and lower functional status.[18]

Most falls in nursing homes occur when a resident transfers from a bed, chair, or wheelchair or attempts to proceed to or from the bathroom. Environmental factors that contribute to falls include floors that are wet, poor lighting, improper bed height, and low nurse staffing during shift changes or breaks.[19]

In a one-year retrospective study, Gurwitz described adverse and unexpected events reported by the staff of a 703-bed long term care facility.[20] Circadian patterns in the incidence of these events, as related to the resident's level of care, included falls, fall-related injuries, and non-fall-related injuries. During the study year, 3,390 adverse and unexpected events were reported. The most frequently reported incidents were falls (52.2 percent), non-fall-related injuries (41.9 percent), and medication-related events (4.6 percent). Wandering, physical assaults, aspirations, inappropriate performance of a procedure, and suicide attempts were less frequently reported.

Falls occurred most often during ambulation (46.8 percent). Nearly 70 percent of the falls did not result in injury. Bruises and skin tears were the most frequently reported fall-related injuries, occurring in 26 percent of these instances, and fractures occurred in 3 percent of falls. Bruises and skin tears were also the most frequently reported non-fall-related injuries (95.8 percent), followed in frequency by burns and fractures.

On the basis of a review of seven studies describing the epidemiology of falls in the long term care setting, Rubenstein reported a mean annual incidence rate of 165 falls per hundred beds, or 1.65 per bed.[17] Rates for falls and fall-related injuries were substantially higher during daytime hours. For residents of semidependent care units, there was a substantial increase in incidence rates for falls and fall-related injuries during the midmorning hours—a period generally characterized by awakening from sleep, transferring from bed, toileting, dressing, and ambulating to the dining room for breakfast. A second peak occurred during the evening hours, potentially related to activities associated with preparation for bed.

These findings suggest that a systematic evaluation of adverse events should direct special attention to the relationship between multifactorial risk factors and the time of the day of the occurrence to identify risk reduction activities. Furthermore, investigations suggest that risk factors for falls can be modified through exercise,[21] a review of medication profiles, elimination of medications that may increase the risk of falling, and the use of environmental safety devices such as hand rails.[22]

Nursing homes represent one of the industries earmarked for emphasis in OSHA's strategic plan. OSHA began a seven-state initiative in 1996 to address injury and illness concerns in nursing homes and personal care facilities, which was then absorbed into the agency's site-specific targeting inspection program in 2002. The program will focus outreach efforts and inspections mainly on hazards that are most prevalent: ergonomics primarily related to resident handling; exposure to blood and other potentially infectious materials; exposure to tuberculosis; and slips, trips, and falls. Issues of violence will also be addressed.

Resident handling and slips, trips, and falls account for the majority of injuries suffered by nursing home residents and employees. In 2002, OSHA notified institutions whose injury rates were higher than average and suggested sources of help to lower them.[23] Efforts to reduce the risk from fall-related injuries should be directed at the development of a prevention program that identifies those at greatest risk and the actions to modify their risk factors. For unpreventable falls, there should be efforts to reduce the risk of disabling consequences through appropriate medical care evaluation and prompt intervention.

Medication Risks

For a variety of physiological and sociomedical reasons, the elderly are particularly susceptible to adverse drug events.[24] The inappropriate prescribing of medication in nursing homes is common, according to Beers's study of 12 nursing homes in Los Angeles.[25] Both male and female residents of large nursing homes are at greater risk of receiving an inappropriate prescription. In this prospective cohort study of 1,106 nursing home residents, the average number of prescriptions per resident was 7.2. A group of 13 experts came to consensus on the criteria for the appropriateness of medication prescriptions and found that 40 percent of the residents received one inappropriate medication; 10 percent received two or more inappropriate medications; and seven percent of all prescriptions were inappropriate. These findings suggest significant potential iatrogenic harm. While Beers's study is significant in its own right, the investigation may contribute to further risk identification related to medication prescriptions in nursing homes and other nursing facilities.

The results of a Massachusetts study reported in 2000 project 350,000 adverse drug events (ADES) yearly among the national nursing home population, with more than half considered preventable. Further, nearly 20,000 fatal or life threatening ADEs occur, 80 percent of which are preventable. This calculates to an ADE rate of 1.89 per 100 resident-months and a preventable ADE rate of 0.96 per 100 resident-months. Nursing home staff identified and reported almost 20 percent of these errors, and the rest were found through record reviews. Most errors, including wrong dosage and failure to act on or adequately monitor laboratory results, occurred at the ordering and monitoring stages.[26]

Between 50 and 80 percent of residents in long term care have some degree of confusion or cognitive impairment, possibly related to Alzheimer's disease and/or dementia. However, in many cases the impairment may be attributable to the adverse side effects of medications.[27] Confusion, disorientation, and memory loss are recognized side effects that accompany more than one-third of the 200 most prescribed medications. These side effects are identified in more than 50 percent of the top 50 most prescribed medications and in just under 50 percent of all the most prescribed medications.[22]

Inappropriate dosages, adverse drug reactions, omissions, incorrect administration of medications, and polypharmacy can, in and of themselves, present "risks." These factors can also predispose residents to other risks with compounding effects. To avoid common, but often preventable problems, there must be early recognition of drug-related cognitive impairment through careful observation of residents, informed prescribing practices, and careful monitoring of cognitive performance when new drugs are prescribed.[28]

Infection Control

To date, no national guidelines exist for infection control practices specific to long term care facilities, although the standard policy of universal precautions should be adopted. Facility-associated nosocomial infections are prevalent in approximately 15 percent of long term care residents, and studies indicate that each resident is likely to acquire an average of two infections per year.[28] An older person's immune system is considered to be more compromised than that of a younger person; consequently, the incidence of infection increases dramatically with age. While infectious disease is not a normal part of aging, prevalence and death rates from many infectious diseases increase with aging. Nosocomial infections threaten not only the affected resident, but also other residents and staff. Symptoms associated with nosocomial infections range from fever to septic shock to death. Smith reviewed infections that commonly occur in nursing homes, such as in the urinary tract and respiratory tract, and with *Staphylococcus aureus*, and he proposed control programs to prevent the spread of infectious diseases.[29]

Infection control programs in nursing homes and facilities are mandated by the Conditions of Participation in Medicare and Medicaid programs, the Occupational Safety and Health Administration (OSHA), and the JCAHO. Guidelines have been established by both private and government agencies such as the Association for Practitioners in Infection Control, the American Geriatrics Society, and the federal Centers for Disease Control and Prevention. State and local standards governing nursing homes and facilities may vary depending on the location and the purpose of the government regulations. OSHA regulations focus on protecting employees, while local regulations may emphasize protecting the resident.

Infection control risks arise in a variety of ways related to the enforcement of preventive measures: hand washing; proper disposal of sharps; monitoring and control of staff and visitors who may bring infectious diseases into the facility; isolation of residents when indicated; wearing of gloves, goggles, and gowns when caring for infectious patients; moving and repositioning patients who are bedridden or always in wheelchairs; and education of staff in infection control policies.

In an analysis of lawsuits involving a total of $14,418,770 in compensation for 35 plaintiffs, it was estimated that if the American Geriatrics Society Clinical Practice Guidelines of "Pressure Ulcers in Adults: Prediction and Prevention" were followed, about $11,389,989 might have been saved in 20 cases. In addition, if these guidelines were used in court as the standard of care against the defendant health care professionals, four of the 14 defense verdicts might have changed.[30]

Under the 1987 OBRA legislation, the federal Health Care Financing Administration (HCFA) developed an outcome-oriented survey process. That process aimed to ensure that residents received the highest quality of care while maintaining their highest obtainable level of functioning. Through the OBRA regulations, the required infection control committee was replaced with a newly mandated quality assessment committee that was given a broader scope of responsibility. Specifically, the current survey process concentrates on the infection control techniques utilized by staff in the provision of care to residents.[29] Generally, the HCFA (renamed the Center for Medicare and Medicaid Services, or CMS) federal regulations for infection control set a minimum standard of care for nursing homes and facilities. These regulations are designed to establish and maintain an infection control program that:

- Investigates, controls, and prevents infections in the facility.
- Decides what procedures to apply to an individual resident.
- Documents infection incidents and corrective actions.

Federal regulations for infection control cover areas such as the design of basic infection control programs, dietary services, pressure sores, isolation, urinary catheters, and environmental or facility cleanliness. During the survey process, the determination as to whether quality care has been rendered is made by the surveyor's direct observation and interviews with residents, families, and staff.

Prudent risk managers in nursing homes and facilities should aim to develop programs that exceed the minimum standard of care. Development, implementation, and ongoing evaluation of written infection control policies and procedures can foster a well-informed, well-educated, and well-trained staff to protect residents and staff from infection while limiting liability.

Risks in Caring for Patients with Dementia

Currently, about four million persons are affected with dementia disorders, and this number is projected to be 12 to 14 million by the year 2040.[31] Patients with dementia pose challenges and risks to the long term care provider, who is required to protect these residents who are unable to protect themselves. Unfamiliar environments or changes within surroundings place these residents at greater risk for wandering and falls, and may trigger exaggerated reactions or adverse sexual behaviors. Management of residents with dementia is most appropriate in self-contained special care units able to enhance the resident's quality of life within a comfortable and secure setting.

Because residents with dementia often place themselves in dangerous situations, personal safety becomes a major risk liability. Programs and the physical design of special care units must address the unique need for controlled levels of stimulation, for personalized sequential structuring of daily events based on the resident's individualized care plan, and for the provision of verbal and visual guides to assist residents as they move from one activity to another. Care for these residents must be planned, monitored, and adjusted to accommodate any cognitive impairments. Program design should strive for the elimination of chemical and physical restraints in caring for residents with dementia, and should include appropriate policies and procedures and proper documentation of restraints, when used.

Wandering is a common behavior among residents with dementia. The usual risk management strategies apply to the physical environment for these residents, but in addition, program designs should incorporate the following:[31]

- Activities to distract or redirect wanderers.
- Controlled exploration, such as secured wandering paths.
- Activities to meet the residents' need for physical activity.
- Technology such as wristbands and satellite tracking.

About 60 percent of people with Alzheimer's disease have been known to wander, and it is estimated that about 125,000 incidents in the community are reported nationwide each year. In the mid-Atlantic states, one in five searches ends in a fatality.[32]

Comprehensive orientation, support, and education of staff working with the special care residents are essential in minimizing risk and reducing stress. These measures help protect residents from potential abuse and exploitation.[31]

Restraints Are a Controversial Issue

A physical or mechanical restraint is any manual method or physical device, material, or equipment attached or adjacent to a patient's body that restricts freedom of movement or normal access to one's body.[32] Evans and Strumpf estimated that 25 to 85 percent of all nursing home residents were physically restrained at some time.[33] Risks of restraints include injury from falls, accidental death by strangulation, contractures, pressure sores, anxiety, social isolation, and functional decline.[34]

Nursing home staff frequently cite fear of litigation as a reason for applying physical restraints, but no institution has been successfully sued simply for failure to restrain. Conversely, legal liability has been identified for the improper application of restraints.[35]

Patient autonomy must be considered in the use of physical restraints. One of the provisions in the 1987 OBRA legislation mandates, "The resident has the right to be free of, and the facility must ensure freedom from any restraints imposed or psychoactive drug administrations for the purpose of discipline or convenience, and not required to treat the resident's medical symptoms." These regulations require documentation of indications for restraint use as well as informed consent. Under this pressure, use of restraints in nursing homes has decreased almost 50 percent, from 20 percent in 1993 to about 11 percent in 1999.[37]

Creative and innovative substitutes for restraints include: binders that restrict access to abdominal tubes by confused patients, the redesign of furniture, accessible call lights, and beds close to the floor without siderails.

A risk manager's restraint reduction program must keep medical, nursing, and administrative staff informed of FDA product alerts regarding safety problems with restraining devices and must direct facilities in developing and adopting written policies and procedures regarding the use of restraints. Policies should address the periodic evaluation of residents who are restrained or secluded, including a maximum time between observations and appropriate documentation in the medical record, and they should conform to the standards of CMS and JCAHO.

Elopement and Wandering

"Elopement" and "wandering" refer to the unauthorized movement of long term care residents within or from the premises of a health care facility, including intentional or unintentional absences by the patients. Whereas a wanderer moves around the facility but does not attempt to leave the facility, an eloper makes overt or purposeful attempts to leave (see Box 12-3).

No facility can afford to be without a risk management plan that aims to reduce the possibility of elopement by any resident (see Box 12-4). When the resident who elopes is disoriented or suffers from dementia, the potential for disaster increases accordingly. Nationwide claim statistics reveal possible elopement and/or wandering outcomes:[35]

- Seventy-nine percent of elopement cases resulted in death.
- Forty-five percent of cases occurred within the first 48 hours of admission.
- Eighty percent of cases were known chronic wanderers with prior elopements.

BOX 12-3

Police found a 70-year-old man who had walked out of (eloped from) a New Brighton (Staten Island, N.Y.) nursing home the previous night. He was in critical condition after spending about five hours in frigid temperatures without a jacket.[38]

BOX 12-4

Liability claims for resident elopement account for 10 percent of the total claims against health care facilities. . . . The average elopement claim costs a health care facility about $100,000 in indemnity and defense costs alone. This figure does not take into account staff time expended by the facility to assist in the defense.[39]

At admission, a resident assessment must accurately evaluate the resident's mental capacity and the propensity for wandering behavior.

As part of their risk management program, institutions must develop, implement, and adhere to a resident elopement limitation plan. This plan must differentiate between the wanderer, who tends to remain on the premises, and the eloper, who opts to leave the site. Factors in developing an elopement risk management plan to minimize exposure to liability are as follows:[40]

- On admission, assess the resident's past history related to elopement and wandering, and periodically reassess any resident whose mental status changes.
- Distribute a document that provides a full explanation to the resident, family members, and/or substitute decision-maker of the facility's policies on control measures such as the use or nonuse of restraints, personal elopement devices, and secure units.
- Educate the staff, conduct drills, and identify the responsibility of each staff member in the event of an elopement.
- Establish a limited number of egress points with continuous surveillance, and install activated alarms on exits and stairwells.
- Initiate a rapid investigation of every alarm activation.

Environmental considerations, such as innovations in design, can result in the attentive care of wanders while accomplishing risk management objectives for providers.

Risks in Related Institutional Services

In the area of dietary services, long term care facilities face potential liability risks from improper handling of food or sanitation procedures, use of outdated foods, lack of training or lack of documentation of the training of feeders, lack of documentation of prescribed therapeutic diets, or failure to meet each patient's nutritional standards. These risks may predispose the resident to further risks, such as the exacerbation of a diabetic or cardiac condition, the spread of infectious diseases, or the development or delayed healing of pressure ulcers related to malnourishment. Facilities must have explicit standards of care, specific to the institution's population, to make nutritional interventions relevant to patient medical outcome and to the quality of care while being attractive and acceptable.[42]

Many therapeutic modalities in rehabilitation services also pose a potential hazard to patients. Burns, scarring, and deformities from inappropriate use of technologies such as electrical stimulation, heat applications, hot water, and plaster casting are potential liabilities. Utilization of occupational therapy, physical therapy, and therapeutic recreation resources each have associated risks for residents. Policies and education of staff in each therapeutic area should be emphasized to alert them to the potential hazardous risks of their respective modalities and the need for documentation of treatments, incidents, and adverse events (see Box 12-5).

Along with rising costs, allegations of billing abuses by rehabilitation companies and nursing homes began to proliferate in 1990. In 1997, Medicare charges for physical therapy and occupational therapy were approximately $7.9 billion:

- Medicare reimbursed nursing homes almost $1 billion for improperly billed physical and occupational therapy and $331 million for care that was "virtually impossible to verify."[43]
- Purchase costs on the Medicare fee schedule for I-V poles exceeded $110, while bulk purchases by nursing homes yielded a cost of $33 per I-V pole.
- Custom-fitted orthotic body jackets, for which Medicare paid $14 million in 1992, were more properly categorized as seat cushions. "Suppliers, rather than physicians, initiated the orders for the nonlegitimate jackets."[44]

Complaints from beneficiaries and their families frequently focus on unnecessary, overpriced, or unprovided services, or on nonexistent phantom employees. These allegations are the target of inquiries by the Department of Health and Human Services Office of the Inspector General, the Department of Justice, Medicare contractors, and HCFA regional offices. Whatever triggers the investigations, they typically reveal overcharges (see Box 12-6). A Department of Justice investigation for four northern Georgia rehabilitation companies led to a grand jury indictment of one individual for filing false claims. Additional charges included mail fraud, wire fraud, and money laundering related to the therapy business. Further complicating the flagrant abuses of Medicare and third-party payers is the complicity of physicians pressured to approve nursing home resident evaluations regardless of whether the rehabilitation services are medically necessary.

Disaster Planning and Fire Safety

Natural and human disasters can occur within and outside the facility. Long term care facilities are required to prepare plans to deal with disasters affecting the building that arise internally or externally. Written plans must exist, and they must include simulation drills. Documented fire safety plans should cover issues such as who is designated to respond, each respondent's responsibilities to protect residents and staff, and specific steps for containment, evacuation, evaluation, and drills.

BOX 12-5

A paraplegic physical reconditioning patient in Tennessee fell from her wheelchair while unattended. This 22-year-old had made great progress during her first month of training, which increased her self-esteem and hope for the future. However, after the accident caused a fractured femur, she experienced severe major depression and great emotional distress about the loss of opportunity and independence. She received a case settlement of $140,000.[41]

BOX 12-6

- "I am writing you concerning a bill that was charged to my mother who was a patient at . . . nursing home in . . . North Carolina. At the time of this speech therapy, my mother was 95 years old and could not communicate with anyone so how they could give her speech therapy is beyond me. . . . They were paid $2,550 for doing nothing."[45]

Environmental factors in the community affect health care facilities in situations such as hurricanes, tornados, floods, electrical power failures, or explosions. Internal building disasters include power failures, bombs and explosions, fires, collapsing walls or floors, elevator mishaps, or catastrophes in the parking areas. Individual patients have created threatening situations by smoking in bed or in bathrooms, by immolating themselves, and by causing ravaging fires and damages.

Physical damage to the facility engenders repair costs, although that expense may be possibly mitigated by appropriate insurance coverage. Other potential losses include reduced revenue if patient bed space is lost for any period of time. Liability estimates should include these factors along with the potential patient, employee, or visitor harm and community service impact that occur in any disaster.

Risk management activities relate to ensuring the training and effectiveness of staff in responding to disasters and fires, as well as the availability and functional status of equipment needed to respond to each type of situation. Disaster and fire safety plans should document drills and the testing and readiness of necessary equipment. Insurance coverage concerning the premises, restoration and equipment replacement, and business interruption should be reviewed.

ELDER ABUSE AND VIOLENCE

Statistically, elder abuse occurs slightly less frequently than child abuse. Abuse of the elderly, in the community or institutional setting, often goes unnoticed or is ignored because of ignorance, fear, or lack of concern. It is estimated that 10 percent of older adults experience multiple types of abuse:

- neglect, whether intentional or unintentional (49 percent)
- emotional: the willful infliction of anguish through threats, intimidation, humiliation, or isolation (35 percent)
- physical abuse resulting in pain, impairment, or bodily injury (25 percent)[46]

In the two-year period ending in January 2001, 30 percent of the nursing homes in the United States were cited for an abuse violation that could place residents in immediate jeopardy of death or serious injury. Reports of state and federal inspections describe appalling physical, sexual, and verbal abuse of patients.[47] Signs of abuse may include unexplained bruises, bruises or fractures in various sages of healing, and alleged repeated falls. Signs of neglect and mistreatment could include malnourishment, poor hygiene, unsafe environment, and decubitus ulcers.

Violence in long term care facilities occurs in different degrees between staff and residents (elder abuse), or among residents. Repeated staff exposure to the same patients, in contrast to the limited interaction in short stay acute hospitals, engenders a social relationship that is complementary to the quality of care of the residents (see Box 12-7). However, continual interaction between staff and residents with known dementia, reduced capacity, paranoia in their new surroundings, or acting out behavior, can result in verbal assaults and physical injury to staff by residents. Residents have bitten, kicked, punched, used their canes as weapons, and deliberately rammed their wheelchairs into staff. Similar violent behavior occurs between residents after heated arguments about what TV show to watch.

Sequelae of these violent actions should be attended to, documented in the medical record, and reported in the risk manage-

BOX 12-7

- Ten percent of nursing assistants reported that they had committed at least one act of physical abuse in the preceding year, and 40 percent reported committing at least one act of physiological abuse.[48]
- A New Jersey elder care facility was found liable for a certified nurse assistant's sexual assault on a 70-year-old woman, a "violation of the right to safe and decent living environment and respectful care."[49]

ment program. Staff members should be taught to have enhanced sensitivity concerning these issues. Medical evaluation of the appropriate level of care, medications, and alternative methods to understand and meet the needs of these special patients is imperative to prevent further incidents.

EMPLOYEE RISKS

Employee risks arise out of administrative failure to comply with federal equal employment opportunity practices, failure to properly screen applicants before hiring, failing to check credentials of professionally licensed personnel, and failure to prevent work-related injuries. A prominent labor relations attorney warned nursing home operators that "a triple whammy of the Americans with Disabilities Act, the Civil Rights Act of 1990, and the feminist movement could put you out of business."[50] As of 1994, the federal Violent Crime Control and Law Enforcement Act mandates security background checks for employees providing care to children, the elderly, the disabled, home health care patients, or patients in other types of long term care. This Act prompts the states to require background checks relative to a job applicant's criminal convictions that might affect the provider's fitness to render care to vulnerable individuals.[49]

In 2002, New York Governor Pataki urged "background checks to block hiring of criminals" in nursing homes. A *New York Daily News* investigation found 457 criminals (92 of them felons) working in nursing homes. At present, 39 states require some type of criminal background check and fingerprint checks on nurse's aides, according to the National Coalition for Nursing Home Reform.[51]

Ergonomics is now OSHA's top priority for standard-setting. Health care is the first industry targeted for a new comprehensive plan to reduce musculoskelatal disorders (MSD) injuries. The American Nurses Association's[52] strong data have revealed the problems of overexertion injuries in hospitals, nursing homes, and home care: 67 percent of disabling injuries to employees that occur in nursing homes are due to MSD. In addition, nurses' lost-time rate due to MSDs is equivalent to 24.5 injuries per 1,000 full-time-equivalent workers, and nursing aides had 74.2 lost-time MSD injuries per 1,000 workers.[53]

There was major opposition to the costs of implementing the new standards that were proposed, and during March 2001 the House, Senate, and president nullified the ergonomics regulations. However, OSHA still has the enforcement power and a record-keeping policy that requires that ergonomic "illness" be documented, and therefore OSHA has leverage on the industry to pay attention to and minimize ergonomic-related hazards.[54]

Other occupational risks are associated with preventing needlesticks, protecting against bloodborne pathogens, preventing exposure to tuberculosis, and the need for appropriate policies, procedures, and plans to eliminate, control, and reduce hazards.

SUBACUTE CARE

> Nursing homes are punching out walls, hanging new signs and hiring new staff. Sometimes, they just relabel old wards in a mad scramble to capture this new type of transitional patient.[55]

Increasingly, long term care facilities are designing units to accommodate patients who previously have received rehabilitation or skilled medical care in an acute care hospital. Subacute care units return patients to independent living more quickly and save money by decreasing acute care lengths of stay. Economically, long term care facilities that have subacute care units gain through the financial incentive of a higher Medicare reimbursement than that generated by a typical nursing home patient. Although subacute care may be financially attractive, providing this care poses increased risks.[56]

In Texas, a recent study indicated that since the average hospital length of stay of Medicaid recipients was 6.79 days, moving a patient to a subacute setting could affect continuity of care and, consequently, compromise quality of care. In addition, in Texas no significant cost savings would be obtained if subacute care services were implemented.[57]

Traditionally, malpractice risks in long term care were minimal in contrast to risks in acute care. Analysts believe that subacute care exposes long term care facilities to claims activity similar to that experienced by hospitals that provide both acute and subacute care.[58] Exposure increases for a number of reasons: subacute care patients are younger and juries consider earning capabilities and expected life span when assessing damages due to negligence; a length of stay is relatively short and may affect treatment practices; and patient improvement is expected to be measurable. All of these factors can lead to unmet expectations, which often lead to lawsuits.[59]

To mitigate risk liability in providing subacute care, long term care facilities must direct and supervise the attending staff. Medical record documentation of care for subacute patients must be more frequent than for other types of patients and should mirror the in-depth documentation of acute care institutions, rather than the scant annotations entered for the typical nursing home patient. Professionally established standards of care should be recorded in documentation similar to the forms and checklists utilized in acute care facilities. Miles offers the following essential risk management criteria for facilities providing subacute care:[59]

1. A comprehensive resident care program specifying employee supervision.
2. Direction by the physician or specialist clinician in concert with the medical director to assure regulatory compliance.
3. A specific program management process.
4. Case management with quality control.
5. Criteria targeting the specific care needs of a patient population identified through market research.
6. Individualized resident care plans developed by a team of specialists in the targeted area of care.
7. Facility enhancement to meet subacute care needs.
8. Care with measurable outcomes aimed at returning individuals to the community.

Because subacute care renders services for a limited period of time, the development of positive long term relations with residents and families is jeopardized. Furthermore, care expectations of subacute residents and their families about services and staff differs from those of the typical long term care patient. Both of these factors pose a significant challenge to subacute care providers. Investigations clearly indicate that a key risk management strategy in avoiding claims is ensuring client satisfaction.[59]

Some states have developed flexible health insurance programs allowing people the option of using home health care services or applying a subsidy to purchase services from agencies, individually employed workers, or even family members.[60] As hospitalization declines, the use of excess hospital beds for subacute care may challenge the position of nursing homes with subacute care units.

HOME HEALTH CARE

Home health care continues to be a rapidly growing segment within the health care industry. With the steady increase in the Medicare population, a continued expansion of home health services is anticipated.[61] Home health care satisfies the nursing and medical needs of elderly persons with disabilities and chronic illnesses who do not require acute hospital care. Changing patterns of reimbursement make it cost effective to provide services in the home. On average, daily home health costs are considerably less than the cost of a day in an acute hospital, a subacute care unit, or a long term care facility. Cost containment efforts to reduce hospital stays have helped to spur the utilization of home health care after patients are discharged.

A "hospital without walls" can be set up in the patient's own home and includes sophisticated home infusion therapy, high technology equipment, and powerful chemotherapy. "Hospitals without walls," which include both home health care and hospice care, are defined in terms of the type of care provided, with reimbursement tied to the illness. Home health care aims to promote, maintain, or restore health while maximizing the recipient's level of functioning, limiting the illness or disability effects, and reducing the need for hospitalization.

Hospice services provide palliative and supportive care for terminally ill persons, their families, and significant others. Comprehensive services include attention to pain control, comfort, physical, psychological, social, and spiritual care offered in either the home or in an inpatient setting, by a combination of providers, or in a managed care setting.[55] Family members and/or friends may be responsible for continuity, for monitoring the equipment, and for providing coverage for a substantial portion of direct patient care.[62]

Identifying and controlling liability risks in home health care include multiple aspects, such as: meeting regulatory and voluntary standards; patient management; informed consent for care and termination; product and equipment failure; patient and employee safety; and employee hiring, classification, and training. Administrators and risk managers must recognize home health care liability risks and develop plans, policies, and procedures to mitigate these risks. Of particular risk significance in home health care, providers may contract or subcontract with various similar agencies to deliver services, or specialized services, in isolated locales. Individual employees may not be under the direct supervision and control of the home health agency. When a contract for home health care services is prepared, risk managers should seek to transfer the liability risk to the contractor agency and "hold harmless" the home health agency. Moreover, agencies rendering care in them must be held accountable for written reports on the patient's condition and for participation in the physician's treatment plan.

Currently, more than 22,000 agencies provide home care services to over eight million patients. Spending for home health care has risen from $3.5 billion in 1990 to $3.6 billion in 1999.[63] Approximately two-thirds of the recipients are women and about two-thirds are over age 65. Medicare is the largest single payer of home care services. In 1997, Medicare accounted for almost 40 percent of the total home health care expenditure (see Box 12-8).[64]

REGULATION OF HOME HEALTH CARE

Public and voluntary regulatory mechanisms ensure the quality of home health care services. Provider agencies must be licensed by the individual states and afterward may be certified by a combination of entities: Medicare or Medicaid; the Community Health Accreditation Program (CHAP), a subsidiary of the National League for Nursing (NLN); or the Joint Commission on Accreditation of Healthcare Organizations (JCAHO).

Medicare reimburses for home health care services for eligible persons 65 years and older, and for persons under 65 who are disabled or have chronic renal disease. Care is defined by Medicare regulations as to the specific services that will be reimbursed. People eligible for Medicaid can also receive medically related home health care services depending on their individual state Medicaid regulations. While federal Medicaid law does not define "home health services," Medicaid regulations require states to include a minimum range of services in their coverage. Generally, Medicaid programs follow Medicare's regulations and require home health care agencies to meet the federal conditions of participation. In 1993, approximately 84 percent of the 7,400 home health care agencies were Medicare certified and 83 percent were Medicaid certified.[61]

BOX 12-8

Providers of Home Health Care:[65]

- Home health agencies
- Homemaker and home care aide agencies
- Pharmaceutical and infusion therapy companies
- Durable medical equipment and supply dealers
- Staffing registries and private duty agencies
- Independent providers

Additional regulatory mechanisms have emerged. In 1986, the American Nurses Association published standards for home health nursing practice. Two years later, JCAHO issued its standards and began accrediting voluntary home health care organizations. In 1988, HCFA proposed that the freestanding home health care agencies accredited by the NLN and the hospital-based agencies accredited by JCAHO be deemed to have also met Medicare certification requirements.[61]

Federal and state quality control regulations are increasing through Medicare certification and through state licensure. This increased emphasis on quality control in home health care may result in greater risk exposure when related to provision of substandard care and aspects surrounding the delivery of care.

The acceptance of illegal kickbacks, overt falsification of participation requirements in Medicare or Medicaid programs, knowing and willful overcharging or accepting of excess Medicare payments, illegal patient referrals, unnecessary prescriptions, and falsified patient care plans have serious consequences for home health care agencies.[67] Billing procedures, receipts, referral agreements, and subcontracting agreements must be carefully scrutinized with appropriate documentation to avoid risk exposure for the agency. Under the Social Security Act and the False Claims Act, false, fictitious, or fraudulent claims submitted to the U.S. government can result in fines of $25,000 and up to five years in prison (see Box 12-9).[68] Home health care organizations could be barred from participating in Medicare and other service programs.[71] Federal antitrust legislation imposes severe penalties for unfair competitive practices among home health care agencies.[68] Fraud in the home health care industry may be poisoning the system and prompting a call for increased government regulation.[72]

WHO RECEIVES HOME HEALTH CARE?

For patients receiving home health care, the three most common primary admission categories of diagnoses were: diseases of the circulatory system; injury or poisoning; and endocrine, nutritional and metabolic, or immunity disorders. Neoplasm was the primary admission diagnosis for 71 percent of the hospice patients. Within this category, cancer of the lungs, breast, colon, and prostate accounted for 60 percent of the diagnoses.[61]

By law and in program regulation, physicians are required to authorize home health care services and to prepare a written treatment plan. Yet, a survey of U.S. medical schools reported that only 54 percent offered some type of home health care training. Investigators commented that "the present system of medical education in the United States prepares students inadequately to care for patients in the home."[73]

BOX 12-9

- A self-employed licensed practical nurse was indicted by a Suffolk County, N.Y., grand jury for inflating the number of hours of home care she worked. She billed Medicaid while on vacation and for days when not assigned to work. She faces up to seven years in prison if convicted.[69]
- The owners of a home health agency in Iowa, who were reimbursed more than $10 million by Medicare, pleaded guilty to submitting false invoices and were sentenced to time in federal prison.[70]
- A federal grand jury in Chicago indicted a former hospice operator on charges of defrauding Medicare and others of more than $28 million.[70]

PATIENT MANAGEMENT

Risk identification and reduction in home health care must begin with the home health agency assessing the patient's health care needs and the patient's and family's ability to participate in care. The environment in which the care will be delivered should be assessed for safety—particularly for fire hazards. Recently JCAHO reported 11 sentinel events in home care in which seven patients died and four others suffered loss of function or permanent disfigurement because of fires to which cigarette smoking was a contributing factor. Risk factors for these fires included lack of smoke detectors, nonfunctional smoke detectors, living alone, cognitive impairment, an identified history of smoking while oxygen is running, and flammable clothing. Plans are needed for assessing homes and testing evacuation plans for patients.[74]

In addition, to safeguard against allegations of abandonment, the contract should include how and when services may be terminated and the conditions for substitution of regular staff with equally qualified staff.[75]

Agencies must ensure that the appropriate level of health care provider is assigned to the patient. Not only must the appropriate provider be selected, but that provider must also be properly trained and supervised while rendering the necessary care.

Informed Consent to Care

> With expansion in the complexity of home health care services provided in the home has come an increased necessity to ensure that patients are properly informed, and that documentation of informed consent is obtained and on file in the home care department.[76]

Patients accepted by a home health care agency must officially consent to the care the agency will provide. An unanswered dilemma is "who" is obligated to obtain and document consent before a home health care patient receives treatment. Home health care challenges the historical tradition, supported by ethics and law, that only physicians can obtain and document a valid informed consent by the patient. "To date there are no cases on the obligation of home health care staff that have come to trial. Nor has it been identified whether consent obtained by a nonphysician is valid."[76]

Although the issue of informed consent remains a moot point, home health care risk managers need to be attentive to the inherent potential risks and develop a policy to systematically mitigate this risk. One suggestion is that home health care nurses "present the process in terms of appearing to confirm with what the patients' physicians have already told them."[76] At the time of the informed consent process, the home health care nurse can review everything in the event the physician missed something. This process is extremely important in relation to the Patient Self-Determination Act and implementation of the health care proxy so that patients and families may fully exercise their rights under this law, and refuse treatment with full knowledge of the consequences if they so wish. Home health care agencies need to develop and implement appropriate policies to notify patients of their rights within state law to safeguard adherence to the patient's wishes in the area of these advance directives.

Termination of Care

Both the acceptance of new patients and the termination of care carry risks for the agency. Reasons for a home health agency to terminate care include: problems in the delivery of care or services; nonparticipating patients and families; patients too sick to remain in the home; abusive patients and families; and insufficient resources to cover the cost of care.[77] Agencies must be familiar with state regulations regarding the discharge of patients. Termination of care should be outlined in the patient's service contract. When it is anticipated that care will be terminated for any reason prior to the contracted period, adequate notification must be given to the patient and family and other caregivers. They should be advised: (1) when services will terminate; (2) whether continued services should be obtained; and (3) that any records will be forwarded to the new agency. Any decision by the patient or family to terminate services must be documented. Policies and procedures for termination of services can help agencies protect themselves from allegations of abandonment—the unilateral termination of a professional relationship without affording the patient reasonable notice and opportunity to replace health care services.[75]

Within agency policies and procedures, the issue of patient and family nonparticipation or noncompliance in the physician's plan of care must be addressed. Consistent nonparticipation may be an indication that a pediatric or elderly patient is being neglected or abused by the family, friends, or other caregivers.[78]

Incident Reporting

Inevitably, adverse incidents will occur in the provision of care to patients in the home. Home health care agencies should facilitate the reporting of any incident that represents a risk exposure to the agency. A format and policy for collecting information, as well as time frames for reporting that are based on the magnitude of the incident, are necessary. Staff must be given clear guidelines for all incidents that must be reported. Incidents that may be outside of the staff's responsibilities, such as dangerous or unsanitary conditions in the home or potentially abusive patients or family members, are included. Clearly, it is better for staff to overreport than to neglect to report adverse incidents.

Home health care employees provide a wide variety of care: blood pressure, temperature, and respiration readings; skin care; catheter care; colostomy and other "ostomy" care; dressing changes; administration of medications; assistance with exercise; monitoring durable medical equipment and devices; and assistance with activities of daily living such as bathing, feeding, toileting, and ambulation.[79] Each of these tasks my enhance the opportunity for an adverse incident or occurrence that is risk noteworthy.

Personal property of patients or family may be broken or damaged, and there may be allegations of theft of jewelry, bankbooks, or even food. Those who provide relief or continued care may not appear in the home in a timely manner so that staff may go home after completion of their shift. Incidents need to be investigated, documented, and communicated to patient and/or family members to reduce dissatisfaction with the care plan or services, or with the assigned staff.

Staff need to develop patient information files in the home that include emergency and nonemergency telephone numbers, as well as emergency plans. Personnel need to be knowledgeable about modifying the home to prevent accidents, increasing bed mobility and positioning the patient to prevent skin deterioration, transferring patients, safely using bathroom and bathtub equipment, administering medication, and using technical devices.

There should be unequivocal communication and documentation of a plan developed by the patient and family regarding who the home health care provider may allow into the home and how visitors will be monitored while there (see Box 12-10).

Falls in the Home Health Care Population

It may be difficult to pinpoint the exact cause of falls in the home health care population. However, studies compared fallers and non-fallers and found specific risk factors: functional status and use of assistive devices, polypharmacy, and medical history. Home health care providers should evaluate the fall potential of patients and develop strategies for fall prevention. Strategies can include minimizing environmental risks, teaching or reteaching adaptive behaviors,

BOX 12-10

A home health care nurse allowed an air conditioner repair man into the home as scheduled. In casual conversation, the repair man asked about the patient and the patient's medications. Although she had given no information, the nurse felt uncomfortable and went to telephone the police. Before she could do so, however, the patient needed care. While she was busy, the repair man rushed out of the house. In checking, the nurse found that the patient's narcotics were missing.[80]

and reducing accompanying risk factors such as changes in visual acuity. Careful assessment of the patient's home and necessary remedial intervention help to decrease liability risk that may arise out of a patient injury.[81]

High Technology Home Health Care: Product and Equipment Failure

Modern medical technology, coupled with advances in health care delivery, have created opportunities for patients to receive complex care at home. With each high technology activity an agency adds, there is increased risk. Greater utilization of high technology home health care may also reflect the provision of care to a younger population. In terms of legal remuneration for damages as a result of negligence, these younger people generally receive higher monetary awards based on longevity. As this younger population becomes more commonplace in home health care, there will be increased risks to agencies providing their care.

Enactment of the federal Safe Medical Device Act of 1990 defined specific applications to home health care organizations. A mini-hospital set up in the home may involve the use of a variety of sophisticated medical equipment and products, which increases liability risks. High technology equipment includes dialysis units, infusion therapy, phototherapy, apnea monitors, respiratory volume ventilators, gaseous oxygen, massage, heating and cooling mattresses or pads, and an assortment of other devices to aid in the care of the patient.

Advances in telecommunications and computer technologies also have applications in home care: electronic devices for measuring patient physiologic processes; electronic devices for administering or monitoring oxygen, drug, and other therapies in the home; personal emergency response systems to monitor smoke or fire, or to signal police or ambulance; video-phones for direct visualization and communication, etc. Every type of technology in use has major advantages for patient care but potential risk, and home health care agency employees must be taught to be aware of potential problems with equipment being used by their patients. Portable medical equipment may present major safety risks for home health care patients. It is incumbent upon home health care agencies to select and use responsible equipment vendors[82] and to train employees in the responsible use of selected technologies. Agencies should develop policies on troubleshooting equipment, equipment maintenance and replacement, and emergency action plans in the event of equipment malfunction or failure.

Safety of Employees

Home health care employees encounter liability risks related to their own safety as they provide services, as illustrated in Box 12-11. Employees must be acutely aware of hazards in the environment and safeguard themselves. An increase in illicit drug use, easily available weapons, and violence in the community places home health care workers, and the agencies they work for, at greater risk. Home health care organizations need to have policies and procedures regarding the safety of workers in the

BOX 12-11

A man grabs the gold chain worn by a therapist and runs away with it; a home health aide is bitten by a patient's dog and requires stitches; during a home visit a nurse and escort are threatened with a gun by the patient's husband.[83]

community and the use of security escorts in unsafe neighborhoods. There should be an ongoing program to develop community relationships and to assess the community to ensure employee safety.[83]

To prevent physical injury to themselves, employees must learn safe transferring, lifting, and positioning techniques. Although infection control policies in home health care are designed to mirror hospital or institutional care policies, a random sample of 600 home health care agencies indicated that 18 percent did not have written infection control policies.[84] Furthermore, OSHA guidelines require employers to provide personal protective wear and hepatitis B vaccine to employees at risk of acquiring body fluid and blood-borne pathogens. Home health care agencies need to have infection control policies that are reviewed and updated on a regular basis to reflect current professional protocols, and employees must be educated about universal precautions.

Employees must be made aware of the extent of the home health care agency's insurance coverage in the event of an injury. Already expansive, employee activities in home health care are continually increasing. Agencies must regularly review all insurance policies to identify and safeguard against gaps in coverage. Does the insurance coverage apply if employees perform a task outside of their job description, such as taking the patient's child to school after their assigned working hours? (See Box 12-12.)

BOX 12-12

Question: Can home health aides recover benefits after an accident en route to their assignments?

Answer: Employees cannot receive workers' compensation benefits if they are hurt while going to or from work. An exception exists when employees travel at the expressed wish of the employer, or when the travel benefits the employer.[85]

HOME HEALTH CARE EMPLOYEES

Between 1992 and 2005, about 500,000 jobs are expected to be added to the home health care workforce, three times the rate of growth of health care as a whole.[86] Home health care agencies are exposed to a multitude of diverse risks that surround the hiring, employment, or contracting for professional and allied home health care providers.

Home health care agencies are particularly vulnerable regarding liability for the actions of their employees or contractors (see Box 12-13). Simply put, the employees provide care "in the field," away from the consistent watchful supervision of supervisors and administrators. Thus, agencies must pay special attention to their hiring policies and procedures to help mitigate this aspect of employee-related risk (see Box 12-14).

An industrywide survey indicated that 75 percent of employers fail to check references before hiring. In home health care, negligent hiring can be lethal, since this poor practice exposes agencies to a host of liability risks. Sussman and Siegel recom-

BOX 12-13

Courts have ruled that employers are responsible for the actions of their employees, whether those actions are within the scope of their job duties, outside the scope of their job duties, or even contrary to their job description.[75]

BOX 12-14

A nurse who cared for multimillionaire tobacco heiress Doris Duke in her mansion was arrested and charged with stealing $439,000 in valuables from Duke and five others.[87]

mend the following documentation for hiring new applicants:[88]

- Applicant interview that includes a review of employment history and an assessment of skills.
- Verification of legally accepted permission to work, such as citizenship, residency, or working visa.
- Verification of health clearance, including immunization, TB and hepatitis B status.
- Assessment of current license or certification status.
- Evidence of state and/or agency requirements, such as infection control training and CPR certification.
- Verification of malpractice insurance.
- Applicant's permission to check references.
- Background check through public records for criminal convictions or reports of patient abuse. (This review is mandated by the federal Violent Crime Control and Law Enforcement Act of 1994.)

As it relates to professional negligence, the law measures a person's overall conduct in an alleged negligent situation by evaluating whether the care delivered is consistent with what is customary and usual in the profession and whether the care is delivered in a caring, compassionate, and humane way.[89] Therefore, the onus is on home health care agencies to use accepted standards of practice and continuously update their policies.

Toward this end, home health care agencies must develop unambiguous job descriptions for personnel that indicate responsibilities as well as limitations. Staff must be highly qualified, dedicated, and reliable. Home health care agencies must assess and supervise the work of all caregivers by periodic field visits and by surveying patients and families. These data must be documented, and plans must be developed and implemented where the need for improvement is identified. Ongoing performance evaluations of staff are fundamental to patient safety. Documentation should specify objective recommendations for continuous staff development and detail plans for improvement, with implementation and time frames for expected results.

Organizations must comply with all federal, state, and local laws and regulations regarding employee reimbursement. Employee wages and hours worked must be recorded in accordance with the regulatory mandates. Because of the nature of the industry, employee reimbursement practices in home health care agencies are being scrutinized by federal and state audits regarding minimum wages, overtime, and record keeping (see Box 12-9).

Negligence Related to Failure to Instruct

Legally, employers can be held accountable for the actions of their employees, regardless of whether the actions are in keeping or even contrary to their job description.[65] A U.S. Supreme Court ruling found that an entity's failure to properly train its personnel can be considered "deliberate indifference" and can result in charges of negligence and civil actions.[68]

Home health care relies on staff to provide care and anticipates the participation of the patient, family, and significant others in maintaining the continuity of care between the provider's visits. Even though teaching is not reimbursable, the home health care provider's ability to train the staff and those who will provide this interim care is critical to the control of risks. Culturally sensitive training should be documented, signed by the patient and/or caregiver, and kept in the patient's record. Training of patients, employees, family members, and other caregivers cannot be a one-time educational requirement, especially when high technology equipment is being used. Home health care agencies must ensure appropriate training, retraining, and competency for the home health care providers. Staff members must be instructed on how to train, retrain, and verify that patients and caregivers understand the procedures. In addition, all of these aspects of staff and caregiver education should be documented.[76]

Independent Contractor versus Employee

Home health care agencies are subject to federal Internal Revenue Service (IRS) investigations and to liability for misclassification of home health care providers. Liability for misclassification of an employee as an independent contractor could include repayment of all associated taxes with interest, civil fines up to $500,000, and criminal charges resulting in up to five years in prison. According to the IRS, the critical point in employee classification is the "right of control" that the agency has over the individual.[76] Prudent home health care organizations should apply the "right of control" test and use IRS definitions to determine the employment classification of home health care workers to minimize liability risks.

HOSPICE CARE

Risk exposure in hospice care mirrors the liability risks in home health care and the institutional setting in which the care is provided.[90] According to the National Association for Home Care, there are more than 2,200 hospices participating in the Medicare program and an additional 200 volunteer hospices. In 1998, more than 400,000 patients received hospice care through Medicaid programs. Most hospice patients are age 65 or older, and the most common terminal illnesses among them are lung cancer and prostate cancer.[91]

Because of the distinctive nature of hospice care, symptom control, specifically pain management, is critical to patient care. Home administration of controlled substances to alleviate pain, such as morphine, is a definite risk exposure. Hospice care agencies must minimize the risk of potential diversion of controlled substances by staff, family members, significant others, or anybody who may enter or be in the household. Policies and procedures for the administration of controlled substances must comply with federal and state laws regarding storage, administration, discarding of unused medication, and documentation. Organizational policies must affirm actions that will be taken if controlled substances are diverted by staff members. Furthermore, that policy must comply with the laws that govern disabled employees.[92]

GROWING INDUSTRY, GROWING RISKS

Because long term care need increases with age, especially after age 85, significant demand for care can be expected well into the twenty-first century as the baby boomer generation ages. Researchers contend that medical advances may actually increase the need for long term care, as people live longer and thus survive long enough to develop age-related disabilities such as Alzheimer's disease or survive longer with existing disabilities. In contrast, other investigators maintain that improved treatments for common problems such as strokes and heart disease, or the prevention of disabilities, could mitigate the long term care need.[93]

The availability of informal, unpaid caregivers will also affect the future demand for public long term care services. Greater geographic dispersion of families, smaller family sizes, and the large percentage of women who work outside the home may continue to strain the capacity of informal caregiving. In the short term, large numbers of potential caregivers in the baby boomer generation may ease the strain. But as baby boomers grow old, they may have fewer family members to care for them. Certain states are increasingly emphasizing home and community based services and constraining costly institutional care as they seek more efficient or cost-effective ways to organize and prioritize services.

Serving the needs of the elderly and disabled is a growth industry with anticipation of greater opportunities for misadventure and professional negligence. As home care agencies and hospices are faced with declining revenues from Medicare and demands from managed care plans to reduce utilization and reduce resources, professional liabilities may increase. However, with appropriate attention to admissions for care, care management, and policies for discharge and termination, potential risks can be minimized.[94]

References

1. Long Term Care, Baby Boom Generation Increases Challenge of Financing Needed Services. (2001). GAO Testimony of William J. Scanlon, GAO-01-563T, March 27.
2. Bectel, R. W., and Tucker, N. G. (1998). *Profiles of Long Term Care Systems Across the States,* 3rd edition. Washington, D.C.: American Association of Retired Persons Public Policy Institute.
3. Aon Risk Consultants, Inc. (2002). *Long Term Care General Liability: Professional Liability Actuarial Analysis*. Washington, D.C.: American Association of Retired Persons Public Policy Institute. February 28.
4. Best Company, Inc. (2000). As nursing home liability losses soar, carriers stop writing business. February 7.
5. Pandyra, S. M. (2001). Nursing Homes. Washington, D.C.: American Association of Retired Persons Public Policy Institute.
6. Burns, J. (1994). ProPAC undecided on subacute payments. *Modern Healthcare* 24(3):32.
7. Sahyoun, N. R., Pratt, L. A., et al. (2001). The Changing Profile of Nursing Home Residents: 1985—1997. CDC, Aging Trends #4, March.
8. Allen, J. E. (2000). *Nursing Home Federal Requirements and Guidelines to Surveyors,* 4th edition. New York: Springer Publishing Company.
9. Peterson, I. (2002). New Jersey reviews and fines long-term care center after an autistic boy, 14, dies. *New York Times,* July 11, p. B7.
10. Becker, B. (2002). Keeping score at nursing homes. *New York Times,* Letters to Editor, July 21, p. 11.
11. Miles, F. (1994). Advertising's legal headaches. *Provider* 20(6):45–46.
12. Macknick, F. J. (1998). Two takes on facility marketing. *Long Term Care Management* 47(10):70–73.
13. Allen, J. E. (2003). *Nursing Home Administration,* 4th edition. New York: Springer Publishing Company.
14. Evans, J. G., Williams, T. F., et al. (2000). *Oxford Textbook of Geriatric Medicine,* 2nd edition. New York: Oxford University Press.
15. MDs fear up to 3 million seniors may be alcoholics. (1995). *Star-Ledger* (Newark, N.J.), September 19, p. 2, col. 4; Scherr, P. A. (1992). Light to moderate alcohol consumption in the elderly. *Journal of the American Geriatrics Society* 40(7):651–657.

16. Pallone, Frank, U.S. Representative. (2002). Preventing Elderly Falls: Reports to Seniors. Mass mailing, July.
17. Kanten, D. N., Mulrow, C. D., Gerety, M. B., et al. (1993). Falls: An examination of three reporting methods in nursing homes. *Journal of the American Geriatrics Society* 41(6):662–666; Rubenstein, L. Z., Josephson, K. R., and Robbins, A. S. (1994). Falls in the nursing home. *Annals of Internal Medicine* 121(6):442–451.
18. Powell, L. E. (1993). Situation specific indicators of of falling. Dissertation, MSC degree, University of Waterloo (Canada).
19. Gross, Y. T., Shimamoto, Y., Rose, C. L., and Frank, B. (1990). Why do they fall? Monitoring risk factors in nursing homes. *Journal of Gerontologic Nursing* 16(10):20–25.
20. Gurwitz, J., Sanchez-Cross, M., Eckler, M., and Matulis, J. (1994). The epidemiology of adverse and unexpected events in the long term care setting. *Journal of the American Geriatrics Society* 42(1):33–38.
21. Province, M. A., Hadley, E., Hornbrook, M. C., et al. (1995). The effects of exercise on falls in elderly patients: A preplanned meta-analysis of the FICSIT trials. *Journal of the American Medical Association* 273(17):1341–1347.
22. Tinetti, M. E., Baker, D. I., McAvay, G., et al. (1994). A multifactorial intervention to reduce the risk of fall and risk of falling among elderly people living in the community. *New England Journal of Medicine* 331(12):821–827.
23. OSHA Trade News Release. (2002). OSHA Announces National Emphasis Program for Nursing and Personal Care Facilities. July 15.
24. Noah, B. A., and Brushwood, D. B. (2000). Adverse drug reactions in elderly patients; alternative approaches to post market surveillance. *Journal of Health Law* 33(3):383–454.
25. Beers, M. H., Ouslander, J. G., Fingold, S. F., et al. (1992). Inappropriate medication prescribing in skilled nursing facilities. *Annals of Internal Medicine* 117(8):684–689.
26. Gurwitz, J. H., Field, T. S., et al. (2000). Incidence and preventability of adverse drug events in nursing homes. *American Journal of Medicare* 109:87–94.
27. Katz, I. R., and Streim, J. E. (1994). America's other drug problem. *Provider* 20(11):70–73.
28. Avorn, J., and Gurwitz, J. H. (1995). Drug use in the nursing home. *Annals of Internal Medicine* 123(3): 195–204.
29. Smith, P. W. (1994). *Infection Control in Long Term Care Facilities*, 2d edition. Delmar, N.Y.: Delmar.
30. Goebel, R. H., and Goebel, M. R. (1999). Clinical practice guidelines for pressure ulcer can prevent malpractice lawsuits in older patients. *Journal of Wound, Ostomy and Continence Nursing* 4:175–184.
31. Karcher, K. A. (1993). Is your risk management program designed to deal with Alzheimer's disease? *Nursing Homes* 42(2):34–36.
32. Goldsmith, R. (2001). Wrist devices guard elderly. *Star-Ledger* (Newark, N.J.), December 27, p. 17, col. 2.
33. Foderaro, L. W. (1994). Hospitals seek an alternative to straitjacket. *New York Times*, August 1, p. B2, col. 4; Evans, L. K., and Strumpf, N. E. (1989). Tying down the elderly: A review of the literature on physical restraint. *Journal of the American Geriatrics Society* 37(1):65–74.
34. Tinetti, M. E., Liu, W., and Ginter, S. F. (1992). Mechanical restraint use and fall-related injuries among residents of skilled nursing facilities. *Annals of Internal Medicine* 116(4):369–374.
35. Harrington, C. H., Carrillo, M. S., et al. (2000). Nursing facilities, staffing, residents, and facility deficiencies, 1993 through 1999. University of California at San Francisco, Department of Social and Behavioral Sciences.
36. Coleman, E. A. (1993). Physical restraint use in nursing home patients with dementia. *Journal of the American Medical Association* 270(17):2114–2115.
37. Allen, J. E. (2003). *Nursing Home Administration*, 4th edition. New York: Springer Publishing Company.
38. Patient found out in cold. (1995). *Staten Island Advance* (New York), February 24, p. A2, col. 1.
39. Foxwell, L. G. (1994). Elopement—Exposure and control. *Journal of Long Term Care Administration* 21(4):8–12.
40. Mulrooney, C. P. (1994). Controlling exposure and exposing control. *Journal of Long Term Care Administration* 21(4):14–15.
41. Healthcare Provider Service Organization. (2001). Legal Case Study, October. Paraplegic physical reconditioning patient falls from wheelchair while unattended—fractured femur with depression—$140,000 settlement in Tennessee. *www.hpso.com.../casesprofindex.php3.*
42. Mazzoni, C., and Chylak, N. (1994). Developing a standard of care for patients for long term hospitalization. *Journal of the American Dietetic Association* 94(10):1415–1418.

43. Brown, J. G. (1999). Physical Therapy in Nursing Homes and Cost of Improper Billings to Medicare. Department of Health & Human Services, Office of the Inspector General. August, OEI-09-07-00122.
44. Grob, R. G. (1997). Testimony on Fraud, Waste and Abuse in Nursing Homes before the House Subcommittee on Human Resources, April 16.
45. Ratner, J. (1995). *Tighter Rules Needed to Curtail Overcharges for Therapy in Nursing Homes.* GAO/HEHS-95-23. Washington, D.C.: Government Printing Office, pp. 1–6, 19, 28; Purnick, J. (1995). Cutting nursing home profits, not care. *New York Times,* March 16, p. B8, col. 3.
46. Grey-Vickrey, I. (2001). Protecting the older adult, *Nursing Management,* 32(10):36-40.
47. Waxman, H. A. (2001). Abuse of Residents Is a Major Problem in U.S. Nursing Homes. Special Investigations Division House Committee on Government Reform, July 30.
48. Pillemer, K., and Hudson, B. (1993). A model abuse prevention program for nursing assistants. *Gerontologist* 33(1):128–131.
49. American Health Consultants. (2001). Nursing home found liable for employee's assault. *Healthcare Risk Management* 23(9):106.
50. Peck, R. L. (1994). A nursing home's guide to self defense. *Nursing Homes* 43(2):49–50.
51. Port, B., and Zambito, T. (2002). Governor vows nursing home law. *Daily News* (New York), August 12, p. 8.
52. American Association of Critical Care Nurses. (2001). Public Policy Update, April.
53. Health care becomes first target of OSHA ergo plan. (2002). *Hospital Employee Health,* Hot Topics.
54. OHSA Ergonomics Regulations Nullified. (2002). *www.armstrongteasdale.com/news/news ohsa null TXT.html.*
55. Fritz, M. (1995). Nursing homes eyeing a new lucrative field. *Star Ledger* (Newark, N.J.), March 19, sec. 1, p. 47, col. 3.
56. Wallach, R. M. (1994). Subacute's success story: Making a difference in patient care. *Provider* 20(10):51–59.
57. Subacute Feasibility Study, Report to Legislature. (2000). The Texas Health and Human Services Commission. September 1.
58. Dewease, S. (1994). Paving the road to subacute care: Professional liability issues. *Nursing Homes* 43(4):35–38.
59. Miles, F. (1994). Subacute and civil liability. *Provider* 20(9):63–64.
60. Kane, R. L., and Kane, R. A. (1995). Long term care. *Journal of the American Medical Association* 273(21):1690–1691.
61. Strahan, G. W. (1994). An overview of home health and hospice care patients: Preliminary data for the 1993 national home and hospice care survey. *Advance Data* No. 256, Pub. No. (PHS) 94-1250, July 22.
62. Arras, J. D., and Dubler, N. N. (1994). Bringing the hospital home. *Hastings Center Report* 24(5):S19–28; Peterson, C. (1995). Homing in on home care. *Managed Healthcare* 5(3):20–24.
63. Home Health Care Information California Registry. *http://ww.calregistry.com/inhome/hhealth/HTM.*
64. Home Health Care Statistics. Oregon Health and Science University. (2002). *http://www.ohsuhealth.com/home health/hhstats.asp.*
65. Home Health Care Overview. Oregon Health and Science University. (2002). *http://www.ohsuhealth.com/home health/overview.asp.*
66. Johnson, S. H. (1991). Liability issues. In *Delivering High Technology Home Care,* edited by M. J. Mehlman and S. J. Younger. New York: Springer, pp. 125–159.
67. Burns, J. (1995). Feds come knocking in search of home-care fraud. *Modern Healthcare* 25(3):40–44; Turner, P. C. (1995). Brothers convicted of $750,000 Medicare scam. *Star-Ledger* (Newark, N.J.), June 13, p. 50, col. 2.
68. Harrison, B. A., and Cole, D. S. (1994). Managing risk to minimize liability. *Caring* 13(5):26.
69. Long Island Nurse Pads Work Hours in Home Health Care Fraud. (2001). Press Release, New York State Department of Law, May 11.
70. Health Care Fraud Press Release. (1998). FBI National Press Office, Federal Bureau of Investigation, U.S. Department of Justice. Washington, D.C., October 21.
71. Anders, G. (1995). Health concern could be barred from Medicare. *Wall Street Journal,* March 1, p. B6, col. 4.
72. Himelstein, L., DeGeorge, G., and Schine, E. (1995). Is fraud poisoning home health care? *Business Week* March 14:70–74.
73. Steel, R. K. (1994). Medical schools and home care. *New England Jornal of Medicine* 331(16):1098–1099.
74. American Health Consultants. (2001). Joint commission offers lessons in home care. *Healthcare Risk Management* 23(5):55.

75. Romaine-Davis, A., Boondas, J., and Lenihan, A. (1995). *Encyclopedia of Home Care for the Elderly*. Westport, Conn.: Greenwood Press; Brent, N.J. (1989). Avoiding patient abandonment charges; Balancing the legal and ethical issues. *Home Healthcare Nurse* 7(2):7–8.
76. Documentation, training protect hospital from risk in home care. (1993). *Hospital Risk Management* 15(11):164–167.
77. Dombi, W. A. (1993) Legal issues in home care. *Caring* 10(9):4–12.
78. Hogue, E. (1992). Parental noncompliance in home care. *Pediatric Nursing* 18(6):603–606; Aspen Reference Group. (1994). *Home Health Care Patient Education Manual*. Gaithersburg, Md.: Aspen.
79. Spiegel, A. D. (1987). *Home Health Care*. Norwood, N.J.: Ablex, pp. 24–26.
80. Warding off thieves. (1994). *Nursing94* 24(1):28.
81. Josephson, K. R., Fabacher, D. A., and Rubenstein, L. Z. (1991). Home safety and fall prevention. *Clinics in Geriatric Medicine* 7(4):707–731.
82. Burdick, A. (1995). If you need medical equipment at home . . . *Good Housekeeping* April:209; Woolsey, C. (1993). Home care exposure on the rise. *Business Week* 27(48):67–68.
83. Nadwairski, J. A. (1992). Inner-city safety for home care providers. *Journal of Nursing Administration* 22(9):42–47.
84. Backinger, C. L. (1993). *The Potential for Reducing the Risk of Bloodborne Pathogen Transmission in Home Health Care in the U.S.* Baltimore: University of Maryland.
85. Can home health aide recover benefits after accident on route to her assignment? (1995). *Workers' Compensation Law Bulletin* Special Issue:6.
86. Freeman, L. (1995). Home-sweet-home health care. *Monthly Labor Review* 118:3–11; Foote, J. (1995). Home care workers ill-paid for vital service. *Star-Ledger* (Newark, N.J.), June 11, sec. 6, p. 1, col. 1.
87. Duke nurse charged with robbing heiress. (1995). *Star-Ledger* (Newark, N.J.), October 10, p. 14, col. 3.
88. Sussman, M. L., and Siegel, P. J. (1991). Assessing an agency's risks. *Caring* 10(9):42–45, 67–68.
89. Brent, N. J. (1990). Avoiding professional negligence. *Home Healthcare Nurse* 8(5):45–47.
90. Sullivan, G. (1995). Home care: More autonomy, more legal risks. *RN* 57(5):63–69.
91. Hospice Care Statistics. Oregon Health and Science University. (2002). *http://www. ohsuhealth.com/home health/hosstats.asp*.
92. Brent, N. J. (1989). Administering controlled substances in the home. *Home Health Care Nurse* 7(4):6–7.
93. Ross, J. L. (1995). *Long Term Care: Current Issues and Future Directions*. GAO/HEHS-95-109. Washington, D.C.: Government Printing Office, pp. 15, 20–22.
94. Rhinehart, E., and Wellman, P. (1998). Admission and termination policies minimizing risk and liability. *Caring* 17(10):32–35.

CHAPTER 13 Risk Management in Selected High Risk Hospital Departments

Alice L. Epstein
Gary H. Harding

Each clinical care area and medical specialty brings to patients the hope and promise of successful medical intervention, as well as the potential for poor outcomes and unexpected complications.

There are management issues applicable to all clinical departments that are relevant to the delivery of safe and effective patient care. For example, medical record documentation, competency of staff, and credentialing to perform the tasks necessary to care for the patient are important regardless of the department or medical specialty. Patient monitoring capabilities and technical equipment must be in place and be effective so that staff is always aware of the physiological condition of the patient and is prepared to intercede if and when necessary.

Departments such as pharmacy, radiology, pathology, and laboratory typically do not have their own patients, but they interact with other specialty departments. In many cases, the challenge is even more difficult for the support departments, since requests for services are referred from outside the department. Accurate and timely communication among the departments and the referring physicians is essential. Without effective communications, laboratory tests may be ordered incorrectly, the wrong patient may be identified for a test, test results may be interpreted inappropriately, and needed intervention may be delayed.

Regardless of the clinical specialty, the risks and risk management interventions are often specific to the clinical specialty. Liabilities are inherent within select clinical specialties, particularly those that the medical literature and insurance data identify as posing heightened risk to patients, institutions, and professionals. It is important to note that a recent analysis of claims[1] indicates that new patterns of high risk are emerging. The nursing/patient care category (which includes medical, surgical, and intensive care) is now the leader for total dollar losses, outpacing perinatal, surgery, and emergency services. The analysis suggests that by improving just a few specific risk management practices, patient safety is improved and the cost of claims is lowered. The following selected high risk departments within clinical care deserve special attention: emergency medicine, obstetrics and neonatology, and surgery and anesthesia.

EMERGENCY MEDICINE

Emergency departments care for more than 100 million patients annually and provide accurate and effective diagnoses in well over 99 percent of the cases.[2] Emergency medicine has a unique set of inherent risks. Most patients arriving at an emergency department are in a medical crisis. However, some patients who come to the emergency department are overreacting to a nonemergency situation and thus are not appropriately accessing the medical system—that is, through a primary care provider. As a result, there are problems with the allocation of resources.

According to the American College of Emergency Physicians (ACEP), the most common allegations of malpractice involve the failure to diagnose the following:[3,4]

- Fractures
- Foreign bodies in wounds
- Myocardial infarctions
- Complications of lacerations, including tendons and nerves

The most costly malpractice allegations involve the following conditions:

- Myocardial infarctions
- Meningitis
- Fractures
- Ectopic pregnancies

STANDARDS AND GUIDELINES

Many professional medical organizations developed standards and guidelines regarding the safe and effective delivery of health care in the emergency setting. Such organizations include the American College of Emergency Physicians, American College of Osteopathic Emergency Physicians, Committee on Trauma of the American College of Surgeons, Emergency Nurses Association, Emergency Department Nurses Association, and the National Association of Emergency Medical Technicians.

According to the American Hospital Association, a true emergency is "any condition clinically determined to require immediate medical care."[5] Some courts have defined an emergency as existing when treatment is necessary to alleviate severe pain or to prevent further deterioration or aggravation of the patient's condition. Federal legislation defines an emergency condition as manifested by acute symptoms of sufficient severity that the absence of immediate medical attention could reasonably be expected to result in serious jeopardy to an individual's health, serious impairment to bodily functions, or serious dysfunction of any body organ or part.

All patients, regardless of economic issues, have a right to receive needed emergency care. In 1986, Congress passed the Consolidated Omnibus Reconciliation Act (COBRA), which contains a section titled the Emergency Medical Treatment and Active Labor Act (EMTALA). This legislation was designed, in part, to prevent patients from being transferred solely for economic reasons. COBRA provides that any hospital that receives Medicare funds and that has an emergency department must provide appropriate medical screening to determine if a medical emergency exists or if the patient is in active labor.[5] If possible, the patient must then be examined and stabilized prior to transfer or discharge.

Whereas clinicians and risk managers tend to define emergencies as "life-threatening" situations, lawyers and courts may take a more liberal view. Merely the existence of an emergency department implies an implicit duty to treat any patient who arrives needing immediate attention. Courts have found that a patient-physician relationship commences as soon as the emergency department is offered as a source of treatment to the general public and the public it seeks to serve. An insurance study has demonstrated a 600 percent increase in the cost of an ER claim when risk management practices are not followed.[6]

PREHOSPITAL SERVICES

Time is of the essence in emergency situations. The more rapidly that medical intervention occurs after the medical condition is discovered, the more likely the results will be positive. Delays prior to arrival for treatment in the emergency department contribute to the decrease in successful emergency medical or surgical interventions and an increase in severity of illness.

A thorough understanding of the prehospital emergency services available in the community is necessary because of the widely varied local and state development of these systems. ACEP's policy statement "Medical Direction of Pre-hospital Emergency Services"[7] suggests that all prehospital emergency services be managed by a physician who has authority over patient care and the responsibility to develop and implement medical policies and procedures, and is board certified in emergency medicine and experienced in emergency department management. Emergency medical technicians (EMTs) who respond by ambulance to crisis situations are required by the U.S. Department of Transportation to complete an 81-hour curriculum. Advanced levels of EMT training require from 280 to 1,000 hours. Some regions in the country are fortunate to have hospital-to-field communication systems that allow on-line medical direction in which physicians are directly responsible for orders given to field personnel regarding specific emergency conditions (see Box 13-1).

Risk management concerns the field situation and approach to the medical emergency. Patients may be dead at the site or may arrive DOA (dead on arrival) at the emergency department. During transport to the hospital, the patient may experience cardiac and respiratory arrests and there may be significant changes in prehospital diagnosis and emergency department diagnosis. Ambulances may be required to reroute to a hospital that is further away than the one they originally set out for, due to overcrowding or understaffing at the original facility.

LEVELS OF SERVICE

Emergency departments are divided into categories based on the sophistication of the

BOX 13-1

Disputes and controversy arose when an oxygen tube was improperly inserted by an ambulance crew attending a collapsed fireman, causing brain damage, coma, and death. Volunteer ambulance workers allegedly refused to yield to emergency medical services paramedics and argued at the scene about which hospital to go to.[9]

services provided. Established by the American Medical Association Commission on Emergency Medical Services,[8] these categories relate to availability of care, physician staffing, medical specialties required to be available in the hospital and on call, referral requirements, required biomedical equipment, medication availability, facility design, and support department availability.

Patients often are not aware of the level of services available at the emergency department they choose to access, nor are they aware of the level of services that their medical condition requires. This lack of knowledge on the part of patients places the staff of the emergency department in a precarious position from a legal perspective. Hospitals can be successfully sued when they do not have the services, personnel, or facilities to render the care they have marketed to the community.

Many hospitals have established emergicenters and/or urgi-centers in an attempt to access new markets within the community, provide additional services, and reduce the patient load on the hospital emergency department. Risk management concerns focus on the potential inappropriate public perception that urgi-centers are staffed and equipped to provide full emergency critical care or trauma services.

Security issues are a major concern for emergency departments. Studies and media reports demonstrate that violence in emergency departments has escalated over the last 10 years.[10] During a nine-month period in just one emergency department, staff members were punched, kicked, grabbed, pushed, or spat on, 19 times.[11] Hospital workers may suffer psychological trauma and post-traumatic stress disorder because of the violent acts in emergency departments.[12] Ideally, security personnel should be in close proximity and availability to the emergency department 24 hours a day. Each institution should review the security risks and risk management issues and develop policies to minimize uncontrolled access into other sections of the hospital, to secure medications in controlled areas, and to deal with confiscated weapons.[13]

According to ACEP, emergency departments should be staffed by emergency care physicians and other professionals, along with specialists on call, during all hours of operation, on the basis of the unique needs of the community and the level of emergency care offered.

Often, emergency departments are staffed by contract physicians or residents, who may be training or "moonlighting." Studies have shown that full-time attending physician coverage can result in a decrease in claims filed and claims paid out.[13] If residents are to be used, it is imperative that attending physician supervision be available on-site.[14] A recent study found that "only about half of the nation's 25,000 jobs in medicine are filled by doctors certified to provide emergency care."[15] It is important to realize that the attending physician is the primary physician responsible for the patient. Attending physicians who practice "long distance" supervision of residents, and facilities that allow such practice, may experience greatly increased liability.

Contracted physicians, if used, should be board certified in emergency medicine, credentialed and privileged to practice in the department, and required to adhere to the policies and protocols of the hospital and to participate in quality improvement activities.

In rural facilities, the number of physicians available may be limited, so the nursing staff needs to be able to stabilize the patient until the physician arrives or until adequate transfer conditions and plans have been met. Many hospitals have developed policies that require the on-call physician to be within 30 minutes of the hospital and that they provide guidance for the nursing staff regarding alternate physicians to be contacted. Frequently the emergency department physician is required to cover in-house emergencies. From a risk management perspective, this responsibility must not compromise the availability of rapid medical or physician response to patients coming into the emergency department.

At a change in shift or change in professionals in the emergency department, each physician should be required to write a status note in the medical record regarding the patient, and the responsibility for patient care should be formally transferred.

Physicians in the emergency department should not practice outside their scope of training or expertise and are expected to contact the appropriate specialist when needed to reduce the potential for liability.

All physicians providing care in the department are under the jurisdiction of the physician-in-charge, with whom final decisions concerning admission or patient discharge should rest. As soon as it is determined that a patient should be admitted, the attending physician should be notified. In most hospitals, emergency department physicians do not have admitting privileges. It is the attending physician's responsibility to admit the patient and assume further responsibility for the patient's care, after discussing the situation with the emergency physician.

Liability increases when patients receive emergency care, are admitted or discharged, or leave without being evaluated by a physician. In addition, problems arise with unsigned and poorly documented medical records of services, consultations, and discussions between the emergency department physician and the attending physician.

TRIAGE

Once the patient arrives at the hospital, it is the responsibility of the staff to treat the patient as the medical situation dictates. Proper triage classifies patients by level of need:

> **Emergent cases** require immediate medical attention because delaying medical care would be harmful to the patient, since the disorder is acute and potentially threatens life or function. Examples include cardiac arrest, severe head injuries, chest pain with difficulty breathing, and a temperature greater than 105°F.

> **Urgent cases** require medical attention within a few hours of arrival at the hospital because the patient is in danger of acute, but not life threatening problems. Examples include burns, back injuries, fractures, and persistent diarrhea.

> **Nonurgent cases** do not require the resources of an emergency department, because the problem is minor or nonacute, or treatment cannot effect outcome or suffering. Examples include nondebilitating headaches, minor fractures, or a case in which the patient is dead on arrival.

Risks most commonly related to triage include the failure to determine the existence of an emergency, improper categorization of the patient's status, improper diagnosis, and failure to communicate pertinent information. In addition to initial assessment, every patient should be reassessed prior to being discharged or transferred to another facility.

An advisory panel of the National Heart Attack Alert Program found that emergency departments could be doing more to quickly identify and treat patients with myocardial infarction.[14] During triage, opportunities also exist to identify battered women,[15] as well as cases of child abuse and neglect that require certain reporting and special social service interventions (see Box 13-2).[16]

Managed care insurance introduced the concepts of the physician gatekeeper, preauthorization of services, and limiting patients to the use of facilities approved by their insurance company. Decisions to assess and treat a patient should not be made on the basis of payment by managed care organizations, Medicaid, or Medicare. Emergency care must be rendered as appropriate to the medical condition, regardless of the patient's ability to pay. Prior approval for payment purposes should not delay assessment or the provision of necessary emergency treatment.

Telephone advice also presents risk management concerns in the emergency department. Frequently, patients and family members telephone the emergency department seeking advice on whether they should come to the emergency department or how they can treat an injury or illness at home. The ACEP position statement "Providing Telephone Advice from the Emergency Department" established some guidelines.[18] Some emergency departments provide this service; others do not.

Some hospitals respond to these calls with a set of physician-developed clinical algorithms designed to facilitate a telephone triage process to determine whether the patient should be brought to the emergency department. If telephone calls are being responded to, a log should be maintained in the department containing details of the calls and any advice given.

BOX 13-2

The New York City Health Department criticized Woodhull Medical Center (Brooklyn, N.Y.) for failure to provide "considerate and respectful care" to a rape victim, who was left unattended for two hours wearing only a hospital gown in an area where handcuffed male prisoners were also awaiting treatment.[17]

PATIENT–PHYSICIAN RELATIONSHIP

One of the keys to a successful outcome of services is the rapport established by the health care professionals in the emergency department with the patient and the family. Physicians should inform patients of the treatment plan and the recognized accuracy of the diagnostic tests they are to receive, identify factors that pose special risks, and discuss the options. To the extent possible, the patient and/or family should be involved in decisions regarding care. Support staff should keep family members advised of the progress of the patient and of how long they can expect to wait. Sometimes anger expressed by a patient is secondary to the clinical situation and can be appropriately evaluated and refocused. Sometimes, however, the anger results in a lawsuit. It is important that patients be made aware of the fact that, most often, emergency room physicians are not hospital employees.

Risk management should monitor emergency department visits and analyze the trends in specific situations, such as complaints and dissatisfaction about present or past treatment, patients seen for a complication resulting from a previous procedure, or patients who return within 72 hours of a previous admission. Some patients may try to establish disability as a result of the injury and treatment. Other patients may make repeated visits, demanding pain medication immediately upon arrival, and may cover their drug addiction with symptoms that mimic renal colic or cardiac pain.

DOCUMENTATION AND CONSENTS

Documentation is crucial to managing risk in the emergency department. From the point of entry into the system, through triage, assessment, physicians' orders, testing, treatment, test results, and discharge, important pieces of communication need to be recorded. Some hospitals use voice recognition programs for documentation;[19] others have instituted checklists to help ensure that a particular clinical path is followed. Software programs of emergency care clinical practice algorithms are available, as are computerized clinical protocols.

The time of the patient's arrival and departure and tests, as well as consent to procedures and tests, should be in the record, as should be evidence of patient education, transfer forms, and copies of discharge instructions.

Whenever possible, consent for examination, treatment, and invasive procedures or tests should be obtained from the patient or an authorized individual if the patient is unable to consent. However, whenever a life-threatening emergency exists and treatment is required to save a life, the presumption is that consent is implied by the patient's arrival at the emergency department. An additional presumption is that a delay in treatment would seriously increase the hazards to health by precipitating death or a serious impairment. When treating a minor, if an emergency condition exists and the parents of the minor cannot be located, the need for consent is generally obviated. Treatment should be limited to that which is necessary to cope with the emergency. Whenever a parent or guardian provides consent via the telephone, a second hospital representative should monitor the conversation as a witness and document his or her presence in the medical record. Subsequently, the parent or the guardian should be requested to sign the consent authorization.

A competent adult or emancipated minor who is deemed competent has the right to refuse medical and surgical treatment even if brought to an emergency department, unless the state can demonstrate a compelling, overriding interest. Usually, the patient's competency and strength of conviction are considered in such cases presented to the court.

SUPPORT SERVICES

Emergency department physicians are sometimes dependent on the analysis of tests performed outside the department to determine the diagnosis of the patient and how to proceed with the patient's treatment. For example, electrocardiograms reduce the number of missed diagnoses of heart attacks, when properly interpreted.

Accurate interpretation of X-rays is also critical for reliable diagnoses. Emergency physicians have limited training in radiology but may be required to perform an initial reading of the X-ray and prescribe treatment. The radiologist usually interprets the film on the following day or following week, especially in rural facilities. Teleradiology is quickly linking rural emergency departments for real-time radiographic interpretations. In this way, emergency departments without access to radiologists are linked to radiology departments in other hospitals. Missed readings or discrepancies in film interpretation need to be documented in the medical record and brought to the attention of the emergency physician immediately so that the patient can be notified and possible alterations in treatment advised.

Failure to communicate important medical information about a patient to the treating physician may be viewed as negligence, particularly if this information would have changed the physician's orders and assessment. Frequently, nurses contact physicians by telephone to discuss a patient presenting in the emergency department. Because of the recognized potential for information to be incomplete, not appropriately communicated, or misunderstood, risk managers recommend that the responsible physician personally evaluate the patient.

DEPARTURES, DISCHARGES, AND TRANSFERS

Patients who leave the emergency department against medical advice prior to medical evaluation pose special risks to the hospital. Some patients and their families tire of a lengthy wait and decide to leave before being seen by a physician. Other patients may not be pleased with the treatment they receive or may not agree with treatment plans suggested by the physician. Existing organizational protocols should delineate how to handle these patients to reduce the number who leave prematurely. Patients who voice their intent to leave should be advised of the possible medical and health consequences, and such conversations with the patient and the family members should be documented in the medical record. A patient's refusal to sign an AMA (discharge against medical advice) statement should also be noted.

For safe transfer of a patient to another hospital or facility from the emergency department, staff must ensure that the patient is approved and stable for transfer and that the mode of transfer selected is appropriate. A receiving facility must agree to the transfer in advance, and the original facility must provide the receiving hospital with medical records.[20] Many transferring patients (for example, newborns and cardiac or psychiatric patients) require attendance by specialty trained professionals and high-tech group or air ambulances.

A statement authorizing the transfer should be signed by the physician and should detail the medical benefits anticipated at the receiving facility that outweigh the increased risks of transfer (see Box 13-3).

Patients discharged directly from the emergency department may require limited follow-up care. To reduce liability, it is recommended that written discharge instructions be given to the patient and family and that these be available in all of the most commonly used foreign languages in the service community. Discharge instructions should be reviewed with the patient by a nurse[22] or the physician prior to the patient's discharge from the emergency department, and a copy should be filed in the medical record. Follow-up calls should be

BOX 13-3

A 32-year-old chronically homeless man verbally threatened to kill his treating psychologist. When brought to the hospital, he acted violently when told he would be committed to the county psychiatric hospital. Six police officers and additional hospital security personnel restrained the patient. He was involuntarily restrained to a gurney with four-point restraints. He was given a sedative, placed face-down on the gurney, and a backboard was placed over him in order to transfer him to the psychiatric hospital by ambulance. While being wheeled out of the emergency room he was found to not be breathing. Efforts to revive him failed.

The county coroner determined that the cause of death was positional asphyxia, and the death was a homicide. Negligence against the hospital, the emergency room physician, and the ambulance company was alleged. The verdict was a total of $2 million.[21]

made to patients discharged with potentially high risk problems, such as head injury, and such calls should also be documented.

RISK MANAGEMENT OPPORTUNITIES

Risk managers have several opportunities to monitor emergency department services: from medical records, by specific notification by the department, or by complaints. All deaths in the emergency department, or within 24 hours of admission, should be investigated. Similarly, all adverse situations should be reviewed, such as transfer of a patient who requires CPR during the transfer, any DOA case, or a patient who dies within 24 hours of admission at the receiving facility.

Risk management should also monitor the emergency department records of patients who refuse hospitalization or treatment, of patients who leave against medical advice, and of family or patients who disappear from the waiting area. Patients should be seen within a reasonable waiting time to reduce complaints from the waiting area, so the time of arrival and time of treatment should be recorded. Useful information may also be gathered on patients who repeatedly use the emergency department for the same or similar diagnoses within a seven-day period.

OBSTETRICS AND NEONATOLOGY

Reviews of malpractice claims demonstrate that lawsuits related to obstetric and neonatal cases are frequently the most expensive in terms of claims settled and malpractice awards paid. With each birth it is hoped, and often expected, that the prenatal process, labor, and delivery will be uncomplicated and successful—the experience of a lifetime. Similar expectations hold true for the early hours and days of an infant's life. In large part because of these expectations and because of the belief that giving birth is typically a planned event, the physical and emotional impact can be severe when a maternal or neonatal complication or injury occurs. Clearly, this feeling is carried over into courtroom decisions favoring the plaintiff.

OBSTETRICS AND NEONATOLOGY LIABILITY RISKS

Multiple studies of obstetric claims have been performed. A study by the American College of Obstetricians and Gynecologists (ACOG) addressed the impact of professional liability actions and costs on the practice of obstetrics and gynecology between 1990 and 1992, and again in 1999.[23] Of the physicians surveyed, approximately 79 percent had experienced at least one malpractice claim. This statistic represented an increase of more than 8 percent from information derived during the 1987 version of the same survey. Twenty-five percent of the physicians had been sued four or more times, an increase of more than 11 percent form the 1987 survey. More than 50 percent of the claims were carried through court or settlement. Of the claims not dropped or settled without payment, approximately 75 percent were settled with payment. In approximately 22 percent of the cases that went to court, the verdict favored the plaintiff. In terms of number of claims reported, the two most significant primary allegations for obstetric claims were neurological impairment to the infant and stillbirth or neonatal death. Additional allegations included maternal injuries, other infant injuries, failure to diagnose a problem, and maternal death. Labor/delivery and the nursery made up about 5.3 percent of all claims (9.6 percent of all losses in 2001), according to recent St. Paul Fire and Marine Insurance Company data. The average loss was a whopping $798,304.[1]

Primary allegations include for cesarean sections: infant neuromuscular development problems, maternal hemorrhage, and maternal or infant death; for vaginal deliveries: infant neuromuscular development problems, Erb's palsy, retained vaginal sponge, intrauterine and ectopic pregnancies, and circumcision-related problems. Additional related allegations included delay in treatment of fetal distress and failure to obtain consent.[27]

While advanced medical technology has enabled physicians to save infants who may not otherwise have survived, it has simultaneously provided a larger base of complications on which lawsuits can be made. A recent study found that "infants weighing less than three pounds are less likely to die or suffer serious problems if they are born in hospitals with neonatal intensive care units or transferred to such centers immediately after birth."[24] However, those infants who are "saved" are often medically compromised, increasing the likelihood of litigation in response to unsatisfactory results and poor long term prognosis. School-age outcomes in children with birth weights under 750 grams were found to be at high risk for neurobehavioral dysfunction and poor school performance.[25]

Additional factors complicate litigation surrounding obstetrics. A *New York Times* investigative reporter discovered that a 1992 New York City report that was never published listed 64 lawsuits that were the direct result of brain damage to infants resulting from hospital negligence. Many of the worst cases involved obstetric residents in training who had little or no supervision from senior physicians.[26] A study of obstetric malpractice claims in Georgia found that 27 percent of the claims were indefensible because of breaches in the standard of care, problems with documentation, or a combination of both.[27]

Multiple surveys and studies of Florida obstetricians have examined the relationship between the mother's inclination to sue and the prior malpractice experience of the attending physician. A study of claims between 1977 and 1989 by mothers of infants who had incurred permanent injuries or had died identified numerous reasons for filing a malpractice claim: advice from knowledgeable acquaintances to file; recognition of a coverup regarding the care of their infant; financial necessity; recognition that their child would have no future; lack of information as to why their child was injured or died; desire to seek revenge; or desire to protect others from similar harm. This same study found two types of communication problems identified by the mothers: (1) their belief that some physicians had misled them and (2) a failure on the part of the physician to provide sufficient information.[28] However, a second study found no relationship between prior malpractice claim experience and differences in objective or subjective measures of the quality of clinical care provided.[29]

An investigation of mothers who had not filed a malpractice claim but who had experienced viable infants, stillborn infants, or infant deaths found that "a consistent pattern of differences emerged when comparing women's perceptions of care received. Patients seeing physicians with the most frequent numbers of claims, but without high payments, were significantly more likely to complain that they felt abused, never received explanations for tests, and were ignored."[30]

These studies demonstrate the myriad of factors that complicate the delivery process and increase a mother's inclination to sue. There are clinical issues, societal issues, communication problems, and administrative support issues that all may contribute in some manner to initiation of a lawsuit. While skilled caregivers are the most effective agents in managing the risk in obstetrics and neonatology, the physician-patient relationship is prominent. Informed consent and medical record documentation must be actively monitored and maintained if litigation is to be successfully defended.

ETHICAL DILEMMAS

There are significant ethical and legal issues to be considered in the delivery and management of high risk infants. Right to life, quality of life, wrongful life or birth, and right to die are issues that are personal to the parents of the infant and are also of concern to the medical profession. Do the parents have the right to know the status of their fetus, if compromised, and the possible resulting medical conditions in the newborn or as the child matures? To what degree and vigor should physicians prolong the life of hopelessly ill newborns with heroic treatments?

Members of the family should be involved in any ethical decision process. Risk managers agree that parents should be provided with all the available information regarding the condition of their fetus and the potential for development. All involved caregivers should be consulted and an attempt made to achieve consensus on the ultimate decision, if possible.

After an initial decision on care is reached, the matter may be revisited in the event of changes in the mother's or fetus/infant's condition or in response to the expressed desires of the family members. The American Academy of Pediatrics recommends ongoing evaluation of the infant's prognosis, with treatment decisions based strictly on what will benefit the newborn. Many facilities established ethics committees to assist in resolving conflicts in neonatal intensive care units.[31] All ethical discussions and decisions regarding care of the fetus or infant should be documented in the medical record.

STANDARDS AND GUIDELINES

Many professional organizations have developed clinical practice guidelines in obstetrics and neonatology: American Academy of Family Physicians (AAFP), American Academy of Pediatrics (AAP), American Institute of Ultrasound and Medicine (AIUM), American College of Nurse-Midwives, American College of Obstetricians and Gynecologists (ACOG), American College of Radiology (ACR), American Pediatric Society (APS), Association of Women's Health, Obstetrics, and Neonatal Nurses, and National Association of Neonatal Nurses (NANN).

Hospital and department policies and procedures, revised annually and distributed widely, are essential in guiding health care providers in the management of obstetric and neonatal patients. Significant risk management problems can arise if practitioners are not fully aware of, and in agreement with, these policies and procedures.

Levels of Care: Institutional Capabilities

Obstetric and neonatal care services are provided in a wide range of hospital settings with varying capabilities throughout the United States. AAP and ACOG have established staffing, equipment, and support service criteria describing the classifications of the levels of care.[32]

Level I facilities provide services that are the least intensive and designed to treat low-risk mothers and their infants. Even so, a Level I facility is required to provide the following:

- A protocol to identify and transfer high risk patients to a higher level facility.
- The ability to perform a cesarean delivery within 30 minutes of determining the necessity.
- The availability of blood and fresh frozen plasma.
- Twenty-four-hour availability of anesthesia, radiology, ultrasound, electronic fetal heart rate monitoring, and laboratory services.
- Infant and maternal resuscitation capabilities at all deliveries.
- The availability of blood typing, crossmatching, and Coombs' testing.
- A qualified physician or nurse-midwife present at all deliveries.

In addition to meeting Level I criteria, Level II facilities must be able to manage high risk mothers, high risk fetuses, and small, sick neonates. A decision to transfer a high risk or critically ill neonate to a Level III facility rests with the referring physician, in consultation with the Level III neonatologist. Level II facility staff must be able to monitor and maintain critical functions, including cardiopulmonary, metabolic, and thermal status. Staffing requirements include: a board certified obstetrician as chief of newborn services; a board certified anesthesiologist supervising obstetrical anesthesiology; 24-hour availability of a radiologist and clinical pathologist; support staff, including a medical social worker, a physical therapist, a dietitian or nutritionist, and a respiratory therapist; and nursing staff capable of identifying and responding to obstetric complications.

A Level III facility delivers more complex care. In addition to meeting all Level I and II criteria, Level III facilities must provide professional staffing with experience in neonatal medicine, maternal-fetal medicine, obstetric and neonatal diagnostic imaging, advanced nursing specialties, and pediatric subspecialities. In addition, the nurse-to-patient ratio of staff is more intensive than is required in Level I or Level II facilities.

Risk managers should periodically survey their facility to document the level classification and to determine compliance of the obstetric service to the staffing, equipment, and support service requirements established by AAP and ACOG.

Except in emergency situations, and depending on the availability of health care providers, the family's wishes, and the condition of the mother and fetus, the prenatal care and delivery of the infant may be performed by an obstetrician, family practitioner, resident, or nurse-midwife. A report in the *New York Times* stated that nurse-midwives, who are responsible for caring for and delivering the babies of many of the lower-income women at New York City's public hospitals, "routinely exceed the limits of state law to handle high risk delivery cases . . . and that these cases are virtually impossible to defend."[33] Credentialing and privileging of these health care providers should be specific to the clinical tasks they will be required to perform.

In some clinical situations, the family practitioner and nurse-midwife are required to consult with or refer the case to an obstetrician. Hospitals should have policies and procedures for required consultations and referrals, as well as for precipitous deliveries. Emergency departments should have delivery packs on hand and have staff available who are trained in emergency delivery procedures and infant care.

PRENATAL AND PERINATAL CARE

Most physicians agree that prenatal care is paramount to ensuring the health and well-being of the newborn. Unfortunately, not all expectant mothers avail themselves of prenatal care, perhaps because of societal pressures, perceived lack of access, lack of money, or lack of knowledge. Regardless of the reason for foregoing prenatal care, it is imperative that physicians and hospital support staff document whatever steps are taken to ensure adequate prenatal care and record the actual extent of care received by the mother. During the prenatal period a multitude of clinical problems can develop, such as hypertension and diabetes, which may have a future negative impact on the mother and unborn child. Physician counseling of the patient should include a discussion of the level of accuracy of diagnostic procedures and the variability of test result interpretations. Mothers should be informed as to realistic expectations regarding morbidity, mortality, tests, and procedure limitations (see Box 13-4).

An important step in determining the appropriate course of care for the expectant mother is an assessment of the gestational age of the fetus. Once pregnancy has been confirmed, the clinician should determine the appropriate plan for patient management on the basis of a thorough risk assessment, patient and family history, physical examination, environmental history, and findings that result from specialized diagnostic procedures and laboratory tests. One insurance study found that the cost of a claim rose 300 percent when these standards are not followed.[1]

BOX 13-4

A baby was born with profound disabilities. Parents of the newborn alleged negligence in not being adequately informed of the results of a prenatal blood test. Their successful lawsuit claimed damages due to "wrongful birth" and "wrongful life."[34]

Genetic Counseling and Testing

Genetic testing is available to determine the potential and/or occurrence of genetic problems during the perinatal period. The most commonly used tests are chorionic villus sampling, percutaneous umbilical blood sampling, and maternal serum alphafetoprotein testing.

Genetic testing is recommended where familial history or previous obstetric history provides an indication of the potential for a problem. In the general population, the risk of delivering an infant with a serious genetic birth defect has been found to be between three and five percent.

Each genetic test carries identified maternal and fetal risks. Prior to genetic testing, ultrasound studies should be performed to locate the placenta, confirm gestational age, determine fetal viability, and identify multiple fetuses if present. Maternal risks for select genetic tests include spontaneous abortion, abruptio placentae, penetration of the fetal vessels resulting in maternal hemorrhage or death, transient vaginal bleeding, and amniotic fluid leakage. Fetal risks include fetal demise, limb and oromandibular defects, intrauterine growth retardation, premature birth, and Rh isoimmunization.

Genetically at-risk mothers and their families should be given information and advice about the possible consequences of inherited disorders that may or may not be detectable and the various options that are available for diagnosis, management, and prevention. A full and complete informed consent should be obtained from the mother prior to genetic testing acknowledging an understanding of the specific risks of the tests to both herself and the fetus. Infants born with unanticipated congenital abnormalities where there is no documented evidence of genetic counseling and/or testing continue to be a liability risk (see Box 13-5).

Several hospital facilities, insurance companies, and HMOs have developed perinatal case management programs to decrease the number of preterm births.[35] Screening programs are utilized to identify at-risk patients. A perinatal case manager coordinates medical, social, and reimbursement resources, and enhances patient education and communication to facilitate an optimal outcome and to improve the quality of care received.

Antepartum Fetal Surveillance

The ability to monitor the clinical status of both the mother and fetus are important steps in preparing for a safe delivery and ensuring the well-being of the mother and unborn infant. Underlying medical disorders may contribute to a high risk pregnancy. A host of clinical risks and complications can occur during the perinatal period. Adequate assessment of the mother and fetus requires that clinicians recognize which parameters require monitoring, the most effective techniques, and how to interpret normal, abnormal, and interference data. Appropriate equipment must be available and operating properly, and staff must be fully trained. Mothers should be informed of the importance and risks of monitoring and should provide their consent.

BOX 13-5

Failure to diagnose a genetic disorder was the allegation in a Florida malpractice case that allowed recovery for all extraordinary expenses incurred during the child's life expectancy.[36]

Physicians conducting examinations and interpreting tests utilizing sophisticated biomedical equipment should be specifically evaluated for those clinical privileges. Monitoring of the clinical parameters during the antepartum and perinatal periods offers clinicians the opportunity to recognize problems early and to institute early intervention.

Establishment of the expected date of delivery (EDD) is of major importance in being able to determine the gestational age of the fetus, to evaluate fetal growth and maturity, and to plan for delivery. Additionally, medical care of ongoing medical problems or problems new to the pregnancy must be assessed through a review of the history, physical examination, and testing so that the impact on the pregnancy and the fetus is minimized.

Fetal surveillance through antepartum testing indicates the degree of fetal well-being. Results of fetal heart rate monitoring, nonstress testing, and visualization of the intrauterine contents through ultrasound/sonography studies provide the information needed for a "biophysical profile." A quantitative score to evaluate fetal oxygenation and the potential for fetal hypoxia is derived from the following five parameters with a possible total score of 10: (1) fetal breathing movement; (2) fetal body movement; (3) fetal tone, demonstrated by extension and reflexion of fetal limbs; (4) fetal heart rate, measured by a nonreactive stress test; and (5) quantitative amniotic fluid volume. A cumulative score of 8 to 10 is interpreted as a normal infant at low risk for asphyxia. A score of 4 or less strongly suggests asphyxia. If asphyxia persists beyond two hours and is unexplained by other factors, immediate delivery is indicated.[37]

Ultrasound/sonography is a relatively noninvasive diagnostic procedure and is one of the most widely used imaging and monitoring techniques during pregnancy. Ultrasound is performed by obstetricians, perinatologists, and radiologists, as well as by some family practitioners, to assist in determining the gestational age of the fetus at about the eighteenth week, to identify fetal anomalies, to view fetal activity, to aid in amniocentesis, and to evaluate fetal growth in high risk or suspicious situations.

Standards for the use of ultrasound were developed by the American Institute of Ultrasound and Medicine, the American Academy of Pediatrics, and the American College of Radiology, but there is no mandatory training or certification for physicians who perform sonography. Past studies on the quality of ultrasound films revealed failure rates of 65 percent. Films evaluated were considered to be of poor or inadequate image quality and technique,[38] and such inadequate documentation poses risks if the films are needed for a defense.

The nonstress test (NST) is based on the assumption that the fetal heart rate will temporarily accelerate with fetal movement and be a good indicator of fetal autonomic function. Fetal heart rate is monitored externally, and the tracing is evaluated for accelerations. Occasionally, heart rate accelerations may be induced by the use of a vibroacoustic stimulator (VAS) to waken the healthy but sleeping fetus. Actual strips and documentation of the professional interpretation are important parts of the medical record. Some loss of reactivity has been reported to be associated with central nervous system depression, ingestion of alcohol, and fetal acidosis.[39] There are no published contraindications for a nonstress test. By the use of low doses of intravenous oxytocin or nipple stimulation, the contraction stress test (CST) monitors the fetal heart rate response to induced uterine contractions. This test is rarely used at present, but may appear in older medical records. Risks of this test, while rare, include preterm labor, induced fetal hypoxia, and perinatal death.

Blood flow studies have been used to evaluate intrauterine fetal growth, low birth weight, placental insufficiency, and severe pregnancy-induced hypertension. In addition, blood flow studies have been used to monitor Rh isoimmunization, fetal cardiac arrhythmias, and diabetes mellitus. When combined with Doppler techniques, ultrasound can measure the blood flow patterns through the vessels of the umbilical cord or the maternal artery. ACOG noted that there is insufficient data to support the use of Doppler velocimetry in reducing the risk of antepartum fetal demise or in improving neonatal outcomes.[37]

Uterine activity can be monitored in the home with a small, pressure-sensitive electronic device that is placed on the woman's abdomen. Movements associated with uterine contractions are converted into electronic signals for transmission over a telephone line to a computer for printout and evaluation. When the device was introduced to the marketplace, it was believed that it would aid clinicians in the early detection of preterm labor and thereby improve outcomes. In 1993, the Preventive Services Task Force of the U.S. Public Health Service found insufficient evidence of clinical effectiveness to recommend for or against home monitoring of uterine activity.[40] A recent study of 1,300 women also found that the monitor did not specifically aid in the identification of mothers at risk for preterm labor, nor did it improve pregnancy outcomes in terms of factors such as birth weight, gestational age at delivery, or infant complications."[45] Nurses, with or without the information from the uterine activity monitor, were equally as effective in managing preterm labor patients.

For all these surveillance techniques the documentation in the medical record becomes a major defensive tool when a breach of standard practice is alleged. Consent forms need to be present that document the what, when, and who of testing, the results of evaluation, and monitoring outputs. Of particular importance is the medical care responsiveness to tests and clinical evaluations indicating fetal distress and abnormalities and the interventions taken, if possible, to minimize poor outcomes of the pregnancy.

INTRAPARTUM PERIOD

Critical adverse events can occur in the intrapartum period, and the well-being of the mother or the newborn cannot be taken for granted. According to ACOG and AAP, 20 percent of perinatal morbidity and mortality occurs during the intrapartum period with mothers who have had no previous complications during their pregnancy.[42] In obstetric claims, ACOG reports that the most significant perinatal injury is acidosis leading to asphyxia at birth or to death.[43] Usually, the allegation is that the fetus suffered hypoxia or anoxia for a period of time during the labor and delivery process sufficient to cause clinical injury to the brain, kidney, heart, or lung. Systemic symptoms may appear shortly after birth.

Labor can occur early in the pregnancy (preterm), amniotic membranes can rupture prematurely, the fetus may present in a difficult delivery position, or labor may not progress adequately or at all. Fetal heart rate monitoring and fetal blood sampling help determine the appropriate clinical approach.

Preterm Labor

Some mothers experience labor prior to 37 weeks gestation, when the fetus has not had the opportunity to develop fully. In such cases, physicians must decide on the appropriate clinical course of treatment: either suppression of labor, or preterm delivery if it is neither desirable nor possible to suppress labor.

Risk management considerations include policies and procedures requiring the physician to be present in the hospital during the administration of tocolytic (suppression) drugs, continuous monitoring of the mother and fetus, notification of the pediatrician or neonatologist of a potential preterm delivery, and the availability of resuscitation equipment.

Fetal Heart Rate Monitoring

Physicians evaluate the fetal heart rate (FHR) to identify changes that may be associated with problems related to fetal oxygenation and placental perfusion, such as hypoxia, umbilical cord compression, tachycardia, and acidosis. "The ability to interpret FHR patterns and understand their correlation with the fetus' condition allows the physician to institute management techniques including maternal oxygenation, amnioinfusion, and tocolytic therapy."[44]

FHR may be evaluated effectively either by auscultation or by internal or external electronic monitoring. ACOG has not been able to determine the most effective method of FHR monitoring, nor the specific frequency or duration of monitoring to ensure an optimal outcome. However, ACOG has established guidelines for monitoring, interpretation, and patient management, depending on various FHR patterns.

If patient management interventions are not successful in improving fetal oxygenation and placental perfusion, ACOG recommends delivering the fetus by the most expeditious route, whether abdominal or vaginal. Multiple researchers and clinical practitioners have found that continuous FHR monitoring is associated with an increased rate of cesarean deliveries, but a decrease in the incidence of intrapartum stillbirth.[45] Electronic FHR monitoring is presently used in 50 to 70 percent of all U.S. births.[46]

Fetal Blood Sampling

The sampling of capillary blood from the fetal scalp and the evaluation of the fetal response to scalp stimulation have been found useful in intrapartum fetal monitoring for fetal hypoxia and abnormally high blood acidity.

Induction and Augmentation of Labor

ACOG has established guidelines for the induction of labor prior to spontaneous onset and for augmentation of labor to improve the quality of contractions.[47] Prior to induction or augmentation of labor, it is important to determine fetal maturity and assess gestational age and the status of the cervix. ACOG guidelines require that a physician who has cesarean section privileges be readily available and that trained personnel be in attendance to monitor the fetal heart rate and uterine contractions during the administration of the induction drug (oxytocin).

Surgical induction, such as rupturing or stripping the membranes, increases the risk of infection, bleeding, fetal dislodgement, and interference with cord presentation. Medical augmentation with intravenous drugs requires careful administration with an infusion pump or controller that permits precise flow rate control. Hospital policies should address immediate availability of the delivering physician from the outset of induction or augmentation; protocols for use in fetal distress, uterine hyperstimulation, and infusion rates; and required documentation.

THE DELIVERY

Injuries or problems that develop during the perinatal period may be present at birth in addition to specific birth-related injuries or problems (see Box 13-6). Clinical injuries identified in malpractice claims as a result of vaginal delivery include newborn cardiopulmonary problems, neuromuscular developmental problems, shoulder dystocia, infant death, and Erb's palsy. Infants delivered by cesarean section (C-section) may experience the same complications that are reported in vaginal deliveries. Additional maternal complications claimed include poor maternal outcomes, such as hemorrhage, perforation or laceration of tissue, coma, paralysis, and death.

Pain Management and Obstetric Anesthesia

Despite the current fad for natural childbirth, most women accept the concept of "natural childbirth without pain" and agree to epidural anesthesia during labor and delivery. However, there are deliveries in which the administration of other types of anesthesia becomes medically necessary.

BOX 13-6

A series of articles in the *New York Times* on excessive maternal and neonatal morbidity and mortality among patients treated in municipal hospitals prompted the New York State health commissioner to order a review of all municipal obstetric wards and, if necessary, close them.[48]

Anesthetic and analgesic agents act not only on the mother, but may affect the respiratory and cardiovascular status of the fetus as well. Anesthesia and analgesics may be administered for pain management during either a vaginal delivery or a C-section. Options include intravenous analgesia and regional anesthesia, primarily epidural, for labor and vaginal delivery, and general anesthesia or spinal anesthesia for a C-section.

A study using the American Society of Anesthesiologists' Closed Claim Database reviewed malpractice claims filed against anesthesiologists in obstetric cases. The most common complications were, in order of severity: maternal death, newborn brain damage, and maternal headache. Minor complications included backache, pain during anesthesia, and emotional injury. Claims involving general anesthesia were frequently associated with severe injuries and resulted in higher payments than did claims involving regional anesthesia.[49]

The prime focus of anesthesia personnel is to cater to the mother and provide pain relief. Under extreme circumstances, they assist the neonatologist or pediatrician if their help is required or if the baby is compromised and other physicians are not available. Certain families and cultures prefer concentrated efforts on the newborn baby, especially male infants. However, in the United States there are professional and ethical questions regarding the primacy of either the mother or the fetus.

Obstetric anesthesia services should be supervised by an anesthetist with special training in obstetric anesthesia. Any hospital providing obstetric services at a minimum should have a qualified physician or certified registered nurse anesthesiologist (CRNA) readily available, preferably within 15 to 30 minutes, in an emergency. However, it is generally recommended that 24-hour in-house anesthesia coverage be available. Qualifications include the ability of the professional to manage life-threatening respiratory and cardiovascular failure, toxemia, convulsions, and aspirations.

Pre- and postanesthesia evaluations that include both maternal and fetal status should be performed by anesthesia personnel. Decisions to use a particular type of pain relief and route of administration should be discussed with the mother by the professional intending to administer the anesthesia. That discussion should include the advantages, disadvantages, and risk implications to both the mother and fetus. Documentation of the discussion and the mother's consent to anesthesia should be reflected in the medical record.

Vaginal Delivery

Vaginal delivery is the most common route for births. Adequate staffing to care for both the newborn and the mother are required. It is preferred that a pediatrician be available for all deliveries and imperative that a pediatrician or neonatologist be present at all high risk deliveries. C-section, infant resuscitation, and anesthesia services should also be available.

In some deliveries, labor will have to be interrupted and a C-section performed. Breech presentations are often delivered through C-section, although it has been shown that vaginal delivery may be attempted if certain obstetric criteria are met.[50]

Delivering babies underwater in so-called "water births" is now being offered as an option in about 200 hospitals in the United States. Proponents feel that the warm-water bathtub is more comfortable for the mother and less traumatic for the baby because it simulates the uterine environment. At the Oregon Health and Science University program, the neonatologist warns that the immersed baby should be removed from the water quickly to avoid near-drowning and deaths. Caution is advised in developing such new programs because of the high risk.[51]

Dystocia

A difficult birth caused by fetal or maternal abnormalities is known as dystocia. The most common causes of dystocia are cephalopelvic disproportion (the inability of the fetal head to pass through the maternal pelvis) and malpresentation (arrival of the fetus at the opening of the uterus in a position other than the normal head-first position). Each of these complications may indicate the need for a C-section delivery, use of tocolytic agents to relax the uterus, or fetal manipulation. If a vaginal delivery is to be attempted, it is recommended that a second physician be present to assist, anesthesia be readily available, and provision for emergency C-section be made.

Forceps and Vacuum Extraction

Obstetric forceps and vacuum extractors are designed to assist in removing the fetus from the birth canal at delivery when maternal contractions are insufficient. There is significant controversy in the medical literature regarding the use of these techniques. Maternal injuries associated with these adjunctive procedures include mild abrasions to severe lacerations of the vagina, cervix, and uterus. Fetal injuries include bruising; serious scalp, cranial, or brain injury; neurological damage; and eye injury. Litigation claims in neurologically impaired infants point to these techniques as the *prima facie* cause of permanent impairment, despite contrary research findings.

Cesarean Section

C-sections are performed in response to a variety of maternal and fetal indications, including previous cesarean delivery, dystocia, breech presentation, and fetal distress. Medical and legal literature suggests that the rate of C-sections performed is, in large part, dependent on a physician's concerns about malpractice litigation. Although the C-section includes inherent surgical risks, when elective it is a more rapid method of delivery. Studies indicate that the C-section rate has increased since 1997, reversing a former steady decline. A goal of having only 17 percent of births delivered via C-section has not been met, and the national average has risen to 22 percent.[51]

If the physician has decided to proceed with a C-section, it is generally recommended that the gestation be at term and that the mother be in active labor. An anesthesia consult should be obtained, blood should be typed and screened, fetal heart tones should be monitored immediately prior to preparation of the abdomen for surgery, infant resuscitation personnel should be in attendance, and a vaginal examination should be performed.[52]

Vaginal Birth after Cesarean (VBAC)

Many pregnant women and their physicians opt for a trial of labor and a vaginal delivery even after they have had as many as two C-section deliveries. With a VBAC, the medical profession recognizes that the need for anesthesia may decrease, some surgical risk is eliminated, and hospital stays are shorter. Documented risks include those associated with any vaginal delivery, as well as uterine rupture.[55] ACOG has issued a press release regarding the potential risks of VBACs[53] and has developed guidelines for VBACs.[56] It is important that the physician carefully identify appropriate candidates on the basis of limiting maternal or fetal clinical criteria. Past obstetric complications and certain social and geographic issues may justify the patient's electing to have a repeat C-section. Should the patient elect to try a VBAC, however, personnel and facilities for an emergency C-section should be readily available.

INFANT RESUSCITATION AND MANAGEMENT

On occasion, newborns require resuscitation immediately following birth. These compromised infants may be apneic or gasping at delivery. In collaboration with the American Heart Association and the American Academy of Pediatrics, the National Resuscitation Program was implemented to create infant resuscitation guidelines and to provide certification for health professionals. Guidelines recommend that at least one person skilled in resuscitating infants is present at every delivery. It is imperative that prior to the delivery the team be aware of who is designated to be responsible for infant intubation and resuscitation.[56]

Documentation of resuscitation efforts, meconium status, Apgar scores, umbilical cord blood test results, and the placental examination are important risk management issues in cases of compromised neonates, which could lead to litigation.

Meconium Management

Heavy or thick meconium (the first stools of a newborn) can indicate past, recent, or ongoing fetal risk or distress. Meconium should be described in the medical record by color, amount, consistency, and amount of staining of the neonate or placenta. If meconium is observed in the amniotic fluid, a staff member trained in neonatal resuscitation should be present at the delivery.

Management of the newborn is aimed at preventing aspiration of the meconium, and should include immediate suctioning, direct visualization of the trachea, and if necessary, suctioning using an endotracheal tube and meconium aspirator. During this procedure, the infant's heart rate should be monitored. If the heart rate falls, ventilation with 100 percent oxygen is recommended.[56]

Apgar Scoring

Apgar scoring is probably the most commonly used newborn assessment tool. Derived from an assessment of select clinical parameters, the score assists the clinician in determining the degree of infant resuscitation required as well as the effectiveness, over time, of the resuscitation efforts. Many clinicians associate a low Apgar score with subsequent identification of neurological disorder, although AAP and ACOG have recommended against using the Apgar score alone as "evidence of or consequent to substantial asphyxia."[57] Additional factors that should be considered include central nervous system immaturity, maternal sedation, and congenital malformations.

Umbilical Cord Blood Acid-Base Assessment

ACOG and AAP believe that umbilical cord blood acid-base assessment is a more objective measure of the acid-base status of a newborn than is the Apgar score.[58] If there is a question of intrapartum asphyxia or a low Apgar score, the literature recommends performing cord blood sampling. In the depressed newborn, the assessment can exclude intrapartum hypoxia as the cause of the depression. Since the sample may be delayed for up to 60 minutes before testing, the five-minute Apgar score should be determined prior to testing.

Placental Examination

An examination of the placenta can sometimes demonstrate whether an injury to the fetus, fetal maldevelopment, or birth trauma is responsible for asphyxia. It has been suggested that a placental examination "may reveal the cause of preterm labor, premature membrane rupture, fetal undergrowth, or antenatal hypoxia."[59] Several groups have examined the value of the placental examination. When based on specific clinical indicators and guidelines, this examination can prove beneficial as a risk management tool in the handling of claims related to fetal injury.[60]

Indications for pathological placental examinations are based on several maternal, fetal, and placental conditions.[61] Maternal conditions include severe preeclampsia, Rh isoimmunization, substance abuse, and insulin-dependent diabetes. Fetal conditions include fetal distress, meconium staining, suspected sepsis, and seizures. Placental conditions include abruption, masses, and abnormal appearance of the placenta or cord. Physicians can protect themselves from being sued over neurologically impaired newborns by saving the placenta when they suspect something is wrong.[62]

If clinical conditions indicate that a placenta examination may help provide answers to clinical complications, the physician should examine the placenta, document any abnormalities, and forward the placenta to the pathology department for further examination. Placental specimens should be retained for subsequent examination by a placental specialist for possible trial testimony. "The placenta may well be the key to a solid defense for these cases in the courtroom."[63]

MATERNAL EXAMINATION POST DELIVERY

From a risk management perspective, it is important that following the delivery the uterus be checked for retained vaginal sponges and retained placenta fragments. Some obstetricians choose not to explore the uterus following birth, for fear of causing pain or introducing infection, and may use ultrasound for the examination. A jury may find it difficult to understand why a physical examination was not performed.

With the trend toward shortened hospital stays following a normal delivery, mothers should be advised to call immediately if they experience excessive bleeding or discomfort when at home prior to their scheduled follow-up office visit.

FAMILY ATTENDANCE AND VIDEOTAPING OF BIRTH

Attendance of the father, significant others, and siblings has become so commonplace at births, that many clinicians do not associate the act as potentially damaging in the event of a malpractice lawsuit. A videotape of the birth may prove to be even more harmful during court proceedings. Most hospitals have a policy that provides guidance for the physician or nurse to ask visitors attending the birth to leave the delivery room or to stop videotaping. This request may be viewed by the visitors as a sign that something has gone wrong or that the medical team is trying to cover up their actions. In one case, the father's videotape was used to support his contention that errors were made during the delivery.[64] But a jury may view a normal delivery videotape and misinterpret what they see. If hospital staff is not simultaneously videotaping the medical team's actions during the delivery, the father's version of actions taped may be all that is presented in court. Lifesaving actions crucial to the case may not be captured on tape.

Standard practice seems to dictate that it would be impossible to bar visitors and videotaping during deliveries. Hospital policies and guidelines should be available to assist clinicians in directing visitors to turn off the camera and to leave the delivery room when requested. Staff should be reminded that a videotape is a permanent record of what they say and do during the birth and that requests to cease filming without direction to leave may lead to covert filming of subsequent actions. If the staff are interviewed on camera after the event, they must understand that the words they say may be subject to misinterpretation and used against them in a court of law.

Some hospitals and physicians have considered videotaping deliveries as a permanent part of the medical record. This policy could be very expensive and may not be in the best interests of the hospital in the event of an error or deviation from standard practice by the medical team. Other facilities choose to tape selected parts of the delivery or take still photographs of the pathology. Whatever the decision, in the event that visitors and videotaping are permitted, information such as visitors' names and the fact that videotaping occurred should be entered into the medical record. If a visitor is asked to leave the room and/or stop videotaping, this request should also be entered into the medical record.

MEDICAL RECORD DOCUMENTATION

Since legal action may be initiated as long as 21 years following the delivery in the case of an injured newborn, it is important that medical record documentation be accurate, objective, and complete, and provide the rationale to support all patient management decisions, including the decision not to intervene. A medical record should be created for all patients presenting themselves for care. Documentation should include the consent prior to all testing, the results of prenatal examinations and tests, and instructions given over the prenatal course. Testing or treatment refused by the mother, missed appointments, and attempts to contact the mother should also be recorded.

Physicians and risk managers alike have found that to ensure the best continuum of care, "copies of the initial history, physical findings, and laboratory data should be received by the hospital from the delivering physician or midwife soon after the first prenatal visit. At 36 weeks gestation, the patient's prenatal care record at the hospital should be updated and the patient counseled by her physician or a designee with regard to labor instructions and warnings."[39] If there was no prenatal care and there are indications of complications or a possibly difficult pregnancy, case management and risk management personnel should be notified to monitor the outcome of the mother and infant, as well as to facilitate subsequent follow-up. It is important that all events during the labor process and delivery be recorded, even if the mother has signs of early labor and is sent home to await more active labor; this record should include the physician's orders and discharge instructions given to the patient.

Fetal heart monitor tracings are considered a part of the medical record and should be filed in a manner that allows them to be retrieved easily up to 21 years after the birth. Tracings and tracing segments should be marked so that the record clearly reflects the event sequence, physician's interpretations, and assessments. Documentation during the delivery should include the condition of the mother, fetal station, and fetal status. Detailed notes in the medical record should include the indications and rationale for the delivery method selected. All maneuvers used in vaginal delivery, including those related to breech presentation or dystocia, should be listed. A narrative labor and delivery summary note should be recorded for each delivery, especially if there are clinically significant FHR patterns, low Apgar scores, low cord pH values, dystocia, preterm deliveries, fetal demise, or a newborn with significant morbidity. All adverse events or poor outcomes should be reflected through documentation of relevant clinical facts. However, it is vitally important that the caregivers do not speculate in the medical record regarding a poor outcome.

Postpartum documentation should include the postdelivery examination, and clinical indicators such as wound checks, bleeding, vital signs, and pain medications. With the shorter hospital stays for normal deliveries, there is less time for nursing interaction with the mother. Mothers at risk for infant care and self-care problems following discharge should be identified and referred to case management. Many facilities have introduced interactive video programs to facilitate the patient education and discharge process. However, an interactive video does not take the place of patient-nurse or patient-physician interaction. All discharge instructions, as well as planned follow-up for mothers with complications, should be documented in the medical record.

NEONATAL SERVICES

Following birth, infants are admitted to a nursery. The level of nursery service depends on the condition of the infant, the desires of the pediatrician or neonatologist, the availability of beds (for example, radiant warmers, incubators, bassinets), and staffing. In addition to the Level I, II, and III nurseries, many hospitals divide their nurseries into well baby and sick baby nurseries. Neonatal intensive care units (NICUs) are reserved for infants who are medically compromised and in need of complex medical technology and specially trained medical professionals. While providing benefits to the infants, these technologies also pose significant risk due, in part, to the compromised condition of the infant, the invasive nature of some therapies, and the sometimes inherent risks of the medical devices.

For routine births, neonatal services pose few liability risks. But with premature births, the expectation of malpractice claims is heightened. Infants with a low birth weight are biologically compromised and require time to mature and grow. Advances in science and technology have increased the ability of pediatricians and neonatologists to support tiny infants successfully for months with intensive care. During this time, diagnostic evaluation of the biological status of the infant is documented; congenital malformations are detected; corrective or emergency pediatric surgery may be performed; and general support of respiration, nutrition, fluid balance, and physiological functions is provided and monitored.

"Premature or otherwise compromised infants require a significant amount of clinical support during the first few weeks after birth."[64] Continuous observation in a therapeutic milieu with highly trained clinicians and nurses, high-tech equipment, and immediate attention to detectable alterations in status and adverse situations reduce the potential for liability in these units (see Box 13-7).

Risk management with these little babies involves early detection and speedy intervention in identifying conditions. Transient hypoxic events and intraventricular hemor-

BOX 13-7

Because her insurance company would not pay for a longer stay in the New Jersey Shore Medical Center (Neptune), Diane Weber and her newborn son left the hospital 36 hours after his birth. Her son became dehydrated, developed high bilirubin, and ended up in the neonatal ICU. A physician at the hospital said a longer stay would likely have meant that the conditions would have been spotted and treated before they became serious.[66]

rhages, pneumonitis, sepsis, ABO blood incompatibility, and excess bilirubin may not be avoidable, but these conditions should be evaluated with a subsequent appropriate response. Individualized case management and an interdisciplinary team approach are essential to improving medical neurodevelopmental outcome while reducing overall hospital charges.[65]

Detailed documentation of the continuing care in regular nurseries and in intensive care units is extremely important for defense in lawsuits. Daily status and changes, diagnoses, test results, consents from the parents, indicated medications and treatments, and periodic updated care plans are necessary parts of the infant's medical record.

Policies and procedures concerning the care of anencephalic infants and infants with multiple malformations, the use of universal precautions, the isolation of infected babies, routine screening tests, the involvement of parents in caring for the baby, and decision making are crucial.

Appropriate maintenance of equipment and training of staff in the use of and response to alarms and indicated infant problems help solidify the team approach to care. If used inappropriately or if malfunctioning, some equipment may cause unnecessary injury.

In comparison to the normal newborn nursery, where neonates stay only two days, intensive care infants stay for months, and the staff may become emotionally attached, as well as involved with family and visitors (see Box 13-8). Despite the best efforts and highest quality of care, deaths do occur. These serious events may be viewed by staff as personal failures and undermine confidence in their respective professional abilities. Group discussions and opportunities for venting feelings and attitudes should be promoted to reduce staff anxiety, stress, and potential loss of experienced staff to other professional activities.

The prolonged medical attention that babies who are born prematurely or with a very low weight require in order to survive to be discharged home raises issues concerning the quality of life.[68] Developmental delays, behavioral problems, neuromuscular deficits, mental retardation, cerebral palsy, and seizure disorders have been identified as unwanted sequelae and major contributions to the instigation of lawsuits.

When negligence claims are reviewed, it becomes difficult to distinguish among the various contributing factors: obstetric care versus anesthesia care versus neonatal care versus the risk itself of prematurity, which may be primary. Typically, in a scattershot approach, all parties are named in the suit:

BOX 13-8

In a newspaper "debate over care of preemies," a mother said it had never occurred to her and her husband to limit treatment to their premature son, who weighed 2.5 pounds at birth. She said that miracles happen in neonatal intensive care units regularly.[67]

hospital, obstetrician, anesthesiologist, neonatologist, pediatrician, consultants, and other caregivers identified in the medical record. From the risk manager's point of view, every baby treated in the neonatal intensive care unit is a potential liability action.

INFANT TRANSPORT

An infant's medical condition may require transport to a facility where a higher level of care is available. Level II and Level III facilities treat not only the infants born at the respective facilities, but also infants transferred from lower level facilities. Infants being transported are typically medically compromised and in need of specialized support and equipment.

Before transfer can occur, the sending facility must contact the receiving facility to ensure acceptance of the infant. AAP and ACOG have outlined the components of infant transport between facilities, including requirements for communications, staffing, essential equipment, vehicles, patient care, and program evaluation.[32] The referring physician is responsible for providing the receiving physician with pertinent clinical information regarding the infant. Generally, it is preferred that the maternal patient be transferred with the fetus in utero, when possible. It is important to remember that sound clinical judgment, as well as the Emergency Medical Treatment and Active Labor Act (EMTALA), requires that a pregnant patient not be transferred until she has been examined and stabilized and has provided consent. Transport should be ordered only if the risks of the transfer do not outweigh the risks of remaining at the original facility.

Copies of all records, tests, monitor tracings, and clinical status details of the pregnancy, labor, and delivery, as well as information related to the infant's physical examination, diagnostic tests, and therapeutic interventions, should be sent along with the patient. Transport records should include the team names, mode of transport, time of arrival and departure from the sending hospital, and time of arrival at the receiving facility. Procedures performed en route, medication administered, and periodic vital signs should be documented, as well as the condition of the patient upon arrival at the new facility.

Risk management should review transport events and investigate any difficulties during transport or technical and professional problems en route to reduce inherent risks in these transfers.

INFANT ABDUCTION

The mass media has paid a significant amount of attention to infants kidnapped from hospitals. Ninety-seven cases of infants abducted from medical facilities were reported between 1983 and 1997. The number of infant abductions appears to be declining, however, in large part probably because of proactive security measures, educational efforts, and a shortened length of stay in the hospital. In an attempt to circumvent infant abductions, many hospitals have discontinued publishing the names of newborns in the local newspapers.

Abducted infants are typically between a few hours and a few days old. In all documented abductions, the abductor was a female with no past criminal record. Usually, the woman had convinced friends and family that she had been pregnant for the past nine months.[69] The kidnapper typically posed as a medical caregiver and dressed in a hospital uniform. A majority of abductions occurred in the mother's room, followed by nursery, pediatrics, and other on-premise locations. Hospitals with delivery services and thus an increased potential for infant abductions should identify security problem areas, design access control systems, develop emergency procedures for responding to an abduction, and promote staff and patient education to reduce risks. Generally, security measures control entry into the nursery; secondarily, they supplement infection control efforts by minimizing traffic into the nursery. Many nurseries are located behind electronically locked and alarmed doors. Only staff with a need to enter should be provided access to the codes and/or electronic keys. Some hospitals utilize closed circuit television and electronic alarm wrist bands. Other areas to consider securing include stairwell and exit doors to maternity, postpartum, and pediatric units.

Risk management guidelines suggest that all staff who have contact with infants wear a photograph identification badge at all times, which should be checked by other staff, and especially by the mother. Although a difficult public relations issue, visitor control is of paramount importance.

Infant identification plays an important role in decreasing the likelihood of abductions and minimizes the potential for giving the wrong infant to the wrong mother. This process should start in the delivery room and include duplicate banding of the infant, mother, and significant other, along with the footprint, blood typing, photograph, and written assessment noting birthmarks and identifying features. If there is a need to remove the infant's identification band, it should be replaced immediately and the incident should be documented in the medical record.

HOME APNEA MONITORING

A major risk management concern with home apnea monitoring is the documented rate of parental noncompliance. Between 1985 and 1993, the Medical Device Report File of the Food and Drug Administration found that noncompliance or misuse of prescribed infant apnea monitors in the home setting occurred more than 54 percent of the time.[70] Noncompliance or misuse was shown to be more prevalent in homes where there was a lack of food, lack of sufficient financial resources, prevalence of illicit drugs, involvement in gangs, and lack of extended family to assist in child care. Monitor-related problems include false alarms, interference, and power loss. Because of these problems, ideally the selected device should have a secondary monitoring modality, such as heart rate monitoring, electrodes that cannot be inadvertently connected into electrical outlets, power loss alarms and/or low battery alarms, and remote alarm capability.[71]

Identification of mothers at risk for noncompliance should receive intense educational efforts and involve social services. Physician reaffirmation of the need for monitoring is imperative. Apnea monitors are primarily a prescription item available through a durable or home medical equipment supplier whose only roles are to supply the equipment and to provide preventive maintenance for it. It is the responsibility of the prescribing physician, and sometimes of case managers, to ascertain compliance, to monitor progress, and to discontinue use when indicated.

SURGERY AND ANESTHESIA

After ambulatory care in the office or clinic, the inpatient surgery department has the highest volume of claims (see Box 13-9). Approximately 24.2 percent of all claims are for inpatient surgery and 2.8 percent for outpatient surgery, according to the St. Paul's Fire and Marine Insurance Company. The average loss for surgery in the hospital was

BOX 13-9

- A Philadelphia jury awarded $100 million to a plaintiff in a malpractice case involving surgeries and other care to an infant born after only 26 weeks of gestation.
- In West Virginia, a jury awarded $2 million (even though there was a $1 million cap) for a patient who died from complications after anti-reflux surgery.

$115,405, and for the ambulatory care surgicenter it was $73,973.[1] The most frequent allegations related to surgery were:

- Postoperative complications
- Inadvertent acts
- Inappropriate procedures
- Postoperative death
- Unnecessary surgery

The most frequent allegations related specifically to inpatient surgery were:

- Treatment complications or bad results
- Injury adjacent to the treatment site
- Foreign body left in the patient
- Equipment malfunction or failure
- Infection, contamination, or exposure

Of these, the most common allegations were injuries incurred adjacent to the treatment site, infections from orthopedic surgery, and burns during inpatient surgery as a result of laser or cautery equipment failure. In outpatient claims, most allegations fell into the category of treatment problems, complications, or bad results, or involved postoperative infections in orthopedics. Postoperative complications account for 50 percent of the claims and nearly 50 percent of the cost of claims involving surgical issues (see Box 13-10).

BOX 13-10

- In June 1995, the headline read "Physician Erred in Brain Surgery." A neurosurgeon at a world-renowned hospital specializing in the treatment of cancer operated on the wrong side of a patient's head. Mistakenly, the surgeon brought another patient's diagnostic films into the operating room, then opened the wrong side of the surgical field and probed the healthy side of her brain for the tumor.[72]
- In February of 2002, the recurring headline read "Florida Hospital Neurosurgeon Slices Wrong Side of Head."[73]

NEGLIGENCE AND MALPRACTICE

Surgery and accompanying sedation or anesthesia are, by nature, risky. For example, surgical risk includes the potential for inadvertent amputation of the wrong limb, accidental damage to an organ or artery, hemorrhage, infection, or unexpected death or brain damage. Except in elective procedures, the patient undergoing surgery with accompanying anesthesia is usually in a medically compromised condition. However, from a legal perspective, patients of higher medical risk, such as the elderly, do not represent the greatest liability risk. It is the young, otherwise healthy, patient having elective or semi-elective surgery for whom damages can be considerable.

There are a plethora of surgical specialties, each with inherent risks and specialized technologies. Many hospitals require mandatory consultation and referrals for each specialized area. Surgery may be performed in various clinical settings, including tertiary teaching hospitals, community hospitals, ambulatory surgery centers, and physicians' offices.

Liability in the ambulatory surgery center rests on many of the same legal principles that apply to the inpatient setting.[78] As a result, it is imperative that consents are documented, adequate and complete preoperative assessments are made, and diagnostic testing and discharge instructions are provided to the patient (see Box 13-11).

SURGICAL SERVICES STAFF

Legally, the surgeon is considered the "captain of the ship" and works closely with teams to accomplish high-quality services. Surgical teams may consist of general surgeons, specialty surgeons, family practice physicians, podiatrists, anesthesia personnel, nursing staff, surgical technicians and assistants, surgical and anesthesia residents, heart-lung pump technicians, and radiology technicians, to name a few. Each team member is trained to perform specific tasks. Their actions may or may not be regulated by national certification or state licensure. With the advent of new procedures and technologies, it is imperative that all members of the specific surgical team for the surgery contemplated have appropriate training. Team members should perform only those procedures for which they have clinical privileges as provided by the medical staff bylaws and department regulations. Risk managers recommend that surgical operating room scheduling managers be provided with the list of hospital surgeons and their approved privileges to ensure that inappropriate surgeries are not scheduled.

Sales representatives who promote new equipment and technology present a host of risk management concerns. Physicians recognize the wealth of specific technical knowledge that these sales representatives have gained in areas such as implantable cardiac pacemakers or balloon pumps. However, the sales representative should only provide technical advice and not be allowed to scrub or to operate any equipment in the operating suite.

A continuing risk management issue for rural hospitals concerns the credentialing of "outreach" surgeons. Guidelines for the use of outreach surgeons were developed by the American Hospital Association's Division of Medical Affairs.[79] These surgeons should be credentialed and privileged in the same manner as all other medical staff members. Specific procedures appropriate for outreach surgery should be determined in advance by the medical staff, with approval by the hospital board of directors. Outreach surgeons should be included in the preoperative assessment of the patient and be instrumental in the decision to operate. Attending physicians should also be com-

BOX 13-11

- A review of 146 medical malpractice cases involving surgery of the lumbar spine disclosed that unintended "incidental" durotomy (23 cases) occurred with perioperative morbidity and long term sequelae.[74]
- For colon and rectal surgeons, causes of malpractice litigation in 98 cases from 103 allegations fell into five major categories: failure to diagnose colorectal cancer and appendicitis (43%); iatrogenic colon injury (24%); iatrogenic medical complications of diagnosis or treatment (15%); sphincter injury (10%); and lack of informed consent (8%).[75]
- Four-year-old Desiree Wade bled to death four days after undergoing a tonsillectomy. The New York State Health Department initiated a full-scale investigation into the death.[76]
- A District of Columbia ophthalmologist lost a malpractice action for allegedly failing to diagnose adenocarcinoma of the lacrimal duct.[77]

petent in the skills required for postoperative care.

PREOPERATIVE ASSESSMENT AND TREATMENT

Successful surgery requires quality clinical and technical skills of the surgical team and effective preoperative assessment, treatments, and diagnostic testing that ready the patient for surgery. The Joint Commission on Accreditation of Healthcare Organizations (JCAHO) states that surgery may be performed only "after a history, physical examination, any indicated diagnostic tests, and the preoperative diagnosis have been completed and recorded in the patient's medical record."[80] Both aggressors and defense factors should be included in the assessment.[81] Aggressors include the type of surgical procedure and anesthesia, carcinoma, infection, medications, chemotherapeutic agents, and radiation. Defense factors include the immune system, nutritional condition, and physiological status.

Preoperative treatments may prepare the physiological state of the patient to deal with factors of aggression. Yet one study, based on a population of more than 2,500 patients in New York, found that nearly 40 percent of patients undergoing inpatient surgical procedures may not have received antibiotics in the proper time frame to be most effective. Medical literature indicates that 25 percent of all postoperative nosocomial infections occur at the site of the surgical incision.[82]

Risk managers must be concerned that often insufficient attention is paid to preoperative protocols. Patient education about what to expect as a result of the surgery, with an emphasis on what the patient's responsibilities are for care and monitoring, can improve the preoperative preparation of the patient.

INTRAOPERATIVE RISK ISSUES

Risk management should be notified of all unusual occurrences in surgical patients and the operating room suite, such as: surgery on the wrong patient; performance of the wrong procedure; medication error; patient return to surgery for repair or removal of an organ or body part damaged in surgery or subsequently; and unexpected patient return to surgery or unplanned readmission to hospital (see Box 13-12). No operation or procedure should be performed for which the surgeon does not have clinical privileges.

Many intraoperative issues are of high risk and pervade several surgical specialties: anesthesia services, blood contact, implants, retained foreign bodies, and burns.

Sedation and Anesthesia

In their many forms, sedation and anesthesia remove the patient's ability to control his or her own actions—in some cases introducing paralysis of limbs, cessation of unassisted breathing, and inability to

BOX 13-12

- An 83-year-old woman with carpal tunnel syndrome was operated on the wrong wrist.[83]
- Comedian Dana Carvey settled a $7.5 million law suit against New York Hospital and his cardiothoracic surgeon when CABG surgery in 1998 bypassed the wrong artery. He had three prior angioplasty surgeries and was subsequently successfully treated with another angioplasty in California.[84]
- An intravenous line was preoperatively inserted into the radial nerve of a 29-year-old woman admitted for outpatient, elective nose reconstruction. The arbitration award was $155,000.[85]

respond to pain. Responsibility for assuring quality of life, viability, and a minimum of pain remains with the surgeon, anesthesiologist, and surgical support team. Anestheisa services may be provided by anesthesiologists, certified registered nurse anesthetists (CRNAs), and in some rural facilities, by general surgeons and obstetricians.

Perioperative complications resulting from anesthesia include hypetension; myocardial ischemia or infarction, and arrhythmias or cardiac arrest; oliguria; hypothermia; malignant hyperthermia; and respiratory arrest or anoxic episodes.[86] On the basis of more than 3,000 cases over a nine-year period, from 1986 to 1995, the American Society of Anesthesiologists Closed Claims Project indicated that the frequency of anesthesia-related claims for adverse respiratory events and the frequency of claims involving death and brain injury were both decreasing.[87]

Because of the complex and life support nature of anesthesia equipment, the Food and Drug Administration (FDA) introduced recommendations for anestheisa apparatus checkout in 1986. In 1993, the use of a revised FDA checklist or a similar one was recommended to inspect the anesthesia system prior to each use.[88] The inspection checklist includes:

- Emergency backup equipment
- Anesthesia machine
- Waste gas scavenging system
- Oxygen supplies
- Oxygen pressure failure system
- Flow meters
- Warning systems
- Accessory equipment
- Machine or breathing equipment leaks
- Ventilator
- Patient suction aparatus
- Electronic monitors
- Airway pressure alarms
- Volume monitor alarms
- Central and cylinder supplies of nitrous oxide and other gases

A preanesthesia assessment should be based on the patient's medical, anesthesia, and medication history; an appropriate physical examination; a review of diagnostic data; and the formulation and discussion of the anestheisa plan with the patient. Provision of detailed information about the risks of complications of general anesthesia on the eve of surgery generally does increase the patient's knowledge without increasing the patient's level of anxiety.[89] Patients must also be reevaluated immediately before the induction of anesthesia.

Noninvasive patient monitoring during anesthesia usually includes blood pressure, pulse, respiratory efforts, skin color, temperature, and electrocardiograms. Capnometry is used on expired gas to measure the concentration of end tidal carbon dioxide as a reflection of patient oxygenation, whereas pulse oximetry can provide an indication of arterial oxygen saturation. Electro-encephalography (EEG) and evoked potentials, although not widely in use, have been used as indicators of unacceptable changes in brain activity as a measure of oxygen perfusion. Invasive monitoring, such as central venous pressure, continuous arterial blood pressure, or pulmonary artery monitoring, is typically used for critically ill patients and for complex surgical procedures (for example, bypass surgery) that allow and require a more continuous method of monitoring.

If intravenous sedation, also called conscious sedation, is frequently administered to patients undergoing outpatient surgery, and there are no anesthesia staff present, there should be strict protocols in place regarding the types of cases and clinical parameters to be monitored by nurses, and steps to be taken in the event of complications.

Prevention of hypothermia is an important aspect of anesthesia management. Some methods used for its prevention, such as warmed intravenous fluid bags or bottles, cause cutaneous burns and are not recommended.[90] Adverse results of anesthesia can result from injury during intubation or extubation; allergic reaction to drugs or transfusions; and equipment failure. Death during surgery implicates surgeons and anesthesia personnel, as well as all other members of the team.

Perioperative Blood Contact

A major risk to surgical team members includes perioperative blood contact and sharps injuries. Blood exposure is associated with increased risk of infection from blood-borne pathogens, including hepatitis B, hepatitis C, HIV, and AIDS. Several authors believe that the incidence of blood exposure among surgical team members has been vastly underreported (see Box 13-13).[91]

A study of more than 8,500 surgical cases in nine hospitals showed that more than 10 percent of the cases resulted in one or more instances of blood contact. Of these contacts, two percent were the result of punctures. Other studies found percutaneous blood exposure of almost five percent and glove perforation as high as 50 percent, although the surgeons were only aware of 15 percent of the perforations.[92] Blood contact included blood soaking through surgical attire and onto the skin of the team member, mucous membrane contact, blood spatter on the face or neck, and sharps lacerations or punctures. Blood exposure is a two-way street. Staff members need to protect themselves from the patient, but the patient also needs to be protected from staff (see Box 13-14).

Risk management should include careful attention to the requirements of universal precautions as recommended by the federal Centers for Disease Control and Prevention and mandated by the Occupational Safety and Health Administration (OSHA). However, reputable authorities have commented that careful adherence to the OSHA recommendations alone may not be effective in reducing exposure risks, since constant vigilance is not possible to maintain or expect. Many facilities are using fully fluid-resistant surgical gowns rather than gowns with fluid-resistant panels; double gloving, or replacement of surgical gloves at intervals throughout the surgery; protective eye wear such as face shields or splatter guards; "no touch" instrument passing; blunted instruments; and careful attention to sharps management.

Whenever possible, needleless systems should be used.[94] Self-sheathing or blunting needles and appropriate sharps waste disposal units should be available. Vaccinations, such as for hepatitis B, should be encouraged for staff. Protocols for responding to an exposure should be in place and

BOX 13-13

A surgeon who put patients at risk by operating on them while knowing he was a hepatitis B carrier was sentenced to one year of imprisonment.[93]

BOX 13-14

In *Faya v. Almaraz*, a Maryland appellate court ruled that a surgeon who was HIV-positive had an obligation to inform patients, thus suggesting the opportunity for recovery of damages by patients even if they had not been infected.[95]

understood by all. In some types of surgery, it is important to understand the potential "sharpness" of patient anatomy. A fractured bone end poses a risk to a finger probing in an open fracture or surgical wounds.

Surgical teams must be vigilant and recognize and report risk events such as major breaches of sterile technique, or blood contact with patients at high risk for bloodborne pathogens.

Biomedical Implants

Medical implants are a significant concern in surgical liability. Breast augmentation has become the most often performed plastic surgery; conservative estimates are that one million procedures have been performed in the United States.[96] Implant materials, such as some polymers, have been alleged to contribute to systemic and local clinical complications that arise years after the implant surgery (see Box 13-15).

Implants of all types may also wear excessively, break or fracture, and be useless years after the surgery. The question of whether to remove an implant is one of great concern to the medical community. Although there are potentially serious risks to allowing the defective implant to remain *in situ*, there are also serious concerns about the clinical hazards of removing the implant.

Mandates of the Safe Medical Devices Act (SMDA) require tracking of specific medical implants from point of purchase through the implant's end of life. Implants that require tracking are:[97]

- Replacement heart valve (mechanical only)
- Implantable cardiac pacemaker pulse generator
- Implanted diaphragmatic or phrenic nerve stimulator
- Implantable infusion pump
- Vascular graft prosthesis
- Implanted cerebellar stimulator
- Cardiovascular permanent cardiac pacemaker electrode
- Temporomandibular joint (TMJ) prosthesis
- Glenoid fossa prosthesis
- Mandibular condyle prosthesis
- Abdominal aortic aneurysm stent grafts
- Dura mater
- Automatic, implantable, cardioverter defibrillator

Since hospitals, licensed practitioners, and ambulatory surgical facilities are required to participate in this program, they should have policies that require tracking and that designate staff responsibility for tracking. Information must be sent to the manufacturer about the implant, the physician, and the patient at the time of receipt, implantation, and the end of the implant's useful life. Failure of permanently implantable devices could have serious adverse health consequences.

BOX 13-15

Brenda Toole, a woman who had to undergo three operations to have silicone removed from her body after her breast implants ruptured, was awarded $6 million in her lawsuit against the implants' manufacturer, the Baxter Healthcare Corporation.[98]

Retained Foreign Bodies

Defense of cases involving a retained foreign body after surgery are very difficult. Courts expect surgeons to be aware of what they use on the patient in the operating room as well as what is removed from the patient. In an effort to minimize the risk of leaving these items in the surgical cavity, the American Association of Operating Room Nurses has developed recommended practices regarding sponge, sharps, and instrument count procedures.[99] If the initial and final counts are not in agreement, an X-ray of the surgical field is recommended prior to the patient's leaving the surgical table. Incorrect instrument, sponge, or sharp counts may necessitate further exploration at the surgical site (see Box 13-16).

Claims of foreign objects or material found following surgery should initiate a thorough investigation by risk management of the medical record to identify lapses in procedure and to prevent further occurrences.

Patient Burns and Pressure Injuries

During surgery, a patient may experience what appears to be a chemical or thermal burn or a pressure injury. Chemical burns may result from the fluid used to clean the surgical site prior to the surgical procedure or the adhesive conductive gel used under the dispersive electrode of an electrosurgical unit (ESU). Thermal burns may result if the patient is placed too close to a surgical light, if an operating microscope is reassembled incorrectly, or if an ESU is used. Pressure injuries, which mimic the appearance of burns, may result from sustained normal pressure during surgery, from body weight, and from external objects that reduce or impede local circulation.[101] Vascular insufficiency may also contribute to pressure injuries. Incorrect positioning of the patient may lead to neural injuries or impairment. Additional risks are inherent in surgical patients who are elderly, who are malnourished or obese, or whose delicate skin is compromised by their basic medical status.

Since a majority of the patient's body is beneath surgical drapes and not visible to the surgical team, constant attention to placement of the patient's extremities is important. Meticulous attention to detail in positioning the patient, pressure distribution devices, and padding, and careful clamping of towels may help eliminate some pressure injuries. Inspection, maintenance, and appropriate placement of electrical accessories and use of devices will reduce unintended burns and future patient discomfort. Documentation of positioning and placement of electrodes protects staff from allegations of poor practices.

Any type of patient injury, reddening of the skin, or break in skin integrity not identified prior to surgery or noticed immediately after surgery or during postoperative recuperation should be examined, treated, and documented in the medical record, as well as thoroughly investigated and reported to risk management.

BOX 13-16

- A blue towel and part of her colostomy bag were left behind in the body of a woman after two separate operations in a city-owned hospital. She was awarded a settlement of $125,000.[83]
- Eight surgical patients required second operations to retrieve sponges, cotton, or metal instruments left inside their bodies.[100]

Laser Surgery

Laser surgery has introduced new and specialized risks to the surgical team and the patient. To ensure safe laser practices, guidelines were developed by the American National Standards Institute (ANSI) the Association of Operating Room Nurses (AORN), the American Society for Laser

Medicine and Surgery (ASLMS), and the Laser Institute of America (LIA).

According to the ANSI, the most common accidents related to laser medicine are burns and eye injuries to the surgical team members, fires, patient burns, and accidental laser activation. The FDA reported that the most common cause of laser-related incidents was mechanical malfunction.[102] Malpractice claims associated with laser surgery have included allegations of lack of informed consent, improper usage, fire, explosion, nerve damage, scarring, disfigurement, and infection. Safety protocols typically include the use of nonflammable surgical drapes, nonreflective surgical instruments, skin preparation of the surgical site with nonflammable agents, endotracheal intubation with tubes made of nonflammable materials specific to laser type, and the use of nonflammable anesthetics.

Several recent newspaper series relative to elective plastic surgery in the *Sun Sentinel* (Florida),[103] the *Philadelphia Inquirer*,[100] and the *Boston Globe*[104] exposed the problems of unexpected deaths, scars, burns, and disfigurements from laser surgeries. Most of these procedures are done in outpatient offices in the community, but the patients are then seen in the hospital after trouble erupts. Some practitioners are unqualified for the procedures they perform.

Physicians should be credentialed and privileged prior to using lasers in surgery. Privileging should encompass specific laser types, as well as types of laser surgery to be performed. Access to the laser and the activation mechanisms should be controlled, and protective eye wear and/or in-line eye protective measures should be provided to staff. Adequate smoke evacuation and filtering is important, as is the availability of a secondary means to control bleeding. Potentially reflective surfaces should be identified and steps taken to minimize the risk. The availability and application of operational safety guidelines and manufacturer's protocols for staff will help reduce the risks inherent in this technology.[100]

POSTOPERATIVE RECOVERY CARE

Following surgery, patients are transported to the postanesthesia/recovery room or intensive care unit for monitoring and stabilization by specially trained physicians, nurses, and ancillary staff. The patient's postoperative status should be assessed on admission to the unit and reassessed prior to discharge. Monitoring should include the patient's physiological and mental status such as vital signs and level of consciousness; pathological findings; medication, fluid, blood, or blood components administration; and unusual events or postoperative complications, as well as management of those complications.[90]

Postoperative risk management issues concern serious adverse clinical events during transfer to the recovery area; adverse results of anesthesia; medication or transfusion reactions; cardiac or respiratory arrest or death; and postoperative neurological deficits not present on admission (see Box 13-17).

BOX 13-17

Following seven hours of surgery to correct a congenital heart condition on a 2-1/2 year-old, the girl was weaned from a respirator, developed difficulty breathing, turned blue, and was revived. The surgeon was sued for negligent postoperative care because the lack of oxygen left the child clinically blind and mentally retarded. Seventeen years later, the jury awarded $5 million to the girl's family.[106]

It is usually the responsibility of the anesthesia personnel to discharge a patient from the recovery room, but some facilities permit the nursing staff to use discharge criteria protocols. Such protocols are developed through the joint efforts of anesthesia, surgical, and nursing staff, and should have the approval of the medical board.

INFORMED CONSENT

Consent is of particular importance when discussing risk management in surgery and anestheisa. Because of the significant potential for injury, the invasiveness of the procedures, and the medical alternatives sometimes available, there is general consensus that the patient and/or legal medical guardian is entitled to an understanding of the procedure, including risks and benefits, as well as alternatives to the procedure. Although requirements for the level of information to be afforded to the patient are highly dependent on state consent laws, there are universally accepted principles expected by risk management and the legal community.

Achieving an informed consent from the patient is primarily the responsibility of the health care practitioner delivering the service. While the surgeon is responsible for the consent discussion with the patient regarding the surgical procedure to be performed, it is the anesthesiologist's responsibility to discuss anesthesia risks and to obtain consent from the patient for anesthesia services. Consent forms are viewed by the court as administrative evidence that health care practitioners had a consent discussion with the patient, not that consent was fully achieved. A witness who signs the consent form is attesting to the signature of the patient, not to the patient's informed consent to proceed with the procedure.

Of particular interest to surgical and anesthesia personnel is the issue of advance directives and whether they are to be honored during surgical procedures or while the patient is under the influence of anesthesia. Many facilities addressed this dilemma through their ethics committees.

MEDICAL RECORD DOCUMENTATION

Medical record documentation concordant with surgical procedures requires that documentation of the preoperative stage include diagnosis, review of the patient's history and physical status, preoperative nursing, review of diagnostic test results, assessment of the risks and benefits of the procedure, the need to administer blood or blood components, consent, and preanesthesia documentation. A plan of care should be generated to include the nursing care, the operative plan, the level of postsurgery care, and the need for additional diagnostic testing or monitoring. Documentation should also reflect the anesthesia process, as well as the nursing and medical course of the surgery.

Postoperative documentation must reflect the care delivered to the patient and the patient's condition in the recovery room and/or intensive care unit, as well as the clinical parameters monitored. Medical records must identify who provided direct patient care nursing services and who supervised that care if provided by someone other than a qualified registered nurse. Daily charting of the physician's assessment of the patient's progress, monitoring and testing, dressing changes and medications, and plans for discharge are necessary. Medical records should also note the name of the licensed, independent practitioner responsible for the discharge, and record discharge instructions for care and follow-up services.

JCAHO requires that the patient's medical record contain evidence of known advance directives, informed consent for procedures for which informed consent is required by hospital policy, and documentation of all operative procedures performed. JCAHO also requires that the medical record of patients undergoing operative procedures and/or anesthesia include the following elements:[90]

- The name of the licensed, independent practitioner who is responsible for the patient, as well as the name of the primary surgeon and all assistants.
- The preoperative diagnosis documented by the licensed, independent practitioner responsible for the patient.
- Operative reports dictated or written in the medical record immediately following surgery.
- The operative report that includes the findings, technical procedures used, specimens removed, and postoperative diagnosis.
- Authentication of completed operative report by the surgeon as soon as possible.
- An operative progress note in the event that there is a delay in placing the operative report in the medical record.

IT'S A RISKY BUSINESS

All the contacts between a patient and the multiple professionals and ancillary personnel involved in the provision of health care services should be meticulously documented. This documentation is the major defense against allegations of medical negligence or incompetence when there has been no breach of community accepted standards of care. Although accidents and misadventures are not entirely avoidable, the organization's and risk manager's objective is to provide high-quality services, to prevent medical disasters, and to limit damages resultant from, and incidental to, unintended untoward happenings.

References

1. *Health Care Update*. (2002). Hospital Issues. The St. Paul's Health Care Claims Analysis. The St. Paul Companies: St. Paul, Minn.
2. Mayer, T. A. (1995). Emergency diagnoses are mostly accurate. *Wall Street Journal*, June 12, p. A13, col. 1.
3. Rogers, J. T. (1985). *Risk Management in Emergency Medicine*. Dallas: American College of Emergency Physicians, pp. 1–36.
4. St. Paul's Fire & Marine Insurance Co. (1993). Patient care area, emergency and inpatient surgery generate most hospital claims. *Hospital Update* Annual Report, St. Paul, Minn.
5. American Hospital Association, Special Member Briefing. (1992). *Emergency Medical Treatment and Active Labor Act Requirements and Investigation*. Chicago: American Hospital Association, pp. 1–12.
6. Centers for Disease Control and Prevention. (2002). Emergency Department Statistics. Washington, D.C.: United States Department of Health and Human Services.
7. American College of Emergency Physicians. (1987). *Policy Statement on Medical Control of Pre-hospital Emergency Medical Services*. Dallas: ACEP.
8. American Medical Association Commission on Emergency Medical Services. (1989). *Guidelines for the Categorization of Hospital Emergency Capabilities*. Chicago: AMA, CEMS, pp. 7–29.
9. Sexton, J. (1995). Differing accounts of a firefighter's care. *New York Times*, March 8, p. B6, col. 4.
10. Reigner, W. (1993). Escalating risk: Violence in the ED. *QRC Advisor* 9(8):1–4.
11. Foust, D., and Rhee, K. J. (1993). The incidence of battery in an urban emergency department. *Annals of Emergency Medicine* 22(3):583–585.
12. Managing traumatic stress. (1994). *Occupational Hazard* 56(10):212.
13. Protection from Physical Violence in the Emergency Department. (2001). *Clinical Policies*. Irving, Tex.: American College of Emergency Physicians.

14. Hobgood, C. D., John, O., et al. (2000). Emergency medicine resident errors: Identification and educational utilization. *Academic Emergency Medicine* 7(11):1317–1320.
15. ED doctors don't always have the right skills. (1994). *American Medical News* 37(37):11.
16. Reilly, B. M. (2002). Impact of a clinical decision rule on hospital triage of patients. *Journal of the American Medical Association* 288:342–350.
17. Hevesi, D. (1994). State assails mistreatment by hospital in rape case. *New York Times,* December 31, p. A29, col. 1.
18. American College of Emergency Physicians, Professional Liability Committee. (1989). *Providing Telephone Advice from the Emergency Department: Position Statement*. Dallas: ACEP, PLC.
19. Clark, S. (1994). Implementation of voice recognition technology at Provenant Health Partners. *Journal of American Health Information Management Association* 65(2):34–37.
20. Principles of appropriate patient transfer. (1990). *Annals of Emergency Medicine* 19(2):337–338.
21. Healthcare Providers Service Organization. (2001). Case of the Month, May. *http//www.hpso.com/case.*
22. Mantel, D. L. (1995). The legal perils of patient discharge. *RN* 58(3):49–51.
23. American College of Obstetrics and Gynecologists (ACOG). (2002). Nation's Obstetrical Care Endangered by Growing Liability Crisis. News release, May 6.
24. Bronstein, J. M., Capilouto, E., Carlo, W. A., et al. (1995). Access to neonatal intensive care for low-birthweight infants: The role of maternal characteristics. *American Journal of Public Health* 85(3):357–361.
25. Hack, M., Taylor, H. G., Klein, N., et al. (1994). School-age outcomes in children with birth weights under 750 grams. *New England Journal of Medicine* 331(12):753–759.
26. Failing our babies. (1995). *Neonatal Intensive Care* 8(3):11.
27. Ward, C. J. (1991). Analysis of 500 obstetric and gynecologic malpractice claims: Causes and prevention. *American Journal of Obstetrics & Gynecology* 165(2):298–303.
28. Hickson, G., Clayton, E. W., Githens, P. B., and Sloan, F. A. (1992). Factors that prompted families to file medical malpractice claims following perinatal injuries. *Journal of the American Medical Association* 268(11):1359–1363.
29. Entman, S. S., Glass, C. A., Hickson, G. B., et al. (1994). The relationship between malpractice claims history and subsequent obstetrical care. *Journal of the American Medical Association* 272(20): 1588–1591.
30. Hickson, G. B., Clayton, E. W., Entman, S. S., et al. (1994). Obstetricians' prior malpractice experience and patients' satisfaction with care. *Journal of the American Medical Association* 272(20):1583–1587.
31. American College of Obstetricians and Gynecologists (ACOG). (2001). Code of Ethics. Washington, D.C.
32. Frigoletto, F. D., and Little, G. A. (1992). *Guidelines for Perinatal Care,* 3d edition. Elk Grove Vilage, Ill.: American Academy of Pediatrics and the American College of Obstetricians and Gynecologists, pp. 37–47.
33. Midwife care generates NY ruckus. (1995). *Medical Liability Monitor* 20(5):5, 8.
34. Capen, K. (1995). New prenatal screening procedures raise specter of more "wrongful-birth" claims. *Canadian Medical Association Journal* 152(5): 734–737.
35. Kotula, C. (1994). High risk pregnancy. *Continuing Care* 13(3):16–19, 28.
36. Statute of repose runs from time of negligence. (1995). *American Medical News* 38(11):19.
37. American College of Obstetrics and Gynecology. (1994). Antepartum fetal surveillance. *Technical Bulletin* No. 188 (January):3.
38. Evans, H. (1995). Technology: Docotors who perform fetal sonograms often lack sufficient training and skill. *Wall Street Journal,* June 20, p. 2, col. 13.
39. Maley, R. A., and Epstein, A. L. (1993). *High Technology in Health Care: Risk Management Perspectives.* Chicago: American Hospital Publishing, pp. 235, 244.
40. U.S. Department of Health and Human Services, Public Health Service, Preventive Services Task Force. (1993). Home uterine activity monitoring for preterm labor: Policy statement. *Journal of the American Medical Association* 270(3):369–370.
41. McClinton, D. H. (1995). Monitoring devices are not essential for improving birth. *Continuing Care* 14(2):5.
42. Catanzarite, V. A., Perkind, R. P., and Pernoll, M. L. (1987). Assessment of fetal well-being. In *Current Obstetric & Gynecologic Diagnosis & Treatment.* Norwalk, Conn.: Appleton & Lange, p. 286.
43. American College of Obstetrics and Gynecology. (1992). Fetal and neonatal neurologic injury. *Technical Bulletin* No. 163 (January).

44. American College of Obstetrics and Gynecology. (1995). Fetal heart rate patterns: Monitoring, interpretation and management. *Technical Bulletin* No. 207 (July).

45. Petrikovsky, B. (1993). Is fetal heart rate monitoring during labor and delivery justified? *Neonatal Intensive Care* 6(4):19–20, 48.

46. Curran, C. (1993). The fetal monitoring position. Second source. *Biomedical Bulletin* 7(3):28.

47. American College of Obstetrics and Gynecology. (1991). Induction and augmentaiton of labor. *Technical Bulletin* No. 157 (July):1–3.

48. Frankel, D. H. (1995). New York's obstetric mess. *Lancet* 345(8951):716.

49. Chadwick, H. S., Posner, K., Caplan, R. A., et al. (1991). A comparison of obstetric and nonobstetric anesthesia malpractice claims. *Anesthesiology* 74(2): 242–249.

50. American College of Obstetrics and Gynecology. (1986). Management of breech presentation. *Technical Bulletin* No. 95 (August).

51. Report says water-birth may be risky. (2002). *Home News Tribune* (New Brunswick, N.J.), August 6, 7:1.

52. American College of Obstetrics and Gynecologists (ACOG). (2000). OB-Gyns Issue Recommendations on Cesarean Delivery Rate. News release.

53. American College of Obstetrics and Gynecologists (ACOG). (2001). ACOG Addresses Latest Controversies in Obstetrics: When Planning for Vaginal Delivery May Not Be Appropriate. News release.

54. Marta, M. R. (1994). Current topics in obsterical risk management, Part II. *Journal of Healthcare Quality* 6(6):6.

55. American College of Obstetrics and Gynecology, Committee on Obstetric Practice. (1991). Guidelines for vaginal delivery after a previous cesarean birth. *Committee Opinion* No. 64.

56. Osbourne, S. E., and Kassity, N. A. (1993). Neonatal resuscitation program update. *Neonatal Intensive Care* 6(6):32–33.

57. American College of Obstetrics and Gynecology, Committee on Obstetric Practice and American Academy of Pediatrics, Committee on Fetus and Newborn. (1991). *Use and Misuse of the Apgar Score.* ACOG/AAP Committee Opinion. Washington, D.C.: ACOG.

58. American College of Obstetrics and Gynecology, Committee on Obstetric Practice and American Academy of Pediatrics, Committee on Fetus and Newborn. (1994). *Utility of Umbilical Cord Acid-Base Assessment.* ACOG/AAP Committee Opinion. Washington, D.C.: ACOG.

59. Marta, M. R. (1994). Current topics in obstetrical risk management, Part 1. *Journal of Healthcare Quarterly* 6(5):7.

60. Stoeckmann, A. (1994). Placental examination as a risk management tool. *Journal of Healthcare Risk Management* 14(1):9–14.

61. Arizona Medical Association, Placental Project. (1992). *Enhancing Placental Examination: The Vision and the Professional Opportunity.* Phoenix: AMA.

62. Clements, B. (1994). Don't get sued. *American Medical News* 37(29):15–17.

63. Schindler, N. R. (1991). Importance of the placenta and cord in the defense of neurologically impaired infant claims. *Archives of Pathology & Laboratory Medicine* 115(7):685–687.

64. OB/GYN claims: Analysis and advice. (1994). *Forum* 4(5):105

65. Als, H., Lawhon, G., Duffy, F. H., et al. (1994). Individualized developmental care for the very low-birthweight preterm infant. *Journal of the American Medical Association* 272(11):853–858; Merenstein, G. B. (1994). Individualized developmental care: An emerging new standard for neonatal intensive care units? *Journal of the American Medical Association* 272(11):890–891.

66. Shaheen, J. (1995). Longer stay needed, a mother says. *New York Times,* March 5, p. 14, col. 5.

67. Umansky, A. B. (1994). Parents thankful for tiny miracles. *Wall Street Journal,* December 8, p. A19, col. 1.

68. Solomon, S. D. (1995). Suffer the little children. *Technology Review* 98(3):42–51.

69. Colling, R. L. (1994). Code pink—code pink. *Continental Rx* 6(2):4.

70. McIntyre, C. H. (1995). Monitoring compliance. *Home Health Care Dealer/Supplier* 6(2):51.

71. Picciano, L. D., and Keller, J. P. (1993). Hospital and home apnea documentation systems: Device acquisition and application. *Neonatal Intensive Care* 6(4):28–31.

72. McShane, L. (1995). Physician erred in brain surgery. *Philadelphia Inquirer,* June 23, p. A18, col. 3.

73. *Naples Daily News.* (2002). February 27.

74. Goodkin, R., and Laska, L. L. (1995). Unintended "incidental" durotomy during surgery of the lumbar spine: Medicolegal implications. *Surgical Neurology* 43(1):4–12.

75. Kern, K. A. (1993). Medical malpractice involving colon and rectal disease: A 20 year review of U.S. civil court litigation. *Diseases of the Colon & Rectum* 36(6):531–539.

76. Rosenthal, E. (1995). Full inquiry into death of girl, 4. *New York Times*, April 4, p. B3, col. 6.

77. "Migraine sinus" was lacrimal gland cancer. (1995). *American Medical News* 38(9):19.

78. Quan, K. P., and Wieland, J. B. (1994). Medicolegal considerations for anesthesia in the ambulatory setting. *International Anesthesiology Clinics* 32(3):145–169.

79. McCormick, B. (1989). Hospital policy on outreach surgery. *Trustee* January:17.

80. Joint Commission on Accreditaiton of Healthcare Organizations. (1995). *Accreditation Manual for Hospitals*, vol. 1: *Standards*. Oakbrook Terrace, Ill.: JCAHO, pp. 6–7, 16–17, 58–59.

81. Gagner, M. (1991). Value of pre-operative physiologic assessment in outcome of patients undergoing major surgical procedures. *Surgical Clinics of North America: Complications of General Surgery* 71(6):1141–1150.

82. Surgical patients in New York hospitals may not receive optimum antibiotic treatments. (1994). *Island Peer Review Organization Quality Initiatives* Summer:10.

83. Why it matters: The medical system is a leading killer. (2002). *Medical Errors and Malpractice*. Minneapolis, Minn. The Association of Health Care Journalists.

84. Falcon, M. (2001). Heart operation no laugh for Dana Carvey. *USA Today*, Health Spotlight. November 5.

85. Delegal, M. K. (2001). IV inserted to nerve results in radial nerve injury: $155,000 arbitration award. *Legal Review & Commentary Supplement, Healthcare Risk Management*. January.

86. Entrup, M. H., and Davis, F. G. (1991). Periopeative complications of anesthesia. *Surgical Clinics of North America: Complications of General Surgery* 71(6):1151–1174.

87. Saidman, L. J. (1995). Anesthesiology. *Journal of the American Medical Association* 273(21):1661.

88. U.S. Department of Health and Human Services, Food and Drug Administration. (1994). *Anesthesia Apparatus Checkout Recommendations*. Rockville, Md.: FDA.

89. Inglis, S., and Farnill, D. (1993). The effects of providing preoperative statistical anaesthetic-risk information. *Anaesthesia & Intensive Care* 21(6): 799–805.

90. Cheney, F. W., Fosner, K. L., Caplan, R. A., and Gild, W. M. (1994). Burns from warming devices in anesthesia: A closed claims analysis. *Anesthesiology* 80(4):806–810.

91. Lynch, P., and White, M. C. (1993). Perioperative blood contact and exposures: A comparison of incident reports and focused studies. *American Journal of Infection Control* 21(6):357–363.

92. Noera, G. (1994). Blood contact during open heart operations: Reducing the risk. *Annals of Thoracic Surgery* 57(3):785–786.

93. Choo, V. (1994). Jail for putting patients at risk of hepatitis B. *Lancet* 344(8928):1012.

94. Needlestick Safety and Prevention Act (House of Representatives 5178) H.R. 5178. Passed November 6, 2000. United States Congress: Washington, D.C.

95. Patients can recover from HIV-positive doctor. (1995). *American Medical News* 38(10):19.

96. Moran, T. (1995). Battle scars. For plastic surgeons, psychological effects linger from silicone breast implant controversy. *Texas Medicine* 91(1):30–34.

97. Low, N., and Wollerton, M. A. (1992). Food and Drug Administration user facility reporting. *FDA Medical Bulletin* 3(Winter):6.

98. $6 million award in implant suit. (1995). *New York Times* February 5, p. 18, col. 4.

99. Association of Operating Room Nurses, Recommended Practices Committee. (1995). *Proposed Recommended Practices for Sponge, Sharp and Instrument Counts*. Denver: AORN.

100. Gerlin, A. (1999). Medical mistakes. *Philadelphia Inquirer*. A series starting Sept. 12.

101. Gendron, F. S. (1990). *Unexplained Patient Burns: Investigating Iatrogenic Injuries*. Brea, Calif.: Quest.

102. Carl, L. (1992). The health care team approach to laser medicine risk management. *Laser Nursing* 6(1):6–8.

103. Schulte, F., and Bergal, J. (1998). Plastic surgery: The risks you take. *Sun-Sentinel* (Florida). A series starting Nov. 29.

104. Tye, L. (1999). Patients at risk. *Boston Globe*. A series starting March 14.

105. Harding, G. H. (1993). Laser surgery. In *High Technology in Health Care: Risk Management Perspectives*, edited by R. A. Maley and A. L. Epstein. Chicago: American Hospital Publishing, pp. 149–150.

106. Schwaneberg, R. (2001). $5 million award stands against MD. *Star-Ledger* (Newark, N.J.), April 20, p. 53, col. 1.

CHAPTER 14

Risk Management in Managed Care Organizations

David E. Manoogian

INTRODUCTION

Risk managers in a managed care organization (MCO) will see more challenges than any other employee in the health care industry. As MCOs become more prevalent and more complex, the role of the risk manager is increasing dramatically in scope and complexity.[1]

There are numerous reasons why the risk manager's role will increase: (1) The increased consumer pressure to maintain quality while controlling the cost of health care. (2) Continued friction between regulation by the states and regulation by the federal government. (3) No centralized, consistent, published, and widely accepted set of laws [that] sets forth clearly what is expected of an MCO. (4) At present, there is no federal law to which the risk manager can look for guidance on legal issues. (5) Generally, state law is more specific but is rapidly changing. Many MCOs operate in multiple states with conflicting state laws that frequently become a bane rather than a boon. (6) Certification standards are starting to emerge, but do not yet meaningfully assist the risk manager of an MCO, thus creating a legal vacuum. (7) Growth in size and complexity makes the management of an entire organization more difficult than the management of each component part of that organization. Each new added component must interface and coordinate with every other component. Usually, the components are in different geographical locations and vary in size from a single doctor's office to an acute care hospital. With this MCO growth, the exposure to risks and the difficulty of managing risks between the components burgeon.[2]

PRESSURES ON MCOs

A variety of forces exert pressure on the operation of an MCO: old and new, internal and external, and complementary and contradictory. All these pressures can be summarized as follows: keep the quality of care up, keep the cost of care down, and reduce the exposure to litigation of any type.

There is no doubt that legal claims against MCOs, and the success of those claims, are increasing and will continue to increase. This trend results not only from the increasing number of MCO subscribers, but also from the sophistication by plaintiffs' lawyers and from subscribers' knowledge of their legal rights.

PUBLIC PERCEPTION OF MCOs AND LITIGATION

Is there a discrepancy between the public's perception of MCOs and reality? In reality, managed care is a large part of the health care market and is growing in market share. However, the public's perception lags behind reality. Usually, the MCO member expects the benefits and prerogatives of an "old-fashioned" indemnity health insurance plan while enjoying the reduced cost of an MCO. Until perception and reality are reconciled, risk managers must deal with an increase in litigation against MCOs.

Negative perceptions about MCOs encourage people to sue. MCOs are perceived as "deep pockets" with greater dollar amounts of insurance coverage than the average physician. A patient may hesitate to sue an individual doctor for fear of causing financial ruin. No such inhibition exists when an MCO is the target. In addition to the usual doctor, nurse, or hospital defendants, an MCO may be another defendant to a lawsuit. Corporate MCOs are perceived as impersonal defendants. MCO members never have the same "warm" feeling about an MCO that they have toward their personal physician. Commonly, MCO members don't comprehend, or they actively reject, the concept of cost containment. This perception that an MCO restricts access to health care providers often generates intensely negative public attitudes toward MCOs.[3] This negativity continues despite the fact that the U.S. Supreme Court has, in a published opinion, recognized that rationing care is the essence of managed care.[4] Collectively, these attitudes make the risk manager's job difficult.

In this new environment, a risk manager must be especially cautious because the law regarding the legal risks of MCOs is new and rapidly evolving. Many questions have no clear answer; some questions have no answer at all. Moreover, many answers are relatively new and may change again in the near future.

MCO STRUCTURE AND LIABILITY

To comprehend the potential liability risks, it is absolutely imperative that the risk manager understand the legal structure of the specific MCO. Laws and legal precedents clearly binding on one MCO model may be irrelevant and inapplicable to another type. Until the legal community matures in its sophistication about MCOs, the risk manager should expect some confusion. Even attorneys may be confused regarding the structure of an MCO and the significance of that structure to a particular risk or legal liability.

Relative to the risks, an MCO is defined as a health care delivery system that is an alternative to the traditional indemnity type of insurance. An MCO consists of voluntarily enrolled subscribers or enrollees entitled to comprehensive health care by providers who are either employed by or have contracted with the MCO. A subscriber's comprehensive health care is provided by the MCO for a prepaid fixed monthly fee, without regard to the actual amount of medical services utilized by the members. Depending on the relationship between the MCO and the subscriber and between the MCO and the health care provider, an MCO may have some, but not all, of the characteristics of a regular business corporation, such as an insurance company, a hospital, or a mixture of corporate models. Risk managers should expect claimants/plaintiffs to characterize the MCO in the form most favorable to the claimant (for example, as a health care provider). In contrast, the risk manager must depict the MCO most favorably to the defense of the risk (for example, as a regular business corporation).

Given the number and complexity of the risks facing the risk manager of an MCO, it is impossible to state one general rule that applies at all times and at all places. However, a vital rule in assessing and managing any risk is the *degree of control* that the MCO exercises in any given situation. MCO control may be established in three ways:

- A contract with the subscriber, the health care provider, a component, etc.
- Actual control, with or without a contract.
- The appearance of control, even without a contract or actual control.

In establishing MCO exposure to risk, the actual or perceived amount of MCO control is extremely critical. Appearance of control is every bit as important as actual control. Risk managers must be sensitive to both. In addition, risk managers must be extremely sensitive to the existence and content of documents that either create or evidence control (e.g., provider contracts, mandatory treatment pathways, etc.).

MODELS OF MCOs

There are three traditional models of MCOs: (1) staff, (2) group, and (3) individual practice association (IPA). In addition, a variety of hybrids exist. When applying theories of liability or defense to a particular risk, the model and operational characteristics of the MCO are extremely important.

Staff Model

Staff model MCOs are the simplest in organizational structure. Health care providers are employed directly by the MCO, are salaried employees, are MCO staff members, and routinely practice at a facility owned or operated by the MCO. Generally, staff models engender a typical employer-employee relationship, give the MCO the greatest degree of control, and increase MCO liability for the conduct of health care providers.

Group Model

In a group model, the MCO either employs or contracts with providers, typically a large multispecialty group, to provide health care services to the MCO subscribers. However, the group's practice may not be limited solely to MCO enrollees. Often, the group practices at a facility that is either owned or operated by the MCO. Generally, the group is reimbursed on a prepaid basis, called capitation, for services. The group may consist either of multispecialty practitioners or of primary care physicians with limited authority to refer enrollees to an approved list of specialists.[5]

A vital task of the risk manager is to assess the MCO's degree of control, either actual or apparent, because the MCO's exposure to liability is based on the conduct of the health care providers. An MCO's exposure to liability increases as the MCO exercises more control over the providers.

IPA Model

In the IPA model, medical care is rendered by private physicians under the umbrella of an MCO. An IPA can act as an intermediary between the MCO and the providers by contracting with primary care or specialist solo practitioners or groups to render health care to subscribers. In turn, the IPA contracts with the MCO to provide administrative services and to receive payment for services rendered. IPA physicians work in their own offices, utilize their own equipment, and keep their own records. In the IPA model, the degree of control by the MCO over a specific provider is more tenuous. When an intermediary IPA is not utilized, the MCO contracts directly with individual practitioners to render health care services to the MCO subscribers. As MCOs create "networks," each IPA physician becomes a "component" to be generally supervised and to be accountable to the MCO for administrative procedures and quality of care.

Of the three traditional MCO models, the IPA presents the most difficulty in assessing the degree of control over the individual provider. As with the other two models, the more control the MCO exerts, the greater its exposure to liability for the conduct of an individual IPA member. Control by the MCO over the physician may not always be obvious. For example, administrative directives, mandatory treatment pathways, or treatment directives may all be forms of control.

Hybrids, New Models, and Networks

Hybrid MCO models, which are increasing dramatically, combine characteristics of the traditional types with new, previously unknown characteristics. As MCOs perceive a need in the marketplace for a particular form of managed care, they respond by devising innovative organizational structures, with or without networks, such as:

PPOs (preferred provider organizations), which allow subscribers to obtain health service from any approved provider. Frequently, the list of providers is quite large in any given marketplace.

PHOs (physician-hospital organizations), which are cooperative efforts between a group of physicians and one or more hospitals to deliver health care services in a given marketplace. PHOs may have a wide variety of characteristics and may be owned or dominated either by the hospital or by the physicians.

POSs (point of service plans), sometimes called "out of plan" options, which allow subscribers to obtain health services from almost any provider, but at a reduced benefit in their insurance coverage.

"Consumer-driven" health plans have become extremely popular recently. In these plans, the individual consumer decides what benefits he or she would like to have (e.g., a lower premium in exchange for a higher co-pay). These plans are so new (and so rapidly evolving) that there are few laws about them.

These examples are not exhaustive, and variations are being created constantly. However, the one constant element that the risk manager must recognize and analyze is degree of control. Who controls whom, and to what degree is that entity controlled? In simplistic terms, as control increases, exposure to liability increases, especially if there is documentation that creates or evidences that control.

MCOs can be owned by hospitals, and conversely hospitals can be owned by MCOs. Physicians can own a corporation, which in turn owns an MCO that contracts with those physicians, as well as others, to render health care services. In this complex administrative arrangement, the degree of control by the owner physicians may be quite high, although not readily apparent. Even if the lines of control are obscure and subtle, the risk manager must understand the complex control linkage to discern the degree of exposure to risk.

STATUTES AND ADMINISTRATIVE REGULATIONS

To minimize risks, an MCO must identify and comply with all statutes and administrative regulations. Statutes are laws enacted by a federal, state, or local legislative body. Administrative regulations have the force of law and are established by an executive body such as the insurance commission or health department, under an enabling statute passed by the legislature.

Failure to comply with either a statute or an administrative regulation can create legal liability for the MCO. However, compliance with the statute or regulation is not as easy as it might seem. An MCO must comply with both federal and state statutes and regulations. Most of the states have enacted MCO regulations in a patchwork fashion, creating internal inconsistencies that make compliance difficult. Some jurisdictions, such as the District of Columbia, have enacted no statutes regulating MCOs. California and Florida have enacted comprehensive MCO regulations. State MCO statutes run the gamut from thorough to nonexistent. Generally, state regulations are not centralized in one location and may be contradictory or inconsistent. Despite these pitfalls, a risk manager must review the entire state legislative and administrative regulatory enactment as a starting point in analyzing risk exposure.

Federal and state statutes are published in the code of the specific jurisdiction. Both state and federal codes and administrative regulations are now widely available on the Internet. While these authorities used to be somewhat difficult to locate, they can now generally be found quite easily online. In addition, the state and federal codes are readily available at almost any law library and at many public libraries. On the other hand, administrative regulations (if not on the Internet) may be difficult to locate and are not widely promulgated. If the MCO can't find the administrative regulations and comply, its potential for risk increases. A risk manager's understanding of the MCO's exposure to legal liability must begin with the federal statutes and regulations and follow through with the statutes and regulations of the states in which the MCO operates.

Federal HMO Statute

The Federal HMO (health maintenance organization) law was originally passed in 1973 and is contained in the *United States Code, Annotated,* Title 42, Section 300e, which is cited as 42 USCA 300e (1982). Federal regulations are in the *Code of Federal Regulations,* commonly called the CFR. General and organizational requirements are detailed regarding the health care services to be made available to HMO members. CFR regulations relate primarily to the administration of a federally qualified HMO and indirectly to malpractice or legal liability. To encourage the development and proliferation of HMOs and MCOs as affordable, alternative health care delivery systems, the federal HMO statute authorized the secretary of the Department of Health and Human Services to make or guarantee loans for initial operational costs. Federal administrators are directing Medicare beneficiaries[6] and Medicaid recipients[7] into MCOs.

While it is arguable that the administrative requirements imposed by federal HMO law constitute a "standard of care" for a state malpractice action, this theory does not appear ever to have been raised in litigation.

State Statutes

Almost every state has enacted statutes relating to the creation and operation of MCOs. Specific details in these state statutes vary by state. Since the statutes are not centralized in one location, risk managers may have to consult several sections of the state code to gain an effective overview of all the state statutes. Usually, the state statutes fall into four categories: (1) the creation of an MCO or HMO found under the insurance commission, (2) the regulation of an MCO under the department of health, (3) the regulation of health care providers, to the extent that the MCO is a provider under state law, and (4) the regulation of corporations. Only by consulting all of these statutory schemes, and others, applicable under specific state law, can the risk manager identify statutes relating to MCO operation.

Under most state laws, the MCO is created by a Certificate of Authority from the state insurance commission. The MCO must obtain this Certificate of Authority before issuing any contracts of membership to subscribers. In Maryland, this requirement is found in the Maryland Code, Health-General, Section 19-707. As in most other states, only the Maryland Commissioner of the State Insurance Commission has the authority to issue, suspend, or revoke an MCO's Certificate of Authority. In operational MCOs, the basic organizational aspects, including a Certificate of Authority, have already been resolved. However, the risk manager should ascertain that the MCO was properly formed and is operating in compliance with state law. If an MCO is sued, a failure to be properly created and/or operated can have catastrophic results.

State Administrative Regulations

When states have statutes regulating MCOs, there are also administrative regulations adopted either by the insurance commission or by the secretary of health. As federal regulations appear in the CFR, state administrative regulations are in a volume or volumes of state regulations. In Maryland, for example, these regulations are called the Code of Maryland Administrative Regulations (COMAR). All states with MCO statutes have a collection of regulations like COMAR.

Typically, the insurance commission has regulations concerning insurance aspects of an MCO, such as: (1) the Certificate of Authority, (2) advertising, (3) marketing, (4) termination of business, and (5) general operations, frequently including member complaints.

A health department regulates health-related aspects of an MCO, such as: (1) services to be offered as a minimum benefit, (2) quality assessment, (3) peer review, (4) medical record content and maintenance, (5) statistical information, (6) access and availability of services, (7) physician availability, (8) required policies and protocols, and (9) advisory committees, frequently including consumers.

In an ideal world, regulations from the insurance commission and health department would be integrated and consistent. Such is not always the case in the real world. These regulations are adopted by different agencies, by different persons, at different times, for different purposes, and with the intent to remedy different perceived dangers. Frequently, the resultant regulations overlap and are not entirely consistent.

Risk managers should be familiar with all state regulations and ensure that someone in the MCO is responsible for compliance with these regulations.

MCO Practice of Medicine under State Law

Despite the fact that MCOs are almost always organized as regular corporations, most states specifically exempt an MCO corporation from any prohibition against the corporate practice of medicine. Risk managers should confirm that their MCO is in full compliance with the state statute or regulation regarding the corporate practice of medicine. In Maryland, a specific statute exempts MCOs, referred to as HMOs, from the corporate practice of medicine: "[A] health maintenance organization may operate as authorized by this subtitle not withstanding any prohibition against the corporate practice of medicine."[8] Operational MCOs may have already resolved this issue, but newer MCOs must address this basic point. If an operating MCO is expanding from a traditional HMO to a more all-inclusive network, the risk manager should confirm that the network is in compliance with any state statute or regulation applying to the corporate practice of medicine. Even if the corporate practice of medicine is allowed by state statute or regulation, an MCO may not necessarily be defined as a health care provider. Risk managers should determine whether the MCO meets the definition of "health care provider" under the state's statutes and/or regulations. A Maryland state statute defines a health care provider, but in a lengthy definitional section about a "health care provider," MCOs and HMOs are not mentioned.[9] Judicial rulings of the appellate courts have not inserted MCOs into this section.[10]

There are advantages and disadvantages to being a health care provider. An advantage of not being a health care provider is that it weakens the possibility of a claim for direct medical malpractice. A disadvantage of not being a health care provider is the loss of certain "tort reform" remedies designed to benefit health care providers. Mandatory arbitration, a cap on damages, and a shortened statute of limitations (the time limit for filing a lawsuit) favor health care providers. Many states have enacted a much shorter statute of limitations solely for health care providers. If the MCO were not a health care provider, it would be subject to the longer statute of limitations for general civil claims. In litigation, it is strategically significant for the risk manager to know whether or not the MCO is a health care provider.

Even if state law does not define an MCO as a health care provider, the legislation may allow the possibility of a malpractice claim against an MCO as permitted against a traditional health care provider. In Maryland, MCOs are not within the definition of a health care provider, but Section 19-710(j) of the Health-General statute (the HMO must "provide evidence of adequate insurance coverage or an adequate plan for self-insurance to satisfy claims for injuries that may occur from providing health care") and Section 31.12.06.02 of the COMAR regulations both require an MCO to maintain adequate liability insurance coverage or adequate self-insurance to satisfy claims for injuries that may occur from providing health care. Clearly, the Maryland statutes and regulations imply that an MCO can be liable for medical malpractice, even though it is not a health care provider.

Risk managers should fully expect that in states where MCOs operate, there will be a statutory and / or regulatory schema similar to Maryland's.

Corporate Laws, Both General and Special

MCOs are subject to the state's general corporate laws, as well as to special laws for MCOs only. Risk managers should be aware of and secure compliance with both sets of laws.

General corporate laws apply because most MCOs are organized as corporations. Although the MCO's component parts, such as a doctor's office, may be organized as a partnership, sole proprietorship, or other forms, the MCO itself is almost always a general corporation. Subsequently, the MCO must comply with all of the state's laws that apply to any general corporation. Risk managers must ensure that the MCO complied with all statutes relating to the creation and operation of a general corporation: annual reports, annual renewal fees, directors' meetings, and routine technical corporate matters. Failure to comply with general corporate law could significantly harm the MCO's ability to defend itself in a lawsuit.

In addition to the state's general corporate laws, the MCO is required to comply with special laws that apply only to MCOs, such as the insurance requirement. This special insurance requirement is significant in litigation, since the plaintiff knows that the MCO must have adequate insurance or self-insurance, by statute. Except for the mandatory automobile insurance that exists in some states, there is virtually no other area of the law in which the plaintiff knows that the defendant, the MCO, is required by law to carry insurance.

Many state statutes appear to create liability, at least malpractice liability, for MCOs, whether or not that was the intent of the statute when enacted. A Maryland HMO statute contains two sections that, when read in conjunction with each other, raise the probability that an MCO is responsible for the malpractice of a treating physician. One section requires that all patient evaluations be "under the direction of a physician . . . who provides continuing medical management."[11] Another section requires MCO care to "meet reasonable standards of quality of care that are applicable to the geographic area to be served."[12] In combination, these two statutes clearly suggest that the MCO has a statutory duty to direct a physician to meet reasonable standards of quality of care. A claimant can easily assert that, after a physician mistreats a patient, the responsibility rests with the MCO for failure to give direction. This Maryland statutory scheme is by no means unique.

THEORIES OF MCO LIABILITY OTHER THAN NEGLIGENCE

Theories of liability against an MCO can be divided into three groupings: (1) theories based on negligence, (2) theories based on statutes, and (3) theories based on claims other than negligence. In a typical medical malpractice case, negligence is the alleged "failure to meet the standard of care." Liability theories other than negligence tend to focus on the contractual duties between the MCO and its members, as well as the benefits provided or withheld under the plan. These include breach of contract, breach of warranty, fraudulent misrepresentation, deceptive trade practices, bad faith, unfair insurance practices, breach of fiduciary duty, and intentional infliction of emotional distress.

Breach of Contract

Risk managers should review and be fully conversant with all contracts to provide services to subscribers. The MCO has a duty to perform pursuant to its contract with the member. That contract is stated in plan documents such as a "summary plan description," "evidence of coverage," or other document. Most commonly, a claim for breach of contract alleges a failure to provide a benefit covered under the plan or a failure to provide "quality" health care.

Breach of Warranty

A warranty is a promise or guarantee that certain conditions will be met. A failure to perform this promise becomes a breach of warranty. Warranties may either be express (specifically stated) or implied (inferred from the language or conduct of the promising party). MCOs would be ill advised to make express warranties. When providing medical care, it is very difficult to guarantee any result. More dangerous for MCOs, however, are implied warranties inferred from sales literature or advertising brochures. While a doctor's oral statement to a patient can also constitute a warranty or promise, most doctors are sufficiently cautious and do not make such statements (see Box 14-1).

Risk managers should review and approve all advertising literature promulgated by the MCO because it is the MCO's duty to perform any promises made in its marketing literature. Thus, advertising promises can become warranties made to the members. If the MCO marketing literature promises more than it can deliver, the MCO has opened the door for legal liability. MCO marketing materials containing assurances of high-quality health care that can be interpreted as a promise may be considered a warranty (see Box 14-2). Thus, potential tensions between the marketing department and risk management are obvious.

Mere puffery is not enough to impose liability. "Puffery" refers to sales representations which are so grossly exaggerated that any reasonable person would realize they are not true. A classic example of puffery is a used car advertisement that describes a used car as "perfect." Any reasonable customer would be expected to realize that a used car is not perfect. In the health care context, puffery is not so clear. A representation that "our doctors are the best" or "our care is state of the art" almost certainly will not be regarded as puffery. Any representations as to quality should thus be carefully monitored.

Fraudulent Misrepresentation

In fraudulent misrepresentation, contracts or marketing materials knowingly misrepresent or omit existing facts to induce the patient to join the MCO or to submit to a certain medical treatment. For example, an MCO declares that it has a facility or service available for "complete" cardiac care but

BOX 14-1

A court held that an MCO could be vicariously liable for breach of an express contract if a physician promised a particular result, the patient consented to the medical treatment in reliance on that promise, and the promised result did not occur.[13]

BOX 14-2

A court ruling allowed a case to go forward with regard to whether the plaintiff had received HMO literature that guaranteed or assured the quality of care to its subscribers.[14]

does not even have cardiac catheterization capability. Such a fraudulent misrepresentation could lead to liability. However, there is a high burden of proof in fraudulent misrepresentations, making it a difficult claim for a plaintiff to prove. Nonetheless, as consumers become more demanding, risk managers should expect an increase in this type of litigation. Simply stated, when an MCO representative says something that is known to be untrue, a fraudulent representation may have occurred. Risk managers should monitor all representations to the public to make sure that they are true.

Deceptive Trade Practices

Almost every state has a statute that prohibits trade practices regarded as deceptive, likely to mislead the consumer. State statutes regarding deceptive trade practices are fairly basic in their requirements. A seller of goods or services is not allowed to misrepresent those services or otherwise deceive the consumer into purchasing the services. As regular corporations, MCOs are fully subject to these trade practice statutes. Particularly because deceptive trade practice litigation against MCOs has been increasing, risk managers should be aware of all applicable deceptive trade statutes and the conduct necessary to comply with them.

Bad Faith

Common law requires that all business dealings, including the business of providing health care, be conducted in good faith. Good faith is defined as fair dealing and candor. Obviously, bad faith is the converse. In the case of MCOs it entails withholding information or being less than candid in business dealings, most likely with subscribers, but also possibly with health care providers. Most risk managers are familiar with bad faith claims against an insurance company for failure to settle a legal claim. For similar reasons, MCOs should expect bad faith claims against them for failure to deal fairly or candidly.

Unfair Insurance Practices

Almost every state has an insurance statute that prohibits unfair insurance practices. State statutes list a number of activities prohibited as unfair: false information about policy terms, false advertising, unfair criticism of one's competitors, unfair comparisons of one's own product to the product of competitors, improper rebates, or charging a premium for coverage that is not actually issued. Although MCOs are not insurance companies in most states, they may still be subject to regulation of insurance practices. Risk managers should review the unfair insurance practices statute and compare it to the MCO's operations to ensure compliance.

Breach of Fiduciary Duty

A fiduciary relationship is one that is based on unusual trust, confidence, or responsibility. In a "normal" business relationship, each party vigorously advances its own economic interests at the expense of the other side. However, a fiduciary relationship requires the fiduciary to use complete good faith to make sure that the transaction is equally fair to all sides. An MCO fiduciary cannot advance its own economic interests by being less than completely candid and fair with the other contracting parties. This fiduciary duty is significantly higher than the duty to avoid bad faith.

A fiduciary relationship between the MCO and its subscribers may exist if subscribers rely on the MCO to provide qualified health care providers. There is a relationship of special trust and confidence, since the subscribers rely on the MCO to do what they cannot do for themselves: decide which providers are clinically competent and professionally reliable. If the MCO allows incompetent professionals to provide services, the alleged wrong may go beyond simple "negligence" and be elevated to a fiduciary duty. To avoid negligence, the risk manager need only ensure that the MCO performs "reasonably." To meet a fiduciary standard, however, the risk manager must ensure that the MCO deals with subscribers in complete candor, withholding no significant information.

A risk manager can assist the MCO in avoiding fiduciary duties by helping to ensure that sales promotions and plan documents do not encourage subscribers to place undue trust or confidence in the MCO's selection of health care providers. Even though such precautions may prevent the MCO's being considered a fiduciary, sales personnel will almost certainly exert pressure to be allowed to make such representations to prospective customers. The U.S. Supreme Court, in *Pegram v. Herdrich*,[25] which is also cited below, discussed fiduciary duties of HMO physicians in the context of making eligibility and treatment decisions. Fiduciary duties may also exist under the federal Employee Retirement and Income Security Act (ERISA) statute; these potential duties are discussed in the section for ERISA, below.

Intentional Infliction of Emotional Distress

Claims for the intentional infliction of emotional distress are increasingly popular and have resulted in extremely large verdicts for plaintiffs. A claim of intentional infliction of emotional distress requires the plaintiff to prove the following elements: (1) extreme and outrageous conduct that is intentional or in reckless disregard of the plaintiff's emotions; this conduct must be so outrageous in character and so extreme in degree as to go beyond all possible bounds of decency or must be atrocious and utterly intolerable in a civilized community; (2) a direct and causal relationship between the alleged infliction and the plaintiff's claimed damages; and (3) damage or harm to the plaintiff, usually severe mental anguish or emotional distress. Boxes 14-3 and 14-4 illustrate this liability risk.

To protect the MCO from a claim of intentional infliction of emotional distress, the law states that there must be an objective and articulable good faith basis for any action taken, including but not limited to the denial of benefits. Since the MCO is required to provide only those benefits agreed upon in the contract, some subscriber claims will have to be denied. Risk managers should ensure that the MCO denies claims by specific reference to the plan documents rather than by subjective whim of a benefits coordinator or, worst of all, to increase the MCO's profits. As long as a risk manager ensures that the MCO is meeting its

BOX 14-3

An MCO denied coverage of a bone marrow transplant for treatment of breast cancer, even though the plaintiff's treating physicians requested the coverage. Evidence showed that the denial was made by an MCO executive who received bonus compensation for limiting expensive medical procedures. Among other claims, the plaintiff asserted reckless infliction of emotional distress. A jury verdict awarded her $12.2 million in compensatory damages, $77 million in punitive damages, and $212,000 in breach of contract damages. After the verdict, a confidential settlement was reached.[15] Two years later, the New Jersey legislature passed a law requiring insurance companies to offer coverage for bone marrow transplants.[16]

BOX 14-4

After the medical director reported her to the authorities for child abuse and neglect, the plaintiff filed a claim against the MCO for intentional infliction of emotional distress. The plaintiff's daughter suffered from a rare life-threatening genetic disorder requiring 24-hour skilled nursing care. After the MCO terminated home nursing coverage, the parents appealed. An MCO medical director notified the child welfare authorities that the plaintiff suffered from Munchausen syndrome, a psychological disorder in which the parents inflict injury or illness because they wish to be associated with the health care profession. Prior to trial, the parties reached a confidential settlement.[17]

requirement of good faith and fair dealing, the MCO should be at minimal risk for claims of intentional inflictment of emotional distress. MCOs should document the basis for their decisions in their records.

STATUTORY LIABILITY

Statutory Liability under EMTALA: Antidumping Law

The federal Emergency Medical Treatment and Active Labor Act (EMTALA)[18] imposes liability on hospitals that fail to provide emergency screening and stabilization to patients who are in an "unstable medical condition" or are in active labor. Antidumping claims have been brought against MCOs for refusing to authorize emergency screening and stabilization services at hospitals that are not under contract with the MCO (see Box 14-5). Lawsuits under this statute should be expected to increase as MCOs expand from the traditional managed care entity to networks involving provider contracts with acute care hospitals. State statutes may also prohibit patient dumping.

BOX 14-5

An MCO subscriber in unstable medical condition went to a hospital. Because the MCO did not have a contract with the hospital, authorization was denied. This subscriber was transferred to three other hospitals before she arrived at an MCO-affiliated hospital. As a result of the delay in treatment and transfers, she claimed to have suffered permanent neurological damage. The plaintiff alleged a violation of the Florida antidumping statute. In dismissing the case on the grounds that it arose under the Federal Employee Retirement and Income Security Act (ERISA), the court said that ERISA does not provide a remedy for medical malpractice.[19] Although this case was preempted by ERISA, the court established the concept that an MCO may be sued under an alleged violation of an antidumping statute.

Under EMTALA, all MCO networks will have to make arrangements for emergency room services or face potential suit. If the emergency room is an integral part of the MCO network, the risk manager can directly secure emergency department compliance with EMTALA. If the emergency department is not an integral part of the MCO network, the challenge to the risk manager becomes greater. In that situation, the risk manager must require the contracting hospital to provide proof of compliance with EMTALA. This proof is vital, since the MCO faces potential liability for the hospital's conduct, especially if the MCO requires subscribers to go to that hospital.

Statutory Liability under ERISA

Under the federal Employee Retirement and Income Security Act (ERISA),[20] an MCO may face liability for the wrongful denial of benefits, as well as potential liability for breach of fiduciary duty. Although ERISA was enacted in 1974, its scope and application are still being actively litigated and its full ramifications are not yet known.[21] Risk managers must be sensitive to liability issues such as wrongful denial of benefits and breach of fiduciary duty.

Liability for Wrongful Denial of Benefits

Section 1132(a)(1)(B) of ERISA authorizes a plan participant or beneficiary to bring a civil action to "recover benefits due under the terms of the plan, to enforce rights under the terms of the plan, or to clarify rights to future benefits under the terms of the plan." However, the subscriber's relief is limited to the benefits provided in the contract, possible attorney's fees, and costs of the action. All that is required of the MCO to comply with this section of ERISA is to give the subscribers those benefits to which they are rightfully entitled. Thus, the risk manager may need to educate the benefits department, especially if the MCO is large and offers multiple plans.

Liability for Breach of Fiduciary Duty

According to Section 1002(21)(A) of ERISA, a fiduciary is any person who exercises any discretionary authority or control with regard to the management of the plan, management or disposition of plan assets, or administration of the plan. Courts have ruled that insurance companies and MCOs that administer claims for employee welfare benefit plans and have authority to grant or deny claims are plan fiduciaries. If the risk manager's MCO performs any of these tasks, the MCO is a plan fiduciary and faces legal responsibility for fiduciary misconduct. If the MCO is a plan fiduciary, any subscriber may file suit alleging a breach of fiduciary duty. Section 1132(a)(1)(B) of ERISA authorizes any plan participant or beneficiary to bring a civil action against a plan fiduciary for breach of a fiduciary duty as defined in Section 1109(a) of the statute, but any damages recovered must inure to the plan.

Even though ERISA will not allow the subscriber to profit personally in fiduciary duty cases, it does allow the subscriber to attempt to control the plan's operation. To avoid this type of subscriber-imposed control, the risk manager must ensure that the plan provides the agreed-upon benefits.

MCO liability for an alleged breach of ERISA fiduciary duty has been considered in the two cases presented in Box 14-6. In both cases, the courts allowed the plaintiffs to request a court order controlling the plan's use and disposition of discounts. In another case, the court allowed the subscribers to request an injunction controlling the plan.[24]

The U.S. Supreme Court has decided two major cases that have significant implications for fiduciary duties under ERISA. On

BOX 14-6

- The plaintiffs alleged that Blue Cross and Blue Shield of Ohio breached a fiduciary duty by not passing along the savings of "secretly" negotiated provider discounts to plan participants, causing the participants to overpay. Importantly, the court would not allow plaintiffs to profit personally from their lawsuit. Rather, the court required that any recovery must be for the benefit of the entire plan.[22]
- The plaintiffs alleged that Humana, Inc., breached an ERISA fiduciary duty by failing to pass along negotiated discounts. A court ruling would not allow the plaintiffs to personally profit.[23]

June 12, 2000, the U.S. Supreme Court decided a major case on the scope of fiduciary duties, *Pegram v. Herdrich*.[25] In the *Pegram* case, the Court held that when an HMO doctor is making "mixed eligibility and treatment" decisions (i.e., not only whether the care in question is a covered benefit under the plan but also whether the treatment is medically necessary), those decisions are not fiduciary decisions under ERISA. While the *Pegram* case is still being analyzed by the legal community, it is generally regarded as narrowing the scope of fiduciary duties under ERISA.

On June 20, 2002, the Supreme Court decided the case of *Rush Prudential HMO v. Moran*.[26] While the issue in *Rush* was simply the application of a state law requiring second opinions to ERISA plans, the case may have implications for the scope of fiduciary duties.

Statutory Liability under ADA

As applied to MCOs, the Americans with Disabilities Act (ADA)[27] is a new and undefined theory of liability. Although the ADA received almost no publicity during its enactment and implementation, parts of the ADA clearly appear to create some risk of liability for MCOs. Up to now, only a few cases under the ADA have applied to MCOs. The most serious risk to an MCO is being considered an extension of the employer.

Defining "Employer"

Title I of the ADA prohibits employers of more than 15 employees from discriminating against employees on the basis of disability in the provision of health benefits. Recent case law defined "employer" for the purposes of ADA in such a way as to open the door for MCOs to be liable under Title I of the ADA. However, two cases did not expand the definition of employer (see Box 14-7). These are two cases that provide a general discussion of the ADA definition of employer.[28]

The four cases that expanded the employer definition represent a trend under ADA Title I, "Employers," to expand the scope and application of the ADA regulations (see Box 14-8). This type of expansion can be expected to continue in the future.

Public Accommodation

As Title I of the ADA applies to employers, Title III applies to places of public accommodation. Ordinarily, "public accommodation" is interpreted to pertain to physical structures such as buildings and parks. At least one recent case indicates that public accommodations may encompass the provision of health benefits. Again, the court decisions are divided. In two cases, the court refused to expand public accommodations.[35,36] The court ruling in both cases specifically required physical use of a place or service before Title III would apply. One case expanded public accommodations by including the design, inclusions and exclusions, of the health benefit plan.[37] This is a particularly dangerous ruling for MCOs because the court decreed that public accommodation is not limited to physical

BOX 14-7

- An administrator of a benefits plan was not deemed an agent of the employer solely because the plan administered the employee benefits.[29]
- A court held that an insurance agency was not an employer under ADA. However, the value of this case is questionable, since the plaintiffs were federal employees and the U.S. government is excluded from the definition of "employer" under the ADA.[30]

BOX 14-8

- A court ruling expanded "employer" to include the trustees of a pension fund. By extension of this logic, an MCO health plan could also be an employer. This litigant was denied membership in the pension fund because he was a diabetic.[31]
- An employee sued a health benefits provider after it reduced the lifetime benefits for AIDS treatment to $25,000 but left lifetime benefits for all other conditions at $1 million. For purposes of Title I of the ADA, the court held that a self-funded health benefits plan may be considered an employer. Furthermore, the court held that health benefits are an important aspect of an individual's employment and are under the ADA. Additionally, the court articulated a detailed definition of employer, which could include many MCOs.[32]
- A court held that a pension fund was covered under the ADA. If a pension fund were covered under the ADA, an MCO health plan could also be covered. This pension fund excluded certain employees who had disabilities from obtaining pension benefits.[33]
- On behalf of the trust fund beneficiaries, the Equal Employment Opportunity Commission filed suit becuase of the denial of coverage for AIDS and AIDS-related conditions. In the ruling, the court held that a self-funded union pension plan could be an employer.[34]

structures, but may include the design of products such as health benefits.

Risk managers can take the following actions to ensure that the MCO is not in violation of either Title I or Title III of the ADA:

1. Make sure the MCO develops underwriting guidelines that are objective, nondiscriminatory, and supported by valid actuarial data. Seriously outdated or incomplete data are not valid data.
2. Ensure that guidelines for coverage are cost-based, not diagnosis-based.
3. Impose benefits limitations equally on all conditions. Do not place lower caps on only certain diseases, such as AIDS.
4. Apply exclusions based on preexisting conditions uniformly. For example, do not exclude coverage for preexisting diabetes while covering preexisting eczema.
5. Exercise special caution with self-funded or self-administered plans, since they appear to be at greater risk for being considered an employer.
6. Educate sales personnel about the ADA. When marketing to small groups, the salesperson cannot design a benefits package intended to exclude one expensive member who could seriously affect the group's premiums.

Statutory Liability under RICO

The Racketeering Influenced and Corrupt Organizations Act (RICO)[38] was enacted to combat organized crime in America by preventing "known mobsters" from infiltrating legitimate businesses. This statute establishes severe criminal penalties and civil remedies against parties who operate a legitimate business activity or enterprise through a pattern of racketeering. Because RICO's statutory language is extremely broad, civil RICO actions are not limited merely to cases involving organized crime. RICO has rarely been used as a theory of liability against an MCO, and it has not yet been used successfully. However, the issue has arisen in several cases (see Box 14-9) and will no doubt arise again.

RICO Claims Barred by the McCarran-Ferguson Act

The McCarran-Ferguson Act[39] established the relationship between state and federal

BOX 14-9

- MCO subscribers brought a class action suit alleging that the MCO's failure to disclose its financial incentives to participating physicians discouraged referrals to specialists, in violation of RICO. Subscribers claimed they would not have enrolled in the plan had they known of the financial incentives. Although the court dismissed the RICO claims, plaintiffs were allowed to allege fraud.[40]
- A provider whose contract was not renewed alleged that there were RICO violations involving fraud in the contract bidding process. On the grounds that there was no pattern of racketeering or collection of unlawful debts, the court dismissed the RICO claims.[41]
- Subscribers sued, alleging various RICO violations for nondisclosure of a "secret" agreement for discounts between the MCO and a participating hospital. They claimed that the MCO used wire and postal services to intentionally conceal and misrepresent the discount agreement. Because the plaintiffs failed to demonstrate a "concrete financial injury" as required by RICO, the court granted summary judgment in favor of the MCO.[42]

laws regulating insurance. This act precludes the application of any conflicting federal law over a state law regulating the business of insurance, based upon weighing a three-pronged test (assuming the federal law in question does not specifically regulate insurance):

1. The regulation has the effect of transferring or spreading a policyholder's risk.
2. The regulation is an integral part of the policy relationship.
3. The regulation is limited to entities within the insurance industry.

It is not necessary to meet all of the three prongs in order for the law to be one that "regulates insurance."[43] The factors are to be weighed and none is necessarily determinative in itself. The Supreme Court also considered when a law "regulates insurance" in the ERISA context in another case,[44] giving the term a broad application.

The Supreme Court has also held that a claimant may file suit under both state insurance laws and the federal RICO statute, if the federal statute does not invalidate, impair, or supercede that state insurance law,[45] which has the practical effect of broadening the relief available to a plaintiff since the plaintiff may claim both state and federal relief.

No ruling has coordinated McCarran-Ferguson (state law prevails over federal law) with ERISA (state laws are preempted by federal law); it is only a matter of time until the issue is raised.

Although the description of activities as "racketeering influenced" is frightening, almost all of the activities prohibited by RICO are also illegal under other laws. Racketeering activities under RICO can include fraud, concealment, collection of an unlawful debt, and the use of wire communication or the postal service to further these wrongs. RICO should not represent a significant new danger to the risk manager. If the risk manager ensures compliance with other laws, compliance with RICO should follow.

CORPORATE NEGLIGENCE

Selection, Rejection, and Termination of Providers

The selection, rejection, and termination of providers are especially perilous for the risk manager because any misstep can result in potential liability for the MCO. If the MCO selects a provider who is not clinically competent, it faces liability for negligent selection. If the MCO excludes a competent provider, it faces liability for wrongful rejection. And once providers are in the plan, it is frequently difficult to terminate them. Legislation forcing an MCO to employ "any willing provider" makes the entire process more difficult.

Legal risks related to selection, rejection, and termination apply to all types of health care providers, not just physicians. Allied health professionals such as chiropractors, physician's assistants, speech therapists, family counselors, and social workers are equally controlled by the rules regarding selection, rejection, and termination.[46]

Selection of Providers

Because the MCO limits the patient's choice of providers, the MCO has an obligation to properly select and credential health care providers. This duty is closely related to hospital liability for negligent credentialing of medical staff. Negligence in this duty can be (1) an alleged failure to properly review and investigate the credentials of provider applicants (see Box 14-10) or (2) an alleged failure to take corrective action when the MCO knows or should know that a provider is not clinically competent (see Box 14-11).

Four elements must coexist for there to be liability for negligent selection: (1) negligent selection of a provider by the MCO, (2) medical malpractice or other actionable misconduct by the provider, (3) a direct and proximate causal relationship between the negligent selection of the provider and the injuries alleged by the claimant, and (4) harm to the patient. If the provider is not clinically competent in procedure X but injures the patient with procedure Z, in which the provider is competent, it is questionable whether there is a causal relationship between the negligent selection of the provider and the claimed injury.

Although there have been only a few legal cases on the negligent selection of

BOX 14-10

One MCO's selection criteria required that the physician hold a medical license, have admitting privileges to a hospital, and be licensed to dispense narcotics. No reference checks or personal interviews were conducted. The plaintiff filed a medical malpractice claim against the independent contractor physician and against the MCO. To prevent a foreseeable risk of harm, the plaintiff maintained that the MCO should have investigated the doctor's competence to discover the doctor's existing malpractice record. The court ruled that when the MCO limits the choice of doctors, the MCO has a common law duty to conduct a reasonable investigation into the doctor's competence.[47] The plaintiff's claim against the MCO was dismissed on a statutory technicality. Nonetheless, the case establishes the legal concept of suing an MCO for failure to investigate its providers.

BOX 14-11

- A malpractice claim alleged negligent selection and retention of the provider. In its decision, the court held that the MCO had a nondelegable duty to select and retain only competent primary care physicians. This duty was breached by the MCO because it failed to exercise reasonable care in the selection, retention, and/or evaluation of its providers.[49]
- In another case, an appellate court ruled that the plaintiff was entitled to a trial in which he could attempt to prove that the HMO had violated a duty to supervise physicians, in the same manner that a hospital does.

providers, it appears clear that the courts will hold an MCO liable for negligent selection as appropriate.

Criteria for Provider Selection

Even for risk managers with experience in hospitals, credentialing for an MCO is a new and more demanding endeavor. Usually, MCOs are larger and more geographically diverse.

Both the Joint Commission on Accreditation of Healthcare Organizations (JCAHO) and the National Committee for Quality Assurance (NCQA) have adopted standards and guidelines for the credentialing of provider members.[48] In addition, the risk manager should ensure that the MCO has an adequate amount of liability insurance to cover its responsibilities regarding the selection, rejection, and termination of providers. Furthermore, the credentialing process should be proportionate to the amount of choice allowed to plan members. As subscribers become more restricted in their provider choices, the credentialing process should become more thorough. Drawing on the JCAHO and NCQA standards,[51] as well as on additional sources,[52] risk managers can adapt the following provider selection guidelines to lessen the likelihood of liability:

1. Selection criteria should be written and reviewed periodically.
2. Final authority to credential should reside with the governing body or network leaders.
3. A specifically designated committee should be formed to make recommendations regarding credentialing.
4. Criteria should apply to all physicians and licensed independent practitioners such as therapists, social workers, chiropractors, and podiatrists.
5. Minimum information collected should include: verification of a current, valid license; verification of clinical privileges in good standing; a valid DEA (Drug Enforcement Agency) certificate; and verification of education, work history, malpractice insurance, and liability claims history. NCQA requires the MCO to obtain primary verification of this information.
6. Information should be obtained from the applicant regarding: physical and mental status; any impairment due to chemical dependency or substance abuse; any criminal history; a report of any disciplinary activity, loss of license, or reduction of privileges; and an attestation as to the completeness and accuracy of the application.
7. If the MCO is allowed to query the National Practitioner Data Bank about the provider's malpractice history, it should do so. Additionally, the MCO should consult the State Board for Medicine and check for any sanctions by Medicare or Medicaid.
8. The offices of potential primary care physicians, OB/GYNs, and other high-volume specialists should be visited.

Rejection of Providers

Granting that the MCO uses reasonable standards that are consistently applied, the MCO still risks a suit by a rejected, or not accepted, provider. Several liability theories apply, including antitrust, discrimination, or "any willing provider" statutes,[53] which are discussed in more detail below. MCOs should make a proper decision either to accept or not to accept a provider and be prepared to defend it.

For many providers, exclusion from a particular MCO will mean serious economic consequences. In such a situation, the provider's only choices are to accept the rejection without resistance or to file a lawsuit. Many will sue, as the examples in Box 14-12 attest.

Despite the court cases, the MCO risk manager can feel reasonably safe in rejecting a provider *if* the MCO has a well-articulated credentialing process that is applied fairly. Yet, as managed care becomes more dominant in the marketplace, suits by rejected providers will undoubtedly increase.

Termination of Providers

After providers are part of the MCO, terminating them is a difficult process with a high potential for legal liability, especially when the terminated provider will be reported to the National Practitioner Data Bank. Clearly, the better course for the risk manager is for the MCO to admit only qualified providers and avoid the termination problem. Court rulings have affirmed that the terminated provider is entitled to notice and basic fairness (see Box 14-13).

The two cases outlined in Box 14-13 indicate that the courts are willing to inject themselves into the termination process to make sure that terminated providers are treated fairly. It should be expected that other courts will follow the same thought process.

Financial Incentives to Physicians

An allegation that has received a great deal of attention recently is that MCOs are giving financial incentives to their physicians, either employed or contracted. It is alleged that the incentives encourage doctors to withhold care in order to increase either the doctor's personal income or the profitability of the MCO, or both. Some court cases

BOX 14-12

- Before a hospital could be excluded from a PPO (preferred provider organization), the court required a thorough, comparative evaluation.[54] This case involved the exclusion of a hospital, but the basic concept of a required evaluation has broad application.
- On appeal, the court reviewed a surgeon's application for privileges that the MCO had denied. Following denial, the surgeon filed suit. An appellate court held that it was proper for a court to review whether the hospital's governing body followed its own bylaws in accordance with the principles of basic fairness. Such a review of the bylaws was not held to be an invasion of the hospital's review of medical competence. In its decision, the court held that the surgeon's rights to due process had been violated by the hospital.[55]

BOX 14-13

- A neurosurgeon filed suit after a hospital terminated his staff privileges. In ruling, the court held that the doctor was entitled to notice of the charges against him and a hearing process in compliance with the hospital bylaws, including an opportunity to be heard. Since there had been substantial, although not strict, compliance with the bylaws, the termination was upheld.[56]
- Two dentists sued after their fee schedule was changed. To protect professionals from arbitrary exclusion or expulsion, even in private organizations if those organizations control important economic interests, the court held that the dentists had a common law right to fair procedures. Because the dentists had had a fair review process, the court upheld the change in fee schedule.[57]

have already considered this issue, with varying results. One case held that the court rejected the plaintiff's claim that an MCO had a duty under ERISA Section 404, 29 U.S.C. 1104 to disclose its physician compensation scheme; the plaintiff claimed the duty to disclose was broad and required disclosure even absent specific request or inquiry from the member.[58]

In another case, the court allowed a financial incentive allegation to proceed. The plaintiff maintained that the MCO was directly and vicariously liable for the death of the member since it imposed financial disincentives on the doctor, which discouraged the doctor from recommending additional treatment. The court held that these claims were not completely preempted under ERISA since the claims implicated the propriety of care and not the administration of benefits; to the extent that a mixed eligibility decision implicated the quality of care given, it was not preempted.[59]

"Any Willing Provider" Laws

"Any willing provider" laws are divided into two basic types: (1) "freedom of choice" statutes that allow a subscriber to see any provider, but at a reduced benefit; and (2) laws that require an MCO to accept any provider willing to meet the MCO's terms and conditions, including the payment schedule. Generally, these statutes can permit almost every provider to join an MCO panel.

"Any willing provider" legislation makes the rejection and termination of providers more difficult for a risk manager. Rejection is difficult if subscribers have freedom of choice and any provider can join the MCO. Termination is almost impossible if the laws open the MCO panel to any provider and the risk manager must prove that the termination was not arbitrary. However, "any willing provider" statutes should not affect rejections and/or terminations for a lack of clinical competence, for a bad claims history, or for professional discipline reasons. If the risk manager can make a *bona fide* case that a particular practitioner lacks clinical competence, almost all courts will defer to the MCO's medical judgment. Nevertheless, even rejections for a lack of clinical competence must include a fair hearing process. An initial protective strategy is for the risk manager to confirm that the MCO has adequate liability coverage to protect it from suits over rejection and/or termination.

A rejection process should include a clear statement by the MCO of why a particular provider was rejected. Providers must have an opportunity to present their side of the story. MCOs must fairly observe the credentialing process. While the court has allowed substantial, rather than strict, compliance (see the first case in Box 14-13), the risk manager should make sure that the credentialing process is carefully followed.

In terminations, the MCO's written procedures should detail the process, including an opportunity for providers to present their case. An MCO may have different "termination tracks," such as termination for matters of clinical competence as opposed to termination for failure to follow the MCO's business and billing practices. There should be a clear statement of the charges against the provider, the basis for those charges, an opportunity for the provider to respond, and most likely a hearing for the provider to argue the case orally. Legal counsel should be allowed. A hearing may be held before a committee, but the final decision should be made by the governing board of the MCO.

A major recent development in the law of "any willing provider" statutes occurred on June 29, 2002, when the U.S. Supreme Court agreed to review the application of ERISA to "any willing provider" statutes.[60] This case could decide whether "any willing provider" statutes apply to ERISA plans; i.e., whether an ERISA plan is required to comply with a state "any willing provider" law by admitting to the MCO panel any doctor who wants to join the panel and who is willing to meet the MCO's terms and conditions. Predicting what the Supreme Court will do is always risky, but given the Court's recent ruling in *Pegram* and *Rush Prudential*, it certainly appears possible that the Court will determine that even ERISA plans must comply with state laws relating to "any willing provider" requirements. If such a ruling were to occur, it would dramatically change the process by which MCOs could select or terminate the providers who are on their panels. The Court agreed to review this case, so oral argument has not been scheduled, nor have any briefs been filed. In the normal course of the Court, a decision will be issued.

Supervision of Providers

An MCO has a duty to reasonably supervise the medical care provided to subscribers by its providers, including allied health professionals. This liability can, and does, extend to potential liability for treatment by plan doctors in their private offices. Furthermore, liability can extend to nurses working for plan doctors in the doctor's private offices. The MCO incurs liability when it unreasonably fails to detect the provider's incompetence or fails to take steps to correct problems after securing information that raises or should raise concerns about risks to patients.

Supervision and the Type of MCO Model

Supervision duties vary with the type of MCO model; they are highest in a staff model and lower in IPAs and group models. Even in hybrid MCO models, the legal duty to supervise providers exists. Regardless of the MCO type, accreditation standards require supervision of providers. It is unimaginable that the courts would tolerate an MCO that exercised no effort to supervise or monitor its providers.

Two landmark cases (see Box 14-14), one in a hospital and one in an MCO, concern the duty to supervise.

Statutory Liability

While state statutes are in flux, the trend is to require greater responsibility by MCOs regarding the quality of providers operating in their network. The Maryland HMO Act mandates that an HMO "evaluate . . . the quality of health care provided to its mem-

BOX 14-14

- A high school football player fractured his leg and went to a hospital emergency room. He sued the hospital after his leg had to be amputated as a consequence of the emergency room practitioner's treatment. The court found the hospital negligent as a result of its failure to assure the competence of a nonemployee orthopedic surgeon. A foreseeable risk of harm evolved from the hospital's failure to investigate the doctor's qualifications.[61]
- A court held that an MCO had a nondelegable duty to retain only competent providers, since the MCO must formulate, adopt, and enforce adequate rules and policies to ensure the quality of care to its subscribers.[62]

bers."[63] It is only a matter of time before litigation is filed under these statutes.

As in other areas, the risk manager's first protective strategy is to have liability insurance in adequate limits to cover this risk. Until the scope of the risk is better defined by case law, the MCO should be well insured.

Risk managers should establish and implement a written procedure to monitor the clinical performance of all providers: physicians and allied health professionals.[64] Monitoring processes should consider significant variables such as the level of risk and the degree of sickness of patients, to ensure statistically accurate and reliable data. After the statistical data are compiled, the risk manager must take action in response to negative data. If the data identify a problem, the risk manager must deal with that problem; it cannot simply be ignored. Responses to the problem move through a hierarchy of corrective procedures such as counseling, monitoring, required education, required supervision, private reprimand, public reprimand, and ultimately, termination. In extreme cases, termination could be the first action.

Procedures to review clinical quality must incorporate the same basic fairness and due process required in termination proceedings. An MCO's quality review procedures reflect the MCO's opinion of what is "fair." Is it fair to consider an isolated catastrophic result better or worse than several moderately bad results? Although there may be good faith differences on what constitutes "fair," the risk manager should ensure that the MCO has an established policy to review quality issues and to deal with identified problems in a fair and consistent manner.

Negligent or Abusive Cost Containment Procedures

An MCO has a duty to exercise cost containment in a fair and reasonable manner consistent with the plan documents. There should be no unfair preference for the MCO's financial interest over the patient's care. An MCO can incur liability by making medically inappropriate decisions that emanate from defects in the design or implementation of a cost containment mechanism. For example, an MCO that arbitrarily ignores, unreasonably disregards, or simply overrides appeals on a patient's behalf incurs legal liability. There must be a causal connection between the decision to withhold or deny treatment and harm to the patient. Unless there is a causal connection, there is no legal liability. Concurrent and retrospective medical record reviews are most likely to uncover legal liability because the notations indicate whether care was withheld from the patient. Causation is usually easier to prove.[65]

Contradictory pressures are obvious. Even though cost containment is the heart of an MCO business, costs cannot be controlled by rendering substandard care. When physicians have a financial incentive to restrict a patient's care by making fewer referrals to specialists, the MCO program can be especially dangerous from a litigation viewpoint.

A recent U.S. Supreme Court decision explicitly recognized the necessity for cost containment in managed care.[66] This opinion has done a great deal to add legitimacy to what most knowledgeable commentators already recognized: In order to control costs, MCOs must be able to control the amount of care given as well as which provider gives that care. At one point in its opinion, the Court said:

> "HMOs became popular because fee-for-service physicians were thought to be providing unnecessary or useless services; today, many doctors and other observers argue that HMOs often ignore the individual needs of a patient in order to improve the HMOs' bottom lines. Although it is true that the relationship between sparing medical treatment and physician reward is not a subtle one under the HMO scheme, no HMO organization could survive without some incentive connecting physician reward with treatment rationing. The essence of an HMO is that salaries and profits are limited by the HMOs's fixed membership fees. This is not to suggest that the schemes in this case are as socially desirable as some other HMO organizational schemes; they may not be. But whatever the HMO, there must be rationing and inducement to ration."[67]

Two of the best-known legal cases on negligent or abusive cost containment procedures are from California (see Box 14-15). In one case the MCO was found liable; in the other, it was not.

Both of the California cases described in Box 14-15 were decided by the same court, but by a different panel of judges. Despite the conflict between these cases, risk managers should anticipate that utilization review decisions that harm the patient may lead to litigation, with an adverse outcome. Risk managers should also be aware that several courts have held that utilization review claims are preempted by ERISA; examples are:

- Denial of hospitalization to a pregnant woman, whose fetus died while she was at home unattended.[68]
- Denial of precertification for cardiac surgery so that by the time surgery was approved, the patient had deteriorated.[69]
- Denial of autologous bone marrow transplant that led to death.[70]

BOX 14-15

- An MCO consultant physician denied authorization for continued hospitalization over the objection of the treating doctor. That denial resulted in the amputation of the patient's leg. Because the treating doctor cannot delegate his responsibility for patient care to an MCO consultant, the court held that the MCO was not liable. A doctor must follow his own medical judgment even if it conflicts with the MCO's utilization review policy. This treating doctor did not appeal the denial.[71]
- An MCO was held liable for the consequences of a utilization review decision that was a substantial causal factor in the patient's death.[72]

If a case is preempted by ERISA, there is no recovery against the MCO. Risk managers should make sure that all cases that are removable under ERISA are actually removed. The following protective risk management strategies can help reduce potential liability:[73]

- Obtain professional liability insurance coverage with adequate limits for conduct arising from utilization review activities.
- Establish and adhere to standard utilization review procedures.
- Design cost containment systems consistent with prevailing medical standards. Decision-makers should examine the patient, review the medical records, and/or discuss the patient's condition with the treating physician.
- Continually monitor the utilization review program to ensure that it is being consistently and fairly administered.
- Clearly document denials and reasons for denial.

- Make prompt determinations to avoid unnecessary delays in medical treatment and to avoid angering the treating physician.
- Do not deny a medical treatment over the attending physician's adamant objections. Although recommendations of alternatives are encouraged, it is not wise to completely override the treating physician's medical judgment.
- Do not require preadmission certification for emergency care.
- Ensure that utilization review appeals are reviewed by a physician specializing in the applicable field of medicine.
- Provide plan physicians with a written copy of the appeal mechanism and ensure that the appeal process is clearly communicated.
- When utilization review functions are contracted to a separate organization, investigate and continually monitor that organization's solvency and insurance coverage, obtain appropriate indemnification and insurance coverage, and determine if the organization has policies and procedures consistent with the applicable standard of medical care.
- Investigate and analyze policies, contracts, consent forms, record release forms, marketing materials, utilization review manuals, and monitoring systems to ensure sufficient appeal procedures.
- If investigation reveals any documents or contracts that create the impression that the MCO is governing the level of medical care for patients, take corrective action immediately.
- Include a disclaimer in utilization review manuals and other materials distributed to physicians stating that the physician bears the sole responsibility for medical decisions.
- Provide written guidelines to the MCO's marketing and advertising departments to avoid the possibility that sales materials will create the unintended impression that the MCO utilization review program governs the level of medical care for the patients.
- Ensure that all utilization review determinations are made by personnel who possess the requisite state license.
- Whenever denying a medical service, try to obtain the concurrence of the treating physician. Use utilization review as a tool to educate physicians about the appropriate use of resources.
- Place greater weight on quality assessment programs such as professional education, credentialing, reference verification, and licensing.
- Conduct patient satisfaction surveys.

VICARIOUS LIABILITY

Respondeat Superior

Respondeat superior establishes the responsibility of an employer for the wrongful acts of its employees. This doctrine may be known as "master/servant" or "principal/agent" or other names in different jurisdictions. Whatever the name, the concept remains the same: the MCO employer is legally responsible for the wrongful acts of its employees committed in the scope of their employment. Elements of *respondeat superior* include: (1) medical malpractice by a health care provider; (2) an employment relationship between providers and the MCO, as opposed to an independent contractor relationship; and (3) providers acting within the scope of their employment. *Respondeat superior* is most likely to be found when the MCO pays salary and benefits to its own providers and utilizes its own medical facilities, such as in a staff model HMO.[74]

Traditionally, *respondeat superior* was applied to physicians in medical malpractice cases. It had to be determined whether the doctor was an employee of a company, usually a hospital, wherein the employer was responsible for the malpractice of the doctor. In managed care, however, the doctrine of *respondeat superior* applies to employed physicians as well as employed allied health professionals. Basically, the MCO employer is responsible for the negligence of all its employees, physician or otherwise, acting within the scope of their employment.

Determining Status as an Employee

An individual who is paid a salary and benefits by an MCO is obviously the MCO's employee. In other cases, however, the employment relationship is not so easily determined. Courts look at the following elements in deciding whether an individual is an employee:

- Right of control by the MCO.
- Degree to which MCO control is exercised.
- Actual day-to-day relationships between providers and the MCO.
- Whether providers obtain a majority of their patients from the MCO.
- Manner of provider selection by the MCO.
- Whether providers comply with rigorous MCO utilization review procedures.
- Industry custom.
- Skill of worker.
- Method of payment.
- Right of discharge by the MCO.
- Whether providers re-negotiate their contract on a yearly basis.
- Ownership of facilities and instrumentalities used to perform work.

Respondeat Superior without an Employment Relationship

Usually, *respondeat superior* is applied only when health care providers are MCO employees. However, one court applied the *respondeat superior* doctrine even though the physician was not formally employed (see Box 14-16), because the MCO clearly exercised a substantial degree of control over its "independent contractor" physicians.

Protective strategies to negate *respondeat superior* are few and dangerous. Health care providers can be converted from formal employees to independent contractors. However, if the MCO still maintains substantial control over the provider's conduct, the MCO will continue to be responsible under the doctrine of ostensible, or apparent, agency. The MCO could convert providers into independent contractors *and* significantly lessen its control over the providers. But lessened control is potentially inconsistent with state law as well as with accreditation standards that require supervision. It is highly debatable whether an uncontrolled independent contractor is a prudent idea for an MCO.[75] The only effective antidote to liability under *respondeat superior* is to ensure that the employed providers meet the standard of care and are not otherwise negligent.

BOX 14-16

Although the doctor was formally an independent contractor, he worked at the HMO's office, could not reject patients, was paid on a capitated basis, and was under the control of the HMO. Despite the absence of formal employment, the court held that the doctor could be considered a direct employee, triggering the doctrine of *respondeat superior*.[76]

Ostensible/Apparent Agency

An MCO is responsible for its own employees as well as for those individuals who appear to be its employees, even though they are not actually its employees. Because these individuals "appear" to be employees, the liability doctrine is called apparent agency or ostensible agency. Ostensible and apparent agency applies to IPA and group model MCOs. At times, only a fine line separates *respondeat superior* (actual employees) from apparent agency (apparent employees). In some cases, it is a close call as to which doctrine the plaintiff will claim and the court will apply.

Elements of Ostensible/Apparent Agency

For ostensible/apparent agency to apply, the following situations must exist:

1. An MCO presents the doctor to the public as its employee and the patient reasonably believes that the doctor is the MCO's employee.
2. Patients reasonably look to the MCO for health care.
3. Reliance by the patient on the representations or conduct of the MCO has resulted in actual detriment.

Factors Creating Apparent Agency

While there are no hard-and-fast rules as to what creates apparent agency, trends have emerged from court rulings. If the answer to most of the following questions is yes, it is likely that the health care provider will be found to be the apparent agent of the MCO, even if the provider is formally an independent contractor.

- Does the doctor work out of the MCO's office?
- Does the doctor's name appear on the MCO's stationery, bills, consent forms, and marketing brochures?
- Does the MCO assert in written documents that the doctor is competent or is subject to quality control?
- Does the medical group do very high volume work for a single MCO?
- Is the doctor's name listed under the MCO listing in the telephone Yellow Pages?
- Does the name of the MCO appear on the medical office building?
- Are MCO marketing or informational materials present and on display in the medical office?

Relevant Factors for Subscriber Reliance on the MCO for Medical Care

For apparent or ostensible agency to apply, the subscriber must *reasonably* rely on the MCO for medical care. In deciding whether subscribers acted reasonably in relying on the MCO, the courts consider the following situations:

- The degree to which patients can choose their own doctor.
- The number of providers from which the patient may choose.
- Whether the patient can choose to use nonparticipating providers.

The case described in Box 14-17 is important because it is probably the first case that held an HMO responsible for an independent contractor doctor.

A number of courts ruled an MCO liable for the conduct of its independent contractors under the doctrine of apparent or ostensible agency (see Box 14-18).

BOX 14-17

Although an MCO is not ordinarily liable for the negligence of its independent contractors, the court held that the MCO is vicariously liable when the independent contractor is the ostensible agent of the MCO. An ostensible agent relationship existed because the patient's primary care physician was selected by the MCO and the MCO had made determinations to authorize payments for specific medical services.[77]

Risk managers can utilize a number of protective strategies to limit the MCO's liability from claims of apparent or ostensible agency:[82]

- Obtain professional liability insurance coverage to protect the MCO from misconduct by apparent agents.
- Use varied communication techniques to make sure that subscribers understand the difference between MCO employees and nonemployees.
- On letterheads and signs, make the doctor's name more prominent than the MCO name. Better yet, omit the MCO's name.
- Place written notice in plan documents such as "summary description" and "evidence of coverage" that the treating physicians are not employees and that the MCO is not responsible for any wrongful conduct by the physicians.
- Clearly specify in written contracts that the providers are independent contractors.
- Convert all oral contracts to writing to avoid any misunderstanding that the providers are independent contractors.
- Have the independent contractors use separate consent forms with proper notation of the independent contractor status printed on the form.

BOX 14-18

- An appellate court held the hospital responsible for the physician's conduct because he was under the control of the hospital. In part, the court said: "Patients entering the hospital through the emergency room could properly assume that the treating doctors and staff of the hospital were acting on behalf of the hospital. Such patients are not bound by secret limitations as are contained in a private contract between the hospital and the doctor."[78]
- Even though the physician was employed by a practice group having the contract for the emergency room, the court held the hospital responsible for the doctor's conduct. Because the emergency room was located in the hospital building and appeared to be part of the hospital, the patient had a right to rely on those appearances.[79]
- Even though the HMO contracted with an IPA, which in turn contracted with specific doctors to provide health services to HMO subscribers, the court held the HMO responsible for the malpractice of a treating doctor. This decision relied heavily on the fact that the HMO appeared to present the doctor as its employee, along with other factors.[80]
- An MCO was held liable for the conduct of a consulting specialist on the grounds that the referral was made by a salaried HMO provider. Factors considered relevant by the court included the following: the HMO referring provider had the right to discharge the consultant, the consultant was providing health care services, providing health care services was part of the HMO's normal business, and the consultant reported to the HMO referring provider.[81]

- Enact policies and procedures and take measures designed to inform the patient of the exact relationship between the provider and the MCO.
- Analyze existing contracts, referral policy, marketing materials, billing procedures, signage, stationery, manner of employee, independent contractor address, and consent forms. If any of these can lead to a reasonable inference of an unintended employment relationship, make immediate corrections.
- Include in any referral policies a provision for employees and independent contractors to advise the patient that the specialist to whom the patient is referred is not an employee.
- Avoid advertising campaigns that may imply an unintended employment relationship.
- Provide written guidelines to the marketing and advertising departments.

MCO DEFENSE

Independent Contractor Status of Physicians

Generally, MCOs are not liable for the conduct of their independent contractors. If the elements of ostensible / apparent agency are absent, the MCO is not liable. In an extensive opinion, the court did not hold an HMO responsible for the alleged malpractice of an independent contractor physician, for the following reasons:[83]

1. The HMO had no control over the independent contractor physicians. Even though the physicians had to comply with the HMO rules and regulations, the HMO did not review the medical practice and decisions of the physicians to ensure accuracy.
2. The HMO did not advertise or hold itself out as exerting control over the physicians.
3. HMO subscribers were told that the HMO did not directly furnish medical care and could not make medical judgments.
4. The plaintiff did not demonstrate a reasonable detrimental reliance on the HMO to provide quality medical care.
5. All HMOs require subscribers to choose a primary physician from a list selected by the HMO, and that does not form a reasonable basis for reliance.

Medical Group Employees

Usually, the MCO will not be liable if the health care provider is employed by a medical group that in turn contracts with the MCO (see Box 14-19). In this case the MCO is not directly employing the physicians. In another, more convoluted case (see Box 14-20), the facts also indicate an absence of MCO liability for independent contractors. Using the protective strategies regarding liability under *respondeat superior* and apparent agency, risk managers should take maximum advantage of the independent contractor defense.

BOX 14-19

An HMO was not liable for the conduct of a treating doctor who was employed by an IPA because the treating physicians were not paid or supervised by the HMO, the treating physicians had no contract with the HMO, and the treating physicians were paid and supervised by the medical association that contracted with the HMO.[84]

BOX 14-20

An HMO contracted with IPA #1, which in turn contracted with IPA #2, which in turn hired physicians. A physician allegedly committed malpractice, and the HMO was sued. Because neither the HMO nor IPA #1 had the power to hire or fire individual physicians, or to set their salaries, their work schedules, or their terms of employment, the court held that the HMO was not liable. Actual control rested with IPA #2, which had not been sued.[86]

Exhaustion of Contractual Remedies

Courts will generally enforce MCO contracts that require internal resolution of subscriber or provider disputes (see Box 14-21). However, the dispute resolution procedures must be fair, impartial, and reasonable.

Exception to Exhaustion Requirement: Futility

Historically, courts have not forced a person to engage in a futile act solely for the purpose of fulfilling a meaningless formality. If MCO members can demonstrate that every internal appeal results in a ruling in favor of the MCO, the court can rule that the members are relieved of the obligation to process their claim through the internal process. A recent case had a good discussion of the futility doctrine.[85]

BOX 14-21

A court held that a contractual provision requiring that provider disputes be submitted to the membership committee for resolution was enforceable. Providers could seek judicial review of the decision only if Delta Dental violated their fair procedure rights to an impartial tribunal.[87]

To take maximum advantage of the requirement that the subscriber exhaust contractual remedies, the risk manager should apply these protective strategies:

- Draft subscriber and provider contracts to require compliance with internal dispute resolution procedures before any court action.
- Provide adequate due process in dispute resolution procedures, including: (1) resolution by an impartial review committee or board having the power to grant an adequate remedy, (2) an opportunity for members to be heard, to argue their case by written submissions, oral argument, or both, and with the assistance of an attorney, (3) provision for an internal appeal of an adverse decision.
- Possibly require binding arbitration after an internal review.
- Apply dispute resolution procedures fairly and in good faith.
- Avoid making the dispute resolution process a "rubber stamp" for pro-management decisions.
- Apply the terms of a plan consistently from member to member.

Exhaustion of Administrative Remedies

Many state statutes require subscriber disputes to be submitted to a specialized administrative agency before being taken to court (see Box 14-22). In Maryland, that agency is the Insurance Commission. Almost universally, the courts defer to the specialized administrative agency requirements because: (1) the agency officials are considered to possess superior expertise in the subject matter and (2) the administrative review is considered part of a comprehensive regulatory scheme requiring judicial deference. If the administrative agency has

BOX 14-22

Failure of an HMO subscriber to exhaust the administrative remedies provided by the Maryland Health Maintenance Organization Act prevented the court from exercising jurisdiction over the plaintiff's denial of a benefits claim.[89]

the power to grant an adequate remedy, the courts are more likely to defer to the agency. These administrative agency reviews are useful to the risk manager because the agencies are more predictable and tend to be less pro-plaintiff than the average jury.

Limited Judicial Review

Generally, the scope of judicial review of administrative decisions is limited to whether the agency complied with the procedural requirements.

ERISA Preemption

ERISA (the Employee Retirement and Income Security Act)[88] regulates employee welfare benefit plans including employer-sponsored health benefits plans. Since ERISA is a federal law, the legislation was deemed a comprehensive statute that preempts any and all state laws that "relate to" employee benefit plans.

Preemption under ERISA has a number of legal and strategic advantages for the MCO defendant. Because ERISA severely limits the relief a plaintiff can obtain, preemption is a tremendously useful defense. ERISA preemption is so favorable to the MCO defendant that it should be requested in every case to which ERISA applies. ERISA applies in most cases in which subscribers obtained their MCO membership as a work-related benefit.

ERISA's scope is by no means settled. There is still vigorous dispute in the courts and the legal community about the parameters of ERISA preemption. Until the scope of ERISA preemption is finally settled by the U.S. Supreme Court or the Congress by legislative amendment, risk managers should use ERISA preemption as aggressively as possible.

Exceptions to ERISA

ERISA does not apply to every MCO membership obtained through employment. This statute does not apply to church plans, government plans, plans maintained to comply with workers' compensation, unemployment compensation or disability plans, plans maintained outside of the United States for the purpose of providing benefits to nonresident aliens, and unfunded excess benefit plans. But at least one court found an exception to the exception (see Box 14-23).

"Relates to" Test for Preemption

A claim under ERISA, including a claim for medical malpractice, must be shown to "relate to" the employee benefit plan. Several arguments can be made to support the ERISA preemption:

- By virtue of employment-based health benefits, the plaintiff was enrolled in the MCO.

BOX 14-23

Although a county government plan is normally exempt from ERISA, the court held that this one was not exempt because nongovernment employees could belong to the plan. Since the plan was not exempt from ERISA, the federal courts possessed exclusive jurisdiction.[90]

- "But for" the participation in the employment-based health benefits plan, the plaintiff would not have had a relationship with the MCO.
- A medical malpractice verdict or award against the MCO affects the assets of the MCO and, therefore, "relates to" the plan.
- A contract defines the quality and scope of medical care provided to the plaintiff by the MCO and, therefore, "relates to" the plan.

Exhaustion of Internal Remedies

ERISA requires benefit plans to provide internal dispute resolution procedures for participants whose benefits claims were denied. Courts have decreed that a plaintiff asserting a claim under ERISA must first exhaust these internal administrative remedies unless it would be futile to do so. Risk managers should insist that internal remedies be exhausted in claim situations. Requiring the exhaustion of internal remedies has a number of advantages: (1) Frivolous ERISA claims may be minimized. (2) The process may promote consistent treatment of benefit claims. (3) Internal remedies can be a nonadversarial dispute resolution process. (4) Money and time may be saved, especially if a final resolution is reached, making court unnecessary.

Plaintiff's Remedies Limited to ERISA Provisions

In an ERISA case, the plaintiff can recover only what the statute allows: restitution and equitable relief to recover benefits under the plan; enforcement of contractual rights under the plan; clarification of future rights under the plan; or recovery for a breach of fiduciary duty. In addition, the statute grants discretionary authority to the court to award attorney's fees and costs of the action. There is no provision for a money award to the plaintiff. This law is fairly clear, since the U.S. Supreme Court has ruled on the scope of remedies in two cases. One decision stated that inclusion of some remedies and exclusion of others within ERISA is based on legislative policy choices and should be honored.[91] In the other, the Court said that the carefully integrated civil enforcement provisions of ERISA provide strong evidence that Congress did not intend to authorize other remedies that it simply forgot to incorporate expressly.[92]

Remedies Not Available under ERISA

Several remedies not available under ERISA are commonly available under state civil law. These include punitive damages,[93] damages for emotional distress,[94] possibly no remedy for medical malpractice,[95] and no monetary damages against a nonfiduciary.[96] Risk managers can immediately understand the significance of trying cases under the ERISA law where there are no punitive damages and no damages for emotional distress. Absence of these damages under ERISA makes ERISA very helpful to the defense.

MCOs can limit their potential liability exposure by avoiding fiduciary status. ERISA fiduciary status applies only to entities that possess discretionary authority in the administration or management of plan assets. MCOs must take the position that they execute duties in strict compliance with directives from the plan administrator and do not possess discretionary authority. As mentioned above, a recent case from the U.S. Supreme Court has limited fiduciary liability when an HMO physician is making mixed eligibility and treatment decisions.[97]

No Right to a Jury Trial

There is virtually universal agreement that a plaintiff is not entitled to a jury trial. Federal courts interpreting the statute have held that since ERISA provides only equitable relief, the standard of review for benefits decisions is "arbitrary and capricious." In proceedings in which the standard of review is arbitrary and capricious, the U.S. Supreme Court has held that there is no right to a jury trial.[98] Actions to recover benefits under employee benefit plans are governed by the common law of trusts, an equitable proceeding, and there is no right to a jury trial in equity. Availability of a jury trial is based on congressional intent. Congress' silence on its intent caused the case of *Berry v. Ciba-Geigy Corporation* to be decided by the Fourth Circuit Court of Appeals according to the common law of trusts, where there is no jury trial.[99] Another case also held that there is no right to a jury trial under ERISA.[100] When the claim is for breach of a fiduciary duty, there is no right to a jury trial under ERISA.[101] Of course, there is always a court decision to the contrary: A U.S. district court for the District of Columbia held that claims for the denial of benefits are legal in nature, since they seek monetary relief, and there is a right to a jury trial.[102] However, this opinion appears to be one in an isolated minority.

Risk managers will immediately appreciate the significance of avoiding a trial by jury. In many jurisdictions, especially large cities, juries have awarded large malpractice verdicts. To avoid a jury trial, risk managers can use the valuable defense tactic of applying the ERISA statute.

ERISA Plans Cannot Be Orally Modified

Health benefits contracts that are provided pursuant to an ERISA plan cannot be orally modified. In the leading case on this issue (see Box 14-24), the court held that the statutory language of ERISA unambiguously requires that all plans and modifications be written. In its decision, the court stated: "Based on this statutory scheme, any modification to a plan must be implemented in conformity with the formal amendment procedures and must be in writing. Oral or informal written modifications to a plan . . . are of no effect."[103] Therefore, the scope of covered benefits, the requirement for preauthorization, and the use of participating providers cannot be modified by oral representations by a subscriber, an employer, an employee of the MCO, or a treating physician. This defense is especially important when the subscriber or employer seeks to receive services not provided by the terms of the benefits contract. Frequently, this defense is used in denial of benefit cases and increasingly in medical malpractice cases.

Denial of Benefits Claims Are Removable

The law is well settled that claims for denial of health benefits, even if tried in state court, are preempted by ERISA. These claims are deemed to be founded in contract and "relate to" the plan. Primary U.S. Supreme Court cases established the ERISA preemp-

BOX 14-24

The plaintiff sought payment for medical expenses incurred after the termination of an ERISA benefits plan. In her claim, the plaintiff stated that employees of the insurer had made verbal representations and had written her letters stating that the medical expenses would be covered. The plaintiff claimed that these representations superceded and modified the written terms of the plan.[104]

tion doctrine.[105,106,107] The court decisions appear to be almost completely unified in the statement that a claim within ERISA's Section 1132(a)(1)(B) to recover, enforce, or clarify benefits is completely preempted under ERISA and will be tried in federal court without a jury.

The Court's Flexible Powers

In addition, the ERISA statute provides some flexibility in the powers the courts can exercise. ERISA allows the court to grant appropriate relief, even though the relief is not specifically stated in the statute. Since the powers of the federal court are not specifically defined in the ERISA statute, an opportunity exists for the court to exercise its discretion to create new remedies, consistent with the congressional intent in passing ERISA. Although this flexibility leaves the door open for federal courts to provide a remedy for medical malpractice, the courts have not yet done so.

Examples of ERISA Preemption

Although ERISA law is rapidly evolving, various courts have already applied ERISA to preempt a wide variety of claims against MCOs. Some examples include:

- Utilization review claim that denied treatment.[108]
- Denial of precertification.[109]
- Denial of autologous bone marrow transplant.[110]
- State antidumping claim.[111]
- State antideception claim.[112]
- State Uncompensated Care Pool Act.[113]

ERISA Removal of Medical Malpractice Claims against MCOs

The law is especially unsettled on whether ERISA allows the removal of medical malpractice claims against MCOs. Some cases have granted removal; others have denied removal. Although no clear trend has developed, the courts seem to be moving toward allowing the removal of malpractice cases.[114] Cases allowing the removal of medical malpractice cases against MCOs included a variety of claims:

- Vicarious liability claim for the medical malpractice of the treating MCO provider.[115]
- Wrongful death claim against an insurance company that provided employment-based health and life insurance benefits.[116]
- Medical malpractice claim against a utilization review company that denied inpatient hospitalization for a pregnant woman, allegedly resulting in the death of the fetus.[117]
- Medical malpractice claim against an HMO that denied certification for surgery, allegedly resulting in the death of the subscriber.[118]
- Medical malpractice claim against an HMO on grounds of vicarious liability for negligence of treating doctors.[119]
- Joint venture liability claim against an MCO for medical negligence by the entity that provided mental health services to HMO subscribers.[120]
- Medical negligence claim against an MCO.[121]
- Medical negligence and wrongful death claim against an HMO.[122]
- Direct liability claim against an HMO for failure to supervise the care and medical treatment provided by its doctors, and a vicarious liability claim against an HMO for the medical negligence of the treating doctor.[123]
- Vicarious liability claim against an HMO for medical negligence and wrongful death, allegedly caused by a denial of benefits, and a vicarious liability claim

against an HMO for medical negligence of the treating doctor.[124]

- Direct and vicarious medical negligence claims against an HMO.[125]

Strategies of ERISA Removal

At this point, the importance of ERISA removal should be apparent. Any time the risk manager has the slightest chance of bringing a case under the ERISA statute, the risk manager should vigorously exploit that possibility. Under ERISA, there may be no jury trial, no punitive damages, no emotional distress damages, and required internal review.

Application of case law in support of ERISA not providing any relief for medical malpractice can result in a case dismissal. Clearly, this is a result risk managers should seek to achieve. In addition, many plaintiffs are discouraged by the prospect of having to deal with ERISA. In some cases, plaintiffs have dismissed the MCO from the case to avoid the ERISA issues and limitations, including removal. Ultimately, either the U.S. Supreme Court or Congress will have to clarify the uncertainty in ERISA. Until there is clear and definite law, the risk manager should press the use of ERISA vigorously.

Federal Employees Health Benefits Act (FEHBA)

ERISA does not apply to government employees, including federal government employees. However, the Federal Employees Health Benefits Act (FEHBA)[126] provides some of the same benefits, such as limitations on damages, for MCO subscribers who are federal government employees. There may also be state statutes that are equivalents to FEHBA or ERISA. As with ERISA, the risk manager should vigorously press all possible rights under FEHBA.

Courts have held that FEHBA preempts state law contract and tort claims that allege inadequate health care provided under an MCO plan if (1) the state law claims attempt to expand the MCO's obligations under the plan, and (2) the state law claims are inconsistent with the plan.[127]

Limitations of Damages under FEHBA

FEHBA limits damages to the amount of contract benefits that are in dispute plus simple interest and court costs.

State Law Contract and Tort Claims Preempted by FEHBA

One court held that all of a plaintiff's contract and tort claims, including medical negligence, were preempted by FEHBA because the plaintiff's participation in the MCO was provided as a benefit of her federal employment.[128]

FEHBA Strategies

FEHBA is not as broad in its application as is ERISA and has not been used in as many cases as ERISA. Nevertheless, risk managers should try to have cases involving federal government employees tried under FEHBA.

MCO CRYSTAL BALL GAZING

The MCO's liability is increasing on several fronts: the old "traditional" legal theories and the "new" approaches. In the future, plaintiffs are expected to seek to expand the boundaries of the old theories and increasingly raise new theories of liability against MCOs. In essence, managed care policies limit the patient's choice of providers and medical options while restricting the physician's clinical autonomy. The goals of management, providers, and patients may conflict under an MCO. These conflicting goals deal with cost containment, utilization of resources, increasing efficiency, eliminating unnecessary treatments, the range of services, informed consent, denial of care, and the quality of care.[129] Financial incentives for physicians to limit services is a particularly disturbing MCO objective.[130] The conflicting stances could certainly lead to potential risks, and liability insurers are already adjusting to the MCO growth.[131]

This scenario is not entirely somber. As the courts come to understand how an MCO operates (as the Supreme Court did in *Pegram*), it is expected that traditional and innovative defenses will be accepted by the courts. As the public comes to understand the operation of an MCO, there should be some hope for reductions in liability and verdicts. For the immediate future, however, the judicial system may not be particularly friendly to MCOs. An experienced MCO lawyer concluded: "I predict that there will be more lawsuits, but that the MCOs will do what the classic defendants in lawsuits have learned to do, which is to adapt to them. . . . MCOs will practice better medicine or practice better medical management as a result of the lawsuits being around."[132] At this time, the future is uncertain.

References

1. Fiesta, J. (1995). Managed care: Whose liability? *Nursing Management* 26(2):31–32.
2. Manoogian, D. E. (1993). The role of the HMO risk manager in medical malpractice cases. *Journal for Healthcare Quality* Part 1, 15(4);34–36; Part 2, 15(5):20–25, 33.
3. Yarmolinsky, A. (1995). Supporting the patient. *New England Journal of Medicine* 332(9):602–603.
4. *Pegram v. Herdrich,* 120 S.Ct. 2143 (2000).
5. Mitka, M. (1994). Managed care plays a big role in group practice. *American Medical News* 37(42):10.
6. Kertesz, L. (1995). Medicare: The final frontier for HMOs. *Modern Healthcare* 25(14):76–84.
7. Washburn, L. (1995). Health care shakeup. Medicaid heads to managed plans. *News Tribune* (Woodbridge, N.J.), July 16, p. 1, col. 6.
8. Maryland Code, Health-General, Sec. 19–704.
9. Maryland Code, Courts & Judicial Proceedings, Sec. 3-2A-01(e).
10. *Group Health Association v. Blumenthal,* 295 Md. 104 (1983); *Wedig v. Tabler,* 83 Md. App. 488 (1990).
11. Maryland Code, Health-General, Sec. 19-710(g)(1).
12. Maryland Code, Health-General, Sec. 19.710(g).
13. *Depenbrok v. Kaiser Foundation Health Plan, Inc.,* 79 Cal. App. 3d 167, 144 Cal. Rptr. 724 (1978).
14. *Boyd v. Albert Einstein Medical Center,* 377 Pa. Super. 609, 547 A. 2d 1229 (1988).
15. *Fox v. HealthNet of California,* No. 219692 (Cal. Super. Ct. Dec. 23, 1993); Patient's family wins $77M. Penalty ordered for denail of treatment. (1993). *Staten Island Advance* (New York), December 29, p. A9, col. 3.
16. Mendez, I. (1995). New law requires insurers to offer bone marrow transplant coveage. *Star-Ledger* (Newark, N.J.), May 10, p. 22, col. 4.
17. *Couture v. Health New England,* Civil No. 93-30089-F (D. Mass. 1993).
18. 42 U.S.C. 1395dd.
19. *Dearmas v. AvMed, Inc.,* 814 F. Supp. 1103 (S.D. Fla. 1993).
20. 29 U.S.C. 1001 *et seq.*
21. Top court rules firms have right to revise insurance, benefit plans. (1995). *Star-Ledger* (Newark, N.J.), March 7, p. 47, col. 1; Somerville, J. (1995). Reform battle turns to ERISA. *American Medical News* 38(4):3, 21–22; Voelker, R. (1995). States face rocky road to reform. *Journal of the American Medical Association* 273(4):187–188.
22. *Everson v. Blue Cross and Blue Shield of Ohio,* No. 93 CV 7534 (N.D. Ohio June 15, 1994).
23. *Forsyth v. Humana, Inc.,* 827 F. Supp. 1498 (D. Nev. 1993). On other grounds, the U.S. Ninth Circuit reversed *Forsyth v. Humana* 114 F.3d 1467 (9th Cir., 1997). The U.S. Supreme Court affirmed the Ninth Circuit but did not consider the ERISA issue, *Humana v. Forsyth* 119 S. Ct. 710 (1999).
24. *Drinkwater v. Metropolitan Life Insurance Co.,* 846 F. 2d 821 (1st Cir.), cert. denied, 488 U.S. 909, 109 S. Ct. 261, 102 L. Ed. 2d 249 (1988).
25. *Pegram v. Herdrich,* 120 S.Ct. 2143 (2000).
26. *Rush Prudential HMO v. Moran* 122 S.Ct. 2151 (2002).

27. 42 U.S.C. 12101 et seq.
28. *Equal Employment Opportunity Commission*, No. IP 00-014-Misc., 2000 WL 724004, at *2–*4 (D. Ind. May 17, 2000); *Devito v. Chicago Park District*, 83 F. 3d 878 (7th Cir. 1996).
29. *Pappas v. Bethesda Hosp. Ass'n*, 861 F. Supp. 616 (S.D. Ohio 1994).
30. *Dodd v. Blue Cross and Blue Shield Ass'n*, 835 F. Supp. 888 (E.D. Va. 1993).
31. *Holmes v. City of Aurora*, 1995 U.S. Dist. WL 21606 (N.D. Ill. Jan. 18, 1995).
32. *Carparts Distrib. Ctr., Inc. v. Automative Wholesaler's Ass'n of New England, Inc.*, 37 F. 3d 12 (1st Cir. 1994).
33. *United States v. State of Illinois*, No. 93 C7741, 1994 U.S. Dist. LEXIS 12890 (N.D. Ill. Sept. 12, 1994).
34. *EEOC v. Mason Tenders Welfare Trust Fund*, No. 93 CIV 3865 JES (S.D. N.Y. 1994).
35. *United States v. State of Illinois*, No. 93 C7741, 1994 U.S. Dist. LEXIS 12890 (N.D. Ill. Sept. 12,1994).
36. *Parker v. Metropolitan Life*, 1995 WL 48471 (W.D. Tenn. Jan. 17, 1995).
37. 29 U.S.C. 1001 *et seq.*
38. 29 U.S.C. 1961 *et seq.*
39. 15 U.S.C. 1011 *et seq.*
40. *Teti v. U.S. Healthcare, Inc.*, No. 88-9808, 88-9822 1989 U.S. Dist. LEXIS (E.D. Pa. Dec. 28, 1989), affirmed 904 F. 2d 696 (3d Cir. 1990).
41. *Plymouth Healthcare Sys., Inc. v. Keystone Health Plan East, Inc.*, No. 91-7551, 1992 U.S. Dist. LEXIS 13428 (E.D. Pa. Sept. 2, 1992), affirmed 993 F. 2d 878 (3d Cir.), cert. denied, 114 S. Ct. 180, 126 L. Ed. 2d 139 (1993).
42. *Forsyth v. Humana, Inc.*, 827 F. Supp. 1498 (D. Nev. 1993).
43. *UNUM v. Ward* 119 S.Ct. 1380 (1999).
44. *Rush Prudential HMO v. Moran* 122 S.Ct. 2151 (2002).
45. *Humana v. Forsyth* 119 S. Ct. 710 (1999).
46. Bloom, R. (1992). Physician credentialling in managed care. *Annals of Health Law* 1:93–98.
47. *Harrell v. Total Health Care, Inc.*, 781 S. W. 2d 58 (Mo. 1989).
48. JCAHO guidelines are specified in their "Human Resources," HR 1.0–6.4. NCQA specifications are their "Standards for Credentialing," CR 1.0–13.0.
49. *McClellan v. Health Maintenance Organization of Pa.*, 413 Pa. Super. 128, 604 A. 2d 1053 (1992), appeal denied, 531 Pa. 664, 616 A. 2d 985 (1992).
50. *Shannon v. McNulty*, 718 A. 2d 828, 835–836 (Pa. Super. Ct. 1998).
51. JCAHO guidelines are specified in their "Human Resources," HR 1.0–6.4. NCQA specifications are their "Standards for Credentialing," CR 1.0–13.0.
52. Mickelsen, R. A. (1994). Managed care credentialling and provider selection. Paper presented at the Managed Care Law Institute: Legal and Structural Issues, National Health Lawyers Association, Washington, D.C., December.
53. Ten states OK "any willing provider" law. (1995). *ACP (American College of Physicians) Observer* 15(3):13.
54. *HCA Health Services of Va., Inc. v. Aetna Life Insurance Co.*, No. 92-574-A, 1994 U.S. Dist. LEXIS 6080 (E.D. Va. Mar. 4, 1994).
55. *Kiester v. Humana Hospital Alaska, Inc.*, 843 P. 2d 1219 (Alaska, 1992).
56. *Owens v. New Britain General Hospital*, 627 A. 2d 1373 (Conn. App. Ct. 1993).
57. *Delta Dental Plan of California v. Banasky*, 33 Cal. Rptr. 2d 381.
58. *Ehlmann v. Kaiser* 198 F. 3d 552 (5th Cir., 2000)
59. *Lazorko v. Pennsylvania Hospita*l 237 F. 3d 242 (3d Cir., 2000).
60. *Kentucky Association of Health Plans v. Miller U.S. Supreme Court No. 00-1471* (on *certiorari* from the United States Sixth Circuit).
61. *Darling v. Charleston Community Memorial Hospital*, 50 Ill. App. 2d 253, 200 N.E. 2d 149 (1964), affirmed, 33 Ill. 2d 326, 211 N.E. 2d 253 (1965), cert. denied, 383 U.S. 946 (1966).
62. *McClellan v. Health Maintenance Organization of Pa.*, 413 Pa. Super. 128, 604 A. 2d 1053 (1992), appeal denied, 531 Pa. 664, 616 A. 2d 985 (1992).
63. Maryland Code, Health-General, Sec. 19-705.1(e).
64. Oberman, L. (1995). HMOs pushing clinical guidelines use by physicians. *American Medical News* 38(4):8.
65. Hinden, R. A. (1992). Utilization review: Managed care's appeal also its biggest liability? *Medical Malpractice Law & Strategy* 9(2):1, 4, 6.
66. *Pegram v. Herdrich*, 120 S.Ct. 2143 (2000).
67. *Pegram v. Herdrich*, 120 S.Ct. 2143 at 2149 and 2150 (2000).
68. *Corcoran v. United Health Care, Inc.*, 965 F. 2d 1321 (5th Cir. 1992), cert. denied, 113 S. Ct. 812, 121 L. Ed. 2d. 684 (1992).

69. *Kuhl v. Lincoln Nat'l. Health Plan of Kansas City, Inc.*, 999 F. 2d 298 (8th Cir. 1993), cert. denied, 114 S. Ct. 694, 126 L. Ed. 2d 661, 62 U.S.L.W. 3451 (1994).

70. *Spain v. Aetna Life Ins. Co.*, 11 F. 3d 129 (9th Cir. 1993) cert. denied, 114 S. Ct. 1612, 128 L. Ed. 2d 340, 62 U.S.L.W. 3703 (1994).

71. *Wickline v. California*, 183 Cal. App. 3d 1064, 228 Cal. Rptr. 661, review granted, 231 Cal. Rptr. 560, 727 P. 2d 753 (1986), review dismissed, remanded, ordered published, 239 Cal. Rptr. 805, 741 P. 2d 613 (1987).

72. *Wilson v. Blue Cross of So. Ca.*, 222 Cal. App. 3d 660, 271 Cal. Rptr. 876 (2d Dist. 1990), review denied, Oct. 11, 1990.

73. Hinden, R. A. (1992). Protecting against corporate negligence liability. *Medical Malpractice Law & Strategy* 9(2):5–7; Quality assurance programs are key to relieving MCO's legal liability, attorney says. (1994). *Managed Care Law Outlook* 3(11):3–4.

74. *Sloan v. The Metro. Health Council of Indianapolis, Inc.*, 516 N.E. 2D 1104 (Ind. Ct. App. 1987).

75. Stahl, D. A. (1995). Managed care contracting: An art or a science? *Nursing Management* 26(2):16–17.

76. *Dunn v. Praiss*, 256 N.J. Super. 180, 606 A. 2d 862 (Sup. Ct. App. Div.), cert. denied, 130 N.J. 20, 611 A. 2d 657 (1992), appeal after remand, 271 N.J. Super. 311, 638 A. 2d 875, cert. granted, 137 N.J. 308, 645 A. 2d 137 (1994).

77. *Elsessor v. Hospital of the Philadelphia College of Osteopathic Medicine*, 802 F. Supp. 1286 (E.D. Pa. 1992).

78. *Mduba v. Benedictine Hosp.*, 52 A.D. 2d 450, 384 N.Y.S. 2d 527 (1976).

79. *Mehlman v. Powell*, 378 A. 2d 1121 (Md. 1977).

80. *Boyd v. Albert Einstein Medical Center*, 377 Pa. Super. 609, 547 A. 2d 1229 (1988).

81. *Schleier v. Kaiser Found. Health Plan of the Mid-Atlantic States*, 876 F. 2d 174 (D.C. Cir. 1989).

82. Hinden, R. A. (1992). Ostensible agency: Managed care entities face vicarious liability. *Medical Malpractice Law & Strategy* 9(6):5–6.

83. *Raglin v. HMO Illinois, Inc.*, 230 Ill. App. 3d 642, 595 N.E. 2d 153 (1992).

84. *Pickett v. Cigna Health Plan of Texas, Inc.*, No. 01-92-00803-CV, 1993 WL 209858 (Tex. App. June 17,1993) (not reported in S.W. 2d).

85. *D'Amico v. CBS Corporation*, 3d Cir., No.01-3956, filed July 18, 2002.

86. *Chase v. Independent Practice Association, Inc.*, 31 Mass, App. Ct. 661, 583 N.E. 2d 251 (1991).

87. *Delta Dental Plan of California v. Banasky*, 33 Cal. Rptr. 2d 381.

88. 29 U.S.C. 1001 et seq.

89. *King v. Healthcare Corp.*, No. 93181081/CL166791 (Md. Cir. Ct. (Balt. City) Oct. 18, 1993).

90. *Nord Community Mental Health Ctr. v. Lorain*, 93 Ohio App. 3d 363, 638 N.E. 2d 623 (1994).

91. *Pilot Life Ins. Co. v. Dedeaux*, 481 U.S. 41, 107 S. Ct. 1549, 95 L. Ed. 2d 39 (1987).

92. *Massachusetts Mutual Life Ins. Co. et al. v. Russell*, 473 U.S. 134, 105 S. Ct. 3085, 87 L. Ed. 2d 96 (1985).

93. *Massachusetts Mutual Life Ins. Co. et al. v. Russell*, 473 U.S. 134, 105 S. Ct. 3085, 87 L. Ed. 2d 96 (1985).

94. *Corcoran v. United Health Care, Inc.*, 965 F. 2d 1321 (5th Cir. 1992), cert. denied, 113 S. Ct. 812, 121 L. Ed. 2d. 684 (1992).

95. *Schleier v. Kaiser Found. Health Plan of the Mid-Atlantic States*, 876 F. 2d 174 (D.C. Cir. 1989).

96. *Mertens v. Hewitt Assoc.*, 113 S. Ct. 2063, 124 L. Ed. 2d 161(1993).

97. *Pegram v. Herdrich*, 120 S.Ct. 2143 (2000).

98. *Chauffers, Teamsters & Helpers Local No. 391 v. Terry*, 494 U.S. 558 (1990).

99. *Berry v. Ciba-Geigy Corp.*, 761 F. 2d 1003 (4th Cir. 1985).

100. *Quesinberry v. Individual Banking Group Accident Ins. Plan*, 737 F. Supp. 90 (W.D. Va. 1990), affirmed in part, reversed in part, and remanded, 987 F. 2d 1017 (4th Cir. 1993).

101. *Tragert v. Group Hosp. & Medical Servs., Inc.*, No. 92-0180-LFO (D.D.C. March 29,1994).

102. *McDonald v. Artcraft Supply Co.*, 774 F. Supp. 29 (D.D.C. 1991).

103. *Coleman v. Nationwide Life Insurance Co.*, 969 F. 2d 54 (4th Cir. 1992), cert. denied, 113 S. Ct. 1051, 122 L. Ed. 2d 359 (1993).

104. *Coleman v. Nationwide Life Insurance Co.*, 969 F. 2d 54 (4th Cir. 1992), cert. denied, 113 S. Ct. 1051, 122 L. Ed. 2d 359 (1993).

105. *Pilot Life Ins. Co. v. Dedeaux*, 481 U.S. 41, 107 S. Ct. 1549, 95 L. Ed. 2d 39 (1987).

106. *Metropolitan Life Ins. Co. v. Taylor*, 481 U.S. 58, 107 S. Ct. 1542, 95 L. Ed. 2d 55 (1987).

107. *Shaw v. Delta Airlines, Inc.*, 463 U.S. 85, 103 S. Ct. 2890, 77 L. Ed. 2d 490 (1983).

108. *Corcoran v. United Health Care, Inc.*, 965 F. 2d 1321 (5th Cir. 1992), cert. denied, 113 S. Ct. 812, 121 L. Ed. 2d. 684 (1992).

109. *Kuhl v. Lincoln Nat'l. Health Plan of Kansas City, Inc.*, 999 F. 2d 298 (8th Cir. 1993), cert. denied, 114 S. Ct. 694, 126 L. Ed. 2d 661, 62 U.S.L.W. 3451 (1994).

110. *Spain v. Aetna Life Ins. Co.*, 11 F. 3d 129 (9th Cir. 1993) cert. denied, 114 S. Ct. 1612, 128 L. Ed. 2d 340, 62 U.S.L.W. 3703 (1994).

111. *Dearmas v. AvMed, Inc.*, 814 F. Supp. 1103 (S.D. Fla. 1993).

112. *Anderson v. Humana Inc.*, 24 F. 3d 889 (7th Cir. 1994).

113. *New England Health Care Employees Union District 1199, SEIU AFL-CIO v. Mount Sinai Hosp.*, 846 F. Supp. 190 (D. Conn. 1994).

114. Sanderson, B. (1995). HMOs can be sued. Court breaks new ground. *News Tribune* (Woodbridge, N.J.), April 19, p. A3, col. 6.

115. *Altieri v. Cigna Dental Health, Inc.*, 753 E Supp. 61 (D. Conn. 1990).

116. *Settles v. Golden Rule Ins. Co.*, 927 F. 2d 505 (10th Cir. 1991).

117. *Corcoran v. United Health Care, Inc.*, 965 F. 2d 1321 (5th Cir. 1992), cert. denied, 113 S. Ct. 812, 121 L. Ed. 2d. 684 (1992).

118. *Kuhl v. Lincoln Nat'l. Health Plan of Kansas City, Inc.*, 999 F. 2d 298 (8th Cir. 1993), cert. denied, 114 S. Ct. 694, 126 L. Ed. 2d 661, 62 U.S.L.W. 3451 (1994).

119. *Ricci v. Gooberman*, 840 F. Supp. 316 (D.N.J. 1993).

120. *Tolton v. American Biodyne, Inc.*, 854 F. Supp. 505 (N.D. Ohio 1993).

121. *Randolph v. Prudential Health Care Plan, Inc.*, No. 9316207, 1993 WL 326560 (N.D. Ill. 1993) (not reported in F. Supp.).

122. *Nealy v. U.S. Healthcare HMO*, 844 F. Supp. 966 (S.D. N.Y. 1994).

123. *Butler v. Wu*, 853 F. Supp. 125 (D.N.J. 1994).

124. *Lancaster v. Chandra*, No. 93-C-2717, 1994 WL 33962 (N.D. Ill.) (not reported in F. Supp.).

125. *Pomeroy v. Johns Hopkins Medical Servs., Inc.*, No. MJG-94-2236 (D. Md. Oct. 18, 1994).

126. 5 U.S.C. 8901 *et seq.*

127. *Grazel v. Nazari*, No. 92-CV-1471, 1992 WL 122913 (E.D. Pa.) (not reported in F. Supp.).

128. *Fink v. Delaware Valley HMO*, 417 Pa. Super. 287, 612 A. 2d 485 (1992).

129. Rodwin, M. A. (1995). Conflicts in managed care. *New England Journal of Medicine* 332(9):604–607.

130. Council on Ethical and Judicial Affairs. (1995). Ethical issues in managed care. *Journal of the American Medical Association* 273(3):330–336.

131. McCormick, B. (1995). Integration shakes the liability insurers. *American Medical News* 38(23):l, 22–23.

132. McBride, S. (1995). Does MCO now stand for "malpractice case overload?" *Managed Healthcare* 5(4):39–44.

CHAPTER 15 Integrated Health Care Delivery Systems

Risk Management Issues, Challenges, and Solutions

Robin A. Maley

As a means to ensure their continued viability, a large and growing number of health care organizations have merged, acquired, or formed alliances with individual physicians, group practices, managed care organizations, and a variety of other health care operations. The success of their efforts depended largely on their ability to develop seamless alignments and linkages among the various components of their systems and their ability to convince network participants to work collaboratively toward sharing risks and rewards.

OVERVIEW OF INTEGRATED NETWORKS

Integrated health care systems, also referred to as integrated networks, community care networks, or accountable health plans, are considered to be the third generation of managed care organizations. Systems including at least one systemwide managed care entity and a minimum of three components of care, including an acute care hospital, a physician component, and one other delivery component, are considered highly integrated. There were a total of 330 integrated delivery systems in the United States in 2001. Of this number, 55 had six or more delivery components, 95 had five or more delivery components, 119 had four or more delivery components, and 61 had three or more delivery components. Initiators of integrated systems as of 2002 are as follows: hospitals (71.2 percent); physicians (3.3 percent); HMOs/PPOs (2.4 percent); PHOs (0.6 percent); universities, clinics, and local, state, and federal governments (5.5 percent); and combinations of these (17.0 percent).[1]

Like their managed care predecessors, integrated health care delivery systems combine the financing of insurance risk and the delivery of a wide variety of services designed to meet their health care needs.

Networks will look different in each community, in accordance with local needs for health care services. However, characteristics common to networks include their focus on providing greater information to the public regarding their operations and performance (for example, via report cards on their quality of care, administration of health promotion programs, and work with community agencies), their commitment to easy network access and the transfer of information among network components, and their use of financial incentives to avoid over-utilization of facilities and services.[2]

Networks are organized generally under an umbrella institution that takes responsibility for integrating and managing each of the component agencies. Most commonly, organizational models for hospital-physician integration include the physician-hospital organizations (PHOs), management services organizations (MSOs), foundations, and group practices without walls.

Physician-Hospital Organizations

A physician-hospital organization (PHO) is an agent that represents hospitals and physicians for the purpose of contracting with HMOs, insurance carriers, employers, and other third-party payers.[3] Combining forces achieves greater contract negotiation and purchasing power and decreases administrative costs. A PHO may be structured to share the risk of contracting between the hospitals and physicians. In some cases, the PHO may actually own an HMO or PPO (preferred provider organization), or vice versa.[4] As the financial and reimbursement interests of the hospital and physicians are aligned, there is generally increased cooperation to achieve mutual goals, greater efficiency, and increased profitability.[3] Under the PHO arrangement, physicians lose little autonomy and do not typically change their practice locations or the ownership of their assets.[4]

Management Services Organizations

A management services organization (MSO) is a legally separate entity owned by a hospital or a PHO that provides management services and administrative systems to one or more medical practices, such as a large group, physician practice, or hospital.[3] MSOs assume the financial risk associated with health care management by purchasing the assets (for example, facilities, equipment, and supplies) of a professional corporation and leasing them back to the corporation. In addition, MSOs provide physicians with administrative services and often employ the nonprofessional staff supporting the medical practices. MSOs may also offer physicians financial support by transferring hospital capital to them in exchange for assets, expanded clinical services, and more affordable administrative systems. An MSO is not considered a *provider* of medical care, since the physicians who sold their assets to the MSOs retain ownership of their clinical practices and medical records. MSOs are usually classified as joint venture partnerships or corporations in which the hospital is a participant, partner, or shareholder.[4]

Foundations

Foundations are nonprofit, tax-exempt organizations through which physicians and hospitals can integrate health care services. Foundations are often affiliates of hospitals within the networks.[5]

Group Practices without Walls

A group practice without walls is a network of physicians who have formed a single legal entity but maintain their individual practices.[3] The integrated health care delivery system parent may provide central management and administrative support but may not necessarily acquire the assets of the individual physicians' practices. This model is appealing to physicians who are not ready to or who do not wish to become fully integrated.

As integrated health care systems have emerged to provide full-spectrum medical services, the new organization's vision, mission, and strategies should take risk management issues into consideration and support measures to promote financial solvency and patient safety. Ultimately, the success of an integrated health care delivery system will be predicated on its financial strength, its structural soundness, and its ability to provide high-quality patient care, obtain patient satisfaction, and secure buy-in from network partners.

RISK MANAGEMENT ISSUES, CHALLENGES, AND SOLUTIONS

Several issues can create risks during the process of integration and lead to integration failure, financial distress, and unsafe patient care: culture clashes, management experience, physician leadership, financial vulnerability, budgeting, assumption of liabilities, incident reporting systems, information systems, legal issues, network formation, and areas of exposure.

Culture Clashes among Integrated Health Care Network Components

At the outset of network negotiations, the need to evaluate the various cultures of the component parts of the integrated health care network and their perceptions and expectations of the new organization are important considerations. Establishing guidelines and job descriptions for professionals and clear lines of communication will help greatly to deter risks and aid in resolving conflicts regarding perceived or actual responsibilities, goals, and objectives.

Medical practice has changed dramatically over the past 10 to 15 years, and the extent of control physicians have over their environment and their degree of autonomy have been severely impacted. Most physicians who began practicing medicine before the increased popularity of managed care have developed very individualistic, independent styles of practicing medicine. These practice methods contrast with those that are necessary to practice within the integrated health care system and that require flexibility, cooperation, and new group dynamics.

Physicians will be further challenged as they find it increasingly difficult to maintain the revenue streams they have had in the past. Threatening the stability of their incomes are continued reimbursement modifications by the government under Medicare Part B and Medicaid; declining insurance payments as managed fee schedules reduce costs; rising personnel expenses; expenses related to compliance with regulatory requirements, for example, Office of Safety and Health Administration (OSHA) and Clinical Laboratory Improvement Amendments (CLIA); and administrative costs associated with managed care contracting. Adding even more pressure on physicians are patient expectations, which may be inflated or unrealistic because of marketing campaigns, media, or other image-enhancing vehicles.

Opportunities and challenges for physicians, and the emerging new health care entities, will relate to the ability of each to work with the other as they forge multiple practice models. Reaching system and individual productivity and profit goals will require cooperation by the providers; implementation of solid recruitment and retention policies; efficient administration of information systems, claims, and contracts; and realistic, targeted marketing plans. It will be important for all involved parties to acknowledge that networking means more than just assembling individual groups under one umbrella entity. Cultures that ignore the business aspects of medicine and potential risk areas and that focus on revenue versus costs will not be able to achieve the goals and efficiency of successfully integrated operations (see Box 15-1).

Quality initiatives implemented across an integrated health care network frequently develop problems and fail. Fetterolf[6] offers the following list of fatal flaws that may be present alone or in combination:

- Failure of the organization to quickly develop a reality-based, accurate mission or vision of its purpose
- Lack of focused, operationally oriented leadership
- Failure to articulate what the real benefit of an integrated network will be
- Lack of real, achievable, short-term outcomes
- Inherent conflict among the parties involved
- Political pressures
- Insufficient information technology capabilities
- The high cost of producing and distributing information
- Clinical heterogeneity
- Legal concerns
- Confidentiality unequally specified
- Apathy

BOX 15-1

University of North Carolina (UNC) Health Care System Hospitals:

UNC Memorial Hospital
North Carolina Women's Hospital
North Carolina Neurosciences Hospital
North Carolina Burn Center

UNC Physicians and Associates (Chapel Hill School of Medicine)

Rex Hospital (Raleigh)

Physicians' practices in counties: Orange, Wake, Durham, Chatham, Lee, Vance, and Alamance

A new system to enhance billing-office efficiency through tight integration of patient accounting is being implemented. Cost savings, increased communication, and higher patient satisfaction are anticipated.[7]

The risks associated with physician practices that may become part of the integrated health care delivery system should be assessed *before* their acquisition and/or acceptance into the network. Factors contributing to the degree of risk within the system include the size of the practice, the scope of services provided, arrangements for inpatient coverage, the amount of time dedicated to administration of the practice, the roles of generalists versus specialists, and the roles of any mid-level providers. Although physicians' autonomy may be limited and their practices industrialized to an extent, physicians may still be held individually liable and accountable for their professional actions.

Recruitment of physicians should be based on a comprehensive systematic plan that considers the needs of the integrated health care delivery system. Compensation guidelines, benefits packages, appointment and credentialing, and clinical privilege processes and orientation proceedings should be well documented, fair, and easy to access.

Compensation packages should be reviewed by legal counsel and include, at least, the following elements: salary and bonus plans; leave (sick, vacation, family medical, holidays, bereavement, educational); personal and professional insurance; pension issues; professional development; and other issues such as loans and relocation expenses.[8]

Having a strong retention plan, as well as a recruitment plan, will promote loyalty and the satisfaction of health care providers within the integrated health care delivery system, to reduce risks associated with job dissatisfaction, anger, or confusion. Procedures and activities supporting strong communications among providers and administrators regarding organizational strategies and direction will assist practitioners in the transition from being independent to being members of a large network of providers. Policies and procedures requiring that productivity demands, work loads, on-call requirements, and other characteristics of the work environment be made clear to network members should also be in place to curb risk.

When networks form, there are often duplicative credentialing systems in place, for example, at the hospitals, group practices, clinics, and so on, and these should be streamlined to avoid confusion, inefficiencies, and false assumptions regarding responsibility. Privileging mechanisms should be devised that address venues of practice, in addition to the practitioner's ability or limitations to perform certain procedures and data regarding provider satisfaction, turnover, member satisfaction, referrals for employment, productivity, and the degree of voluntary participation in network operations and events.

Management Experience

Leading a truly integrated health care delivery system is a major challenge to even the most experienced health care executives. Risks are inherent in the process, since most board members and administrators contemplating and forming integrated health care delivery systems have not done so before. These new systems require a great deal of commitment, leadership, and business savvy. It is important that empowering leaders change their focus and think "system" versus independent organizations (for example, hospitals, home care agencies, etc.). Leadership is necessary to structure continuums of care that de-emphasize reliance on specialists and acute care services and that focus on the utilization of primary care providers and nonacute care services.

Risk management professionals can be helpful in evaluating the management strengths and weaknesses of each network component on the basis of existing managers' credentials, past performance, commitment, and skills. Each component affects the others, and the ability of the leadership to work toward the benefit of the whole system will be a critical success determinant.

Physician Leadership

Supporting the chances for success of integrated delivery systems are means to identify physician leaders. Leaders chosen should be dynamic, competent, and respected by their peers, and should express a willingness to become involved in meetings, discussions, the ongoing development of the network, and the education of other health care delivery system members. Communicating key decisions to system members and implementing new processes should be the responsibilities of leaders.

The scope of health care team members' responsibilities should be evaluated, tested, and documented. As health care utilization patterns shift and patients are treated in primary care areas on a more frequent basis, more attention must be given to establishing general standards, policies, and procedures at the corporate level of systems that can then be modified to fit various places of practice and/or service. The input of physician leaders and overall physician buy-in and conformance to established guidelines will be critical to risk avoidance and containment.

Financial Vulnerability

Financial integrity of the network will be contingent on many factors, which should be meticulously analyzed. Credentials and references of financial advisors, actuaries, accountants, lawyers, and other consultants utilized should be checked and verified. Information regarding past experience should be requested and evaluated by those responsible for structuring the integrated health care delivery system, including the risk manager.

Competitors' strategies should also be evaluated carefully. Their methods for achieving cost savings may be shortsighted, less efficient than advertised, and financially risky when their ultimate impact on outcomes is analyzed. Therefore, these strategies should not be duplicated quickly in an effort to appear competitive in the marketplace.

Risk managers should be actively involved in the evaluation of the match between customer needs and the array of products and services that will be available. Mismatched product lines and services, or their unavailability or inaccessibility, could lead patients to misuse services or to have difficulty in "making it through the system." Whether a truly "user-friendly" continuum of care exists must be evaluated. The increased likelihood of accidents when such a continuum does not exist and patient expectations are not met increases the potential for future litigation.

Financial Forecasting or Budgeting

Financial forecasting or budgeting should take into consideration the historic financial experiences of each component of the integrated health care delivery system: premium, product, managed care enrollments, and mix of services and provider changes. One-time expenditures should be identified and long-term benchmarks for monitoring financial performance and quality established. Risk implications of actions to be taken must be identified, analyzed, and factored into financial plans and operational strategies. Risk managers, as well as clinical professionals, should be integral players and can be invaluable in pointing out areas of potential liability that could negatively affect the bottom line.

Assumption of Liabilities

The risk manager should consider the liabilities from the various components of the system that may need to be assumed by the network. These may include outstanding environmental or malpractice claims, tax payments, unfunded pension plans, labor liabilities for past or ongoing EEOC (Equal Employment Opportunity Commission) problems, and billing and collection problems. Estimating expenses for handling assumed liabilities is an area where companies can meet. Incurred but not reported claims can be particularly hazardous if underestimated. To determine future payouts, it is also prudent to review and consider actuarial data, historical rates of claim reporting, past liabilities incurred, and the current legal environment. Assumed liabilities need to be evaluated carefully in order to determine their overall impact on the network's financial status and the types of insurance and future risk management interventions needed. Inventories should be performed to find outstanding claims and other potential liability situations. Insurance and risk management programs will vary according to the structure, complexity, and locations of the components of the integrated health care delivery system.

Incident Reporting Systems

Although systems for identifying and controlling risks are usually in place in hospitals and large clinics, they are seldom found to be in force in more remote health care settings, such as radiology centers or physicians' offices. One of the major challenges for risk managers at integrated health care delivery systems is to establish a network-wide incident reporting system. Policies and procedures should be written to encompass all component locations with instructions defining what constitutes a reportable incident or occurrence, as well as reasons, methods, and time frames within which reports must be made. Providing educational programs to all levels of health care providers is highly recommended to ensure compliance with policies and procedures.

The risk manager should review all incidents and follow up on each one to ensure that actions to control, monitor, and treat risks are implemented. Incidents should also be reviewed by medical supervisory personnel and designated liaisons at the various components of the integrated health care delivery system.

Information Systems

Inferior, incompatible, or duplicative information systems can pose serious risks for integrated health care networks. For example, the incomplete transmission of critical patient information can have devastating results, such as misdiagnoses or improper treatments. Duplicative information systems may further stress networks financially. Network information systems should be designed to accomplish the following:

- Facilitate member enrollment and determination of plan eligibility.
- Demonstrate the proper administration of defined benefits.
- Document the medical necessity of care, including how, where, and how long it is given.
- Measure the impact of cost-sharing arrangements.
- Maintain provider credentialing information.
- Yield information regarding providers' adherence to payment policies and their responses to payment incentives.
- Track the effects of treatment provided, by measuring clinical outcomes.
- Support member and provider relations by providing access to data necessary to answer member questions and promote the easy transfer of information among providers.
- Produce management reports.
- Provide decision support tools.
- Collect and categorize adverse incidents and claims.

As of 2002, 92.9 percent of integrated systems components/users are connected to a common intranet, 82.2 percent of providers can access information from any system site, and 35.7 percent are linked real-time to central medical records.[1]

Merging information systems in preparation for integration can be an overwhelming and expensive task, but it must be done if the system is to be managed well from financial, quality, and utilization standpoints. The ability to evaluate particularly the performance of physicians, collect data regarding patients' use of inpatient and outpatient services, and track and monitor claims is critical to strategic planning and customer satisfaction.

If reliable and accurate data can be used to demonstrate trends to physicians, their behavior can be more easily directed to meet the integrated delivery system's business goals and objectives. Providers can be compared both internally and externally to benchmark their performance against that of competitors and to make improvements. Risks, both financial and clinical, can be monitored and the impact of risk reduction efforts evaluated. This task requires acknowledgment of the importance and complexity of reporting.

Data source integration problems, poor data quality, or data unavailability can create numerous problems that should concern the risk manager. For instance, costs of providing care or claims payments may be inaccurate and, thus, financial projections off base; or patient care may be affected by clinicians' reliance on incomplete medical information, and demonstrations that quality care is being provided may be impossible. Service and patient satisfaction may also be affected if there are delays in transmitting pertinent information.

It is particularly hard to demonstrate quality if data are not well organized and relationships between actions and outcomes are difficult to access and compare. The organization of data should eliminate to the highest degree possible the potential for their misinterpretation. A dedicated, user-friendly decision support system will:

- Promote data source integration.
- Detect errors and make corrections.
- Incorporate processes to map data and make changes as new variables come into play.
- Standardize data.
- Organize data.
- Build medical intelligence and use expert logic systems to tag certain patients and to enhance reporting capabilities.

Implementation of appropriate information systems will allow direct access to data and rapid retrieval (see Box 15-2). Such systems will also accommodate standard system applications, such as Health Plan Employer Data and Information Set (HEDIS), and produce flexible, user-friendly reports. To reduce the long hospital admission procedure, an immediate-response electronic data exchange allows hospitals to discover within six seconds if a patient has insurance and what the out-of-pocket expenses are, if any.[10] Taking care in choosing an information system vendor is of the utmost importance. Researching various options and then matching the needs of the integrated health care delivery system with available resources are imperative to risk containment.

BOX 15-2

Intermountain Health Care (IHC), headquartered in Salt Lake City and with branches in Utah and Idaho, is an integrated health care system that has contracted for software that will capture, store, index, and make available one million radiology studies generated annually internally. Images will be distributed through the IHC electronic medical record system of 22 hospitals and 5,000 to 8,000 medical practitioners with secure authenticated access.[9]

LEGAL ISSUES

Risk managers involved with integrated health care delivery systems need to be aware of requirements for the legal formation of such systems, and the extension of existing theories of liability to the integrated health care delivery system setting.

Network Formation

Integrated health care delivery systems must adhere to all relevant federal, state, and local laws concerning formation, corporate structure, licensing guidelines, and so on. If the corporate form for the system is for-profit, capitalization will require adherence to both state and federal securities laws. Not-for-profit entities will have to ensure complete compliance with both local and federal guidelines for the formation and maintenance of such a corporation that also has the benefit of tax exemption (see Box 15-3).

It is particularly important to be aware of the antitrust problems that may arise as a result of the corporate structure that has been chosen and the role that the system will play in the provision of health care in a relevant market.[12] The federal antitrust statute, the Sherman Antitrust Act,[13] prohibits acts in restraint of trade, and forbids the formation of market monopolies.[14] If a system engages in price setting or other anticompetitive behavior, both federal and state antitrust regulations could be implicated.[15] Similarly, restrictive credentialing and hiring protocols can have antitrust implications.[16] U.S. Senator Howard M. Metzenbaum strongly supported maintaining the antitrust laws to protect the best interests of consumers.[17] Others have been more moderate, calling for a tailoring of antitrust enforcement to the promotion of consumer welfare.[18] A specific investigation focused on hospital mergers and joint ventures and an appeal by the American Hospital Association to immunize such agreements from federal antitrust scrutiny.[19]

BOX 15-3

The Veterans Health Administration (VHA) is the largest integrated health care system in the United States, with more than 1,300 sites of care currently divided into 21 integrated networks.[11]

AREAS OF LIABILITY EXPOSURE

With the development of integrated delivery systems has come, of course, the application of basic theories of liability and recovery to these networks. A variety of doctrines have been applied.

System Liability as It Relates to Provider Selection and Services

Most systems set out to attract the most qualified, prestigious practitioners to join their organizations, and the manner in which providers are selected and the services they render are critical issues for risk management. An integrated health care delivery system can be found liable not only for the procedures through which it selects or monitors the services rendered by the providers in its network, but also, in certain circumstances, for the very acts or omissions of those providers. Mechanisms to ensure that professionals within the system are properly selected, credentialed, and monitored are critical to reducing the potential liability of the system as it relates to provider care.

In situations involving employees, the integrated health care delivery system could be held liable for their negligence under the theory of *respondeat superior*. Independent contractors, on the other hand, are considered nonemployees and, as such, the system has no legal right to control the manner in which those providers deliver patient care. Thus, the theory of *respondeat superior* would not apply. To determine liability, courts look to the actual relationship of the provider to the system, management control, the manner of payment, and the understanding between the parties as to their legal relationship.[20]

However, an integrated health care delivery system, similar to a hospital, may be held liable for negligent patient care by contracted providers if the selection and control of these providers are performed in a negligent manner. Courts have found that a hospital has a duty to its patients to exercise due care in the selection of its providers and to ensure the competence of its medical staff and personnel, including independent contractors.[21]

Corporate negligence theory was extended to HMOs and PPOs as it relates to the hiring and retention of staff.[22] To date, there have been no reported cases holding an integrated health care delivery system liable for improperly credentialing its providers; however, it is quite possible that the corporate liability theory will be extended to these systems in the future. Integrated health care delivery systems could be perceived to be involved in the delivery of health care to their clients by directing subscribers to specific providers or restricting their choice of providers. The networks, it would be argued, have a duty to ensure that these providers are competent.

Under the theory of ostensible agency, the integrated health care system may be held liable for the acts or omissions of contracted providers if the patient believes that the provider is the HMO's employee on the basis of acts of the HMO that could reasonably lead the patient to rely on the reputation of the HMO and the apparent relationship between the provider and HMO.[23] In 1999, 189 HMOs were part of integrated health care systems, with over 60 percent of them being not-for-profit.[24] The amount of control an integrated health care delivery system exerts over the patient's choice of provider or the control it has over provider practice patterns would be factors reviewed to determine its liability for the negligence of contracted providers under the ostensible agency theory.

A whole range of theories of recovery could be applied to the integrated health care delivery system, arising out of claims surrounding issues regarding the failure of providers to follow the system's explicit procedures or to provide benefits described in the system's contracts and marketing brochures. When written materials or verbal communications to patients that contain express or implied representations and/or warranties to provide a certain type and/or quality of service are breached, the system could be held liable for misrepresentation, fraud, and/or breach of warranty.[25]

In establishing procedures for the selection of providers, it is important to be aware of "any willing provider" statutes, which exist in different forms in most states. Opponents of the "any willing provider" laws, including the Federal Trade Commission, argue that these laws defeat the intent of "managed" care by creating an anticompetitive environment leading to a decrease in the quality of care and a rise in health care costs. Those in favor counter that these laws prevent the exclusion of qualified practitioners who are willing to participate in the plans.

Liability and the System's Services

Traditional theories of liability, where acts or omissions of the providers cause harm, can be applied to integrated health care systems. If resultant harm can be traced to the mechanisms utilized by the system, from credentialing to cost containment procedures, the systems themselves can be found liable.

Integrated health care delivery systems may be held liable for injuries to patients that stem from errors resulting from defects in the structure or implementation of cost containment provisions of the system.[26] Systems may also be held liable for the utilization management program decisions of a contracted third party, for adverse outcomes of negligence on the part of the decision-maker, or for defects in the design or implementation of the program.[27]

ADDITIONAL LEGAL ISSUES

Other legal issues the risk manager should be cognizant of when dealing with integrated health care delivery systems involve federal law under the Employee Retirement Income Security Act (ERISA),[28] as well as requirements set forth by the Health Insurance Portability and Accountability Act (HIPAA) in regard to the transmission and confidentiality of patient information.

ERISA Preemption

Under ERISA, federal law sets forth a comprehensive regulatory structure for the governance of employee benefit plans. ERISA nullifies many traditional state court causes of action (generally limiting claimants to seeking lost benefits, and not other types of damages), and displaces a broad range of state laws as they relate to such plans, placing disputes concerning benefit plans within the ERISA framework and ultimately before federal courts.[28]

The extent to which the ERISA preemption, "that portion of ERISA that displaces state laws and claims of recovery," applies to state laws regulating benefit plans, and state claims against such plans will depend on whether "the disputes in question arise out of or relate to the plan."[29] Preemption will apply to shield a benefit plan if the disputes arising between the claim and a plan administrator can be traced to the benefit plan.[30]

Confidentiality of Patients' Medical Information

Federal and state laws and regulations require that confidentiality of patient medical records be maintained, and staff should be aware of these laws and regulations. Provider contracts, as well as bylaws, rules, and regulations, should reinforce confidentiality requirements. To avoid liability to a patient for a breach of confidentiality, the integrated health care delivery system should obtain releases from patients whenever information regarding their care is released to a third party. Federal regulations also require that there be specific language contained within releases for drug and alcohol treatment records.[31]

To further ensure confidentiality and preservation of medical record contents, they should be maintained within a secure environment that precludes unauthorized access or use, loss, destruction, or tampering, and is within the guidelines of HIPAA.

Underwriting Considerations

Risk managers should be aware of underwriting guidelines used by insurers or plan administrators of managed care operations, since they will clearly influence who is part of the insurance program and to what extent they bear risk. Risk managers should consult with the actuarial staff developing rates to ensure that they have a full appreciation and knowledge of the services being offered, the composition and expertise of providers within the networks, and the demographics of the patient population being served. Risks associated with treating large numbers of obstetrical patients versus older adults, children, and geriatric patients vary. Arrangements made by contracted employer groups using the integrated health care delivery system's services will influence market share, penetration, and utilization patterns. Whereas plans containing lower-priced options with limited benefits will attract young, healthy customers, broader benefit packages will appeal to families.

Another risk management goal should be to help underwriters develop systems to capture healthy, predictable markets. Exposures to adverse selection and undesirable risks need to be identified so that insurance premiums can be set accordingly. Risk managers should support the development of profiles that complement the business goals, objectives, marketing strategies, and corporate values of the integrated health care delivery system. Reviews of rating methodologies, such as utilization management guidelines and protocols, are also means of assessing risks for more appropriate underwriting.

Insurance Program Structure

The integration of hospitals with physicians and managed care organizations brings forth numerous challenges in structuring insurance programs to best protect the risks of each while doing business together and separately. Having the means to assess current and future insurance needs, insurance coverages in place, the ability to combine coverages, and options for risk financing is important. Insurance assessment can be performed internally by finance, insurance, and risk management experts or in conjunction with insurance agents, brokers, or consultants.

Several factors affect the selection and ultimate structure of a risk financing arrangement. Foremost, a full assessment of the nature of the operations at the integrated health care delivery system is important. As the structure of integrated health care delivery system models varies to meet community needs and regulatory requirements in particular geographic locations, so does the insurance program. The extent to which the system operates as a health care service provider, insurer, and third-party claim administrator will be a major factor in determining corresponding potential liabilities and insurance coverage needs. The employment status of providers must also be determined, and their employer (hospital? MCO? group practice? subsidiary or joint venture?) must be identified.

Experts suggest that the following coverages be encompassed within the insurance programs of integrated health care delivery systems:

Corporate Professional and General Liability coverage for one or more institutional health care providers who may or may not be from the same economic family.

Physician Professional and General Liability coverage.

Managed Care Liability and Third-Party Administrators Errors and Omissions coverage.

Insurance Company Errors and Omissions coverage.

Provider Excess coverage.

Employer Medical Stop Loss coverage.

Employment Practices Liability/Wrongful Termination coverage.

HMO Reinsurance coverage.

It is important for the risk manager to stay abreast of changes in health care delivery patterns, since they may significantly impact risk and the variety and amount of insurance coverage needed. It is difficult to assess the costs and liabilities associated with integrated health care systems because they are still evolving. Premiums for primary care specialists and allied health professionals may rise as their responsibilities increase, while specialist services and insurance costs may decrease accordingly.

A trend that may affect future insurance buying practices is the increase in the number of capitation agreements being signed and the need for stop loss policies. By 1998, 40.9 percent of group practices were deriving revenue from capitation contracts.[32] Under capitation, if the care provided by the provider is less than the fixed payment, the provider makes money; if the care provided costs more, the provider loses money. There has been fear expressed that misapproximations in potential income or poor performance in general could result in huge financial losses. MCOs with more than 10,000 members are thought to be at risk.[32] Stop loss policies help stem the risks accompanying capitated agreements and assuming risk for services that exceed a specific amount.

In addition to considering the issues previously mentioned, the risk manager must evaluate the ability of the insurance carrier to meet the needs of the integrated health care system both at the present time and in the future.

Questions relevant to selecting an insurance carrier include:

- What is the size and financial stability of the carrier?
- Is the carrier willing to provide coverage for the various components of the integrated delivery system?
- What level of risk will the carrier assume?
- Does the carrier have adequate capacity to provide the requested limits?
- Does the carrier have an "A" rating?
- Who actually bears the risk?
- What influence do reinsurers have on the business practices of the carrier?
- Are underwriting approaches flexible and creative?
- What is the availability of funding options?
- Is the carrier a direct writer or is the product coming through a broker or managing general agent?
- Will arrangements to cover nonemployed physicians by bringing them into the hospital's malpractice program be considered?
- Are the carrier's representatives familiar with issues surrounding health care integration and managed care?
- How long has the carrier been underwriting coverages for managed care organizations and/or integrated health care systems?
- What are the carrier's claims-handling philosophies? Capabilities? Reputation?
- What risk management services are available? Are they included in the premium or purchased separately?

Questions relevant to evaluating insurance coverage options include:

- What coverages will be needed to adequately and best protect parties that make up the newly formed integrated health care delivery system?
- What are the variety and terms of insurance coverages already in place?
- Should the policy be claims made or occurrence coverage?
- Should the policy be commercially purchased or self-insured?

- Can there be other arrangements, such as captives?
- How is "tail" coverage treated in the policy?
- Is there coverage for physicians?
- How does the option fit among various policies?
- Are there renewal practices/provisions?

AFLOAT IN UNCHARTED WATERS

Risk management will become increasingly important as the health care delivery system in the United States moves from a private acute care-based fee-for-service system to a managed integrated health care network utilizing alternate payment arrangements such as capitation to reduce costs.[33] Lack of support for risk management programs will place formerly secure entities in jeopardy for financial loss and poor patient outcomes in the new administrative configurations. A successful integrated delivery system would be based on the following strategic elements:[34]

1. Participating parties must learn to trust each other.
2. Participants should address all concerns openly.
3. Assessment of market conditions should favor collaboration.
4. Potential participants should know each other well.
5. Organizational roles, responsibilities, and the decision-making process should be clearly delineated beforehand.
6. All participants should be aware of the advantages and disadvantages in participating in the network.
7. An implementation plan should be developed jointly.

Professionals who want to survive these burgeoning challenges must work as a team to contain liability risks as the new organizations and alliances evolve to form the health care industry's backbone.[35]

References

1. Managed Care Digest. (2002). Aventis Pharmaceuticals, Inc.: Bridgewater, N.J. *http://www.managedcaredigest.com/edigets/hm2002.*
2. Kremer, B. K. (1994). Integrated networks: The new direction for managed care in the 1990s. *Technology News* 7(4):1–2, 9–13.
3. United Health Care Corporation. (1994). *The Managed Care Resource.* Minnetonka, Minn.: UHCC, pp. 37, 46, 57.
4. Fine, A. (1995). *Integrated Health Care Delivery Systems Manual.* New York: Thompson, tabs 100, 800.
5. McKissock, W. J., and Hoffman, P. C. (1995). Liability issues in managed care. Presentation at Group Health Institute, Winterhaven, Florida, April 20.
6. Fetterolf, D. E. (2002). Editorial: Why do multiorganizational quality initiatives usually fail? *American Journal of Medical Quality* 17(2).
7. AMS Media Contacts news release. (2001). University of North Carolina healthcare systems to implement AMS's healthcare solutions. July 17. *http://www3.amsinc.com/CMC/newsroom.msf/pr.*
8. Group Health Association of America. (1995). GHHA Conference on Understanding Managed Care, Seattle, Wash., August 2–5.
9. Amicus, Inc. (2002). Signs, Salt Lake City, Basch Intermountain Health Care press release. May 6. *http://www.amicas.com/press/2002/5_06_02asp.*
10. Radosevich, L. (1994). Network eases pain of hospital visits. *Computerworld* 28(5):59–60.
11. Veterans Administration. (2002). *Cares.* August 14. *http://www.VA.gov/cares/ renewed/updates.*
12. *Ball Memorial Hospital v. Mutual Hospital Insurance Inc.,* 784 F. 2d 1325 (7th Cir. 1986).
13. 15 U.S.C. 1 *et seq.*
14. Waxman, J. M. (1995). Antitrust and integrated delivery systems: The safety zone. *Health Care Innovations* 5(1):16–18.
15. *Reazin v. Blue Cross/Blue Shield of Kansas, Inc.,* 899 F. 2d 951 (10th Cir.), cert. denied, 497 U.S. 1005 (1990).
16. *Patrick v. Burget,* 486 U.S. 94 (1988); *Hassan v. Independent Pratice Assoc's, P.C.,* 698 F. Supp. 679 (E.D.

Mich. 1988); *Brown v. Blue Cross & Blue Shield of Alabama*, 898 F. 2d 1556 (11th Cir.) cert. denied, 498 U.S. 1040 (1990).

17. Metzenbaum, H. M. (1993). Antitrust enforcement: Putting the consumer first. *Health Affairs* 12(3): 137–143.
18. Bloch, R. E., and Falk, D. M. (1994). Antitrust competition and health care reform. *Health Affairs* 13(1):206–223.
19. Jaggar, S. F. (1994). Federal and State Antitrust Actions Concerning the Health Care Industry. GAO/HEHS-94-220. Washington, D.C.: Government Printing Office.
20. *Schleier v. Kaiser Foundation Health Plan*, 876 F. 2d 174 (D.C. Cir. 1989); *Gugino v. Harvard Community Health Plan*, 380 Mass. 464, 403 N.E. 2d 1166 (1980).
21. *Johnson v. Misericorida Community Hospital*, 99 Wis. 2d 708, 301 N.W. 2d 156 (Wis. Sup. Ct. 1981); *Elam v. College Park Hospital*, 132 Cal. App. 3d 332, 183 Cal. Rptr. 156 (1982); *Darling v. Charlestown Community Memorial Hospital*, 33 Ill. 2d. 326, 211 N.E. 2d 253 (Ill. Sup. Ct. 1965).
22. *McClellan v. HMO of Pennsylvania*, 604 A. 2d 1053 (Pa. Super. Ct. 1992), appeal denied, 616 A. 2d 985 (1992).
23. *Albain v. Flower Hospital*, 55 Ohio State 3d 251, 553 N.E. 2d 1938 (Sup. Ct. Ohio 1990); *Boyd v. Albert Einstein Medical Center*, 547 A. 2d 1229 (Pa. Super. Ct. 1988).
24. Managed Care Digest. (2000). Bridgewater, N.J.: Aventis Pharmaceuticals, Inc. *http://www.managedcaredigest.com/edigests/hm2000*.
25. *Depenbrok v. Kaiser Foundation Health Plan*, 79 Cal. App. 3d 167, 144 Cal. Rptr. 167 (1978); *Pulvers v. Kaiser Foundation Health Plan*, 99 Cal. App. 3d 560, 160 Cal. Rptr. 392 (1980).
26. *Wickline v. State of California*, 22 Cal. App. 3d 660, 271 Cal. Rptr. 876 (1990).
27. *Taylor v. Prudential Life Insurance Co.*, 775 F. 2d 1457 (11th Cir. 1985).
28. *Pilot Life Ins. Co. v. Dedeaux*, 481 U.S. 41 (1987); *Ingersoll-Rand Co. v. McClendon*, 498 U.S. 133 (1990); *Salley v. E. DuPont de Nemours & Co.*, 966 F. 2d 1011 (5th Cir. 1992).
29. *Metropolitan Life Ins. Co. v. Massachusetts*, 471 U.S. 724 (1985): *Corcoran v. United Healthcare, Inc.*, 965 F. 2d 1325 (5th Cir.), cert. denied, 113 S. Ct. 812 (1992).
30. *Settles v. Golden Rule Insurance Co.*, 927 F. 2d 505 (10th Cir. 1991); *Visconti by Visconti v. U.S. Healthcare*, 857 F. Supp. 1097 (E.D. Pa. 1994); *Dukes v. U.S. Healthcare Systems of Pennsylvania*, 848 F. Supp. 35 (E.D. Pa. 1994); *Ricci v. Gooberman*, 840 F. Supp. 316 (N.D. N.J. 1993); *Altieri v. CIGNA Dental Health, Inc.*, 753 F. Supp. 61 (D. Conn. 1990).
31. 42 C.F.R. Part 2.
32. Kreig, J. (1995). Stemming the risk of capitated contracts: What providers should consider when buying stop loss insurance. *Health Care Innovations* 5(2):12–16.
33. Findlay, S. (1993). Networks of care may serve as a model for health reform. *Business & Industry* 11(2):27–31.
34. Integrated health care systems: Strategic considerations. (1994). *Managed Care Reporter* December:1–8.
35. COR Healthcare Resources. (1995). *Building Integrated Delivery Networks*. Santa Barbara, Calif.: COR Healthcare Resources.

Index